PHILOSOPHERS AT WORK

Issues and Practice of Philosophy

SECOND EDITION

PHILOSOPHERS AT WORK

Issues and Practice of Philosophy

SECOND EDITION

ELLIOT D. COHEN

Indian River Community College

WADSWORTH
CENGAGE Learning™

Australia • Brazil • Japan • Korea • Mexico • Singapore • Spain • United Kingdom • United States

WADSWORTH
CENGAGE Learning

Philosophers at Work: Issues
and Practice of Philosophy,
Second Edition
Elliot D. Cohen

For product information and
technology assistance, contact us at **Cengage Learning
Customer & Sales Support, 1-800-354-9706**

For permission to use material from this text or product,
submit all requests online at **www.cengage.com/permissions**
Further permissions questions can be e-mailed to
permissionrequest@cengage.com

Library of Congress Control Number: 99-62462

ISBN-13: 978-0-15-505599-5

ISBN-10: 0-15-505599-2

Wadsworth Cengage Learning
20 Davis Drive
Belmont, CA 94002-3098
USA

Cengage Learning is a leading provider of customized learning
solutions with office locations around the globe, including
Singapore, the United Kingdom, Australia, Mexico, Brazil,
and Japan. Locate your local office at:
www.cengage.com/global

Cengage Learning products are represented in Canada by Nelson
Education, Ltd.

To learn more about Wadsworth, visit
www.cengage.com/wadsworth

Purchase any of our products at your local college store or at our
preferred online store **www.cengagebrain.com**

Printed in the United States of America
4 5 6 7 8   17 16 15 14 13

To My Students

PREFACE

Philosophers at Work is intended as a comprehensive introduction to philosophy. Its approach is a distinctive one. Each chapter is divided into two main parts, an Issues section and a Practice section. The Issues section contains lively and lucid discussions by prominent philosophers of key theoretical problems arising in such areas as ethics, social philosophy, logic, philosophy of religion, and political philosophy.

The Practice sections have been written by philosophers who work, or have worked, in such diverse realms as business, medicine, government, education, psychology, art, historiography, social services, criminal justice and religion. Within each Practice section, the philosopher practitioner shows by a first person account and analysis of his or her own work experiences, how the respective issues (those raised in the first part of chapter) can arise and be philosophically addressed within the actual work context. Through this approach, students are not only exposed to the range of traditional problems, theories, and methods of philosophy; they are also provided with a window through which to view philosophers at work in diverse practical regions of life. Thereby they can be afforded a comprehensive, stimulating, and credible encounter with philosophy.

One caveat is in order here. Although the Issues sections aim at comprehensive coverage of the key perspectives on philosophical issues (usually in the form of the juxtaposition of selections containing sharply contrasting viewpoints), the perspectives taken by the philosopher practitioners in their Practice articles are not necessarily the only ones that can be taken. Students should be encouraged to consider alternative perspectives, in the light of their readings, and to engage their own critical and creative thinking. Many of the discussion questions at the end of each chapter have been prepared with this goal in mind.

In addition to the general introduction to the text, each chapter has its own introduction which summarizes the chapter's contents and emphasizes some key issues and problems. The Practice section of each chapter has been written in the light of the selections contained in its Issues section, and students may want to read the Issues section before reading the corresponding Practice section. On the other hand, reading the Issues section in the light of the corresponding Practice section can be helpful to set the Issues discussions in a meaningful context. The two sections are thus mutually supportive and students may benefit by reading, and re-reading, each in the light of the other. This mutuality has been corroborated through the experiences of the many students who have used the first edition of this text.

Instructors need not follow the order in which areas, or chapters within areas, are herein presented. For example, some instructors may prefer to start with "Truth and Knowledge" or with "Logic and Science" rather than with "Ethics and the Professions." However, since the Issues section of Chapter 1 provides background on normative ethical theories, it might be helpful to assign it before assigning subsequent work in ethics or social and political philosophy.

With the realization that different instructors will have different interests and areas of concentration, much effort has been made to include enough material to satisfy a wide range of individual concerns. It is not expected, therefore, that everything contained in this text will be viewed by all instructors with the same degree of urgency.

Further considerations in the selections of theoretical material for this text may have been clarity of presentation and student accessibility. Within these parameters, primary source materials have been incorporated into many of the Issues sections throughout each part of the text. Thus, in addition to secondary source readings, students will be afforded an ample opportunity to read and explore edited selections from important works of classical thinkers.

Many of the Practice sections in this second edition have been modified to include more practice articles. Students now get further, clear examples of philosophers at work while instructors get more pedagogical material for engaging students in class discussion. Toward this goal, the range as well as quantity of discussion questions have been expanded to cover the new practice articles.

This second edition has also expanded applications of philosophy to practice areas at the cutting edge of the twenty-first century such as computer programming and artificial intelligence. The breadth of philosophical issues covered is also greater. For example, there is coverage of the problem of evil in the chapter on religion including traditional as well as more recent perspectives. The chapters on ethics and social philosophy have been expanded to cover virtue ethics, care ethics, and feminist perspectives. A chapter on "Lawyer's Ethics" has been included which presents lively practice discussions on the ethics of defending and prosecuting cases of date rape and homicide.

Philosophers at Work owes its existence to many contributors, a number of whom have written their articles especially for the book. Moreover, many authors of Practice papers have also provided substantial input into the selection of Issues papers as well as the formulation of discussion questions. To all of these authors, a special acknowledgement is due. In addition, I wish to acknowledge and thank the reviewers of the second edition: David Felder; Evelyn Pluhar, Pennsylvania State University–Fayette; and David Smith, University of North Carolina–Asheville. I also wish to thank my many students, who throughout the years, have provided constructive suggestions, a number of which have been incorporated into this second edition. Finally, I wish to thank the staff at Harcourt Brace, and especially Katie Frushour, Developmental Editor, and David Tatom, Executive Editor, for their support in bringing this project to fruition.

TABLE OF CONTENTS

PREFACE   vii

1. THE ACTIVITY OF PHILOSOPHY   1
   What Philosophy Is   1
   Elliot D. Cohen
   The Origins of Applied Philosophy   9
   Richard T. DeGeorge

I. ETHICS AND THE PROFESSIONS 15

2. HEALTH CARE ETHICS   17
   Issues
   Ethical Theory and Mental Health Practice   21
   Elliot D. Cohen
   Utilitarianism   35
   John Stuart Mill
   The Categorical Imperative   43
   Immanuel Kant
   Practice
   The Philosopher as Ethics Consultant in a Psychiatric Ward   49
   Clifton B. Perry
   Ethics Consulting in a Multicultural Setting: Quality Care and the Wounds of Diversity   58
   Kenneth Kipnis
   Prescribing Viagra: Ethical Issues in Urologic Practice   64
   Muriel R. Friedman
   Discussion Questions   72

3. LAWYER'S ETHICS   74
   Issues
   Virtue Ethics   77
   Aristotle
   The Lawyer as Friend   84
   Charles Fried

Pure Legal Advocates and Moral Agents: Two Concepts of a
    Lawyer in an Adversary System   93
    Elliot D. Cohen

Practice

The Philosopher as Public Defender:
    In Defense of a Rapist   111
    Steven Wasserman

The Philosopher as Prosecutor: An (Unlawful) Prosecution
    of a Guilty Man   115
    William Heffernan

Discussion Questions   127

II. SOCIETY AND POLITICS 129

4. WOMEN'S RIGHTS AND SOCIAL WORK   131
    Issues

        The Natural Inferiority of Women   135
            Aristotle

        Women in Love   137
            Simone de Beauvior

        The Subjection of Women   142
            John Stuart Mill

    Practice

        The Philosopher as Social Worker   155
            Janice K. Wilkerson

        Letter from a Battered Philosophy Student   165
            Anonymous

    Discussion Questions   168

5. CRIMINAL JUSTICE: PRISONS AND CORRECTIONS   170
    Issues

        The Deterrence Theory of Punishment   173
            Martin P. Goulding

        The Retributive Theory of Punishment   175
            Robert Nozick

        Punishment versus Therapy   183
            Herbert Morris

    Practice

        The Philosopher as Corrections Officer: Doing Time
            in a Participatory Democracy   187
            Bill Puka

    Discussion Questions   201

6. POLITICAL THEORY AND PRACTICE   202
    Issues

        Dictatorship   205
            Thomas Hobbes

Rule by the Majority   211
  John Locke

Communism   216
  Karl Marx and Friedrich Engles

Practice

  The Philosopher in Representative Government:
   Applying Classical Theories   224
   Stanilaus J. Dundon
Discussion Questions   240

III. LOGIC AND SCIENCE   241

 7. LOGIC AND COMPUTER PROGRAMMING   243
  Issues

   The Scope of Logic   248
    Wesley C. Salmon

   Aristotelian Logic   254
    Howard Kahane

   The Logic of Truth Functions   260
    Stephen Barker

  Practice

   The Philosopher as Software Developer   265
    Gregory Tropea
  Discussion Questions   288

 8. SCIENTIFIC METHOD: MEDICAL RESEARCH   291
  Issues

   Science and Hypothesis   292
    Irving M. Copi

  Practice

   The Philosopher as Physician: Testing Clinical
   Hypotheses   306
    Reidar K. Lie
  Discussion Questions   315

IV. TRUTH AND KNOWLEDGE   317

 9. PERSPECTIVES ON TRUTH: ART, HUMANITIES,
  AND SOCIAL SCIENCE   319
  Issues

   Truth as Extra-Sensible Reality   327
    Plato

   Sense-Experience as the Standard of Truth   333
    Alfred Jules Ayer

   The Pragmatist's Approach to Truth   338
    William James

Practice

*The Philosopher as Dancer: In Consideration of Plato's
Theory of Truth 344
Maxine Morphis*

*The Philosopher as Historian: The Correspondence
Approach to Truth 357
Alfred L. Castle*

*The Philosopher as Journalist: A Pragmatic Approach
to Truth 366
Deni Elliot*

*The Philosopher as Psychologist: Truth and the
Schizophrenic Patient 373
Victor Guarino*

Discussion Questions 386

10. THEORIES OF KNOWLEDGE AND ELEMENTARY
SCHOOL EDUCATION 389

Issues

*Rationalism 394
René Descartes*

*Empiricism 400
John Locke*

*Epistemological Idealism 406
George Berkeley*

*The Empirical Grounds of Causal Reasoning 411
David Hume*

Practice

*The Philosopher as Elementary School Teacher:
Epistemology Applied to Fourth-Grade Education 414
Matthew Lipman*

Discussion Questions 430

V. MINDS AND MATTER 431

11. FREE WILL, DETERMINISM, AND PHILOSOPHICAL
COUNSELING 433

Issues

*Behaviorism 440
B. F. Skinner*

*Existentialism 444
Jean-Paul Sartre*

*Theories of Counseling and the Free Will–Determinism
Issue 449
Gale S. Cohen*

Practice

*The Philosopher as Counselor 457
Elliot D. Cohen*

Discussion Questions 467

12.   MINDS, BODIES, AND ARTIFICIAL INTELLIGENCE   468

    Issues

        Mind-Body Dualism: The Interactionist Theory   472
          Baruch A. Brody

        Materialism: The Identity Theory   479
          Jerome A. Shaffer

        Minds, Bodies, and Computers   486
          John Searle

    Practice

        Simulating Human Thinking: An Empirical Approach
          to the Mind-Body Problem   494
          Herbert A. Simon

    Discussion Questions   518

VI. RELIGION AND MYSTICISM   519

13.   THEISM, ATHEISM, AND THE CLERGY   521

    Issues

        The Ontological Proof of God's Existence: The A Priori
          Approach   526
          St. Anselm

        Five Ways of Proving God's Existence: The A Posteriori
          Approach   528
          St. Thomas Aquinas

        Why God's Existence Cannot Be Proven   530
          Søren Kierkegaard

        I and Thou   533
          Martin Buber

        Human Existence Without God   538
          Friedrich Nietzche

        The Problem of Evil: The Free Will and Soul-Building
          Arguments   540
          John H. Hick

        Evil and the Limits of God: Jewish Perspectives   546
          Neil Gillman

    Practice

        The Philosopher as Priest: Applying Proofs of God's Existence
          to the Case of a Dying Cancer Patient   555
          Fr. Robert R. Gerl

        The Philosopher as Rabbi: Confronting Evil in the Face of the
          HIV/AIDS Pandemic   563
          Rabbi Allen I. Freehling

    Discussion Questions   575

14.   MYSTICISM AND COSMIC CONSCIOUSNESS   578

    Issues

        The Authority of Mystical Experience   581
          William James

Mysticism as Metaphysically Mistaken   588
  Bertrand Russell

Practice

*The Philosopher as Mystic: Experiencing and Interpreting Cosmic
  Consciousness*   593
  Alan W. Watts

Discussion Questions   599

GLOSSARY   601

PHILOSOPHERS AT WORK

Issues and Practice of Philosophy

SECOND EDITION

I

THE ACTIVITY OF PHILOSOPHY

ELLIOT D. COHEN

WHAT PHILOSOPHY IS

The word "philosophy," which is derived from the Greek *philein* (love of) and *sophia* (wisdom), has in fact two distinct though related uses. It may be used to refer to certain philosophical theories, principles, or systems of belief, as, for example, when one says, "Today in class we studied the philosophy of Immanuel Kant." Or it may be used to refer to a certain kind of *thinking activity,* as, for example, when your philosophy teacher says "Today in class we are going to *do* some philosophy."

Actually, philosophy as a thinking activity is the primary meaning of philosophy. That is, there would be no philosophy to study (no philosophy of Immanuel Kant, for example) if there were no philosophical activity of thinking.

What, then, is involved in the thinking activity of philosophy?

PHILOSOPHY AS A THINKING ACTIVITY

Philosophers have not always agreed on the precise ways in which philosophical thinking activity should be carried out, but there are certain broadly definable aspects of this activity to which, since ancient times, they have subscribed.

Justifying What One Thinks

One very important aspect of this thinking enterprise is the need to *justify* what one thinks, which means to give *reasons* for what one thinks. Moreover, in the process of providing such reasons, one can be said to be *arguing* for one's claim or, alternatively, to be advancing a *logical argument* for it.

For example, in his famous *Essay Concerning Human Understanding,* the English philosopher John Locke (1632–1704) considers (and ultimately rejects) the following logical argument for the claim that there are certain principles or truths that are *innately* known by all human beings—that is, known from the time of birth:

> There are certain principles [e.g., "Whatever is, is" and "It is impossible for something to be and not to be"], universally agreed upon by all mankind: which therefore . . . must needs be constant impressions which . . . they bring into the world with them, as necessarily and really as they do any of their inherent faculties.[1]

The claim that there are innate principles is thus, in the above excerpt, justified or defended by *arguing* that some principles (those cited) are universally assented to, which, *presumably,* would not be the case if such principles were not native to the human mind itself. Notice, however, that it is not sufficient for a philosopher to simply provide some reason for his or her claim, as in the above. Such reasons must *themselves* survive a careful examination. This leads, then, to a second aspect of philosophical thinking activity.

The Analysis of the Argument

Let us continue with the above example. Locke himself was not prepared to accept the foregoing argument. His strategy was rather to attack the claim that some principles are universally assented to, and thus to shatter the argument for innate principles.

Locke argued that there are not really, after all, any principles to which everybody gives assent. To establish this, he maintained that even regarding such persuasive principles as "Whatever is, is" and "It is impossible for something to be and not to be," it is, nonetheless, "evident that all *children* and *idiots* have not the least apprehension or thought of them."[2] Therefore, they are not *universally* assented to.

Of course, in the light of such *counterexamples* to the proffered argument, a philosopher could attempt to "tighten up" his or her argument. As Locke acknowledged, to avoid his counterexamples of children and idiots, a proponent of the original argument might offer the following *revised* argument:

> All men know and assent to them [those principles cited] *when they come to the use of reason;* and this is enough to prove them innate.[3]

Notice, however, that this revised argument merely *assumes* that any principle that is assented to by all men, "when they come to the use of reason," must be innate. This, in turn, points to another important aspect of the analysis of arguments, namely, the importance of *exposing and examining any assumptions* which underly the argument.

As a philosopher, Locke could not simply accept this assumption. Rather, he carried his analysis even deeper, concentrating on another fundamental aspect of philosophical thinking activity, namely the need *to clarify or define terms.*

The Clarification or Definition of Important Terms

Locke saw that the phrase "when they come to the use of reason" was ambiguous and needed some clarification. As he saw it, it could either mean that the principles in question come to be known "as soon as" a person acquires reason, or merely that, with the aid of reason, anybody would be able to discover such principles.

However, when understood in the first way, argued Locke, the argument would break down, for there are people, namely "illiterate people and savages," who "pass many years, even of their rational age" without even knowing such principles. On the other hand, if taken in the second way, argued Locke, the argument would still break down. For even principles which are clearly *not* innate could be discovered by the aid of reason; for example, mathematical theorems which can be derived from axioms only by constructing very intricate proofs. Therefore, he concluded that on either understanding of the term "when they come to the use of reason," the argument for innate principles should be dismissed.[4]

There were, indeed, those of Locke's contemporaries who were not moved by his attempt to refute the doctrine of innate principles. (Leibnitz is a case in point.) In fact, seldom is it the case in philosophy that philosophical arguments go unchallenged.

Enough has been said, however, to yield some sense of what philosophy as a thinking activity is about. It is about arguing carefully and clearheadedly for what one believes. And it is about challenging the arguments of others one believes to be mistaken, and, in turn, arguing carefully and clearheadedly against such other arguments.

THE TRADITIONAL AREAS OF PHILOSOPHY

Traditionally, philosophers have applied their thinking skills to *basic* issues and problems[5] which, broadly speaking, may be classified under four related headings: epistemology, logic, metaphysics, and axiology.

Epistemology

The term "epistemology" is derived from the Greek *episteme* (knowledge) and is appropriately called the theory of knowledge. In this area are included such basic concerns as the definition of knowledge, the kinds of knowledge that are possible, the justification of our claims to know, the relation between perception and the external world, and the standards of truth and falsehood. Within this area, more specialized areas can be located such as the philosophy of science and of mathematics. The example presented earlier of Locke's inspection of the claim that there are innately known principles provides us with one example of an epistemological inquiry.

Logic

This area, insofar as it may be considered distinct from epistemology, may be defined as "the study of the methods and principles used to distinguish good (correct) from bad (incorrect) reasoning."[6] It has, itself, two general divisions, namely *deductive* logic and *inductive* logic. In chapter 5 of this text, for example, you will have the opportunity to study some of the traditional methods and principles of deductive logic that were first devised by the ancient Greek philosopher Aristotle.

Metaphysics

Metaphysics, from the Greek *meta* (beyond) and *physica* (nature), is concerned with the nature of reality itself. Metaphysical issues and problems include such ones as the nature of the mental and the physical and their relationship (the so-called "mind-body problem"), the question of whether human beings have free will (the "free will versus determinism" problem), the existence of God, and the nature and origin of the cosmos ("cosmology"). The areas referred to as the philosophy of mind and the philosophy of religion are included within this area.

Axiology

Axiology is the theory of *value* and, broadly interpreted, includes such areas as ethical theory, social and political philosophy, and aesthetics. In ethical theory basic questions about *moral* values are raised (for example, the nature and grounds of morally right and wrong conduct). In social and political philosophy, basic questions about social and political values are raised (for example, the limits of personal liberty, the problems of just or equitable treatment of individuals in society). In aesthetics, basic questions about art and its value are raised (the nature of beauty, the quest for a definition of art, for instance).

PHILOSOPHICAL THEORIES AND SYSTEMS

Philosophical thinking about basic issues and problems in the traditional areas mentioned above has historically given rise to *philosophical theories*. Such theories are, in effect, beliefs which have undergone a process of justification, analysis, and conceptual elucidation—the marks of philosophical thinking activity discussed earlier.

For example, when Locke set out to refute the doctrine of innate principles, it was for purposes of clearing the way for his own philosophical theory, which could be true only if the doctrine of innate principles was false. In a famous passage, Locke states, "Let us then suppose the mind to be, as we say, white paper void of all characters, without any ideas. How comes it to be furnished? . . . To this I answer, in one word, from *experience*. In that all our knowledge is founded; and from that it ultimately derives itself."[7] Locke's *Essay* is then devoted to a justification, analysis, and conceptual elucidation of this philosophical theory. Moreover, in the process, Locke's thoughts emerge as a *system* of coherent beliefs about the "original, certainty, and extent of human knowledge, together with the grounds and degrees of belief, opinion, and assent."[8]

Philosophical theories may thus take the form of well-worked-out systems of belief in which each belief fits in with the others much like the bricks of a carefully constructed building, the cement that holds the structure together being the logical arguments in which the individual beliefs figure. Although not all philosophers are, or have been, interested in building such systems of belief, some have erected grandiose systems which attempt to address basic issues and problems from all of the traditional areas of philosophy—epistemology, logic, metaphysics, and axiology. Spinoza and Kant are good examples of such philosophers.

PHILOSOPHY AND PROBLEM SOLVING

Philosophy, its methods of thinking as well as its theories, may be employed toward the solution or clarification of two distinct, although related, sorts of problems: intellectual problems and practical problems.

Philosophy within the Context of Intellectual Problem Solving

When philosophy is primarily aimed at answering or clarifying the question of what to *think* or *believe* about some basic issue or problem arising in a traditional philosophical area, it can be said to be employed with respect to an intellectual problem. An intellectual problem is thus, roughly speaking, a problem about what to think or believe. For example, when Locke argued that all knowledge was ultimately derived from experience, he was tackling an intellectual problem through philosophical thinking and theorizing. He was trying to justify a certain *belief* about the genesis of all knowledge.

The use of philosophy in the context of such intellectual problem solving is sometimes called "pure" or "academic" philosophy. Many philosophers throughout the history of philosophy have looked upon such "pure" philosophy as being the most valuable kind of philosophy. For example, Aristotle considered this sort of intellectual pursuit to be the "highest" and most "divine" of human activities.[9]

Philosophy within the Context of Practical Problem Solving

In contrast to pure philosophy, which focuses upon matters of thought, philosophy may also be conversant about *what to do* about human problems arising in the various spheres of life. Philosophy which aims primarily at answering or clarifying questions about what to do (what *actions* to take), and not merely about what to think, is sometimes called "applied" or "practical" philosophy.

Although applied philosophers do not typically deny the value of pure philosophy, they see philosophy as having as well the practical mission of helping to solve or clarify problems of human action. They seek to ameliorate life or to make aspects of practical existence more manageable through the use of philosophy. For instance, Karl Marx summarized the applied philosopher's creed when he stated that hitherto "the philosophers have only interpreted the world differently: the point is, however, to change it." [10]

Marx himself was concerned with the problem of social oppression, and he conceived of his philosophical activities as a means to the end of alleviating this problem. The applied philosopher's creed is then one of action or "changing things," and not only one of thought or "interpretation."

There are two ways in which philosophy may be "applied" within the context of practical problem solving: (1) the *thinking activities* of philosophy—justifying, analyzing, and clarifying—may themselves be applied within the context of practical problem solving; and (2) the *theories* of philosophy may be applied within this context.

Applying Philosophical Thinking Activities

Kai Nielsen has offered the following example of the first of the above applications of philosophy within a context of medical ethical problem solving:

> Suppose, to take a much discussed example, a doctor has a patient who is a Jehovah's Witness and who categorically refuses a blood transfusion. . . . It is not, even remotely, enough for the physician to say I must not harm my patient and not giving him the transfusion is to harm him. In the first place, the notion of "harming the patient" needs disambiguation. "Harming," in the most mundane and straightforward contexts, refers to not damaging the person physically. It can, and should be, extended to not damaging him mentally or emotionally. The physician who takes a paternalistic line is likely to be thinking of only that most manifest sense of "harm." But "harm" can also refer to not showing respect for the patient's person. . . . What a moral philosopher can and should do in a medical context is firmly to draw these distinctions and refine them sufficiently to make the moral point that needs to be made against medical paternalism. [11]

By defining and clarifying different senses of the term "harming the patient" within a medical context, a philosopher may thus aid in the making of a practical decision, one about a patient's life. The applied philosopher may not thereby *solve* the problem, but he or she may nevertheless help in facilitating a clear-headed and enlightened approach toward its solution.

As a further example of applying philosophical thinking activities, let us consider the lawyer's code of professional ethics as set forth in the American

Bar Association's *Model Rules of Professional Conduct* (1983). According to rule 1.6 governing "Confidentiality of Information":

   (a) A lawyer shall not reveal information relating to representation of a client unless the client consents after consultation, except for disclosures that are impliedly authorized in order to carry out the representation, and except as stated in paragraph (b).

   (b) A lawyer may reveal such information to the extent the lawyer reasonably believes necessary:

      (1) to prevent the client from committing a criminal act that the lawyer believes is likely to result in imminent death or substantial bodily harm; or

      (2) to establish a claim or defense on behalf of the lawyer in a controversy between the lawyer and the client, to establish a defense to a criminal charge or civil claim against the lawyer based upon conduct in which the client was involved, or to respond to allegations in any proceeding concerning the lawyer's representation of the client.

The *Model Rules* also contains another rule, rule 3.3, governing "Candor Toward the Tribunal," which states (in part):

A lawyer shall not knowingly fail to disclose a material fact to a tribunal when disclosure is necessary to avoid assisting a criminal or fraudulent act by the client.

However, upon analysis, it becomes clear that rule 3.3 is *inconsistent* with rule 1.6, for 1.6 requires confidentiality of information in all but those cases mentioned in paragraph (b). But rule 3.3 requires that lawyers disclose clients' fraudulent testimony (perjury) to the affected tribunal, even when this information is confidential. This, though, contradicts 1.6 since the case of client perjury does not fall under the permitted exceptions given in paragraph (b). Applied philosophical analyses like the above one can affect legal practice itself by pointing the way to needed changes in the lawyer's code of professional ethics. After all, a lawyer cannot possibly both reveal and not reveal confidential information. It could then be argued that, if the code requires the impossible, it should be changed.

Applying Philosophical Theories

As mentioned, the other way in which philosophy can be applied within the context of practical problem solving is through the application of *philosophical theories* within such contexts.

For example, consider Jean Paul Sartre's idea that, for human beings, "existence precedes essence"; that human beings do not have any preestablished nature but rather define themselves through their own freely chosen actions. As you will see in chapter 9, such an "existential" philosophy can be used as a basis for psychotherapy in situations where clients have lost control over their own lives as a result of strong socialization.

Another example of the application of philosophical theories to practical problem solving can be instanced in the use of the principles and methods of logic for constructing personnel examinations. As you will see in chapter 5, the United States government employs applied philosophers who use the principles and methods of logic in preparing examinations that are administered to prospective government personnel for hiring purposes.

THE INTERDEPENDENCE OF "PURE" AND "APPLIED" PHILOSOPHY

We have noted that pure philosophy is concerned primarily with intellectual problems (problems about what to *believe*), whereas applied philosophy is concerned primarily with practical problems (problems about what actions to take). However, belief and action are, themselves, intimately bound up. What one believes obviously influences how one acts. This is especially true of our axiological convictions. Consider, for example, the incongruity of a man's claiming that the treatment of women as inferior human beings is "unjust" but nevertheless refusing to allow his wife equal say in family decisions. This would indeed be odd since if a man sincerely *believed* in women's rights, we would expect him, other things being equal, to *act* as though he did. Therefore, it should be apparent why pure philosophy, which concerns belief, bears substantially upon applied philosophy, which concerns action.

Conversely, applied philosophy also bears substantially upon pure philosophy. As Norman Bowie has made clear,[12] applied philosophers do not "straightforwardly apply" philosophical theories. Rather, they must take account of the contexts in which they are working. To use Bowie's example, within limits lawyers are permitted to harm the interests of others in order to advance their clients' interests. Thus, within the context of our legal system, a moral theory that proffered an obligation to treat the claims of everybody equally could not be "straightforwardly applied." Rather, the theory would itself have to be changed or revised in light of the practical realities of legal practice. In this sense, applied philosophy bears substantially upon pure philosophy.

Furthermore, the philosophical thinking activities employed by pure philosophers are, in general, the same as those employed by applied philosophers. Both attempt to build logical arguments, engage in logical analyses of arguments, examine assumptions of such arguments, and define key terms. Applied philosophy and pure philosophy are thus also related in point of methodology.

It is a premise of this text that applied philosophy and pure philosophy cannot be separated without creating a false impression. This is why each chapter in this text contains both a "pure" part (an Issues section) and an "applied" part (a Practice section). Many traditional texts which neglect the applied counterpart are apt to leave the student with a false impression about the practical uses of philosophy. Given the interdependence of pure and applied philosophy, both sides deserve a hearing.

It is also a premise of this text that those philosophers who are themselves intimately involved in the areas of *praxis* on which they are speaking are likely to have something of importance to say to us all, philosopher and layperson alike. For this reason, all of the Practice sections have been prepared by philosophers who have actually worked in those practical areas on which they are writing. As such, these philosophers, all of whom have graduate credentials in philosophy, are able to call upon their own experiences and expertise in the areas in question in order to provide a most penetrating and provocative look at philosophy within the context of practical problem solving.

NOTES

1. John Locke, *An Essay Concerning Human Understanding,* I, ii, 2.
2. Locke, *Essay,* I, ii, 5.
3. Ibid., 6.
4. Ibid., 7, 8, 12.
5. By a *basic* issue or problem we mean one of a general sort which underlies a wide range of particular issues or problems. For example, in this sense, "What causes cancer?" raises a particular issue or problem, whereas "What is a cause?" raises a basic issue or problem.
6. Irving Copi, *Introduction to Logic,* 7th ed. (New York: Macmillan, 1986), p. 3.
7. *Essay,* II, i, 2.
8. Locke, *Essay,* I, i, 2.
9. Aristotle, *Nichomachean Ethics,* Bk. X, ch. 8, $1178^{b}21-22$.
10. Karl Marx, *Theses on Feuerbach* (Eleventh Thesis).
11. Kai Nielsen, "On the Need for Moral Experts: A Test Case for Practical Ethics," *The International Journal of Applied Philosophy,* Vol. 2, No. 1 (Spring 1984): 72–73.
12. Norman E. Bowie; "Applied Philosophy—Its Meaning and Justification," *Applied Philosophy,* Vol. 1, No. 1 (Spring 1982): 10–11.

RICHARD T. DEGEORGE

THE ORIGINS OF APPLIED PHILOSOPHY

"Applied philosophy" may sound like a contradiction in terms to some people both in and out of professional philosophical circles. And indeed, if the term "philosophy" is taken narrowly enough, it would be a contradiction. Those outside of academic philosophy who perceive philosophy to be an esoteric, jargon-filled, impractical discipline concerned with how many angels can dance on the head of a pin or other equally arcane topics would see no point in attempting to apply to the world in which they live the answers one might get to such questions. Ironically, many people who hold such a view of philosophy will, at the least provocation, be willing, even anxious, to detail their personal "philosophy of life," which amounts to applied philosophy. Those in professional philosophical circles who believe that philosophy is properly concerned only with logical connections and a priori thinking might admit that what they do is relevant to the world; but they would maintain that when one applied what they do to the world, one is then engaged in some enterprise other than philosophy.

There is no need to restrict philosophy in either of these two ways. Although the endless debates about what philosophy is will continue, there is a fairly good consensus about who in the history of philosophy are to be considered philosophers. Any view of philosophy that excluded Socrates, Plato, Aristotle, Aquinas, Descartes, Locke, Spinoza, Berkeley, Hume, Leibniz, Kant, Hegel, Russell, Wittgenstein, or Heidegger would be too restricted a view to have much currency. And philosophy refers to the topics they addressed: the nature of reality, the validity of knowledge, the determination of right and wrong, the delineation of the beautiful, and so on.

Applied philosophy in one sense is as old as philosophy itself. In another sense it is a relatively new phenomenon. Both senses deserve some discussion.

Following an Aristotelian distinction, we can divide philosophy into two broad types—theoretical and practical. What Aristotle called "practical" can be taken as equivalent to "applied." For him practical philosophy concerned action rather than thinking. The practical areas of philosophy *par excellence* were ethics and politics. Ethics was the task of deriving and defending the rules that ought to govern human action and the goods worth seeking in human life. Aristotle begins his ethics with the statement that every art, inquiry, action, and pursuit aims at some good—a doctrine he defends in his theoretical philosophy. Thus the two types of philosophy are not distinct but related, and the practical builds on the theoretical. Politics concerns how to properly govern a state. Poetics, another area of practical philosophy, concerns how to properly construct a drama. Each of these builds on a human activity and constructs justification for principles that ought to govern that activity.

Applied philosophy, if considered as practical philosophy, is that portion of philosophy concerned with governing human activity. Although we can understand this in a rough and ready way, the supposed bounds of applied philosophy expand once we begin to push the notion of human activity. Since thinking is itself a human activity, logic, or the rules that ought to govern human thinking of a deductive or inductive nature, turns out to be practical as opposed to theoretical philosophy.

Historically a case can be made for the thesis that as an area of philosophy became more and more applied so that it was concerned with what is, as determined by empirical research and experimentation, it broke off from what was considered philosophy. A clear case would be the field of psychology. The study of the psyche, the soul, or mind was for a long time the province of philosophy. What we know as modern psychology broke off from philosophy when its emphasis became empirical—not in the sense of going to experience, which philosophy also did—but in the sense of relying on experimentation and the collection and systematization of data.

In a similar manner what we call political science broke off from the theoretical aspect of political philosophy, even though political philosophy for Aristotle belonged in the area of practical philosophy. Aristotle was concerned with theory and with a discussion of how best to govern. Political science has a much greater concern with the description of how political systems actually work and how practice deviates from theory and from abstract models.

Despite the fact that a large number of the disciplines we recognize today had their roots in ancient and medieval philosophy and have broken off from philosophy as they became more empirically and experimentally oriented, each of them has theoretical bases and presuppositions which can still appropriately be described as philosophical. The study of these bases and presuppositions, as well as of the methodologies employed by these disciplines, makes up such areas of philosophy as the philosophy of science and the philosophy of the social sciences (or of individual social sciences such as the philosophy of psychology, the philosophy of anthropology, the philosophy of economics, and so on). To some interpreters, these branches of philosophy are practical or applied areas as opposed to central theoretical areas such as theory of knowledge or metaphysics.

Clearly the divisions are to some extent arbitrary. Although there are clear cases of one or another kind of philosophy, the distinctions break down in two ways. First they break down at the borders. Drawing neat lines dividing philosophy of mind, philosophical psychology, philosophy of psychology, and psychology itself from one another becomes an arbitrary exercise, even though in a rough way we can distinguish each of these from the others.

The other way the distinction breaks down is within each of the so-called empirical or practical or theoretical areas themselves. Insofar as they are coherent bodies of knowledge and constitute fields, they each have theoretical foundations and components. Any neat division between theory and practice within the field will be as arbitrary as a neat division among fields.

The second sense of "applied philosophy" is the contemporary sense. In this sense it is almost a technical term, even though it emerged from an ordinary meaning of "applied." In this sense applied philosophy has a relatively short history and its domain is still in the process of self-definition.

The contemporary sense of applied philosophy has its origins in the 1960s and grows out of a certain historical situation in American philosophy. In the 1940s three different and in some ways competing strands stood out from the many strands then and still represented in American philosophy. One of these, the instrumentalism of John Dewey, which had been especially influential in the 1930s, took a pragmatic approach to philosophy in general and was influential on popular issues, especially education and politics. Dewey and his followers, of whom there were many, engaged in applying philosophy to all areas of life, as well as in dealing with strictly philosophical issues.

A second trend, developed in Europe after the Second World War and imported into the United States, became known as the existential-phenomenological approach to philosophy and was sometimes referred to as "continental philosophy." With existentialism came questions of the meaning of life and death, of the lived world, and other topics with an existentialist and so a practical import. Such questions reentered metaphysical discourse, and were considered aspects of applied metaphysics; whether God exists and what this means for our lives are questions of applied philosophical theology. The phenomenological aspect has survived even more strongly and has influenced other areas—especially psychology and the other social sciences. Its methodology was applied by practitioners in this area, funneling into what has become applied philosophy.

The third trend, which became dominant in the 1950s and 1960s in the United States, was known as "analytic philosophy"; following what has become known as "the linguistic turn," it concerned itself primarily with language, logic, and meaning. Its practitioners were not concerned with the application of philosophy to practical problems and even in the field of ethics were concerned primarily with the meaning of moral terms and the logic of moral reasoning, or with what is called "meta-ethics." Political philosophy was generally ignored and its practitioners were found not in philosophy departments but in departments of political science.

To some extent applied philosophy emerged as a reaction to the narrowing of philosophy represented by analytic philosophy as practiced in the 1950s and early 1960s, although it also grew out of analytic philosophy in the sense that many of those who do applied philosophy consider themselves analytic philosophers.

The three trends converged in the 1960s. The application of philosophy to practical issues also took place in response to forces outside of philosophy. The 1960s was a period of great ferment and student activism. The Vietnam War was a focus for popular dissent, and reaction against the war led to attacks on the military-industrial complex, the establishment, and the universities, which were seen as bastions of tradition and authority. Partially in response to student interests and concerns, professors began turning their attention to practical and pressing demands and issues, and began to bring their philosophical skills to bear on them.

In 1972 John Rawls' *A Theory of Justice* appeared to great acclaim. That a respected Harvard analytic philosopher could turn to topics with a practical import for moral issues, politics, law, and social problems was taken as a signal by some within the philosophical establishment that applied philosophy was academically respectable and acceptable. In a period of declining college enrollments, philosophy departments also found that they could attract more students to courses that applied philosophy to practical problems than to courses that dealt only with the traditional, abstract aspects of philosophy. Many other issues emerged about the same time. Discussions of the morality of nuclear war fueled interest in applied philosophy, as did the Supreme Court decisions on abortion (*Roe v. Wade*) and affirmative action. New advances in medicine led to the emergence of medical ethics, and scandals in business led to courses in business ethics.

The application of logic to the analysis of everyday discourse, to speeches and editorials, to the uncovering of fallacies and the analysis of everyday arguments became acceptable. Once applied to everyday thinking, a movement started to introduce logic—a topic once reserved for college courses—into the grade schools. Another area that had spun off from applied philosophy at the grade-school level was "values clarification," a movement as well as a course that attempted to teach children the difference between facts and values and to help them choose their values.

Once the development of applied philosophy began there were no a priori limits anyone could place on it. Applied philosophy took on a life of its own, and philosophy found application in a wide variety of areas. Applied ethics found its way into not only medicine and business but also into engineering, architecture, journalism, law, and a number of other fields. Aesthetics also came to be applied, as did logic. Even such traditional areas as philosophy of mind and theory of knowledge came to be applied to practical endeavors by computer scientists interested in artificial intelligence.

In its contemporary sense applied philosophy does not correspond to the old sense of practical philosophy. Nor is it simply the application of theoretical philosophy. Applied philosophy not only borrows from theoretical philosophy; it also makes contributions to theoretical philosophy. The relation between the two is one of active interrelation. As people started applying theoretical philosophy, they found that they were in fact testing the validity and completeness of the theory. In some cases they found that the theory had ignored a variety of possibilities and problems that had not emerged until someone tried to apply the theory. In still other cases they found that applications made a difference to what one should or could hold and that a given theory took on different shapes depending on the area in which it was applied.

Philosophers also found that doing applied philosophy usually meant learning a good deal about the area in which the application took place. One could not do medical ethics, for instance, without knowing something about medicine; and many serious practitioners found themselves learning a great deal about medicine, making rounds with doctors in hospitals, and taking part in the dramatic and difficult weighing of right and wrong, good and bad that takes place in medicine when lives are at stake.

Applied philosophy, however, remains philosophy. It still involves a good deal of theory and abstract reasoning. Although its aim is practical, those engaged in it still seek clarity in argument, and still try to decide issues on the basis of the validity of the arguments that can be mustered in their favor. Applied philosophy is not a repudiation of philosophy. At its best it is a revitalization of it and a recapturing of a unity of theory and practice that some feel had been lost as philosophy became too removed from life and its problems, too academic, too rigid, and too obscurantist.

Applied philosophy does not designate a particular way of doing philosophy, since, as we have seen, pragmatists, phenomenologists, and analytic philosophers—as well as those with other orientations—all engage in it. Nor can it be defined by a specific subject matter, since it cuts across the traditional areas of philosophy as well as across traditional branches of knowledge. To say that it is still in the process of self-definition is an indication that no limits have been set on it and that its nature (and perhaps even its validity) is still debated. Some of the work that goes under the name of applied philosophy is shoddy and poor. But any field deserves to be judged not by the worst but by the best work done in it. And there is enough first-rate applied philosophy that it deserves study, cultivation, and dissemination.

As a new area or field, applied philosophy has developed the trappings of academic respectability—learned societies, journals, textbooks, and a group of vocal supporters and active practitioners. Included in the number are many who would not identify themselves as applied philosophers and might not even call what they do applied philosophy, preferring to think of themselves as philosophers and of what they do as philosophy. That is entirely appropriate. For applied philosophy is philosophy, and applied philosophers are philosophers. The dispute about the name is insignificant. What is important is that the work is done, that the research is carried on, that the articles and books get published, and that the results are available not only to the audience of professional philosophers but also to society at large. Philosophy has traditionally been an attempt to make sense out of individual and collective human experience. Applied philosophy is one aspect of that endeavor, and represents a conscious attempt to make philosophy once again relevant to society and to those who live in it. The growing body of high-quality literature appropriately called applied philosophy is testimony to the success of that endeavor.

I

ETHICS AND THE PROFESSIONS

2

HEALTH CARE ETHICS

Ethics may generally be defined as the study of morality. There are principally two distinct but related ways in which we might study morality. One is the manner in which a social scientist might go about it. This would amount to giving a *description* of different moral outlooks or systems of morality as subscribed to by different cultures, subcultures, or groups. Thus, we would study morality in this way if we were to investigate and report on the views on sexual morality generally held by the people of Sweden, or the views of Eskimos on the care of the elderly, or the views of Jehovah's Witnesses on the acceptability of blood transfusions. We could also study morality *philosophically*.

The philosophical study of morality is that branch of ethics that is concerned with the clarification or solution of *moral problems*. A moral problem is a *practical* problem (see chapter 1) which raises a question of the form, "What, morally speaking, ought a subject (oneself, society, a certain institution, a certain profession, etc.) to do about such and such (abstract or concrete) issue? For example: Ought people ever break their promises? Ought society to accept physician-assisted suicide as a legal option? Ought a physician to disclose confidential information about the HIV positive status of a patient in order to protect the life of the patient's unsuspecting sexual partner? Ought pornography over the Internet to be censored by government? In taking a philosophical approach, we would be concerned with morally evaluating or assessing viewpoints and not merely with describing them (although we would obviously need to do the latter in order to assess them), and with making and defending our own moral judgments. For example, we might try to determine whether the Oregon Death with Dignity Act, which makes physician-assisted suicide a legal option in Oregon in certain cases, is morally acceptable. We might defend our own moral position on suicide in order to make the determination.

When the philosophical study of morality is directed to problems arising in the professions—health care practice, law, business, journalism, engineering, and so on—it is called *professional ethics*. Since the present and subsequent chapters of this book respectively address moral problems of health care practice and legal practice, they fall within the domain of professional ethics.

The philosophical study of morality also includes the study and application of *ethical theories*. An ethical theory is a general standard (or set of standards), complete with a reasoned defense of why it should be respected, intended to assist in resolving moral problems. Historically, there have been numerous *ethical theories*. In the first selection of this chapter, "Ethical Theory and Mental Health Practice," some major ethical theories are examined and applied to moral problems occurring in the context of mental health practice.

Ethical theories may be divided into virtue ethics, rule ethics, and care ethics. Virtue ethics emphasize character, and defines what a morally good *person* is. This type of ethics will be considered in the next chapter.

Rule ethics provide general rules for resolving moral problems. Two such theories that have dominated contemporary discussions of ethics are *utilitarianism* and *Kantian ethics*. Included in this chapter are two primary source selections representing each of these currents. The first is by the nineteenth-century British utilitarian, John Stuart Mill, excerpted from his *Utilitarianism*. The second is a selection by the eighteenth-century German philosopher, Immanuel Kant, excerpted from his *Groundwork of the Metaphysics of Morals*.

There are, in general, two ways in which a utilitarian standard can be applied: (1) to acts directly and (2) to acts indirectly through the medium of *rules*. Roughly speaking, according to the former, an act is morally justified when, and only when, it is calculated to maximize human happiness; and, roughly speaking, according to the latter, an act is morally justified when, and only when, it is required by a *rule or policy* that is itself calculated to maximize human happiness. An example of the application of the utilitarian standard to an act is that of a physician who decides not to tell a patient that she is going to die because, after weighing the "pros" and "cons," he considers this to be, on balance, best. An example of the application of a utilitarian standard to a rule is that of a physician who routinely resuscitates all patients in cardiac arrest (without considering in each instance whether this would be best, on balance) because there is a hospital policy requiring that all such patients be resuscitated. The policy itself is justified on the grounds that steadfast adherence to it will maximize human happiness in the long run.

Utilitarian ethics determines right and wrong action exclusively in terms of the *consequences or results* of actions and, for that reason, has sometimes been dubbed "teleological" (from the Greek *teleos* meaning "end" or "purpose"). On this approach, the moral worth of an action is itself a function of a *further* (nonmoral) value, that of the happiness it produces. While classical utilitarians have identified happiness with *pleasure,* it is noteworthy that the value of pleasure itself has been understood differently by different utilitarians. For example, for Jeremy Bentham, the founder of utilitarianism, there is no difference in value between different types of pleasure. Pleasure is pleasure and the more of it one can get, the better. Thus, if one gets more pleasure out of playing a child's game or indulging one's physical appetites (say, eating a candy bar or having sex) than engaging in an intellectual pursuit (say, playing chess or philosophical contemplation), then the former must be considered more valuable than the latter. In contrast, according to John Stuart Mill, the famous student of Bentham, intellectual pleasures in comparison to physical ones are of a higher quality and worth more even *if* (what may be contrary to fact) they yield less pleasure in the long run. "It is better," says Mill, "to be a dissatisfied Socrates than a happy pig."

Of course, one may still wonder how qualitative differences among pleasures can be numerically quantified so that they can figure in the weighing up and balancing of pleasures within a calculus as the utilitarian standard seems to require. In speaking exclusively in terms of *quantities* of pleasure, Bentham may have avoided this problem.

Kantian ethics takes the notion of *duty for duty's sake* as the core basis for determining the moral quality of actions. It has accordingly been dubbed "deontological" (from the Greek *deontos* meaning "duty"). In contrast to utilitarians, Kant thinks actions done for the sake of consequences may be expedient, but what is expedient is not the same as what is moral. Instead moral action is a function of a "good will," a will which conforms to a rational formula he calls "the categorical imperative."

As discussed in the first selection of this chapter, Kant gives several formulations of this principle. In one important formulation Kant states, "Always treat humanity, whether in your own person or that of another, as an end in itself and never as a means only." In this and all other formulations, Kant recognizes a right of human beings in their capacity as rational beings to freely determine their own fate, even if this is likely to be contrary to their future happiness or welfare. For example, physicians should not lie to patients about their illnesses even if done for patients' own good. In contrast to utilitarianism, such respect for the rational autonomy (self-determination) of persons has *intrinsic* merit, that is, worth that is not affected (neither augmented nor diminished) by any positive or negative consequences that may accrue from it.

Care ethics, a more recent approach, takes concrete interpersonal relationships as the primary concern of ethics. On this view, which is represented by the work of Carol Gilligan as discussed in the first selection of this chapter, morality cannot be a mere matter of weighing up of consequences as utilitarians hold, or a dispassionate, rational judgment as Kant holds. Rather, it is a process of perception that is infused with emotions of caring and empathetic regard for the plights of all concerned.

To embrace an ethics of care need not, however, be to deny the value of other approaches including rule-based ones. Indeed, these approaches may offer guidance and direct attention to what is of moral significance. For example, the fact that an action will have negative consequences cannot be divorced from caring; nor can the fact that a patient is, in Kant's terms, treated "as a mere means" (that is, like an object) by a failure to get his or her consent to treatment. Thus, in coming to an enlightened moral decision one might benefit from an eclectic consideration of several approaches.

In the first Practice section of this chapter, Clifton Perry applies Kantian and utilitarian ethics to an intriguing case he confronted while working as a philosopher on Ethics Grand Rounds in the Department of Psychiatry at the University of Tennessee Medical School.

The case Perry discusses is that of a thirty-three-year-old manic who, after being restored to "competency," refused further medication for his manic condition on the grounds that he preferred his "manic-high" to being "straight." It is in this context that utilitarian considerations (harm to third parties, effects of the drug regime on the patient, the patient's "high" itself) and Kantian considerations (specifically, the right of persons to refuse medical treatment) are brought into play. The question Perry focuses upon is, "Should a manic, who might very well be restored to mental health, be allowed to refuse that treatment necessary for continued competence?"

By drawing comparisons between the case in point and a further case concerning a Jehovah's Witness who refuses a blood transfusion, Perry arrives at a Kantian argument that, paradoxically, casts its vote *against* permitting the patient the autonomy to refuse treatment. Perry's stand is, broadly, that a person's right to act autonomously cannot, without self-defeat, include the giving up of one's autonomy for the sake of giving it up. The case in point is thus, for Perry, one in which the Kantian right of autonomy is pushed beyond its logical limits: "if the right of autonomy actually included the freedom to place oneself intentionally in a position of incompetency for *that very purpose*, then one would be a nonautonomous being by design." Indeed, given the high premium Kant placed on rationality as the grounds of autonomy, and as the locus of "personhood," it is plausible that Kant himself may have found such a case for the limits of autonomy convincing. (Is it rational to relinquish, forever, one's rationality *for the very purpose* of becoming irrational?) Nevertheless, as Perry would acknowledge, the utilitarian might still see things differently.

In the second Practice paper, Kenneth Kipnis, a professor of philosophy at the University of Hawaii at Manoa and a medical ethics consultant for area hospitals, discusses an ethics consult concerning an elderly Korean man who refused lifesaving treatment. In the case at hand, the patient distrusted and feared his physicians because they were Japanese, a result of having associated them with Japanese oppression of Koreans during the earlier half of the twentieth century.

Against a background of multiculturalism where "all of us are minorities," this case brings into focus a conflict of values between the utilitarian concern for patient welfare and the Kantian duty to respect the inherent dignity of others. On the one hand, by refusing to get the patient a non-Japanese physician, respect for the dignity of the Japanese physicians would be preserved; however, the patient would die. On the other hand, by replacing the physicians, the patient might live, but not without underwriting invidious discrimination.

In the final analysis, Kipnis would resolve this dilemma by giving priority to the patient's life. On the other hand, Kantian principles would appear to militate against engaging in discriminatory practice, regardless of the outcome for the patient. This is so because no rational, self-determining person would choose to become a recipient of prejudice, stereotypes, and hateful discrimination. Nor would a rational, self-determining person choose to be made an instrument for the propagation of such.

Still, ethics of care would resist conceptualizing the moral problem in terms of a *dilemma* in which someone's interests must inevitably be sacrificed. It would instead stress trying hard to work through individual differences, foster empathetic regard for the feelings of physician and patient alike (realizing how one might feel if one were in the patient's/physician's own subjective shoes), break down barriers of ignorance and fear that sustain stereotypes, and open up lines of interpersonal communication in the hope (although not the certainty) that no one will have to suffer. Alas, ethics of care would aim to dispel discrimination and hatred while at the same time seeking to preserve patient welfare.

In the final Practice selection, Muriel R. Friedman, M.D., drawing from her experience as a woman urologist in a predominantly male profession, shows how the emergence of an effective impotence treatment such as Viagra has made urgent the need for a more enlightened social perspective on the problem of male impotence. In her view, sexual outlooks that have been propagated through socialization, pharmaceutical company advertisements and slogans, and by medical practitioners themselves, have misrepresented the actual needs and desires of men and women. Women, she argues, generally prefer the intimacy of a warm caring relationship to that of mere sex. Similarly, men who are impotent need to locate their self-esteem in other human characteristics besides an erect penis. In her view, impotence is not merely a mechanical problem but an interpersonal one. She has accordingly worked with her patients to overcome social barriers that interfere with meaningful interpersonal relationships.

Because Dr. Friedman's approach to dealing with human problems— among which impotence is one—is to start with concrete interpersonal relationships, her ethics appear to be largely one of care. If, as Carol Gilligan suggests, women incline towards such ethics, this is not surprising. Yet in a male-dominated profession, where the rule is to repair the mechanical malfunction and send the patient on his way, the injection of ethics of care into the treatment modality may be just what the doctor should have ordered.

ISSUES

ELLIOT D. COHEN

ETHICAL THEORY AND MENTAL HEALTH PRACTICE

Ethical theory is a branch of philosophical ethics that formulates general criteria or standards for distinguishing the morally good from the morally bad. It is this branch that provides general directions for avoiding evil and for living the

SOURCE: From *The Virtuous Therapist: Ethical Practice of Counseling and Psychotherapy*, 1st ed., by E. Cohen and G. Cohen. © 1999. Reprinted with permission of Wadsworth Publishing, a division of International Thompson Publishing.

(morally) good life. One form of ethical theory that has dominated Western philosophy is *rule (or principle) ethics,* which philosophically defends certain rules or principles of moral conduct. A more recent variety of ethical theory is *care ethics,* which, as developed by feminist thinkers, takes relationships of caring to be central to the mission of ethics. This selection will examine, relate, and illustrate these two types of approaches in the context of mental health practice.

RULE ETHICS

One variety of rule ethics is "utilitarianism" (or the ethics of utility). Formulated in the nineteenth century, this theory has come to be a major current in contemporary ethical theory. According to this theory, actions (or types of action) are morally justified (right) or morally unjustified (wrong) according to the amount of good and evil they can be expected to bring into the world by their performance. When the conduct in question can be expected to produce more good over evil than any available alternative course of action, then it is morally justified; otherwise it is wrong. Thus the principle of utility emerges as the sole standard of moral action.

In its classical form, as formulated by the English philosophers Jeremy Bentham and John Stuart Mill, utilitarianian ethics was hedonistic (from the Greek root *hedone,* meaning "pleasure") in its theory of the good. That is, it took "good" to signify "pleasure"; and its contrary "evil" to signify "pain." So understood, the moral rightness of actions could be calculated by determining their overall tendency to produce pleasure and prevent pain.

For the classical utilitarians, moreover, the pleasures and pains of *all those affected* by the action in question were to be taken into account and counted equally in the "hedonic calculus." Thus, as a principle of *social* utility, the theory went beyond the narrow self-serving concern for the agent's (actor's) own pleasures and pains (or those of significant others), and sought to equally consider the welfare (the pains and pleasures) *of others.*

There are two types of utilitarianism that have been distinguished. They are (1) *act* utilitarianism and (2) *rule* utilitarianism. While the former—act utilitarianism—requires that a separate calculus be undertaken for each individual action that is contemplated, the latter—rule utilitarianism—applies the principle of utility toward the justification of rules and, thus only indirectly, to acts.

Consider, for example, the case of John, a client experiencing suicidal ideation:

> John had unsuccessfully attempted suicide two months prior to entering therapy with Dr. Weinick. The suicidal attempt was precipitated by his having been fired from his job subsequent to his wife having divorced him. John had taken both of these events as proof of his own self-worthlessness and futility of going on with his life. He had been in therapy for just three weeks when he requested to see his counseling records. While state laws normally entitled clients to view their records, Dr. Weinick was convinced that revealing the clinical diagnoses contained in these records—which included "Borderline Personality

Disorder"—would be viewed by John as further confirmation of his own worthlessness and could, at this early stage in therapy, not only jeopardize prospects for successful therapy but could very likely precipitate a second suicide attempt. What was Dr. Weinick to do?

If Dr. Weinick were to apply the act utilitarian principle, he would approach this question by considering whether *in this instance* the disutility (pain, frustration, and potential loss of life) resulting from permitting the client to see his records would be an overriding reason not to permit the client such access. On the one hand, Dr. Weinick would need to decide, on the basis of this client's prior history and clinical assessment, what the probabilities of another suicide attempt would be if this client were permitted to view the records as written. On the other, he would also have to consider the probable outcomes of all other possible alternatives, from that of outright refusing to reveal the records to selectively "editing" the records before revealing them. This calculus would also need to take account of the effects of each option on all those concerned, including the therapist himself. For example, Dr. Weinick would need to consider whether there were legal risks involved in altering these records and whether the harm prevented to his client was worth undertaking such risks.

From a *rule* utilitarian perspective the challenge would be to formulate a professional rule governing client access to records which could be justified by virtue of its tendency to maximize overall utility, at least in the long run, when generally obeyed. Given such a rule, Dr. Weinick could find out what to do without first having to perform a complex "utility calculus."

Of course, it is possible that *two* such rules might, in a given situation, conflict. For example, in the present situation a general rule prescribing respect for client self-determination would seem to require disclosing the records to the client at his request. On the other hand such a rule would appear to conflict with one proscribing doing harm to clients. Given that *each* of these rules is utility maximizing, which rule should take precedence?

One classical response to this question, proposed by J. S. Mill (who appears to have been a rule utilitarian), is to appeal directly to the "first principle" of utility in case of conflict between two "secondary rules." According to Mill, "if utility is the ultimate source of moral obligations, utility may be invoked to decide between them when their demands are incompatible. . . . We must remember that only in these cases of conflict between secondary principles is it requisite that first principles should be appealed to." [1] Thus where the obligation to respect clients' autonomy in viewing their own records conflicts with the obligation not to harm clients, the psychotherapist may appeal directly to the principle of utility to resolve the conflict. However, in situations where no such conflict exists, says Mill, such a utility calculus is not necessary, and appeal to a secondary rule—such as a rule granting clients autonomy in viewing their own records—will suffice.

In formulating utility-maximizing rules, it would also appear that exceptions to the rules may be made *a part of* the rules themselves. For example, a rule permitting client access to records may be more apt to maximize overall utility if it included a qualification excepting cases where such access would (or probably would) cause serious psychological or physical harm to clients. It is, however, unlikely that all exceptions may be conceived of and built into a rule in advance; and such an approach may still sometimes require *some* utility calculation in order to determine whether an exception to the rule actually applies in the first place. For example, Dr. Weinick would still need to assess the risk of harm to John in permitting him to view his counseling records.

Nevertheless, the recognition of exceptions to rules, including legal ones, is important from a rule utilitarian perspective. Consider, for example, the case of Jeannie, a fifteen-year-old female who was two months pregnant:

> When Jeannie first began therapy, she told her therapist, Dr. Jamieson, that the pregnancy was due to having had sexual intercourse with her boyfriend. However, as therapy progressed, she revealed to Dr. Jamieson that she had lied about how she had gotten pregnant, that she never even had a boyfriend, and that the pregnancy was really the result of having been sexually molested by her father, who had repeatedly done so since she was a little girl. Moreover, Jeannie said that her father had threatened her about revealing this fact to anybody and had forbidden her, on religious grounds, from getting an abortion despite her pleas for one. In the state in which Jeannie resided, however, parental consent was required of a minor before being permitted to have an abortion. Thus, Jeannie was being forced, against her protests, into having the child.

While a legal rule requiring parental consent for minors to receive abortions may arguably be held to maximize utility in the majority of cases, it can also be argued that such a rule may overlook important exceptions in which much disutility — pain and suffering — is generated. This would appear to be true in Jeannie's case. Thus, from the rule utilitarian perspective, a better rule, that is, a rule that more closely attained the goal of maximal utility, would be one that avoided the disutility of requiring parental consent in cases where the parent from whom consent is required was also the prospective father of the unborn child. How such a rule could be formulated and practically implemented, however, raises difficulties for the rule utilitarian, for the process of proving in the first place that the minor's father is also the prospective father of the unborn child, and even that of proving that the father sexually molested his daughter, must itself proceed in a manner promoting maximal utility. Inasmuch as the rule in question is part of a larger system of rules, it is the system itself that must be examined for its conduciveness to human happiness. Hence, avoiding the disutility of such exceptional cases may demand changes in other parts of the system — for example, changing standards for proving sexual abuse. What might have seemed to be a simple utility adjustment can thus end up being a rather complex attempt to balance a number of rules within a system of rules.

One criticism of *act* utilitarianism has been its purported ability to justify unjust acts so long as they maximized overall utility. For example, suppose conducting a psychological experiment on certain clients would stand a good chance of providing valuable insights that would, in the long run, benefit many clients suffering from serious psychopathology. However, imagine that the experimental design required that these clients not be informed that they were being used as experimental subjects, and imagine also that there were substantial risks that a certain drug administered (under false pretenses) to these subjects would cause irreversible brain damage resulting in mild intelligence deficits. Nevertheless, given that the experiment would be likely to benefit many mentally ill clients, the theory of act utilitarianism could still justify conducting the experiment. However (so the criticism goes), such action would be unjust, for it would be a violation of the right of these clients not to be made subjects of the experiment without their freely given, informed consent.

Rule utilitarians have, however, responded to the above criticism by maintaining that such unjust acts could never be justified by a system of utility-maximizing rules, since such a system would never contain any rule legitimizing the conducting of psychological experiments on clients without their freely given, informed consent. Indeed, were such a rule to exist, many individuals in need of psychotherapy would be deterred from seeking such therapy for fear of becoming the unwitting "guinea pigs" of experiments.

A further criticism of utilitarianism—which would appear to apply to *both* act and rule forms—has been its insistence that the consequences of actions alone are (ultimately) a sufficient standard of moral action. It is argued that an adequate assessment of the morality of action must also consider the *motive* from which the action proceeds. For example, a person who helps the police rescue a kidnapped child for purposes of collecting a reward—and who, without promise of such reward, would have just as well let the abductors kill the child—produces good results by his deed. Nonetheless, it is questionable that an act so ill motivated could be called "morally good." While the consequences of such an action could reasonably be called "good," the ascription of the term "moral" or "morally good" to such an ill-disposed act is not as clear-cut.

Some utilitarians, for instance, Mill, have responded to this criticism by maintaining that the principle of utility is a standard for assessing the morality of action, not one for assessing the morality of motives or character.[2] However, this response merely assumes that it is possible to morally assess actions independently of their motives; and it is precisely this assumption that some wish to deny.

Immanuel Kant, the famous eighteenth-century German philosopher, proposed a rule-based ethics that emphasized motive exclusive of consequences.[3] While utilitarians try to assess the morality of action exclusively in terms of consequences, Kantians go to the opposite extreme of trying to assess the morality of action exclusively in terms of motive. Thus, for Kant, neither the intention to bring about results nor the actual results of action are relevant to assessing moral worth. Rather, moral action proceeds from a "good will" as manifested in action performed *for the sake of duty*.

According to Kant, an act is performed for the sake of duty when motivated by respect for an unconditional command of reason known as "the categorical imperative." In one form, this principle of duty prescribes acting only in ways that any rational being could consistently accept as universally binding:

"Act as if the maxim of your action were to become through your will a universal law of nature."[4] For example, suppose that a psychotherapist, moved by the desire for money, extended the duration of a client's therapy beyond its usefulness. For Kant, to expose the impropriety of such conduct the therapist in question need only ask whether her "maxim" (motive) of action—in order to make money I will provide services whether needed or not—could be accepted as a "universal law of nature" by any rational being. Since no rational being would herself consent to being so treated were she a client—inasmuch as a client would need to trust her therapist in order for therapy to be useful—no rational being could consistently accept such a practice as universally binding.

Consider, for example, the case of Dr. Schneider, a fifty-seven-year-old male psychologist with a thriving practice:

> Dr. Schneider has recently gone through a divorce after thirty-two years of marriage. Experiencing depression over the ending of his marriage, he has found it difficult to keep his attention focused on what his clients tell him in session. While his case notes have in the past been quite accurate and complete, he has begun to fill them out in a cursory fashion adding further to his lack of recall of case details. On the one hand, Dr. Schneider regrets the present state of his ineptness in treating clients. On the other, the mere thought of referring his present clients only seems to add to his feelings of despair and forlornness. He wonders whether he can get through the present crisis without sacrificing any of his practice, yet he still has the conscience to ask himself if attempting to do so would even be right.

As stated, from Kant's perspective, the moral propriety of actions must be assessed in terms of motive alone. However, if Dr. Schneider were to give up (all or some of) his clients out of concern for their welfare, he would still not—contrary to utilitarianism—be acting morally. Nor would he be acting morally if he were to give up any of his caseload out of a "guilty conscience." While, for Kant, such acts might be expedient, and even *in accordance with* what his duty requires (assuming it is his duty to give up clients), these actions would lack *moral* worth since they would not be done *for the sake of duty*. To accomplish the latter, Dr. Schneider would need to transcend mere expedience and emotionality, and to act out of respect for what *reason*—in the form of the categorical imperative—would prescribe. In looking rationally and dispassionately at his own problem, Dr. Schneider would see that he could not make a universal law out of his maxim—in order to work through my own psychological difficulties, I will provide psychological services inferior to what my clients could obtain elsewhere. Instead, this maxim would be inconsistent with the way any rational being, including Dr. Schneider himself, would want to be treated. Accordingly, *to be moral,* Dr. Schneider would have to surrender his present maxim no matter how emotionally trying for him this might be. This, in turn, might require referring present clients for more competent services as well as not taking on new clients until satisfactorily working through the present crisis.

In ceasing to perceive his clients as mere psychological "crutches," Dr. Schneider would have begun to treat his clients with the respect that they as persons deserve. That is, for Kant, only motives that can be rationally made into universal laws respect the inherent dignity of persons. Kant accordingly accepts a further formulation of his categorical imperative: "Act in such a way that you always treat humanity, whether in your own person or in the person of any other, never simply as a means, but always at the same time as an end." [5] As in the case of Dr. Schneider, to present inferior or unnecessary services on pretense of providing competent therapy would be to treat clients as *objects used or manipulated* ("mere means") instead of as *rational, self-determining agents* ("ends in themselves").

One difficulty of Kantian ethics is its failure to recognize the importance of *context* in ethical decision making. For example, Kant has argued that suicide for self-interested reasons such as to end one's own suffering is *always* wrong since a universal law of destroying life in order to improve it would be self-contradictory.[6] Nevertheless, against Kant, it is arguable that *in some extreme situations* of unmitigated pain and suffering, the disutility of continued existence makes suicide both a reasonable and moral option. Thus Kant's attempt to settle ethical questions—such as whether suicide is ever justified—by abstract calculations without careful consideration of concrete situations appears to oversimplify the realities of ethical decision making.

Consider, for example, the case of Larry, a person with AIDS:

> Larry has been seeing his therapist, Dr. Adler, for eight years. During this time, Dr. Adler has seen Larry's health progressively decline. He has witnessed his wasting away from a robust man to one of virtual skin and bone. He has seen the ravages of Kaposi's sarcoma and the rise of other opportunistic infections, and currently, early signs of cognitive/motor deterioration associated with HIV encephalopathy. It is evident to Dr. Adler that Larry has made his peace with himself and his loved ones and is prepared to die. Larry explains to Dr. Adler his well-organized plan to end his own life before the ravages to his brain foreclose this opportunity. Dr. Adler considers Larry's desire to be a reasonable one under his special circumstances, and he sees no point to try to stop him. Rather, Dr. Adler is deeply sympathetic towards the plight of this client whom he has come to know and respect.

Not only is Dr. Adler's complacent attitude toward Larry's intentions to end his own life legally unclear, the moral question is also not cut-and-dried. Yet, Kant's view leaves little to argument. On that view, Dr. Adler is effectively condoning and permitting an unreasonable and immoral act. There is no allowing for the context in which Larry and his therapist find themselves, and no accounting for the dignity that accrues from taking control of one's own death.

Nor is there any accounting for Dr. Adler's compassion for his client as a basis for noninterference with Larry's suicide, for Kant's theory does not recognize *feelings and emotions* as morally legitimate motives of action. While some philosophers (for example, Hume) have made sentiments such as sympathy the foundation of morality, for Kant an action performed out of such a motive "however right and however amiable it may be, has still no genuine moral worth." [7] By emphasizing reason to the exclusion of emotion, Kant has, indeed, made moral action out to be an affair of cool and dispassionate calculation. However, moral actions occur within the context of interpersonal relations, and such relations are often emotionally charged. While *intense* emotions can destroy moral "objectivity" (as when one flies into a rage), emotional detachment can produce insensitivity toward, and lack of regard for, the welfare, interests, and needs of others. Thus *some* degree of emotional engagement (within reason) would appear relevant to moral action.

According to a third formulation of Kant's "categorical imperative," we should "act always on the maxim of such a will in us as can at the same time look upon itself as making universal law."[8] In other words, our actions should be rationally autonomous, grounded in "universal laws" that we rationally and freely choose. Consider, for example, the case of Kathy, a forty-year-old housewife and mother:

> Kathy is in therapy with Dr. Lipkin for depression. As she explains, "It is as though I am going through the motions of living without feeling like anything really matters. I don't know what's wrong with me. I have a husband who takes good care of me, and three lovely children, but I'm still not happy." While Kathy had earlier hoped to attend college to become a high school Spanish teacher, she got married after graduating from high school, became pregnant, and did not attend college. When Dr. Lipkin asked her if she considered going back to school for teaching, she declared, "It is more important for the man to have a career than the woman anyway. The woman should be at home with the kids." When, however, Dr. Lipkin asked her why it was more important for the man to have a career, and why women and men could not share in parental duties, she became agitated. Eventually, however, she admitted to not being sure why men's careers should be considered more important than women's except that this is what her mother had repeatedly told her when she was a young girl.

From Kant's perspective, in Kathy's uncritical acceptance of male and female gender roles, she had not autonomously and rationally conformed her will to "universal law." Rather, she was moved by forces of emotion and socialization. For Kant, such determination is bondage, not freedom. On the other hand, by beginning to see an inconsistency—"double standard"—in the differential social treatment of women and men, she had begun to transcend these forces, to fashion her will according to universal law rationally determined, and, accordingly, to assert her freedom.

Indeed, for Kant, it is only through such conformity of the will to reason that one can attain freedom and realize one's nature as an end in itself. For him, we are otherwise no different than physical objects (mere means) that are acted upon and completely determined by external forces. However, while some rational engagement may be requisite to our freedom, we need not suppose that emotional engagement or the acceptance of cultural norms cannot themselves be rational and free. While Kant issues an important reminder to avoid being carried away by blind emotion or blind adherence to social rules, this does not mean that a will that is at least partly moved by such extrinsic factors must always be unfree. Kant's emphasis on *pure* reason as the ground of human freedom may thus be unrealistic.

RULE ETHICS AND THE CONCEPT OF A RIGHT

In the context of discussing moral problems, it is not uncommon for one to argue for or against a particular ethical stance by appealing to rights. For example, one might argue against abortion on the grounds that the unborn has a right to life. Talk about rights can only be understood within the context of *rule* ethics. In general, *a right is an interest that is protected by a rule.* To say that a person has a right to something of interest implies that there is a rule that prohibits others from interfering with that interest. Thus, one has a right to life because there is a rule that forbids others from taking away one's life. When the rule in question is a legal rule, then the right in question can be considered a *legal right;* whereas the right is a *moral right* when the rule in question is a moral one. For example, a client may have a legal right to refuse to disclose confidential information in a court of law in a state that recognizes such privilege by statute. This is the so-called legal right of *privileged communication.* On the other hand, in a state where no such statute exists, no such legal right exists. But, it is possible to argue that one has a moral right to such privileged communication even if there is no corresponding legal right. This is possible because one could argue that courts (morally) *should* respect clients' private communications with their therapists.

Insofar as a theory of ethics accommodates rules, talk about rights makes sense from that theoretical perspective. For example, according to *rule* utilitarianism, one has (or should have) a right to something of interest *when general conformity to a rule forbidding interference with that interest can be calculated to maximize overall happiness.* Thus we have a right to life, from this perspective, because general respect for life maximizes overall happiness. Such utilitarian rights are sometimes called *instrumental* or *extrinsic* rights because their recognition depends upon and is a means to the production of (maximal) happiness. On the other hand, Kantian ethics would countenance a right to life because such a rule or maxim can be turned into a universal law of nature and it is just what is required in order to treat others as "ends in themselves." Since Kantian rights are neither dependent upon nor a means to the production of anything further (such as maximal happiness), they are sometimes called *intrinsic* rights.

Because intrinsic rights attach to persons by virtue of their being persons (that is, rational, autonomous beings), such rights have an *inalienable* quality. In contrast, utilitarian rights have a *contingent* character since they are a function of the production of happiness. For example, for Kantians, it would be a violation of rights to apply the death penalty to speeders in order to deter motorists from speeding. Indeed, this would be to treat them as "mere means." Yet, if it could be proven that this would cut down significantly on loss of life on the roadways without generating any overriding negative results, then there would be no basis for recognizing a utilitarian right against such a penalty. Of course, utilitarians may argue that a rule like the one in question would cause overriding distress among motorists. Nevertheless, this is an empirical claim and is always subject to possible disconfirmation.

Because *act* utilitarianism does not accommodate rules, it cannot provide *any* theory of rights. On this brand of utilitarianism, we are supposed to use the utility standard to justify *concrete actions,* not abstract rules or maxims. For example, a particular promise should be kept if it is best on the whole to keep it, not because promise keeping *as a rule* is justified. A further type of ethics that also does not accommodate rules, and accordingly cannot entertain a theory of rights, is *care ethics,* to which we now turn.

CARE ETHICS

While Kantian ethics proposes a master rule (categorical imperative) for the abstract calculation of morality, care ethics links morality to the concrete situation. As advanced by the Harvard psychologist Carol Gilligan, care ethics perceives morality in terms of concrete interpersonal relationships that can only be understood by people who have compassion and empathy for the predicaments of other people. It is about the preservation of such relationships and the prevention of human suffering. In care ethics the primary motive is "the wish not to hurt others and the hope that in morality lies a way of solving conflicts so that no one will get hurt."[9] Caring does not mean that nobody ever actually gets hurt, however, since in the real world our capacity to help others may be limited by time and circumstances. "Although inclusion is the goal of moral consciousness, exclusion may be a necessity of life."[10]

Although care ethics resembles act utilitarianism in its concentration on context (as against abstract rules and talk about rights) and on the consequences of action, it denies that morality is a matter of rational calculation or adding up of pleasures and pains. Rather, moral action involves a sense of what is right in a given situation, a kind of perception as opposed to the product of applying an algorithm. Thus, an ethics of care would not justify wholesale sacrifice of welfare, interest, or needs of any individual(s) because doing so could be calculated to maximize overall utility.

Moreover, unlike the act utilitarian calculation, the act of caring is infused with emotion. In clarifying the notion of caring, Lawrence N. Hinman states:

> Caring has an irremediably emotive component to it. To care about someone is not just to act in particular ways; it is also, and necessarily, to *feel* in particular ways. There would be something odd if a parent tried to add up impersonally all the hedons and dolors for a particular choice that will affect the family. Part of caring is to feel something for the other person.[11]

Consider, for example, the case of Dr. Engle, a psychologist in private practice:

> Mrs. Johnston, a single mother of a thirteen-year-old female, Cindy, called Dr. Engle and explained that Cindy had threatened to commit suicide after she

received news of a close friend having attempted suicide. Mrs. Johnston said that she worked three jobs and that Cindy was often left on her own after school and evenings. She also stated that Cindy was now very distraught over the possibility of being involuntarily placed in an inpatient facility for evaluation, but that no other therapist had agreed to see her on an outpatient basis. Mrs. Johnston was crying and indicated that, although she had no insurance and could not afford Dr. Engle's usual fee of $125, she did not know what to do if Dr. Engle refused to help her. Dr. Engle recalled her own sense of futility and quiet desperation when, as a young adolescent, a close friend of hers committed suicide. As a mother as well as an experienced professional, she also understood what Mrs. Johnston was going through, the pain of watching her baby suffer, the anxiety of not knowing how to make the suffering go away, the feeling of helplessness and loss of control over something so precious. While Dr. Engle could not see Cindy that same day without imposing upon other clients, she was willing and able to see Cindy before regular hours at seven o'clock the following morning at a substantially reduced fee. She advised Mrs. Johnston not to go to work that evening and to keep a close watch on her daughter.

In this case, Dr. Engle did not simply weigh up the pluses and minuses of seeing Cindy on an outpatient basis. Had she done so, she may well have advised Mrs. Johnston to involuntarily check Cindy into a free psychiatric facility. Dr. Engle's response to Mrs. Johnston's desperate plea was itself infused with emotion. She was emotionally in tune with both mother and daughter, and with her own feelings. She really cared, and such caring could not be extracted from such emotionality and relegated to a purely rational process of abstract calculations. She was not simply performing a utility calculus in which the welfare of one person was balanced over that of another. Nor did she consult pure reason in the form of the categorical imperative to find out what her duty was. Rather, her motive was to address the needs of all parties concerned—Cindy, Mrs. Johnston, her other clients—without sacrificing anyone's needs.

While such caring involves an "irremediably emotive component" this should not be taken to mean that it therefore does not also include a rational component. Thus according to Maxine Morphis and Christopher Riesbeck, the ethics of care may be viewed as a function of "case-based reasoning" as opposed to "rule-based reasoning." For example:

> A rule-based model of planning a dinner party might use rules to calculate when to have the party, who to invite, what level of formality to impose, what food to serve, and so on. A case-based approach, on the other hand, would use previous dinner parties as a model, and make modifications based on those experiences. Thus, unfortunate combinations of guests would be avoided, the kind of food that has been popular before would be an obvious option, realistic starting and ending times would be assumed, and so on.[12]

Similarly, in confronting Mrs. Johnston's plea for help, Dr. Engle did not simply apply ethical principles or other prepackaged rules—for example, "If a prospective client can't afford your services, then make a referral" or "If you can't see a potentially suicidal client immediately, then advise placement in an inpatient facility for evaluation." Instead, in coming to a conclusion about how to respond to Mrs. Johnston's plea for help, she began with her own past experiences—as a child in a similar situation, as a mother, as a professional in dealing with similar crises. While these past experiences were infused with emotion, they also provided rational bases for proceeding in the present case. Indeed, these experiences provided reliable information *precisely because* they were emotional. Much as understanding colors requires *seeing in color,* understanding the present case—which was emotional—called for *emotional understanding,* not just cold (dispassionate) perception.

Carol Gilligan provides a further illustration of the case-based nature of care ethics in contrast to a rule-based perspective. In discussing the short story "A Jury Of Her Peers" by Susan Glaspell, in which the character of Minnie Foster is suspected of killing her husband, Gilligan relates the following:

> A neighbor woman and the sheriff's wife accompany the sheriff and the prosecutor to the house of the accused woman. The men representing the law seek evidence that will convince a jury to convict the suspect. The women, collecting things to bring Minnie Foster in jail, enter in this way into the lives lived in the house. Taking in rather than taking apart, they begin to assemble observations and impressions, connecting them to past experience and observations until suddenly they compose a familiar pattern. . . . Discovering a strangled canary buried under pieces of quilting, the women make a series of connections that lead them to understand what happened. The logic that says you don't kill a man because he has killed a bird, the judgment that finds these acts wildly incommensurate, is counterposed to the logic that sees both events as part of a larger pattern—a pattern of detachment and abandonment that led finally to the strangling. . . . Mrs. Peters, the sheriff's wife, recalls that when she was a girl and a boy killed her cat, "If they hadn't held me back I would have—" and realizes that there had been no one to restrain Minnie Foster. . . . Seeing detachment as the crime with murder as its ultimate extension, implicating themselves, and also seeing the connection between their own and Minnie Foster's actions, the women solve the crime. . . .[13]

According to Morphis and Riesbeck a case-based understanding of care ethics helps to explain its contextual as well as its "intuitive" nature.[14] Since case-based reasoning must pay close attention to the *details* of the individual contexts in which interpersonal relationships occur, in order to make *comparative* judgments of present contexts with past ones, such reasoning is indisolubly *contextual* in nature rather than abstract. For example, in order to compare Minnie Foster's life to her own, Mrs. Peters first had to absorb intimate details of the way in which Minnie Foster lived, and by parity of reasoning, Mrs. Peters was then able to put together ("intuit") what really happened. This ability to see deeply into the situation required that Mrs. Peters exercise her powers of *empathetic understanding* to sense what Minnie Foster sensed. It also required what feminist thinkers have recently characterized as *connected knowing,* a way of knowing based upon a commitment to understand the views of others rather than to look for flaws in them.[15] These concepts will be examined in chapter 3. As will become apparent, the ability of therapists to relate personally to intimate aspects of clients' lives—including clients' feelings and emotions— is fundamental to a viable counseling ethic.

The comparative or analogical structure of case-based reasoning may be contrasted to rule-based reasoning insofar as the latter *begins with rules* and (deductively) applies them to specific contexts in order to reach conclusions. For example, from the rule that "You don't kill a man because he has killed a bird," it follows that Minnie Foster must have had other motives for killing her husband. As Gilligan suggests, such abstract and detached logic would have failed to reach a true conclusion.[16] On the other hand, in case-based reasoning, prior cases (such as Mrs. Peters's own experience of what it felt like to have her cat's life destroyed by another human being) stand as *precedents* for adducing conclusions about present cases; thus such reasoning *begins with cases,* rather than with rules.

Nevertheless, in care ethics, rules may still serve heuristically, as guidelines. For example, the Kantian rule of treating persons as ends in themselves and not as mere means may help to call attention to a moral problem inherent in treating persons in a certain way, for example, a therapist's lying to a client, or perhaps (as in the previous example) Dr. Engle's treating Mrs. Johnson or Cindy in a way she herself would not want to be treated. From the perspective of care-based ethics, moral rules provide only a "moral minimum" to moral action. The rest must be provided by attention to the nuances and relevant details of individual contexts such as facts about the lives of concrete persons affected by contemplated actions, appeals to one's own prior experiences, observations, and emotions. In general, moral action must be informed by sensitivity to relevant factors that may be too complex or by their nature not readily captured and formulated by a (prearranged) set of rules. Such a set of rules may thus be "only as good as its role in the correct articulation of the concrete."[17] As Gilligan suggests,

> moral judgment must be informed by "growing insight and sympathy," tempered by the knowledge gained through experience that "general rules" will not lead people "to justice by a ready-made patent method, without the trouble of exerting patience, discrimination, impartiality, without any care to assure whether they have the insight that comes from . . . a life vivid and intense enough to have created a wide, fellow feeling with all that is human."[18]

And, as Morphis and Riesbeck suggest, caring itself is

> not definable by a set of conditions, but rather will be repeatedly tested and will evolve with individuals and with families as well as with culture and with technology. Caring is an art, not a science.[19]

As first proposed by Carol Gilligan, care ethics was intended to call attention to differences between the ways males and females approach morality (as well as the distinct developmental stages women go through in reaching moral maturation). Thus, while morally mature men have been characterized as tending to settle ethical problems by impartially applying universal rules (for instance, Kantian ones) protective of human rights,[20] morally mature women have been characterized in terms of the informal, concrete "injunction to care, a responsibility to discern and alleviate the 'real and recognizable trouble' of this world."[21] Moreover, this injunction to care does not exclude self-regard. Indeed, for Gilligan, what distinguishes morally mature women from many who lack such maturity is appreciation that responsibility to care includes caring about *oneself* as well as about others.[22]

Nevertheless, as Gilligan herself maintains, "development for both sexes . . . would seem to entail an integration of rights and responsibilities through the discovery of the complementarity of these disparate views."[23] Thus an ethics of care need not be viewed as the exclusive domain of women. Indeed, "men can have both masculine and feminine dimensions to their moral voices just as women can have both."[24]

As stated, care ethics perceives morality in terms of the preservation of concrete interpersonal relationships. However, while some relationships may be worthy of maintaining, others such as abusive marriages may not be. Thus it might be argued that care ethics, with its focus upon preservation of relationships, may promote the preservation of even those relationships that are better off terminated.[25]

For example, a marriage counselor who perceives his primary professional goal to be the preservation of the marital relationship, may tend to view it as a professional failure when counseling ends in divorce. Such singlemindedness may accordingly be incompatible with the well-being of a client involved in an abusive or otherwise untenable relationship. Given the proclivity of abuse victims to remain in abusive relationships, any cue from the therapist to the effect that divorce should be avoided if at all possible, the client may, to her detriment, continue in the relationship.

While the above suggests a potential problem in applying care ethics to psychotherapy, it should be borne in mind that care ethics also stresses the responsibility to prevent pain and suffering. Insofar as abusive relationships promote pain and suffering, preservation of such relationships would appear to be, at bottom, inconsistent with the ethics of care.

NOTES

1. J. S. Mill, "Utilitarianism," *Mill: Utilitarianism: Text and Critical Essays,* ed. Samuel Gorovitz (New York: Bobbs-Merrill, 1971), 30.
2. Mill, "Utilitarianism," 25, no. 3.
3. Immanuel Kant, "The Categorical Imperative," *Groundwork of the Metaphysic of Morals,* trans. H. J. Paton (New York: HarperCollins, 1964).
4. Kant, "Categorical Imperative," 89.
5. Ibid., 96.
6. Ibid., 89.
7. Ibid., 66.
8. Ibid., 100.
9. C. Gilligan, "In a Different Voice: Women's Conception of Self and Morality," *Philosophy: History and Problems,* ed. S. Stumpf (New York: McGraw Hill, 1994), 728.

10. C. Gilligan, *In a Different Voice: Psychological Theory and Women's Development* (Cambridge, Mass.: Harvard University Press, 1982), 148.

11. L. M. Hinman, *Ethics: A Pluralistic Approach to Moral Theory* (Fort Worth, Texas: Harcourt Brace, 1981), 336.

12. M. Morphis and C. K. Reisbeck, Feminist ethics and case-based reasoning: A marriage of purpose, *International Journal of Applied Philosophy* 5(2) (1990): 16.

13. C. Gilligan, "Moral Orientation and Moral Development," *Applied Ethics: A Multicultural Approach*, ed. L. May and S. C. Sharratt (Englewood Cliffs, N.J.: Prentice Hall, 1994), 270.

14. M. Morphis and C. K. Reisbeck, Feminist, 20.

15. Goldberger

16. C. Gilligan, "Moral Orientation," 270.

17. M. C. Nussbaum, *Love's Knowledge: Essays on Philosophy and Literature* (New York: Oxford University Press, 1990), 95.

18. C. Gilligan, "Different Voice."

19. M. Morphis and C. K. Reisbeck, Feminist, 23.

20. C. Gilligan, "Moral Orientation," 264.

21. C. Gilligan, "In a Different Voice: Women's Conception of Self and Morality," *Philosophy: History and Problems*, ed. S. Stumpf (New York: McGraw Hill), 731 and C. Gilligan "Moral Orientation," 264.

22. C. Gilligan, "Different Voice," 731.

23. C. Gilligan, "Different Voice," 731.

24. Hinman, *Ethics*, 334.

25. G. R. Beaubot and D. J. Wennemann, *Applied Professional Ethics* (Lanham, Md.: University Press of America), 42.

JOHN STUART MILL

UTILITARIANISM

A passing remark is all that needs be given to the ignorant blunder of supposing that those who stand up for utility as the test of right and wrong use the term in that restricted and merely colloquial sense in which utility is opposed to pleasure. An apology is due to the philosophical opponents of utilitarianism for even the momentary appearance of confounding them with anyone capable of so absurd a misconception; which is the more extraordinary, inasmuch as the contrary accusation, of referring everything to pleasure, and that, too, in its grossest form, is another of the common charges against utilitarianism: and, as has been pointedly remarked by an able writer, the same sort of persons, and often the very same persons, denounce the theory "as impracticably dry when the word 'utility' precedes the word 'pleasure,' and as too practically voluptuous

SOURCE: John Stuart Mill, "Utilitarianism." Reprinted from *Utilitarianism with Critical Essays*, ed. Samuel Gorovitz. (New York: Bobbs-Merrill Company, Inc., 1971), pp. 17–30.

when the word 'pleasure' precedes the word 'utility.'" Those who know anything about the matter are aware that every writer, from Epicurus to Bentham,
who maintained the theory of utility meant by it, not something to be contra-
distinguished from pleasure, but pleasure itself, together with exemption from
pain; and instead of opposing the useful to the agreeable or the ornamental, have
always declared that the useful means these, among other things. Yet the common herd, including the herd of writers, not only in newspapers and periodi-
cals, but in books of weight and pretension, are perpetually falling into this
shallow mistake. Having caught up the word "utilitarian," while knowing nothing whatever about it but its sound, they habitually express by it the rejection
or the neglect of pleasure in some of its forms: of beauty, of ornament, or of
amusement. Nor is the term thus ignorantly misapplied solely in disparagement,
but occasionally in compliment, as though it implied superiority to frivolity and
the mere pleasures of the moment. And this perverted use is the only one in
which the word is popularly known, and the one from which the new generation are acquiring their sole notion of its meaning. Those who introduced the
word, but who had for many years discontinued it as a distinctive appellation,
may well feel themselves called upon to resume it if by doing so they can hope
to contribute anything toward rescuing it from this utter degradation.[1]

The creed which accepts as the foundation of morals "utility" or the
"greatest happiness principle" holds that actions are right in proportion as they
tend to promote happiness; wrong as they tend to produce the reverse of happiness. By happiness is intended pleasure and the absence of pain; by unhappiness, pain and the privation of pleasure. To give a clear view of the moral
standard set up by the theory, much more requires to be said; in particular, what
things it includes in the ideas of pain and pleasure, and to what extent this is
left an open question. But these supplementary explanations do not affect the
theory of life on which this theory of morality is grounded—namely, that pleasure and freedom from pain are the only things desirable as ends; and that all
desirable things (which are as numerous in the utilitarian as in any other scheme)
are desirable either for pleasure inherent in themselves or as means to the pro-
motion of pleasure and the prevention of pain.

Now such a theory of life excites in many minds, and among them in some
of the most estimable in feeling and purpose, inveterate dislike. To suppose that
life has (as they express it) no higher end than pleasure—no better and nobler
object of desire and pursuit—they designate as utterly mean and groveling, as
a doctrine worthy only of swine, to whom the followers of Epicurus were, at a

---

[1] The author of this essay has reason for believing himself to be the first person who brought the word
"utilitarian" into use. He did not invent it, but adopted it from a passing expression in Mr. Galt's
Annals of the Parish. After using it as a designation for several years, he and others abandoned it
from a growing dislike to anything resembling a badge or watchword of sectarian distinction. But
as a name for one single opinion, not a set of opinions—to denote the recognition of utility as a
standard, not any particular way of applying it—the term supplies a want in the language, and offers, in many cases, a convenient mode of avoiding tiresome circumlocution.

very early period, contemptuously likened; and modern holders of the doctrine are occasionally made the subject of equally polite comparisons by its German, French, and English assailants.

When thus attacked, the Epicureans have always answered that it is not they, but their accusers, who represent human nature in a degrading light, since the accusation supposes human beings to be capable of no pleasures except those of which swine are capable. If this supposition were true, the charge could not be gainsaid, but would then be no longer an imputation; for if the sources of pleasure were precisely the same to human beings and to swine, the rule of life which is good enough for the one would be good enough for the other. The comparison of the Epicurean life to that of beasts is felt as degrading, precisely because a beast's pleasures do not satisfy a human being's conceptions of happiness. Human beings have faculties more elevated than the animal appetites and, when once made conscious of them, do not regard anything as happiness which does not include their gratification. I do not, indeed, consider the Epicureans to have been by any means faultless in drawing out their scheme of consequences from the utilitarian principle. To do this in any sufficient manner, many Stoic, as well as Christian, elements require to be included. But there is no known Epicurean theory of life which does not assign to the pleasures of the intellect, of the feelings and imagination, and of the moral sentiments a much higher value as pleasures than to those of mere sensation. It must be admitted, however, that utilitarian writers in general have placed the superiority of mental over bodily pleasures chiefly in the greater permanency, safety, uncostliness, etc., of the former—that is, in their circumstantial advantages rather than in their intrinsic nature. And on all these points utilitarians have fully proved their case; but they might have taken the other and, as it may be called, higher ground with entire consistency. It is quite compatible with the principle of utility to recognize the fact that some kinds of pleasure are more desirable and more valuable than others. It would be absurd that, while in estimating all other things quality is considered as well as quantity, the estimation of pleasure should be supposed to depend on quantity alone.

If I am asked what I mean by difference of quality in pleasures, or what makes one pleasure more valuable than another, merely as a pleasure, except its being greater in amount, there is but one possible answer. Of two pleasures, if there be one to which all or almost all who have experience of both give a decided preference, irrespective of any feeling of moral obligation to prefer it, that is the more desirable pleasure. If one of the two is, by those who are competently acquainted with both, placed so far above the other that they prefer it, even though knowing it to be attended with a greater amount of discontent, and would not resign it for any quantity of the other pleasure which their nature is capable of, we are justified in ascribing to the preferred enjoyment a superiority in quality so far outweighing quantity as to render it, in comparison, of small account.

Now it is an unquestionable fact that those who are equally acquainted with and equally capable of appreciating and enjoying both do give a most marked preference to the manner of existence which employs their higher faculties. Few human creatures would consent to be changed into any of the lower animals for a promise of the fullest allowance of a beast's pleasures; no intelligent human being would consent to be a fool, no instructed person would be an ignoramus, no person of feeling and conscience would be selfish and base, even though they should be persuaded that the fool, the dunce, or the rascal is better satisfied with his lot than they are with theirs. They would not resign what they possess more than he for the most complete satisfaction of all the desires which they have in common with him. If they ever fancy they would, it is only in cases of unhappiness so extreme that to escape from it they would exchange their lot for almost any other, however undesirable in their own eyes. A being of higher faculties requires more to make him happy, is capable probably of more acute suffering, and certainly accessible to it at more points, than one of an inferior type; but in spite of these liabilities, he can never really wish to sink into what he feels to be a lower grade of existence. We may give what explanation we please of this unwillingness; we may attribute it to pride, a name which is given indiscriminately to some of the most and to some of the least estimable feelings of which mankind are capable; we may refer it to the love of liberty and personal independence, an appeal to which was with the Stoics one of the most effective means for the inculcation of it; to the love of power or to the love of excitement, both of which do really enter into and contribute to it; but its most appropriate appellation is a sense of dignity, which all human beings possess in one form or other, and in some, though by no means in exact, proportion to their higher faculties, and which is so essential a part of the happiness of those in whom it is strong that nothing which conflicts with it could be otherwise than momentarily an object of desire to them. Whoever supposes that this preference takes place at a sacrifice of happiness—that the superior being, in anything like equal circumstances, is not happier than the inferior—confounds the two very different ideas of happiness and content. It is indisputable that the being whose capacities of enjoyment are low has the greatest chance of having them fully satisfied; and a highly endowed being will always feel that any happiness which he can look for, as the world is constituted, is imperfect. But he can learn to bear its imperfections, if they are at all bearable; and they will not make him envy the being who is indeed unconscious of the imperfections, but only because he feels not at all the good which those imperfections qualify. It is better to be a human being dissatisfied than a pig satisfied; better to be Socrates dissatisfied than a fool satisfied. And if the fool, or the pig, are of a different opinion, it is because they only know their own side of the question. The other party to the comparison knows both sides.

It may be objected that many who are capable of the higher pleasures occasionally, under the influence of temptation, postpone them to the lower. But this is quite compatible with a full appreciation of the intrinsic superiority of the higher. Men often, from infirmity of character, make their election for the nearer good, though they know it to be the less valuable; and this no less when the choice is between two bodily pleasures than when it is between bodily and mental. They pursue sensual indulgences to the injury of health, though perfectly aware that health is the greater good. It may be further objected that many who begin with youthful enthusiasm for everything noble, as they advance in years, sink into indolence and selfishness. But I do not believe that those who undergo this very common change voluntarily choose the lower description of pleasures in preference to the higher. I believe that, before they devote themselves exclusively to the one, they have already become incapable of the other. Capacity for the nobler feelings is in most natures a very tender plant, easily killed, not only by hostile influences, but by mere want of sustenance; and in the majority of young persons it speedily dies away if the occupations to which their position in life has devoted them, and the society into which it has thrown them, are not favorable to keeping that higher capacity in exercise. Men lose their high aspirations as they lose their intellectual tastes, because they have not time or opportunity for indulging them; and they addict themselves to inferior pleasures, not because they deliberately prefer them, but because they are either the only ones to which they have access or the only ones which they are any longer capable of enjoying. It may be questioned whether anyone who has remained equally susceptible to both classes of pleasures ever knowingly and calmly preferred the lower, though many, in all ages, have broken down in an ineffectual attempt to combine both.

From this verdict of the only competent judges, I apprehend there can be no appeal. On a question which is the best worth having of two pleasures, or which of two modes of existence is the most grateful to the feelings, apart from its moral attributes and from its consequences, the judgment of those who are qualified by knowledge of both, or, if they differ, that of the majority among them, must be admitted as final. And there needs be the less hesitation to accept this judgment respecting the quality of pleasures, since there is no other tribunal to be referred to even on the question of quantity. What means are there of determining which is the acutest of two pains, or the intensest of two pleasurable sensations, except the general suffrage of those who are familiar with both? Neither pains nor pleasures are homogeneous, and pain is always heterogeneous with pleasure. What is there to decide whether a particular pleasure is worth purchasing at the cost of a particular pain, except the feelings and judgment of the experienced? When, therefore, those feelings and judgment declare the pleasures derived from the higher faculties to be preferable *in kind,* apart from the question of intensity, to those of which the animal nature, disjoined from the higher faculties, is susceptible, they are entitled on this subject to the same regard. . . .

I must again repeat what the assailants of utilitarianism seldom have the justice to acknowledge, that the happiness which forms the utilitarian standard of what is right in conduct is not the agent's own happiness but that of all concerned. As between his own happiness and that of others, utilitarianism requires him to be as strictly impartial as a disinterested and benevolent spectator. In the golden rule of Jesus of Nazareth, we read the complete spirit of the ethics of utility. "To do as you would be done by," and "to love your neighbor as yourself," constitute the ideal perfection of utilitarian morality. As the means of making the nearest approach to this ideal, utility would enjoin, first, that laws and social arrangements should place the happiness or (as, speaking practically, it may be called) the interest of every individual as nearly as possible in harmony with the interest of the whole; and, secondly, that education and opinion, which have so vast a power over human character, should so use that power as to establish in the mind of every individual an indissoluble association between his own happiness and the good of the whole, especially between his own happiness and the practice of such modes of conduct, negative and positive, as regard for the universal happiness prescribes; so that not only he may be unable to conceive the possibility of happiness to himself, consistently with conduct opposed to the general good, but also that a direct impulse to promote the general good may be in every individual one of the habitual motives of action, and the sentiments connected therewith may fill a large and prominent place in every human being's sentient existence. If the impugners of the utilitarian morality represented it to their own minds in this its true character, I know not what recommendation possessed by any other morality they could possibly affirm to be wanting to it; what more beautiful or more exalted developments of human nature any other ethical system can be supposed to foster, or what springs of action, not accessible to the utilitarian, such systems rely on for giving effect to their mandates.

The objectors to utilitarianism cannot always be charged with representing it in a discreditable light. On the contrary, those among them who entertain anything like a just idea of its disinterested character sometimes find fault with its standard as being too high for humanity. They say it is exacting too much to require that people shall always act from the inducement of promoting the general interests of society. But this is to mistake the very meaning of a standard of morals and confound the rule of action with the motive of it. It is the business of ethics to tell us what are our duties, or by what test we may know them; but no system of ethics requires that the sole motive of all we do shall be a feeling of duty; on the contrary, ninety-nine hundredths of all our actions are done from other motives, and rightly so done if the rule of duty does not condemn them. It is the more unjust to utilitarianisin that this particular misapprehension should be made a ground of objection to it, inasmuch as utilitarian moralists have gone beyond almost all others in affirming that the motive has nothing to do with the morality of the action, though much with the worth of the agent. He who saves a fellow creature from drowning does what is morally right, whether his motive be duty or the hope of being paid for his trouble; he who betrays the friend that trusts him is guilty of a crime, even if his object be to serve another friend to whom he is under greater obligations. But to speak only of actions done from the motive of duty, and in direct obedience to principle: it is a misapprehension of the utilitarian mode of thought to conceive it as implying that people should fix their minds upon so wide a generality as the world, or society at large. The great majority of good actions are intended not for the benefit of the world, but for that of individuals, of which the good of the world is made up; and the thoughts of the most virtuous man need not on these occasions travel beyond the particular persons concerned, except so far as is necessary to assure himself that in benefiting them he is not violating the rights, that is, the legitimate and authorized expectations, of anyone else. The multiplication of happiness is, according to the utilitarian ethics, the object of virtue: the occasions on which any person (except one in a thousand) has it in his power to do this on an extended scale—in other words, to be a public benefactor—are but exceptional; and on these occasions alone is he called on to consider public utility; in every other case, private utility, the interest or happiness of some few persons, is all he has to attend to. Those alone the influence of whose actions extends to society in general need concern themselves habitually about so large an object. In the case of abstinences indeed—of things which people forbear to do from moral considerations, though the consequences in the particular case might be beneficial—it would be unworthy of an intelligent agent not to be consciously aware that the action is of a class which, if practiced generally, would be generally injurious, and that this is the ground of the obligation to abstain from it. The amount of regard for the public interest implied in this recognition is no greater than is demanded by every system of morals, for they all enjoin to abstain from whatever is manifestly pernicious to society. . . .

We not uncommonly hear the doctrine of utility inveighed against as a *godless* doctrine. If it be necessary to say anything at all against so mere an assumption, we may say that the question depends upon what idea we have formed of the moral character of the Deity. If it be a true belief that God desires, above all things, the happiness of his creatures, and that this was his purpose in their creation, utility is not only not a godless doctrine, but more profoundly religious than any other. If it be meant that utilitarianism does not recognize the revealed will of God as the supreme law of morals, I answer that a utilitarian who believes in the perfect goodness and wisdom of *God* necessarily believes that whatever God has thought fit to reveal on the subject of morals must fulfill the requirements of utility in a supreme degree. . . .

Again, defenders of utility often find themselves called upon to reply to such objections as this—that there is not time, previous to action, for calculating and weighing the effects of any line of conduct on the general happiness. This is exactly as if anyone were to say that it is impossible to guide our conduct by Christianity because there is not time, on every occasion on which anything has to be done, to read through the Old and New Testaments. The answer to the objection is that there has been ample time, namely, the whole past duration of the human species. During all that time mankind have been learning by experience the tendencies of actions; on which experience all the prudence as well as all the morality of life are dependent. People talk as if the commencement of this course of experience had hitherto been put off, and as if, at the moment when some man feels tempted to meddle with the property or life of another, he had to begin considering for the first time whether murder and theft are injurious to human happiness. Even then I do not think that he would find the question very puzzling; but, at all events, the matter is now done to his hand. It is truly a whimsical supposition that, if mankind were agreed in considering utility to be the test of morality, they would remain without any agreement as to what *is* useful, and would take no measures for having their notions on the subject taught to the young and enforced by law and opinion. There is no difficulty in proving any ethical standard whatever to work ill if we suppose universal idiocy to be conjoined with it; but on any hypothesis short of that, mankind must by this time have acquired positive beliefs as to the effects of some actions on their happiness; and the beliefs which have thus come down are the rules of morality for the multitude, and for the philosopher until he has succeeded in finding better. That philosophers might easily do this, even now, on many subjects; that the received code of ethics is by no means of divine right; and that mankind have still much to learn as to the effects of actions on the general happiness, I admit or rather earnestly maintain. The corollaries from the principle of utility, like the precepts of every practical art, admit of indefinite improvement, and, in a progressive state of the human mind, their improvement is perpetually going on. But to consider the rules of morality as improvable is one thing; to pass over the intermediate generalization entirely and endeavor to test each individual action directly by the first principle is another. It is a strange notion that the acknowledgment of a first principle is inconsistent with the admission of secondary ones. To inform a traveler respecting the place of his ultimate destination is not to forbid the use of landmarks and direction-posts on the way. The proposition that happiness is the end and aim of morality does not mean that no road ought to be laid down to that goal, or that persons going thither should not be advised to take one direction rather than another. Men really ought to leave off talking a kind of nonsense on this subject, which they would neither talk nor listen to on other matters of practical concernment. Nobody argues that the art of navigation is not founded on astronomy because sailors cannot wait to calculate the Nautical Almanac. Being rational creatures, they go to sea with it ready calculated; and all rational creatures go out upon the sea of life with their minds made up on the common questions of right and wrong, as well as on many of the far more difficult questions of wise and foolish. And this, as long as foresight is a human quality, it is to be presumed they will continue to do. Whatever we adopt as the fundamental principle of morality, we require subordinate principles to apply it by; the impossibility of doing without them, being common to all systems, can afford no argument against any one in particular; but gravely to argue as if no such secondary principles could be had, and as if mankind had remained till now, and always must remain, without drawing any general conclusions from the experience of human life is as high a pitch, I think, as absurdity has ever reached in philosophical controversy.

The remainder of the stock arguments against utilitarianism mostly consist in laying to its charge the common infirmities of human nature, and the general difficulties which embarrass conscientious persons in shaping their course through life. We are told that a utilitarian will be apt to make his own particular case an exception to moral rules, and, when under temptation, will see a utility in the breach of a rule, greater than he will see in its observance. But is utility the only creed which is able to furnish us with excuses for evil-doing and means of cheating our own conscience? They are afforded in abundance by all doctrines which recognize as a fact in morals the existence of conflicting considerations, which all doctrines do that have been believed by sane persons. It is not the fault of any creed, but of the complicated nature of human affairs, that rules of conduct cannot be so framed as to require no exceptions, and that hardly any kind of action can safely be laid down as either always obligatory or always condemnable. There is no ethical creed which does not temper the rigidity of its laws by giving a certain latitude, under the moral responsibility of the agent, for accommodation to peculiarities of circumstances; and under every creed, at the opening thus made, self-deception and dishonest casuistry get in. There exists no moral system under which there do not arise unequivocal cases of conflicting obligation. These are the real difficulties, the knotty points both in the theory of ethics and in the conscientious guidance of personal conduct. They are overcome practically, with greater or with less success, according to the intellect and virtue of the individual; but it can hardly be pretended that anyone will be the less qualified for dealing with them, from possessing an ultimate standard to which conflicting rights and duties can be referred. If utility is the ultimate source of moral obligations, utility may be invoked to decide between them when their demands are incompatible. Though the application of the standard may be difficult, it is better than none at all; while in other systems, the moral laws all claiming independent authority, there is no common umpire entitled to interfere between them; their claims to precedence one over another rest on little better than sophistry, and, unless determined, as they generally are, by the unacknowledged influence of consideration of utility, afford a free scope for the action of personal desires and partialities. We must remember that only in these cases of conflict between secondary principles is it requisite that first principles should be appealed to. There is no case of moral obligation in which some secondary principle is not involved; and if only one, there can seldom be any real doubt which one it is, in the mind of any person by whom the principle itself is recognized.

IMMANUEL KANT

THE CATEGORICAL IMPERATIVE

[CLASSIFICATION OF IMPERATIVES.]

All *imperatives* command either *hypothetically* or *categorically*. Hypothetical imperatives declare a possible action to be practically neccessary as a means to the attainment of something else that one wills (or that one may will). A categorical imperative would be one which represented an action as objectively necessary in itself apart from its relation to a further end. . . .

SOURCE: Immanuel Kant, "The Categorical Imperative." Reprinted from Immanuel Kant, *Groundwork of the Metaphysic of Morals*, trans. H. J. Paton (New York: Harper and Row, 1964). Reprinted with permission from Hutchinson Publishing Group.

[THE FORMULA OF UNIVERSAL LAW. . . .]

When I conceive a *hypothetical* imperative in general, I do not know before-hand what it will contain—until its condition is given. But if I conceive a *categorical* imperative, I know at once what it contains. For since besides the law this imperative contains only the necessity that our maxim* should conform to this law, while the law, as we have seen, contains no condition to limit it, there remains nothing over to which the maxim has to conform except the universality of a law as such; and it is this conformity alone that the imperative properly asserts to be necessary.

There is therefore only a single categorical imperative and it is this: '*Act only on that maxim through which you can at the same time will that it should become a universal law.*'

Now if all imperatives of duty can be derived from this one imperative as their principle, then even although we leave it unsettled whether what we call duty may not be an empty concept, we shall still be able to show at least what we understand by it and what the concept means. . . .

[ILLUSTRATIONS.]

We will now enumerate a few duties, following their customary division into duties towards self and duties towards others and into perfect and imperfect duties.**

1. A man feels sick of life as the result of a series of misfortunes that has mounted to the point of despair, but he is still so far in possession of his reason as to ask himself whether taking his own life may not be contrary to his duty to himself. He now applies the test 'Can the maxim of my action really become a universal law of nature?' His maxim is 'From self-love I make it my principle to shorten my life if its continuance threatens more evil than it promises pleasure'. The only further question to ask is whether this principle of self-love can become a universal law of nature. It is then seen at once that a system of nature by whose law the very same feeling whose function (*Bestimmung*) is to stimulate the furtherance of life should actually destroy life would contradict itself

---

*A *maxim* is a subjective principle of action and must be distinguished from an *objective principle*—namely, a practical law. The former contains a practical rule determined by reason in accordance with the conditions of the subject (often his ignorance or again his inclinations): it is thus a principle on which the subject *acts*. A law, on the other hand, is an objective principle valid for every rational being; and it is a principle on which he *ought to act*—that is, an imperative.

**It should be noted that I reserve my division of duties entirely for a future *Metaphysic of Morals* and that my present division is therefore put forward as arbitrary (merely for the purpose of arranging my examples). Further, I understand here by a perfect duty one which allows no exception in the interests of inclination, and so I recognize among *perfect duties*, not only outer ones, but also inner. This is contrary to the accepted usage of the schools, but I do not intend to justify it here, since for my purpose it is all one whether this point is conceded or not.

and consequently could not subsist as a system of nature. Hence this maxim cannot possibly hold as a universal law of nature and is therefore entirely opposed to the supreme principle of all duty.

2. Another finds himself driven to borrowing money because of need. He well knows that he will not be able to pay it back; but he sees too that he will get no loan unless he gives a firm promise to pay it back within a fixed time. He is inclined to make such a promise; but he has still enough conscience to ask 'Is it not unlawful and contrary to duty to get out of difficulties in this way?' Supposing, however, he did resolve to do so, the maxim of his action would run thus: 'Whenever I believe myself short of money, I will borrow money and promise to pay it back, though I know that this will never be done'. Now this principle of self-love or personal advantage is perhaps quite compatible with my own entire future welfare; only there remains the question 'Is it right?' I therefore transform the demand of self-love into a universal law and frame my question thus: 'How would things stand if my maxim became a universal law?' I then see straight away that this maxim can never rank as a universal law of nature and be self-consistent, but must necessarily contradict itself. For the universality of a law that every one believing himself to be in need can make any promise he pleases with the intention not to keep it would make promising, and the very purpose of promising, itself impossible, since no one would believe he was being promised anything, but would laugh at utterances of this kind as empty shams.

3. A third finds in himself a talent whose cultivation would make him a useful man for all sorts of purposes. But he sees himself in comfortable circumstances, and he prefers to give himself up to pleasure rather than to bother about increasing and improving his fortunate natural aptitudes. Yet he asks himself further 'Does my maxim of neglecting my natural gifts, besides agreeing in itself with my tendency to indulgence, agree also with what is called duty?' He then sees that a system of nature could indeed always subsist under such a universal law, although (like the South Sea Islanders) every man should let his talents rust and should be bent on devoting his life solely to idleness, indulgence, procreation, and, in a word, to enjoyment. Only he cannot possibly *will* that this should become a universal law of nature or should be implanted in us as such a law by a natural instinct. For as a rational being he necessarily wills that all his powers should be developed, since they serve him, and are given him, for all sorts of possible ends.

4. Yet a *fourth* is himself flourishing; but he sees others who have to struggle with great hardships (and whom he could easily help); and he thinks 'What does it matter to me? Let every one be as happy as Heaven wills or as he can make himself; I won't deprive him of anything; I won't even envy him; only I have no wish to contribute anything to his well-being or to his support in distress!' Now admittedly if such an attitude were a universal law of nature, mankind could get on perfectly well—better no doubt than if everybody prates

about sympathy and goodwill, and even takes pains, on occasion, to practise them, but on the other hand cheats where he can, traffics in human rights, or violates them in other ways. But although it is possible that a universal law of nature could subsist in harmony with this maxim, yet it is impossible to *will* that such a principle should hold everywhere as a law of nature. For a will which decided in this way would be in conflict with itself, since many a situation might arise in which the man needed love and sympathy from others, and in which, by such a law of nature sprung from his own will, he would rob himself of all hope of the help he wants for himself. . . .

[THE FORMULA OF THE END IN ITSELF.]

The will is conceived as a power of determining oneself to action *in accordance with the idea of certain laws*. And such a power can be found only in rational beings. Now what serves the will as a subjective ground of its self-determination is an *end;* and this, if it is given by reason alone, must be equally valid for all rational beings. What, on the other hand, contains merely the ground of the possibility of an action whose effect is an end is called a *means.* The subjective ground of a desire is an *impulsion (Triebfeder);* the objective ground of a volition is a *motive (Bewegungsgrund).* Hence the difference between subjective ends, which are based on impulsions, and objective ends, which depend on motives valid for every rational being. Practical principles are *formal* if they abstract from all subjective ends; they are *material,* on the other hand, if they are based on such ends and consequently on certain impulsions. Ends that a rational being adopts arbitrarily as *effects* of his action (material ends) are in every case only relative; for it is solely their relation to special characteristics in the subject's power of appetition which gives them their value. Hence this value can provide no universal principles, no principles valid and necessary for all rational beings and also for every volition—that is, no practical laws. Consequently all these relative ends can be the ground only of hypothetical imperatives.

Suppose, however, there were something *whose existence* has *in itself* an absolute value, something which as *an end in itself* could be a ground of determinate laws; then in it, and in it alone, would there be the ground of a possible categorical imperative—that is, of a practical law.

Now I say that man, and in general every rational being, *exists* as an end in himself, *not merely as a means* for arbitrary use by this or that will: he must in all his actions, whether they are directed to himself or to other rational beings, always be viewed *at the same time as an end.* All the objects of inclination have only a conditioned value; for if there were not these inclinations and the needs grounded on them, their object would be valueless. Inclinations themselves, as sources of needs, are so far from having an absolute value to make them desirable for their own sake that it must rather be the universal wish of every rational being to be wholly free from them. Thus the value of all objects that can *be produced* by our action is always conditioned. Beings whose existence depends, not on our will, but on nature, have none the less, if they are non-rational beings, only a relative value as means and are consequently called *things*. Rational beings, on the other hand, are called *persons* because their nature already marks them out as ends in themselves—that is, as something which ought not to be used merely as a means—and consequently imposes to that extent a limit on all arbitrary treatment of them (and is an object of reverence). Persons, therefore, are not merely subjective ends whose existence as an object of our actions has a value *for us:* they are *objective ends*—that is, things whose existence is in itself an end, and indeed an end such that in its place we can put no other end to which they should serve *simply* as means; for unless this is so, nothing at all of *absolute* value would be found anywhere. But if all value were conditioned—that is, contingent—then no supreme principle could be found for reason at all.

If then there is to be a supreme practical principle and—so far as the human will is concerned—a categorical imperative, it must be such that from the idea of something which is necessarily an end for every one because it is an *end in itself* it forms an *objective* principle of the will and consequently can serve as a practical law. The ground of this principle is: *Rational nature exists as an end in itself*. This is the way in which a man necessarily conceives his own existence: it is therefore so far a *subjective* principle of human actions. But it is also the way in which every other rational being conceives his existence on the same rational ground which is valid also for me; hence it is at the same time an *objective* principle, from which, as a supreme practical ground, it must be possible to derive all laws for the will. The practical imperative will therefore be as follows: *Act in such a way that you always treat humanity, whether in your own person or in the person of any other, never simply as a means, but always at the same time as an end*. We will now consider whether this can be carried out in practice. . . .

[THE FORMULA OF AUTONOMY.]

This principle of humanity, and in general of every rational agent, *as an end in itself* (a principle which is the supreme limiting condition of every man's freedom of action) is not borrowed from experience; firstly, because it is universal, applying as it does to all rational beings as such, and no experience is adequate to determine universality; secondly, because in it humanity is conceived, not as an end of man (subjectively)—that is, as an object which, as a matter of fact, happens to be made an end—but as an objective end—one which, be our ends what they may, must, as a law, constitute the supreme limiting condition of all subjective ends, and so must spring from pure reason. That is to say, the ground for every enactment of practical law lies *objectively in the rule* and in the form of universality which (according to our first principle) makes the rule capable of being a law (and indeed a law of nature); *subjectively*, however, it lies in the *end;* but (according to our second principle) the subject of all ends is to be found in every rational being as an end in himself. From this there now follows our third practical principle for the will—as the supreme condition of the will's conformity with universal practical reason—namely, the Idea *of the will of every rational being as a will which makes universal law.*

By this principle all maxims are repudiated which cannot accord with the will's own enactment of universal law. The will is therefore not merely subject to the law, but is so subject that it must be considered as also *making the law* for itself and precisely on this account as first of all subject to the law (of which it can regard itself as the author).

[The Exclusion of Interest. . . .]

Once we conceive a will of this kind, it becomes clear that while a will *which is subject to law* may be bound to this law by some interest, nevertheless a will which is itself a supreme lawgiver cannot possibly as such depend on any interest; for a will which is dependent in this way would itself require yet a further law in order to restrict the interest of self-love to the condition that this interest should itself be valid as a universal law.

Thus the *principle* that every human will *is a will which by all its maxims enacts universal law**—provided only that it were right in other ways—would be *well suited* to be a categorical imperative in this respect: that precisely because of the Idea of making universal law it is *based on no interest* and consequently can alone among all possible imperatives be *unconditioned.* Or better still—to convert the proposition—if there is a categorical imperative (that is, a law for the will of every rational being), it can command us only to act always on the maxim of such a will in us as can at the same time look upon itself as making universal law; for only then is the practical principle and the imperative which we obey unconditioned, since it is wholly impossible for it to be based on any interest.

We need not now wonder, when we look back upon all the previous efforts that have been made to discover the principle of morality, why they have one and all been bound to fail. Their authors saw man as tied to laws by his duty, but it never occurred to them that he is subject only to *laws which are made by himself* and yet are *universal,* and that he is bound only to act in conformity with a will which is his own but has as nature's purpose for it the function of making universal law. For when they thought of man merely as subject to a law (whatever it might be), the law had to carry with it some interest in order to attract or compel, because it did not spring as a law from *his own* will: in order to conform with the law his will had to be necessitated by *something else* to act in a certain way. This absolutely inevitable conclusion meant that all the labour spent in trying to find a supreme principle of duty was lost beyond recall; for what they discovered was never duty, but only the necessity of acting from a certain interest. This interest might be one's own or another's; but on such a view the imperative was bound to be always a conditioned one and could not

---

*I may be excused from bringing forward examples to illustrate this principle, since those which were first used as illustrations of the categorical imperative and its formula can all serve this purpose here.

possibly serve as a moral law. I will therefore call my principle the principle of the *Autonomy* of the will in contrast with all others, which I consequently class under *Heteronomy*.

PRACTICE

CLIFTON B. PERRY

THE PHILOSOPHER AS ETHICS CONSULTANT IN A PSYCHIATRIC WARD

From January 1981 through March 1981, and again from July 1982 through July 1983, I held fellowships in clinical medical ethics at the University of Tennessee Medical School with the Program on Human Values and Ethics. My role as a medical ethics fellow was that of student and consultant. As a student I was permitted to go on working and teaching rounds and see first hand the problems that arise within the medical context. As a consultant I participated in the activities of working and teaching rounds and periodically conducted what are known as Ethics Grand Rounds.

Ethics Grand Rounds were generally conducted once a month and were held in the medical school's various core departments, for example, internal medicine, surgery, psychiatry, and the like. The purpose of such rounds is to investigate the ethical problems that *actually arise* within a particular clinical setting. During one Ethics Grand Round I was asked to comment on a case I had previously confronted on teaching rounds.[1]

In preparation for going on rounds in the Department of Psychiatry, I had learned that certain affective disorders are associated with compromised or diminished cognitive and emotional capacities and, thus, with one's ability to act as a fully autonomous individual. Some of the personality problems, for example, paranoia, schizophrenia, hysteria, depression, and agoraphobia, have been treated successfully, to varying degrees, through sundry drug regimes: neuroleptics, such as Haldol; phenothiazines, such as Thorazine and Stelazine; tricyclic antidepressants, such as Pertegrane and Sinequan, for example. Rather dramatic therapeutic results, I discovered, have been achieved in the treatment

SOURCE: This paper is based upon an earlier paper entitled "A Problem with Refusing Certain Forms of Psychiatric Treatment" which appeared in *Soc. Sci. Med* (1985) Vol. 20, No. 6, pp. 645–648. The author also wishes to acknowledge and thank Elliot Cohen and Marcia Rossi for their help with this paper.

Clifton B. Perry received his Ph.D. in philosophy from the University of California, Santa Barbara, in 1976, and is presently professor of philosophy at Auburn
University. Dr. Perry has published numerous articles in diverse areas of applied
philosophy. His work experience in applying philosophy includes conducting
in-service programs on nursing ethics at St. Jude's Children's Research Hospital in
Memphis, Tennessee; conducting Ethical Grand Rounds in the Department of Internal Medicine, Psychiatry, Pediatrics, and Surgery at the University of Tennessee
Medical School; and working as a congressional aide (through an American Philosophical Association congressional fellowship) in the United States Congress. Recently earning his Juris Doctorate, Dr. Perry was admitted to the Alabama and New
Mexico Bars. Also intrigued by federal Indian law and tribal law, he has taken and
passed the Navajo Nation bar exam (1997) and the Jicarilla Apache Nation bar
exam (1998).

of mania from the administration of lithium carbonate.[2] Continued treatment
with lithium has in many cases been successful in rendering previously incompetent manic patients fully capable of competent self-governance.

While on rounds in the Department of Psychiatry, I encountered a case that
posed a very perplexing problem. A thirty-three-year-old male[3] was admitted
to a local emergency room for a fractured radius suffered while playing foot-
ball. Lab and physical exams revealed no renal, cardiac, or neurological problems and no fluid or electrolyte imbalances. Still, the patient exhibited excessive
excitement, mood elevation, psychomotor overactivity, overproduction of ideas,
and delusions of grandeur. Hospital records revealed that the patient had been
previously diagnosed as manic, a diagnosis subsequently corroborated by the
Brief Psychiatric Rating Scale. Records also indicated that he had been successfully treated with a psychotropic medication named lithium carbonate. The

patient was given Phenolthiazone and 500 mg. of Lithium t.i.d. and transferred to the psychiatric ward. In ten days, he scored within acceptable levels on the *Brief Psychiatric Rating Scale* with no toxic reactions to the lithium. At this juncture, the patient, while fully rational, said, "I rather enjoy my prior state. Being straight is a bore; I don't want any more lithium."

I realized that there is considerable reluctance to allow *incompetent* individuals the freedom to refuse either life-preserving medical treatment[4] or that psychiatric treatment deemed essential for achieving self-determination.[5] By contrast, there seems to be much less reluctance to allow *competent* individuals the freedom to refuse life-saving medical attention.[6] It is out of respect for personal autonomy that *competent,* as opposed to *incompetent,* individuals are allowed to be self-directed even if *patient death* is the result of such patient directives. But is such respect for the competent individual's autonomy to be granted carte blanche? Should a manic, who might very well be restored to mental health, be allowed to refuse that treatment necessary for continued competence?[7]

I thought a contrasting case might help answer this question. If we have our "ethical feet" on a second case and the manic case is analogous to the second, then we shall be able to reasonably respond to the problem posed by the manic. Fortunately, one of my colleagues was a consultant in a case that I thought might prove analogous and within which the ethical dimensions were fairly worked out. In that case a forty-three-year-old male was admitted to an emergency room at a local hospital, for internal bleeding after a tree had fallen on him. It was determined that the patient required whole blood transfusions. Nevertheless, when given an informed consent sheet, he refused to sign it, arguing, "I very much want to live, but I do not want to be denied the opportunity to enjoy everlasting life." The patient was a Jehovah's Witness.

I thought it could be argued that forcing a presently *incompetent* patient to undergo psychiatric treatment could be considered permissible for two reasons. First, there is the *utilitarian* consideration of concern for overall happiness. The manic may cause harm to others or to himself.[8] Second, the psychiatric treatment, that is, lithium, is designed to restore that patient's capacity to engage in self-regulating behavior.

But can we force the presently *drug-induced competent* patient to continue that therapy necessary to retain his competent state after he has refused such therapy? There may be, of course, very good utilitarian reasons for not forcing a presently drug-induced competent patient to continue that psychiatric treatment necessary for his continued state of competency, for example, the possible deleterious effects due to long-term use of the drug. However, what if there are no such deleterious effects? Shall we pay respect to the decision made by the now drug-restored competent patient who rationally weighs the benefit of being a responsible self-directive individual (with all of its attendant joys and sorrows) against the elation of a manic-high and decides that being mildly psychotic is better? That is, shall we allow our manic patient, in the absence of deleterious or otherwise untoward sequellae of the drug regimes and the absence of any possibility of harm to third parties, to refuse to continue that psychiatric therapy necessary for his continued competency in favor of the incompetent manic-high? If there are no known utilitarian counterconsiderations, what reasons could possibly be promulgated in support of forcing our presently competent psychiatric patient to continue the psychiatric treatment necessary for continued competency if during the period of competency, the patient refused further treatment?

Our analysis may initially appear to favor the manic's request. The manic might argue that there is no transgression of other's rights in allowing him to return to his manic state, and there may indeed be more happiness propagated by allowing him to be truly happy with no harm to others than to make him unhappy with no harm to others. Moreover, the manic might point out that if the refusal of life-saving blood by the Jehovah's Witness will be respected because of his *Kantian* grounded right of autonomy, then, by analogy, the presently competent manic's refusal to continue appropriate treatment should likewise be respected. Conforming to the respective refusals of each patient demonstrates a respect for patient autonomy. That the manic's subsequent autonomous and competent behavior is achieved in many cases through drugs is irrelevant to whether or not each patient is currently fully autonomous.

The manic, I suspect, might be able to argue that the cases of refusing life-preserving treatment and refusing modifying drugs are analogous in that each demonstrates respect for patient autonomy *at the expense of* patient well-being. Although the Jehovah's Witness, who is allowed to die, may have his *personal interests* furthered, it is doubtful that his well-being is furthered.[9] Respecting the refusal of blood is to respect patient autonomy at the expense of patient well-being. It might likewise be maintained that allowing the presently competent manic to refuse further psychiatric therapy is to show respect for patient autonomy at the expense of patient well-being. Respect for patient autonomy, as manifested through respecting the patient's considered wishes, would demand parity of treatment in each case. If the essential blood transfusion would be withheld from the unconscious Jehovah's Witness through the substitution of the previously expressed refusal by the competent individual, then the same substitutional respect for patient autonomy would dictate withholding lithium from the manic who refuses, while competent, the psychiatric treatment necessary for the continuance of his competent state.

If *utililarian* considerations, for example, patient welfare, were to mitigate respect for patient autonomy, it would seem more reasonable that it should do so in the case of the Jehovah's Witness, where harm to the patient is complete and irreversible, rather than in the case of the manic, where the harm is only partial and reversible. Therefore, the manic might argue that, not only does the Kantian respect for patient autonomy, when conjoined with the principle of fairness, demand parity of treatment in each case, but also that if transgressions of patient autonomy are going to be made in the name of the utilitarian concern for patient welfare, it should more easily occur in the case of refusing life-saving treatment than in the case of refusing psychiatric treatment.

One physician argued that the manic who refuses that therapy necessary for continued competency eventually places himself in the ineluctable position of having the psychiatric therapy administered since an incompetent patient is usually treated according to the utilitarian principle of beneficence. That is, it may well seem that after the manic returns to the diminished state, it is the psychiatrist's duty to administer the necessary therapeutic treatment since it is the medical provider's obligation to treat the incompetent in accordance with what is in the patient's best interests or welfare.

This argument might initially be criticized as omitting reference to the prior competently considered wishes of the manic. It is not as though the manic simply became incompetent without previously expressing, while ephemerally competent, his desires. If he had, then the utilitarian principle of beneficence would dictate the administration of the necessary psychiatric therapy. However, the manic did express, while competent, a wish not to be treated. If it would be improper because of respect for one's intrinsic right of autonomy to transgress the expressed wishes of the Jehovah's Witness who refused necessary medical treatment and subsequently became incompetent, then would it not likewise be morally improper to transgress the expressed wishes of a competent manic who refused necessary psychiatric treatment and subsequently became incompetent?

Something did, however, strike me as puzzling about the manic's request, and in fairness to the psychiatrist's concern, I considered more seriously the argument raised by the physician. Could there possibly be a Kantian argument in addition to the utilitarian concerns raised which might contravene the manic's position? We might first suggest that the Jehovah's Witness' refusal of life-saving medical treatment is not completely like the manic's refusal of that drug therapy necessary for continued competent behavior. The major difference between each patient's refusal is that the Jehovah's Witness competently wishes only to alter his physical state of pain and/or disablement, not his state of competency. Unlike the manic, the Jehovah's Witness does not deny that condition necessary to refuse further medical attention, namely, his capacity for self-determination. He may, of course, lose his capacity for self-direction but this would surely be an adventitious result of his decision not to receive further medical attention, not the direct or intended result of such a decision. He may lose his ability to be self-governing but this would be the result of his deteriorating physical state and in spite of, not in virtue of, his intended goal. The manic, on the other hand, desires a state where the capacity necessary for the exercise of self-governance is lost. The manic wishes both to govern his life and lose the capacity to govern. Indeed, the manic desires the former *only* as a means to achieve the latter.

It is the manic's desire to relinquish his autonomy as part of his right of self-determination which seemingly causes the problem. Does one's right to govern freely one's life include the freedom to relinquish one's freedom to govern one's life for the sake of being enslaved? Perhaps as the rules of a game dictate what constitutes an appropriate move but *not* the viability of the rules themselves, one's right of autonomy guarantees the freedom to do or not to do a prodigious variety of things within the limits of the law, but abnegating one's freedom to do or not do such things for the sake of not being able to do them is not protected by one's right of autonomy. "The principle of freedom cannot require that he (anyone) should be free not to be free," [10] "The law of contracts similarly refuses to recognize as valid contracts to sell oneself into slavery." [11]

We might continue to argue that construing the right to autonomy as being such that it might justify the intentional enslavement of oneself for *that* very purpose makes little sense. If the right of autonomy actually included the freedom to place oneself intentionally in a position of incompetency for *that very purpose,* then one would be a nonautonomous being by design. In such a situation, in order to circumvent being treated only in accordance with the principle of beneficence, one would have to retain a position of control over one's life. But this control seems to be just what the drug-restored competent manic relinquishes when he refuses the therapy necessary for continued competency in order to enjoy the incompetency of a psychotic high. In other words, in wishing to be a nonautonomous being, the manic gives up the very control over his life necessary to circumvent the administration of therapy and remain nonautonomous. If such a conclusion is viable, then insofar as the same patient cannot also retain that which he abnegates, the alleged right to relinquish forever the capacity to act autonomously results in a *reductio ad absurdum.*

If this argument is not spurious, then there was something insightful in the physician's argument. Either the manic may forever relinquish that capacity necessary for self-governance for the purpose of achieving incompetency or he may not. If he can, then given the above, he will be covered by the utilitarian principle of beneficence and therapeutically treated accordingly. If he cannot, then he will also be therapeutically treated accordingly. But in each case, the Kantian right of autonomy is not violated. In the former case, the manic intentionally becomes constitutionally incompetent and is treated according to the utilitarian principle of beneficence. In the latter case, the patient's right of self-regulation simply does not apply. In either case, the manic will receive therapy.

The proposed action of the manic who refuses the medication necessary for his continued competency seems similar to that of one who freely places himself into slavery. The manic intends forever to relinquish his autonomy. Nonetheless, this would appear not to be permitted by the Kantian right of self-determination as a right possessing intrinsic value. Given the utilitarian notion of rights as having instrumental value, such a conclusion may not be required. Therefore, not allowing the patient to refuse that therapeutic measure designed to keep him in a competent state may not be to contravene his freedom when incompetence is his desired state since there appears at least *prima facie* reason for thinking that under the Kantian theory no one has the freedom to place himself intentionally and forever in such a state for such a purpose. Of course, a Kantian might note that irrespective of the utilitarian's concern with promoting social welfare, one might be free to escape disease and thereby lose one's freedom, but it does not follow that one is free to lose one's freedom for the *sake* of not being free.

Interestingly enough, the psychiatrists noted at this point that it was indeed fortunate that concern for third-party welfare was operative so that the manic could be induced to take lithium, since my Kantian argument was too strong. First, cannot one justifiably relinquish forever one's right of self-governance in order to circumvent greater evils, for example, death and the possibly lethal iatrogenic effects of therapy?

Against the psychiatrists, I argued that, for the manic, the abnegation of autonomy is done freely and for its own sake. In the case of the coerced abnegation in order to circumvent death, the abnegation is neither freely done nor is it done for its own sake. In the case of relinquishing one's autonomy in order to circumvent the undesirable sequellae of the therapy necessary for retaining one's autonomy, the abnegation is not done for its own sake; that is, it is not done because one wishes to be incompetent, but rather because one does not wish to futher endanger his health.

But is not the Kantian argument still too strong? If it were accepted one could not, by appeal to one's right of self-determination, even ephemerally allow another to make decisions on one's behalf or freely become intoxicated.

Again, that such behavior is not disallowed and may indeed be justified under the right of autonomy seems correct. After all, to force someone to exercise his right of autonomy may be construed as paternalistic and therefore as an interference with that right. Nevertheless, could it not be argued that this counterargument confuses the failure to exercise one's autonomy at a certain level of decision making while maintaining it at another level, *with* exercising it at a certain level so as to lose it at all levels?[12] It is only the latter which is proscribed by the Kantian right of autonomy. In the case of intoxication, one exercises autonomy so as to lose it at all levels but only for a certain period. One does not with intoxication, as one does in the manic case, forever place oneself in a position where autonomous choice is not possible. Indeed, in the case of allowing others decision-making powers and in the case of intoxication, one's competency may or will be recaptured. Both the individual who relinquishes decision-making powers to others and the individual who becomes intoxicated make autonomous decisions at various future junctures; for example, the former decides whether or not to continue allowing another such power and thus exercises autonomy at that level, while the latter similarly decides whether or not to once more place himself in that intoxicated state. Such decisions are not open to the manic after the rejection of the necessary therapy.

If my argument is plausible, then a distinction can be made between the Jehovah's Witness who refuses life-saving medical treatment and the manic who intentionally refuses medication essential for maintaining competence for the purpose of securing nonautonomy. The patient who refuses medical life-saving therapy need not wish to lose his capacity to engage in free autonomous behavior and, in fact, generally wishes otherwise. Such a patient may lose the questioned capacity secondary to behaving according to an obligation, for example, not to receive blood, or in the attempt to discontinue an impaired physical state, for example, through the removal of "extraordinary medical means." By contrast, the manic psychiatric patient who refuses that therapy necessary for competency with the goal of becoming incompetent denies the capacity necessary for the exercise of the right of autonomy. Such a patient, therefore, freely abnegates his status as an autonomous being. But since it is at least suspect that one has the freedom to abnegate one's autonomy for its own sake, no violation of patient autonomy need be perpetrated by not allowing the psychiatric patient to refuse the medications necessary for autonomous behavior.[13] Nevertheless, there may be *other* reasons, for instance, fear of deleterious iatrogenic effects of the drug regime, which might justify the presently drug-induced competent patient's refusal of that therapy essential for continued competency.

The Kantian intrinsic value of autonomy, but not necessarily the utilitarian's instrumental value of such, is what might unfavorably confront the manic in his quest to achieve incompetency. For the Kantian, since autonomy is not valued because of other ends, its relation to such is nongermane to its status. Thus, there is nothing inconsistent in maintaining that the manic cannot intentionally abnegate his autonomy even if he would achieve a more desired end. The utilitarian, on the other hand, would have to consent to the manic's demand so long as it might empirically be demonstrated that more happiness is produced, in particular or in general, by allowing the manic his refusal.

In the end, the manic in question was "persuaded" to take the lithium carbonate because he was not going to be allowed to place innocent parties in jeopardy. I do not know whether the psychiatrists would have resorted to my Kantian argument to deny the manic's request if there were no arguable risk to third parties. If there was a reluctance to employ the Kantian argument, it may, of course, have been because they found it unpersuasive, but it also may have been because of policy consideration regarding ease of administration. In other words, even if the psychiatrists had been persuaded of at least the feasibility of the Kantian argument, they might have allowed the manic's request simply because, in the absence of third-party harm, it is easier (and less risky from a legal perspective) not to challenge the patient's wishes. But what may be the "easier" thing to do need not, of course, be the "right" thing to do. This should not, therefore, vitiate the importance of consistently applying ethical theories toward the solution of perplexing concrete, ethical problems like that which I have considered here.

NOTES

1. Oddly enough, although I confronted this case at the University of Tennessee Medical School, I conducted this Ethics Grand Round at the University of Arkansas Medical School in Little Rock.

2. A. G. Gilman, L. S. Goodman, and A. Gilman, eds., *The Pharmacological Basis of Therapeutics*, 6th ed. (New York: Macmillan, 1980), pp. 408–442. See also G. L. Klerman, "Psychotropic Drugs as Therapeutic Agents," *Hastings Center Report*, Vol. 2 (1974): 81–93. We are, of course, talking about therapeutic levels for patients for whom the drugs are not counterindicated.

3. The subject was married, without children, employed for an hourly wage, and had no criminal record.

4. *In the matter of Karen Quinlan*, 355 A. 2d 647 (3-31-76). *Superintendent of Belchertown State School v. Saikewica*, 370 N.E. 2d 417 (1977). *In the matter of Earle Spring*, 405 N.E. 2d 115 (Mass. 1980). *Eichner v. Dillon*, 420 N.E. 2d 64 (1981)

5. G. Annas, "Refusing Medication in Mental Hospitals," *Hastings Center Report*, Vol. 10 (February 1980); 21–22; and R. Macklin, "Refusal of Psychiatric Treatment: Autonomy, Competency, and Paternalism," in *Psychiatry and Ethics*, ed. R. Edwards (Buffalo, N.Y.: Prometheus Books, 1982), pp. 331–340.

6. *In re Quackenbush*, 156 N.J. Super. 282, 353 A. 2d 785 (1978).

7. S. H. Rockford, "More on the Right to Refuse Treatment: Brother Fox and the Mentally Ill in New York," *Law, Medicine, and Health Care*, Vol. 11, No. 1 (February 1983): 19–21.

8. Macklin, op. cit. The type of harm generally associated with mania is overgenerosity. That is, the manic is inclined to give away all of his belongings and even the belongings of others. If depressed, there is the danger that the manic will harm himself. The manic in this case did not experience periods of depression.

9. See, for instance, *Mercy Hospital v. Jackson*, 489 A. 2d 1130 (1982). In cases where the court went against the decision, unorthodox religious or quasi-religious views were cited. See *Sampson v. Taylor*, 29 N.Y. 2d 900, 328 N.Y.S. 2d 686 (1972); *In re Carstairs*, 115 N.Y.S. 2d 314 (Fam. Ct. 1952); *In re Rotkowitz*, 175 Misc. 948, 25 N.Y.S. 2d 624 (Dol. Rel. Ct. 1941); *Mitchell v. Davis*, 205 S.W. 2d 812 (Tex. Civ. App. 1947). See also P. J. Kearney, "Leukemia in Children of Jehovah's Witnesses: Issues and Priorities in a Conflict of Care," *Journal of Medical Ethics*, Vol. 4 (1978): 32–35; T. Ackerman, "The Limits of Beneficence: Jehovah's Witnesses and Childhood Cancer," *Hastings Center Report*, Vol. 10 (August 1980): 13–18; and C. Perry, "Jehovah's Witnesses and the Quality of Life," *Westheimer Institute Review*, Vol. 2, No. 4 (Summer 1983): 8–10.

10. J. S. Mill, *On Liberty. A Norton Critical Edition*, ed. D. Spitz (New York: W. W. Norton, 1975), pp. 95 (text), 229 (comment by D. Spitz).

11. J. Feinberg, *Social Philosophy* (Englewood Cliffs, N.J.: Prentice-Hall, 1973), pp. 46–47.

12. M. Golding, "Towards a Theory of Human Rights," *Monist*, Vol. 52 (January 1968): 521–549; and J. Deigh, "On the Right to Be Punished: Some Doubts," *Ethics*, Vol. 94 (January 1984): 191–211.

13. It should perhaps be noted that since no violation of the patient's autonomy occurs by not allowing him to refuse that psychiatric treatment necessary for maintaining competency, and such interference may be paternalistic, some paternalistic acts directed toward competent individuals may fail to violate a patient's right of autonomy. For a somewhat different view on this general issue, see G. C. Graber and F. H. Marsh, "Ought a Defendant Be Drugged to Stand Trial?" *Hastings Center Report*, Vol. 9 (February 1979): 8–10.

KENNETH KIPNIS

ETHICS CONSULTING IN A MULTICULTURAL SETTING: QUALITY CARE AND THE WOUNDS OF DIVERSITY

Since 1982 I have done ethics consultation at a number of hospitals in the state of Hawaii. Uniquely separate from the mainland, situated in an isolated part of the mid-Pacific, many of us who have been transplanted here find ourselves developing something of a planetary perspective as we remain in these islands. There is no majority population here: We are all minorities. Often accustomed to being a majority, Caucasians like myself represent only about a third of the population. There are almost as many Japanese Americans. The balance is a cosmopolitan blend of Chinese, Filipinos, Hawaiians, Samoans, Koreans, Puerto Ricans, Native Americans, African Americans and other groups. About 40 percent of our current marriages are interracial. It is an unusual place to be doing ethics.

Several years ago I was called to a hospital to assist in a case involving an older Korean gentleman. I was told he had a difficult medical condition: hard to diagnose and treat. As a consequence he had steadily gotten worse despite the vigorous efforts of the medical and nursing staffs. At last the doctors felt they knew what the problem was and offered the patient a treatment plan that promised a better than 50 percent chance of recovery with only minimal risks. Nonetheless the patient refused further treatment. He said that, having suffered enough already, he did not want the doctors to do anything else. Though there had been an earlier history of mental illness, there was no evidence that it was playing any role in this refusal. He plainly understood his options as these had been explained and appreciated the consequences of his choice. This refusal was properly charted and the staff awaited the expected terminal trajectory.

Had nothing else occurred, I would not have been called in, and the Korean gentleman would likely have expired as expected. But when he was asked the hospital's routine questions about code status, he had replied by requesting full support! That had generated the call for an ethics consult. Following a telephone conversation with the patient's attending physician, I went to the bedside and joined up with a hospital ethics consultant—a very experienced nurse.

SOURCE: Kipnis, Kenneth. Previously appeared in *Clinical Ethics Report* 10, no. 4 (1996): 5–8. Reprinted in the *Newsletter of the American Philosophical Association*, Spring 1998. Reprinted by permission of the author.

Kenneth Kipnis is a professor of philosophy at the University of Hawaii at Manoa. Born in New York City, he studied philosophy at Reed College, the University of Chicago, and Brandeis University. He has done consultations in Honolulu hospitals since 1982 and has written broadly on ethical issues in medicine, engineering, early childhood education, law, nursing, and higher education. He is the author of *Legal Ethics* (Prentice Hall, 1986) and an editor of six other books.

She had just finished reviewing his chart. The task for the two of us was to understand the glaring discrepancy between his informed refusal of potentially life saving treatment and his firm request for cardioversion if he went into arrest. The latter was a burdensome procedure that could prolong his life for, at best, only a brief interval. Why was he rejecting the promising treatment while requesting the code? What was making the difference for him?

For at least forty minutes the two of us conversed with the patient, questioned him, gently pressed him, and still the discrepancy remained opaque. Finally, perhaps caving in to our persistence, he quietly asked if we would mind if he said something embarrassing. We encouraged him to go on. In the most timorous of voices, the Korean gentleman asked if we had noticed that all of his doctors had been Japanese?

I was stunned by an instantaneous appreciation of what was going on. For most of the first half of the twentieth century, Imperial Japan had ruthlessly tyrannized Korea very much as Nazi Germany had oppressed Poland during

World War II. Exploited as inferiors, many Koreans still retain powerful anti-Japanese sentiments. This unfortunate man perceived himself as exquisitely vulnerable, surrounded by his too-familiar oppressors.

As it happened, neither of us at the bedside had noticed that the gentleman's doctors had been Japanese. The physician I had spoken with on the telephone was a woman with an unexceptional accent and a non-Japanese last name. The nurse working with me had never met the attending. We did, however, know enough recent Korean-Japanese history to appreciate the patient's concerns. He "knew" why he kept getting worse. The Japanese doctors were not trying to make him better. What we were seeing as failures to improve, he saw as successful attempts to worsen his condition. To make things even worse, he was familiar enough with Western ideals of toleration, equality, and individualism to know that, in Hawaii, it was politically incorrect to express his candid opinion of Japanese physicians. There was a cryptic note in the chart that he had once asked a nurse if he could have a doctor in a three-piece suit. He had noticed, we later learned, that all the Japanese doctors wore white coats but many of the other doctors wore three-piece suits. When this ploy failed, he had then tried to evade the deadly ministrations of his Japanese physicians by refusing their offers of treatment. Of course he would want a prompt emergency response if he went into an immediately life-threatening condition. After all, he wanted to live. Paradoxically, he was refusing lifesaving treatment in order to save his life.

It seemed plain to us that the patient needed to see a non-Japanese physician. The nurse-ethicist relayed our findings to a very cooperative attending who readily agreed with our recommendation. Within a few hours another doctor—a non-Japanese physician wearing a three-piece suit—was at the bedside persuading the patient to accept treatment.

In the years since, I have often reflected on what happened that afternoon. On many occasions I have recounted the story to medical and nursing students and to clinical staff. I have used the case to show that ethics consultation can be critically important in patient care. Here was an instance in which a patient's life may have been saved by an ethics consult. I have used it to illustrate the importance of understanding the patient's underlying value commitments. There are times when our job isn't done until the patient's decision makes sense to us against the background of the patient's reasonably stable personal values. Here the two of us kept up the questioning until the patient's process of decision came into focus. In retrospect it was important that we took the time to understand how to treat him with dignity. And I have used the case to illustrate the importance of understanding cultural differences. Perhaps the two of us—and the hospital staff as well—should have been more appreciative of Korean cultural sensibilities.

But more recently I have been troubled by another aspect of this case.

The history of the United States can easily be read as a dramatic succession of cultural collisions. From the prototypical "Columbian encounter," to the westward expansion into lands occupied by Native Americans, to our social and political responses to race-based slavery, and up to our current divisions around immigration and affirmative action, we have wrestled mightily with the painful legacies—the wounds—of cultural diversity. While much of this history is unbecoming, there is also cause to take credit for the progress that has been made in overcoming prejudice and eliminating discrimination. Schools that formerly barred the entry of women and minority groups now strive for diversity. Social institutions now commonly express and often honor their commitments to nondiscrimination. Prejudicial slurs and racial stereotypes, when they are advanced, are frequently challenged. These familiar features of American life are new. For many—perhaps most of us—they are welcome.

Even so, clinicians still see patients who demand accommodation on the basis of racist beliefs and attitudes. Prejudice and stereotypical thinking patterns may be dominating a patient's preferences when, for example, a southern white male in an emergency room refuses to be treated by a black resident, or a Vietnam veteran objects to being attended by a Southeast Asian doctor. While on the one hand, clinicians have a professional concern to promote patient comfort, that value can be in conflict both with the deontological obligation to refrain from becoming an instrument of invidious discrimination and the collegial obligation to stand up for the professional dignity of one's colleagues.

What has bothered me about my role in the case of the Korean gentleman was that, until recently, these aspects of the case had completely escaped my attention. Notwithstanding the painful history of Japan and Korea during the first half of the twentieth century, I had no reason to believe that physicians of Japanese ancestry, currently practicing in Hawaii, had it in for their Korean patients. Both the nurse-ethicist and I viewed the gentleman's misgivings as wholly baseless. Although we did not discuss the matter with the patient (as perhaps we should have), we took it for granted that even though Japanese occupation forces had historically mistreated Korean nationals, it did not follow that Japanese doctors in Hawaii were now mistreating Korean patients. Yet instead of challenging the patient's beliefs on the basis of our own experience, the two of us left them unquestioned. Not only that; despite the absence of any reason to doubt the fidelity and honor of the gentleman's Japanese physician, we successfully affected her withdrawal in keeping with what we believed to be the patient's baseless prejudices. Was it right for us to do this? If it was, when is it appropriate to accommodate patient prejudice and when is it not?

One route might be to distinguish between prejudicial beliefs that are the consequence of past victimization and those that emerge purely as an integral aspect of the processes of oppression. It seems easy to sympathize with a Jewish survivor of the Nazi concentration camps who is severely distressed at the prospect of being treated by a German physician. It is much more difficult to sympathize with an anti-Semitic skinhead who does not want to be seen or touched by a Jewish physician. In similar fashion, one might suppose that the Korean gentleman's sentiments are grounded in his painful memories of the brutal Japanese occupation and, with that pedigree, perhaps worthy of accommodation. But the Vietnam veteran's objection to treatment by a Southeast

Asian points up the difficulty with this approach. Is the veteran a victim or an oppressor? Strong cases might be made both ways. Without in the least diminishing the seriousness of the damage they may do, racists themselves may lead profoundly diminished lives, spiritually and socially crippled by the attitudes they have absorbed. Alas, the world does not divide neatly into victims and oppressors; and, accordingly, a refusal to accommodate a prejudice-based preference may merely reflect the limits of our moral imagination.

At least one colleague has asked me whether I knew—really knew—that the Japanese physicians were not trying to harm the Korean gentleman. In related discussions I have encountered vigorous disagreement about whether women who ask for female gynecologists are merely prejudiced against men or merely knowledgeable about the relative merit of women. Although there was agreement in that debate that some male ob-gyns were sensitive and considerate and some female ob-gyns were not, there appeared also to be consensus (among those in a position to know) that female ob-gyns were a better bet. Is this a prejudice or not? Having never been a Korean patient of a Japanese physician (or, for that matter, a female patient of an ob-gyn), my experience is an inferior source of data. Perhaps on this basis, we should routinely defer to patient preferences. Maybe they know something we do not.

On the other hand, these preferences are very like those that have historically created institutionalized practices of sexism and racism. Until the 1960s many American owners of hotels and restaurants assumed—perhaps reasonably—that white customers would not want to dine and lodge with black customers. The presence of widespread prejudice can have the result of excluding stigmatized groups from careers and opportunities that are routinely open to others. Perhaps the distinction between accommodatable and unaccommodatable prejudice turns on the severity of the cumulative effects of accommodation. The Japanese doctors working at the hospital did not, it seemed, suffer discernable losses as a consequence of Korean prejudice. The case I reported may have been unique. However the historically broad reticence among white patients to accept the ministrations of black physicians may have contributed to unjust exclusionary practices. We may be better off as a consequence of saying that the preferences of others cannot be used to justify hiring on the basis of sex or race. Female sports reporters now have equal access to men's locker rooms. The utilitarian concern to overcome the damaging effects of discrimination can, it seems, give us a weighty reason to refuse to accommodate prejudice-based preferences. Perhaps it is this social injustice that should properly limit accommodation.

But recollect that the Korean gentleman was existentially prepared to die rather than accept treatment by his Japanese doctor. One supposes that, besides Koreans, other groups may be equally willing to live out equally firm commitments to prejudice-based preferences. Consider for the moment only those cases in which the accommodation to prejudice-based preference does significant damage to the interests of stigmatized groups. Should HMOs, hospitals, and health-care professionals be prepared to sacrifice the lives of vulnerable patients on the altar of tolerance and nondiscrimination? One can perhaps envision an institutional or professional commitment to offer high-quality services, but if a vulnerable patient refuses these on the basis of a health-care professional's race, sex, religion, and the like, that is the patient's choice: The patient's death is not our responsibility, and we respect both the patient's dignity and the dignity of the caregiver.

And yet a commitment to quality care can involve a commitment to providing that care in ways that patients can accept. In these cases one cannot evade responsibility by showing that quality care was offered but refused. Responsibility is there when (1) the reason the care was refused had to do with how it was offered, and (2) the care could have been offered in a way that would have led to acceptance. How do we deal with vulnerable patients whose prejudice-based existential preferences are damaging to our deepest senses of justice and human dignity? The dilemma involves a conflict between the physician's clear utilitarian duty to minister as best one can to the patient's pressing health care needs and the equally clear deontological prohibition on becoming an instrument of injustice. Vulnerable patients with societally damaging, prejudice-based existential preferences force us to make a choice.

I confess I am not confident about how these values should be prioritized. While it is sometimes a mark of success merely to have stated a problem clearly, a few tentative suggestions can be made in closing. In the first place, it would surely be ethically prudent to try to finesse the issue. Perhaps the southern white male in the ER could be persuaded to accept treatment from the black resident. And it seems that there is good reason to confront the patient directly: at a minimum to defend the capabilities and integrity of one's black colleague and to make it clear for the record that one does not share the patient's opinion. Perhaps in some cases tactics like these will suffice to make the problem disappear.

But if they do not and one has to choose, I believe it should be on behalf of the patient and his or her physical well-being. For it is that value that, above all, informs the practices of health care: its distinctive skills, knowledges, and technologies. It may be wise to consider health-care professionals as having a deontological duty to the community to promote the utilitarian value of physical well-being. In modern societies, only these licensed professionals are legally permitted to apply a broad range of therapeutic interventions. Given those privileges, health-care professionals arguably owe a reciprocal duty to the community to provide the distinctive forms of care they profess to be uniquely able to provide.[2] Training programs for doctors and nurses are not concerned with assessing the claims of those aggrieved and wounded by history and, in consequence, shared expertise in the healing arts is not accompanied by a distinctive professional understanding of social justice. Accordingly, it would appear that the focus of professional attention ought to be on the patient's well-being.

It is inevitable that health care—like all human pursuits—will be practiced in a profoundly imperfect world and that these imperfections will implicate practitioners and clients alike. In the face of all these painful shortcomings, there is something to be said for mindfully striving to treat vulnerable patients with dignity and respect, even when their views are hateful.

NOTES

1. The author is indebted to the contributors to the Medical College of Wisconsin Bioethics Listserv for their helpful and illuminating discussion on some of the issues raised by this case. Early versions of this paper appeared in the *Newsletter of the American Philosophical Association* and *Clinical Ethics Report*.
2. Kenneth Kipnis, "Professional Responsibility and the Responsibility of Professions" in Wade L. Robison, Michael S. Pritchard, and Joseph Ellin, eds., *Profits and Professions* (Clifton: Humana Press, 1983), pp. 9–22.

M U R I E L   R.   F R I E D M A N

PRESCRIBING VIAGRA: ETHICAL ISSUES IN UROLOGIC PRACTICE

As a urologist, I am a surgical specialist who treats obstructions, tumors, infections, and other conditions of the urinary tract in both sexes, as well as male genital problems. One of those problems is impotence. I believe there is a large but underappreciated psychosocial aspect to this very personal region of the body and have brought a more holistic, care-oriented approach into my practice.

Impotence is a very real problem for millions of men. The introduction of Viagra (sildenafil citrate) in April 1998 as the first effective oral medication has been a godsend to many men. Yet it raises numerous issues that have ethical implications and that are poorly dealt with in medical and lay arenas. Some of these issues include incomplete or false notions of what is being treated, the risk of death, the obligations of physicians, and allocation of resources. In this paper I will discuss these issues within their historical and social contexts.

IMPOTENCE: HISTORICAL BACKGROUND

Impotence is generally defined as the inability to have an erection sufficient for intercourse, but the interpretation varies. The term "impotence" is as pejorative as the mercifully obsolete "frigidity" was for women. In medical literature, "impotence" is being replaced with the more accurate "erectile dysfunction." For many years, impotence was thought to be psychological in the majority of cases. By the 1970s it was recognized that hardening of the arteries supplying blood to the penis was the cause or major contributing factor in most men with erection difficulties. However, no treatment other than psychotherapy was available. Penile prostheses which could be surgically implanted in the penis reached the point of development adequate for use in the mid-1970s. Through the

Muriel R. Friedman, M.D., practices urology at the Western Montana Clinic in Missoula. Having majored in history at the University of California, Berkeley, she finds medical ethics and medical humanities an intrinsic part of her job. She attended New York Medical College and received her urology training at Columbia-Presbyterian Medical Center in New York. She has been a member of the ethics committee at St. Patrick Hospital since 1993 including two years as chair. She is a board member of the Institute of Medicine and Humanities, a joint project of the hospital and the University of Montana-Missoula. She also serves on the board of directors of the Missoula Demonstration Project/The Quality of Life's End. In 1982 she became the seventh woman board-certified in urology.

1980s, penile prostheses, particularly inflatable prostheses, were perfected and became popular.

In the early 1980s, at the American Urological Association annual meeting in Las Vegas, in one of the greatest medical spectacles of all times, an andrology researcher dropped his trousers and produced an erection by injecting his penis with a drug called papaverine. Pharmacologic injection therapy became the first nonsurgical treatment option. Around that time, after years of trying, an engineer finally persuaded the urologic establishment that his invention, a plastic cylinder with a pump on one end, could suck blood into the flaccid penis sufficient to cause an erection, which could then be maintained by slipping a constriction ring onto the base of the penis. Vacuum erection devices offered a simpler treatment for impotence than either injection therapy or penile prostheses. Surgical procedures to alter the arterial or venous blood supply to the penis were developed and generally abandoned because of the poor long-term results.

Also in the 1980s, Canadian urologists tested yohimbine, an herb with alleged aphrodisiac properties derived from the bark of an African tree, and found it effective in about 30 percent of patients who took it chronically. The field of sex therapy also flourished in the 1980s, but few patients were willing to see psychologists, and their success rate was disappointing as well. By 1990, impotence was well understood by urologists, patients were becoming less reluctant to discuss impotence with their physician, and various treatments were available, even though all treatment options had significant disadvantages.

IMPOTENCE AND SOCIETAL EXPECTATIONS

My patients and colleagues all agree that the ideal treatment for impotence would be a drug that could be taken by mouth or applied to the skin of the penis to cause a rapid, reliable, and safe erection. Viagra originally was conceived as a drug for angina, but when test subjects reported improved erections, the direction of research changed. Viagra was brought to market in April 1998; two different drugs are expected to be released by the end of 1999.

While those in the know expected a great deal of attention to Viagra once it was released, nobody anticipated the immense clamor and sensation that ensued. Viagra became a media darling that lasted far beyond the typical nine-day public attention span. Cartoons and jokes abounded. Millions of prescriptions were written, a record-setting over $300 million of the drug was sold in the first month, and Pfizer even sent urologists a stamp pad after hearing complaints that their hands were getting tired from writing Viagra prescriptions. Drug representatives reported thefts of samples from their supply bags. Straight and gay men and women without sexual dysfunction eagerly sought information and samples to see if Viagra might enhance their sex lives. More importantly, however, the advent of an effective treatment took impotence—and sexual insecurity in general—out of the closet. There could finally be dialogue.

Dialogue often starts with jokes. One cartoon showed an elderly man telling the pharmacist he'll need some Viagra while his wife says, "I'll need some Mace." In another cartoon a smiling man marks notches on the bedroom wall while his wife dumps a bottle of pills down the kitchen sink. Clearly, men's and women's desires and expectations vary. Most urologists seem to assume that men are good lovers, women want sex, and the goal in treating impotence is to restore erections. Alternatively, the normative view of sexual activity according to ethicist Deni Elliott is a conversation between two people, not a goal-oriented event. What and who are erections for anyway?

The penis, like guns and cars, allows its possessor to feel powerful. Indeed, the definition of potency is "to have power or the ability to effect a certain result." Boys learn that having a penis gives them certain privileges in society. Feminist critics of Freud have stated that what women envy is not a penis but the benefits of having one. Once reproduction is no longer the goal, potency, from nature's standpoint, is as expendable as menses are for women. Male socialization teaches boys that a man needs all his weapons, even if they are never used; erectile potential bestows membership in the group. The loss of hair, vision, hearing, and mobility have nowhere near the social implication of loss of sexual potential. Impotence is more akin to being forced to give up one's driver's license or move into a nursing home. Men whose erections fail them generally suffer from major loss of self-esteem because they feel unworthy of being in the club.

SEXUAL STEREOTYPES VERSUS REALITY

Prescribing a pill and sending the patient home is easy: the doctor feels good, the patient feels good, and the obvious problem is solved. However, most couples have unspoken, unresolved discrepancies in sexual desires and expectations resulting from male and female socialization and life experience. Until recently, society expected men somehow to know how to please a woman even if he had little experience. Women were not supposed to touch themselves or talk about what they wanted, and men could expect a compliant partner because "men have their needs." The sexual revolution of the 1960s debunked these expectations, but they never disappeared. While few boys fail to discover masturbation, many or most girls still believe their bodies are dirty or shameful and do not experiment. Current social pressure is such that being without a boyfriend is worse than becoming pregnant or acquiring a sexually transmitted disease. Thus we have the climate of girls submitting to sexual activity they do not want, derive little pleasure from, and which potentially exposes them to much pain and serious consequences.

The reality is that while many women fully enjoy sexual activity, many others do not. According to the 1994 National Health and Social Life Survey, 8 percent of women never or rarely have orgasms during sexual activity and an additional 21 percent only sometimes do. Postmenopausal women often experience pain with sexual activity because of the thinning of genital tissue due to lack of female hormones. Far too many women have endured rape or emotional, sexual, or physical abuse at some time in their lives, which may make sexual activity unpleasant at best. Many women are secretly thrilled when their husbands become impotent so they can stop doing their wifely duty without having a confrontation. What women generally do want is communication, affection expressed as kissing, holding, and hugging, and being treated with respect. Women only half-jokingly ask, "Is there a pill that will make him talk to me?"

IIMPOTENCE AND RESPECT FOR PERSONS

When I first see a man for impotence, I perform a history and physical examination to determine the likely cause, contributing factors, possible avenues for further testing, and direction for treatment. Most urologists treat impotence as a mechanical problem unless there is an obvious psychologic reason, such as the recent death of the wife. Unfortunately, most urologists reinforce male socialization about the way the man views both himself and his partner. A patient brochure by one of the vacuum device manufacturers admonishes men to ask themselves "tough questions," and urges, "To stand a better chance for success, you should define yourself as eager or very eager to resume sexual activity on a regular basis. . . . Conviction, strong emotion and basic masculine motivation are needed to resolve sexual dysfunction problems." In other words, the brochure seems to challenge, "Are you man enough?" Another patient brochure addressed to wives seems a throwback to wifely duties and satisfying male egos. It warns wives against negative attitudes that "may undermine the success of any medical or psychological intervention," and advises them to "verbally acknowledge your share of responsibility for the problem." A Pfizer television ad tells viewers, "We help people love one another."

In the early 1980s, a new patient of mine was quite nonplused when he realized the urologist he was seeing for impotence was a woman. But at the end of his visit, he told me, "I'm really glad I came to see you. Those guys [male urologists] don't care; theirs work. You care." What I tell patients is that one's manhood has nothing to do with his penis but rather the sort of person he is, that women want a nice guy who treats them well, and an erect penis is only one way to please a woman. I encourage kissing and foreplay. I reframe the problem in terms of men not being able to fake arousal like women can, how society sets harsh standards for men, and why all men with impotence feel bad about themselves. I encourage men to discuss with their equally reticent partners what both of them feel and want. In short, I try to give the man back his self-esteem and show him how both verbal and sexual communication can help. In my view, Viagra and the other treatments are adjuncts.

PHYSICIANS' RESPONSIBILITY IN THE TREATMENT OF IMPOTENCE

What is my responsibility as the physician treating impotence: to restore erections, to explore and improve the relationship of the two partners, or to improve a man's relationship with himself? Unfortunately, most urologists view sexual dysfunction as a narrow mechanical problem and consider only the former to be their professional duty. While I discuss all three areas with my patients, do I have a duty to society to teach my colleagues?

Men frequently say they want erections so they can please their partner, although they may not have one. Sometimes (but too often) I have heard the reply to my encouragement for noncoital activity, "I don't want to start anything I can't complete." The younger wife of one such patient tearfully told me that the last time he kissed her was the day they got married, asserting, "Now that I've got you, I don't have to do that." Such men are using their partners as objects for their own ends, namely male orgasm, and female orgasm, if it occurs, is to provide the man a feeling of accomplishment. This very much violates

Kant's imperative to "treat humanity as ends in themselves rather than as mere means." I fear the former attitude continues to be far too common, even in young men. In truth, each partner is responsible for his/her own orgasm, with the help of the partner in a mutually agreed-upon manner and with concern for the other person as a person.

THE PROBLEM OF DANGER

While it is generally quite a safe drug, Viagra is dangerous for men who take nitroglycerin-type medications. A growing number of deaths have occurred when men take nitroglycerin after experiencing chest pain from sexual exertion. This is not surprising because men with impotence are typically in their 60s or older and have at least some degree of atherosclerosis or other health problems which might increase their risk. Pfizer has tried to educate physicians not to give Viagra to patients who might need nitroglycerin, but some physicians may not be aware of the danger, and some emergency personnel might not know that the patient has taken Viagra and administer nitroglycerin in an otherwise appropriate manner. Many other drugs have been brought to market, only to be withdrawn when enough deaths occur to become a liability or ethical issue for the pharmaceutical company. When it was learned that the popular weight-loss drug combination Fen-Phen caused serious heart valve disease, the drugs were taken off the market. Clearly, the reason Viagra is still on the market is the ancient and utilitarian hue and cry for a drug to enhance sexual pleasure and self-esteem despite small but potentially lethal risks.

While "dying in the saddle" like Nelson Rockefeller has a certain mystique, is a chance to have sex again worth dying for? Is risking death from Viagra really a form of suicide akin to Russian roulette? Is it fair for a woman to risk losing her husband because he wants to feel better about himself—even if she wants sexual intercourse too? An elderly neighbor of mine in poor health asked me about Viagra shortly after its introduction. Knowing he was taking nitrates, I told him it wasn't safe and he seemed to accept my answer. When he mentioned it to his normally caring, articulate wife, she responded, "You silly old man." I was saddened to hear that she (and likely thousands of other women) was so insensitive in dismissing something important to him without discussion.

What is the responsibility of the physician toward the 30–50 percent of patients who are not improved by Viagra? Not only have their erections failed them, but the wonder drug that helps most other men has bypassed them, perhaps adding to the isolation they feel. I am aware of no study that examines why many couples stop using other impotence aids including previously implanted penile prostheses. Could it be that both partners realize intercourse is not as important as they had thought? All of these people could benefit from additional information or help which is not forthcoming. In a normative system, training of urologists should encompass many of the issues I have raised. This is not currently the case.

PROBLEMS OF ALLOCATION

After a drug has been approved, it is legal and not unethical for a physician to prescribe it for other purposes or indications; many drugs have multiple uses, only some of which may have gone through the arduous and expensive licensing process. Viagra is approved only for men with erectile dysfunction, but there is evidence that it helps women who cannot achieve orgasm and that many people without sexual dysfunction experience enhanced sexual pleasure. A patient of mine in his fifties requested Viagra because he had trouble achieving erections at night after late restaurant meals with either of his two girlfriends, even though he had no trouble in the morning. Before Viagra, I would have told him to wait until morning. Should I refuse to give him the drug, knowing he would find a doctor who would? Who am I to judge that he should not receive a drug that could enhance his pleasure? Is it appropriate for physicians to control access to reasonably appropriate treatment, beyond evaluating the cause for his difficulty, in this case fatigue and wine, and making sure medication is not contraindicated? I prescribed the drug.

Columnist Ellen Goodman and other women have written about the injustice of insurance coverage of Viagra when oral contraceptives are not covered. Insurance companies typically do not pay for treatment deemed not medically necessary, such as cosmetic surgery and, variably, infertility or sterilization treatments. Viagra initially cost about $10 a pill, about the price of a bottle of wine or a movie, something an affluent man could afford. Is it fair to ask a man of modest means, perhaps without insurance—and his family, which would forgo potentially more necessary purchases—to pay this arbitrary price? Private insurance pays for most prescription drugs. Why should Viagra be different? If a man has impotence on a psychogenic basis, should Viagra not be covered, while a man with organic impotence has his medication covered? If a young man has impotence caused by diabetes or a spinal injury, should his medication be covered if nobody else's is? Other impotence treatments are generally covered by insurance; why shouldn't Viagra? If insurance premiums for everyone have to rise to pay for the seemingly infinite "need" for Viagra, should it be covered?

The Pentagon estimates that it will spend $50 million a year on Viagra, mostly for retired personnel. A former alcoholic in his fifties with Medicaid benefits came to me requesting Viagra. There were no medical reasons not to prescribe it. It angered me that my state had approved seven Viagra tablets a month for Medicaid patients—$840 a year—while many poor people have no Medicaid coverage at all. At the same time, the state limited my autonomy: I could not ethically deny him a drug to which the state said he was entitled. Even more basic than oral contraceptives, immunizations, and preventive care are often not covered by insurance. Why should taxpayers or other third parties pay for sexual pleasure?

Most urologists perform their job in treating patients with impotence adequately from a standard-of-care perspective. However, on the basis of care ethics I believe they fall short. Impotence is not simply a mechanical problem but a crisis deeply affecting both partners. Physicians treating impotence should be knowledgeable about and sensitive to the various factors involved in human sexuality. They should base treatment on maximally improving the patient's relationship with himself and his partner while minimizing the emotional, not just physical, harm done. Patients then could have reasonable goals without taking undue risks. With better knowledge and more realistic expectations, society can make better decisions about allocation of taxpayer and insurance resources.

DISCUSSION QUESTIONS

1. Discuss the utilitarian ethics of John Stuart Mill. Explain the difference between act and rule utilitarianism. In your estimation, does Mill embrace act or rule utilitarianism? Justify your view.

2. What is hedonism and how is it related to utilitarianism?

3. Do you agree with Mill's claim that intellectual pleasures are of a higher quality and have more value than bodily pleasures? On what grounds does he propose that we assess the value of each? "Few creatures," Mill states, "would consent to be changed into any of the lower animals for a promise of the fullest allowance of a beast's pleasures." Do you agree? Defend all your responses.

4. Describe the theory of ethics presented by Kant. What fundamental difference exists between utilitarian and Kantian ethics?

5. Explain the difference between the way a utilitarian would view rights and the way in which a Kantian would view them.

6. Describe some cases (for example, from history, your own personal encounters) in which you think the right of persons to act autonomously has been wrongfully violated. Can you also think of any cases in which persons have been justly prevented from exercising this right?

7. What is care ethics? How does it differ from utilitarianism? How does it differ from Kantian ethics? What advantages, if any, do you see in relying on a care ethics to confront ethical problems? What disadvantages, if any, are there?

8. Suppose that you are a physician. A biopsy reveals that your patient has progressed cancer and has only a few months to live. The patient's immediate family members have unequivocally requested that you not disclose this information to the patient. They argue that the patient, who has a history of attempted suicide, will become depressed and in all probability will attempt suicide again if this information is disclosed to him. What would act utilitarianism, as applied to this case, tell you to do? What would rule utilitarianism say? What would Kantian ethics say? What would care ethics say? What would you say?

9. Do you think Jehovah's Witnesses should ever be disallowed the autonomy to refuse lifesaving blood transfusions? Defend your answer.

10. What similarities and differences does Perry see between the case of the Jehovah's Witness who refuses the blood transfusion and that of the manic who refuses the lithium? Do you think that comparing these two cases in the ways Perry does helps to shed any moral light on the question of whether to allow the manic to refuse treatment? If so, why? If not, why not?

11. Discuss Perry's Kantian argument against allowing the manic to refuse treatment. Do you think the physicians should have adopted it? Defend your answer.

12. Some existentialist thinkers, notably Jean-Paul Sartre, emphasize the importance of living the "authentic existence," that is, living the way one chooses to live and not the way society, through its various rules, roles, and institutions, stipulates. Suppose that allowing the manic to refuse the lithium did not present any signifi-

cant risk of harm to third parties. Do you think the physicians should have then allowed the manic to live his "authentic existence"? Defend your answer.

13. In the case presented by Kenneth Kipnis, was the decision to provide the Korean gentleman with a non-Japanese physician morally right? Defend your answer in terms of the ethical theories presented in this chapter. What counterarguments might be advanced against your view from a different theoretical standpoint? How would you respond to these arguments?

14. In what ways does urologist Muriel Friedman apply care ethics in her practice of treating impotent men? All other things being equal, would you be more comfortable with a urologist/gynecologist who took a care-based approach like Friedman or with a physician who simply viewed your problem as a mechanical one? Should the gender of the physician ever figure in your choice of a urologist/gynecologist? Explain.

15. In your view, should insurance policies cover the cost of Viagra? Defend your response in terms of an ethical theory(ies).

16. Friedman describes a case of a patient of hers in his fifties who requested Viagra "because he had trouble achieving erections at night after late restaurant meals with either of his two girlfriends, even though he had no trouble in the morning." If you were the physician, would you have agreed to prescribe the drug? Defend your answer in terms of an ethical theory(ies).

3

LAWYERS' ETHICS

In this chapter, questions concerning the ethics of lawyers' practice in an adversary system will be examined. One such question that appears to ungird many others is that of whether good lawyers can also be *good* or *virtuous* people. As will become apparent, this question is particularly difficult with respect to criminal defense attorneys, especially public defenders. One the one hand, such lawyers are expected to be officers of the court dedicated to the ideals of truth and justice. On the other, they are expected to be zealous clients' advocates. As advocates, they may be permitted, if not required, to do such things as defend clients they know to be (in fact) guilty of heinous offenses, to cross-examine rape complainants, whom they know to be telling the truth, in order to destroy their credibility, and to invoke "legal technicalities" in order to defeat just causes against their clients. This question is difficult here because such actions may appear to be incompatible with the ordinary understanding of a *morally* good or virtuous person.

In the first selection of this chapter, excerpted from his *Nicomachean Ethics,* the ancient Greek philosopher Aristotle provides an analysis of what it means to be virtuous. Aristotle's view rests upon the assumption that every activity, action, and pursuit has its proper end or purpose. For example, the end of medicine, he says, is health and that of shipbuilding a vessel. Similarly, there is an ultimate human end or purpose, a determinable human nature, according to which human happiness (prosperity, virtue, or excellence) can be defined. According to Aristotle, this nature can be found in that which uniquely distinguishes human beings from all other animals. Upon careful consideration, he comes to the conclusion that this nature lies in the human ability to reason. It is life according to reason, he concludes, that uniquely defines the proper end of all human activity and which, therefore, provides the standard of human virtue.

Human virtue, however, is for Aristotle, of two kinds, intellectual and moral. Whereas intellectual virtue concerns the proper functioning of theoretical or scientific reasoning, moral virtue concerns the proper functioning of practical reasoning as it relates to character. Moral virtue, he maintains, is a state of character that comes about as a result of *habit.* "We become just by doing just acts, temperate by doing temperate acts, brave by doing brave acts."

Such acts that produce virtuous states of character are performed according to a general rule. According to Aristotle, this rule is one of choice that avoids excess and deficiency with respect to our *passions or appetites*. Virtuous action, he says, involves choosing the mean between excess and deficiency in the exercise of passion. For instance, fear, confidence, anger, pity, pleasure, and pain "may be felt both too much and too little, and in both cases not well; but to feel them at the right times, with reference to the right objects, toward the right people, with the right motive, and in the right way is what is both intermediate and best, and this is characteristic of virtue." For example, *courage* is the mean in the way of having fear, the avoidance of extremes of foolhardiness and cowardice, and *temperance* is the mean between extremes in the way of indulging bodily appetites such as desire for food or sex.

Determination of the mean depends upon the situation and is thus "relative to us." For example, while courage is the mean between cowardice and foolhardiness, where such a mean lies will depend upon the context of action; what is brave in one context may be foolhardy in another. Thus risking one's life may be a brave act if done to save another life, but it may be foolhardy if done needlessly.

Determination of the mean, Aristotle believes, is a matter of perception of particular circumstances informed by experience accrued from having lived. It is the kind of judgment exercised by a prudent individual, someone who knows how to accomplish his or her ends, but who chooses only proper ends and ways to accomplish them. This should not be confused with the *clever* person who is good at accomplishing his or her goals, but who cares little about being just or brave or temperate, or other virtues. Accordingly, in Aristotle's view, "virtue is a state of character concerned with choice, lying in a mean, i.e. the mean relative to us, this being determined by a rational principle, and by that principle by which the man of practical wisdom would determine it."

Using Aristotle's definition of virtue as a standard against which to judge lawyers' conduct may, for some, raise a question about its appropriateness as applied to the professional life of a lawyer. Do lawyers in their professional capacity have a morality that is distinct from that by which we judge individuals in their private lives?

In the second selection entitled "The Lawyer as Friend," Charles Fried advances a moral defense of the traditional conception of a lawyer's role as zealous client's advocate. By construing the traditional conception on the analogy of a kind of "special-purpose friendship," he attempts to show that it exemplifies, "at least in a unilateral sense," such intrinsic goods as trust and personal care as well as assuring "the due liberty of each citizen, before the law"; and that, accordingly, "there is a vocation and a satisfaction even in helping Shylock obtain his pound of flesh or in bringing about the acquittal of a guilty man."

Applying elements of Aristotle's analysis of virtue to legal practice, the next selection, excerpted from my article on "Pure Legal Advocates and Moral Agents: Two Concepts of a Lawyer in an Adversary System," argues that lawyers can be morally good or virtuous persons provided they incorporate into their practice specific *prima facie* moral principles which guide the actions of morally good persons. For example, lawyers can (and should) incorporate principles of truthfulness, nonmaleficence, and moral courage into their practices. It is argued that, if lawyers are to practice as moral agents, then they must be permitted the autonomy to weigh up and strike moral balances between competing moral interests; for example, not harming third parties and keeping clients' confidences, which may sometimes come into conflict. Conversely, it is argued that lawyers who practice as "pure legal advocates" get into or reinforce habits opposite to virtuous states of character.

The present chapter includes two Practice discussions, one from the perspective of a defense attorney and the other from the perspective of a prosecutor. In his paper on "The Philosopher as Public Defender," Steven Wasserman, a former philosophy professor turned public defender, discusses a case in which he was instrumental in affecting the acquittal of a rape defendant whom he had good reason to believe was guilty.

In the final selection entitled "The Philosopher as Prosecutor," William C. Heffernan, editor of the prominent journal *Criminal Justice Ethics*, discusses a manslaughter case he confronted as a prosecutor at the appellate level. In this case Heffernan found himself faced with the need to weigh up and strike a moral balance between two competing moral claims: the (legal as well as moral) fight to a fair trial, and the demand that those actually guilty of heinous crimes be punished.

Wasserman's and Heffernan's papers together provide a realistic basis upon which to approach the question of whether a good lawyer can be a good person. They also show the possible problems of attempting to apply any one theoretical perspective to all areas of legal practice. For example, since, as Heffernan points out, the client of prosecutors (if there is one at all) is "the abstract entity of the 'people' of the state in which they work," there may be a special problem in construing prosecutors on the analogy of a "friend" to the client. Such a perspective may well be more illuminating when applied to the criminal defense attorney. Still, since *public* defenders are required to "take all comers," as Wasserman states, there are, in this case, constraints upon a lawyer's degree of autonomy, which may arguably present a problem in applying the moral agent concept to public defenders. In any case, the readings in this chapter, taken collectively, help to show how theoretical perspectives can enlighten the practice of lawyers, and conversely, how the practice itself can enlighten the theory.

ISSUES

ARISTOTLE

VIRTUE ETHICS

BOOK I

Every art and every inquiry, and similarly every action and pursuit, is thought to aim at some good; and for this reason the good has rightly been declared to be that at which all things aim. But a certain difference is found among ends; some are activities, others are products apart from the activities that produce them. Where there are ends apart from the actions, it is the nature of the products to be better than the activities. Now, as there are many actions, arts, and sciences, their ends also are many; the end of the medical art is health, that of shipbuilding a vessel, that of strategy victory, that of economics wealth. But where such arts fall under a single capacity—as bridle-making and the other arts concerned with the equipment of horses fall under the art of riding, and this and every military action under strategy, in the same way other arts fall under yet others—in all of these the ends of the master arts are to be preferred to all the subordinate ends; for it is for the sake of the former that the latter are pursued. It makes no difference whether the activities themselves are the ends of the actions, or something else apart from the activities, as in the case of the sciences just mentioned.

If, then, there is some end of the things we do, which we desire for its own sake (everything else being desired for the sake of this), and if we do not choose everything for the sake of something else (for at that rate the process would go on to infinity, so that our desire would be empty and vain), clearly this must be the good and the chief good. Will not the knowledge of it, then, have a great influence on life? Shall we not, like archers who have a mark to aim at, be more likely to hit upon what is right? If so, we must try, in outline at least to determine what it is, and of which of the sciences or capacities it is the object . . .

Let us again return to the good we are seeking, and ask what it can be. It seems different in different actions and arts; it is different in medicine, in strategy, and in the other arts likewise. What then is the good of each? Surely that for whose sake everything else is done. In medicine this is health, in strategy victory, in architecture a house, in any other sphere something else, and in every

---

SOURCE: Aristotle, *Nicomachean Ethics*. Reprinted from the *Basic Works of Aristotle* ed. Richard McKeon, Trans. W. D. Ross (New York: Random House, 1941).

action and pursuit the end; for it is for the sake of this that all men do whatever else they do. Therefore, if there is an end for all that we do, this will be the good achievable by action, and if there are more than one, these will be the goods achievable by action. . . .

Now such a thing happiness, above all else, is held to be; for this we choose always for itself and never for the sake of something else, but honour, pleasure, reason, and every virtue we choose indeed for themselves (for if nothing resulted from them we should still choose each of them), but we choose them also for the sake of happiness, judging that by means of them we shall be happy. Happiness, on the other hand, no one chooses for the sake of these, nor, in general, for anything other than itself. . . .

Presumably, however, to say that happiness is the chief good seems a platitude, and a clearer account of what it is is still desired. This might perhaps be given, if we could first ascertain the function of man. For just as for a flute-player, a sculptor, or any artist, and, in general, for all things that have a function or activity, the good and the 'well' is thought to reside in the function, so would it seem to be for man, if he has a function. Have the carpenter, then, and the tanner certain functions or activities, and has man none? Is he born without a function? Or as eye, hand, foot, and in general each of the parts evidently has a function, may one lay it down that man similarly has a function apart from all these? What then can this be? Life seems to be common even to plants, but we are seeking what is peculiar to man. Let us exclude, therefore, the life of nutrition and growth. Next there would be a life of perception, but *it* also seems to be common even to the horse, the ox, and every animal. There remains, then, an active life of the element that has a rational principle; of this, one part has such a principle in the sense of being obedient to one, the other in the sense of possessing one and exercising thought. And, as 'life of the rational element' also has two meanings, we must state that life in the sense of activity is what we mean; for this seems to be the more proper sense of the term. Now if the function of man is an activity of soul which follows or implies a rational principle, and if we say 'a so-and-so' and 'a good so-and-so' have a function which is the same in kind, e.g. a lyre-player and a good lyre-player, and so without qualification in all cases, eminence in respect of goodness being added to the name of the function (for the function of a lyre-player is to play the lyre, and that of a good lyre-player is to do so well): if this is the case, [and we state the function of man to be a certain kind of life, and this to be an activity or actions of the soul implying a rational principle, and the function of a good man to be the good and noble performance of these, and if any action is well performed when it is performed in accordance with appropriate excellence: if this is the case,] human good turns out to be activity of soul in accordance with virtue, and if there are more than one virtue, in accordance with the best and most complete.

But we must add 'in a complete life'. For one swallow does not make a summer, nor does one day; and so too one day, or a short time, does not make a man blessed and happy.

Let us serve as an outline of the good; for we must presumably first sketch it roughly, and then later fill in the details. . . .

BOOK II

Virtue . . . being of two kinds, intellectual and moral, intellectual virtue in the main owes both its birth and its growth to teaching (for which reason it requires experience and time), while moral virtue comes about as a result of habit, whence also its name *ethike* is one that is formed by a slight variation from the word *ethos* (habit). From this it is also plain that none of the moral virtues arises in us by nature; for nothing that exists by nature can form a habit contrary to its nature. For instance the stone which by nature moves downwards cannot be habituated to move upwards, not even if one tries to train it by throwing it up ten thousand times; nor call fire be habituated to move downwards, nor can anything else that by nature behaves in one way be trained to behave in another. Neither by nature, then, nor contrary to nature do the virtues arise in us; rather we are adapted by nature to receive them, and are made perfect by habit.

Again, of all the things that come to us by nature we first acquire the potentiality and later exhibit the activity (this is plain in the case of the senses; for it was not by often seeing or often hearing that we got these senses, but on the contrary we had them before we used them, and did not come to have them by using them); but the virtues we get by first exercising them, as also happens in the case of the arts as well. For the things we have to learn before we can do them, we learn by doing them, e.g. men become builders by building and lyre-players by playing the lyre; so too we become just by doing just acts, temperate by doing temperate acts, brave by doing brave acts.

This is confirmed by what happens in states; for legislators make the citizens good by forming habits in them, and this is the wish of every legislator, and those who do not effect it miss their mark, and it is in this that a good constitution differs from a bad one.

Again, it is from the same causes and by the same means that every virtue is both produced and destroyed, and similarly every art; for it is from playing the lyre that both good and bad lyre-players are produced. And the corresponding statement is true of builders and of all the rest; men will be good or bad builders as a result of building well or badly. For if this were not so, there would have been no need of a teacher, but all men would have been born good or bad at their craft. This, then, is the case with the virtues also; by doing the acts that we do in our transactions with other men we become just or unjust, and by doing the acts that we do in the presence of danger, and being habituated to feel fear or confidence, we become brave or cowardly. The same is true of appetites and feelings of anger; some men become temperate and good-tempered, others self-indulgent and irascible, by behaving in one way or the other in the appropriate circumstances. Thus, in one word, states of character arise out of like activities. This is why the activities we exhibit must be of a certain kind; it is because the states of character correspond to the differences between these. It makes no small difference, then, whether we form habits of one kind or of another from our very youth; it makes a very great difference, or rather *all* the difference. . . .

First . . . let us consider this, that it is the nature of such things to be destroyed by defect and excess, as we see in the case of strength and of health (for to gain light on things imperceptible we must use the evidence of sensible things); both excessive and defective exercise destroys the strength, and similarly drink or food which is above or below a certain amount destroys the health, while that which is proportionate both produces and increases and preserves it. So too is it, then, in the case of temperance and courage and the other virtues. For the man who flies from and fears everything and does not stand his ground against anything becomes a coward, and the man who fears nothing at all but goes to meet every danger becomes rash; and similarly the man who indulges in every pleasure and abstains from none becomes self-indulgent, while the man who shuns every pleasure, as boors do, becomes in a way insensible; temperance and courage, then, are destroyed by excess and defect, and preserved by the mean.

But not only are the sources and causes of their origination and growth the same as those of their destruction, but also the sphere of their actualization will be the same; for this is also true of the things which are more evident to sense, e.g. of strength; it is produced by taking much food and undergoing much exertion, and it is the strong man that will be most able to do these things. So too is it with the virtues; by abstaining from pleasures we become temperate, and it is when we have become so that we are most able to abstain from them; and similarly too in the case of courage; for by being habituated to despise things that are terrible and to stand our ground against them we become brave, and it is when we have become so that we shall be most able to stand our ground against them. . . .

The question might be asked, what we mean by saying that we must become just by doing just acts, and temperate by doing temperate acts; for if men do just and temperate acts, they are already just and temperate, exactly as, if they do what is in accordance with the laws of grammar and of music, they are grammarians and musicians.

Or is this not true even of the arts? It is possible to do something that is in accordance with the laws of grammar, either by chance or at the suggestion of another. A man will be a grammarian, then, only when he has both done something grammatical and done it grammatically; and this means doing it in accordance with the grammatical knowledge in himself.

Again, the case of the arts and that of the virtues are not similar; for the products of the arts have their goodness in themselves, so that it is enough that they should have a certain character, but if the acts that are in accordance with the virtues have themselves a certain character it does not follow that they are done justly or temperately. The agent also must be in a certain condition when he does them; in the first place he must have knowledge, secondly he must choose the acts, and choose them for their own sakes, and thirdly his action must proceed from a firm and unchangeable character. These are not reckoned in as conditions of the possession of the arts, except the bare knowledge; but as a condition of the possession of the virtues knowledge has little or no weight, while the other conditions count not for a little but for everything, i.e. the very conditions which result from often doing just and temperate acts.

Actions, then, are called just and temperate when they are such as the just or the temperate man would do; but it is not the man who does these that is just and temperate, but the man who also does them *as* just and temperate men do them. It is well said, then, that it is by doing just acts that the just man is produced, and by doing temperate acts the temperate man; without doing these no one would have even a prospect of becoming good.

But most people do not do these, but take refuge in theory and think they are being philosophers and will become good in this way, behaving somewhat like patients who listen attentively to their doctors, but do none of the things they are ordered to do. As the latter will not be made well in body by such a course of treatment, the former will not be made well in soul by such a course of philosophy.

Next we must consider what virtue is. Since things that are found in the soul are of three kinds—passions, faculties, states of character, virtue must be one of these. By passions I mean appetite, anger, fear, confidence, envy, joy, friendly feeling, hatred, longing, emulation, pity, and in general the feelings that are accompanied by pleasure or pain; by faculties the things in virtue of which we are said to be capable of feeling these, e.g. of becoming angry or being pained or feeling pity; by states of character the things in virtue of which we stand well or badly with reference to the passions, e.g. with reference to anger we stand badly if we feel it violently or too weakly, and well if we feel it moderately; and similarly with reference to the other passions.

Now neither the virtues nor the vices are *passions*, because we are not called good or bad on the ground of our passions, but are so called on the ground of our virtues and our vices, and because we are neither praised nor blamed for our passions (for the man who feels fear or anger is not praised, nor is the man who simply feels anger blamed, but the man who feels it in a certain way), but for our virtues and our vices we *are* praised or blamed.

Again, we feel anger and fear without choice, but the virtues are modes of choice or involve choice. Further, in respect of the passions we are said to be moved, but in respect of the virtues and the vices we are said not to be moved but to be disposed in a particular way.

For these reasons also they are not *faculties*; for we are neither called good nor bad, nor praised nor blamed, for the simple capacity of feeling the passions; again, we have the faculties by nature, but we are not made good or bad by nature; we have spoken of this before.

If, then, the virtues are neither passions nor faculties, all that remains is that they should be *states of character*.

Thus we have stated what virtue is in respect of its genus.

We must, however, not only describe virtue as a state of character, but also say what sort of state it is. We may remark, then, that every virtue or excellence both brings into good condition the thing of which it is the excellence and makes the work of that thing be done well; e.g. the excellence of the eye makes both the eye and its work good; for it is by the excellence of the eye that we see well. Similarly the excellence of the horse makes a horse both good in itself and good at running and at carrying its rider and at awaiting the attack of the enemy. Therefore, if this is true in every case, the virtue of man also will be the state of character which makes a man good and which makes him do his own work well.

How this is to happen . . . will be made plain . . . by the following consideration of the specific nature of virtue. In everything that is continuous and divisible it is possible to take more, less, or an equal amount, and that either in terms of the thing itself or relatively to us; and the equal is an intermediate between excess and defect. By the intermediate in the object I mean that which is equidistant from each of the extremes, which is one and the same for all men; by the intermediate relatively to us that which is neither too much nor too little—and this is not one, nor the same for all. For instance, if ten is many and two is few, six is the intermediate, taken in terms of the object; for it exceeds and is exceeded by an equal amount; this is intermediate according to arithmetical proportion. But the intermediate relatively to us is not to be taken so; if ten pounds are too much for a particular person to eat and two too little, it does not follow that the trainer will order six pounds; for this also is perhaps too much for the person who is to take it, or too little—too little for Milo, too much for the beginner in athletic exercises. The same is true of running and wrestling. Thus a master of any art avoids excess and defect, but seeks the intermediate and chooses this—the intermediate not in the object but relatively to us.

If it is thus, then, that every art does its work well—by looking to the intermediate and judging its works by this standard (so that we often say of good works of art that it is not possible either to take away or to add anything, implying that excess and defect destroy the goodness of works of art, while the mean preserves it; and good artists, as we say, look to this in their work), and if, further, virtue is more exact and better than any art, as nature also is, then virtue must have the quality of aiming at the intermediate. I mean moral virtue; for it is this that is concerned with passions and actions, and in these there is excess, defect, and the intermediate. For instance, both fear and confidence and appetite and anger and pity and in general pleasure and pain may be felt both too much and too little, and in both cases not well; but to feel them at the right times, with reference to the right objects, towards the right people, with the right motive, and in the right way, is what is both intermediate and best, and this is characteristic of virtue. Similarly with regard to actions also there is excess, defect, and the intermediate. Now virtue is concerned with passions and actions, in which excess is a form of failure, and so is defect, while the intermediate is praised and is a form of success; and being praised and being successful are both characteristics of virtue. Therefore virtue is a kind of mean, since, as we have seen, it aims at what is intermediate.

Again, it is possible to fail in many ways (for evil belongs to the class of the unlimited, as the Pythagoreans conjectured, and good to that of the limited), while to succeed is possible only in one way (for which reason also one is easy and the other difficult—to miss the mark easy, to hit it difficult); for these reasons also, then, excess and defect are characteristic of vice, and the mean of virtue;

For men are good in but one way, but bad in many.

Virtue, then, is a state of character concerned with choice, lying in a mean, i.e. the mean relative to us, this being determined by a rational principle, and by that principle by which the man of practical wisdom would determine it. Now it is a mean between two vices, that which depends on excess and that which depends on defect; and again it is a mean because the vices respectively fall short of or exceed what is right in both passions and actions, while virtue both finds and chooses that which is intermediate. Hence in respect of its substance and the definition which states its essence virtue is a mean, with regard to what is best and right an extreme.

But not every action nor every passion admits of a mean; for some have names that already imply badness, e.g. spite, shamelessness, envy, and in the case of actions adultery, theft, murder; for all of these and suchlike things imply by their names that they are themselves bad, and not the excesses or deficiencies of them. It is not possible, then, ever to be right with regard to them; one must always be wrong. Nor does goodness or badness with regard to such things depend on committing adultery with the right woman, at the right time, and in the right way, but simply to do any of them is to go wrong. It would be equally absurd, then, to expect that in unjust, cowardly, and voluptuous action there should be a mean, an excess, and a deficiency; for at that rate there would be a mean of excess and of deficiency, an excess of excess, and a deficiency of deficiency. But as there is no excess and deficiency of temperance and courage because what is intermediate is in a sense an extreme, so too of the actions we have mentioned there is no mean nor any excess and deficiency, but however they are done they are wrong; for in general there is neither a mean of excess and deficiency, nor excess and deficiency of a mean. . . .

As we say that some people who do just acts are not necessarily just, i.e. those who do the acts ordained by the laws either unwillingly or owing to ignorance or for some other reason and not for the sake of the acts themselves (though, to be sure, they do what they should and all the things that the good man ought), so is it, it seems, that in order to be good one must be in a certain state when one does the several acts, i.e. one must do them as a result of choice and for the sake of the acts themselves. Now virtue makes the choice right, but the question of the things which should naturally be done to carry out our choice belongs not to virtue but to another faculty. We must devote our attention to these matters and give a clearer statement about them. There is a faculty which is called cleverness; and this is such as to be able to do the things that tend towards the mark we have set before ourselves, and to hit it. Now if the mark be noble, the cleverness is laudable, but if the mark be bad, the cleverness is mere smartness; hence we call even men of practical wisdom clever or smart. Practical wisdom is not the faculty, but it does not exist without this faculty. And this eye of the soul acquires its formed state not without the aid of virtue, as has been said and is plain; for the syllogisms which deal with acts to be done are things which involve a starting-point, viz. 'since the end, i.e. what is best, is of such and such a nature', whatever it may be (let it for the sake of argument be what we please); and this is not evident except to the good man; for wickedness perverts us and causes us to be deceived about the starting-points of action. Therefore it is evident that it is impossible to be practically wise without being good.

CHARLES FRIED

THE LAWYER AS FRIEND

Can a good lawyer be a good person? The question troubles lawyers and law students alike. They are troubled by the demands of loyalty to one's client and by the fact that one can win approval as a good, maybe even great, lawyer even though that loyalty is engrossed by overprivileged or positively distasteful clients. How, they ask, is such loyalty compatible with that devotion to the common good characteristic of high moral principles? And whatever their views of the common good, they are troubled because the willingness of lawyers to help their clients use the law to the prejudice of the weak or the innocent seems morally corrupt. The lawyer is conventionally seen as a professional devoted to his client's interests and as authorized, if not in fact required, to do some things (though not anything) for that client which he would not do for himself.[1] In this essay I consider the compatibility between this traditional conception of the lawyer's role and the ideal of moral purity—the ideal that one's life should be lived in fulfillment of the most demanding moral principles, and not just barely within the law.

THE THESIS

I will argue in this essay that it is not only legally but also morally right that a lawyer adopt as his dominant purpose the furthering of his client's interests— that it is right that a professional put the interests of his client above some idea, however valid, of the collective interest. I maintain that the traditional conception of the professional role expresses a morally valid conception of human

SOURCE: Charles Fried, 1976 The Lawyer as Friend. Reprinted by permission of the Yale Law Journal Company and Fred B. Rothman & Company from *The Yale Law Journal*, 85:1060–1089.

conduct and human relationships, that one who acts according to that conception is to that extent a good person. Indeed, it is my view that, far from being a mere creature of positive law, the traditional conception is so far mandated by moral right that any advanced legal system which did not sanction this conception would be unjust.

How can it be that it is not only permissible, but indeed morally right, to favor the interests of a particular person in a way which we can be fairly sure is either harmful to another particular individual or not maximally conducive to the welfare of society as a whole?

The resolution of this problem is aided, I think, if set in a larger perspective. Charles Curtis made the perspicacious remark that a lawyer may be privileged to lie for his client in a way that one might lie to save one's friends or close relatives. I do not want to underwrite the notion that it is justifiable to lie even in those situations, but there is a great deal to the point that in those relations—friendship, kinship—we recognize an authorization to take the interests of particular concrete persons more seriously and to give them priority over the interests of the wider collectivity. One who provides an expensive education for his own children surely cannot be blamed because he does not use these resources to alleviate famine or to save lives in some distant land. Nor does he blame himself. Indeed, our intuition that an individual is authorized to prefer identified persons standing close to him over the abstract interests of humanity finds its sharpest expression in our sense that an individual is entitled to act with something less than impartiality to that person who stands closest to him—the person that he is. There is such a thing as selfishness to be sure, yet no reasonable morality asks us to look upon ourselves as merely plausible candidates for the distribution of the attention and resources which we command, plausible candidates whose entitlement to our own concern is no greater in principle than that of any other human being. Such a doctrine may seem edifying, but on reflection it strikes us as merely fanatical.

This suggests an interesting way to look at the situation of the lawyer. As a professional person one has a special care for the interests of those accepted as clients, just as his friends, his family, and he himself have a very general claim to his special concern. But I concede this does no more than widen the problem. It merely shows that in claiming this authorization to have a special care for my clients I am doing something which I do in other contexts as well.

THE UTILITARIAN EXPLANATION

I consider first an argument to account for fidelity to role, for obligation, made most elaborately by the classical utilitarians, Mill[2] and Sidgwick.[3] They argued that our propensity to prefer the interests of those who are close to us is in fact perfectly reasonable because we are more likely to be able to benefit those people. Thus, if everyone is mainly concerned with those closest to him, the distribution of social energies will be most efficient and the greatest good of the greatest number will be achieved. The idea is that the efforts I expend for my friend or my relative are more likely to be effective because I am more likely to know what needs to be done. I am more likely to be sure that the good I intend is in fact accomplished. One might say that there is less overhead, fewer administrative costs, in benefiting those nearest to us. I would not want to ridicule this argument, but it does not seem to me to go far enough. Because if that were the sole basis for the preference, then it would be my duty to determine whether my efforts might not be more efficiently spent on the collectivity, on the distant, anonymous beneficiary. But it is just my point that *this* is an inquiry we are not required, indeed sometimes not even authorized, to make. When we decide to care for our children, to assure our own comforts, to fulfill our obligations to our clients or patients, we do not do so as a result of a cost-benefit inquiry which takes into account the ease of producing a good result for our friends and relations.

What we must look for is an argument which shows that giving some degree of special consideration to myself, my friends, my clients is not merely instrumentally justified (as the utilitarians would argue) but to some degree intrinsically so.[4]

I think such an argument can be made. Instead of speaking the language of maximization of value over all of humanity, it will speak the language of rights. The stubborn ethical datum affirming such a preference grows out of the profoundest springs of morality: the concepts of personality, identity, and liberty.

SELF, FRIENDSHIP, AND JUSTICE

Consider for a moment the picture of the human person that would emerge if the utilitarian claim were in fact correct. It would mean that in all my choices I must consider the well-being of all humanity—actual and potential—as the range of my concern. Moreover, every actual or potential human being is absolutely equal in his claims upon me. Indeed, I myself am to myself only as one of this innumerable multitude. And that is the clue to what is wrong with the utilitarian vision. Before there is morality there must be the person. We must attain and maintain in our morality a concept of personality such that it makes sense to posit choosing, valuing entities—free, moral beings. But the picture of the moral universe in which my own interests disappear and are merged into the interests of the totality of humanity is incompatible with that[5] because one wishes to develop a conception of a responsible, valuable, and valuing agent, and such an agent must first of all be dear to himself. It is from the kernel of individuality that the other things we value radiate. The Gospel says we must love our neighbor as ourselves, and this implies that any concern for others which is a *human* concern must presuppose a concern for ourselves. The human concern which we then show others is a concern which first of all recognizes the concrete individuality of that other person just as we recognize our own.

Therefore, it is not only consonant with, but also required by, an ethics for human beings that one be entitled first of all to reserve an area of concern for oneself and then to move out freely from that area if one wishes to lavish that concern on others to whom one stands in concrete, personal relations. Similarly, a person is entitled to enjoy this extra measure of care from those who choose to bestow it upon him without having to justify this grace as either just or efficient. We may choose the individuals to whom we will stand in this special relation, or they may be thrust upon us, as in family ties.

In explicating the lawyer's relation to his client, my analogy shall be to friendship, where the freedom to choose and to be chosen expresses our freedom to hold something of ourselves in reserve, in reserve even from the universalizing claims of morality. These personal ties and the claims they engender may be all-consuming, as with a close friend or family member, or they may be limited, special-purpose claims, as in the case of the client or patient. The special-purpose claim is one in which the beneficiary, the client, is entitled to all the special consideration *within* the limits of the relationship which we accord to a friend or a loved one. It is not that the claims of the client are less intense or demanding; they are only more limited in their scope. After all, the ordinary concept of friendship provides only an analogy, and it is to the development of that analogy that I turn.

SPECIAL-PURPOSE FRIENDS

How does a professional fit into the concept of personal relations at all? He is, I have suggested, a limited-purpose friend. A lawyer is a friend in regard to the legal system. He is someone who enters into a personal relation with you—not an abstract relation as under the concept of justice. That means that like a friend he acts in your interests, not his own; or rather he adopts your interests as his own. I would call that the classic definition of friendship. To be sure, the lawyer's range of concern is sharply limited. But within that limited domain the intensity of identification with the client's interests is the same. It is not the specialized focus of the relationship which may make the metaphor inapposite, but the way in which the relation of legal friendship comes about and the one-sided nature of the ensuing "friendship." But I do insist upon the analogy, for in overcoming the arguments that the analogy is false, I think the true moral foundations of the lawyer's special role are illuminated and the utilitarian objections to the traditional conception of that role overthrown. When I say the lawyer is his client's legal friend, I mean the lawyer makes his client's interests his own insofar as this is necessary to preserve and foster the client's autonomy within the law. This argument does not require us to assume that the law is hostile to the client's rights. All we need to assume is that even a system of law which is perfectly sensitive to personal rights would not work fairly unless the client could claim a professional's assistance in realizing that autonomy which the law recognizes.

The lawyer acts morally because he helps to preserve and express the autonomy of his client vis-à-vis the legal system. It is not just that the lawyer helps his client accomplish a particular lawful purpose. Pornography may be legal, but it hardly follows that I perform a morally worthy function if I lend money or artistic talent to help a pornographer flourish in the exercise of this right. What is special about legal counsel is that whatever else may stop the pornographer's enterprise, he should not be stopped because he mistakenly believes there is a legal impediment. There is no wrong if a venture fails for lack of talent or lack of money—no one's rights have been violated. But rights *are* violated if, through ignorance or misinformation about the law, an individual refrains from pursuing a wholly lawful purpose. Therefore, to assist others in understanding and realizing their legal rights is always morally worthy. Moreover, the legal system, by instituting the role of the legal friend, not only assures what it in justice must—the due liberty of each citizen before the law—but does it by creating an institution which exemplifies, at least in a unilateral sense, the ideal of personal relations of trust and personal care which (as in natural friendship) are good in themselves.

STAYING WITHIN THE LAW

I have defined the lawyer as a client's legal friend, as the person whose role it is to ensure the client's autonomy within the law. Although I have indicated that the exercise of that autonomy is not always consonant with the public interest, it does not at all follow that the exercise of that autonomy, therefore, must also violate the law. If the legal system is itself sensitive to moral claims, sensitive to the rights of individuals, it must at times allow that autonomy to be exercised in ways that do not further the public interest. Thus, the principle that the lawyer must scrupulously contain his assistance and advocacy within the dictates of the law seems to me perfectly consistent with my view of the lawyer as the client's friend, who maintains the client's interests even against the interests of society.

To be sure, there may have been and may still be situations where the law grossly violates what morality defines as individual rights; and there have been lawyers who have stood ready to defy such laws in order to further their client's rights—the rights which the law should, but did not, recognize. Whatever might be said about those cases, the lawyer's conduct in them travels outside the bounds of legal friendship and becomes political friendship, political agitation, or friendship *tout court*. But that is not the case I am examining. The moral claims which a client has on his lawyer can be fully exhausted though that lawyer contains his advocacy strictly within the limits of the law.

IMMORAL MEANS

I come to what seems to me one of the most difficult dilemmas of the lawyer's role. It is illustrated by the lawyer who is asked to press the unfair claim, to humiliate a witness, to participate in a distasteful or dishonorable scheme. I am assuming that in none of these situations does the lawyer do anything which is illegal or which violates the ethical canons of his profession; the dilemma arises if he acts in a way which seems to him personally dishonorable, but there are no sanctions—legal or professional—which he need fear.

It is not wrong but somewhat lame to argue that the lawyer like the client has autonomy. From this argument it follows that the lawyer who is asked to do something personally distasteful or immoral (though perfectly legal) should be free either to decline to enter into the relationship of "legal friendship" or to terminate it.[6] And if the client can find a lawyer to do the morally nasty but legally permissible thing for him, then all is well—the complexities of the law have not succeeded in thwarting an exercise of autonomy which the law was not entitled to thwart. So long as the first lawyer is reasonably convinced that another lawyer can be found, I cannot see why he is less free to decline the morally repugnant case than he is the boring or poorly paid case. True, but lame, for one wants to know not whether one *may* refuse to do the dirty deed, but whether one is morally *bound* to refuse—bound to refuse even if he is the last lawyer in town and no one else will bail him out of his moral conundrum.

If personal integrity lies at the foundation of the lawyer's right to treat his client as a friend, then surely consideration for personal integrity—his own and others'—must limit what he can do in friendship. Consideration for personal integrity forbids me to lie, cheat, or humiliate, whether in my own interests or those of a friend, so surely they prohibit such conduct on behalf of a client, one's legal friend. This is the general truth, but it must be made more particular if it is to do service here. For there is an opposing consideration. Remember, the lawyer's special kind of friendship is occasioned by the right of the client to exercise his full measure of autonomy within the law. This suggests that one must not transfer uncritically the whole range of personal moral scruples into the arena of legal friendship. After all, not only would I not lie or steal for myself or my friends, I probably also would not pursue socially noxious schemes, foreclose on widows or orphans, or assist in the avoidance of just punishment. So we must be careful lest the whole argument unravel on us at this point.

Balance and structure are restored if we distinguish between kinds of moral scruples. Think of the soldier. If he is a citizen of a just state, where foreign policy decisions are made in a democratic way, he may well believe that it is not up to him to question whether the war he fights is a just war. But he is personally bound not to fire dumdum bullets, not to inflict intentional injury on civilians, and not to abuse prisoners. These are personal wrongs, wrongs done by his person to the person of the victim. So also, the lawyer must distinguish between wrongs that a reasonably just legal system permits to be worked by its rules and wrongs which the lawyer personally commits. Now I do not offer this as a rule which is tight enough to resolve all borderline questions of judgment. We must recognize that the border is precisely the place of friction between competing moral principles. Indeed, it is unreasonable to expect moral arguments to dispense wholly with the need for prudence and judgment.

Consider the difference between humiliating a witness or lying to the judge on one hand, and, on the other hand, asserting the statute of limitations or the lack of a written memorandum to defeat what you know to be a just claim against your client. In the latter case, if an injustice is worked, it is worked because the legal system not only permits it, but also defines the terms and modes of operation. Legal institutions have created the occasion for your act. What you do is not personal; it is a formal, legally-defined act. But the moral quality of lying or abuse obtains both without and within the context of the law. Therefore, my general notion is that a lawyer is morally entitled to act in this formal, representative way even if the result is an injustice, because the legal system which authorizes both the injustice (e.g., the result following the plea of the statute of limitations) and the formal gesture for working it insulates him from personal moral responsibility. I would distinguish between the lawyer's own wrong and the wrong of the system used to advantage by the client.

The clearest case is a lawyer who calls to the attention of the court a controlling legal precedent or statute which establishes his client's position even though that position is an unjust one. (I assume throughout, however, that this unjust law is part of a generally just and decent system. I am not considering at all the moral dilemmas of a lawyer in Nazi Germany or Soviet Russia.) Why are we inclined to absolve him of personal moral responsibility for the result he accomplishes? I assert it is because the wrong is wholly institutional; it is a wrong which does not exist and has no meaning outside the legal framework. The only thing preventing the client from doing this for himself is his lack of knowledge of the law or his lack of authority to operate the levers of the law in official proceedings. It is to supply that lack of knowledge or of formal capacity that the lawyer is in general authorized to act—and the levers he pulls are all legal levers.

Now contrast this to the lawyer who lies to an opposing party in a negotiation. I assume that (except in extreme cases akin to self-defense) an important lie with harmful consequences is an offense to the victim's integrity as a rational moral being, and thus the liar affirms a principle which denigrates his own moral status.[7] Every speech act invites belief, and so every lie is a betrayal. However, may a lawyer lie in his representative capacity? It is precisely my point that a man cannot lie just in his representative capacity; it is like stabbing someone in the back "just" in a representative capacity. The injury and betrayal are not worked by the legal process, but by an act which is generally harmful quite apart from the legal context in which it occurs.

There is an important class of cases which might be termed "lying in a representative capacity." An example is the lawyer presenting to the court a statement by another that he knows to be a lie, as when he puts a perjurious client-defendant on the stand. There is dispute as to whether and when the positive law of professional responsibility permits this,[8] but clearly in such instances it is not the lawyer who is lying. He is like a letter carrier who delivers the falsehood. Whether he is free to do that is more a matter of legal than personal ethics.

A test that might make the distinction I offer more palpable is this: How would it be if it were known in advance that lawyers would balk at the practice under consideration? Would it not be intolerable if it were known that lawyers would not plead the defense of the statute of frauds or of the statute of limitations? And would it not be quite all right if it were known in advance that you cannot get a lawyer to lie for you, though he may perhaps put you on the stand to lie in your own defense?

A more difficult case to locate in the moral landscape is abusive and demeaning cross-examination of a complaining witness. Presumably, positive law and the canons of ethics restrict this type of conduct, but enforcement may be lax or interpretation by a trial judge permissive. So the question arises: What is the lawyer *morally* free to do? Here again I urge the distinction between exposing a witness to the skepticism and scrutiny envisaged by the law and engaging in a personal attack on the witness. The latter is a harm which the lawyer happens to inflict in court, but it is a harm quite apart from the institutional legal context. It is perhaps just a matter of style or tone, but the crucial point is that the probing must not imply that the lawyer believes the witness is unworthy of respect.

The lawyer is not morally entitled, therefore, to engage his own person in doing personal harm to another, though he may exploit the system for his client even if the system consequently works injustice. He may, but must he? This is the final issue to confront. Since he may, he also need not if there is anyone else who will do it. Only if there is no one else does the agony become acute. If there is an obligation in that case, it is an institutional obligation that has devolved upon him to take up a case, to make arguments when it is morally permissible but personally repugnant to him to do so. Once again, the inquiry is moral, for if the law enjoins an obligation against conscience, a lawyer, like any conscientious person, must refuse and pay the price.

The obligation of an available lawyer to accept appointment to defend an accused is clear. Any moral scruples about the proposition that no man should be accused and punished without counsel are not morally well founded. The proposition is intended to enhance the autonomy of individuals within the law. But if you are the last lawyer in town, is there a moral obligation to help the finance company foreclose on the widow's refrigerator? If the client pursues the foreclosure in order to establish a legal right of some significance, I do not flinch from the conclusion that the lawyer is bound to urge this right. So also if the finance company cannot foreclose because of an ideological boycott by the local bar. But if all the other lawyers happen to be on vacation and the case means no more to the finance company than the resale value of one more used refrigerator, common sense says the lawyer can say no. One should be able to distinguish between establishing a legal right and being a cog in a routine, repetitive business operation, part of which just happens to play itself out in court.

CONCLUSION

I do not imagine that what I have said provides an algorithm for resolving some of these perennial difficulties. Rather, what I am proposing is a general way of looking at the problem, a way of understanding not so much the difficult borderline cases as the central and clear ones, in the hope that the principles we can there discern will illuminate our necessarily approximate and prudential quest for resolution on the borderline. The notion of the lawyer as the client's legal friend, whatever its limitations and difficulties, does account for a kind of callousness toward society and exclusivity in the service of the client which otherwise seem quite mysterious. It justifies a kind of scheming which we would deplore on the part of a lay person dealing with another lay person—even if he were acting on behalf of a friend.

It would be absurd to contend that the lawyer must abstain from giving advice that takes account of the client's moral duties and his presumed desire to fulfill them. Indeed, in these situations the lawyer experiences the very special satisfaction of assisting the client not only to realize his autonomy within the law, but also to realize his status as a moral being. I want to make very clear that my conception of the lawyer's role in no way disentitles the lawyer from experiencing this satisfaction. Rather, it has been my purpose to explicate the less obvious point that there is a vocation and a satisfaction even in helping Shylock obtain his pound of flesh or in bringing about the acquittal of a guilty man.

NOTES

1. See, e.g. J. Auberback, *Unequal Justice* (1976); M. Green, *The Other Government* (1975).

    Lord Brougham stated the traditional view of the lawyer's role during his defense of Queen Caroline: [A]n advocate, in the discharge of his duty, knows but one person in all the world, and that person is his client. To save that client by all means and expedients, and at all hazards and costs to other persons, and, among them, to himself, is his first and only duty; and in performing this duty he must not regard the alarm, the torments, the destruction which he may bring upon others. Separating the duty of a patriot from that of an advocate, he must go on reckless of consequences, though it should be his unhappy fate to involve his country in confusion.

    Trial of Queen Caroline 8 (J. Nightingale ed. 1821). A sharply contrasting view was held by law professors at the University of Havana who said that "the first job of a revolutionary lawyer is not to argue that his client is innocent, but rather to determine if his client is guilty and, if so, to seek the sanction which will best rehabilitate him." Berman, *The Cuban Popular Tribunals*, 69 Colum. L. Rev. 1317, 1341 (1969), and a Bulgarian attorney has been quoted as saying, "In a Socialist state where is no division of duty between the judge, prosecutor and defense counsel . . . the defense must assist the prosecution to find the objective truth in a case." J. Kaplan, *Criminal Justice: Introductory Cases and Materials* 264–65 (1973).
2. Mill, "Utilitarianism," in *The Philosophy of John Stuart Mill* 321, 342–44 (M. Cohen ed. 1961).
3. H. Sidgwick, *The Methods of Ethics* 252 (7th ed. 1907).
4. See generally D. Lyons, *Forms and Limits of Utilitarianism* (1965); J. Smart & B. William, *Utilitarianism: For and Against* (1973); Harrod, "Utilitarianism Revised," 45 *Mind* 137 (1936); Mabbott, "Punishment," 48 *Mind* 152 (1939).
5. See generally C. Fried, *An Anatomy of Values*, 203–06; Rawls, *The Independence of Moral Theory*, 48 Am. Phil. Ass'n 17–20 (1975) (Kantian theory, as compared to

utilitarianism, takes seriously basic moral fact of primacy of notion of individual personality).

6. DR 2-100(B)(1) of the *Code of Professional Responsibility* makes withdrawal *mandatory* if the attorney "knows or it is obvious that his client is bringing the legal action, conducting the defense, or asserting a position in the litigation, or is otherwise having steps taken for him, merely for the purpose of harassing or maliciously injuring a person." DR 2-110 (C) (1) (c) and (a) (d) *permit* a lawyer to seek withdrawal if the client either "[i]nsists that the lawyer pursue a course of conduct that is illegal or that is prohibited under the Disciplinary Rules" or "[b]y other conduct renders it unreasonably difficult for the lawyer to carry out his employment effectively." For an argument that an attorney should make his own moral judgments about whether and how to represent clients, see M. Green, *supra* note 1, at 268–89. See also J. Auberback, *supra* note 1, at 279–82.

7. Here I follow Augustine, *Lying,* In Treatises on Various Subjects (R. Deferrari ed. 1952), and I. Kant, *The Metaphysical Principles of Virtue* 90–93 (J. Ellington trans. 1964).

8. Compare M. Freedman, Lawyers' Ethics in an Adversary System, 27–41 (1975), *Advocacy and the Limits of Confidentiality,* 64 Mich L. Rev. 1485 (1966).

ELLIOT D. COHEN

PURE LEGAL ADVOCATES AND MORAL AGENTS: TWO CONCEPTS OF A LAWYER IN AN ADVERSARY SYSTEM

It is sometimes asked whether a good lawyer in an adversary system can also be a good person. We must first notice that there are two different senses of the term *good* employed in this question. In its first occurrence, *good* may be taken in its instrumental sense to mean, roughly, *effective.* In its second occurrence, *good* may be taken in its moral sense to mean *morally good.* Thus the question is whether an effective lawyer can also be a morally good person. And the latter question, it is clear, can be answered only if we have some idea of what we mean by a morally good person, and by an effective lawyer.

Accordingly, in this paper I shall first outline what we take to be salient marks of a morally good person. Second, I shall examine one sense of a lawyer, what we call the *pure legal advocate concept,* in which a good lawyer does *not* satisfy our criteria of a morally good person. Third, I shall examine a further concept of a lawyer, what might be called the *moral agent concept,* according

SOURCE: Elliot D. Cohen, 1985. Pure Legal Advocates and Moral Agents. Reprinted from Pure Legal Advocates and Moral Agents: Two Concepts of a Lawyer in an Adversary System. *Criminal Justice Ethics* (winter/spring):38–59.

to which a good lawyer is, *ipso facto,* a morally good person. Fourth . . ., I shall answer some possible objections to applying the moral agent concept.

MORALLY GOOD PERSONS

Following one tradition, let us say that a morally good person is a person who, through exercise and training, has cultivated certain morally desirable traits of character; the latter traits being constituted by dispositions to act, think, and feel in certain ways, under certain conditions, which are *themselves* morally desirable.[1] What traits of character in particular are morally desirable and to what extent and in what combinations they must be cultivated in order for a person to be morally good are admittedly no settled matters. Still, there are some traits which at least most of us would countenance as being important, if not essential, ingredients of the morally good personality. It is such traits of character with which I shall be concerned, particularly those among them which seem to be the most relevant to legal practice.

What then are some such characteristic marks of a morally good person?

1. We would not ordinarily countenance a person as being morally good if we believed that he was not a *just* person, that is, if we thought that he was not disposed toward treating others justly. There are, however, two senses of *just* and *unjust* in which a person may be said to treat others justly or unjustly.

First, a person may be said to treat others justly when, in distributing some good or service among them, she observes the principle of treating relevantly similar cases in a similar fashion; and she may be said to treat others *unjustly,* in this sense, when she violates this principle. For example, a physician who consistently distributes medical service among the ill on the basis of medical need would, *ceteris paribus,* be acting justly in this sense; whereas one who distributes such service without regard to medical needs, but instead with regard to race or religion, would, in this sense, be acting unjustly. This is so because we typically regard medical need as the controlling factor in distributing health care; whereas race and religion appear to be quite irrelevant in such a context.

We may, however, be said to treat others justly when we are respectful of their legal and moral rights, or when we give to them what they rightfully deserve; and we may be said to treat others unjustly when we intrude upon their legal or moral rights, or when we treat them in ways in which they do not deserve to be treated. For example, one acts justly, in this sense, when he keeps an agreement with an individual who has the right to insist upon its being kept; or a judge acts justly, in this sense, when he hands down a well-deserved punishment to a legal offender; whereas a person perpetrates an injustice upon another, in this sense, when he fails to uphold a binding agreement or when he inflicts injury upon an innocent party.[2]

Let us say, then, that the just person is one who is disposed toward treating others justly in *both* of the above senses. That is, she tends to be consistent in her treatment of others—she does not normally make biased or arbitrary exceptions. But she is also the sort of person who respects individual rights and can usually be counted upon to make good on her obligations to others.

2. Being morally good would also appear to require being *truthful*. By *truthful person* is meant one who is in the habit of asserting things only if he *believes* them to be true. Thus he is in the habit of asserting things with the intention of *informing* his hearers, and not deceiving them, about the truth. An *untruthful* person, on the other hand, is in the habit of asserting things which she *disbelieves;* and this she does with the intention of deceiving her hearers about the truth.[3] Moreover, the untruthful person may deceive not merely through her spoken word, but also by other means. She may, for example, leave false clues or simply remain silent where such measures are calculated to mislead as to the truth.[4] This is not to suggest that such tactics are never justified; it is rather to say that, when they constitute the rule instead of the exception, the person in question has fallen below that level of truthfulness which we should normally require of a morally good person.

3. Being a morally good person would also seem to demand at least *some* measure of *moral courage*. Indeed, it would appear that a person could not be just or truthful if he did not have any such measure; for it often takes courage to be honest or to do what is just. By a *morally* courageous person we mean a person who is disposed toward doing what he thinks is morally right even when he believes that his doing so means, or is likely to mean, his suffering some substantial hardship. As Aristotle suggests, it is "the mark of a brave man to face things that are, and seem, terrible for a man, because it is noble to do so and disgraceful not to do so."[5]

And, therefore, we can say, along with Aristotle, that a person who endures hardship just for the sake of some reward—such as fame or fortune—or for the sake of avoiding some punishment—such as public disfavor or legal sanctions—is not truly acting courageously in this sense, for he acts not because it is morally right to do so, but to gain a reward or avoid a punishment.[6]

4. The moral quality of a person is no doubt often revealed through her monetary habits. Indeed, for some individuals, the making of money constitutes an end in itself for which they willfully transgress the bounds of morally permissible conduct—for example, the pimp, the drug dealer, the thief, and the hit man. And some—those whom we characterize as being stingy, miserly, tight—cling to their money with such tenacity that they would sooner allow great iniquities to occur than surrender a dollar.

The morally good person, on the other hand, would appear to be one who has developed *morally respectable* monetary habits. Such a person Aristotle calls a *liberal* person, one who, he states, "will both give and spend the right amounts and on the right objects, alike in small things and in great, and that with pleasure; he will also take the right amounts and from the right sources."[7] Following Aristotle, let us say then that a morally good person must also be, to some degree, a *liberal* person.

5. We should also expect a morally good person to be *benevolent*. By this we mean that she is disposed to do good for others when she is reasonably situated, and to do no harm. And the concern she has for the well-being of others does not arise out of some ulterior motive but rather *for its own sake*. Furthermore, she is disposed toward *feeling* certain ways under certain conditions—for example, feeling sorrow over another's misfortune or taking pleasure in another's good fortune or in helping another.[8]

It is not supposed, however, that in order to be a morally good person one must be disposed toward benefiting others at great sacrifice to oneself; nor is it supposed that such a person must go very far to benefit or feel sympathetic toward those who do not stand in any concrete personal relation such as friendship or kinship. Still, a person who does not go an inch to benefit *anyone*—unless justice demands it—and who sympathizes with no one is perhaps at most a minimally good person. But one who intentionally harms others, as a matter of course, with pleasure or without regret, cannot normally be regarded as being benevolent. Indeed, such is a mark of a malevolent or morally base person.

6. So too, would we expect to find *trustworthiness* in a morally good person. That is, we should expect such a person to be in a habit of keeping the confidences and agreements which he freely accepts or enters upon. Indeed, the person who breaks faith for no good reason is not just being dishonest; he is also being a "traitor" or a "double-crosser."

This, however, is not to suppose that an individual must *never* breach a trust if he is to be a morally good person. There are, undoubtedly, some extenuating circumstances in which breaking a trust would be the morally right thing to do—as when keeping it involves working some greater injustice upon someone than that involved in breaking it.[9] Nor is it to be supposed that trustworthiness is a *sufficient* condition of being morally good. There may be loyalty among thieves, for instance, but we should not, for that reason alone, take their lot to be morally good.

7. A morally good person, I would suggest, is one who is regularly disposed to do her *own* moral thinking—that is, to come to her own decisions about moral issues on the basis of her own moral principles; and then, in turn, to *act* upon her considered judgment. Kant expressed this fact by saying that the will of a morally good person (that is, a morally good will) is one which is determined "autonomously."[10] Following his usage, let us say then that a morally good person is a person who possesses *moral autonomy*.

Being such a person is undoubtedly no easy matter, for moral decisions are frequently difficult ones to make. For instance, in cases of conflict between one's moral principles, one must weigh one principle against another and then "strike a moral balance"—as, for instance, in a case where keeping a promise involves inflicting harm upon another; or when, in determining the value of the consequences of an act, one must balance the good consequences against the bad ones. And such determinations are clearly no mere matter of logical deduction. All that one can reasonably be expected to do in such cases is to try one's level best. But it is a mark of a morally autonomous person, and thus of a morally good person, that he actually *makes* such an earnest effort.

Keeping the foregoing criteria of a morally good person in mind, let us now turn to an analysis of lawyers.

THE PURE LEGAL ADVOCATE CONCEPT

Following one traditional usage, we can say that the concept of a lawyer is a *functional* concept—that is, it may be defined in terms of the function or role which a lawyer *qua* lawyer is supposed to perform, in an analogous manner in which a watchdog may be defined in terms of its function of guarding property, or in which a carpenter's hammer may be defined in terms of *its* function of driving in nails. Hence, just as a good (effective) watchdog may be defined as a dog which performs well the function of guarding property, so too may a good (effective) lawyer be defined as a person who performs well the function or role of a lawyer.[11] What, then, we may ask, *is* the function or role of a lawyer?

One sense of *lawyer* is that in which the role of a lawyer is restricted to that of the client's legal advocate, and in which a good lawyer is thus conceived as being *simply* an effective legal advocate. This sense, which we shall hereafter call the *pure legal advocate concept* is exemplified in the classic statement made by Lord Brougham when he was defending Queen Caroline against George IV in their divorce case before the House of Lords. He states:

> An advocate, in discharge of his duty, knows but one person in all the world, and that person is his client. To save that client by all means and expedients, and at all hazards and costs to other persons, and, amongst them, to himself, is his first and only duty.[12]

The pure legal advocate concept is also more recently suggested by Canon 15 of the ABA *Canons of Professional Ethics,* which states that

> the lawyer owes "entire devotion to the interest of the client, warm zeal in the maintenance and defense of his rights and the exertion of his utmost learning and ability," to the end that nothing be taken or be withheld from him, save by the rules of law, legally applied.[13]

This concept is also suggested, among other places, in *The Ethics of Advocacy* by Charles P. Curtis.[14]

Given the pure legal advocate concept, it is easy for one to conclude that the necessary and sufficient mark of a good lawyer is her tendency to win cases by all legal means. For, as was said, this concept supposes that a good lawyer is simply an effective legal advocate; and it is easy to suppose that the necessary and sufficient mark of an effective legal advocate is her tendency to legally win cases. A good lawyer hence emerges as a legal technician skillful in manipulating legal rules for the advancement of her clients' legal interests; in this sense, the good lawyer is no different than a skillful chess player able to manipulate the rules of chess to win *his* game.

Furthermore, given this concept, a lawyer may, and indeed is required, to do certain kinds of things on behalf of his client which would ordinarily be regarded as being morally objectionable. In such instances all that matters, so far as lawyering is concerned, is that such acts are legal means of advancing the client's legal interests. For instance, a defense attorney in a rape case may cross-examine the prosecutrix, whom he knows to be telling the truth, about her chastity for purposes of casting doubt upon her truthful testimony. Or, he may permit his client to take the stand knowing full well that the client will perjure himself. Or, a lawyer in a civil case may invoke a legal technicality (for example, the statute of limitations) on behalf of his client in order to defeat a just cause against him. Or, a corporate lawyer on a continuing retainer may represent a client who seeks to keep a factory in operation which creates a public health hazard by emitting harmful pollutants into the air.[15]

However, some who countenance the pure legal advocate concept—namely, those sometimes referred to as rule utilitarians—hold that such immoralities as the above-mentioned ones are the necessary evils of maintaining an adversary system which itself does the greatest good. The working assumption here is that the adversarial form of legal administration, wherein two zealous advocates are pitted against each other before an impartial judge, constitutes the best-known way of maximizing truth and justice; and that, furthermore, this system works best when lawyers disregard their personal moral convictions and thereby restrict their professional activities to the zealous legal representation of their clients.[16]

If the rule utilitarian is correct, then lawyering, so conceived, can be said to be a morally justified function, notwithstanding that, on that view, a lawyer may be required to engage in conduct which, by common standards, is morally objectionable. Thus, when seen in this light, the lawyer emerges as a promoter of the highly prized ends of justice and truth, and as an individual who, because of her service to society, is worthy of praise and admiration. Indeed, she begins to seem like a morally good person.

Nevertheless, I want to suggest that the appearance is deceiving, that, on the contrary, the lawyer, so conceived, will inevitably fall short of our marks of a morally good person. Moreover, I want to suggest that, as a result of such shortcomings, there is substantial disutility in the pure legal advocate concept of lawyering which its utilitarian exponents rarely take into account in their utilitarian justification of it.

Let me emphasize that I am supposing, along with Aristotle, that it takes exercise and training to cultivate the character traits of a morally good person: one is not simply born with them.[17] My claim is, accordingly, that the legal function as construed under the pure legal advocate concept, with its emphasis on suppression of the individual lawyer's personal moral convictions, does not allow for the cultivation of these traits and is, in fact, quite conducive to their corresponding vices.

Furthermore, I am supposing that a lawyer cannot easily detach his professional life from his private life and thereby cannot easily be one sort of person with one set of values in the one life, and a quite different sort with quite different values in the other life.[18]

The latter supposition is justified by the substantial amount of empirical evidence that now exists correlating the personality traits of individuals with their specific vocations.[19] One ambiguity, however, is whether individual vocations influence personality traits,[20] or personality traits influence choice of vocation, or some combination of both; for any one of these hypotheses would explain the correlation.

Some studies have supported the hypothesis that personality traits influence choice of profession—that is, that people with certain personalities are attracted to certain professions in order to satisfy their individual needs.[21] But even *if* this hypothesis is true, and the other above-mentioned hypotheses are false, it is clear that the kind of person found in a profession will remain a function of the way the profession itself is conceived. Specifically, on the hypothesis in question: We would expect the personalities of those choosing careers in law to depend upon their conception of a lawyer. But, if I am correct, then legal practice as construed on the pure legal advocate model could seem attractive only to those individuals contemplating a career in law who would feel comfortable in a professional climate which discourages, rather than promotes, the personality traits of a morally good person as here understood.

MORAL SHORTCOMINGS OF THE PURE LEGAL ADVOCATE

1. It appears that a lawyer, on the pure legal advocate concept, will inevitably fall short of being a *just* person. For although she does not violate the principle of treating relevantly similar cases similarly when she gives special preference to her client—inasmuch as being a client would appear to be a *relevant* dissimilarity for the purposes of an adversary system—she does, indeed, work injustices through the violation of the *moral rights* of individuals. For on this concept the lawyer's fundamental professional obligation is to do whatever she can, within legal limits, to advance the legal interests of her clients. But from this basic obligation there derives a more specific one which, contra Kant, may be expressed thus: "Whenever legally possible treat others not as ends but as means toward winning your case."

For example, the criminal defense lawyer is thereby authorized to knowingly destroy the testimony of an innocent rape victim in order to get an acquittal for his client; and a civil lawyer is authorized to knowingly deprive another of what he rightfully deserves by invoking the statute of limitations for the purpose of furthering his client's interests. But we shall concur with Kant in maintaining that lawyers, like anyone else, have a duty to treat others with the respect which they, as persons, have a right to insist upon.

2. Nor will the pure legal advocate meet the mark of *truthfulness*. For, from her cardinal obligation there derives the secondary obligation of being *un*truthful where doing so can legally contribute toward winning the case. An example of a lawyer who complies with this obligation is one who remains silent when she knows that her client has, under oath, lied to the court. The lawyer, by wittingly saying nothing, engages in deceptive behavior—she contributes to the court's being deceived as to the truth—and is on that count *herself* guilty of being untruthful. Indeed, scrupulous adherence to *this* obligation could hardly support anything but an untruthful habit.

3. Nor does the concept in question support *moral courage.* For, according to it, the personal moral convictions of a lawyer are irrelevant to his function and should not serve as reasons for zealous representation of clients, or for any sacrifices—of time, money, reputation, and the like—which he may make on their behalf. Indeed, if he is to do his job well, then he must get into the habit of *not* being influenced by his moral outlook. Rather, any sacrifice he may make should be for the sake of obtaining a legal victory, be it a moral one or not. It is plausible to suppose, however, that where morality takes a back seat, ulterior motives, such as the self-aggrandizement obtained through winning, will serve as the primary motivation.

4. Nor does the pure legal advocate concept support liberality; for the pure legal advocate, through her unconcern with the moral character of her clients and the purposes for which they hire her, gets into the habit of taking money from dishonorable individuals for unsavory purposes. She thus emerges as a professional who can be hired, for a good sum, to do the dirty work of a villain or a scoundrel. Indeed, she then begins to sound more like a hired assassin than like the liberal person whom Aristotle had in view. The high-priced corporate lawyer who wittingly helps her corporate client to market a dangerous product provides us with one example of such a lawyer; and the high-priced criminal lawyer who specializes in defending mass murderers is another.

5. Furthermore, the pure legal advocate concept does not appear to satisfy the minimum condition of benevolence—that is, the nonmalevolence expected of a morally good person. For, from his primary obligation, there derives the secondary obligation to employ even such means to forward a client's interests as are injurious to others, so long, of course, as they are legal. But this also means that a lawyer must learn to put off sympathetic feelings which a benevolent person would normally have. In particular, he must get used to working injury upon others without having any strong feelings of guilt, sorrow, or regret. For, to be sure, such feelings could only serve to interfere with the execution of his basic obligation to his client. The result is thus a callous attitude in his dealings with others. As Charles Curtis puts it, the lawyer "is required to treat others as if they were barbarians and enemies." [22] And, notwithstanding the benefits the lawyer may confer upon his clients, we should not want to call such a person benevolent.

6. Prima facie, it appears that the morally desirable character trait of *trustworthiness* receives strong support from the pure legal advocate concept. For, indeed, it appears that a lawyer cannot put on the most effective representation

of her client's interests unless she is also prepared to hold in confidence the secrets entrusted to her by her client. A problem with this view, however, arises in the case in which there is a conflict between a lawyer's obligation to keep her client's confidence and some other *moral* obligation—for instance, that of not harming innocent persons. In such a case, the restricted lawyer is required to keep her client's confidence so long as it is legally possible and in her client's best interest to do so. Her considered judgment as to what is, under the circumstances, morally best is then quite irrelevant. But it is a mark of a morally good person to choose what she thinks is, all things considered, the *morally right* thing to do in such a situation. Hence, whereas a morally good person sees his obligation to keep confidences as one among several moral principles which may at times override one another, the pure legal advocate sees *her* professional obligation to keep her clients' confidences as binding upon her quite independently of the moral propriety of doing so in any particular case.

In any event, even *if* it is admitted that the pure legal advocate concept reinforces trustworthiness which, *in itself,* is a morally good trait, this still does not show that the good lawyer, on this conception, can be a morally good person. For, as we have seen, there are *further* requisites of a morally good life.

7. I have suggested that an important quality of a morally good person is that he has *moral autonomy*. However, the pure legal advocate concept offers no stimulus to the cultivation of this trait. For, as we have seen, the pure legal advocate inhabits a world in which his moral judgment is quite beside the point. If morality is relevant, it is so at the level of the judge or the legislator, but it is quite outside the purview of the lawyer's function. The lawyer must know the law and must know that he owes his undivided allegiance to his client. Given the latter he can easily accommodate himself to the requirements of the law. His decisions are, in effect, made *for him* by the system he serves. He is more like a cog in a machine and less like a person. But the moral world is inhabited by *persons*—that is, individuals who autonomously confront their moral responsibilities; so that, for a lawyer who has grown comfortable with passing the buck of moral responsibility, there is little hope of his aspiring to the morally good life.

THE MORAL AGENT CONCEPT

If I am correct, then it appears that the pure legal advocate who scrupulously adheres to her restricted role, far from being a morally good person, will be given ample opportunity for becoming—if she is not already—quite the opposite. For she will thereby be placed in a professional climate conducive to her being unjust instead of just; untruthful instead of truthful; unmotivated by a moral outlook instead of morally courageous; illiberal instead of liberal; callous instead of benevolent; morally irresponsible instead of morally autonomous. In short, she will fall well below the minimum standards of a morally good person.

But if all this is right, then there will, it seems, be a good deal of *disutility* in the pure legal advocate concept which, indeed, any utilitarian exponent of it ought to consider in computing its overall balance of utility. For it appears that such personality traits as those mentioned above, when associated with our concept of a lawyer, can serve only to bring disrespect upon the legal profession and, by association, upon the legal system as a whole. And this low regard may well lead to a commonplace view of the adversary system as a haven for the guilty and the wicked and as something of which the innocent and the morally good ought to steer clear. It can very well serve to discourage persons of strong moral character from entering the legal profession.[23] It is also quite plausible that pure legal advocates who, by virtue of their knowledge of, and relation to, the law, are uniquely situated to contribute to needed changes in unjust laws, will disconcern themselves with such moral reformation. Moreover, add to these the disutility involved in the unsavory acts performed by pure legal advocates on behalf of their clients in the normal course of discharging their professional obligations—the injuries thereby done to individual litigants as well as to others—and there is at least a strong prima facie case for abandoning the adversary system entirely in favor of a different model (an inquisitorial model for instance) or for adopting a concept of a lawyer in an adversary system which avoids these disutilities.

Fortunately, there *is* a further concept of a lawyer which, while *not* abandoning the adversarial approach, serves to avoid much of the distitility mentioned above.

This further sense, hereafter called the *moral agent concept,* is exemplified, for example, in the remarks on advocacy made by Lord Chief Justice Cockburn, in the presence of Lord Brougham, at a dinner given in honor of M. Berryer on November 8, 1864. He stated:

> My noble and learned friend, Lord Brougham, whose words are the words of wisdom, said that an advocate should be fearless in carrying out the interests of his client: but I couple that with this qualification and this restriction—that the arms which he wields are to be the arms of the warrior and not of the assassin. It is his duty to strive to accomplish the interest of his clients *per fas,* but not *per nefas;* it is his duty, to the utmost of his power, to seek to reconcile the interests he is bound to maintain, and the duty it is incumbent upon him to discharge, with the eternal and immutable interests of truth and justice.[24]

The moral agent concept was also expressed, more recently, by John Noonan when he remarked that

> a lawyer should not impose his conscience on his client; neither can he accept his client's decision and remain entirely free from all moral responsibility, subject only to the restraints of the criminal law. The framework of the adversary system provides only the first set of guidelines for a lawyer's conduct. He is also a human being and cannot submerge his humanity by playing a technician's role.[25]

And this concept is suggested elsewhere by Richard Wasserstrom, Jeremy Bentham, and *The Report of the Joint Conference on Professional Responsibility.*[26]

Given the moral agent concept, we may no longer say that the good lawyer is *simply* the effective legal advocate; he is, rather, one who is effective in *morally as well as legally* advocating his client's cause. Hence, one cannot infer from this concept that the good lawyer is one who tends to win his cases. For, on this concept, he is not merely a good legal technician; he is also one who conducts himself in the manner of a *morally good person*—that is, as a person with morally desirable character traits.

It is evident, however, that a lawyer cannot so conduct herself unless she also subscribes to the *moral principles* to which a morally good person would subscribe were she to participate in an adversarial process. If our analysis of a morally good person is supposed, then such principles would need to be ones supportive of the personality traits set forth in that analysis. To wit, from these character traits we may derive a corresponding set of moral principles which are adjusted to an adversarial context. I suggest the following formulations, although other similar formulations are possible:

- Treat others as ends in themselves and not as mere means to winning cases. (Principle of Individual Justice)
- Treat clients and other professional relations who are relevantly similar in a similar fashion. (Principle of Distributive Justice)
- Do not deliberately engage in behavior apt to deceive the court as to the truth. (Principle of Truthfulness)
- Be willing, if necessary, to make reasonable personal sacrifices—of time, money, popularity, and so on—for what you justifiably believe to be a morally good cause. (Principle of Moral Courage)
- Do not give money to, or accept money from, clients for wrongful purposes or in wrongful amounts. (Principle of Liberality)
- Avoid harming others in the process of representing your client. (Principle of Nonmalevolence)
- Be loyal to your client, and do not betray his confidences. (Principle of Trustworthiness)
- Make your *own* moral decisions to the best of your ability and act consistently upon them. (Principle of Moral Autonomy)

We can say that the above principles, or ones like them, at least in part *constitute or define* the moral agent concept of a lawyer; for they are principles to which a lawyer's conduct must to some extent conform if he is to function not simply as a legal advocate but also as a morally good person.

I am *not* suggesting that these principles are unconditional ones. Indeed, to say so would be unrealistic since they will inevitably come into conflict with each other when applied to specific contexts, thereby making it impossible for the lawyer to satisfy all principles at once. (That is, in order to be truthful, a lawyer may need to betray a client's trust, and conversely.) Rather, what I am suggesting is that such principles impose upon a lawyer *conditional*—or prima facie—obligations which, in cases of conflict, must be weighed, one against the other, by the lawyer in question in the context in question.

Let me offer an example which will illustrate the difference between applying, in conflict situations, the above multi-principle model and the pure legal advocate model. In *Lawyer's Ethics in an Adversary System,* Monroe Freedman cites the following:

> In a recent case in Lake Pleasant, New York, a defendant in a murder case told his lawyers about two other people he had killed and where their bodies had been hidden. The lawyers went there, observed the bodies, and took photographs of them. They did not, however, inform the authorities about the bodies until several months later, when their clients had confessed to those crimes. In addition to withholding the information from police and prosecutors, one of the attorneys denied information to one of the victims' parents, who came to him in the course of seeking his missing daughter.[27]

According to Freedman, the lawyers in the above-cited case were simply discharging their *unconditional* professional obligation to represent their clients' legal interests. However, if the moral agent concept is supposed, then it is clear that the above lawyers could have revealed where the bodies were buried. Admittedly, according to the Principle of Trustworthiness, a lawyer has a (prima facie) obligation to keep his client's confidences. But he also has further (prima facie) obligations such as those of Truthfulness, Individual Justice, and Non-malevolence. I think that a plausible case can be made that the latter principles were sacrificed to some extent by the lawyers in the Lake Pleasant case at least insofar as their treatment of the relatives of the deceased was concerned. And it is plausible, I believe, to argue that the moral weight of the latter principles, taken collectively, outweighed that of the Principle of Trustworthiness taken by itself in the situation in question. This need *not* have been what the lawyers in the cited case should have finally decided to be the correct balancing of principles. The point I want to make is rather that the lawyers *did have* in the first place, on the conception in question, the *moral autonomy* (as legitimized by our Principle of Moral Autonomy) to make such a judgment on the matter. It is just such moral autonomy—with its weighing of competing moral principles, one against the other—that the pure legal advocate concept disallows.

Of course, if lawyers are allowed such autonomy, there arises the difficulty of providing *criteria* for arbitrating between conflicting principles. This difficulty, we have seen, does not arise on the pure legal advocate model since the pure legal advocate is, in effect, insulated from making moral trade-offs by her unconditional allegiance to her client's legal interests.

One normative view regarding how a lawyer, in accordance with the moral agent concept, might go about solving moral dilemmas takes the form of a "pure" utilitarianism. According to such an ethic, all eight of our principles are to be understood as receiving their ultimate justification from the principle of utility. Hence, in case of conflict the final court of appeal will be the principle of utility itself.

I do not think, however, that such a basis for solving lawyers' moral dilemmas would be adequate. My objection is that which has traditionally been made against utilitarian ethics which are not tempered by justice considerations. Suppose, for example, a criminal lawyer is defending an influential politician accused of rape. Suppose also that the politician admits his guilt to his attorney but nevertheless informs her of his intention to testify under oath (to that which is false) that the defendant first made sexual advances toward him. Now suppose that the politician in question is in the process of bringing about a change in taxation which would mean substantial tax reductions for millions of Americans, and that, furthermore, these efforts would most likely be defeated if the politician in question were convicted of rape. On the pure utilitarian criterion, it would appear that the attorney in question would be committed to allowing the politician to perjure himself notwithstanding the defeat of the true rape claim; for the greatest good would (*ex hypothesi*) be served by allowing the politician to escape the charge of rape through his perjured testimony. But in such a case it would seem unjust (by the Principle of Individual Justice) to sacrifice the well-being of the truthful rape victim for the tax reduction. Indeed, in doing so, the lawyer would arguably be committing a grossly immoral act. But, if so, the principle of utility untempered by some principle(s) of justice—such as the Principle of Individual Justice or the Principle of Distributive Justice—would be an inadequate criterion for settling lawyers' moral dilemmas.

A modified utilitarian approach would be to construct a meta-level rule telling lawyers which principle is to receive priority in cases of conflict. The meta-level rule is then to be justified on the basis of the utility of having such a rule. For example, it could be held that the greatest good is ultimately served by requiring lawyers, as a matter of course, to give priority to truthfulness over nonmalevolence.

I do not think, however, that such a position would be tenable. First, like rule utilitarianism in general, it leads to a kind of rule worship where lawyers are asked to abide by a rule even in contexts where the greatest good would not be served by subscribing to it or in which justice considerations would seem to proscribe acting in accordance with it. Furthermore, the view in question is inconsistent with the Principle of Moral Autonomy which legitimizes a lawyer's acting according to his own considered moral judgments. Indeed, in one of its forms—the one in which the Principle of Trustworthiness is unconditionally ranked above all other principles—this view would seem to be extensionally equivalent to the pure legal advocate model according to which a lawyer is asked to ignore his personal moral convictions.

How then is a lawyer, on the moral agent conception, to resolve antimonies arising between these principles? Although I do not see any formula for doing so, this is not to suggest that one resolution is just as respectable as any other. For one thing, there is a difference between the ethical judgment of a lawyer that is *factually enlightened* and one that is not. For example, the judgment of a lawyer who allows trustworthiness to override harm in a particular case without adequate knowledge of the nature and extent of the harm is less respectable than the judgment of a lawyer who takes account of such facts.

Still, once the facts are known a decision must be made in their light; and I think it would be intellectually dishonest to suggest that there is some principle(s) from which we may logically deduce our decision. Principles take us just so far, leaving the final verdict in our hands.

It is the lack of clear noncontroversial criteria for resolving moral dilemmas, and the ensuing feeling that ethics is, in the end, a matter of "fiat" or "personal preference," that may make some feel uncomfortable about giving lawyers moral autonomy. However, it should be kept in mind by those who worry about the "gray" areas of ethics that the making of ethical decisions is already an accepted and unavoidable part of the role of *some* officials in our legal system. For example, given the "open-textured" quality of legal rules and precedents themselves, judges often need to rely upon their own *moral* evaluations in deciding whether a given set of facts falls under a given legal rule or precedent.[28] But if judges can handle their moral problems—and I believe that, in general, they *do* handle them—then there appears to be less reason to fear that lawyers cannot or will not handle *their* moral problems. . . .

I have already argued that the alternative to the moral agent concept—that is, the pure legal advocate concept—can have unwelcome effects upon the moral character of lawyers and that this, in turn, can have a significant measure of social disutility which *any* utilitarian calculus (whether this calculus be "pure" or mixed with deontological considerations) should consider. Yet there are also arguments *against* this conception. I will now discuss what seem to me to be two very common ones.

THE MORAL AGENT CONCEPT:
SOME ARGUMENTS AGAINST IT ANSWERED

According to one argument, if lawyers are given the autonomy to break confidences with clients in those situations in which they judge further serious moral principles to be overriding, then the obligation lawyers have to keep their clients' confidences will be destroyed. As a result, clients will cease to confide in their lawyers and thus will withhold information necessary for an adequate defense of their legal interests. The final result will then be the demise of the adversary system itself and its accompanying benefits. For example, according to Monroe Freedman,

> the adversary system, within which the lawyer functions, contemplates that the lawyer frequently will learn from the client information that is highly incriminating and may even learn, as in the Lake Pleasant case, that the client has in fact committed serious crimes. In such a case, if the attorney were required to

divulge that information, the obligation of confidentiality would be destroyed, and with it, the adversary system itself.[29]

First, the argument in question rests upon the unfounded assumption that the obligation of confidentiality will be destroyed if lawyers are allowed to take exception to it in serious moral conflicts. That is, because lawyers in general are allowed to make such exceptions does not mean that they will no longer see themselves as being under an obligation to keep their clients' confidences. To argue thus is like arguing that if certain exceptions to the proscription against killing are permitted—such as self-defense—then people will no longer see themselves as having a duty not to kill others. The fall down the slippery slope does not necessarily occur.

Second, those who advance the argument in question do not provide adequate evidence to support the claim that clients in general will cease to confide in their lawyers if they are not given an unconditional guarantee by their lawyers that all information conveyed, no matter what, will be taken confidentially. Indeed, even such intimate bonds as friendship, to which the lawyer-client relation has sometimes been compared,[30] have their moral limits. We do not typically expect our friends to surrender their moral integrity for our security. Yet that fact does not serve to destroy the bond of trust existing in such a relation. The claim that the bond of trust existing between lawyer and client will be destroyed if lawyers are given their moral autonomy appears to be equally as unfounded.

Third, even if it is admitted that according lawyers such moral autonomy will cause *some* clients, even some innocent ones, to omit information necessary for their adequate defense, this fact does not entail that the problem will be so widespread and serious as to lead to the destruction of the adversary system. It must also be kept in mind that an unconditional bond of confidentiality also generates difficulties. (Consider, for example, those resulting from the lawyers' actions in the Lake Pleasant case.) Moreover, there are favorable consequences of according lawyers moral autonomy which must also be taken into account. Thus, for example, Bentham suggests that one such consequence would be "that a guilty person will not in general be able to derive quite so much assistance from his law advisor, in the way of concerting a false defense, as he may do at present.[31]

In short, there is simply no clear proof that the effects of according lawyers the autonomy to take moral exception to the confidentiality principle would be so dramatic as to destroy the adversary system.

It is sometimes argued that, if lawyers were permitted the power of accepting or refusing employment or of retaining or withdrawing from cases, according to their personal moral judgments as to the guilt of a party or as to the goodness of a cause, then the role of the judge would be usurped; the lawyer, in effect, would become the judge. And this could, in turn, present serious moral difficulties, particularly for defendants in criminal cases. For there it may be argued that, if an individual defendant seems guilty enough, then no criminal lawyer will take his case, and, as such, he will be deprived of his constitutional right to counsel and to his day in court. Moreover, it is often difficult for a criminal lawyer to withdraw from a case he has already undertaken without leaving the impression that his ex-client is guilty. And, of course, it is always possible that a person who seems guilty is not *actually* guilty.[32]

I do not think, however, that the above argument succeeds in destroying the moral agent concept. For one thing, it depends upon the untenable assumption that if the moral agent concept is generally accepted, then *no* criminal lawyer will defend seemingly guilty individuals. It is more realistic to suppose that, no matter *what* concept is adopted, there will always be *someone* to take up such a cause.

But more importantly, the argument appears to be attacking a straw man. For there is no inconsistency between a criminal lawyer's defending an apparently guilty client and her accepting the moral agent concept. None of our eight moral principles constituting that concept would, in fact, militate against her doing so. Indeed, it appears that an adequate understanding of our principle of distributive justice would demand that criminal lawyers *not* allow individuals, no matter how guilty they might *seem* to be, to be deprived of their constitutional right to counsel. Moreover, it often takes *moral courage* to represent clients who have come under public disfavor (see EC 2-27). Hence the moral agent concept appears to support criminal lawyers' defense of the guilty rather than to proscribe it.

Nor do I think that there is any solid support for the claim that, if lawyers accept the moral agent concept with its insistence upon lawyers' moral autonomy, the role of the judge will be usurped by the lawyer. For such autonomy is not tantamount to license. The autonomous lawyer is still his client's advocate; it is his job to defend his client's legal interests and to present them in the clearest and most forceful light. But he must accomplish this task within the parameters of morality—that is, without forfeiting his moral integrity. It is not at all clear, therefore, why such a conception must lead to usurpation of the judge's role by the lawyer.

Concluding Remarks

Again we return to the question whether a good lawyer, in an adversary system, can be a morally good person. In answering this, a great deal depends upon our concept of a lawyer. For it is our full conception of the role of a professional which sets the parameters on the kind of personality compatible with that role and which serves to shape the personalities of its participants accordingly, or to invite those sorts who would fit it. I do not mean to suggest by this that there are not currently practicing lawyers who fit our criteria of morally good persons. This would be an absurd suggestion. Yet it is, I think, probable that most of these individuals have adopted the moral agent concept in some form or other.

If the legal profession is to move further in the direction of the moral agent concept, some changes must be made in its understanding. . . .

The spirit of this concept will need to be *internalized*, as well, through the appropriate education. Above all, law schools and prelaw curricula will need to provide prospective lawyers with the facilities for cultivating an understanding of, and sensitivity to, moral problems. For the lawyer's ability to deal sensibly with such moral problems is an essential part of his professional function. It is beyond the scope of this paper to outline in detail what such curricula would consist of, but they would, undoubtedly, include diverse courses in applied ethics and legal philosophy.[33]

Presently, the legal profession is, I think, on a course toward the moral agent concept. Conceptual shifts of this magnitude, however, do not spring up full blown overnight; they take time and occur in stages. But, to be sure, it is a process worth nurturing, not just for the good of the legal profession itself, but for the good of all of us, whom the profession so vitally serves.[34]

NOTES

1. *See* ARISTOTLE, NICOMACHEAN ETHICS, Bk. II. All quotations in this paper from ARISTOTLE's ETHICS are from 9 THE WORKS OF ARISTOTLE (W. D. Ross ed. 1963).

2. *Compare* Joel Feinberg's distinction between "comparative" and "noncomparative" senses of justice in his SOCIAL PHILOSOPHY 98–99 (1973). *Compare also* John Stuart Mill's discussion of justice in his UTILITARIANISM ch. 5.

3. *See* Chisholm & Feehan, *The Intent to Deceive,* 74 J. OF PHIL. 143–59 (1977).

4. *Compare* C. FRIED, RIGHT AND WRONG 57–58 (1978).

5. ARISTOTLE, *supra* note 1, at 1117a16.

6. *Id.* at 1116a15–b3.

7. *Id.* at 1120b29–31.

8. *Compare* H. SIDGWICK, THE METHODS OF ETHICS 238–39 (1962); *compare also* A. SMITH, THE THEORY OF MORAL SENTIMENTS 345 (1966).

9. *Compare, e.g.,* the discussion of justified violations to the rule of confidentiality between a physician and his patient in T. L. BEAUCHAMP & J. F. CHILDRESS, PRINCIPLES OF BIOMEDICAL ETHICS 214–17 (1979).

10. I. KANT, GROUNDWORK OF THE METAPHYSIC OF MORALS 98–99 (H. J. Paton trans. 1964).

11. A person can admittedly perform the function of a lawyer without actually *being* a lawyer, in an analogous manner in which a rock can serve the function of a hammer without actually being a hammer. Further conditions must also be satisfied— for example, a lawyer must have gone to law school and passed the bar. For this complication in the analysis of functional concepts—which is here ignored for the sake of simplicity—see G. H. VON WRIGHT, THE VARIETIES OF GOODNESS 20–22 (1968).

12. M. H. FREEDMAN, LAWYER'S ETHICS IN AN ADVERSARY SYSTEM 9 (1975).

13. AMERICAN BAR ASSOCIATION, CANONS OF PROFESSIONAL ETHICS (1908).

14. *See* Curtis, *The Ethics of Advocacy,* 4 STAN. L. REV. 3–23 (1951).

15. The cited examples appear, respectively, in FREEDMAN, *supra* note 12 at ch. 4, esp. 48–49; Freedman, *Professional Responsibility of the Criminal Defense Lawyer: The*

Three Hardest Questions, 64 Mich. L. Rev. 1474–78 (1966); Fried, *The Lawyer as Friend: The Moral Foundations of the Lawyer-Client Relation*, 85 Yale L. J. 1064 (1976); Wasserstrom, *Lawyers as Professionals: Some Moral Issues*, 5 Hum. Rts. 8 (1975).

16. "Are there no limits (short of violating criminal laws and rules of court) to the partisan zeal that an attorney should exert on behalf of a client who may be a murderer, a rapist, a drug pusher, or a despoiler of the environment? Is the lawyer never to make a conscientious judgement about the impact of the client's conduct on the public interest and to temper the zealousness of his or her representation accordingly? I believe that the adversary system is itself in the highest public interest . . . and that it is, therefore, inconsistent with the public interest to direct lawyers to be less than zealous in their roles as partisan advocates in an adversary system." Freedman, *Are There Public Interest Limits on Lawyers' Advocacy?* 2 J. of the Legal Prof. 47 (1977).

17. Aristotle, *supra* note 1 at 1103a15–b1.

18. *Compare* Richard Wasserstrom's suggestion that the behavior engaged in by the Watergate lawyers on behalf of Richard Nixon—lying to the public, dissembling, stonewalling, tape-recording conversations, playing dirty tricks, etc.—was "the likely if not inevitable consequence of their legal acculturation," *supra* note 15 at 15.

19. For example, *see generally*, *Factors and Theories of Career Development*, in B. Shertzer & S. Stone, Fundamentals of Guidance ch. 12 (1981).

20. *See, e.g.*, the discussions of studies on the influence of vocations upon personality traits in Komarovsky & Sargent, *Research into Subcultural Influences upon Personality*, in Culture and Personality 145–48 (S. S. Sargent and M. W. Smith eds. 1949).

21. *See, e.g.*, Teevan, *Personality Correlates of Undergraduate Fields of Specialization*, 18 J. of Consulting Psychology 212–14 (1954).

22. Curtis, *supra* note 14 at 5.

23. *See* Teevan, *supra* note 21.

24. Costigan, *The Full Remarks on Advocacy of Lord Brougham and Lord Chief Justice Cockburn at the Dinner to M. Berryer on November 8, 1964*, 19 Calif. L. Rev. 523 (1931).

25. Noonan, *The Purposes of Advocacy and the Limits of Confidentiality*, 64 Mich L. Rev. 1492 (1966).

26. *See*, respectively, Wasserstrom, *supra* note 15; J. Bentham, Rationale of Judicial Evidence, bk. 9, ch. 5, in 7 The Works of Jeremy Bentham (J. Bowring ed. 1843); American Bar Association and the Association of American Law Schools, *Professional Responsibility: Report of the Joint Conference*, 44 A.B.A. J. 1161 (1958).

27. M. Freedman, *supra* note 12 at 1.

28. *Compare* Jones, *Legal Realism and Natural Law*, in The Nature of Law (M. P. Golding ed. 1966).

29. M. Freedman, *supra* note 12 at 5.

30. *See, e.g.*, Fried, *supra* note 15.

31. J. Bentham, *supra* note 26 at 474.

32. *Compare generally*, M. Freedman, *supra* note 12.

33. Investigations of this sort are already in progress. *See, e.g.*, The Council for Philosophical Studies, S. Gorovitz & B. Miller, Professional Responsibility in the Law: A Curriculum Report from the Institute on Law & Ethics (Summer 1977).

(The Center for Philosophy and Public Policy at the University of Maryland has also recently announced the availability of a model course on "Ethics and the Legal Profession" prepared by Professor David Luban. A copy can be obtained by sending $2.50 for postage and handling to Maryland Courses, Center for Philosophy and Public Policy, Woods 0123, University of Maryland, College Park, MD 20742.)

34. I am thankful to Professor Walter Probert and Judge Charles Smith for their assistance in obtaining important references. I am also thankful to Gale Spieler Cohen and an anonymous referee of *Criminal Justice Ethics* for their contribution to some of the ideas contained herein.

PRACTICE

STEVEN WASSERMAN

THE PHILOSOPHER AS PUBLIC DEFENDER: IN DEFENSE OF A RAPIST

As a public defender, my job is to represent those who are accused of crimes and cannot afford an attorney. Clients are assigned to me if they are arrested during my tour of duty at the courthouse. I must take all comers. While some of the charges against my clients are petty, pathetic, or amusing, many of them are accused of serious, ugly crimes.

Regardless of the charges, I am required to do everything the law allows to help my clients achieve the best possible outcome for themselves. Occasionally, conflicts have arisen between my responsibilities as an advocate for my clients, and my reponsibility, as a human being, for the results of my actions. This essay concerns a conflict between professional ethics and personal morality, a case in which it was my job to participate in a miscarriage of justice.

Sam was a handsome young laborer in his 20s who was accused of rape by Doris, a pretty, well-spoken woman of the same age who had taken a ride with Sam in his car. Both would testify that they had met on a cool autumn night while walking down the main street of their poor neighborhood in Brooklyn, New York. Having both come from very religious backgrounds, they somehow struck up a conversation about church, and eventually, they decided to get into his car and go for a midnight snack. This is where their tales diverge.

Doris said that Sam drove her to a secluded area instead of a restaurant, and then forced himself on her by nearly strangling her. Sam said Doris had agreed to have sex for money, but had become enraged at the small amount of money, and affection, that he had offered her afterward. Both Sam and Doris said she had accepted a ride home. When Sam was arrested at work the following day, her phone number was found in his pocket. There were no marks on her throat, and no other signs of trauma.

Steven B. Wasserman is an attorney with the Criminal Defense Division of the New York City Legal Aid Society and an Adjunct Associate Professor of Law and Ethics in the Graduate Program at the John Jay College of Criminal Justice, C.U.N.Y. He received a Ph.D. in philosophy from Yale in 1974 and has combined teaching ethics with the practice of law for the past twenty years.

Both Sam and Doris had some discrediting information in their backgrounds. Doris had a history of youthful pregnancies and family strife that had led to her placement in a foster home. Sam had twice before been arrested on similar complaints by other women. In both of Sam's cases, the charges had later been dropped, and the public records sealed. Because none of the above information about Sam or Doris was legally admissible,* the jury would not learn about it. This would be a pure contest of credibility; a case of "my word against yours".

It would also be a contest between two attorneys. The prosecutor would assume the role of Doris' coach. She would help her to be convincing, effective under questioning, and generally appealing to the jury. And she would do her utmost to make Sam appear mendacious and unsympathetic. Correspondingly,

---

*In general, the New York rules of evidence prohibit inquiry into the sexual history of a rape complainant, unless it involves convictions for prostitution or conduct with the accused. They also prohibit a prosecutor from inquiring into arrests that do not result in convictions. Although juries are likely to be influenced by such information, jurists agree that these rules are sound, because they keep the emphasis of the trial upon the evidence of the crime, and off the character of the witnesses, which is only somewhat relevant. The rules incidentally reduce the moral problems of advocacy, by diminishing the obligation to attack and embarrass witnesses.

my role was to discredit Doris, and to coach Sam to be convincing, and to withstand cross-examination. After the testimony, the prosecutor and I would address the jury personally, and use our powers of persuasion to bring about the desired verdict.

This typical credibility contest presented me with no moral conflicts. To be sure I was disturbed by Sam's prior arrests, just as the prosecutor should have been disturbed by Doris' history, and her imprudence with a stranger. Still, as defense attorneys are fond of saying, I was not present at the scene, and neither was the prosecutor. We did not know what happened. The parties were entitled to our professional assistance, and the jury could only benefit from a full exploration of every facet of the incident. And, after all, it was probably Sam's track record that inspired the prosecutor to seek this indictment in the first place. Therefore I had a moral duty to assure that Doris' complaint was credible.

But after I examined my office's confidential files on Sam's previous arrests, I became convinced that I was defending a guilty man. I discovered to my shock and disgust that his prior cases were identical to this case; not only in the overt behavior that was alleged, but in the smallest details and phrases with which Sam recounted his version to his former attorneys. It was apparent from our files that Sam was a charming and clever psychopath, and that Doris was a typical victim of what criminologists have termed the "date-rape".

Date-rape victims are always vulnerable to a skillful cross-examination. It would be especially difficult for a woman of Doris' religious background to acknowledge the normal romantic impulses that led her to give Sam her telephone number and to enter his car. But if she dissembled, or misrepresented her feelings, she would be even more vulnerable to cross-examination. Mine was the unappetizing task of exploiting her embarrassment in order to discredit her complaint; a complaint about which I had no doubts. Moreover, I was employed in the service of a persistent rapist, whose chances for acquittal were not bad.

DISCUSSION

Before turning to the difficult question of my moral responsibility, let's consider a comparatively easy question: Was I under a professional duty to stay with this case, and to work for Sam's acquittal?

There simply was no respectable way for a public defender to be excused from Sam's case. No judge could relieve a lawyer from a criminal defense assignment merely because the lawyer has lost faith in his client's defense, or because of the repugnance of the charges. Were it otherwise, far too many defendants, especially poor ones, would find themselves completely shunned and abandoned. Moreover it is especially inappropriate for a public defender, as an attorney of last resort, to avoid cases like Sam's. After all, if I won't take such cases, who will?

So my beliefs about Sam's guilt, however well founded, were not a good reason to be relieved of his case. Anyway, I was prohibited from disclosing the reasons for my beliefs, which were confidential interviews with a client of my office. I might have been dismissed, if not disbarred, for explaining why I was so convinced of his guilt.

But believing what I did, was I required to defer to Sam's decision to go to trial and proclaim his innocence? Or was I permitted to influence him to plead guilty, and to try for a lenient sentence? As his advocate, concerned only with promoting his objectives, my advice to him would surely have been to stand trial. He had a good chance of winning, and moreover New York's six year minimum sentence for rape was unacceptably long for him.

On the other hand, the code of legal ethics does not require me to adopt my client's value system. I am entitled to give moral advice to a client, even if it is unsolicited. Should I have tried to persuade Sam, by confronting him with the unbelievably identical prior incidents, to "come clean" and to take his punishment? For my own conscience, could I have tried to avoid participation in a likely miscarriage of justice?

I did not try to talk Sam out of standing trial, because to do so, as a practical matter, was incompatible with being his advocate. It would surely have undermined his confidence in my loyalty, and compromised our ability to collaborate at his trial. I could not risk subverting his trust on the slight chance that I could induce a change of heart. Even were he to confess, moreover, it would surely have been out of despair at my abandonment of him, rather than out of remorse.

I might have advised confession, if Sam were a paying customer who could have taken "his business elsewhere", in case my advice displeased him. But as the only lawyer he was going to have, it was important to me that his poverty not deprive him of the benefits enjoyed by those who can fire their lawyer. Those who pay thousands of dollars are in a position to command fidelity to their objectives. The paying customer is seldom obliged to endure exhortations to confess. To place our clients on an equal footing with those who can pay, public defenders must be especially careful not to discourage those who wish to assert their rights.

So there was a trial, at which the jury, unaware of Sam's grisly career, acquitted him because of their reasonable doubts; doubts which I will never share.

If my role as Sam's attorney required me to seek his acquittal, does it follow that I was morally justified in doing so? Philosophically, the only sound answer is "not necessarily"; not until I have considered the question of whether my role in the criminal justice system, and indeed the system itself, is morally justifiable.

Before I began my legal career, I was a professor of Philosophy, with a specialty in Ethics. While much of what interested me then seems less important to me now, I still subscribe to an idea that was expressed by Jean Paul Sartre and other Existentialists: the roles which we assume in life never relieve us of our full moral responsibility for each action that we take. Although we may feel at times that our commitments have left us with no choice, we always have the choice, difficult and awkward as it may be, of rejecting or opting out of an assumed role, whenever it requires us to do the wrong thing.

Thus I do not believe that my advocacy for Sam or for anyone is morally justified, simply because my job requires it. It is an open question whether I ought to remain a public defender, if it requires me, as I believe it occasionally does, to work for the acquittal of psychopaths. Indeed, I believe that it is *wrong* to do this work unless the role that requires it is essential to a system of criminal justice that is itself justifiable.

A full justification of the system is more than I can undertake. Indeed, I am not sure that it *is* ultimately justifiable. But surely, a public defender must have either enormous faith or utter indifference to the justifiability of our criminal system. Only with enormous faith can a public defender believe that a transcendent ideal is advanced, while he assumes the personal martyrdom of humiliating a rape victim and achieving a predator's release. With utter indifference, the responsibility for false verdicts can be shifted onto the jury, the defender's job, or some other abstract entity. Although it is philosophically untenable, utter indifference is a characteristic posture of many effective defense attorneys.

Those of us who believe in our role have reasons that stand above and beyond the system's tendency to produce correct verdicts. We are also dedicated to its preoccupation with fair and uniform procedures, chief among which are those which guarantee every accused a full opportunity to challenge his accusers and to present his defense. As Sam's case illustrates, there is no preestablished harmony between adherence to these procedures and correct verdicts; but many believe that there is an impressive correlation. As true devotees of our system, public defenders uphold the procedures almost for their own sake, believing that strict and habitual adherence to them will promote concern and respect for all parties, and thus prevent the more avoidable and tempting errors to which verdicts are subject. Without some justifying belief, it would not be possible for me to serve this system by taking all comers.

WILLIAM C. HEFFERNAN

THE PHILOSOPHER AS PROSECUTOR: AN (UNLAWFUL) PROSECUTION OF A GUILTY MAN

Under what circumstances, if any, should a prosecutor seek affirmance of a criminal conviction he knows to have been obtained in violation of the law? It is disquieting even to pose a question such as this, for one of the premises of criminal justice is that a conviction can fairly be obtained only according to procedures set by law. Certainly I never expected to confront such a question when I started out as an assistant district attorney. Furthermore, had I been told before assuming the position that I would have to confront this issue, I would

William C. Heffernan is an associate professor of law at John Jay College of Criminal Justice and the Graduate Center, the City University of New York. He is co-
editor of *Criminal Justice Ethics*. He has edited two books on ethical issues in
criminal justice: *Police Ethics: Hard Choices in Law Enforcement* (New York: John
Jay Press, 1985) and *From Social Justice to Criminal Justice: Poverty and the
Administration of Criminal Law* (New York: Oxford University Press, 1999). His
publications on legal issues have appeared in numerous law reviews.

never have expected that I would take it seriously, that I would consider the
possibility of seeking to keep a defendant in prison when I knew he had been
denied a basic legal right at his trial. The essay that follows explains how this
issue arose and the factors I took into account in trying to resolve it.

Because of prior experience I had had in writing and research, my first assignment as a prosecutor was to the appeals bureau of my new office. The assignment was somewhat unusual, since most of my peers started out in the
office's criminal court bureau. Had I been sent to that bureau, I would have
worked on the initial stages of the criminal process—on writing up complaints,
representing the state at arraignments, conducting plea bargains for misde-
meanors, and so on. My work in the appeals bureau placed me at the other end
of the criminal process. Most of the cases that reached the appeals bureau had
already gone to trial and had resulted in convictions, although an occasional
appeal had to do with the terms of a plea bargain or the results of a pretrial suppression motion. As a junior member of the appeals bureau, I dealt with the
most elementary issues presented to it. The dramatis personae in my appeals
cases were always interesting: disappointed lovers, a good many drug addicts,
an occasional robber or burglar, and so on. The legal problems at stake were

not particularly complicated, though. My superiors wanted to make sure I learned my craft thoroughly; that meant I had to begin with elementary problems and progress to more difficult ones.

Not only were the legal issues relatively easy to handle at the onset, the moral issues I confronted in my first few months of work were also not as difficult as those faced by more experienced lawyers. In applying for a position in prosecutors' offices I was—among other things—trying to avoid the kind of morally troubling situations criminal defense attorneys often encounter in the course of their work. The best-known of these is also perhaps the most difficult: providing an aggressive defense for a client an attorney knows or has good reason to believe to be guilty. Other difficulties arise when a defense attorney finds himself required to preserve a confidence or to cross-examine an opposing witness he believes to be telling the truth. Even before I began looking for a job, I knew of possible justifications for these practices. I was more skeptical of those justifications than I am now. I am convinced even now, though, that some of the practices criminal defense attorneys are professionally allowed to engage in are nonetheless not morally justifiable.

By contrast, the prosecutor's world appeared to be less riddled with moral dilemmas. I was aware of course of the kinds of unconscionable practices that prosecutors sometimes engage in. I knew, for instance, that some District Attorneys and United States Attorneys pursue highly publicized prosecutions in order to seek higher office, that prosecutors have on occasion covered illegal police practices, that they have provided special deals for favored defendants. The office I entered had never been tarnished with such scandals; its District Attorney presented himself to the public—and was accepted by the newspapers—as a person who ran an apolitical operation. That image turned out to be accurate. In the time I served as prosecutor, I encountered no incidents that could be classified as gross abuses of office.

On beginning my new job, I knew as well that subtler moral dilemmas could often arise in the course of a prosecutor's work. What I appreciated about the prosecutor's role was the opportunity it would give me to approach those dilemmas from a broader perspective than the one defense attorneys—even morally conscientious defense attorneys—can employ when they encounter the same dilemmas from their side of the table. Among the dilemmas facing prosecutors are these:

- *Agreeing to a simple plea bargain* Given overcrowding in the courts, most criminal sentences are arrived at by plea bargaining rather than trials. One of the functions of the trial is to test the strength of the prosecutor's case—to make sure there is proof beyond a reasonable doubt of a defendant's guilt. In the absence of a trial, a prosecutor has to ask himself whether such proof would be possible and—if he's uncertain it would be—whether he still wants to seek a guilty plea to a criminal charge.

- *Agreeing to more complex bargains* Occasionally bargains are sought not so much to expedite the disposition of cases but to gain testimony that can be sided against even more serious wrongdoers. Proof beyond a reasonable doubt of the lesser wrongdoing is usually clear in such situations—otherwise the lesser wrongdoer would be unwilling even to consider a bargain. What a prosecutor must consider, though, is whether the wrongdoing he considers greater actually is greater—and whether it's so much greater that it warrants a light penalty for the person who is seeking a plea bargain in exchange for testimony.

- *Planning undercover operations* Current law allows the government to carry out a broad range of deceptive undercover operations. The kind of deception available can pose a problem (agents can, for instance, deceptively engender relations of friendship or love in order to discover wrongdoing), and so can the selection of targets (there is no legal threshold of suspicion that must be crossed before an undercover operation can be undertaken). Sound judgment as to what is morally legitimate is thus required given the broad range of activity that has been declared legally legimate for government agents.

- *Exploiting procedural rules of law* Procedural rules are often created not to guarantee that justice be done in individual cases but to promote efficient operation of the entire legal system. Efficiency-enhancing devices are undoubtedly necessary in a legal system as complicated as ours, but their application can sometimes lead to disturbing outcomes in individual cases. Lawyers for criminal defendants, for instance, can sometimes fail to make timely objections to rulings by trial courts, and the legal effect of a failure to object is to hold that a defendant has waived the right in question. The rule is a useful one in that it encourages trial lawyers to notify trial judges of legal errors at the time they are made. If a defense lawyer fails to object, though, should his client be made to pay the price by foregoing what often is a significant legal right? The decision concerning this will often rest with the prosecutor, who can—if he wishes—not insist that a right has been waived. Whether a prosecutor should make this concession is one of the difficult moral decisions that can come with the job.

In what sense, though, can prosecutors be said to take a broader view of their tough choices than do defense attorneys of theirs? The answer lies in the different concepts conscientious defense attorneys and prosecutors bring to their roles. The conscientious defense attorney must, I think, be client-oriented in his concerns. How far an attorney should go in defending a client is a critical issue, but given the absence of other people who can aid the client and given the important consequences of losing liberty a defense attorney must give serious weight to the immediate interests of his client. By contrast, a prosecutor has the public as a client, and conscientious prosecutors have tended to assume that the public requires them to seek just outcomes of cases rather than the exploitation of all the legal advantages that are available to them. Prosecutors' offices often overstate their willingness to forgo tactical advantages in the interests of justice. I found, for instance, that my office required more vigorous prosecution of cases that had reached the media than of cases that hadn't. I also learned that the exploitation of legal advantages was less likely to be frowned on than appeals to conscience—although it should be added that my colleagues valued neither the person who was invariably hard-nosed nor the one who consistently emphasized the importance of forgoing advantages. If these caveats are borne in mind, then it is fair to say that the lawyers in my office had far more leeway to consider the justness of ultimate outcomes than did their counterparts in the criminal defense bar. The broader perspective available to prosecutors made the job seem particularly appealing to me.

I'd like to turn now to the issue I raised at the beginning of this essay. When considered from a moral point of view, the case that posed the issue was by far the most difficult I handled. The others seemed to me to raise no serious doubts about either guilt or the punishment that should be imposed. These questions weren't at issue in the difficult case either; instead, the hard problem for me centered on the moral justification of denying a defendant's legal right. The right at stake was the right to have a jury pass on a defendant's claim of self-defense, and the moral problem the case posed was whether my office should agree to retrial because of the judge's refusal to let the jury pass on this claim.

The defendant in the case had been charged with murder. There was uncontradicted testimony from the victim's girlfriend that the defendant had been making a play for her in the weeks that preceded the incident and that she had rebuffed him. Furthermore, the victim's girlfriend and the storekeeper who had observed the incident both testified that the killing had occurred in the following way. The victim and the defendant had gathered as they usually did, on a streetcorner with a number of other people and had talked and joked throughout the day. (The trial transcript made it clear that the key participants in the incident were unemployed and given to spending substantial parts of the day in streetcorner conversations with their friends.) At the end of the afternoon, the victim, his girlfriend, and the defendant walked over to a grocery store. While in the store, the defendant suddenly demanded that the girlfriend leave with him alone. The victim immediately spoke up and said his girfriend didn't have to if she didn't want to. As the two began to quarrel, the storekeeper intervened and told them to move outside. They did, but the quarrel only became worse. From within the store, the girlfriend and storekeeper saw the defendant deliver what appeared to be a punch to the victim's chest. The victim stumbled backwards and fell to the ground. The defendant then came back into the store carrying a knife that was stained with what appeared to be blood and demanded that the girlfriend leave with him. She did. Fortunately, shortly after they started walking down the street together, they encountered a police officer, and after the girlfriend sought his help the officer placed the defendant under arrest.

A compelling case for either murder or manslaughter thus seemed to have been made. Not only did the stories told by the girlfriend and the storekeeper support one another, the medical examiner also took the stand to testify that the victim had died from a single knifewound to his chest. There was one major difficulty, however. After the prosecution had presented its case, the defendant took the stand and testified—contrary to everything else that had been said—that he hadn't had a knife on the day in question, that he hadn't lunged at the victim, and that he had merely raised his hands in self-defense when the victim had struck out in anger at him. According to the defendant, it was the victim who took out a knife and brandished it in a threatening manner. The defendant testified he'd said he wanted nothing to do with knives and stated he'd then tried to move away from the victim. The defendant said the victim nonetheless lunged forward. The defendant sought to protect himself by grabbing the hand holding the knife. A struggle ensued over the knife, and the defendant testified it was possible the victim might have stabbed himself during the struggle.

Whatever strength this testimony might have had was weakened by the prosecutor's cross-examination of the defendant, which revealed that the defendant had been convicted on a number of assault crimes and one attempted murder in the past. Theoretically, such evidence is admissible not to show that a defendant is likely to act in a similar way again but to impeach his credibility as a witness. In fact, though, its effect is almost always to convince jurors that a defendant would act in a similar way again.

Not only was it likely that the jurors were impressed by what had been brought on cross-examination, I was impressed with it as well. In fact, after reading the transcript and the defendant's file, I concluded that he was a person who was acutely prone to violence, someone who lurched from one street fight to another, seeking each occasion to vindicate his honor against those he imagined to be challenging it. I also found the defendant's self-defense story quite incredible. Two witnesses—one of whom had no reason to favor either the victim or the defendant—had given similar accounts of the killing. Their accounts also dovetailed with the medical's statement that the knife which had killed the victim had gone four inches into his chest, a fact that was hard to reconcile with the defendant's suggestion that the victim might have accidentially stabbed himself in the course of a struggle over the knife. Furthermore, I was also aware the one other witness to the incident had corroborated the story told by the girlfriend and the storekeeper. This witness had testified before the grand jury but had disappeared between the time of the grand jury hearing and the trial. No one supported the defendant's version of events; all accounts pointed toward another version which, if true, established his guilt. I thus found myself in hearty agreement with the jury's verdict that the defendant was guilty of manslaughter in the first degree—that is, that he had intended to cause the victim serious bodily harm and, in the course of carrying out this intention, had killed him.

I wasn't the trier of fact, though. That was the jury's role, and the legal difficulty posed by the case centered on the question of whether the jury had been allowed to perform its role properly. Whatever its credibility, the defendant's story did at least conform to the legal definition of self-defense: that is, he stated that the victim had attacked him, that he'd tried to avoid this attack, and that on finding this impossible he'd defended himself against the use of deadly force by using deadly force himself. What's more, the law of the jurisdiction in which I worked stated that a defendant is entitled to have a jury consider the defense of justifiable use of deadly force as long as the defendant provides evidence that satisfies the legal definition of the defense. The *credibility* of the evidence provided is for the trier of fact to determine. As long as evidence satisfying the legal definition is produced, a trial judge is obligated to instruct the jury concerning the justifiable use of deadly force and to allow it to decide whether a defendant has told the truth about an incident.

In this case, though, the defendant's attorney had requested that an instruction be given concerning the use of deadly force and that instruction had been denied. The trial judge announced that the defendant's story lacked the basic credibility which is needed for a question of fact to be presented to a jury. Intriguing as such a rationale is, it is strongly at variance with the law. As I reviewed the case law bearing on this point, I discovered that the trial judge had made a fundamental legal error. I couldn't find a single reported case in which an appeals court within my jurisdiction had failed to reverse a criminal conviction after a judge had improperly omitted a requested instruction concerning the justifiable use of deadly force. As I expected, the reported cases focused not on the plausibility of defendants' stories of self-defence—appeals courts seemed to realize that many of these were made up—but on the importance of the right to have a jury rather than a judge pass on the plausibility of these stories. The trial judge in this case had failed to grasp this elementary point, thus laying the foundation for the dilemma I faced.

To understand why the dilemma was a serious one, though, one other factor must be taken into account. In the adversary setting of the appellate process, a lawyer can often count on courts to make informed, morally defensible judgments about difficult issues that are presented to them. In this instance, though, I was dealing with an appeals process that was stacked strongly in favor of prosecutors. It was true that the *reported* appeals cases strongly favored the defendant. But it was also true that the intermediate appellate court that would hear the case was well-known within the legal community in which I worked for using its power to affirm the judgments of lower courts without explaining why those judgments were legally correct. The consequence was that the appeals court improved a rough, extra-legal justice on criminal defendants. If the appeals court believed a criminal defendant deserved punishment or if the judges on the court, each of whom had to run for re-election, feared the adverse publicity of reversing a conviction, then an affirmance would be entered in a given case. The affirmance would, on the one hand, leave the law on the books intact; on the other hand, though, it would deny the benefit of the law to the defendant in that case. Legal ideas could thus be preserved and at the same time a significant number of defendants could actually be denied the rights that supposedly flow from those ideals.

Whatever the merits of this practice (and I think they are few), its conse-quence was to make prosecutors decisive figures in the appeals process. When-ever a convicted defendant looked unsavory but still had a strong legal claim, a prosecutor's decision to challenge the defendant's appeal would usually be sufficient to guarantee that the defendant's conviction would be upheld—*with-out an opinion.* That certainly appeared to be likely here. There was enough in the trial transcript to make it very likely that the appellate court required to hear the case would reverse because the defendant's legal rights had been vio-lated. During cross-examination of the defendant, for instance, the prosecution had established how many violent crimes he had been convicted of in the past. The victim's girlfriend had provided testimony that indicated how violent the defendant could become once he believed his honor to be at stake. While such evidence is not supposed to influence an appellate court, it was common knowl-edge among the experienced lawyers in my office that the court that would hear my case routinely used its power to affirm without opinion to unavoid unwel-comed applications of the law. If I argued for the state, it was likely the defen-dant would stay in prison—and be denied an important legal right. If I conceded the validity of the appeal, he would then (and probably only then) be granted a new trial—but the new trial might very well result in his release despite the strength of the evidence against him.

This last point is an important one, and it would be best to consider it now before reviewing the more general moral issues I took into account in deciding what to do. Legally, the most the defendant could have obtained by winning at the appellate stage would have been a retrial of his case. In this instance, how-ever, the prosecution would have been at a severe disadvantage at his retrial, for all of the witnesses who testified for the prosecution about the incident would have been difficult to locate for a retrial. It will be recalled that one of the wit-nesses who testified before the grand jury disappeared by the time of the trial. Another—the victim's girlfriend—had been available for the trial. Like the vic-tim and the defendant, though, she was given to a life of streetcorner drinking and so would probably have been difficult to find for a retrial given the year and a half that had elapsed between the trial and the appeal. Finally, the storekeeper had already left the jurisdiction by the time of the trial (he had moved to Israel), and his testimony had been taken at a special pretrial hearing and read to the trial jury by officers of the court. The prosecution could of course have had the testimony of *all* of its chief witnesses read to the jury at a new trial. This would hardly have made for a compelling case, though, since the defendant—and the defendant alone—would then have been the sole witness to the incident to take the stand on retrial.

What, then, was the right thing to do? Three questions seemed to me to be central. First, should a prosecutor concern himself at all with the moral issues bearing on a case, or should he seek merely to maximize the legal advantages available to his side? Second, assuming moral considerations are important, what consequences can a prosecutor be morally accountable for given the duty of an appellate court hearing a case to render a just decision under law? And third, if a prosecutor can be held morally accountable for the ultimate disposition of a case such as the one discussed here, what factors should he consider in deciding how it should be resolved?

As I've already indicated, the first issue was not in fact a problem for those working in my office, nor in my opinion should it pose a difficulty for anyone who properly conceives his role as a prosecutor. From the moment I was interviewed for a job as a prosecutor, I was bombarded with questions about what would be the right—as opposed to the expedient—thing to do in this situation or that. The questions were sometimes disingenuous; as I've noted, in highly publicized cases, the prosecutors with whom I worked sometimes did exploit all possible legal advantages (and ignore the moral implications at stake) for the sake of political expediency. The unfortunate exception aside, though, there was simply no inclination among my peers to win cases or legal points simply for the sake of winning.

As far as prosecutors are concerned, this is as it should be. If prosecutors have a client at all, that client is the abstract entity of the "people" of the state in which they work. The law makes it clear that prosecutors do not *represent* victims; they often *speak for* victims and, in speaking for them, often satisfy victims' desires to get even with those who have harmed them. "Getting even" should never be more than an incidental consequence of prosecution, however, and there will be many occasions when a victim would like a tougher charge or stiffer sentence than a prosecutor deems appropriate. It is these latter instances that the independent role of the prosecutor becomes clear. The prosecutor must be certain that the charge and the sentence sought are fair. He must also make sure that the procedures employed by agents of the state are proper. Finally, he should make sure the results obtained are obtained according to law. It is understandable that crime victims will be less concerned than prosecutors about each of these factors. What sets off the prosecutor as a moral agent is his independent concern with all of them.

To suggest that the prosecutor as moral agent should give strong weight to the justness of a final disposition is not to suggest, though, that a defense attorney as moral agent should weigh the justice of a final disposition equally strongly in his deliberations. The question of what weight a defense attorney should give to the justness of a disposition is a vexing one, and I shall touch on it here only to emphasize a possible asymmetry between the conscientious prosecutor and the conscientious defense attorney. It can at least plausibly be maintained that even when they work from similar premises about desert and punishment, a conscientious defense attorney *should* give less weight to these premises than should a conscientious prosecutor. To argue in this way is not to say that the attorneys would reach different conclusions about deserved punishment if they were serving as, say, judges on a case. According to this argument, though, it would be morally appropriate for the defense attorney to give less *weight* to the issue of deserved punishment than would a prosecutor. If this point is true, then the idea of moral agency can constitute only a starting point for analysis of advocacy in the criminal process, for a defense attorney might agree with a prosecutor not only on their status as moral agents but also on the concepts of desert relevant to a case but still give different weight to the idea of desert than would the prosecutor and so properly work for a different outcome than would a prosecutor.

To speak of a prosecutor as a moral agent, however, is not to say what he is actually accountable for in an adversary setting. Among other things, moral accountability has to do with the structure of the world in which we function as moral agents. We may be concerned with a number of issues of moral significance but may have no capacity to influence their resolution and so will often not be accountable for whatever the ultimate resolution of those issues may be. Alternatively, we can find ourselves in settings where a division of labor prevails and where some individuals can address themselves to one set of morally significant concerns with confidence that others will address themselves to other concerns of moral significance. The adversary system often provides a division of moral labor of this kind. A criminal defense attorney, for instance, may sometimes be in a position where he can reasonably count on the judge and jury hearing his case to assign his arguments from a morally valid point of view. When this is so, then the defense attorney can concern himself with vigorous assertion of claims on behalf of his client and can at the same time rely on other agents of the adversary system to perform a screening role in assessing the moral worth of those claims. If, for some unexpected reason, the screening role is *not* performed in a given case (a clearly guilty person might unexpectedly be acquitted, for instance), then the defense attorney cannot be held accountable for the result that has been reached. Provided he had a reasonable basis for believing that a division of moral labor would prevail in the adversary system, he cannot be held accountable for an undesirable result because the division of moral labor did *not* prevail on a specific occasion.

Was I in a position to count on a division of moral labor in the appellate process? In many instances, an advocate can in fact count on this. The cases that reach the appeals stage are frequently close ones, and lawyers often can reasonably expect the courts hearing those cases to use uninformed moral judgment in disentangling the issues they present. This is certainly the ideal context for arguing appeals, if only because judges are better situated than advocates to determine the best disposition of a case. This was not, however, the context in which my appeal could be brought. Given the reputation of the court before which I was to appear, it seemed very unlikely that even an effort to gain affirmance of the conviction would be sufficient to guarantee its affirmance. My position was in this sense a decisive one, and if I didn't consider carefully the justifiability of the ultimate disposition of the case, it was improbable anyone else would.

The justifiability with which I was concerned had to do partly with a moral right, partly with the moral significance of deterring future violations of that right, and partly with the importance to be attached to my strong belief that the defendant was guilty of at least manslaughter. The moral right at stake was the right an individual possesses to have his legal claims adjudicated according to law. *Why* this is a moral right seems to me to depend on a more general right we possess to have our legitimate reliance on promises vindicated. The state has in effect promised that we will be tried in a certain way when we are charged with wrongdoing. Among other things, it has promised that a jury will determine the truth of our stories at any criminal trial. A perhaps troubling consequence of that promise is that individuals can lie in order to lay claim to the right to have a jury assess the truth of a defense they present. The consequence would be fatal, however, only if we always had access to the actual truth concerning a situation and so could always know when a defendant was lying and when he was not. If this were possible, then the jury system would deserve to be replaced and a state which fostered reliance on it would be negligent at best and corrupt at worst. In the absence of such perfect knowledge, though, it makes sense to grant a legal right to a jury trial, and once this legal right is granted there is also a moral right to have it vindicated in particular situations. The defendant had such a right here, a right that had been denied because of the judge's refusal to instruct the jury concerning the justifiable use of deadly force.

A quite different consideration in my mind had to do with the importance of deterring practices such as the failure to give a requested jury instruction. From a deterrence standpoint, my concern was not with *this* defendant but instead with defendants in the future who might be denied instructions if this conviction were not corrected. My colleagues have told me they had encountered errors of this kind before. Their conversations with me also indicated that the formal appellate process offered little hope of deterrence; in fact, I came to understand that the appellate process—with its "affirmed without opinion" option—provided a means of covering up errors made at trial. Concession on the part of the prosecutor could have an impact throughout the legal community in which I worked—on the trial judge who'd made the error, on his peers, and on other prosecutors engaged in trial work. The deterrent effect on concession, I concluded, could only serve to buttress the rights of future defendants in criminal trials.

I had to weigh against these considerations, though, the seriousness of the crime with which the defendant stood charged and the risk that he would go unpunished if there were another trial. In the end, these latter considerations proved to be decisive in my mind. I stated before that I thought the defendant had a moral right to have his claim of self-defense adjudicated according to law. I didn't think, though that the right should be given precedence over the punishment deserved for so heinous an act as manslaughter. The latter conclusion depended on a number of premises. Two were factual: that the defendant actually was guilty of manslaughter and that there was a good chance he could avoid punishment for it on retrial. Both points seemed then—and seem now—to be warranted. Some key moral premises were at stake as well. One had to do with the concept of deserved punishment, a concept that had troubled me in many instances but that seemed easiest to defend in situations where harm had been wantonly inflicted on someone else. Another premise had to do with the overriding of moral rights. I certainly believed that the right to jury consideration of the defendant's claim was an important one. Assuming though, that he was guilty of the offense charged and that there was a good chance he would escape punishment for it on retrial, vindication of that right at the expense of deserved punishment seemed to me to be too high a price to pay.

What, though, could be said about the difference rationale for conceding the appeal? My answer to this was simple: because there was a good chance the witnesses could not be reassembled and the case thus lost on retrial, this was not the case in which to deter judicial errors in formulating jury instructions. I understood there was an irony to this decision about deterrence, an irony that in fact surrounds all reflections on deterrence, for the more painful a consequence for the audience to be deterred, the more likely it is to have a deterrent effect on the audience. The concession in this case would have been *more* painful than in one where the witnesses would have been easier to gather again or where the crime was less serious. Furthermore, failure to concede would send a signal that errors about jury instructions (and perhaps other matters) may be tolerable when all other factors go against a defendant. These points are important ones. A deterrent effect is never a certainty, however; it's possible, for instance, that our concession wouldn't have been widely publicized or that the facts underlying the concession would have been misunderstood. And the principle underlying deterrence—the greater the pain, the greater the deterrent effect—is, in any case, hard to swallow when the pain involved is our moral indignation about the evasion of deserved punishment. Deterrence, I decided, should wait for another day; punishment seemed to be the paramount consideration.

I thus went ahead with the appeal, and events unfolded as expected. Both sides submitted written briefs concerning the case. When the time came for oral argument, the appeals court questioned opposing counsel sharply. Even though my office's position was very weak legally, I was asked virtually no questions when my turn came to present our case. About four weeks later, the appeals court affirmed the conviction without opinion. Defense counsel then sought leave to appeal to the highest court of the state. The court, however, denied leave to appeal, and there the matter came to an end, with rough justice having been done, but not justice according to law.

DISCUSSION QUESTIONS

1. What does Aristotle mean when he says the following: "Neither by nature nor contrary to nature . . . do the virtues arise in us; rather, we are adapted by nature to receive them, are made perfect by habit." Do you agree with him? Defend your answer.

2. Explain Aristotle's doctrine that "virtue is a kind of mean." What does he mean when he says that such a mean is "relative to us"? Explain and illustrate Aristotle's claim that "there is neither a mean of excess and deficiency, nor excess and deficiency of a mean."

3. What is an adversary system? What rationale is there for having a lawyer-client bond of confidentiality in such a system? In your view, should lawyers have autonomy to make *any* exceptions to keeping clients' confidences? If so, what exceptions would be warranted? Defend your answer.

4. Discuss Charles Fried's analogy of a lawyer as a friend. What similarities exist between lawyers' and (clients') friends? What differences exist? Do you think that this analogy is enlightening? Defend your answer.

5. What is Fried's criticism of utilitarianism? Do you agree with it? Explain.

6. Explain Fried's distinction between institutional wrongs and personal wrongs. Do you think that this distinction is a useful one for helping lawyers deal with their moral problems? Defend your answer.

7. Discuss the merit of the following claim made by Fried: When a lawyer presents "to the court a statement by another that he knows to be a lie, as when he puts a perjurious client-defendant on the stand . . . it is not the lawyer who is lying. He is like a letter carrier who delivers the falsehood."

8. What, according to Cohen, are some "characteristic marks" of a morally good person? In your opinion, are all of these personality traits consistent with being an effective clients' advocate? Defend your answer.

9. Describe briefly Cohen's "moral agent" and "pure legal advocate" concepts of a lawyer. Compare and contrast each with Fried's concept of a "lawyer as friend."

10. Discuss the merit of the following statement of Cohen's: "I am supposing that a lawyer cannot easily detach his professional life from his private life and thereby cannot easily be one sort of person with one sort of values in the one life, and a quite different sort with quite different values in the other life."

11. What do you think Aristotle might say about a lawyer who adopted and practiced according to Fried's concept of a "lawyer as friend"? Would such a lawyer qualify as a virtuous person with Aristotle's criteria? Is it even warranted to apply Aristotle's criteria to a profession such as lawyer, or does the latter require an independent morality with its own distinct set of virtues?

12. Explain the distinction Aristotle makes between a clever person and a person with practical wisdom. In your view, must a lawyer possess practical wisdom or is cleverness enough? Defend your answer.

13. If you were a defense lawyer in the Lake Pleasant case (as discussed in Cohen's article) what would you have done if the parents of one of your client's victims came to you asking about the whereabouts of their daughter whom you knew to be one of the victims? Justify your answer, and respond to objections that would probably be made from an opposing perspective.

14. Why was Steven Wasserman so sure that his client was guilty? Could he have been mistaken?

15. Why didn't Wasserman ask the judge to assign Sam a lawyer who believed in his case?

16. Why was Wasserman not permitted to ask Doris about her pregnancies? Why was the prosecutor not permitted to ask Sam about his prior arrests? Do you think such questions should be permitted? Defend your answer.

17. Why was Wasserman prohibited from disclosing (to judge or jury) the evidence which convinced him of his client's guilt? Do you think that such a disclosure should have been permitted? Defend your answer.

18. Should Wasserman have confronted Sam with his account of the two prior incidents with women? Should he have asked Sam to account for the "coincidence" that led three women to make the same "false" accusations? What do you think of his reasons for not doing so?

19. Did Wasserman's defense of Sam contribute to a just society or was it merely a second criminal attack on Doris? Defend your answer.

20. Is Wasserman a "pure legal advocate" as Cohen would define this term? Explain. In your opinion, can a public defender be a "moral agent" in Cohen's sense? Defend your answer.

21. Describe the dilemma which confronted Heffernan. How did the judge's error give rise to this dilemma? What other factors contributed to the dilemma?

22. How, and on what basis, did Heffernan finally resolve the dilemma he faced as prosecutor? Do you agree with his reasoning? Defend your answer.

23. What does Heffernan mean by a "division of moral labor" as it exists in our adversary system? Were there significant differences in the "division of moral labor" which existed in the case described by Wasserman and that described by Heffernan? For instance, Heffernan argues that his seeking affirmance of the defendant's criminal conviction was, in the given case, predictably decisive in determining the outcome of the appeal. Was Wasserman in a similar situation as Heffernan regarding his ability to influence the outcome of his client's trial?

II

SOCIETY AND POLITICS

4

WOMEN'S RIGHTS AND SOCIAL WORK

The belief that women are naturally inferior to men is one that has had a long and unfettered history. Nor has this view of women been confined to the vulgar or the unsophisticated, for it is also expressed in the writings of some of the revered philosophers. For example, Aristotle, the great ancient Greek philosopher, unequivocally held that the relationship between husband and wife "involves an inequality between parties" wherein the husband rules "in virtue of his superiority," and in which "the better [the male] gets more of what is good and each gets what befits him." The man is a natural ruler who leads by "the exercise of mind" and the woman, his natural subject who by her body "gives effect to such foresight." Even such a liberal democratic thinker as John Locke *assumed* the natural inferiority of women when he wrote that "the last determination" of an issue on which a husband and wife disagree "naturally falls to the man's share, as the abler and the stronger." In the first selection of this chapter, excerpted from Book I of Aristotle's *Politics,* this time-honored perspective is represented.

Aristotle's view about the inferiority of women depends upon his *teleological* metaphysic. Aristotle held that everything has its proper *teleos* (Greek meaning "end" or "purpose") in relation to which its virtue can be assessed. Human beings are, by definition, *rational* animals. As distinct from all other animals, their *teleos* resides in their capacity for living rationally. Insofar as human beings live according to reason, they are virtuous. Thus one human being is, as such, superior to another if the one can live more rationally than the other.

All Aristotle needed to add in order to rank women inferior to men was the premise that women (in general) are less capable of living rationally than men. Of course, Aristotle never says this, for he states that each gender has its proper moral virtues, which means that there is a sense in which women's wills must conform to reason; but he maintains that, unlike her male counterpart, "silence is a woman's glory." This implies that there is a deficit in a woman's "higher order" reasoning capacity, that is, the kind of reasoning needed for command.

While Aristotle's teleology is philosophically controversial, the premise that women are less capable of (higher order) rationality than men is an empirical claim that requires confirmation. Perhaps women, as a matter of fact, tend to rely more on their emotions (or passions) than do men. However, from this premise alone it does not follow that they are less rational. What is also needed is the assumption that reason and emotion are contraries (like black and white) which exclude one another. Aristotle appears to accept this assumption, for he states that "appetite [emotion] is contrary to choice" and that "choice involves a rational principle and thought." [1]

As Aristotle's characterization of choice suggests, rational decision making is always a process involving the application of universal rules or principles to particular situations. This process is defined by Aristotle in terms of a form of *deductive* reasoning known as a *syllogism*. [2]

According to Aristotle, the ability to reason deductively from universal premises to conclusions is what distinguishes human beings from "the lower animals" "who have no universal judgment but only imagination and memory of particulars." [3] Aristotle's model of rationality is thus one of deductive, rule-based logic. Indeed, this should not surprise us since Aristotle was the founder of deductive logic.

However, as suggested by Carol Gilligan and other feminist thinkers, women's thinking may tend to be less rule based and deductive and more *case-based* and *analogical*. (In this text, see chapter 2 for a discussion of care ethics in "Ethical Theory and Mental Health Practice.") That is, rather than coming to the fore of concrete situations with preconceived rules that are then applied to the situation, women may tend to rely more than men on their "imagination and memory of particulars." They may tend to draw conclusions about what to do in present cases based upon comparisons made with previous situations. They may tend to rely more than men on their emotions in sizing up situations, perceiving details, and reaching decisions; and they may focus more on preserving concrete interpersonal relationships. This mode of thinking did not fit Aristotle's paradigm of rationality; so it is not surprising that he viewed women as being inferior to men.

Recognition of a *difference* between men's and women's ways of thinking does not entail that one mode is any better than the next. Nevertheless, the male model of rule-based, deductive thinking appears to have reigned supreme within Western philosophical tradition. No wonder, since virtually all of the great classical thinkers have been men.

One woman philosopher who represents a break with this tradition is Simone de Beauvoir. In the next selection on "Women in Love," excerpted from *The Second Sex*, de Beauvoir, writing in the mid-twentieth century, draws out the practical implications that a view such as Aristotle's has for a woman in love. In such love, as she describes it, a woman surrenders her identity to a man, and thereby lives in his shadow. As her master, she is nonexistent without him. But since she has sacrificed her identity for him, she must live through him, demanding his total attention and devotion, always, "She hates his sleep." He is her "hero" and he must continually prove his worthiness. On the other hand, the man wants his independence and does not want to "squander his existence on her." He wants to take possession of her without abdicating his own freedom.

This picture de Beauvoir paints does little to commend such a model of love to either sex. Still, on de Beauvoir's view, there is a double standard that favors men, for although they also suffer in love, "their pangs are either short lived or not overly severe" whereas a woman, in "accepting a total dependence, creates a hell for herself." In de Beauvoir's view, it is not until a woman can love without relinquishing her independence that love will be a value worthy of her pursuing. While de Beauvoir's observations were made a half-century ago, one may still question whether this time has yet arrived.

It is ironic that the tradition of male domination as reflected in Aristotle's thought and in de Beauvoir's portrayal of women in love, should have been so fervently and eloquently challenged by a male philosopher writing from a patently male philosophical orientation. In the next selection, excerpted from his treatise on *The Subjection of Women*, John Stuart Mill, the English utilitarian philosopher, argues that the legal subordination of women by men should be replaced by "a principle of perfect equality, admitting no power or privilege on the one side, nor disability on the other." It is noteworthy that, although Mill wrote his treatise in 1861, he postponed publishing it until 1869 for fear that the "revolutionary" ideas it contained might be so ill received as to do more harm than good. Indeed, when it was finally published, although it was met with enthusiasm by some, it was also met with extreme hostility by others who saw it as morally and socially subversive.

As a utilitarian, Mill approaches the issue of women's rights from the perspective of human welfare. His strategy is, roughly, to ask what benefits are obtained by a social system in which there is an inequality of rights between men and women. His answer is that no such benefits are obtained. Rather, according to Mill, such a system merely keeps women from making important contributions to society, by preventing them from entering "the more elevated social positions," for "any limitation of the field of selection deprives society of some chances of being served by the competent without ever saving it from the incompetent."

Furthermore, according to Mill, women are not *naturally* inferior to men, but are instead socialized into a kind of "willful slavery." That is, they have been "brought up from their earliest years" to believe that their "ideal of character" is "submissiveness and yielding to the control of others," that "it is their nature to live for others, to make complete abnegation of themselves, and to have no life but in their affections." This "willful slavery" (what Janice K. Wilkerson calls the "victim mentality"), in turn, leaves the door open for serious abuse of women at the hands of their husbands; for, then, even "the vilest male-factor has some wretched woman tied to him, against whom he can commit any atrocity except killing her, and if tolerably cautious, can do that without much danger of the legal penalty."

Add to the foregoing evils the loss of *human freedom* among women which after food and raiment is "the first and strongest want of human nature"—as well as the "weariness, disappointment, and profound dissatisfaction with life, which are so often the substitute for it," and Mill has carved out a strong utilitarian argument for dispensing with a male-dominated social structure and for opting for a system that affords equal rights.

It is under the theoretical auspices of Mill's utilitarian perspective that Janice K. Wilkerson, an applied philosopher-social worker, has taken up the banner of women's rights. In her paper in the Practice section of this chapter, Wilkerson exemplifies the evils, addressed by Mill, of a male-dominated social structure as they occur in the context of *domestic violence*. Through two extremely provocative case studies, she sets out to display the relevance of Mill's nineteenth-century indictment of the model of male dominance to present-day society. In particular, she attempts to demonstrate how our system, with its built-in sexist bias toward males, offers the victim of physical or sexual abuse little or no legal protection against the abuser—and how it, in fact, is instrumental in delivering the victim back into the clutches of the husband or parent who abused her; and how, against what Mill insists upon, the burden of proving one's innocence in litigation inevitably falls upon the abused, rather than upon the abuser. In general, she attempts to show the vicious circularity of a system that teaches women to be weak, victimizes them because they *are* weak, and then punishes them for being so weak.

Whether or not the reader agrees entirely with Wilkerson's sharp condemnation of our current social structure, he or she is bound to be moved by the persuasive arguments of a social philosopher who not only theorizes about the social oppression of women, but who also "seeks out the patients suffering from these social ills, and using the skills of applied philosophy to perform social surgery, cuts out the tumors of violence that threaten us with death."

In the final selection of this chapter, "Letter from a Battered Philosophy Student," a student from an introductory philosophy class, sends a message to her classmates after class assignments to read the Aristotle, Mill, and Wilkerson selections in this chapter. The letter, anonymously sent to the instructor with a note to read to the class, provides us all with a vivid reminder that the subjection of women and attendant violence do not simply happen to "someone else." Physical and emotional abuse persist across all population boundaries and, as this student demonstrates, need not exempt the college student sitting in the next seat over.

Notes

1. Aristotle, "Virtue Ethics," *Nicomachean Ethics*, ed. Richard McKeon, trans. W. D. Ross (New York: Random House, 1941), bk. 3, chap. 2, 1111b15, 1112a16.
2. Ibid., bk. 7, chap. 3, 147a. See also this text chapter 7.
3. Aristotle, "Virtue Ethics," bk. 7, chap. 3, 1147b5.

ISSUES

ARISTOTLE

THE NATURAL INFERIORITY
OF WOMEN

Some people think that the qualifications of a statesman, king, householder, and master are the same, and that they differ, not in kind, but only in the number of their subjects. For example, the ruler over a few is called a master; over more, the manager of a household; over a still larger number, a statesman or king, as if there were no difference between a great household and a small state. . . .

But all this is a mistake; for governments differ in kind. . . . As in other departments of science, so in politics, the compound should always be resolved into the simple elements or least parts of the whole. We must therefore look at the elements of which the state is composed, in order that we may see in what the different kinds of rule differ from one another, and whether any scientific result can be attained about each one of them.

He who thus considers things in their first growth and origin, whether a state or anything else, will obtain the clearest view of them. In the first place there must be a union of those who cannot exist without each other; namely, of male and female, that the race may continue (and this is a union which is formed, not of deliberate purpose, but because, in common with other animals and with plants, mankind have a natural desire to leave behind them an image of themselves), and of natural ruler and subject, that both may be preserved. For that which can foresee by the exercise of mind is by nature intended to be lord and master, and that which can with its body give effect to such foresight is a subject, and by nature a slave; hence master and slave have the same interest. Now nature has distinguished between the female and the slave. For she is not niggardly, like the smith who fashions the Delphian knife for many uses; she makes each thing for a single use, and every instrument is best made when intended for one and not for many uses. But among barbarians no distinction is made between women and slaves, because there is no natural ruler among them: they are a community of slaves, male and female. Wherefore the poets say,—

"It is meet that Hellenes should rule over barbarians";

as if they thought that the barbarian and the slave were by nature one.

SOURCE: Aristotle, *Politics*, Book 1, tr. Benjamin Jowett, in *The Works of Aristotle*, ed. J. A. Smith and W. D. Ross (Oxford: Oxford University Press, 1966). Reprinted by permission of the publisher.

Out of these two relationships between man and woman, master and slave, the first thing to arise is the family, and Hesiod is right when he says,—

"First house and wife and an ox for the plough,"

for the ox is the poor man's slave. The family is the association established by nature for the supply of men's everyday wants, and the members of it are called by Charondas "companions of the cupboard," and by Epimenides the Cretan, "companions of the manger."

. . . A husband and father, we saw, rules over wife and children, both free, but the rule differs, the rule over his children being a royal, over his wife a constitutional rule. For although there may be exceptions to the order of nature, the male is by nature fitter for command than the female, just as the elder and full-grown is superior to the younger and more immature. But in most constitutional states the citizens rule and are ruled by turns, for the idea of a constitutional state implies that the natures of the citizens are equal, and do not differ at all. Nevertheless, when one rules and the other is ruled we endeavor to create a difference of outward forms and names and titles of respect. . . .

. . . The relation of the male to the female is of this kind, but there the inequality is permanent. The rule of a father over his children is royal, for he rules by virtue both of love and of the respect due to age, exercising a kind of royal power. And therefore Homer has appropriately called Zeus "father of Gods and men," because he is the king of them all. For a king is the natural superior of his subjects, but he should be of the same kin or kind with them, and such is the relation of elder and younger, of father and son.

. . . A question may indeed be raised, whether there is any excellence at all in a slave beyond and higher than merely instrumental and ministerial qualities— whether he can have the virtues of temperance, courage, justice, and the like; or whether slaves possess only bodily and ministerial qualities. And, whichever way we answer the question, a difficulty arises; for, if they have virtue, in what will they differ from freemen? On the other hand, since they are men and share in rational principle, it seems absurd to say that they have no virtue. A similar question may be raised about women and children, whether they too have virtues: ought a woman to be temperate and brave and just, and is a child to be called temperate, and intemperate, or not? So in general we may ask about the natural ruler, and the natural subject, whether they have the same or different virtues. For if a noble nature is equally required in both, why should one of them always rule, and the other always be ruled? Nor can we say that this is a question of degree, for the difference between ruler and subject is a difference of kind, which the difference of more and less never is. Yet how strange is the supposition that the one ought, and that the other ought not, to have virtue! For if the ruler is intemperate and unjust, how can he rule well? If the subject, how can he obey well? If he be licentious and cowardly, he will certainly not do his duty. It is evident, therefore, that both of them must have a share of virtue, but varying as natural subjects also vary among themselves. Here the very constitution of the soul has shown us the way; in it one part naturally rules, and the other is subject, and the virtue of the ruler we maintain to be different from that of the subject;—the one being the virtue of the rational, and the other of the irrational part. Now, it is obvious that the same principle applies generally, and therefore almost all things rule and are ruled according to nature. But the kind of rule differs;—the freeman rules over the slave after another manner from that in which the male rules over the female, or the man over the child; although the parts of the soul are present in all of them, they are present in different degrees. For the slave has no deliberate faculty at all; the woman has, but it is without authority, and the child has, but it is immature. So it must necessarily be supposed to be with the moral virtues also; all should partake of them, but only in such manner and degree as is required by each for the fulfillment of his duty. Hence the ruler ought to have moral virtue in perfection, for his function, taken absolutely, demands a master artificer, and rational principle is such an artificer; the subjects, on the other hand, require only that measure of virtue which is proper to each of them. Clearly, then, moral virtue belongs to all of them; but the temperance of a man and of a woman, or the courage and justice of a man and of a woman, are not, as Socrates maintained, the same; the courage of a man is shown in commanding, of a woman in obeying. And this holds of all other virtues, as will be more clearly seen if we look at them in detail, for those who say generally that virtue consists in a good disposition of the soul, or in doing rightly, or the like, only deceive themselves. Far better than such definitions is their mode of speaking, who, like Gorgias, enumerate the virtues. All classes must be deemed to have their special attributes; as the poet says of women,

"Silence is a woman's glory,"

but this is not equally the glory of man.

SIMONE DE BEAUVOIR

WOMEN IN LOVE

The word *love* has by no means the same sense for both sexes, and this is one cause of the serious misunderstandings that divide them. Byron well said: "Man's love is of man's life a thing apart; 'Tis woman's whole existence." Nietzsche expresses the same idea in *The Gay Science:*

> The single word love in fact signifies two different things for man and woman. What woman understands by love is clear enough: it is not only devotion, it is a total gift of body and soul, without reservation, without regard

SOURCE: Reprinted from *The Second Sex* by Simone de Beauvoir; translated and edited by H. M. Parshley. Copyright 1952, 1980 by Alfred A. Knopf, Inc. Reprinted by permission of the publisher.

for anything whatever. This unconditional nature of her love is what makes it a *faith*,[1] the only one she has. As for man, if he loves a woman, what he *wants*[1] is that love from her; he is in consequence far from postulating the same sentiment for himself as for woman; if there should be men who also felt that desire for complete abandonment, upon my word, they would not be men.

Men have found it possible to be passionate lovers at certain times in their lives, but there is not one of them who could be called "a great lover";[2] in their most violent transports, they never abdicate completely; even on their knees before a mistress, what they still want is to take possession of her; at the very heat of their lives they remain sovereign subjects; the beloved woman is only one value among others; they wish to integrate her into their existence and not to squander it entirely on her. For woman, on the contrary, to love is to relinquish everything for the benefit of a master. As Cecile Sauvage puts it: "Woman must forget her own personality when she is in love. It is a law of nature. A woman is nonexistent without a master. Without a master, she is a scattered bouquet."

The fact is that we have nothing to do here with laws of nature. It is the difference in their situations that is reflected in the difference men and women show in their conceptions of love. The individual who is a subject, who is himself, if he has the courageous inclination toward transcendence, endeavors to extend his grasp on the world: he is ambitious, he acts. But an inessential creature is incapable of sensing the absolute at the heart of her subjectivity; a being doomed to immanence cannot find self-realization in acts. Shut up in the sphere of the relative, destined to the male from childhood, habituated to seeing in him a superb being whom she cannot possibly equal, the woman who has not repressed her claim to humanity will dream of transcending her being toward one of these superior beings, of amalgamating herself with the sovereign subject. There is no other way out for her than to lose herself, body and soul, in him who is represented to her as the absolute, as the essential. Since she is anyway doomed to dependence, she will prefer to serve a god rather than obey tyrants— parents, husband, or protector. She chooses to desire her enslavement so ardently that it will seem to her the expression of her liberty; she will try to rise above her situation as inessential object by fully accepting it; through her flesh, her feelings, her behavior, she will enthrone him as supreme value and reality: she will humble herself to nothingness before him. Love becomes for her a religion. . . .

The supreme happiness of the woman in love is to be recognized by the loved man as a part of himself; when he says "we," she is associated and identified with him, she shares his prestige and reigns with him over the rest of the world; she never tires of repeating—even to excess—this delectable "we." As one necessary to a being who is absolute necessity, who stands forth in the world seeking necessary goals and who gives her back the world in necessary form, the woman in love acquires in her submission that magnificent possession, the absolute. It is this certitude that gives her lofty joys; she feels exalted to a place at the right hand of God. Small matter to her to have only second place if she has *her* place, forever, in a most wonderfully ordered world. So long as she is in love and is loved by and necessary to her loved one, she feels herself wholly justified: she knows peace and happiness. Such was perhaps the lot of Mlle Aïsse[3] with the Chevalier d'Aydie before religious scruples troubled his soul, or that of Juliette Drouet in the mighty shadow of Victor Hugo.

But this glorious felicity rarely lasts. No man really is God. The relations sustained by the mystic with the divine Absence depend on her fervor alone; but the deified man, who is not God, is present. And from this fact are to come the torments of the woman in love. Her most common fate is summed up in the famous words of Julie de Lespinasse:[4] "Always, my dear friend, I love you, I suffer and I await you." To be sure, suffering is linked with love for men also; but their pangs are either of short duration or not overly severe. Benjamin Constant wanted to die on account of Mme Récamier: he was cured in a twelvemonth. Stendhal regretted Métilde for years, but it was a regret that perfumed his life without destroying it. Whereas woman, in assuming her role as the inessential, accepting a total dependence, creates a hell for herself. Every woman in love recognizes herself in Hans Andersen's little mermaid who exchanged her fishtail for feminine legs through love and then found herself walking on needles and live coals. It is not true that the loved man is absolutely necessary, above chance and circumstance, and the woman is not necessary to him; he is not really in a position to justify the feminine being who is consecrated to his worship, and he does not permit himself to be possessed by her.

An authentic love should assume the contingence of the other; that is to say, his lacks, his limitations, and his basic gratuitousness. It would not pretend to be a mode of salvation, but a human interrelation. Idolatrous love attributes an absolute value to the loved one, a first falsity that is brilliantly apparent to all outsiders. "*He* isn't worth all that love," is whispered around the woman in love, and posterity wears a pitying smile at the thought of certain pallid heroes, like Count Guibert. It is a searing disappointment to the woman to discover the faults, the mediocrity of her idol. Novelists, like Colette, have often depicted this bitter anguish. The disillusion is still more cruel than that of the child who sees the father's prestige crumble, because the woman has herself selected the one to whom she has given over her entire being.

Even if the chosen one is worthy of the profoundest affection, his truth is of the earth, earthy, and it is no longer this mere man whom the woman loves as she kneels before a supreme being; she is duped by that spirit of seriousness which declines to take values as incidental—that is to say, declines to recognize that they have their source in human existence. Her bad faith[5] raises barriers between her and the man she adores. She offers him incense, she bows down, but she is not a friend to him since she does not realize that he is in danger in the world, that his projects and his aims are as fragile as he is; regarding him as the Faith, the Truth, she misunderstands his freedom—his hesitancy and anguish of spirit. This refusal to apply a human measuring scale to the lover explains many feminine paradoxes. The woman asks a favor from her lover. Is it granted? Then he is generous, rich, magnificent; he is kingly, he is divine. Is it refused? Then he is avaricious, mean, cruel; he is a devilish or a bestial creature.

One might be tempted to object: if a "yes" is such an astounding and superb extravagance, should one be surprised at a "no"? If the "no" discloses such abject selfishness, why wonder so much at the "yes"? Between the superhuman and the inhuman is there no place for the human?

A fallen god is not a man: he is a fraud; the lover has no other alternative than to prove that he really is this king accepting adulation—or to confess himself a usurper. If he is no longer adored, he must be trampled on. In virtue of that glory with which she has haloed the brow of her beloved, the woman in love forbids him any weakness; she is disappointed and vexed if he does not live up to the image she has put in his place. If he gets tired or careless, if he gets hungry or thirsty at the wrong time, if he makes a mistake or contradicts himself, she asserts that he is "not himself" and she makes a grievance of it. In this indirect way she will go so far as to take him to task for any of his ventures that she disapproves; she judges her judge, and she denies him his liberty so that he may deserve to remain her master. Her worship sometimes finds better satisfaction in his absence than in his presence; as we have seen, there are women who devote themselves to dead or otherwise inaccessible heroes, so that they may never have to face them in person, for beings of flesh and blood would be fatally contrary to their dreams. Hence such disillusioned sayings as: "One must not believe in Prince Charming. Men are only poor creatures," and the like. They would not seem to be dwarfs if they had not been asked to be giants.

It is one of the curses afflicting the passionate woman that her generosity is soon converted into exigence. Having become identified with another, she wants to make up for her loss; she must take possession of that other person who has captured her. She gives herself to him entirely; but he must be completely available to receive this gift. She dedicates every moment to him, but he must be present at all times; she wants to live only in him—but she wants to live, and he must therefore devote himself to making her live. . . .

Acceptance is in fact an obligation that is binding on the lover, without his having even the benefit of seeming to be a giver; the woman requires him to accept gratefully the burdens with which she crushes him. And her tyranny is insatiable. The man in love is tyrannical, but when he has obtained what he wants he is satisfied; whereas there are no limits to woman's exigent devotion. A lover who has confidence in his mistress feels no displeasure if she absents herself, is occupied at a distance from him; sure that she is his, he prefers to possess a free being than to own a thing. For the woman, on the contrary, the absence of her lover is always torture; he is an eye, a judge, and as soon as he looks at anything other than herself, he frustrates her; whatever he sees, he robs her of; away from him, she is dispossessed, at once of herself and of the world; even when seated at her side reading or writing or whatever, he is abandoning her, betraying her. She hates his sleep. . . .

The god must not sleep lest he become clay, flesh; he must not cease to be present, lest his creature sink into nothingness. For woman, man's sleep is selfishness and treason. The lover sometimes awakens his mistress: it is to embrace her; she wakes him up simply to keep him from sleeping, to keep him there, in the room, in the bed, in her arms—like God in the tabernacle. That is what woman wants: she is a jailer. . . .

Genuine love ought to be founded on the mutual recognition of two liberties; the lovers would then experience themselves both as self and as other: neither would give up transcendence, neither would be mutilated; together they would manifest values and aims in the world. For the one and the other, love would be revelation of self by the gift of self and enrichment of the world. . . .

Men have vied with one another in proclaiming that love is woman's supreme accomplishment. "A woman who loves as a woman becomes only the more feminine," says Nietzsche, and Balzac: "Among the first-rate, man's life is fame, woman's life is love. Woman is man's equal only when she makes her life a perpetual offering, as that of man is perpetual action." But therein, again, is a cruel deception, since what she offers, men are in no wise anxious to accept. Man has no need of the unconditional devotion he claims, nor of the idolatrous love that flatters his vanity; he accepts them only on condition that he need not satisfy the reciprocal demands these attitudes imply. He preaches to woman that she should give—and her gifts bore him to distraction; she is left in embarrassment with her useless offerings, her empty life. On the day when it will be possible for woman to love not in her weakness but in her strength, not to escape herself but to find herself, not to abase herself but to assert herself—on that day love will become for her, as for man, a source of life and not of mortal danger. In the meantime, love represents in its most touching form the curse that lies heavily upon woman confined in the feminine universe, woman mutilated, insufficient unto herself. The innumerable martyrs to love bear witness against the injustice of a fate that offers a sterile hell as ultimate salvation.

NOTES

1. Nietzsche's italics.
2. In the sense that a woman may sometimes be called *"une grand amoureuse."*—Tr.
3. An account of her life, with her letters, will be found in *Lettres du XVIIᵉ et du XVIIᵉ Siècle*, by *Eugène Asse* (Paris, 1873).—Tr.
4. Famous intellectual woman of the eighteenth century, noted for her salon and her fervid correspondence with the rather undistinguished military officer and writer Count Guibert, mentioned below.—Tr.
5. In Sartre's existentialist terminology, "bad faith" means abdication of the human self with its hard duty of choice, the wish therefore to become a thing, the flight from the anguish of liberty.—Tr.

JOHN STUART MILL

THE SUBJECTION OF WOMEN

The object of this Essay is to explain, as clearly as I am able, the grounds of an opinion which I have held from the very earliest period when I had formed any opinions at all on social or political matters, and which, instead of being weakened or modified, has been constantly growing stronger by the progress of reflection and the experience of life: That the principle which regulates the existing social relations between the two sexes—the legal subordination of one sex to the other—is wrong in itself, and now one of the chief hindrances to human improvement; and that it ought to be replaced by a principle of perfect equality, admitting no power or privilege on the one side, nor disability on the other.

The very words necessary to express the task I have undertaken show how arduous it is. But it would be a mistake to suppose that the difficulty of the case must lie in the insufficiency or obscurity of the grounds of reason on which my conviction rests. The difficulty is that which exists in all cases in which there is a mass of feeling to be contended against. So long as an opinion is strongly rooted in the feelings, it gains rather than loses in stability by having a preponderating weight of argument against it. For if it were accepted as a result of argument, the refutation of the argument might shake the solidity of the conviction; but when it rests solely on feeling, the worse it fares in argumentative contest, the more persuaded its adherents are that their feeling must have some deeper ground, which the arguments do not reach; and while the feeling remains, it is always throwing up fresh intrenchments of argument to repair any breach made in the old. And there are so many causes tending to make the feelings connected with this subject the most intense and most deeply rooted of all those which gather round and protect old institutions and customs, that we need not wonder to find them as yet less undermined and loosened than any of the rest by the progress of the great modern spiritual and social transition; nor suppose that the barbarisms to which men cling longest must be less barbarisms than those which they earlier shake off.

In every respect the burden is hard on those who attack an almost universal opinion. They must be very fortunate, as well as unusually capable, if they obtain a hearing at all. They have more difficulty in obtaining a trial, than any other litigants have in getting a verdict. If they do extort a hearing, they are subjected to a set of logical requirements totally different from those exacted from other people. In all other cases, the burden of proof is supposed to lie with the affirmative. If a person is charged with a murder, it rests with those who accuse

SOURCE: John Stuart Mill, *The Subjection of Women* (New York: Henry Holt and Company, 1885), excerpted from Ch. 1.

him to give proof of his guilt, not with himself to prove his innocence. If there is a difference of opinion about the reality of any alleged historical event, in which the feelings of men in general are not much interested, as the Siege of Troy for example, those who maintain that the event took place are expected to produce their proofs, before those who take the other side can be required to say anything; and at no time are these required to do more than show that the evidence produced by the others is of no value. Again, in practical matters the burden of proof is supposed to be with those who are against liberty; who contend for any restriction or prohibition; either any limitation of the general freedom of human action, or any disqualification or disparity of privilege affecting one person or kind of persons, as compared with others. The *a priori* presumption is in favor of freedom and impartiality. It is held that there should be no restraint not required by the general good, and that the law should be no respector of persons, but should treat all alike, save where dissimilarity of treatment is required by positive reasons, either of justice or of policy. But of none of these rules of evidence will the benefit be allowed to those who maintain the opinion I profess. It is useless for me to say that those who maintain the doctrine that men have a right to command and women are under an obligation to obey, or that men are fit for government and women unfit, are on the affirmative side of the question, and that they are bound to show positive evidence for the assertions, or submit to their rejection. It is equally unavailing for me to say that those who deny to women any freedom or privilege rightly allowed to men have the double presumption against them that they are opposing freedom and recommending partiality, must be held to the strictest proof of their case, and unless their success be such as to exclude all doubt, the judgement ought to go against them. These would be thought good pleas in any common case, but they will not be thought so in this instance. Before I could hope to make any impression, I should be expected not only to answer all that has ever been said by those who take the other side of the question, but to imagine all that could be said by them—to find them in reasons, as well as answer all I find: and besides refuting all arguments for the affirmative, I shall be called upon for invincible positive arguments to prove a negative. And even if I could do all this, and leave the opposite party with a host of unanswered arguments against them, and not a single unrefuted one on their side, I should be thought to have done little; for a cause supported on the one hand by universal usage, and on the other by so great a preponderance of popular sentiment, is supposed to have a presumption in its favor, superior to any conviction which an appeal to reason has power to produce in any intellects but those of a high class. . . .

The generality of a practice is in some cases a strong presumption that it is, or at all events once was, conducive to laudable ends. This is the case, when the practice was first adopted, or afterward kept up, as a means to such ends, and was grounded on experience of the mode in which they could be most effectually attained. If the authority of men over women, when first established, had been the result of a conscientious comparison between different modes of constituting the government of society; if, after trying various other modes of social organization—the government of women over men, equality between the two, and such mixed and divided modes of government as might be invented—it had been decided, on the testimony of experience, that the mode in which women are wholly under the rule of men, having no share it all in public concerns, and each in private being under the legal obligation of obedience to the man with whom she has associated her destiny, was the arrangement most conducive to the happiness and well-being of both; its general adoption might then be fairly thought to be some evidence that, at the time when it was adopted, it was the best: though even then the considerations which recommended it may, like so many other primeval social facts of the greatest importance, have subsequently, in the course of ages, ceased to exist. But the state of the case is in every respect the reverse of this. In the first place, the opinion in favor of the present system, which entirely subordinates the weaker sex to the stronger, rests upon theory only: for there never has been trial made of any other: so that experience, in the sense in which it is vulgarly opposed to theory, cannot be pretended to have pronounced any verdict. And in the second place, the adoption of this system of inequality never was the result of deliberation, or forethought, or any social ideas, or any notion whatever of what conduced to the benefit of humanity or the good order of society. It arose simply from the fact that from the very earliest twilight of society, every woman (owing to the value attached to her by men, combined with her inferiority in muscular strength) was found in a state of bondage to some man. Laws and systems of policy always begin by recognizing the relations they find already existing between individuals. They convert what was a mere physical fact into a legal right, give it the sanction of society, and principally aim at the substitution of public and organized means of asserting and protecting these rights, instead of the irregular and lawless conflict of physical strength. Those who had already been compelled to obedience became in this manner legally bound to it. Slavery, from being a mere affair of force between the master and the slave, became regularized and a matter of compact among the masters, who, binding themselves to one another for common protection, guaranteed by their collective strength the private possessions of each, including his slaves. In early times, the great majority of the male sex were slaves, as well as the whole of the female. And many ages elapsed, some of them ages of high civilization, before any thinker was bold enough to question the rightfulness, and the absolute social necessity, either of the one slavery or of the other. By degrees such thinkers did arise: and (the general progress of society assisting) the slavery of the male sex has, in all the countries of Christian Europe at least (though, in one of them, only within the last few years), been at length abolished, and that of the female sex has been gradually changed into a milder form of dependence. But this dependence as it exists at present is not an original institution, taking a fresh start from considerations of justice and social expediency—it is the primitive state of slavery lasting on, through successive mitigations and modifications occasioned by the same causes which have softened the general manners, and brought all human relations more under the control of justice and the influence of humanity. It has not lost the taint of its brutal origin. No presumption in its favor, therefore, can be drawn from the fact of its existence. The only such presumption which it could be supposed to have must be grounded on its having lasted till now, when so many other things which came down from the same odious source have been done away with. And this, indeed, is what makes it strange to ordinary ears, to hear it asserted that the inequality of rights between men and women has no other source than the law of the strongest. . . .

Whatever gratification of pride there is in the possession of power, and whatever personal interest in its exercise, is in this case not confined to a limited class, but common to the whole male sex. Instead of being, to most of its supporters, a thing desirable chiefly in the abstract, or, like the political ends usually contended for by factions, of little private importance to any but the leaders; it comes home to the person and hearth of every male head of family, and of every one who looks forward to being so. The clodhopper exercises, or is to exercise, his share of the power equally with the highest nobleman. And the case is that in which the desire of power is the strongest: for every one who desires power, desires it most over those who are nearest to him, with whom his life is passed, with whom any independence of his authority is oftenest likely to interfere with his individual preferences. If, in the other cases specified, powers manifestly grounded only on force, and having so much less to support them, are so slowly and with so much difficulty got rid of much more must it be so with this, even if it rests on no better foundation than those. We must consider, too, that the possessors of the power have facilities in this case greater than in any other, to prevent any uprising against it. Every one of the subjects lives under the very eye, and almost, it may be said, in the hands, of one of the masters—in closer intimacy with him than with any of her fellow subjects; with no means of combining against him, no power of even locally overmastering him, and, on the other hand, with the strongest motives for seeking his favor and avoiding to give him offense. In struggles for political emancipation, everybody knows how often its champions are bought off by bribes, or daunted by terrors. In the case of women, each individual of the subject-class is in a chronic state of bribery and intimidation combined. In setting up the standard of resistance, a large number of the leaders, and still more of the followers, must make an almost complete sacrifice of the pleasures or the alleviations of their own individual lot. If ever any system of privilege and enforced subjection had its yoke tightly riveted on the necks of those who are kept down by it, this has. . . .

Some will object, that a comparison cannot fairly be made between the government of the male sex and the forms of unjust power which I have adduced in illustration of it, since these are arbitrary, and the effect of mere usurpation, while it on the contrary is natural. But was there ever any domination which did not appear natural to those who possessed it? There was a time when the division of mankind into two classes, a small one of masters and a numerous one of slaves, appeared, even to the most cultivated minds, to be a natural, and the only natural, condition of the human race. No less an intellect, and one which contributed no less to the progress of human thought, than Aristotle, held this opinion without doubt or misgiving; and rested it on the same premises on which the same assertion in regard to the dominion of men over women is usually based, namely, that there are different natures among mankind, free natures, and slave natures; that the Greeks were of a free nature, the barbarian races of Thracians and Asiatics of a slave nature. But why need I go back to Aristotle? Did not the slave-owners of the Southern United States maintain the same doctrine, with all the fanaticism with which men cling to the theories that justify their passions and legitimate their personal interests? Did they not call heaven and earth to witness that the dominion of the white man over the black is natural, that the black race is by nature incapable of freedom, and marked out for slavery?—some even going so far as to say that the freedom of manual laborers is an unnatural order of things anywhere. Again, the theorists of absolute monarchy have always affirmed it to be the only natural form of government; issuing from the patriarchal, which was the primitive and spontaneous form of society, framed on the model of the paternal, which is anterior to society itself, and, as they contend, the most natural authority of all. Nay, for that matter, the law of force itself, to those who could not plead any other, has always seemed the most natural of all grounds for the exercise of authority. Conquering races hold it to be Nature's own dictate that the conquered should obey the conquerors, or, as they euphoniously paraphrase it, that the feebler and more unwarlike races should submit to the braver and manlier. The smallest acquaintance with human life in the middle ages shows how supremely natural the dominion of the feudal nobility over men of low condition appeared to the nobility themselves, and how unnatural the conception seemed, of a person of the inferior class claiming equality with them, or exercising authority over them. It hardly seemed less so to the class held in subjection. The emancipated serfs and burgesses, even in their most vigorous struggles, never made any pretension to a share of authority; they only demanded more or less limitation to the power of tyrannizing over them. So true is it that unnatural generally means only uncustomary, and that everything which is usual appears natural. The subjection of women to men being a universal custom, any departure from it quite naturally appears unnatural. But how entirely, even in this case, the feeling is dependent on custom, appears by ample experience. Nothing so much astonishes the people of distant parts of the world, when they first learn anything about England, as to be told that it is under a queen: the thing seems to them so unnatural as to be almost incredible. To Englishmen this does not seem in the least degree unnatural, because they are used to it; but they do feel it unnatural that women should be soldiers or members of Parliament. In the feudal ages, on the contrary, war and politics were not thought unnatural to women, because not unusual; it seemed natural that women of the privileged classes should be of manly character, inferior in nothing but bodily strength to their husbands and fathers. The independence of women seemed rather less unnatural to the Greeks than to other ancients, on account of the fabulous Amazons (whom they believed to be historical), and the partial example afforded by the Spartan women; who, though no less subordinate by law than in other Greek states, were more free in fact; and being trained to bodily exercises in the same manner with men, gave ample proof that they were not naturally disqualified for them. There can be little doubt that Spartan experience suggested to Plato, among many other of his doctrines, that of the social and political equality of the two sexes.

But, it will be said, the rule of men over women differs from all those others in not being a rule of force; it is accepted voluntarily; women make no complaint, and are consenting parties to it. In the first place, a great number of women do not accept it. Ever since there have been women able to make their sentiments known by their writings (the only mode of publicity which society permits to them), an increasing number of them have recorded protests against their present social condition: and recently many thousands of them, headed by the most eminent women known to the public, have petitioned Parliament for their admission to the Parliamentary Suffrage. The claim of women to be educated as solidly, and in the same branches of knowledge, as men is urged with growing intensity, and with a great prospect of success; while the demand for their admission into professions and occupations hitherto closed against them becomes every year more urgent. Though there are not in this country, as there are in the United States, periodical Conventions and an organized party to agitate for the Rights of Women, there is a numerous and active Society organized and managed by women, for the more limited object of obtaining the political franchise. Nor is it only in our own country and in America that women are beginning to protest, more or less collectively, against the disabilities under which they labor. France, and Italy, and Switzerland, and Russia now afford examples of the same thing. How many more women there are who silently cherish similar aspirations, no one can possibly know; but there are abundant tokens how many *would* cherish them, were they not so strenuously taught to repress them as contrary to the proprieties of their sex. It must be remembered, also, that no enslaved class ever asked for complete liberty at once. When Simon de Montfort called the deputies of the commons to sit for the first time in Parliament, did any of them dream of demanding that an assembly, elected by their constituents, should make and destroy ministers, and dictate to the king in affairs of state? No such thought entered into the imagination of the most ambitious of them. The nobility had already these pretensions; the commons pretended to nothing but to be exempt from arbitrary taxation, and from the gross individual oppression of the king's officers. It is a political law of nature that those who are under any power of ancient origin never begin by complaining of the power itself, but only of its oppressive exercise. There is never any want of women who complain of ill usage by their husbands. There would be infinitely more, if complaint were not the greatest of all provocatives to a repetition and increase of the ill usage. It is this which frustrates all attempts to maintain the power but protect the woman against its abuses. In no other case (except that of a child) is the person who has been proved judicially to have suffered an injury replaced under the physical power of the culprit who inflicted it. Accordingly wives, even in the most extreme and protracted cases of bodily ill usage, hardly ever dare avail themselves of the laws made for their protection; and if, in a moment of irrepressible indignation, or by the interference of neighbors, they are induced to do so, their whole effort afterward is to disclose as little as they can, and to beg off their tyrant from his merited chastisement.

All causes, social and natural, combine to make it unlikely that women should be collectively rebellious to the power of men. They are so far in a position different from all other subject classes that their masters require something more from them than actual service. Men do not want solely the obedience of women, they want their sentiments. All men, except the most brutish, desire to have, in the woman most nearly connected with them, not a forced slave but a willing one, not a slave merely, but a favorite. They have therefore put everything in practice to enslave their minds. The masters of all other slaves rely, for maintaining obedience, on fear,—either fear of themselves or religious fears. The masters of women wanted more than simple obedience, and they turned the whole force of education to effect their purpose. All women are brought up from the very earliest years in the belief that their ideal of character is the very opposite to that of men; not self-will and government by self-control, but submission and yielding to the control of others. All the moralities tell them that it is the duty of women, and all the current sentimentalities that it is their nature, to live for others, to make complete abnegation of themselves, and to have no life but in their affections. And by their affections are meant the only ones they are allowed to have—those to the men with whom they are connected, or to the children who constitute an additional and indefeasible tie between them and a man. When we put together three things—first, the natural attraction between opposite sexes; secondly, the wife's entire dependence on the husband, every privilege or pleasure she has being either his gift or depending entirely on his will; and lastly, that the principal object of human pursuit, consideration, and all objects of social ambition, can in general be sought or obtained by her only through him, it would be a miracle if the object of being attractive to men had not become the polar star of feminine education and formation of character. And this great means of influence over the minds of women having been acquired, an instinct of selfishness made men avail themselves of it to the utmost as a means of holding women in subjection, by representing to them meekness, submissiveness, and resignation of all individual will into the hands of a man, as an essential part of sexual attractiveness. . . .

The preceding considerations are amply sufficient to show that custom, however universal it may be, affords in this case no presumption, and ought not to create any prejudice, in favor of the arrangements which place women in social and political subjection to men. But I may go further, and maintain that the course of history and the tendencies of progressive human society afford not only no presumptions in favor of this system of inequality of rights, but a strong one against it; and that, so far as the whole course of human improvement up to this time, the whole stream of modern tendencies, warrants any inference on the subject, it is that this relic of the past is discordant with the future, and must necessarily disappear. . . .

The old theory was, that the least possible should be left to the choice of the individual agent; that all he had to do should, as far as practicable, be laid down for him by superior wisdom. Left to himself he was sure to go wrong. The modern conviction, the fruit of a thousand years of experience, is, that things in which the individual is the person directly interested, never go right but as they are left to his own discretion; and that any regulation of them by authority, except to protect the rights of others, is sure to be mischievous. This conclusion, slowly arrived at, and not adopted until almost every possible application of the contrary theory had been made with disastrous result, now (in the industrial department) prevails universally in the most advanced countries, almost universally in all that have pretensions to any sort of advancement. It is not that all processes are supposed to be equally good, or all persons to be equally qualified for everything; but that freedom of individual choice is now known to be the only thing which procures the adoption of the best processes, and throws each operation into the hands of those who are best qualified for it. Nobody thinks it necessary to make a law that only a strong-armed man shall be a blacksmith. Freedom and competition suffice to make blacksmiths strong-armed men, because the weak-armed can earn more by engaging in occupations for which they are more fit. In consonance with this doctrine, it is felt to be an overstepping of the proper bounds of authority to fix beforehand, on some general presumption, that certain persons are not fit to do certain things. It is now thoroughly known and admitted that if some such presumption exists, no such presumption is infallible. Even if it be well grounded in a majority of cases, which it is very likely not to be, there will be a minority of exceptional cases in which it does not hold: and in those it is both an injustice to the individuals, and a detriment to society, to place barriers in the way of their using their faculties for their own benefit and for that of others. In the cases, on the other hand, in which the unfitness is real, the ordinary motives of human conduct will on the whole suffice to prevent the incompetent person from making, or from persisting in the attempt.

If this general principle of social and economical science is not true, if individuals, with such help as they can derive from the opinion of those who know them, are not better judges than the law and the government, of their own capacities and vocation; the world cannot too soon abandon this principle, and return to the old system of regulations and disabilities. But if the principle is true, we ought to act as if we believed it, and not to ordain that to be born a girl instead of a boy, any more than to be born black instead of white, or a commoner instead of a nobleman, shall decide the person's position through all life—shall interdict people from all the more elevated social positions, and from all, except a few, respectable occupations. Even were we to admit the utmost that is ever pretended as to the superior fitness of men for all the functions now reserved to them, the same argument applies which forbids a legal qualification for members of Parliament. If only once in a dozen years the conditions of eligibility exclude a fit person, there is a real loss, while the exclusion of thousands of unfit persons is no gain; for if the constitution of the electoral body disposes them to choose unfit persons, there are always plenty of such persons to choose from. In all things of any difficulty and importance, those who can do them well are fewer than the need, even with the most unrestricted latitude of choice; and any limitation of the field of selection deprives society of some chances of being served by the competent, without ever saving it from the incompetent. . . .

Neither does it avail anything to say that the *nature* of the two sexes adapts them to their present functions and position, and renders these appropriate to them. Standing on the ground of common sense and the constitution of the human mind, I deny that any one knows, or can know, the nature of the two sexes, as long as they have only been seen in their present relation to one another. If men had ever been found in society without women, or women without men, or if there had been a society of men and women in which the women were not under the control of the men, something might have been positively known about the mental and moral differences which may be inherent in the nature of each. What is now called the nature of women is an eminently artificial thing—the result of forced repression in some directions, unnatural stimulation in others. It may be asserted without scruple, that no other class of dependents have had their character so entirely distorted from its proportions by their relation with their masters; for, if conquered and slave races have been, in some respects, more forcibly repressed, whatever in them has not been crushed down by an iron heel has generally been let alone, and if left with any liberty of development, it has developed itself according to its own laws; but in the case of women, a hothouse and stone cultivation has always been carried on of some of the capabilities of their nature, for the benefit and pleasure of their masters. Then, because certain products of the general vital force sprout luxuriantly and reach a great development in this heated atmosphere and under this active nurture and watering, while other shoots from the same root, which are left outside in the wintry air, with ice purposely heaped all round them have a stunted growth, and some are burnt off with fire and disappear; men, with that inability to recognize their own work which distinguishes the unanalytic mind, indolently believe that the tree grows of itself in the way they have made it grow, and that it would die if one-half of it were not kept in a vapor-bath and the other half in the snow.

Of all the difficulties which impede the progress of thought, and the formation of well-grounded opinions of life and social arrangements, the greatest is now the unspeakable ignorance and inattention of mankind in respect to the influences which form human character. Whatever any portion of the human species now are, or seem to be, such, it is supposed, they have a natural tendency to be: even when the most elementary knowledge of the circumstances in which they have been placed clearly points out the causes that made them what they are. Because a cottier deeply in arrears to his landlord is not industrious, there are people who think that the Irish are naturally idle. Because constitutions can be overthrown when the authorities appointed to execute them turn their arms against them, there are people who think the French incapable of free government. Because the Greeks cheated the Turks, and the Turks only plundered the Greeks, there are persons who think that the Turks are naturally more sincere: and because women, as is often said, care nothing about politics except their personalities, it is supposed that the general good is naturally less interesting to women than to men. History, which is now so much better understood than formerly, teaches another lesson: if only by showing the extraordinary susceptibility of human nature to external influences, and the extreme variableness of those of its manifestations which are supposed to be most universal and uniform. But in history, as in traveling, men usually see only what they already had in their own minds; and few learn much from history, who do not bring much with them to its study.

Hence, in regard to that most difficult question, what are the natural differences between the two sexes—a subject on which it is impossible in the present state of society to obtain complete and correct knowledge—while almost everybody dogmatizes upon it, almost all neglect and make light of the only means by which any partial insight can be obtained into it. This is, an analytic study of the most important department of psychology, the laws of the influence of circumstances on character. For, however great and apparently ineradicable the moral and intellectual differences between men and women might be, the evidence of their being natural differences could only be negative. Those only could be inferred to be natural which could not possibly be artificial—the residuum, after deducting every characteristic of either sex which can admit of being explained from education or external circumstances. The profoundest knowledge of the laws of the formation of character is indispensable to entitle any one to affirm even that there is any difference, much more what the difference is, between the two sexes considered as moral and rational beings; and since no one, as yet, has that knowledge (for there is hardly any subject which, in proportion to its importance, has been so little studied), no one is thus far entitled to any positive opinion on the subject. Conjectures are all that can at present be made; conjectures more or less probable, according as more or less authorized by such knowledge as we yet have of the laws of psychology, as applied to the formation of character. . . .

One thing we may be certain of—that what is contrary to women's nature to do, they never will be made to do by simply giving their nature free play. The anxiety of mankind to interfere in behalf of nature, for fear lest nature should not succeed in effecting its purpose, is an altogether unnecessary solicitude. What women by nature cannot do, it is quite superfluous to forbid them from doing. What they can do, but not so well as the men who are their competitors, competition suffices to exclude them from; since nobody asks for protective duties and bounties in favor of women; it is only asked that the present bounties and protective duties in favor of men should be recalled. If women have a greater natural inclination for some things than for others, there is no need of laws or social inculcation to make the majority of them do the former in preference to the latter. Whatever women's services are most wanted for, the free play of competition will hold out the strongest inducements to them to undertake. And, as the words imply, they are most wanted for the things for which they are most fit; by the apportionment of which to them, the collective faculties of the two sexes can be applied on the whole with the greatest sum of valuable result.

The general opinion of men is supposed to be, that the natural vocation of a woman is that of a wife and mother; I say, is supposed to be, because judging from acts—from the whole of the present constitution of society—one might infer that their opinion was the direct contrary. They might be supposed to think that the alleged natural vocation of women was of all things the most repugnant to their nature; insomuch that if they are free to do anything else—if any other means of living, or occcupation of their time and faculties, is open, which has any chance of appearing desirable to them—there will not be enough of them who will be willing to accept the condition said to be natural to them. If this is the real opinion of men in general, it would be well that it should be spoken out. I should like to hear somebody openly enunciating the doctrine (it is already implied in much that is written on the subject)—"It is necessary to society that women should marry and produce children. They will not do so unless they are compelled. Therefore it is necessary to compel them." The merits of the case would then be clearly defined. It would be exactly that of the slaveholders of South Carolina and Louisiana. "It is necessary that cotton amd sugar should be grown. White men cannot produce them. Negroes will not, for any wages which we choose to give. *Ergo* they must be compelled." An illustration still closer to the point is that of impressment. Sailors must absolutely be had to defend the country. It often happens that they will not voluntarily enlist. Therefore there must be the power of forcing them. How often has this logic been used! and, but for one flaw in it, without doubt it would have been successful up to this day. But it is open to the retort—First pay the sailors the honest value of their labor. When you have made it as well worth their while to serve you, as to work for other employers, you will have no more difficulty than others have in obtaining their services. To this there is no logical answer except "I will not": and as people are now not only ashamed, but are not desirous, to rob the laborer of his hire, impressment is no longer advocated. Those who attempt to force women into marriage by closing all other doors against them lay themselves open to a similar retort. If they mean what they say, their opinion must evidently be, that men do not render the married condition so desirable to women, as to induce them to accept it for its own recommendations. It is not a sign of one's thinking the boon one offers very attractive, when one allows only Hobson's choice, "that or none." And here, I believe, is the clew to the feelings of those men who have a real antipathy to the equal freedom of women. I believe they are afraid, not lest women should be unwilling to marry, for I do not think that any one in reality has that apprehension; but lest they should insist that marriage should be on equal conditions; lest all women of spirit and capacity should prefer doing almost anything else, not in their own eyes degrading, rather than marry, when marrying is giving themselves a master, and a master too of all their earthly possessions. And truly, if this consequence were necessarily incident to marriage, I think that the apprehension would be very well founded. I agree in thinking it probable that few women, capable of anything else, would, unless under an irresistible *entrainement,* rendering them for the time insensible to anything but itself, choose such a lot, when any other means were open to them of filling a conventionally honorable place in life: and if men are determined that the law of marriage shall be a law of despotism, they are quite right, in point of mere policy, in leaving to women only Hobson's choice. But, in that case, all that has been done in the modern world to relax the chain on the minds of women has been a mistake. They never should have been allowed to receive a literary education. Women who read, much more women who write, are, in the existing constitution of things, a contradiction and a disturbing element: and it was wrong to bring women up with any acquirements but those of an odalisque, or of a domestic servant.

Whether the institution to be defended is slavery, political absolutism, or the absolutism of the head of family, we are always expected to judge of it from its best instances; and we are presented with pictures of loving exercise of authority on one side, loving submission to it on the other—superior wisdom ordering all things for the greatest good of the dependents, and surrounded by their smiles and benedictions. All this would be very much to the purpose if any one pretended that there are no such things as good men. Who doubts that there may be great goodness, and great happiness, and great affection, under the absolute government of a good man? Meanwhile, laws and institutions require to be adapted, not to good men, but to bad. Marriage is not an institution designed for a select few. Men are not required, as a preliminary to the marriage ceremony, to prove by testimonials that they are fit to be trusted with the exercise of absolute power. The tie of affection and obligation to a wife and children is very strong with those whose general social feelings are strong, and with many who are little sensible to any other social ties; but there are all degrees of sensibility and insensibility to it, as there are all grades of goodness and wickedness in men, down to those whom no ties will bind, and on whom society has no action but through its *ultima ratio,* the penalties of the law. In every grade of this descending scale are men to whom are committed all the legal powers of a husband. The vilest malefactor has some wretched woman tied to him, against whom he can commit any atrocity except killing her, and if tolerably cautious, can do that without much danger of the legal penalty.

And how many thousands are there among the lowest classes in every country, who, without being in a legal sense malefactors in any other respect, because in every other quarter their aggressions meet with resistance, indulge the utmost habitual excesses of bodily violence toward the unhappy wife, who alone, at least of grown persons, can neither repel nor escape from their brutality; and toward whom the excess of dependence inspires their mean and savage natures, not with a generous forbearance, and a point of honor to behave well to one whose lot in life is trusted entirely to their kindness, but on the contrary with a notion that the law has delivered her to them as their living thing, to be used at their pleasure, and that they are not expected to practice the consideration toward her which is required from them toward everybody else. The law, which till lately left even these atrocious extremes of domestic oppression practically unpunished, has within these few years made some feeble attempts to repress them. But its attempts have done little, and cannot be expected to do much, because it is contrary to reason and experience to suppose that there can be any real check to brutality, consistent with leaving the victim still in the power of the executioner. Until a conviction for personal violence, or at all events a repetition of it after a first conviction, entitles the woman *ipso facto* to divorce, or at least to a judicial separation, the attempt to repress these "aggravated assaults" by legal penalties will break down for want of a prosecutor, or for want of a witness. . . .

Thus far, the benefits which it has appeared that the world would gain by ceasing to make sex a disqualification for privileges and a badge of subjection, are social rather than individual; consisting in an increase of the general fund of thinking and acting power, and an improvement in the general conditions of the association of men with women. But it would be a grievous understatement of the case to omit the most direct benefit of all, the unspeakable gain in private happiness to the liberated half of the species; the difference to them between a life of subjection to the will of others, and a life of rational freedom. After the primary necessities of food and raiment, freedom is the first and strongest want of human nature. While mankind are lawless, their desire is for lawless freedom. When they have learned to understand the meaning of duty and the value of reason, they incline more and more to be guided and restrained by these in the exercise of their freedom; but they do not therefore desire freedom less; they do not become disposed to accept the will of other people as the representative and interpreter of those guiding principles. On the contrary, the communities in which the reason has been most cultivated, and in which the idea of social duty has been most powerful, are those which have most strongly asserted freedom of action of the individual—the liberty of each to govern his conduct by his own feelings of duty, and by such laws and social restraints as his own conscience can subscribe to. . . .

When we consider the positive evil caused to the disqualified half of the human race by their disqualification first in the loss of the most inspiring and elevating kind of personal enjoyment, and next in the weariness, disappointment, and profound dissatisfaction with life, which are so often the substitute for it; one feels that among all the lessons which men require for carrying on the struggle against the inevitable imperfections of their lot on earth, there is no lesson which nature inflicts, by their jealous and prejudicial restrictions on one another. Their vain fears only substitute other and worse evils for those which they are idly apprehensive of; while every restraint on the freedom of conduct of any of their human fellow-creatures (otherwise than by making them responsible for an evil actually caused by it) dries up *pro tanto* the principal fountain of human happiness, and leaves the species less rich, to an inappreciable degree, in all that makes life valuable to the individual human being.

Janice K. Wilkerson received her master's degree in applied philosophy at Bowling Green State University. She also holds criminal justice and paralegal degrees. Her work experience includes child advocate at Turning Point, Marion, Ohio; contract worker for Choices for Victims of Domestic Violence, Columbus, Ohio; legal advocate for Sandusky Valley Domestic Violence Shelter, Fostoria, Ohio; and juvenile probations counselor in the Ohio State Juvenile Court System. Ms. Wilkerson has also been a corrections program specialist at the Marion Correctional Institution in Marion, Ohio.

PRACTICE

JANICE K. WILKERSON

THE PHILOSOPHER AS SOCIAL WORKER

The philosopher as social worker may sound strange at first; however, it should make sense when examined more closely. Social philosophers have always been the elite diagnosticians of our social illnesses. Although they have been read and written and spoken well of among their peers, they have been puzzling to most of the general population. Philosophers have never been the general practitioners who rolled up their sleeves, sterilized their tools, and operated to remove the tumor afflicting the social body. So, in essence, even if the social philosopher had the correct diagnosis for a social ill, the patient, our society, might well die if the cure relied on an applied social surgery or reconstruction that needed to be performed by the philosopher who has studied the problem and mastered the system. It was not the role of traditional philosophers to dirty their hands with the practical applications of their wise theories. It is the current trend toward applied philosophy that lets philosophers bring together their theoretical backgrounds with a chance to make practical and concrete their ideas by way of social action. In what follows, I will illustrate how, by using the theory of John Stuart Mill as a social base for dealing with battered women and children and juveniles involved with the court system, I have become a philosopher who is a social worker as well as a social thinker.

In the first section of this chapter you read a selection from John Stuart Mill's *Subjection of Women* that provided a discussion of power of men over women and the skewed relationships this imbalance causes. One of the initial functions of this essay will be to give you a sense of what Mill is speaking about when he says there is no practical or justifiable basis for "the legal subordination of one sex to the other." We will examine the problems that have a ripple effect as they gradually get more serious as one injustice or inhumane act builds on another.

Through two case studies, you will get a microcosmic view of how the male model of power influences our daily lives. The case studies will illustrate the main points of Mill's writing as they pertain to either the problem of domestic violence and the care of the victims, or the solution that seeks to restore human dignity and integrity. I will show how this all comes together to define a social problem and forms the basis for my work as an applied philosopher doing social work, ever conscious of the social constructs that exist and shape social attitudes.

The first case is taken from my work in a domestic violence shelter where I lived for three months and met a young woman I will call Nancy.

"No matter where I go, he will find me and if I testify against him, he will find me and kill me." This quotation sums up the dilemma Nancy faced as she was brought to the shelter directly from the hospital where she had spent two weeks. She had been severely beaten and her skin broke as it gave way to the pounding and tore open. She had been beaten with the cord of an iron and had a broomstick forced up her vagina. She told me that she could remember how her body began to swell, to the point that she was unable to even fasten her pants. Nancy couldn't get anyone to stop and help her once she got out on the street after the beating, so she walked a mile to her parents' house and was only then taken to the hospital. Her face wore the scars and wrinkles of someone much older than her twenty years. Nancy's history of abuse started by her being sexually assaulted by her father. As a reaction to her pain and confusion, she started to rebel against her father's authority, which got her committed to a juvenile corrections home. Unwilling to submit herself to the rules dictated by her abuser, she was punished and made the victim one more time. When released from the juvenile facility, Nancy refused to return home and chose to live in the street, which is where she met the next man who was to carry on this pattern of violence.

When Nancy came to our shelter on this occasion, she had been involved in an abusive relationship for four years and wore the scars from beatings and from cuts that had received no medical attention. She had received a Grand Jury indictment two years prior, when, at the trial, she was so intimidated by the presence of her abuser in the courtroom that she perjured herself by changing her story and told the court she had lied about the abuse. However, there was an imprint under one of her eyes that matched the insignia of the ring the abuser wore that day. Without her testimony, the state was forced to drop the case, and he walked out of the courtroom—free to abuse again. Nancy explained her failure to testify with the quotation used earlier as she reflected on the hopelessness of her position one more time while she lay aching in a room behind locked doors in a location not known to the general public. *What was happening to the abuser?*

Joe, as I will call him, had been put in jail by a Municipal Court judge, pending his case being bound over to the Court of Common Pleas. His case was bound over and he was released on $500 bond within three hours. Nancy, on the other hand, was unable to go anywhere and was looking at a shelter stay of about six months if she received an indictment and the case went to trial.

In one of my first interviews with Nancy, immediately following Joe's release, she told me that she wanted "to get out, find him, and kill him." I told her that he was not worth the time she would spend in prison for murder, and that indeed this violence would be no more acceptable than the violence that had been inflicted upon her. Nancy's response continued to haunt me as I worked with these victims; she said, "It would be worth it to me because I wouldn't be afraid anymore!" Nancy was not able to find a solution for survival without the constant fear of the man she thought she loved.

I began to work with Nancy on her right to be physically secure, on her need to see herself as capable of doing whatever she wanted to do, and her need to overcome the "victim mentality." I use the phrase "victim mentality" as synonymous with Mill's description of the effects of women being slaves. Mill tells us:

> Men do not want solely the obedience of women, they want their sentiments. All men, except the most brutish, desire to have, in the women most nearly connected with them, not a forced slave but a willing one, not a slave merely, but a favorite. They have therefore put everything in practice to enslave their minds. The masters of all other slaves rely, for maintaining obedience, on fear—either fear of themselves or religious fears. The masters of women wanted more than simple obedience, and they turned the whole force of education to effect their purpose. All women are brought up from the very earliest years in the belief that their ideal character is the very opposite to that of men; not self-will and government by self-control, but submission and yielding to the control of others.

This is an explanation of a state of mind and socialization that makes a certain population, in this case women, feel less capable or even incapable of being equal and cripples their chances of utilizing their abilities. They value their social role and status more than their own physical and mental welfare, because that has been their "acceptable vocation."

Nancy and the assistant prosecutor went back to the Grand Jury to request, once again, an indictment, and the indictment was handed down; however, the abuser remained on the streets and the victim remained locked up. It seemed more and more inevitable to Nancy, as the next three months wore on, that her plight would not be answered by the only system of recourse available. If she went back to Joe she would once again fear being beaten badly or possibly killed. If she did not go back and went on trial with her testimony responsible for a guilty verdict, he would most certainly kill her. Nancy was transferred to another shelter for her protection, but her sense of hopelessness grew as she started her sixth month of hiding. One day she walked away from the shelter. Another court date came and went, but Nancy did not appear. She has not been heard from since that day by anyone at the shelter, and I often wonder if she has found a safe hiding place or if she is even alive.

The messages of social inequity and oppression that Nancy received dictated that the system would seek to favor those in power. This involved factors like the length of time it took for the legal proceedings that caused her life to stand still as she continued to be punished for being female, a system that taught her to be weak, victimized her because she *was* weak, and then punished her for being so weak. Nancy also knew she would never be safe from her abuser and that we would not be able to protect her. This woman, and many others like her, saw society as a disapproving father who blamed them for being victimized because of their socialization that oppressed them with role models of weakness and submissiveness and then blamed them for being victimized by men as they tried to fulfill their social obligations and expectations that kept them in these abusive relationships.

In the excerpt from Mill, we find a section that describes the horrors of this closed system that abuses, punishes, and judges.

> In no other case (except that of a child) is the person who has been proved judicially to have suffered an injury replaced under the physical power of the culprit who inflicted it. Accordingly wives, even in the most extreme and protracted cases of bodily ill usage, hardly ever dare avail themselves of the laws made for their protection: and if, in a moment of irrepressible indignation, or by the interference of neighbors, they are induced to do so, their whole effort afterward is to disclose as little as they can, and to beg off their tyrant from his merited chastisement.

It is worth noting, at this point, that Mill's philosophy was directed at violations or restrictions of liberty for no apparent good reason—and the status of women was a rich source of examples of such blatant assaults on liberty. Not the least of these examples was the history of our laws to govern violence in our homes. Common law told us that women were the property of their husbands, to use as they desired. "The Rule of Thumb" was codified law that said a man could beat his wife with anything as long as it was not thicker than his thumb. Next, the laws permitting and overtly condoning violence disappeared but were not replaced with laws making domestic violence illegal until several years later. Even when these laws came on the books, the police were not required to answer calls to "domestic squabbles." Today these are laws and police *must* go to a home when they get a call reporting domestic violence; however, how they react to each participant once they arrive will be shaped by their own prejudice and bias. Looking at such a history makes it easy to begin to see the complexity of such a social problem as domestic violence and the real need to look at our social and political philosophy through the years.

The problem we are confronted with when we talk about domestic violence is, at the base, how difficult it is to affect widespread and lasting changes in social laws and attitudes. This is especially true if these changes demand an alteration in the distribution of power, and particularly when we are asking families to change their internal structure. I will again draw from my experience to illustrate this problem, and the waste of valuable human resources and sometimes even lives.

In 1983 and 1984 I worked with a nineteen-year-old who had two children, ages one and four. I will call her Deb. Like Nancy's, Deb's victimization traced back to the nuclear family, her father having both physically and sexually assaulted her for five years. She left home at age fifteen and went to live with "Tim," a man seventeen years her senior. It was not long before abuse of Deb began.

At one point, Deb and the two children were held at gunpoint by Tim for twenty-four hours. She was told that if they fell asleep, he would shoot them. Tim brutally beat Deb at the end of the twenty-four-hour period in the presence of both children. It was after this incident that Deb came to the shelter for help and with her came her violent history.

Deb told of being sent out to the streets to sell herself in order to get money to support Tim's drug habit. She wore the scars that were left on her after Tim would carve on her with a knife. He would also sort through her clothes and slash them beyond repair, knowing that her clothes were the only thing Deb knew (or thought she knew) were "hers." Tim would sit playing Russian roulette with a gun pointed at his own hand; he once actually shot himself through the hand in the presence of both children. Tim had even used his four-year-old son to carry drugs for him. These examples contribute to a horror story about the violence visited upon Deb and her children. The most disheartening part of her story is that even with truth on her side, she could not receive justice and support for her plight from the legal system.

Deb was able to get the guilty verdict on the first domestic violence charge, which resulted in a fifty-dollar fine and a thirty-day suspended sentence. This was the only time the system would respond to her plea in any meaningful way.

Deb's real challenge and concern was the visitation privileges available for and being used by Tim to see the children. She was seeking to restrict visitation or even halt it, because she feared for the welfare of the children. She went back to the legal system believing that it would act more auspiciously on their behalf, but through seven hearings, pleas of guilt and allegations by Tim, and eloquent speeches about the best interest of the children, the court refused to restrict visitation in any way. Deb was not married to Tim and the children carried her last name, yet the Court upheld what they considered to be Tim's right to see his children. Deb and the rest of the staff involved with the case felt the court ruled so as to exclude the protection and rights of the children.

This court battle raged on for a year, during which time Deb absorbed the message about being privileged in our society. She eventually went back to living with Tim and tried to put her life back together. Having had so much contact with him through his visitation, she decided to give him the chance to prove he had changed through all the mire of courts, shelters, and harsh feelings. Although things seemed better at first for Deb, Tim, and the children, old patterns again began to emerge and soon their lives mirrored their pasts.

In October 1985, Deb let her older child visit her parent's house for the night; she cleaned her house, did the laundry, and then, with her youngest by her side, shot herself through the head. I was later told that Deb had been suffering abuse from both Tim and her own drug habit, the only way she could (though not forever) survive her hellish life, as each day brought new terror. I believe that Deb just ran out of hope of being heard and lost faith in a social structure that quietly condoned violence, against her and the children she loved so much. The custody of the children has now been awarded to Deb's parents. Maybe she knew it would happen that way, although she had had no indications from the legal system that they would hear any of her screams.

I mourned the loss of another victim's life, but I mourned more for the children who had been cared for so carefully by this young woman as she tried to lull them out of their nightmares of violence. I was left to witness less humanity and more crushing power housed in what I had previously thought to be a system of justice for all people; justice that attempted to carry out its utilitarian mandate of the "greatest good for the greatest number." Mill eloquently brings us to focus on this problem when he says that

> in practical matters, the burden of proof is supposed to be with those who are against liberty; who contend for any restriction or prohibition; either any limitation of the general freedom of human action, or any disqualification or disparity of privilege affecting one person or kind of persons, as compared with others. The *a priori* presumption is in favor of freedom and impartiality. It is held that there should be no restraint not required by the general good, and that the law should be respector of persons, but should treat all alike, save where dissimilarity of treatment is required by positive reasons, either of justice or of policy.

What is most readily noticeable about the way we have, as a society, dealt with domestic violence is that the burden of proof lies not with those who advocate against liberty but indeed those very victims who have been denied equal liberty. The legal system and society have always asked victims of domestic violence to prove that they are not guilty of any wrongdoing that might well be translated as provocation. They are asked to prove their innocence beyond a reasonable doubt, and this cannot be considered just or right in any way.

Now that we have been exposed to Mill's philosophy through *The Subjection of Women* and two case studies that show in stark terms how pervasive this age-old problem is, we can draw out some key issues, all of which support a tradition of violence.

I believe the source of the social problem we call domestic violence is the way women and children are oppressed in our society. White males have created a power structure whose main intent is to perpetuate its own structure even if the loss of human life is to be used as support for this system. When we do not ask them to give up their lives, we ask them to be enslaved—their lives, their bodies, their minds, and their hearts—by an unforgiving master as his whip snaps, tearing away at their layers of dignity and self-will.

We ask women to be obedient and submissive to their husbands and society in general. When they comply, we reward them by calling them weak and less capable, and then punish them for this weakness that we cannot tolerate. This also tends to be the biggest factor in keeping them in abusive relationships, and then we see them as hysterical and usually in need of psychiatric care. Often we say they deserve to be beaten if they are not smart enough or strong enough to leave after the first battering incident. We give them less credibility and refuse them the opportunity to exercise talents other than those needed to be a wife or a mother. This also leaves them unskilled for the work force and financially dependent. Again I look to Mill to describe what has happened to our perceptions of what the nature of a woman is and should be.

> Standing on the ground of common sense and the constitution of the human mind, I deny that any one knows, or can know, the nature of the two sexes, as long as they have only been seen in their present relation to one another. If men had ever been found in society without women, or women without men, or if there had been a society of men and women in which the women were not under the control of the men, something might have been positively known about the mental and moral differences which may be inherent in the nature of each. What is now called the nature of women is an eminently artificial thing—the result of forced repression in some directions, unnatural stimulation in others. It may be asserted without scruple, that no other class of dependents have had their character so entirely distorted from its natural proportions by their relation with their masters; for, if conquered and slave races have been, in some respects, more forcibly repressed, whatever in them has not been crushed down by an iron heel has generally been let alone, and if left with any liberty of development, it has developed itself according to its own laws; but in the case of women, a hot-house and stove cultivation has always been carried on of some of the capabilities of their nature, for the benefit and pleasure of their masters. Then, because certain products of the general vital force sprout luxuriantly and reach a great development in this heated atmosphere and under this active nurture and watering, while other shoots from the same root, which are left outside in the wintry air, with ice purposely heaped all around them have a stunted growth, and some are burnt off with fire and disappear; men, with that inability to recognize their own work which distinguishes the unanalytic mind, indolently believe that the tree grows of itself in the way they have made it grow, and that it would die if one-half of it were not kept in a vapor-bath and the other half in the snow.

> Of all the difficulties which impede the progress of thought, and the formation of well-grounded opinions of life and social arrangements, the greatest is now the unspeakable ignorance and inattention of mankind in respect to the influences which form human character.

We stand as a nation considering ourselves a good judge of the individual and collective natures of people in general. We find ourselves in a world where terrorism strives to prevail and say that these violators of the sanctity of human life are not to be our friends and we condemn their actions while thousands of women are killed annually as they are beaten to death in their homes. (One study suggests 40 percent of all homicides are such and another conservatively says 2000 to 4000 annually.) We have consistently refused to support the sanctity of their lives as we turn our heads and say that what goes on in our homes is private—even if what goes on is life-threatening violence. We offer these victims a system of recourse for the crimes against them that is supposed to offer "liberty and justice for all." What we give them actually is a system of liberty and justice for all those who have power instead of all people.

We have made our social resources unavailable to these victims, because in order for our government to give financial support to violence shelters, we have to first admit that such a problem as domestic violence exists. This is the most crippling myth that has been created because we simply do not want to believe that women (and children) are being beaten in their own homes. The one place where we expect that people will love and care for each other is the one place where some six million women a year are unsafe and living in fear.

When we ask women to serve and never to think of their own desires and ambitions, we lose out as a society on great women philosophers, doctors, scientists, writers, politicians, and judges. As I said earlier, we change their lives from lives of possibility to lives of limitations. As Mill comments:

> If individuals, with such help as they can derive from the opinion of those who know them, are not better judges than the law and the government, of their own capacities and vocation; the world cannot too soon abandon this principle, and return to the old system of regulations and disabilities. But if the principle is true, we ought to act as if we believed it, and not to ordain that to be born a girl instead of a boy, any more than to be born black instead of white, or a commoner instead of a nobleman, shall decide the person's position through all life—shall interdict people from all the more elevated social positions, and from all, except a few, respectable occupations. Even were we to admit the utmost that is ever pretended as to the superior fitness of men for all functions now reserved to them, the same argument applies which forbids a legal qualification for members of Parliament. If only once in a dozen years the conditions of eligibility exclude a fit person, there is a real loss, while the exclusion of thousands of unfit persons is no gain; for if the constitution of the electoral body disposes them to choose unfit persons, there are always plenty of such persons to choose from. In all things of any difficulty and importance, those who can do them well are fewer than the need, even with the most unrestricted latitude of choice; and any limitation of the field of selection deprives

society of some chances of being served by the competent, without ever saving it from the incompetent.

We must also understand that competency has little to do with chronological age, and is just one more way of dividing, conquering, and creating more victims with the victim mentality.

In my work in juvenile probation, I have seen disturbing patterns that show that about 82 to 90 percent of all the females in our system have been victims of violence, particularly incest. Detecting abuse and especially sexual abuse in males is extremely hard, but I am willing to predict we will find a large percentage of abuse among boys also. Both the problems of females displaying their pain through unruly and promiscuous behavior (as defined by men and a male model of justice) and males' inability to express their pain and anger because of their need to be in control arise from the same insidious root as the subjection of women by men as explicated in this paper. Their weaknesses lie in their age or minority, and, again, this is something that is beyond their control. It will be interesting to see the patterns that do develop as we look more closely at the perpetrators of juvenile crimes and begin to pressure the juvenile justice system to adopt a female model of justice that treats boys and girls equally while considering the oppression of women: a model that strives to make them all strong and capable adults not bound by the same ropes of ignorance as we have been bound all our lives.

Through my work in domestic violence shelters and as a juvenile probation counselor, I have tried to invoke a concept of liberty, justice, and human rights that is ever-conscious of the social constructs that deny equal treatment and equal access, so that I might be instrumental in coercing this hostile system to carefully examine its past and current shortcomings that allow it to be a fist landing blows on an already beaten victim. We perpetuate the victim mentality and endanger the lives of millions.

I have worked in shelters as a legal advocate, seeking to secure quality and timely legal representation for these victims. I have had to pressure law enforcement officials and the legal system to answer the mandates of the codified laws that are now seeking to condemn this violence in our homes. I helped them to be good witnesses, by first restoring their sense of themselves, and encouraging them to outlast the slowly grinding wheels of justice.

I have also worked as a children's advocate, attempting to repair lives of children that have been broken as easily as their Christmas toys, as they seek the love, attention, and understanding of parents involved in hurting each other. We as a society do not believe that children have rights and certainly not if they conflict with our rights as parents and adults. We make them feel as if they are without power and not aware of what is really going on around them. When these children are given permission to grieve and tell the family secrets, the pain and confusion rushes out of them as they attempt to make sense of what it all means as they struggle to have normal violence-free relationships. Normalcy is not easy for children who are taught that Dad loves Mom, Mom loves Dad,

Dad beats Mom, so if you are male you are abusive to the females in your life, and if you are female, you will be passive and take whatever comes your way. Unless these children are taught what a healthy relationship is actually like, they will guarantee us another generation of adults who will batter or be battered. We will lose more human resources, more faith in our society, and many more lives as life becomes cheap and expendable. I have tried to teach these children through a belief in a system of children's rights, and a firm belief in each of them as humans capable of endless wonders. This has been done through individual counseling, group counseling, and activities that offered them a break from the pain. All these components were based on equal treatment and equality of the sexes.

My counseling with adult victims starts from this base also. It seeks to find those people who once were capable and ready to accept the challenge of their daily lives and to renew their faith in their abilities to be whatever they choose to be, and to sculpt their lives to a form that only their eyes can see. This means helping these women develop a positive self-image that allows them to know that there are undeniable truths about who they are and who they can be. Helping these victims must start here because they have been made to believe they cannot do anything right, and that it is only right if someone with power says it is right. Instead, they must learn that knowing within themselves that it is right is where the real power emanates from and this demands that people respect such.

I live a feminist philosophy that enables me to strive to make humans deal with each other as equals, and to stop using our efforts and force for oppression and destruction, when we could be constructing better ways and better answers to the social groupings we call family, government, society, and civilization.

I agree with Mill's analysis that says that not until this social inequity that causes an unnatural schism between the sexes is rectified can our society progress beyond its current state. This means that your gender would only determine whether you are called a boy or a girl, but would not dictate that you are weak, strong, rich, poor, powerless, powerful, dominant, or submissive. It would be no barrier to your education, vocation, or economic status, but would serve to be a difference that can bring together all that is good in all people. Not until boys and men are taught that they can cry and express pain openly, or stay home with the children, and not until girls and women are taught that they can be strong, successful in their own right, and not stay home with the children, will we be able to reap the full richness of each member of our society. If, on the other hand, this does not happen, we will continue to kill those we love and need the most and will in the same process destroy all we love and need from our society.

I ask only that we not allow our women and children to be sexually and physically abused, and that we allow each of us human beings to develop our abilities as we see fit. I do not ask society to see women as a population with needs that are more sacred or important than those of the male population but also no less sacred or important. It is to this struggle that I have decided to dedicate my life as an applied philosopher seeking out the patients suffering from these social ills, and using my skills to perform social surgery as I cut out the tumors of violence that threaten us with death.

Only when we as a society seek to empower each individual member by offering the same opportunities to all will we realize the full splendor, rich strength, and beauty that can be achieved as today's distant possibilities become tomorrow's achievements. Only when we as a society refuse to accept violent assaults on any human life will we be able to stop our worst nightmares about our own inhumanity based on no better reason than a born difference in gender and the subordination of women by men.

ANONYMOUS

LETTER FROM A BATTERED PHILOSOPHY STUDENT

After the discussion today on Janice K. Wilkerson's article on domestic violence, there will be a significant number of people in this class doubting the statistics. Some students may believe that domestic abuse happens only to other people . . . certainly not to someone in a philosophy class, who may be sitting right next to them. Educated women of today would never allow violence of this nature. But it has happened to me. I will not attempt to explain the forces that caused me to remain in a relationship with an abusive alcoholic for five years, but I am well aware of the societal, biological and psychological influences that held me there.

It takes the experience of one who has been there to know that as painful as physical abuse can be, psychological abuse can erode the mind and abcess every aspect of a woman's life. A bruise will go away; a black eye will heal fairly rapidly. But the aggressive attack on a woman's "self" plants itself and grows like hot-house flowers in the psyche of her self-awareness.

Society believes that men and women have achieved a certain equality, at least to the point that personal integrity is an inalienable right. In my home, I was not allowed to answer the phone. My calls were screened with such exactness that eventually, the only person who afforded any importance was my mother. I braced myself when someone called and hung up. Undoubtedly, it was a man calling for me. I would have preferred to have been beaten immediately. Instead, he waited for hours. His silence was my reassurance of his inevitable brutality. Still, I tried to act nonchalant, feigning an unawareness of his anger. He was very creative with his attacks. A slap across the face was usually reserved for minor offenses (such as wearing too much make-up). For an anonymous phone call, being locked in a closet was not uncommon. Occasionally, he raped me. Afterwards I was made to sit at his feet with my head down.

He never opened my mail, but I had to read each personal letter aloud. When I first moved in with him, I was a member of a pen-pal club and received mail from all over the country and as far away as Russia. I cherished this correspondence. After each letter, and as his interrogations of my relationships with the writers became more intense, I discontinued all communications. The arguments and accusations didn't merit the trouble of continuing the hobby.

He didn't like the kind of music I listened to. He thought Madonna was a slut, and since I liked her music, I was also a slut. My constant defenses and justifications also did not seem worth the effort. I began to listen to his music.

He carefully chose which outfits I wore to school, opting for skirts and dresses that were unflattering to me. He chose my hairstyles, make-up shades (lipstick was forbidden), and dictated what jewelry was appropriate. Necklaces that were too long were not allowed because they "drew attention" to my breasts. Mini-skirts and shorts were "unlady-like" and were eventually discarded entirely.

Each semester, he decided my course of study. He would not allow courses that promoted self-actualization, or what he called "ugly feminism." These included philosophy, sociology, and psychology. In American History, I drew a research topic on Susan B. Anthony. He was disgusted by her views and by her influence on the woman's movement. He pored over pages and pages of the books that I had chosen for references. He questioned my obedience to him and demanded that I not write a paper that "promoted female equality to men." The more I fought, not for the cause but for my academic success in the class, the more angry he became. Too late to pick another topic, I failed the class.

My political views were analyzed and dissected. He was a staunch Republican; I, a Democrat. He went as far as to suggest that I vote the way he wanted me to vote. My only control was to refrain from voting at all.

Because his drinking made him so unpredictable, I never knew what to expect. While driving home from work I prepared myself for the worst. I took hair combs out of my hair because they could be used to cut me. I removed my earrings because they could be ripped out of my ears. I took my watch off (a present from him after a particularly cruel beating) to keep it from being smashed. He once used a belt I was wearing to tie me to a chair. In the course of this relationship, I learned tricks that occasionally saved my life. Couch cushions could be used to soften the blows of his frustration. I had hiding places, escape routes, and four extra sets of car keys planted in various places outside. They could all work in my favor, or they could work against me.

I suffered hours of emotional abuse. I could not defend myself or counterattack. I could just sit there for the eternity it took him to tell me that I was a whore . . . I was nothing . . . I would never make it without him . . . I deserved what I got . . . I had it better than most women. It never ended. Most often I prayed to be struck. A physical attack is vicious, but it is over much quicker than psychological battery. I never had to agree with a punch. What hurt more was agreeing with his ugly opinion of me. Every time I did, I lost a little bit more of myself.

His well-timed violence hurt, too. I can't deny that. Last year, the night before the CLAST [College Level Aptitude Scholastic Test] exam, I was being hit and tossed and shoved and raped at 4:00 in the morning. I would have taken the CLAST anyway, four hours later, if I had not been in the emergency room having my right arm placed back into its socket. By that time in our relationship, it was all a part of the game of "master" and "slave" and to be frank, I was getting used to it. I knew that he would have proved his masculinity to himself and reestablished my submission, I would get to play "supreme victim," and he would be nice to me until my next infraction.

Ironically, it was a year ago today . . . that I got away from him, but only through the intervention of family and their combined efforts to have me committed to a psychiatric hospital "to rest." During the four weeks of my "incarceration," I lost my job, my home, and failed an entire semester of school. I was medicated and counseled and my mother successfully obtained legal guardianship over me. Against my will I was moved from the city of . . . to . . . and was made to start over again. Nothing happened to him. And still I wonder what it was about me that made him want to hurt me so badly.

His influence remains. I question everything about myself and often find myself longing for his "guidance." It sickens me, too. I tried to remain faithful to my belief that women should let the strong arm of a man lead them, and that faith nearly killed me. I don't blame him. I know that something was inherently wrong with my belief system, and my utter lack of self-esteem fed off his overwhelming control. I try not to be bitter, but looking back, I see now that the relationship was nothing but a twisted game with stupid rules that withstood the odds with the support of society. But I got out. Still, as I nod my head in agreement with the views of Aristotle, and find myself being drawn to chauvinistic men, I have to sincerely question the success of my escape.

DISCUSSION QUESTIONS

1. Aristotle states that one who "can foresee by the exercise of mind is by nature intended to be lord and master, and that which can with its body give effect to such foresight is a subject, and by nature a slave"; and he suggests that men and women fall respectively into these categories. Why do you think Aristotle regarded women's intellect to be, as a rule, inferior to that of men for purposes of leadership? Do you agree with Aristotle? Explain.

2. Simone de Beauvoir suggests that the love of a woman and that of a man are different and engender a double standard. Explain de Beauvoir's view. Do you think that such a double standard still exists today? Defend your answer.

3. In your estimation, does Aristotle's view of the relationship between women and men support or encourage the double standard de Beauvoir describes? Defend your answer.

4. What hypothesis does Mill advance to explain how the male subjection of women in society got started in the first place? Do you agree with Mill? Defend your answer.

5. What, according to Mill, is the difference between the male subjection of women and other forms of "slavery"?

6. Cite some differences (in personality, interests, capabilities) that you think, in general, might presently exist between males and females. In your opinion, are any of these differences *natural* ones or are they all an effect of differences in the ways males and females have been *socialized?* Explain.

7. What are, according to Mill, the major evils arising out of the male's subjection of women? What psychological effects do you suppose the male's subjection of women has on the male himself?

8. In the anonymous letter from the battered philosophy student, the student states that she is still attracted to "chauvinistic men" and still "questions the success of her escape." Why do you suppose her attraction for such men still persists? How would Mill explain this persistent attraction? How would de Beauvoir explain it? How would Aristotle explain it?

9. Mill, as a utilitarian, attempts to justify a system of equal rights for both sexes in terms of the greater utility of having such a system. In contrast to this utilitarian approach, describe how a *Kantian* would approach the issue of women's rights. (Note that utilitarian and Kantian ethics are discussed in chapter 1.) What ethical approach do you, yourself, find acceptable? Justify your response.

10. To what extent do you think Mill's indictment of a male-dominated social structure applies to our society today? What recent advances, if any, do you think have been made in women's rights?

11. What features of our legal system does Janice Wilkerson find particularly distressing?

12. What, in your opinion, can be done to provide better legal protection for the victims of spouse abuse against their abusers?

13. As Wilkerson points out, child abuse, especially sexual abuse, is a widespread problem in our society. Wilkerson sees this problem as a consequence of our system of unequal rights between males and females. Do you agree with Wilkerson about the cause of the problem? Defend your answer. What, in your opinion, can be done to mitigate the problem of child abuse?

14. Do you think that an androgynous society (that is, a society that combines male and female attributes so that no gender differences, except purely physical ones, exist) would be one worth pursuing? Defend your answer.

5

CRIMINAL JUSTICE:
PRISONS AND CORRECTIONS

In this chapter, we will discuss contrasting perspectives on punishment and treatment of criminal offenders.

One classical theory of punishment, which takes a utilitarian approach to the punishment of criminal offenders, is called *deterrence theory*. Broadly speaking, in this theory punishment of an offender is justified insofar as it serves to *deter* others (as well as the offender himself or herself) from committing the same offense *in the future*. Since it concentrates on the forward-looking consequences of acts of punishment, this theory is *teleological* in character. That is, it does not view punishment as being right *in itself* but rather as justified to the extent that it tends to promote the overall happiness or good of society.

However, as Martin Golding makes clear in the first selection in this chapter, deterrence theory is subject to some serious objections deriving from its utilitarian basis. Specifically, it has been argued that the theory might well justify the punishment of an innocent person if such would indeed have a substantial deterrent effect. Moreover, the theory offers no way of guaranteeing that the punishment will always "fit the crime." For example, if parking violations could be deterred by cutting off violators' arms, then that punishment might be justified by the theory. What is needed, Golding argues, is a theory that incorporates some nonteleological and nonforward-looking constraints on punishment such as some consideration of guilt, moral accountability, desert, and blameworthiness.

In the second selection, Robert Nozick outlines such a theory, traditionally known as the *retributive theory of punishment*. According to this theory, as Nozick presents it, a punishment is *deserved* when it equals the magnitude, H, of the wrongness of the act multiplied by the person's degree of responsibility, r, that is, r × H. For example, if the offender was fully responsible for the offense, then the deserved punishment would be 1 × H, or H; where the punishment is then roughly equal (when feasible) in magnitude to the wrong perpetrated by the offender.

According to Nozick, in imposing a deserved punishment (one of the magnitude r × H) upon the offender, all retributive punishment *communicates a message* to the offender, namely "This is how wrong what you did was." Some retributivists, those Nozick terms "teleological retributivists," take the primary purpose of communicating such a message, through punishment, to be the moral improvement of the offender—that is, to bring about the offender's recognition and acceptance of the correct value(s). Such retributivists are "teleological" since they base the value of punishment upon consequences outside of the punishment itself.

Nozick, however, argues that retributive punishment can be viewed "nonteleologically," as having value *in itself*. According to Nozick, insofar as such punishment "connects" the offender with the correct values by giving them "some significant effect in his life," by, so to speak, "hitting him over the head with them," this punishment has value in itself (although, Nozick admits, less overall value than when it also serves to morally improve the offender). Finally, Nozick makes clear that the nonteleological position does not replace the teleological one but rather "goes alongside it."

In the third selection, John Rawls attempts a reconciliation of the deterrence-utilitarian and retributive theories by trying to show that each has a point. Rawls' reconciliation is based on a distinction between justifying a practice or institution as "a system of rules to be applied and enforced" and justifying particular actions falling under such rules. According to Rawls, the institution of punishment itself, including rules assigning specific penalties to particular offenses, can be justified on utilitarian grounds, whereas the assignment of specific penalties in particular cases can be justified on something like retributive grounds. For example, an offender found guilty of shoplifting may be sentenced by a judge in a legally authorized manner. The judge need not look beyond the law itself to determine whether the punishment in question will have general deterrence effects. The punishment is justified because the defendant is guilty of an offense to which the given punishment applies. On the other hand, a *legislator* may well be concerned about whether the penalties provided by law against shoplifting have general deterrence effects. Moreover, according to Rawls, since the utilitarian theory applies to the *institution* of punishment and not to the particular acts failing under it, the earlier-mentioned charge against it, namely that it can justify the punishment of the innocent, is groundless. This is so, Rawls argues, because any institution of punishment which allowed officials (judges) it set up to punish the innocent whenever this seemed to these officials to be in the best interest of society would not *itself* be in the interest of society.

There are, however, some objections which could be raised against Rawls' view. First, it should be noted that when judges sentence criminal offenders, they often have considerable latitude for the exercise of discretion. This tends to blur any "hard and fast" distinction between the judge and the legislator. Moreover, it is not so clear that utilitarianism would not justify at least some rules which led to the punishing of the innocent. To use Golding's example, a legal rule specifying that for certain offenses the punishment should be inflicted on the offender's minor child might have excellent capacity to deter.

In the fourth selection, Herbert Morris argues that we have a right to be punished which derives from "a fundamental human right to be treated as a person." By contrasting an institution of just punishment with one in which offenders are systematically treated therapeutically, instead of being punished, he tries to show the manner in which the former, in contrast to the latter, respects such a fundamental right to be treated as a person. For example, in the punishment model, unlike the therapeutic model, there is an attempt at *proportionality* between the wrongdoing and the punishment meted out. In the punishment model, there is an attempt to maximize individual *freedom of choice* by legally protecting spheres of conduct from interference by others; and by "connecting punishment to a freely chosen act violative of the rules," thus making it plausible to say that "what a person received by way of punishment he himself had chosen." In contrast, in the therapy model, the acts of offenders are viewed as symptomatic of some pathological condition over which the individual has no freedom.

If our choice is exclusively between a thoroughgoing institution of therapy and a thoroughgoing institution of just punishment, then Morris' arguments appear persuasive. Still, in the real world, a viable institution of criminal treatment may inevitably need to recognize *both* punishment and therapy. Indeed, it makes sense to argue that there are offenders who may be more amenable to therapy than to punishment, and conversely. One hard question for criminologists is just where to draw the line. For example, should a kleptomaniac be given therapy or be punished? When can an offender be considered "criminally insane"? Morris' article is an important reminder to take such line-drawing very seriously.

In the Practice section of this chapter, Bill Puka discusses a novel program he participated in for several years at the Niantic State Correctional Facility in Niantic, Connecticut. The program, conducted under the auspices of the Harvard Center for Moral Development, set up a "just community" for thirty inmates who were given the direct mutual responsibility of conducting their own democratic community in which they held "constitutional conventions," out of which "social contracts" assigning aims and responsibilities emerged; resolved conflicts at town meetings; and conducted their own system of disciplinary procedures for offenders.

A central aim of the program was, in Nozick's terms, to "connect" these prisoners with the "correct value"—namely, the ideal of mutual respect—by providing an environment in which they could "spontaneously evolve" cognitively and morally.

Puka's discussion raises some important questions upon which theory and practice converge. Should "moral reform" be construed as a primary goal of punishment? Did the punishment the thirty prisoners incurred satisfy the retributive formula ($r \times H$)? Could such a program meet the demands of the deterrence theorists? Should tax dollars be spent in support of such special programs where costs of incarceration are already so high? Should all prisoners retain their "right to be treated as persons," as the program in question assumes, or do at least some offenders forfeit this right? Although Puka goes some distance in responding to these and other questions, the issues surrounding the treatment of criminal offenders can hardly be viewed as settled.

ISSUES

MARTIN P. GOLDING

THE DETERRENCE THEORY OF PUNISHMENT

The idea that punishment serves as a deterrent to crime or other wrongdoing is, of course, very ancient (see, for example, Deuteronomy 21:21), but probably the oldest statement of the deterrence theory is given in Plato's *Laws* (xi, 934):

> Punishment is not retribution for the past, for what has been done cannot be undone: it is imposed for the sake of the future and to secure that both the person punished and those who see him punished may either learn to detest the crime utterly or at any rate to abate much of their old behavior.

Taking this as an epitome of the justification of legal punishment in terms of deterrence, we see that the theory is teleological in character. Punishment is not good in itself; it is justified by reference to the good consequence (reduction of crime) it presumably brings about. This constitutes the justifying aim or end, and punishment is the means. The deterrence theory is *forward-looking,* because this consequence lies in the future of the time at which a punishment is imposed. Retributivism is usually contrasted with this theory on precisely these points: it affirms the rightfulness, independently of any good consequences that might result, of punishing an offender—but only if he is morally accountable—because he (past fact) committed a crime. Some recent writers [John Rawls, for example] have proposed a kind of amalgamation of both theories. They maintain that the aim of deterrence justifies having the *institution* of legal punishment while backward-looking considerations justify punishing *given individuals* (offenders). The deterrence theory answers to "Why punish at all?" and something like retributivism answers to "Whom shall we punish?" . . .

SOURCE: From *Philosophy of Law* by M. Goulding, © 1975. Reprinted by permission of Prentice Hall, Inc., Upper Saddle River, NJ.

To deal with this objection we need to introduce two distinctions: first, a distinction between the *threat* of punishment and its actual *imposition*. . . .

Now there seem to be good grounds for believing that many people *are* deterred from committing some acts by the threat of punishment. Aside from self-observation, this is supported by crime increase during police strikes and by obedience to regulations promulgated by an occupying power in wartime. It is of course true that the offender who is now being punished was not deterred by that prospect from committing his act, but the threat may well have deterred him from committing more acts of the same kind. (The fact that I have been fined for parking violations does not show that I was never deterred from committing them.) . . .

The second distinction is between *particular* and *general* deterrence. Whether or not an offender's actual punishment will deter *him* from committing future crimes of the same kind—this is what is meant by "particular deterrence"—depends partly on the punishment he gets. If he is executed, the punishment will be completely effective. If he is imprisoned, he is deterred, prevented, during his incarceration, at least. . . .

In any case the main interest of the deterrence theorist is general deterrence—that is, that punishing the offender deters *others* from committing acts of the same kind, thus reducing crime. General deterrence, as Bentham says, is the "chief end" and "real justification" of legal punishment. . . .

But does general deterrence work? Granted that the offender who is incarcerated or executed is prevented from committing crimes, does this deter others? Studies of capital punishment, for example, have at least cast doubt on its effectiveness as a deterrent to murder. Similarly, repeaters and growing crime rates cast general doubt on the punitive approach to the problem of crime; perhaps it would be better to deal with the causes of crime. . . .

This attack on the empirical basis of the deterrence theory has already been partially answered. The evidence against general deterrence is far from conclusive. Moreover, we know precious little about the causes of crime (although there is a high correlation between certain crimes and economic class) and even less about how to eliminate them. . . .

The most ardent supporters of the deterrence justification have been the hedonistic utilitarians. *Hedonistic utilitarianism* is an ethical doctrine which holds that (only) pleasure is intrinsically good and (only) pain is intrinsically bad. The rightness of a particular act or—in some versions—of a type of act depends on its tendency to maintain or increase the balance of pleasure over pain in the society. The only justifiable reason for inflicting pain is that otherwise there would be more pain or less pleasure. Punishment, though itself unpleasant and therefore intrinsically bad, can be justified insofar as it maintains or increases the balance of pleasure over pain by discouraging harmful (pain-producing) behavior. This is the classical *utilitarian-deterrence* theory. In a nutshell, individuals are punished for the good (overall happiness) of society.

The objections to this theory are obvious. First of all, if the reason and only reason for punishing is the good of society—if, as Kant would say, we are justified in using someone as a means to this end—why confine punishment to criminals? Why not punish the innocent? After all, what counts in deterring others from committing crimes is not that the punished person *has* committed an offense but rather the general *belief* that he has. The utilitarian-deterrence theory seems to allow "framing" innocent persons in the name of deterrence. Moreover, although it may be conceded that the criminal law is initially designed to deter the potential offender by threatening him with punishment, why should its imposition be confined to actual offenders if all we are interested in is deterrence? Most parents would be just as deterred from committing crimes if they knew that the threatened consequences would be imposed on their children instead of themselves. In the utilitarian-deterrence view there seems to be nothing wrong with visiting the sins of wicked fathers on innocent sons.

The second kind of objection bears on the issue of how much we should punish. The utilitarian-deterrence theory seems to permit unjust punishments— e.g., severe penalties for minor offenses. It may be possible to deter parking violations by cutting off an arm or by a long prison sentence, but this would be *unjust to the offender.* Punishment should "fit" the crime and be proportionate to the blameworthiness of the offender. . . .

No justification is morally acceptable if it "justifies" injustice, and this is what the theory apparently does. It seems to permit punishing the innocent and punishing the criminal out of proportion to the gravity of his offense. The source of the difficulty is clear: the theory contains no essential reference to such retributivist concepts as guilt, moral accountability, desert, and blameworthiness, which are ingredients of the common concept of punitive justice. Any such reference, moreover, seems barred, for it introduces the sort of nonteleological and nonforward-looking ethical considerations that have no place in hedonistic utilitarianism.

ROBERT   NOZICK

THE RETRIBUTIVE THEORY
OF PUNISHMENT

In what sense is punishment deserved and what purpose does its infliction serve? Is not the notion of deserved punishment, of retribution, primitive—a disguise for vengeful passions? . . .

SOURCE: Reprinted by permission of the publisher from *Philosophical Explanations* by Robert Nozick, Cambridge, MA: The Belknap Press of Harvard University Press, Copyright © 1981 by the President and Fellows of Harvard College.

The punishment deserved depends on the magnitude H of the wrongness of the act, and the person's degree of responsibility r for the act, and is equal in magnitude to their product, r × H. . . .

The punishment (deserved) is to affect the wrongdoer, but not simply as he finds himself after doing the wrongful act; his ill-gotten gains (including psychic ones) are removed or counterbalanced before the infliction of the deserved penalty. Thus, the punishment deserved, r × H, is imposed relative to a baseline that marks the situation the wrongdoer would have been in had he not committed the wrong. . . .

Retributive matching penalties are penalties that not only fit the magnitude of r × H but, when r = 1, do to the wrongdoer the same H to the extent this is feasible, as he has done. . . .

Under retributive punishment for S's act A (I speak here of the fullest and most satisfactory case):

1. Someone believes that S's act A has a certain degree of wrongness
2. and visits a penalty upon S
3. which is determined by the wrongness H of the act A, or by r × H,
4. intending that the penalty be done because of the wrong act A
5. and in virtue of the wrongness of act A,
6. intending that S know the penalty was visited upon him because he did A
7. and in virtue of the wrongness of A,
8. by someone who intended to have the penalty fit and be done because of the wrongness of A
9. and who intended that S would recognize (he was intended to recognize) that the penalty was visited upon him so that 1–8 are satisfied, indeed so that 1–9 are satisfied.

Having set forth the r × H framework, we turn to delineating its rationale. . . .

THE MESSAGE OF RETRIBUTION

Retributive punishment is an act of communicative behavior. Revenge also fits this communicative structure, though with a somewhat different message; this provides an explanation of why the two are so often confused.

What is the message of retributive punishment, and why is it communicated in that especially forceful and unwelcome way? The . . . message is: this is how wrong what you did was. But if our intention is to mean his act was that (magnitude of) wrong, why don't we just say so and spare him the penalty? (Don't say we first must get his attention.) What justifies us in inflicting upon him so unwelcome a mode of communication?

We may view different "theories" of punishment as focusing upon different aspects of communication: the sender of a message, the recipient of this message, the transmission itself. Some have pointed out that punishment has an expressive function, wherein the sender condemns the crime. More frequently, the literature focuses upon the recipient. Under this rubric, we might see punishment as an attempt to demonstrate to the wrongdoer that his act was wrong, not only to mean the act is wrong but to *show* him its wrongness. Some retributive theorists see the showing as having a further goal: the moral improvement of the offender. Punishment is supposed to achieve this goal by bringing home to the offender the nature of what he has done, from which he is to realize its wrongness. Since these theorists see the central purpose of punishment in its further consequences, they have been termed "teleological retributivists."

Someone is shown something by being presented with it directly. If an act is wrong because of what it does to someone else, the most powerful way to show him what it does is to do the same to him. However, there are some things whose wrongness we cannot show by doing the same to him. If his act leads another person to waste his life, to punish such acts in retributive matching fashion would only make things irremediably worse. . . .

To do to someone what he has done to another shows him what he has done. How does it show him that it is wrong? The hope is that the punished person will realize an act A is wrong when it is done to him. It is hoped that he will not universalize "Let A be done!" or distinguish his situation from that of his victim. . . .

Retributive matching punishment thus, in its teleological version, rests on an optimistic hypothesis about what another person will or can come to know. If someone is so far outside the moral community that there is no hope of bringing him to a realization of the wrongness of his acts by showing him them, perhaps there is nothing left to do but deter him. Deterrence theory treats everyone as outside the moral community. . . .

We can now understand the uneasiness retributivists feel about punishing someone who already realizes his act was wrong and is repentant, attempting to make amends, and so forth. The telos of the act of punishing has been removed, so it is left simply as a harmful act. (Note that the deterrence theorist may well recommend a policy of punishing in such circumstances.) . . .

CONNECTING WITH CORRECT VALUES

I wish to present a different view of retributive punishment, conceiving of it nonteleologically, so that it is seen as right or good in itself, apart from the further consequences to which it might lead. These further consequences are not to be dismissed simply; but we shall see them as an especially desirable and valuable bonus, not as part of a necessary condition for justly imposed punishment. Rather, the consequences the teleological theorist seeks we view not as a disconnected bonus but as an intensification of what nonteleological punishment actually involves.

The wrongdoer has become disconnected from correct values, and the purpose of punishment is to (re)connect him. It is not that this connection is a desired further effect of punishment: the act of retributive punishment itself effects this connection.

Consider three ways that correct values can have effect in our lives: (a) We can do acts because they are right or good, we can do them as right or good acts. (b) Having acted wrongly, we can repent, and give this repentance effect in our lives, performing repentant actions and so forth. (c) We can have the connection imposed upon us, via punishment.

This third alternative is worse than the others, but although less desirable it is an alternative of the same sort. It is a way, an inferior one, of falling on the same dimension on which doing something because it is right falls. That dimension is: connecting with correct values.

Correct values are themselves without causal power, and the wrongdoer chooses not to give them effect in his life. So others must give them some effect in his life, in a secondary way. When he undergoes punishment these correct values are not totally without effect in his life (even though he does not follow them), because we hit him over the head with them. Through punishment, we give the correct values, qua correct values, some significant effect in his life, willy-nilly linking him up to them. (Also, by our activity we illustrate and exemplify being connected to value as value, in addition to affecting this in him.)

Such an effect *on* him is not what the teleological retributivist seeks; he aims for an effect *in* the wrongdoer: recognition of the correct value, internalizing it for future action—a transformation in him. Not only is the nonteleological effect on the wrongdoer different, it is of lesser value and not as desirable. Yet still, it is of some considerable value, much better than if the correct values qua correct values had no effect on him at all.

The complicated structure of the nine conditions of retribution are a way to enable and ensure that correct values have an effect on the wrongdoer's life, qua correct values. . . .

There now is no puzzle about why we do not simply speak or telegram the . . . message, without adding a punishment. The punishment is central— that is the way the correct values which he has flouted have a significant effect on his life. . . .

Retributive punishment is to effect two things: (a) connect the wrongdoer to value qua value (b) so that value qua value has a significant effect in his life, as significant as his own flouting of correct values. The punishment part is needed for the effect to be significant (this would not be served merely by telling him he was wrong), while the complex intentions in punishment (described in the nine conditions of retribution) are needed for it to be value qua value that acts through us on him.

The hope is that delivering the message will change the person so that he will realize he did wrong, then start doing things because they are right—thus the teleological position. Yet, if it does not do this, still, punishment does give the values some significant effect on his life (even if not that of guiding his conduct) which is in itself good. The nonteleological position we have formulated does not replace the teleological one; it goes alongside it.

JOHN RAWLS

RECONCILING THE DETERRENCE
AND RETRIBUTIVE THEORIES
OF PUNISHMENT

For our purposes we may say that there are two justifications of punishment. What we may call the retributive view is that punishment is justified on the grounds that wrongdoing merits punishment. It is morally fitting that a person who does wrong should suffer in proportion to his wrongdoing. That a criminal should be punished follows from his guilt, and the severity of the appropriate punishment depends on the depravity of his act. The state of affairs where a wrongdoer suffers punishment is morally better than the state of affairs where he does not; and it is better irrespective of any of the consequences of punishing him.

What we may call the utilitarian view holds that on the principle that bygones are bygones and that only future consequences are material to present decisions, punishment is justifiable only by reference to the probable consequences of maintaining it as one of the devices of the social order. Wrongs committed in the past are, as such, not relevant considerations for deciding what to do. If punishment can be shown to promote effectively the interest of society it is justifiable, otherwise it is not.

I have stated these two competing views very roughly to make one feel the conflict between them: one feels the force of *both* arguments and one wonders how they can be reconciled. . . . The resolution which I am going to propose is that in this case one must distinguish between justifying a practice as a system of rules to be applied and enforced, and justifying a particular action which falls under these rules; utilitarian arguments are appropriate with regard to questions about practices, while retributive arguments fit the application of particular rules to particular cases.

We might try to get clear about this distinction by imagining how a father might answer the question of his son. Suppose the son asks, "Why was J put in jail yesterday?" The father answers, "Because he robbed the bank at B. He was duly tried and found guilty. That's why he was put in jail yesterday." But suppose the son had asked a different question, namely, "Why do people put other people in jail?" Then the father might answer, "To protect good people from bad people" or "To stop people from doing things that would make it uneasy for all of us; for otherwise we wouldn't be able to go to bed at night and sleep in peace." There are two very different questions here. . . .

SOURCE: John Rawls, "Two Concepts of Rules," *Philosophical Review* 64 (1955): 3–13. Copyright © 1955 Cornell University. Reprinted by permission of the publisher and the author.

The father says in effect that a particular man is punished, rather than some other man, because he is guilty, and he is guilty because he broke the law (past tense). In his case the law looks back, the judge looks back, the jury looks back, and a penalty is visited upon him for something he did. That a man is to be punished, and what his punishment is to be, is settled by its being shown that he broke the law and that the law assigns that penalty for the violation of it.

On the other hand we have the institution of punishment itself, and recommend and accept various changes in it, because it is thought by the (ideal) legislator and by those to whom the law applies that, as a part of a system of law impartially applied from case to case arising under it, it will have the consequence, in the long run, of furthering the interests of society.

One can say, then, that the judge and the legislator stand in different directions: one to the past, the other to the future. The justification of what the judge does, *qua* judge, sounds like the retributive view; the justification of what the (ideal) legislator does, *qua* legislator, sounds like the utilitarian view. Thus both views have a point. . . .

The answer, then, to the confusion engendered by the two views of punishment is quite simple: One distinguishes two offices, that of the judge and that of the legislator, and one distinguishes their different stations with respect to the system of rules which make up the law; and then one notes that the different sorts of considerations which would usually be offered as reasons for what is done under the cover of these offices can be paired off with the competing justifications of punishment. One reconciles the two views by the time-honored device of making them apply to different situations.

But can it really be this simple? Well, this answer allows for the apparent intent of each side. Does a person who advocates the retributive view necessarily advocate, as an *institution,* legal machinery whose essential purpose is to set up and preserve a correspondence between moral turpitude and suffering? Surely not. What retributionists have rightly insisted upon is that no man can be punished unless he is guilty, that is, unless he has broken the law. Their fundamental criticism of the utilitarian account is that, as they interpret it, it sanctions an innocent person's being punished (if one may call it that) for the benefit of society.

On the other hand, utilitarians agree that punishment is to be inflicted only for the violation of law. They regard this much as understood from the concept of punishment itself. The point of the utilitarian account concerns the institution as a system of rules: utilitarianism seeks to limit its use by declaring it justifiable only if it can be shown to foster effectively the good of society. Historically it is a protest against the indiscriminate and ineffective use of the criminal law. It seeks to dissuade us from assigning to penal institutions the improper, if not sacrilegious, task of matching suffering with moral turpitude. Like others, utilitarians want penal institutions designed so that, as far as humanly possible, only those who break the law run afoul of it. They hold that no official should have discretionary power to inflict penalties whenever he thinks it for the benefit of society; for on utilitarian grounds an institution granting such power could not be justified. . . .

First, will not a difference of opinion as to the proper criterion of just law make the proposed reconciliation unacceptable to retributionists? Will they not question whether, if the utilitarian principle is used as the criterion, it follows that those who have broken the law are guilty in a way which satisfies their demand that those punished deserve to be punished? To answer this difficulty, suppose that the rules of the criminal law are justified on utilitarian grounds (it is only for laws that meet his criterion that the utilitarian can be held responsible). Then it follows that the actions which the criminal law specifies as offenses are such that, if they were tolerated, terror and alarm would spread in society. Consequently, retributionists can only deny that those who are punished deserve to be punished if they deny that such actions are wrong. This they will not want to do.

The second question is whether utilitarianism doesn't justify too much. One pictures it as an engine of justification which, if consistently adopted, could be used to justify cruel and arbitrary institutions. Retributionists may be supposed to concede that utilitarians *intend* to reform the law and to make it more humane; that utilitarians do not *wish* to justify any such thing as punishment of the innocent; and that utilitarians may appeal to the fact that punishment presupposes guilt in the sense that by punishment one understands an institution attaching penalties to the infraction of legal rules, and therefore that it is logically absurd to suppose that utilitarians in justifying *punishment* might also have justified punishment (if we may call it that) of the innocent. The real question, however, is whether the utilitarian, in justifying punishment, hasn't used arguments which commit him to accepting the infliction of suffering on innocent persons if it is for the good of society (whether or not one calls this punishment). More generally, isn't the utilitarian committed in principle to accepting many practices which he, as a morally sensitive person, wouldn't want to accept? Retributionists are inclined to hold that there is no way to stop the utilitarian principle from justifying too much except by adding to it a principle which distributes certain rights to individuals. Then the amended criterion is not the greatest benefit of society *simpliciter,* but the greatest benefit of society subject to the constraint that no one's rights may be violated. Now while I think that the classical utilitarians proposed a criterion of this more complicated sort, I do not want to argue that point here. What I want to show is that there is *another* way of preventing the utilitarian principle from justifying too much, or at least of making it much less likely to do so: namely, by stating utilitarianism in a way which accounts for the distinction between the justification of an institution and the justification of a particular action failing under it. . . .

Consider the following from Carritt:

> [T]he utilitarian must hold that we are justified in inflicting pain always and only to prevent worse pain or bring about greater happiness. This, then, is all we need to consider in so-called punishment, which must be purely preventive. But if some kind of very cruel crime becomes common, and none of the criminals can be caught, it might be highly expedient, as an example, to hang an innocent man.

Carritt is trying to show that there are occasions when a utilitarian argument would justify taking an action which would be generally condemned; and thus that utilitarianism justifies too much. But the failure of Carritt's argument lies in the fact that he makes no distinction between the justification of the general system of rules which constitutes penal institutions and the justification of particular applications of these rules to particular cases by the various officials whose job it is to administer them. This becomes perfectly clear when one asks who the "we" are of whom Carritt speaks. Who is this who has a sort of absolute authority on particular occasions to decide that an innocent man shall be "punished"? . . . Is this person the legislator, or the judge, or the body of private citizens, or what?

One must describe more carefully what the *institution* is which his example suggests, and then ask oneself whether or not it is likely that having this institution would be for the benefit of society in the long run. . . .

Try to imagine, then, an institution (which we may call "telishment") which is such that the officials set up by it have authority to arrange a trial for the condemnation of an innocent man whenever they are of the opinion that doing so would be in the best interests of society. . . .

Once one realizes that one is involved in setting up an *institution*, one sees that the hazards are very great. For example, what check is there on the officials? How is one to tell whether or not their actions are authorized? How is one to limit the risks involved in allowing such systematic deception? How is one to avoid giving anything short of complete discretion to the authorities to telish anyone they like? In addition to these considerations, it is obvious that people will come to have a very different attitude towards their penal system when telishment is adjoined to it. . . . They will wonder whether the same fate won't at any time fall on them. If one pictures how such an institution would actually work, and the enormous risks involved in it, it seems clear that it would serve no useful purpose. . . .

One reason for this is that punishment works like a kind of price system: By altering the prices one has to pay for the performance of actions, it supplies a motive for avoiding some actions and doing others. The defining features are essential if punishment is to work in this way; so that an institution which lacks these features, for example, an institution which is set up to "punish" the innocent, is likely to have about as much point as a price system (if one may call it that) where the prices of things change at random from day to day and one learns the price of something after one has agreed to buy it.

HERBERT MORRIS

PUNISHMENT VERSUS THERAPY

My aim is to argue for four propositions concerning rights that will certainly strike some as not only false but preposterous; first, that we have a right to punishment; second, that this right derives from a fundamental human right to be treated as a person; third, that this fundamental right is a natural, inalienable, and absolute right; and, fourth, that the denial of this right implies the denial of all moral rights and duties. . . .

The immediate reaction to the claim that there is such a right is puzzlement. And the reasons for this are apparent. People do not normally value pain and suffering. Punishment is associated with pain and suffering. When we think about punishment we naturally think of the strong desire most persons have to avoid it, to accept, for example, acquittal of a criminal charge with relief and eagerly, if convicted, hope for pardon or probation. . . .

Let us first turn attention to the institutions in which punishment is involved. The institutions I describe will resemble those we ordinarily think of as institutions of punishment; they will have, however, additional features we associate with a system of just punishment.

Let us suppose that men are constituted roughly as they now are, with a rough equivalence in strength and abilities, a capacity to be injured by each other and to make judgments that such injury is undesirable, a limited strength of will, and a capacity to reason and to conform conduct to rules. Applying to the conduct of these men are a group of rules, ones I shall label "primary," which closely resemble the core rules of our criminal law, rules that prohibit violence and deception and compliance with which provides benefits for all persons. These benefits consist in noninterference by others with what each person values, such matters as continuance of life and bodily security. The rules define a sphere for each person, then, which is immune from interference by others. Making possible this mutual benefit is the assumption by individuals of a burden. The burden consists in the exercise of self-restraint by individuals over inclinations that would, if satisfied, directly interfere or create a substantial risk of interference with others in proscribed ways. . . .

Connecting punishment with the violation of these primary rules, and making public the provision for punishment, is both reasonable and just. First, it is only reasonable that those who voluntarily comply with the rules be provided some assurance that they will not be assuming burdens which others are unprepared to assume. Their disposition to comply voluntarily will diminish as

SOURCE: *The Monist*, Vol. 52, No. 4 (October 1968): 475–501. Copyright © 1968. Reprinted by permission of the publisher.

they learn that others are with impunity renouncing burdens they are assuming. Second, fairness dictates that a system in which benefits and burdens are equally distributed have a mechanism designed to prevent a maldistribution in the benefits and burdens. Thus, sanctions are attached to noncompliance with the primary rules so as to induce compliance with the primary rules among those who may be disinclined to obey. In this way the likelihood of an unfair distribution is diminished.

Third, it is just to punish those who have violated the rules and caused the unfair distribution of benefits and burdens. A person who violates the rules has something others have—the benefits of the system—but by renouncing what others have assumed, the burdens of self-restraint, he has acquired an unfair advantage. Matters are not even until this advantage is in some way erased. . . . Forgiveness—with its legal analogue of a pardon—while not the righting of an unfair distribution by making one pay his debt is, nevertheless, a restoring of the equilibrium by forgiving the debt. Forgiveness may be viewed, at least in some types of cases, as a gift after the fact, erasing a debt, which had the gift been given before the fact, would not have created a debt. . . .

I want now to sketch an extreme version of a set of institutions of a fundamentally different kind, institutions proceeding on a conception of a man which appears to be basically at odds with that operative within a system of punishment. . . .

In this world we are now to imagine, when an individual harms another his conduct is to be regarded as a symptom of some pathological condition in the way a running nose is a symptom of a cold. Actions diverging from some conception of the normal are viewed as manifestations of a disease in the way in which we might today regard the arm and leg movements of an epileptic during a seizure. . . .

I want to suggest tendencies of thought that arise when one is immersed in the ideology of disease and therapy. First, punishment is the imposition upon a person who is believed to be at fault of something commonly believed to be a deprivation where that deprivation is justified by the person's guilty behavior. It is associated with resentment, for the guilty are those who have done what they had no right to do by failing to exercise restraint when they might have and where others have. Therapy is not a response to a person who is at fault. We respond to an individual, not because of what he has done, but because of some condition from which he is suffering. If he is no longer suffering from the condition, treatment no longer has a point. Punishment, then, focuses on the past; therapy on the present. Therapy is normally associated with compassion for what one undergoes, not resentment for what one has illegitimately done.

Second, with therapy, unlike punishment, we do not seek to deprive the person of something acknowledged as a good, but seek rather to help and to benefit the individual who is suffering by ministering to his illness in the hope that the person can be cured. The good we attempt to do is not a reward for desert. The individual suffering has not merited by his disease the good we seek to bestow upon him but has, because he is a creature that has the capacity to feel pain, a claim upon our sympathies and help.

Third, we saw with punishment that its justification was related to maintaining and restoring a fair distribution of benefits and burdens. Infliction of the prescribed punishment carries the implication, then, that one has "paid one's debt" to society, for the punishment is the taking from the person of something commonly recognized as valuable. It is this conception of "a debt owed" that may permit, as I suggested earlier, under certain conditions, the nonpunishment of the guilty, for operative within a system of punishment may be a concept analogous to forgiveness, namely pardoning. . . .

Fourth, with punishment there is an attempt at some equivalence between the advantage gained by the wrongdoer—partly based upon the seriousness of the interest invaded, partly on the state of mind with which the wrongful act was performed—and the punishment meted out. Thus, we can understand a prohibition on "cruel and unusual punishments" so that disproportionate pain and suffering are avoided. With therapy attempts at proportionality make no sense. It is perfectly plausible giving someone who kills a pill and treating for a lifetime within an institution one who has broken a dish and manifested accident proneness. We have the concept of "painful treatment." We do not have the concept of "cruel treatment." Because treatment is regarded as a benefit, though it may involve pain, it is natural that less restraint is exercised in bestowing it than in inflicting punishment. . . .

In our system of punishment an attempt was made to maximize each individual's freedom of choice by first of all delimiting by rules certain spheres of conduct immune from interference by others. The punishment associated with these primary rules paid deference to an individual's free choice by connecting punishment to a freely chosen act violative of the rules, thus giving some plausibility to the claim, as we saw, that what a person received by way of punishment he himself had chosen. With the world of disease and therapy all this changes and the individual's free choice ceases to be a determinative factor in how others respond to him. . . .

Now, it is clear I think, that were we confronted with the alternatives I have sketched, between a system of just punishment and a thoroughgoing system of treatment, a system, that is, that did not reintroduce a concept appropriate to punishment, we could see the point in claiming that a person has a right to be punished, meaning by this that a person had a right to all those institutions and practices linked to punishment. For these would provide him with, among other things, a far greater ability to predict what would happen to him on the occurrence of certain events than the therapy system. There is the inestimable value to each of us of having the responses of others to us determined over a wide range of our lives by what we choose rather than what they choose. A person has a right to institutions that respect his choices. Our punishment system does; our therapy system does not.

Apart from those aspects of our therapy model which would relate to serious limitations on personal liberty, there are clearly objections of a more profound kind to the mode of thinking I have associated with the therapy model.

First, human beings pride themselves in having capacities that animals do not. A common way, for example, of arousing shame in a child is to compare the child's conduct to that of an animal. In a system where actions are assimilated to happenings, we are assimilated to creatures—indeed, it is more extreme than this—whom we have always thought possessed of less than we. Fundamental to our practice of praise and order of attainment is that one who can do more—one who is capable of more and one who does more—is more worthy of respect and admiration. And we have thought of ourselves as capable where animals are not of making, of creating, among other things, ourselves. The conception of man I have outlined would provide us with a status that today, when our conduct is assimilated to it in moral criticism, we consider properly evocative of shame.

Second, if all human conduct is viewed as something men undergo, thrown into question would be the appropriateness of that extensive range of peculiarly human satisfactions that derive from a sense of achievement. For these satisfactions we shall have to substitute those mild satisfactions attendant upon a healthy well-functioning body. Contentment is our lot if we are fortunate; intense satisfaction at achievement is entirely inappropriate.

Third, in the therapy world nothing is earned and what we receive comes to us through compassion, or through a desire to control us. Resentment is out of place. We can take credit for nothing. . . .

Fourth, attention should also be drawn to a peculiar evil that may be attendant upon regarding a man's actions as symptoms of disease. The logic of cure will push us toward forms of therapy that inevitably involve changes in the person made against his will. . . .

Finally, perhaps most frightening of all would be the derogation in status of all protests to treatment. If someone believes that he has done something right, and if he protests being treated and changed, the protest will itself be regarded as a sign of some psychological condition, for who would not wish to be cured of an affliction? . . . .

When we talk of not treating a human being as a person or "showing no respect for one as a person" what we imply by our words is a contrast between the manner in which one acceptably responds to human beings and the manner in which one acceptably responds to animals and inanimate objects. When we treat a human being merely as an animal or some inanimate object our responses to the human being are determined, not by his choices, but ours in disregard of or with indifference to his. And when we "look upon" a person as less than a person or not a person, we consider the person as incapable of rational choice. In cases of not treating a human being as a person we interfere with a person in such a way that what is done, even if the person is involved in the doing, is done not by the person but by the user of the person. . . .

Bill Puka is professor of philosophy at Rensselaer Polytechnic Institute. He received his Ph.D. at Harvard, working with Robert Nozick, John Rawls, and Lawrence Kohlberg. He has published various articles on ethics, political philosophy, and moral development. In addition, he was the first Congressional Fellow in Philosophy and worked in the office of Senator Gary Hart on legislation concerning employee ownership and urban revitalization. He currently runs a character education program, "Be Your OWN Hero: Careers in Commitment," and an urban revitalization program for the Troy area originally funded by the Sloan Foundation. He is about to publish a book entitled *The Right Choice On Ethical Problem Solving Methods.*

PRACTICE

BILL PUKA

THE PHILOSOPHER AS CORRECTIONS OFFICER: DOING TIME IN A PARTICIPATORY DEMOCRACY

Imagine passing through the guarded gates and checkpoints of a state prison—an intimidating experience. You enter a prison unit housing convicted felons, including thieves and murderers. There you find inmates gathered closely together in a circle, as you may have expected. You approach them tentatively, coming within earshot, to find them vehemently discussing the moral responsibility each owes the other as a concerned member of their prison community, as a coauthor of the "social contract" between them, based on justice and mutual respect. Not what you expected? It wasn't what I expected.

For several years I worked at the Niantic State Correctional Facility, where, under the auspices of Harvard's Center for Moral Development, I facilitated "moral discussion" and "peer-counseling" groups for thirty inmates of the so-called Just Community Unit. Our program aimed to enhance the cognitive and interpersonal competence of inmates, especially regarding a sense of moral responsibility and fair social cooperation. Toward this aim we created a participatory democracy within the prison unit, complete with "constitutional conventions." We also provided various forums for reflection on the more and less responsible uses of this newfound freedom-behind-bars. Inmates and staff (guards) shared responsibilities and decision-making authority on a one-person, one-vote basis. Work duties and internal discipline were determined by the group in concert. Peaceful and open discussion, consensus, and majority rule replaced intimidation and favoritism.

For many inmates, the program provided their first significant experience in social cooperation based on mutual respect and fair play. As such, it helped them gain more of an insider's sense of why it matters to each of us in society that each member plays by the same fair rules. The "just community" experience not only enhanced the moral awareness and commitment of inmates but also engendered a greater sense of why the crimes they committed are deemed legitimately punishable. (In this way our program "connected those being punished with correct values" regarding their crime, as Nozick's retributivism recommends. Yet it did so by helping them change, rather than by harming them in hopes of change.)

Through our program, prisoners also gained a sense of why society's treatment of them could stand some moral improvement itself, even if the crimes committed were unjustified. (Most prison inmates are extremely poor and from minority groups, and therefore often victimized by various social injustices.) Overall, these changes effected in moral outlook appeared to decrease future criminal activity and recidivism for the inmates involved in the program.

We will discuss the methods by which the just community formed and functioned there, to see how the inmates applied the ethics of justified punishment cited in this chapter. Let us begin at the roots of the moral development approach to corrections, tracing its historical decline and recent rebirth.

ROOTS

One of the most outdated ways to view convicted criminals is as moral deficients. Likewise, one of the most anachronistic approaches to corrections seeks to reform the prisoner's moral character. Yet, historically, it was hoped that if convicts were made better people—at least as good as the rest of society was, presumably—they would "sin no more" against society. Moreover, by reforming character, rather than threatening coercion, we would be squelching the evil expressed in criminal action at its source. Eliminating this source of evil, and bringing a lost soul back into the fold, also seems a good and noble deed in itself. It is just the sort of thing a good people would do. And so for the good people of old, this moral rehabilitation approach exerted great moral force.

There are old-fashioned parallels for this ethics of punishment in ethics generally. Ancient Greek and Asian ethics focused on the "perfectibility of man," on the development of virtue. It considered how we could make ourselves better people, living worthier lives, rather than on protecting rights ensuring social justice, or advancing the common welfare. (The religious ethics of Christianity and Hinduism show this focus.) Our modern ethics of punishment, however, build on these latter moral themes—on individual justice and social utility. They protect the rights of innocent citizens against law-breakers (while acknowledging prisoner-rights as well). They also give prisoners what they deserve, erasing the unfair advantage that criminal wrongdoing has gained for them. Moreover, they seek to enhance social stability and safety by deterring future crime, by decreasing the crime rate in society. (These are the themes of Kantian respect for persons, retribution, and utilitarian deterrence discussed in the preceding readings.)

The historical "character reform" perspective on punishment gave way to these newer ethics as we gained insight into the true nature of ethics and its psychological underpinnings. We came to doubt that there is such a pure and simple psychological thing as "moral character." We doubted also that this sort of entity would exert a direct and powerful influence on criminal acts, even if it existed. Criminal behavior seems fueled by a more complex interaction of social and psychological factors, many of them nonmoral. In addition, we came to recognize that law should not punish people for moral wrongs or evils or vices in themselves. It should stay out of the personal lives and minds of social members. The proper focus of legal sanctions should be on violations of publicly agreed upon rules, rules governing public cooperation among social citizens. Many of these rules are primarily practical and economic, not moral. Finally, we came to see how hopeless it was to find one universal standard of moral good and virtue on which we all might agree. We began to wonder if anyone could be given the authority to decide on the one moral truth to be trained into everyone's character.

Too often in human history a certain vision of moral virtue had been used to bend the have nots in society to the will of those in control. Moral education, and reeducation especially, has been used as a guise for mind control, for conformism to the social will. Those in society who are most reluctant to toe the prevailing ideological line, such as law-breakers, are most liable to bear the brunt of social pressures to conform. (Punishment, as a means to reform, is perhaps the ultimate social pressure.) And these pressures are all the more sinister when they work on our insides, shaping our very thoughts and feelings, traits and preferences, rather than merely challenging our behavior. A character re-form approach to corrections, then, is dangerous business, especially when it is forced on social dissidents (including criminals) by the state (in prisons).

Yet at the same time, the actual effects of such historical mind control have not been as significant as we might fear. Trying to get people to think "better" thoughts or hold higher aims is exceedingly difficult. And this is so whether the moral lessons utilized are thrust on them coercively or held up inspirationally from afar, in "Sunday school" fashion. In *adult* prisoners, especially, abstract moral ideals compete poorly with less noble but practical motivations that have become ingrained over years of life "on the street."

Therefore, given the dangers and unlikelihood of successful character re-form in prisons, modern ethics of rehabilitation have become far less ambitious. They merely seek to convey to convicts the need to stay within the law, if only out of self-interest. And they bid us to provide exconvicts with some means for survival within these legal limits, such as education or a job skill. Still, such re-habilitation is only one among several ethics governing modern penal systems.

RESURRECTION

The just community approach seeks to revive the ancient and failed hope of moral reform and character development, giving it priority in penal correc-tions. The effort seems worthwhile given the basic nobility of moral reform logic. Other approaches to corrections are merely justifiable, not fully moral. They assume that society is permitted to harm wrongdoers because of the harm wrongdoers have done it. They assume that we can use wrongdoers harmfully, once we have them, to scare away other potential criminals, or bring down the crime rate. By contrast, the character reform approach utilizes no unnecessary harms or manipulation to achieve its ends. Rather, it helps prisoners rationally choose, and voluntarily effect the goals which harmful punishment hopes to yield—penitence, and a resolve to make amends.

To revive these noble aims of moral reform, however, requires an updated conception of "moral character" and "reform." It also requires a modern ethic that distinguishes the proper spheres of morality and law, and accommodates the modern ethics of just punishment and deterrence, where they are valid.

Character

To fill these bills, our approach first consulted decades of research in moral psy-chology. On this basis it reconceived "moral character" as primarily a kind of cognitive system, a system of reasoning capacities, rather than as habits or virtues such as honesty, courage, or generosity. This cognitive-moral system possesses such competences as the ability to distinguish and interrelate our moral concepts and apply them to social interactions. It also possesses the ability to take the roles of people and relate them, to integrate personal responsibilities with social ones. And out of these abilities it evolves a reasoned commitment to do so, because it is right and just to do so, and because it feels morally competent and gratifying to do so.

Development

Decades of research on how cognitive-moral systems developed were also utilized to recast the notion of moral reform. After consulting the work of Jean Piaget, Lawrence Kohlberg, and others, our approach assumed that most people spontaneously evolve in the same general direction in the basic structure of their moral thought. Cognitively people become less egocentric in the course of their normal interactions with others. They become progressively more able to "see where other people are coming from," and why it matters. They come to see how different levels and institutions of society depend on and benefit each other. Morally, people come to see the legitimacy of mutual respect and fair play (where it is feasible) and the need to maintain group well-being. The deep-seated need to be generally competent in our thinking and interactions with others requires at least these moral developments, regardless of what other social conventions our social life experiences cause us to adopt.

Of course, many of us do not always put what we see or preach into practice. We also evolve a widely diverse set of personal values, personal ethics to live by. But in the basic structure of our moral reasoning, our paths of development seem to coincide. The rate at which we evolve, at the same time, varies for different people.

Reform

This modern, research-based account of moral development militates against traditional moral reform. It casts doubt on attempts to train pet virtues into personal character, where presumed vices now predominate. Modern moral reform need only promote the natural process of moral development already ongoing in the life of prisoners, as they interact with those "inside" and "on the outside." It need only make the social world of inmates safe for this development and its expression. This is accomplished by challenging the way inmates think about their interactions, their social problem solving. It involves calling their attention to the ways other inmates and staff perceive and deal with situations. This is precisely the focus of our moral discussion groups. And the democratic practices of our just community ensure that these thought experiments can go forward freely without intimidation, and with realistic hope of translating into practice. The just community makes the inmates' social environment safe for cognitive-moral development, protecting it from the battering of harsh prison life. It renders developed moral sensibilities practicable there, where they would normally be naive.

Recompense

Protecting morality in this way is especially crucial. Research shows that the rate of moral development is impeded by ill treatment, by authoritarian and unjust social conditions. In fact, research on Niantic prisoners showed them lagging far behind most adults their age in general cognitive competence, as well as in cognitive-moral development. They were not necessarily worse people, just less possessed of the capacities, at present, for figuring out how to be, and do, better. In particular, they were less able to relate their actions to the consequences they would have, especially to remote consequences. They were less able to reason out practical means to desired ends, and to patiently pursue those ends, controlling impulses conceptually and delaying gratification. When frustrations and obstacles entered their path, they were less able to see alternative paths to take.

Across various psychological scales that assess *moral* reasoning, adult inmates showed a level of functional competence typical of early adolescence or of even younger children. They lacked the active ability to put themselves accurately in the place of their victims, or to personalize their victims empathetically. They were less able to see how the operation of social institutions supported personal activities, including criminal activities. (Being a successful thief, after all, depends on laws that successfully protect private property, including stolen property.) These findings support the common belief among corrections officials that prison inmates are not necessarily the worst criminals, only the least competent.

To someone who lacks sufficient cognitive skill generally, including the ability to assess one's options or set high goals one can pursue effectively, the prospect of grabbing a purse or stealing money from a cash register may pose the most feasible of meaningful work opportunity available.

In addition, prison inmates are found to have extremely low self-esteem. They feel a sense of social impotence and alienation rather than belonging and participation. They do not feel capable of contributing or "making it" in society's terms. Indeed, they have little experience at succeeding or being well treated in the nine-to-five world. As a result it is understandable, even predictable, that opportunities to exercise competencies successfully outside that world would hold appeal. (A constant source of amazement among Niantic inmates was that anyone would drive down from Harvard University to hear anything they would have to say.)

The just community seeks to remedy these particular problems as well, by giving inmates the opportunity to run their own society on a "legit" basis, and run it well. Making that society small-scale and manageable, and helping inmates reflect on how it works, affords them the opportunity to assume responsible positions and handle them knowledgeably. It provides social and cognitive support for confronting problems that arise in those positions, seeing matters from different angles, and being able to help other people out through one's solutions. For inmates who feel totally victimized by "the man," this opportunity confronts them with the real question of whether they could do things differently if they were in control.

Ethos

Of course, establishing a just community, even with its democratic procedures, has moral dangers of its own. It is all too easy to *impose* a certain vision of democracy or a slanted vision of moral development, in the name of true democracy and impartial moral reform. And it may turn out easier to raise the general cognitive competence of inmates than their moral capability and resolve. This would only make them more criminally able, harder to detect and corral. Moreover, it is easy to convey the impression, in such a program, that it is the prisoner alone who must change. This ignores their social victimization, in key respects, and the need for social reform in the way poor people and minorities are treated.

From this broader social perspective, our program raises additional ethical worries. Why is it fair to the poor and oppressed who have struggled to stay within the law that we provide such ideal social conditions for those who have not? Why should limited social resources be placed here, into special programs for wrongdoers but not do-gooders? And why should taxpayers have to foot the bill for such special programs, when the cost of mere incarceration is already so high? (It costs about twenty-five thousand dollars a year to punish a convict, not counting costs of arrest and trial.) When prison provides a deterrence for crime, the taxpaying public gets a clear benefit for their investment. But will the threat of doing time in an ideal democracy deter? Most important, how do just community inmates *pay* for their crimes? They have harmed and victimized people, sometimes egregiously. Should the suffering they caused merely be overlooked in an attempt to treat prisoners with *increased* respect despite the ultimate disrespect they showed others?

These are serious questions that deserve careful responses. In a sense, they are objections that alternative ethics of punishment—just desert, deterrence—may raise to the present approach. In the hope of accommodating these other ethics, the just community program takes the following positions. First, regarding retributivism, the prisoner pays for his or her crime by incarceration itself: by being caged like an animal as a disgraced outcast from society; by having almost every aspect of his or her lifestyle, almost every liberty and enjoyment it yields, eliminated or severely curtailed; by having to live only with people in the same deprived and demoralized conditions, many of whom would be the last people anyone would choose for neighbors. (Even during the most inspired periods of our community relations, any prisoner would have traded almost anything just to be free.) If these prison conditions are not much worse than the prisoner knew on the outside, this is more an indictment of society than of our program.

Second, within the confines of such punishment, prisoners have a right to fair treatment and democratic self-determination over their lives, like anyone else. This is a matter of basic respect for persons. As I see it, they have a right to basic cognitive-moral development insofar as this process is akin to a kind of natural psychological growth. They also have a right to be compensated for infringements of this right by society, through special developmental programs. (As noted, evidence shows that inmates lag behind most other people in their spontaneous cognitive development, due, in part, to authoritarian and unjust treatment.) Other victims of such mistreatments and violations, who have not committed crimes, deserve similar compensation. Our prison program is not unfair for compensating the criminal group. Rather, society is unfair for not compensating the noncriminal group. (Just community programs are now in progress in high schools also, especially for poor and minority students in "tough neighborhoods.")

Third, as noted, the just community approach pursues the legitimate forward-looking aims of retributivism and deterrence. It helps inmates recognize voluntarily why what they did was wrong, and resolve to "sin no more" in the future. In fact the approach goes farther. It helps inmates truly understand the logic of crime as a moral and legal wrong. It helps them develop their own committed and well thought out stand against it. And it does this not by stamping some pet vision of virtue on a prisoner's heart and mind, but by supporting the unfolding virtue already found there. Indeed, it focuses not so much on the prisoner's *personal* values as on *public* responsibility and respect for *law*. As noted, this is the only domain of life in which government-run moral education clearly belongs.

Let us now consider the actual functioning of this program, to see its ethical theory in practice.

DEMOCRACY AND RESPONSIBILITY

Informed Consent

In the beginning, inmates and guards at the prison were told of a new program to be created in a particular unit. They were informed that it would try to create a community of inmates and staff, run democratically through group meetings. The distribution of responsibilities, privileges, and disciplinary measures would be jointly determined by the inmates and staff.

They also were told that entering the program would increase burdens of mutual responsibility and accountability. Inmates and guards could not adopt the typical loner attitude, looking out for number one. They could not assume that if they minded their own business they would be left alone. In addition, it was made clear beforehand that the new program was not to be a "pet project" involving special privileges. Rather, it was experimental and would be closely scrutinized by prison officials. It would use certain theories of cognitive development and moral education which would be explained fully to anyone entering the program. Only those inmates and guards who seemed to fully comprehend and accept these conditions were initially admitted. Later admissions were determined democratically by the community.

Constitutional Conventions

Once thirty inmates and a normal staff were "on board," a constitutional convention was held, facilitated by members of the Center for Moral Development. Ultimate ground rules, which would not be up for grabs, were reviewed at the outset. We could not establish rules permitting escape or the commission of crimes within the unit, including "coming to blows" during group discussions. Daily housekeeping chores had to be performed within the unit, and within the roles of inmate and staff. And democratic ideals had to be pursued where possible. Beyond that the basic principles of our social cooperation were left to the discretion of the community. (Normally, virtually every aspect of an inmate's daily routine is scheduled by staff.)

During the marathon meetings of this convention, a wide variety of interests and suspicions was expressed on all sides. Many proposals were put forward with inmates emphasizing individual privileges and staff emphasizing the need for limits, order, and staff control. Facilitators from the Center, such as myself, worked to help clarify the interests being expressed along with the conflicts and shared aims that arose. We tried to get inmates and staff to air the reasons and purposes behind their stated views, including their opposition to or support for the views of others. We tried to get contending parties to see matters from each other's point of view. And over the course of discussion we tried to assure that those comments which upheld the value of community, mutual respect, and fairness were heard. However, we were careful not to explicitly endorse them. (Soon on-line staff took over such facilitative functions at all community meetings.)

Out of these discussions a set of aims and principles for social cooperation was drafted, forming an explicit social contract. In this process, as in all community decision making, consensus was sought above all. Majority vote represented a last resort for achieving agreement. Every so often (at least once a year) additional conventions were held to be sure that all members of the community continued to accept the social contract, and to bring new members on board. Changes in the constitution were also enacted at this time.

Over the course of several conventions, these changes reflected a growing sense of mutual respect in the community. In general, there was a movement away from rigid rules protecting individual turf toward shared aims and responsibilities. This led, surprisingly, to inmates arguing for more social control rather than less—but self-imposed control—for the good of the group as a whole. Rules of fairness originally enacted by inmates because they "sounded good" or "were what the staff wanted to hear" were later elaborated and reaffirmed with understanding and commitment. This change seemed to result from good experiences with the just community, good community relations.

"Town Meetings"

Community meetings were held once a week, although an additional meeting could be called by any member of the unit should a significant issue of relevance to the whole arise. In these meetings, the expression of concerns was encouraged, and conflicts were aired openly. Emphasis was placed by the facilitators on letting participants "get it out" before others in the group "got their two cents in." A typical comment heard was, "Wait a minute, listen to what is being said here." At first inmates played a waiting game, mistrustful of the consequences of speaking out, wary of hidden staff agendas. The staff did the same. But soon, members saw how the group process could work to air gripes and resolve conflicts.

As a member of the community, I voiced concerns and gripes like everyone else. As a staff member and facilitator, however, I performed very much like an ethics professor during class discussion. My comments helped clarify the different concerns being expressed, suggesting that we raise a range of possible solutions to problems. I tried to help distinguish moral considerations—matters of personal and group responsibility or fairness—from pragmatic and seemingly irresponsible ones. In doing so, I emphasized the range of ethical considerations being raised such as individual rights and promise-keeping, fair distribution of benefits and burdens in the group, individual merit or just desert, group solidarity and welfare. However, I did not initiate or explain these points pedagogically. Rather, I reflected on what I heard people saying and on how I felt in response.

The typical problems and concerns raised in the group had strong moral components. They involved people lying to each other, breaking a trust, being two-faced, not living up to their end of an agreement or friendship, not performing the various work duties they had agreed to take on. Many of the problems also concerned being callous and unsociable, failing to help out or show compassion when people were in need. However, the problems considered most serious over time involved social irresponsibility—someone doing something that jeopardized the community or program. Slowly members of our unit came to see that the group could offer them various forms of crucial support. It helped them improve the way they thought about things, felt about themselves and other people, and dealt with interpersonal problems. A sense of protectiveness toward their community developed.

They also came to feel this way about the program as a whole, and what they called "the theory" on which it was based. (Mention of "the theory" came up often in inmate conversation.) As inmates put it, "This idea of letting people have their say, that's good. They choose what they have to do *for themselves,* and they be responsible for themselves. That treats me like I count, like I can do it for myself. These other programs [mental health, behavior modification] just ain't serious. They try to screw around with your mind, so you got to figure out how to get over on them. But here if I get over on 'them' I screw myself up really." (Recall Morris' claims, above, about the failure of mental health programs to respect persons.)

Staff came to feel similarly, being relieved from functioning simply as cops or detectives or "wardens" in the unit. They no longer had to keep their own problems in as "coming with the job." In the just community guards could relate to inmates as fellow citizens, asking for equal consideration, asking that inmates put themselves in staff's place. In this way guards could earn respect without exerting authority.

(Of course, there were many negatives, many failings alongside these positive successes of the program.)

Disciplinary Contracts

As inmates began to take the notion of self-imposed social contract seriously, they applied it to their own disciplinary procedures. If you violated enforceable rules you helped set, you were actually asking for the punishment that enforced them. (Morris discusses this precise notion above.) Here we had a new twist on more popular logic of penal contract, "Don't do the crime if you can't do the time." When inmates were called up for some wrongdoing in the community, great emphasis was placed on urging them to admit it freely, and come to see why it was wrong. The punishment of making amends or losing privileges was actually called a contract. One might be given a contract not to "borrow" someone else's personal goods anymore, or leave chores half done. One might even get a contract to be less nasty or unsociable. Often recalcitrant wrongdoers in the unit were given contracts to "think about what they had done," and why they would not admit it. (Of course, even thought contracts could be appealed on a "not guilty" basis.)

In these proceedings staff members had to walk a thin line. We perceived the disciplinary procedures as exerting undue pressure on fellow inmates, exhorting extravagant confessions and rigid conformity to group norms. Inmate-prosecutors seemed much more harsh and punitive toward each other than staff had been on them. However, once in control, inmates saw us "citizens" and "Harvard types" as "bleeding hearts" who did not see how truly devious and unrighteous inmates truly were.

Small Groups

One of my primary roles on staff was in the small groups. These met twice a week to deal with the more personal concerns and problems of inmates that did not involve the community as a whole. We discussed disputes that inmates had had with relatives or spouses during visits or phone calls. We also discussed jealousies and resentments among friends and lovers in the unit. Much attention was devoted to personal feelings of isolation, depression, anxiety, and sense of failure. Many of these "issues," especially the interpersonal ones, were left over from community meetings. While morally "legitimate" claims usually had been resolved fairly there, personal claims and feelings of resentment often lingered. Members of the community felt that they had not been addressed adequately as people by the impersonal logic of justice and its brand of impartial respect. Thus our psychological discussions of psychological problems also typically involved moral considerations, but along the themes of caring concern rather than mere fairness.

Small groups also were designed to nurture practical skills for living. We worked on the ability to set and pursue goals, to approach others for help and reciprocate in kind, to relate well to others and establish enduring friendships or family relationships. To these ends we discussed a variety of personal and interpersonal situations being confronted by inmates and various ways of dealing with them. Again, an emphasis was placed on trying to see matters from various perspectives, taking the roles of the different parties involved. Often inmates would try out group suggestions for breaking destructive habits in dealing with family and friends. Informal "contracts" might even be put on them to do so, when they agreed that they should, but felt lacking in needed gumption. Again moral issues were raised about what one's responsibilities were to people close to one, and when one should stand up for oneself in these situations. These were intermingled with practical and psychological issues. Indeed, doing the right thing in a given situation depends on having certain psychological insights, motivations, and practical skills to achieve one's noble goals.

Peer Counseling and Caring Aspirations

In my particular small group, great emphasis was placed on peer-counseling skills. I trained both inmates and staff in the basics of client-centered psychotherapy so that they could see each other through the personal crises of prison life. While counseling skills seem primarily psychological, their role in being moral is perhaps even more central. Let us see how, to conclude our discussion.

As noted, the logic of justice in community is based on the attitude of respect for each individual. To respect people is a very difficult thing, requiring that we get a good idea of who they are, what they want or need, what their situation is. Often the ethic of justice has been criticized for emphasizing respectful *behavior* and *treatment* of others, rather than the respectful attitude which should motivate and guide it. Thus respecting people's rights must involve not infringing their liberty. However, it need not involve "giving a damn" about them in any other respects, or about how they use their liberty, or why. Often it is argued that the moral attitude of respect must be complemented by one of concern and compassion. And more emphasis must be placed on the value of relationships and group welfare than on individual rights. It has been argued, in fact, that adequate moral development must include not only a theme of just respect but also relational caring.

As our program shows, justice and respect can encompass concerns for community as well. Still, the good will and goodheartedness of morality often falls short here. I noted this when citing the personal resentments that show up in small groups after community meetings have decided on just policies. Justice can be impersonal and callous. One can show just regard for community welfare as a whole, in the abstract, without establishing a personal relationship with anyone in it. Justice also can be judgmental and punitive, rather than accepting and supportive. An adequate ethic, by contrast, must operate in the modes of both respect and helpfulness.

The skills of peer-counseling convey both moral attitudes, and superbly. The stance one assumes toward others when counseling them is exemplary in its moral regard. It rivets your attention on them and their concerns; it causes you to feel what they feel and know what they know of themselves. It also leads you to appreciate and care about them in a way that prompts you to help. Peer-counseling affords the instant experience of being a preeminently kind and caring person in one's manner of orienting to others.

The main orientations of peer-counseling are as follows: (a) *Attending, listening:* here one learns the skill of focusing one's attention fully on the other person, and listening intently to what they are saying. This may seem a small thing, but we rarely do it well. More often we pay partial attention to others. We listen somewhat distractedly to what they are saying while preparing to offer evaluations or suggestions, or to talk about ourselves. (b) *reflecting, accepting:* this skill involves conveying to people that you have heard what they said and have understood it as they meant it. Such reflection allows them to see themselves, as in a mirror, which affords them a better sense of how they are feeling, It also allows them to feel understood and more ready to open up. By contrast, when we "do things" to what people say—reinterpreting, judging, evaluating—we often close them off to us. We get into verbal disputes. This is because we are showing little regard for them in their own terms, though it appears we are trying to help. (c) *Probing the purpose:* rather than responding to the surface content of what someone says or does, peer-counseling looks for the feelings and motivations that prompted it. It looks to the real meaning and purpose for the person, because it is the person and his or her purposes that count. Philosophical skills, by contrast, are among the least respectful and understanding modes of orienting to others. (This is why they are often confined to the written word.) These skills typically pick at the face value of the content or logic of our statements: "But didn't you say X and Y, and doesn't that imply Z, which is false or contradictory?" (d) *Empowerment:* in peer-counseling one offers a person support by simply confronting and sitting with their problems, once they have come out. One also shares these problems empathetically. Then one helps the person figure out his or her own solutions and develop the ability for doing so, while offering supporting aid. One struggles with the person jointly to find solutions.

In our small group we worked on these skills by role-playing various conversations and situations. We also wrote our responses to typical statements or complaints people voiced in the unit, and read them to each other. Then we reflected on the various ways we each tended to respond in these contexts. Inmates were surprised to see how often they failed to listen well, how often they jumped to judgment and offered unsolicited advice.

Members of small groups who had trained in peer-counseling became much better participants in community meetings. They paid more attention to people. They asked more questions in the hope of getting a better sense of what was really going on. They also were slow to disagree and get into disputes, and more interested in conciliation, consensus, and skirting irresolvable conflict. When they stood up for themselves and others, making claims on the community, they did not alienate their listeners by making claims *against* them. Rather than raising issues of fairness and responsibility judgmentally, or abstractly, they used these ethics to convey personal understanding, respect, and concern for others. In this respect, they promoted a nurturant and caring community, as well as a just democracy.

POSTSCRIPT

When inmates left the just community unit, they faced a much colder and harsher world of compatriots in many respects. As ex-inmates reported, our program had made them more vulnerable to the dangers and harms of the streets in some ways. They were now too ready to trust, and to set unrealistic expectations of fair treatment. They also were less willing to take the path of intimidation and "pay back" that ensures survival. To deal with this serious problem, a half-way house was established in a nearby city. Here new releases could ease back into "real life" during the day, with a just community to return to at night. But even such a home base cannot overcome the harsh reality of not finding economic means of support on the outside. Ex-cons do not get hired; therefore, our program sought to expand its training to include joint entrepreneurial skills. If our graduates could not find jobs, or nonexploitative jobs, perhaps they could go into business jointly for themselves. They might create small cooperative enterprises, run democratically, that would offer low-skill services at low start-up costs. (Examples would be gardening and housecleaning services, fruit and vegetable stands.) Thus far these possibilities remain unexplored. The prospect of ex-con entrepreneurship invokes much skepticism, which we have yet to overcome.

NOTE: For further reading on prison democracy, see *The Just Community Prison Manual*, by L. Kohlberg, K. Kauffman, P. Scharf, and J. Hickey (Center For Moral Development Publications, Larsen Hall, Harvard University, Cambridge, MA 02138). For further reading on moral development, see *Essays in Moral Development*, Vols. I, II, by Lawrence Kohlberg (New York: Harper & Row, 1982, 1984).

DISCUSSION QUESTIONS

1. What does the deterrence theory of punishment assert? What criticisms can be made of this theory?
2. What does the retributivist theory of punishment assert? What criticism might be made of this theory by a deterrence theorist?
3. What is the difference between "teleological retributivism" and "nonteleological retributivism"?
4. How does Rawls attempt to reconcile the deterrence and retributive theories? What virtues does Rawls see in his reconciliation of these theories?
5. What objections might be made against Rawls's position?
6. Why does Morris think we have a right to be punished? What, in particular, does he find objectionable about a system of therapy as compared with that of punishment?
7. If you had a choice between being given therapy and being punished for a legal offense, what would you choose? (Suppose, for purposes of this question, that you have knowledge of how severe the punishment will be or what the therapy will consist of; suppose also that you know nothing about how long either will last.) Defend your answer.
8. Describe Puka's "just community" approach to punishment. How does it differ from the traditional moral reform approach? What (moral) advantages does Puka claim for his approach over retributivism and the deterrence theory?
9. According to Puka, what did research on the Niantic prisoners reveal about their state of cognitive and moral development? How did the just community approach attempt to deal with these findings?
10. What objection, discussed by Puka, would some retributivists have to the just community approach? How does Puka respond to this objection? In your opinion, is his response adequate? Defend your answer.
11. How would a teleological retributivist perceive the just community approach? Explain your answer.
12. What objection, discussed by Puka, would a deterrence theorist have to the just community approach? How does Puka respond to this objection? In your opinion, is his response adequate? Defend your answer.
13. According to Puka, prisoners "have a right to basic cognitive-moral development insofar as this process is akin to a kind of natural psychological growth." Discuss the merit of this argument.
14. Do you think capital punishment is ever justified? Develop your answer in terms of one or more of the theories discussed in this chapter.

6

POLITICAL THEORY AND PRACTICE

The central focus of this chapter will be on classical views about the nature and purpose of state and government as well as the practical relevance of such views to the operation of present-day political institutions such as that of the United States Congress.

The first selection of this chapter is excerpted from *Leviathan* by Thomas Hobbes (1588–1679). Arguing from a pessimistic view of human nature as fundamentally selfish, Hobbes hypothesizes what life would be like in a "state of nature," that is, a precivil state where no organized government exists to maintain the peace and safety of the community. According to Hobbes, given human nature as he portrays it, there would be, in such a precivil state, a condition of "war of all against all" wherein the life of man is "solitary, poor, nasty, brutish, and short." As the necessary means of avoiding such a precarious existence, Hobbes argues for a powerful central government in which sovereign power is vested in one man or an assembly of men, such sovereign power being absolute (unbounded by any further governing body or authority), irrevocable, and nontransferable.

In contrast to Hobbes' concept of absolute government, John Locke, in the second selection of this chapter, excerpted from his *Second Treatise of Government,* argues for government which derives its authority from, and is limited by, the majority rule of the people themselves.

Like Hobbes, Locke employs the notion of a "state of nature" in his reasoning. But, unlike Hobbes, Locke is more optimistic about human nature. For him, the state of nature is not one of complete "license" but rather is governed by a law of nature obliging respect for the "life, health, liberty and possessions of others (what Locke terms, collectively, "property"). Whereas for Hobbes, human beings are fundamentally selfish, for Locke, they are capable of mutual respect and cooperation. This, accordingly, makes feasible the democratic participation of citizens in government. Whereas Hobbes takes the primary end of government to be the survival of the subjects, Locke takes the primary end of government to be the more efficient protection of those property rights which also pervade a state of nature. In light of his pessimistic view of human nature,

Hobbes sees a form of dictatorship as the only viable means toward achieving the primary end of government as he defines it. In light of his more optimistic outlook, Locke sees rule by the majority as the only viable means toward achieving the primary end of government as *he* defines it.

In the third selection of this chapter, excerpted from the *Manifesto of the Communist Party,* Karl Marx (1818–1883) and Friedrich Engels (1820–1895) defend communism as the answer to the problem of government. From the Marxist perspective, the problem with state organizations has always been the exploitation of one social class by another. In modern industrialized societies, this exploitation is carried out through the exploitation of the proletariat (the working class) by the bourgeoisie (those capitalists who own the means of production). Under such a system of capital, laborers are reduced to mere "commodities" or "appendages of machines," manipulated and abused (overworked, undercompensated, and the like) by capitalists for their own profit. For the Marxist, the inevitable outcome of such human automation is the uniting of the proletariat and their eventual revolutionary overthrow of the bourgeoisie. The Marxist solution to the modern problem of class exploitation thus becomes the "abolition of private property" in the form of capital.

Marxists do not believe, however, that the transition from capitalism to a society which permits no class distinctions and thus no class exploitation (communism) occurs directly. Rather, by means of the revolution, the proletariat must first seize state power, establishing itself as "the ruling class" (the so-called dictatorship of the proletariat) and "as such, sweep away by force the old conditions of production" until there is no longer any need for classes in general; and, thereby having, after a time, "abolished its own supremacy as a class." At such time all means of production will be "concentrated in the hands of a vast association of the whole nation," and the existence of class oppression dissolved.

Some reflection will, undoubtedly, call up a common problem inherent in each of the above-mentioned political approaches. Hobbes confronts the problem of the sovereign power emerging as a form of merciless despotism. For Locke the same difficulty is raised by the tyrannical rule of the majority over the minority, for it is quite clear that minorities have not always, throughout history, been treated fairly at the hands of majorities. (Consider, for example, the history of racial oppression.) Finally, the Marxist approach runs the risk of exchanging one form of class exploitation for that of another, namely the "dictatorship of the proletariat."

It is in light of these political theories and his own experience in Washington as a congressional aide that Stanislaus J. Dundon writes the Practice section of this chapter. According to Dundon, a central criticism of congressional politics, as it presently exists, is its lack of a consistent and well-developed purpose or end. Rather, much of the motivation among politicians is provided by a "nonrational (if not irrational) desire to work at important tasks in environments where great power is wielded, great events begun and ended, and worldwide attention is focused, even if one's work is not at that focus." As Dundon views it, such "trivial narcissism" ("Potomac fever," as it has been termed) must be replaced, as a first step, by a "loving" and "knowing" concern for the "common good" understood as the "well-being of the citizens of the state." It is, however, an important point of Dundon's that this goal of the "common good" cannot be articulated a priori by representatives without the active participation of their constituents who possess valuable knowledge about their own needs. Moreover, such an end must govern the means, and political theory and action must draw upon an adequate knowledge of human nature in reaching the end. According to Dundon, Hobbes, Locke, and Marx have equally failed in this regard by resorting to "political pipe-dreams" such as, for example, "omniscient monarchs" and a "selfless working class." Even if Marx had the right idea about the problems inherent in class struggle, his means of rectifying such problems were not based upon a solid understanding of human nature. According to Dundon, what is requisite in politics is "prudence," defined as "the careful study of the available means to achieve some end; informed and unbiased comparison of those means with a view to selecting those with maximum ability to reach the end with minimum costs and undesirable side-effects; and, finally, choice and firm application in action."

Such prudence, argues Dundon, requires that politicians be prepared to relinquish class biases as well as political ideologies for the sake of promoting the "common good." Moreover, it requires that politicians give up their "bureaucratic rationality" or "expertise" in favor of a "learn from the client" or "on-the-job" approach in which government actions are planned and administered as closely as possible to "the field of actual need and use, where the increase in the common good is to occur" (the so-called principle of subsidiarity). Finally, Dundon urges the active cooperation and participation of the citizens themselves in affecting political change within their districts, insofar as "it is the nature of democracy and of the nature of representatives within it that they will respond to the intelligent persistent voices of their constituents who can demonstrate that they represent a considerable voting segment of their districts."

In reading Dundon's critique of representative government it should be borne in mind that his judgments have been formed by his own firsthand experiences in Washington. In this respect, he has himself attempted to respect the principle of getting as close as possible to the actual field of study (that is, congressional politics) before speaking authoritatively. Nevertheless, his own constructive recommendations for politics may themselves raise the specter of the "political pipe-dreams" he claims exist in the classical pronouncements of Hobbes, Locke, and Marx. For example, are politicians within a capitalist social structure in any position to exercise the sort of prudence Dundon urges? Is human nature itself compatible with the political exercise of such prudence? Does (and can) the "average" citizen possess the intelligence, interest, and ability to cooperate that is requisite for playing a viable role in shaping government actions? Indeed, as will become apparent from the readings included in this chapter, philosophers have not always agreed on the answers to such matters; nor have they viewed them with the same optimism.

ISSUES

THOMAS HOBBES

DICTATORSHIP

THE STATE OF NATURE

. . . [I]n the nature of man, we find three principal causes of quarrel. First, competition; secondly, diffidence; thirdly, glory.

The first maketh men invade for gain; the second, for safety; and the third, for reputation. The first use violence, to make themselves masters of other men's persons, wives, children, and cattle; the second, to defend them; the third, for trifles, as a word, a smile, a different opinion, and any other sign of undervalue, either direct in their persons or by reflection in their kindred, their friends, their nation, their profession, or their name.

Hereby it is manifest that during the time men live without a common power to keep them all in awe, they are in that condition which is called *war;* and such a war as is of every man against every man. For war consisteth not in battle only, or the act of fighting, but in a tract of time, wherein the will to contend by battle is sufficiently known: and therefore the notion of *time* is to be considered in the nature of war, as it is in the nature of weather. For as the nature of foul weather lieth not in a shower or two of rain, but in an inclination thereto of many days together: so the nature of war consisteth not in actual fighting, but in the known disposition thereto during all the time there is no assurance to the contrary. All other time is *peace.*

Whatsoever therefore is consequent to a time of war, where every man is enemy to every man, the same is consequent to the time wherein men live without other security than what their own strength and their own invention shall furnish them withal. In such condition there is no place for industry, because the fruit thereof is uncertain: and consequently no culture of the earth; no navigation, nor use of the commodities that may be imported by sea; no commodious building; no instruments of moving and removing such things as require much force; no knowledge of the face of the earth; no account of time; no arts;

SOURCE: Thomas Hobbes, *Leviathan,* in *Great Books of the Western World,* Vol. 23 (1952), pp. 85 – 87, 91, 100–104. © 1952, 1990. Reprinted by permission of Encyclopaedia Britannica, Inc.

no letters; no society; and which is worst of all, continual fear, and danger of violent death; and the life of man, solitary, poor, nasty, brutish, and short.

It may seem strange to some man that has not well weighed these things that Nature should thus dissociate and render men apt to invade and destroy one another: and he may therefore, not trusting to this inference, made from the passions, desire perhaps to have the same confirmed by experience. Let him therefore consider with himself: when taking a journey, he arms himself and seeks to go well accompanied; when going to sleep, he locks his doors; when even in his house he locks his chests; and this when he knows there be laws and public officers, armed, to revenge all injuries shall be done him; what opinion he has of his fellow subjects, when he rides armed; of his fellow citizens, when he locks his doors; and of his children, and servants, when he locks his chests. Does he not there as much accuse mankind by his actions as I do by my words? But neither of us accuse man's nature in it. The desires, and other passions of man, are in themselves no sin. No more are the actions that proceed from those passions till they know a law that forbids them; which till laws be made they cannot know, nor can any law be made till they have agreed upon the person that shall make it.

It may peradventure be thought there was never such a time nor condition of war as this; and I believe it was never generally so, over all the world: but there are many places where they live so now. For the savage people in many places of America, except the government of small families, the concord whereof dependeth on natural lust, have no government at all, and live at this day in that brutish manner, as I said before. Howsoever, it may be perceived what manner of life there would be, where there were no common power to fear, by the manner of life which men that have formerly lived under a peaceful government use to degenerate into a civil war. . . .

To this war of every man against every man, this also is consequent; that nothing can be unjust. The notions of right and wrong, justice and injustice, have there no place. Where there is no common power, there is no law; where no law, no injustice. Force and fraud are in war the two cardinal values. Justice and injustice are none of the faculties neither of the body nor mind. If they were, they might be in a man that were alone in the world, as well as his senses and passions. They are qualities that relate to men in society, not in solitude. It is consequent also to the same condition that there be no propriety, no dominion, no *mine* and *thine* distinct; but only that to be every man's that he can get, and for so long as he can keep it. And thus much for the ill condition which man by mere nature is actually placed in; though with a possibility to come out of it, consisting partly in the passions, partly in his reason.

The passions that incline men to peace are: fear of death; desire of such things as are necessary to commodious living; and a hope by their industry to obtain them. And reason suggesteth convenient articles of peace upon which men may be drawn to agreement. These articles are they which otherwise are called the *laws of nature,* whereof I shall speak more particularly in the two following chapters.

THE LAWS OF NATURE

. . . A *law of nature, lex naturalis,* is a precept, or general rule, found out by reason, by which a man is forbidden to do that which is destructive of his life, or taketh away the means of preserving the same, and to omit that by which he thinketh it may be best preserved. For though they that speak of this subject use to confound *jus* and *lex, right* and *law,* yet they ought to be distinguished, because *right* consisteth in liberty to do, or to forbear; whereas *law* determineth and bindeth to one of them: so that law and right differ as much as obligation and liberty, which in one and the same matter are inconsistent.

And because the condition of man (as hath been declared in the precedent chapter) is a condition of war of every one against every one, in which case every one is governed by his own reason, and there is nothing he can make use of that may not be a help unto him in preserving his life against his enemies; it followeth that in such a condition every man has a right to every thing, even to one another's body. And therefore, as long as this natural right of every man to every thing endureth, there can be no security to any man, how strong or wise soever he be, of living out the time which nature ordinarily alloweth men to live. And consequently it is a precept, or general rule of reason: *that every man ought to endeavour peace, as far as he has hope of obtaining it; and when he cannot obtain it, that he may seek and use all helps and advantages of war.* The first branch of which rule containeth the first and fundamental law of nature, which is: *to seek peace and follow it.* The second, the sum of the right of nature, which is: *by all means we can to defend ourselves.*

From this fundamental law of nature, by which men are commanded to endeavour peace, is derived this second law: *that a man be willing, when others are so too, as far forth as for peace and defence of himself he shall think it necessary, to lay down this right to all things; and be contented with so much liberty against other men as he would allow other men against himself.* For as long as every man holdeth this right, of doing anything he liketh; so long are all men in the condition of war. But if other men will not lay down their right, as well as he, then there is no reason for anyone to divest himself of his: for that were to expose himself to prey, which no man is bound to, rather than dispose himself to peace. . . .

From that law of nature by which we are obliged to transfer another such rights as, being retained, hinder the peace of mankind, there followeth a third; which is this: *that men perform their covenants made;* without which covenants are in vain, and but empty words; and the right of all men to all things remaining, we are still in the condition of war.

And in this law of nature consisteth the fountain and original of *justice.* For where no covenant hath preceded, there hath no right been transferred, and every man has right to everything; and consequently, no action can be unjust. But when a covenant is made, then to break it is *unjust:* and the definition of *injustice* is no other than *the not performance of covenant.* And whatsoever is not unjust is just.

But because covenants of mutual trust, where there is a fear of not performance on either part (as hath been said in the former chapter), are invalid though the original of justice be the making of covenants, yet injustice actually there can be none till the cause of such fear be taken away; which, while men are in the natural condition of war, cannot be done. Therefore before the names of *just* and *unjust* can have place, there must be some coercive power to compel men equally to the performance of their covenants, by the terror of some punishment greater than the benefit they expect by the breach of their covenant, and to make good that propriety which by mutual contract men acquire in recompense of the universal right they abandon: and such power there is none before the erection of a Commonwealth. And this is also to be gathered out of the ordinary definition of justice in the Schools, for they say that *justice is the constant will of giving to every man his own.* And therefore where there is no *own,* that is, no propriety, there is no injustice; and where there is no coercive power erected, that is, where there is no Commonwealth, there is no propriety, all men having right to all things: therefore where there is no Commonwealth, there nothing is unjust. So that the nature of justice consisteth in keeping of valid covenants, but the validity of covenants begins not but with the constitution of a civil power sufficient to compel men to keep them: and then it is also that propriety begins. . . .

The only way to erect such a common power, as may be able to defend them from the invasion of foreigners, and the injuries of one another, and thereby to secure them in such sort as that by their own industry and by the fruits of the earth they may nourish themselves and live contentedly, is to confer all their power and strength upon one man, or upon one assembly of men, that may reduce all their wills, by plurality of voices, unto one will: which is as much as to say, to appoint one man, or assembly of men, to bear their person; and every one to own and acknowledge himself to be author of whatsoever he that so beareth their person shall act, or cause to be acted, in those things which concern the common peace and safety; and therein to submit their wills, every one to his will, and their judgements to his judgement. This is more than consent, or concord; it is a real unity of them all in one and the same person, made by covenant of every man with every man, in such manner as if every man should say to every man: *I authorise and give up my right of governing myself to this man, or to this assembly of men, on this condition; that thou give up thy right to him, and authorise all his actions in like manner.* This done, the multitude so united in one person is called a Commonwealth; in Latin, Civitas. This is the generation of that great Leviathan, or rather, to speak more reverently, of that mortal god to which we owe, under the immortal God, our peace and defense. For by this authority, given him by every particular man in the Commonwealth, he hath the use of so much power and strength conferred on him that, by terror thereof, he is enabled to form the wills of them all, to peace at home, and mutual aid against their enemies abroad. And in him consisteth the essence of the Commonwealth; which, to define it, is: *one person, of whose*

acts a great multitude, by mutual covenants one with another, have made them-
selves every one the author, to the end he may use the strength and means of
them all as he shall think expedient for their peace and common defence.

And he that carryeth this person is called *sovereign,* and said to have *sov-*
ereign power; and every one besides, his *subject.* . . .

THE SOVEREIGN POWER

A Commonwealth is said to be instituted when a multitude of men do agree,
and covenant, every one with every one, that to whatsoever man, or assembly
of men, shall be given by the major part the right to present the person of them
all, that is to say, to be their representative; every one, as well he that voted for it
as he that voted against it, shall authorize all the actions and judgements of that
man, or assembly of men, in the same manner as if they were his own, to the
end to live peaceably amongst themselves, and be protected against other men.

From this institution of a Commonwealth are derived all the rights and faculties of him, or them, on whom the sovereign power is conferred by the consent of the people assembled.

First, because they covenant, it is to be understood they are not obliged by
former covenant to anything repugnant hereunto. And consequently they that
have already instituted a Commonwealth, being thereby bound by covenant to
own the actions and judgements of one, cannot lawfully make a new covenant
amongst themselves to be obedient to any other, in anything whatsoever, without his permission. And therefore, they that are subjects to a monarch cannot
without his leave cast off monarchy and return to the confusion of a disunited
multitude; nor transfer their person from him that beareth it to another man,
or other assembly of men: for they are bound, every man to every man, to own
and be reputed author of all that he that already is their sovereign shall do and
judge fit to be done. . . .

. . . Because every subject is by this institution author of all the actions and
judgements of the sovereign instituted, it follows that whatsoever he doth, it
can be no injury to any of his subjects; nor ought he to be by any of them accused of injustice. For he that doth anything by authority from another doth
therein no injury to him by whose authority he acteth: but by this institution of
a Commonwealth every particular man is author of all the sovereign doth; and
consequently he that complaineth of injury from his sovereign complaineth of
that whereof he himself is author, and therefore ought not to accuse any man
but himself. . . .

. . . [A]nd consequently to that which was said last, no man that hath sovereign power can justly be put to death, or otherwise in any manner by his subjects punished. For seeing every subject is author of the actions of his sovereign,
he punisheth another for the actions committed by himself.

. . . [I]t is annexed to the sovereignty to be judge of what opinions and doctrines are averse, and what conducing to peace; and consequently, on what

occasions, how far, and what men are to be trusted withal in speaking to multitudes of people; and who shall examine the doctrines of all books before they be published. For the actions of men proceed from their opinions, and in the well governing of opinions consisteth the well governing of men's actions in order to their peace and concord. And though in matter of doctrine nothing ought to be regarded but the truth, yet this is not repugnant to regulating of the same by peace.

. . . [I]t is annexed to the sovereignty the whole power of prescribing the rules whereby every man may know what goods he may enjoy, and what actions he may do, without being molested by any of his fellow subjects: and this is it men call *propriety.*

. . . [I]t is annexed to the sovereignty the right of judicature; that is to say, of hearing and deciding all controversies which may arise concerning law, either civil or natural, or concerning fact. For without the decision of controversies, there is no protection of one subject against the injuries of another. . . .

But a man may here object that the condition of subjects is very miserable, as being obnoxious to the lusts and other irregular passions of him or them that have so unlimited a power in their hands. And commonly they that live under a monarch think it the fault of monarchy; and they that live under the government of democracy, or other sovereign assembly, attribute all the inconvenience to that form of Commonwealth; whereas the power in all forms, if they be perfect enough to protect them, is the same: not considering that the estate of man can never be without some incommodity or other; and that the greatest that in any form of government can possibly happen to the people in general is scarce sensible, in respect of the miseries and horrible calamities that accompany a civil war, or that dissolute condition of masterless men without subjection to laws and a coercive power to tie their hands from rapine and revenge; nor considering that the greatest pressure of sovereign governors proceedeth, not from any delight or profit they can expect in the damage or weakening of their subjects, in whose vigour consisteth their own strength and glory, but in the restiveness of themselves that, unwillingly contributing to their own defence, make it necessary for their governors to draw from them what they can in time of peace that they may have means on any emergent occasion, or sudden need, to resist or take advantage on their enemies. For all men are by nature provided of notable multiplying glasses (that is their passions and self-love) through which every little payment appeareth a great grievance, but are destitute of those prospective glasses (namely moral and civil science) to see afar off the miseries that hang over them and cannot without such payments be avoided.

JOHN LOCKE

RULE BY THE MAJORITY

OF THE STATE OF NATURE

To understand political power right and derive it from its original, we must consider what state all men are naturally in, and that is a state of perfect freedom to order their actions and dispose of their possessions and persons as they think fit, within the bounds of the law of nature, without asking leave or depending upon the will of any other man.

A state also of equality, wherein all the power and jurisdiction is reciprocal, no one having more than another; there being nothing more evident than that creatures of the same species and rank, promiscuously born to all the same advantages of nature and the use of the same faculties, should also be equal one amongst another without subordination or subjection; unless the lord and master of them all should, by any manifest declaration of his will, set one above another, and confer on him by an evident and clear appointment an undoubted right to dominion and sovereignty. . . .

But though this be a state of liberty, yet it is not a state of license; though man in that state have an uncontrollable liberty to dispose of his person or possessions, yet he has not liberty to destroy himself, or so much as any creature in his possession, but where some nobler use than its bare preservation calls for it. The state of nature has a law of nature to govern it, which obliges every one; and reason, which is that law, teaches all mankind who will but consult it that, being all equal and independent, no one ought to harm another in his life, health, liberty, or possessions; for men being all the workmanship of one omnipotent and infinitely wise Maker—all the servants of one sovereign master, sent into the world by his order, and about his business—they are his property whose workmanship they are, made to last during his, not one another's, pleasure; and being furnished with like faculties, sharing all in one community of nature, there cannot be supposed any such subordination among us that may authorize us to destroy another, as if we were made for one another's uses as the inferior ranks of creatures are for ours. Every one, as he is bound to preserve himself and not to quit his station wilfully, so by the like reason, when his own preservation comes not in competition, ought he, as much as he can, to preserve the rest of mankind, and may not, unless it be to do justice to an offender, take

SOURCE: John Locke, *The Second Treatise of Government*, ed. Thomas P. Peardon (New York: Macmillan, 1952), pp. 4–6, 16, 17, 19, 54–56, 70–72, 81–82. Reprinted by permission of the Macmillan Publishing Company.

away or impair the life, or what tends to be the preservation of the life, the liberty, health, limb, or goods of another. . . .

OF PROPERTY

Whether we consider natural reason, which tells us that men, being once born, have a right to their preservation, and consequently to meat and drink and such other things as nature affords for their subsistence; or revelation, which gives us an account of those grants God made of the world to Adam, and to Noah and his sons; it is very clear that God, as King David says (Psalm cxv, 16), "has given the earth to the children of men," given it to mankind in common. But this being supposed, it seems to some a very great difficulty how any one should ever come to have a property in anything. I will not content myself to answer that if it be difficult to make out property upon a supposition that God gave the world to Adam and his posterity in common, it is impossible that any man but one universal monarch should have any property upon a supposition that God gave the world to Adam and his heirs in succession, exclusive of all the rest of his posterity. But I shall endeavor to show how men might come to have a property in several parts of that which God gave to mankind in common, and that without any express compact of all the commoners. . . .

Though the earth and all inferior creatures be common to all men, yet every man has a property in his own person; this nobody has any right to but himself. The labor of his body and the work of his hands, we may say, are properly his. Whatsoever then he removes out of the state that nature has provided and left it in, he has mixed his labor with, and joined to it something that is his own, and thereby makes it his property. It being by him removed from the common state nature has placed it in, it has by this labor something annexed to it that excludes the common right of other men. For this labor being the unquestionable property of the laborer, no man but he can have a right to what that is once joined to, at least where there is enough and as good left in common for others. . . .

It will perhaps be objected to this that "if gathering the acorns, or other fruits of the earth, etc., makes a right to them, then any one may engross as much as he will." To which I answer: not so. The same law of nature that does by this means give us property does also bound that property, too. "God has given us all things richly" (1 Tim. vi. 17), is the voice of reason confirmed by inspiration. But how far has he given it us? To enjoy. As much as any one can make use of to any advantage of life before it spoils, so much he may by his labor fix a property in; whatever is beyond this is more than his share and belongs to others. Nothing was made by God for man to spoil or destroy. And thus considering the plenty of natural provisions there was a long time in the world, and the few spenders, and to how small a part of that provision the industry of one man could extend itself and engross it to the prejudice of others, especially keeping within the bounds set by reason of what might serve for his use, there could be then little room for quarrels or contentions about property so established. . . .

Of the Beginning of Political Societies

Men being, as has been said, by nature all free, equal, and independent, no one can be put out of this estate and subjected to the political power of another without his own consent. The only way whereby any one divests himself of his natural liberty and puts on the bonds of civil society is by agreeing with other men to join and unite into a community for their comfortable, safe, and peaceable living one amongst another, in a secure enjoyment of their properties and a greater security against any that are not of it. This any number of men may do, because it injures not the freedom of the rest; they are left as they were in the liberty of the state of nature. When any number of men have so consented to make one community or government, they are thereby presently incorporated and make one body politic wherein the majority have a right to act and conclude the rest.

For when any number of men have, by the consent of every individual, made a community, they have thereby made that community one body, with a power to act as one body, which is only by the will and determination of the majority; for that which acts any community being only the consent of the individuals of it, and it being necessary to that which is one body to move one way, it is necessary the body should move that way whither the greater force carries it, which is the consent of the majority; or else it is impossible it should act or continue one body, one community, which the consent of every individual that united into it agreed that it should; and so every one is bound by that consent to be concluded by the majority. And therefore we see that in assemblies empowered to act by positive laws, where no number is set by that positive law which impowers them, the act of the majority passes for the act of the whole and, of course, determines, as having by the law of nature and reason the power of the whole.

And thus every man, by consenting with others to make one body politic under one government, puts himself under an obligation to every one of that society to submit to the determination of the majority and be concluded by it; or else this original compact, whereby he with others incorporates into one society, would signify nothing, and be no compact, if he be left free and under no other ties than he was in before in the state of nature. For what appearance would there be of any compact? What new engagement if he were no further tied by any decrees of the society than he himself thought fit and did actually consent to? This would be still as great a liberty as he himself had before his compact, or any one else in the state of nature has who may submit himself and consent to any acts of it if he thinks fit.

For if the consent of the majority shall not in reason be received as the act of the whole and conclude every individual, nothing but the consent of every individual can make anything to be the act of the whole; but such a consent is next to impossible ever to be had if we consider the infirmities of health and avocations of business which in a number, though much less than that of a commonwealth, will necessarily keep many away from the public assembly. To which, if we add the variety of opinions and contrariety of interests which un-avoidably happen in all collections of men, the coming into society upon such terms would be only like Cato's coming into the theatre only to go out again. Such a constitution as this would make the mighty leviathan of a shorter dura-tion than the feeblest creatures, and not let it outlast the day it was born in; which cannot be supposed till we can think that rational creatures should de-sire and constitute societies only to be dissolved; for where the majority cannot conclude the rest, there they cannot act as one body, and consequently will be immediately dissolved again.

Whosoever, therefore, out of a state of nature unite into a community must be understood to give up all the power necessary to the ends for which they unite into society to the majority of the community, unless they expressly agreed in any number greater than the majority. And this is done by barely agreeing to unite into one political society, which is all the compact that is, or needs be, between the individuals that enter into or make up a commonwealth. And thus that which begins and actually constitutes any political society is nothing but the consent of any number of freemen capable of a majority to unite and incorporate into such a society. And this is that, and that only, which did or could give beginning to any lawful government in the world. . . .

OF THE ENDS OF POLITICAL SOCIETY AND GOVERNMENT

If man in the state of nature be so free, as has been said, if he be absolute lord of his own person and possessions, equal to the greatest, and subject to nobody, why will he part with his freedom, why will he give up his empire and subject himself to the dominion and control of any other power? To which it is obvi-ous to answer that though in the state of nature he has such a right, yet the en-joyment of it is very uncertain and constantly exposed to the invasion of others; for all being kings as much as he, every man his equal, and the greater part no strict observers of equity and justice, the enjoyment of the property he has in this state is very unsafe, very unsecure. This makes him willing to quit a condi-tion which, however free, is full of fears and continual dangers; and it is not without reason that he seeks out and is willing to join in society with others who are already united, or have a mind to unite, for the mutual preservation of their lives, liberties, and estates, which I call by the general name 'property.'

The great and chief end, therefore, of men's uniting into commonwealths and putting themselves under government is the preservation of their property. To which in the state of nature there are many things wanting:

First, there wants an established, settled, known law, received and allowed by common consent to be the standard of right and wrong and the common measure to decide all controversies between them; for though the law of nature be plain and intelligible to all rational creatures, yet men, being biased by their interest as well as ignorant for want of studying it, are not apt to allow of it as a law binding to them in the application of it to their particular cases.

Secondly, in the state of nature there wants a known and indifferent judge with authority to determine all differences according to the established law; for every one in that state being both judge and executioner of the law of nature, men being partial to themselves, passion and revenge is very apt to carry them too far and with too much heat in their own cases, as well as negligence and unconcernedness to make them too remiss in other men's.

Thirdly, in the state of nature there often wants power to back and support the sentence when right, and to give it due execution. They who by any injustice offend will seldom fail, where they are able, by force, to make good their injustice; such resistance many times makes the punishment dangerous and frequently destructive to those who attempt it.

Thus mankind, notwithstanding all the privileges of the state of nature, being but in an ill condition while they remain in it, are quickly driven into society. Hence it comes to pass that we seldom find any number of men live any time together in this state. The inconveniences that they are therein exposed to by the irregular and uncertain exercise of the power every man has of punishing the transgressions of others make them take sanctuary under the established laws of government and therein seek the preservation of their property. It is this makes them so willingly give up every one his single power of punishing, to be exercised by such alone as shall be appointed to it amongst them; and by such rules as the community, or those authorized by them to that purpose, shall agree on. And in this we have the original right of both the legislative and executive power, as well as of the governments and societies themselves. . . .

These are the bounds which the trust that is put in them by the society and the law of God and nature have set to the legislative power of every commonwealth, in all forms of government:

First, they are to govern by promulgated established laws, not to be varied in particular cases, but to have one rule for rich and poor, for the favorite at court and the countryman at plough.

Secondly, these laws also ought to be designed for no other end ultimately but the good of the people.

Thirdly, they must not raise taxes on the property of the people without the consent of the people, given by themselves or their deputies. . . .

Fourthly, the legislative neither must nor can transfer the power of making laws to anybody else, or place it anywhere but where the people have.

KARL MARX AND
FRIEDRICH ENGELS

COMMUNISM

I. BOURGEOIS AND PROLETARIANS

. . . The means of production and of exchange, on whose foundation the bourgeoisie built itself up, were generated in feudal society. At a certain stage in the development of these means of production and of exchange, the conditions under which feudal society produced and exchanged, the feudal organisation of agriculture and manufacturing industry, in one word, the feudal relations of property became no longer compatible with the already developed productive forces; they became so many fetters. They had to be burst asunder; they were burst asunder.

Into their place stepped free competition, accompanied by a social and political constitution adapted to it, and by the economical and political sway of the bourgeois class.

A similar movement is going on before our own eyes. Modern bourgeois society with its relations of production, of exchange and of property, a society that has conjured up such gigantic means of production and of exchange, is like the sorcerer, who is no longer able to control the powers of the nether world whom he has called up by his spells. For many a decade past, the history of industry and commerce is but the history of the revolt of modern productive forces against modern conditions of production, against the property relations that are the conditions for the existence of the bourgeoisie and of its rule. . . .

The weapons with which the bourgeoisie felled feudalism to the ground are now turned against the bourgeoisie itself.

But not only has the bourgeoisie forged the weapons that bring death to itself; it has also called into existence the men who are to wield those weapons—the modern working class—the proletarians.

In proportion as the bourgeoisie, i.e., capital, is developed, in the same proportion is the proletariat, the modern working class, developed—a class of labourers, who live only so long as they find work, and work only so long as their labour increases capital. These labourers, who must sell themselves piecemeal, are a commodity, like every other article of commerce, and are consequently exposed to all the vicissitudes of competition, to all the fluctuations of the market.

SOURCE: Karl Marx and Friedrich Engels, *The Communist Manifesto* (New York: Pantheon, 1967). Reprinted by permission of Pantheon books, a Division of Random House, Inc.

Owing to the extensive use of machinery and to division of labour, the work of the proletarians has lost all individual character, and, consequently, all charm for the workman. He becomes an appendage of the machine, and it is only the most simple, most monotonous, and most easily acquired knack, that is required of him. Hence, the cost of production of a workman is restricted, almost entirely, to the means of subsistence that he requires for his maintenance, and for the propagation of his race. But the price of a commodity, and therefore also of labour, is equal to its cost of production. In proportion, therefore, as the repulsiveness of the work increases, the wage decreases. Nay more, in proportion as the use of machinery and division of labour increases, in the same proportion the burden of toil also increases, whether by prolongation of the working hours, by increase of the work exacted in a given time or by increased speed of the machinery, etc.

Modern industry has converted the little workshop of the patriarchal master into the great factory of the industrial capitalist. Masses of labourers, crowded into the factory, are organised like soldiers. As privates of the industrial army they are placed under the command of a perfect hierarchy of officers and sergeants. Not only are they slaves of the bourgeois class, and of the bourgeois State; they are daily and hourly enslaved by the machine, by the overlooker, and, above all, by the individual bourgeois manufacturer himself. The more openly this despotism proclaims gain to be its end and aim, the more petty, the more hateful and the more embittering it is.

The less the skill and exertion of strength implied in manual labour, in other words, the more modern industry becomes developed, the more is the labour of men superseded by that of women. Differences of age and sex have no longer any distinctive social validity for the working class. All are instruments of labour, more or less expensive to use, according to their age and sex.

No sooner is the exploitation of the labour by the manufacturer, so far, at an end, than he receives his wages in cash, than he is set upon by the other portions of the bourgeoisie, the landlord, the shopkeeper, the pawnbroker, etc.

The lower strata of the middle class—the small tradespeople, shopkeepers, and retired tradesmen generally, the handicraftsman and peasants—all these sink gradually into the proletariat, partly because their diminutive capital does not suffice for the scale on which Modern Industry is carried on, and is swamped in the competition with the large capitalists, partly because their specialised skill is rendered worthless by new methods of production. Thus the proletariat is recruited from all classes of the population.

The proletariat goes through various stages of development. With its birth begins its struggle with the bourgeoisie. At first the contest is carried on by individual labourers, then by the workpeople of a factory, then by the operatives of one trade, in one locality, against the individual bourgeois who directly exploits them. They direct their attacks not against the bourgeois conditions of production, but against the instruments of production themselves; they destroy imported wares that compete with their labour, they smash to pieces machinery, they set factories ablaze, they seek to restore by force the vanished status of the workman of the Middle Ages.

At this stage the labourers still form an incoherent mass scattered over the whole country, and broken up by their mutual competition. If anywhere they unite to form more compact bodies, that is not yet the consequence of their own active union, but of the union of the bourgeoisie, which class, in order to attain its own political ends, is compelled to set the whole proletariat in motion, and is moreover yet, for a time, able to do so. At this stage, therefore, the proletarians do not fight their enemies, but the enemies of their enemies, the remnants of absolute monarchy, the landowners, the non-industrial bourgeois, the petty bourgeoisie. Thus the whole historical movement is concentrated in the hands of the bourgeoisie, every victory so obtained is a victory for the bourgeoisie.

But with the development of industry the proletariat not only increases in number; it becomes concentrated in greater masses, its strength grows, and it feels that strength more. The various interests and conditions of life within the ranks of the proletariat are more and more equalised, in proportion as machinery obliterates all distinctions of labour, and nearly everywhere reduces wages to the same low level. The growing competition among the bourgeois, and the resulting commercial crises, makes the wages of the workers ever more fluctuating. The unceasing improvement of machinery, ever more rapidly developing, makes their livelihood more and more precarious, the collisions between individual workmen and individual bourgeois take more and more the character of collisions between two classes. Thereupon the workers begin to form combinations (Trades' Unions) against the bourgeois; they club together in order to keep up the rate of wages; they found permanent associations in order to make provision beforehand for these occasional revolts. Here and there the contest breaks out into riots.

Now and then the workers are victorious, but only for a time. The real fruit of their battles lies, not in the immediate result, but in the ever-expanding union of the workers. . . .

The essential condition for the existence, and for the sway of the bourgeois class, is the formation and augmentation of capital; the condition for capital is wage-labour. Wage-labour rests exclusively on competition between the labourers. The advance of industry, whose involuntary promoter is the bourgeoisie, replaces the isolation of the labourers, due to competition, by their revolutionary combination, due to association. The development of Modern Industry, therefore, cuts from under its feet the very foundation on which the bourgeoisie produces and appropriates products. What the bourgeoisie, therefore, produces, above all, is its own gravediggers. Its fall and the victory of the proletariat are very inevitable.

II. PROLETARIANS AND COMMUNISTS

The distinguishing feature of Communism is not the abolition of property generally, but the abolition of bourgeois property. But modern bourgeois private property is the final and most complete expression of the system of producing and appropriating products, that is based on class antagonisms, on the exploitation of the many by the few.

In this sense, the theory of the Communists may be summed up in the single sentence: Abolition of private property.

We Communists have been reproached with the desire of abolishing the right of personally acquiring property as the fruit of a man's own labour, which property is alleged to be the groundwork of all personal freedom, activity and independence.

Hard-won, self-acquired, self-earned property! Do you mean the property of the petty artisan and of the small peasant, a form of property that preceded the bourgeois form? There is no need to abolish that; the development of industry has to a great extent already destroyed it, and is still destroying it daily.

Or do you mean modern bourgeois private property?

But does wage-labour create any property for the labourer? Not a bit. It creates capital, i.e., that kind of property which exploits wage-labour, and which cannot increase except upon condition of begetting a new supply of wage-labour for fresh exploitation. Property, in its present form, is based on the antagonism of capital and wage-labour. Let us examine both sides of this antagonism.

To be a capitalist, is to have not only a purely personal, but a social *status* in production. Capital is a collective product, and only by the united action of many members, nay, in the last resort, only by the united action of all members of society, can it be set in motion.

Capital is, therefore, not a personal, it is a social power.

When, therefore, capital is converted into common property, into the property of all members of society, personal property is not thereby transformed into social property. It is only the social character of the property that is changed. It loses its class-character.

Let us now take wage-labour.

The average price of wage-labour is the minimum wage, i.e., that quantum of the means of subsistence, which is absolutely requisite to keep the labourer in bare existence as a labourer. What, therefore, the wage-labourer appropriates by means of his labour, merely suffices to prolong and reproduce a bare existence. We by no means intend to abolish this personal appropriation of the products of labour, an appropriation that is made for the maintenance and reproduction of human life, and that leaves no surplus wherewith to command the labour of others. All that we want to do away with, is the miserable character of this appropriation, under which the labourer lives merely to increase capital, and is allowed to live only in so far as the interest of the ruling class requires it.

In bourgeois society, living labour is but a means to increase accumulated labour. In Communist society, accumulated labour is but a means to widen, to enrich, to promote the existence of the labourer.

In bourgeois society, therefore, the past dominates the present; in Communist society, the present dominates the past. In bourgeois society capital is independent and has individuality, while the living person is dependent and has no individuality.

And the abolition of this state of things is called by the bourgeois, abolition of individuality and freedom! And rightly so. The abolition of bourgeois individuality, bourgeois independence, and bourgeois freedom is undoubtedly aimed at.

By freedom is meant, under the present bourgeois conditions of production, free trade, free selling and buying.

But if selling and buying disappears, free selling and buying disappears also. This talk about free selling and buying, and all the other "brave words" of our bourgeoisie about freedom in general, have a meaning, if any, only in contrast with restricted selling and buying, with the fettered traders of the Middle Ages, but have no meaning when opposed to the Communistic abolition of buying and selling, of the bourgeois conditions of production, and of the bourgeoisie itself.

You are horrified at our intending to do away with private property. But in your existing society, private property is already done away with for nine-tenths of the population; its existence for the few is solely due to its non-existence in the hands of those nine-tenths. You reproach us, therefore, with intending to do away with a form of property, the necessary condition for whose existence is the non-existence of any property for the immense majority of society.

In one word, you reproach us with intending to do away with your property. Precisely so; that is just what we intend.

From the moment when labour can no longer be converted into capital, money, or rent, into a social power capable of being monopolised, i.e., from the moment when individual property can no longer be transformed into bourgeois property, into capital, from that moment, you say, individuality vanishes.

You must, therefore, confess that by "individual" you mean no other person than the bourgeois, than the middle-class owner of property. This person must, indeed, be swept out of the way, and made impossible.

Communism deprives no man of the power to appropriate the products of society; all that it does is to deprive him of the power to subjugate the labour of others by means of such appropriation.

It has been objected that upon the abolition of private property all work will cease, and universal laziness will overtake us.

According to this, bourgeois society ought long ago to have gone to the dogs through sheer idleness; for those of its members who work, acquire nothing, and those who acquire anything, do not work. The whole of this objection is but another expression of the tautology: that there can no longer be any wage-labour when there is no longer any capital.

All objections urged against the Communistic mode of producing and appropriating material products, have, in the same way, been urged against the Communistic modes of producing and appropriating intellectual products. Just as, to the bourgeois, the disappearance of class property is the disappearance of production itself, so the disappearance of class culture is to him identical with the disappearance of all culture.

That culture, the loss of which he laments, is, for the enormous majority, a mere training to act as a machine.

But don't wrangle with us so long as you apply, to our intended abolition of bourgeois property, the standard of your bourgeois notions of freedom, culture, law, &c. Your very ideas are but the outgrowth of the conditions of your bourgeois production and bourgeois property, just as your jurisprudence is but the will of your class made into a law for all, a will, whose essential character and direction are determined by the economical conditions of existence of your class.

The selfish misconception that induces you to transform into eternal laws of nature and of reason, the social forms springing from your present mode of production and form of property—historical relations that rise and disappear in the progress of production—this misconception you share with every ruling class that has preceded you. What you see clearly in the case of ancient property, what you admit in the case of feudal property, you are of course forbidden to admit in the case of your own bourgeois form of property.

Abolition of the family! Even the most radical flare up at this infamous proposal of the Communists.

On what foundation is the present family, the bourgeois family, based? On capital, on private gain. In its completely developed form this family exists only among the bourgeoisie. But this state of things finds its complement in the practical absence of the family among the proletarians, and in public prostitution.

The bourgeois family will vanish as a matter of course when its complement vanishes, and both will vanish with the vanishing of capital.

Do you charge us with wanting to stop the exploitation of children by their parents? To this crime we plead guilty.

But, you will say, we destroy the most hallowed of relations, when we replace home education by social.

And your education! Is not that also social, and determined by the social conditions under which you educate, by the intervention, direct or indirect, of society, by means of schools, &c.? The Communists have not invented the intervention of society in education; they do but seek to alter the character of that intervention, and to rescue education from the influence of the ruling class.

The bourgeois clap-trap about the family and education, about the hallowed co-relation of parent and child, becomes all the more disgusting, the more, by the action of Modern Industry, all family ties among the proletarians are torn asunder, and their children transformed into simple articles of commerce and instruments of labour.

But you Communists would introduce community of women, screams the whole bourgeoisie in chorus.

The bourgeois sees in his wife a mere instrument of production. He hears that the instruments of production are to be exploited in common, and, naturally, can come to no other conclusion than that the lot of being common to all will likewise fall to the women.

He has not even a suspicion that the real point aimed at is to do away with the status of women as mere instruments of production.

For the rest, nothing is more ridiculous than the virtuous indignation of our bourgeois at the community of women which, they pretend, is to be openly and officially established by the Communists. The Communists have no need to introduce community of women; it has existed almost from time immemorial.

Our bourgeois, not content with having the wives and daughters of their proletarians at their disposal, not to speak of common prostitutes, take the greatest pleasure in seducing each other's wives.

Bourgeois marriage is in reality a system of wives in common and thus, at the most, what the Communists might possibly be reproached with, is that they desire to introduce, in substitution for a hypocritically concealed, an openly legalised community of women. For the rest, it is self-evident that the abolition of the present system of production must bring with it the abolition of the community of women springing from that system, i.e., of prostitution both public and private.

The Communists are further reproached with desiring to abolish countries and nationality.

The working men have no country. We cannot take from them what they have not got. Since the proletariat must first of all acquire political supremacy, must rise to be the leading class of the nation, must constitute itself *the* nation, it is, so far, itself national, though not in the bourgeois sense of the word.

National differences and antagonisms between peoples are daily more and more vanishing, owing to the development of the bourgeoisie, to freedom of commerce, to the world-market, to uniformity in the mode of production and in the conditions of life corresponding thereto.

The supremacy of the proletariat will cause them to vanish still faster. United action, of the leading civilised countries at least, is one of the first conditions for the emancipation of the proletariat.

In proportion as the exploitation of one individual by another is put an end to, the exploitation of one nation by another will also be put an end to. In proportion as the antagonism between classes within the nation vanishes, the hostility of one nation to another will come to an end.

The charges against Communism made from a religious, a philosophical, and, generally, from an ideological standpoint, are not deserving of serious examination.

Does it require deep intuition to comprehend that man's ideas, views and conceptions, in one word, man's consciousness, changes with every change in the conditions of his material existence, in his social relations and in his social life?

What else does the history of ideas prove, than that intellectual production changes its character in proportion as material production is changed? The ruling ideas of each age have ever been the ideas of its ruling class.

When people speak of ideas that revolutionise society, they do but express the fact, that within the old society, the elements of a new one have been created, and that the dissolution of the old ideas keeps even pace with the dissolution of the old conditions of existence.

When the ancient world was in its last throes, the ancient religions were overcome by Christianity. When Christian ideas succumbed in the eighteenth century to rationalist ideas, feudal society fought its death battle with the then revolutionary bourgeoisie. The ideas of religious liberty and freedom of conscience merely gave expression to the sway of free competition within the domain of knowledge.

"Undoubtedly," it will be said, "religious, moral, philosophical and juridicial ideas have been modified in the course of historical development, But religion, morality, philosophy, political science, and law, constantly survived this change."

"There are, besides, eternal truths, such as Freedom, Justice, etc., that are common to all states of society. But Communism abolishes eternal truths, it abolishes all religion, and all morality, instead of constituting them on a new basis; it therefore acts in contradiction to all past historical experience."

What does this accusation reduce itself to? The history of all past society has consisted in the development of class antagonisms, antagonisms that assumed different forms at different epochs.

But whatever form they may have taken, one fact is common to all past ages, viz., the exploitation of one part of society by the other. No wonder, then, that the social consciousness of past ages, despite all the multiplicity and variety it displays, moves within certain common forms, or general ideas, which cannot completely vanish except with the total disappearance of class antagonisms.

The Communist revolution is the most radical rupture with traditional property relations; no wonder that its development involves the most radical rupture with traditional ideas.

But let us have done with the bourgeois objections to Communism.

We have seen above, that the first step in the revolution by the working class, is to raise the proletariat to the position of ruling class, to win the battle of democracy.

The proletariat will use its political supremacy to wrest, by degrees, all capital from the bourgeoisie, to centralise all instruments of production in the hands of the State, i.e., of the proletariat organised as the ruling class; and to increase the total of productive forces as rapidly as possible.

Of course, in the beginning, this cannot be effected except by means of despotic inroads on the rights of property, and on the conditions of bourgeois production; by means of measures, therefore, which appear economically insufficient and untenable, but which, in the course of the movement, outstrip themselves, necessitate further inroads upon the old social order, and are unavoidable as a means of entirely revolutionising the mode of production.

These measures will of course be different in different countries.

Nevertheless in the most advanced countries, the following will be pretty generally applicable.

1. Abolition of property in land and application of all rents of land to public purposes.
2. A heavy progressive or graduated income tax.
3. Abolition of all rights of inheritance.

4. Confiscation of the property of all emigrants and rebels.
5. Centralisation of credit in the hands of the State, by means of a national bank with State capital and an exclusive monopoly.
6. Centralisation of the means of communication and transport in the hands of the State.
7. Extension of factories and instruments of production owned by the State; the bringing into cultivation of waste-lands, and the improvement of the soil generally in accordance with a common plan.
8. Equal liability of all to labour. Establishment of industrial armies, especially for agriculture.
9. Combination of agriculture with manufacturing industries; gradual abolition of the distinction between town and country, by a more equable distribution of the population over the country.
10. Free education for all children in public schools. Abolition of children's factory labour in its present form. Combination of education with industrial production, &c., &c.

When, in the course of development, class distinctions have disappeared, and all production has been concentrated in the hands of a vast association of the whole nation, the public power will lose its political character. Political power, properly so called, is merely the organised power of one class for oppressing another. If the proletariat during its contest with the bourgeoisie is compelled, by the force of circumstances, to organise itself as a class, if, by means of a revolution, it makes itself the ruling class, and, as such, sweeps away by force the old conditions of production, then it will, along with these conditions, have swept away the conditions for the existence of class antagonisms and of classes generally, and will thereby have abolished its own supremacy as a class.

In place of the old bourgeois society, with its classes and class antagonisms, we shall have an association, in which the free development of each is the condition for the free development of all.

PRACTICE

STANISLAUS J. DUNDON

THE PHILOSOPHER IN REPRESENTATIVE GOVERNMENT: APPLYING CLASSICAL POLITICAL THEORIES

In 1980 I was selected by the American Philosophical Association to serve with Bill Puka on the first team of philosophers to work in Congress on its staffs or

Stanislaus J. Dundon, a philosopher and historian of science by training (Ph.D, St. John's University, New York) specializing in early modern physics, became involved in agricultural science and its ethics due to his work at a large agricultural school, Cal Poly, San Luis Obispo. The capacity of agricultural technology to do great harm and even cause hunger in spite of all good intentions seemed a serious paradox. This led to a career of interest in public policy, ethics, and technology. He worked, as a Congressional Science Fellow, for agricultural committees with Congressman George Brown's (D. San Bernardino) office in 1980–81. He returned to his campus and over a decade established several agricultural ethics courses at Cal Poly and University of California, Davis, where he also did short courses and presentations for farmers, farm extension agents, and EPA state administrators. His teaching, now at California State University, Sacramento, includes bioethics and business and computer ethics. He is currently national coordinator of the "Soul of Agriculture," a project aimed at a national consensus statement on the values and ethics of family managed farming.

committees. In this paper I have organized and present the practical philosophic reflections which resulted from that work on the role of citizens in sharing in government.

In the brief scope of this essay, I can only assist a thoughtful and caring citizen who wishes to participate effectively in the guidance of political action toward a good end with a very few basic constant truths and some guides for good political change. I propose to do the following: against the background of the preceding selections from Hobbes, Locke, and Marx, I will describe three things: (1) The activist's need for philosophical theory on the purpose of the state or of government. (2) How to find in that purpose, with the assistance of philosophy on the nature of humankind, both suggestions as to good political tools and limits on those tools. (3) Why those tools depend on grass roots, year-long democracy. My practical recommendations will apply largely to the kind of legislative system we find in the U.S. Congress today.

THE PURPOSE OF THE STATE

I had just received news that I had reached the "finals" of the selection phase when a talented and public-spirited physicist who had served in the same congressional program took me aside to discuss the work. The senator he worked for was on an important energy committee and had assigned the physicist to assist in calculating a complicated pricing policy to encourage new domestic oil sources without producing a "windfall" for the old sources. The normally modest scientist glanced up at me from the figures he was scribbling and said, "It was incredible to be involved in setting energy prices for the whole country." His eyes flashed with the obvious excitement he felt even in remembering it, but he quickly returned to his usual diffidence—"Of course, who knows if they were the right prices?"

I hardly heard anything else he said. I thought to myself: "If a guy with both talent and modesty can still feel that intoxication, how would a less-disciplined ego handle it?" I began to worry about my motives and ability to direct myself to the good purpose I had in mind in entering the competition for this appointment. To do good, I reasoned, I would have to align my purposes with the good purpose of the state itself. But what is that purpose?

It should seem obvious that one cannot conduct any complicated business, make decisions, and act without some purpose. That purpose or goal must be both known and loved. Knowing it provides the main criteria for judging policy choices, namely, their ability to reach the goal. And loving it provides the energy to act at all. And without a single goal, at least vaguely stated, there would be no way to settle on compromises or judge cases except by force.

Excess of Purpose—Potomac Fever

When I got to Washington I found that it did not lack at all for a sense of purpose. In fact, the place seems to suffocate with the feeling that absolutely everything has some ulterior motive, a further purpose, even things which should not have purposes beyond their immediate effect, like friendly smiles, a cheerful greeting on the phone, passing friendships, courtesy, and thoughtfulness. And yet there seems to be a fear of stating what the final purpose of activity is. Food and housing is expensive; the work is hard, often unnoticed, and boring; and the pay, for aides and staffers, is not good. You know that some burning purpose is driving people. The heat of that desire has a name: Potomac Fever. It usually refers to a nonrational (if not irrational) desire to work at important tasks in environments where great power is wielded, great events begun and ended, and worldwide attention is focused, even if one's own work is not at that focus. What this suggests is rather unsettling: much work in Washington is motivated by the desire to continue working there.

Lack of Purpose

On the other hand, the purpose of the work itself is not often stated explicitly enough to be of much use in the actual guiding of legislation. No one would deny that government has a noble purpose beyond the satisfaction of the personal drives and needs of those doing the work. And when there is an immediate small beneficiary class, like hostages or farmers, or narrow goal, like restraining inflation, it will be stated. But one often finds important actors either unwilling or unable to state how those intermediate goals serve some final goal of the state. So a kind of policy chaos can and does exist, in which any temporary consistency in the Heraclitean flux is related to the strength and persistence of petitioners, the lobbyists, rather than any stability of purpose in the policymaker. The motive for acceding to these petitioners comes back partially to the desire to remain in the power structure.

This desire to be creative in important, honored work at the center of action and to enjoy being thought well of for such work are constructive passions. The trouble is that these desires do not direct government in any consistent way to any appropriate end. The end needs to be sought and stated clearly enough to avoid seduction into trivial narcissism or worse deviations. Knowing the goal and loving it is the first step to a creative integrity.

The Common Good

I echo a long line of philosophers in giving the goal of the state as the "common good," defined as the well-being of the citizens of the state. The history of politics and political philosophy resembles two rollercoaster rides of ideals and applications. And on peaks and valleys at different times are the meaning of the common good and the list of persons eligible to be included among the "common." Various theories have limited the "good," so that it does not embrace every kind of good the citizens can experience. Ancient church-state theories confined the state to the "temporal good." Modern libertarian theories attempt to limit it to bodily and property goods among the temporal goods. I would propose that no a priori precision on what is included in "common good" should be set out without argument and agreement among the citizens themselves.

It is a common ploy, perhaps unconscious, for thinkers of one class to develop fancy theories declaring conveniently that the state should be concerned with *providing* only those parts of the common good their class lacks, and protect, but not provide, those parts their class already possesses. Thus one well-known conservative editorialist wants few or no job training programs for the poor, but does want state assistance for rehabilitation and therapy for retarded or handicapped children. He has a Down's syndrome afflicted child, the cost of whose fullest development exceeds the finances even of the upper middle class. Others push for billions to produce marginal improvement in airport landing safety, but object to similar sums for health services to residents of the country's major cities. One class flies at least once a year, the other once or twice a lifetime. And the number of lives saved or significantly improved by the health care is a hundred times that of the improved landing technology. Neither air travel safety nor basic health should be excluded from the meaning of "common good." But whether a certain part of the common good should be today's high-priority government policy should be determined by democratic debate and fairness. "Frequent flyers," however, should remember that their basic health has probably been secured better than those who cannot afford to fly.

Second, many thinkers, including philosophers, have had rather unjustified limitations on who the citizens are. The end of slavery and of various kinds of ethnic or sexual "second-class" citizenry strikes me as evidence that our moral maturity is catching up with the logic of our definitions. Marx recognized that the international character of industrial economy makes the common good, especially referring to the working class, of a single country unattainable and meaningless apart from the condition of workers elsewhere. We see that so well today as jobs leave the United States in search of near-slave labor elsewhere. And finally, modern weaponry is forcing us to see that Hobbesian deterrence of invasion must be replaced by a cooperative pursuit of international common good. This movement does not imply that sovereignty and personal autonomy are not part of the common good. Broadening of "common good" means accommodation to prior elements, not elimination of them.

Such accommodations do require cooperative concessions and law-guided restraint on behavior. It is surprising in Washington to hear refined gentlemen defending lawless behavior by the United States among the community of nations as patriotic, when they would consider allowing such behavior by their own children within their local community equivalent to encouraging delinquency. The lawlessness of other nations is, of course, terrorism. It is only gradually, and with much back-sliding, that opinion and behavior begin to reflect the logic of our definitions.

This movement to broaden the "common good," on two fronts, the goods and the persons to enjoy them, proceeds unevenly in the halls of Congress. The candidate goods today include political freedom; the means to secure basic physical needs, such as employment or productive resources; and equal availability of public facilities, both tax-supported, like schools, hospitals, and parks, and commercial, like housing, restaurants, or athletic facilities. The candidate persons are all humans in the state. It is not difficult to grasp mentally. It has a kind of Fourth of July simplicity. It is a wonder why it is not used as a criterion to sort out legislative proposals. But when I called a Florida congressperson to complain that our office did not want to see the law changed which required that U.S.-funded parathion spraying of Mexican marijuana be accompanied by a bright dye so that the poisoned crop would not be sold, he objected that, in spite of the laid-back attitude of Californians, people aren't supposed to be smoking it anyway. I had to point out that a death penalty for smoking mari-juana is hardly fair, even for Californians. The righteous have to remember that lawbreakers, which most of us are at some time in at least small matters, remain part of the "common."

When you work in political environments, to wear this knowledge and love of the end of the state "on your sleeve" will mark you as arrogant. Very many of your companions will share it without ever telling you. You will really be ar-rogant if you judge their behavior as unfaithful to the goal without under-standing all the factors that went into their decisions.

On the other hand, those who confidently insist that no such goal exists are "the blind leading the blind." They may be more honorable and courageous than most at their duties, with an undoubted virtue derived from excellent up-bringing and natural sensitivity. But in times of great tension and debate, intel-lectual clarity of the state's purpose is needed to sort out all the competing claims and set a consistent course.

A Look at Some Philosophers

In some of the fundamental opinions of Hobbes, Locke, and Marx on the goal of the state we find hints as to why the common good does not effectively guide policy even today in the congressional environment.

Hobbes derived his choice of a type of government in part from a pes-simistic view of human nature. Note how powerfully pessimism functions in his theoretical concept of a prestate "natural condition," the worst features of which the state is erected to prevent. His experience of actual civil unrest may also have been a reason why he made the de facto end of the state the suppression of civil strife, implicitly defining the "common good" as the avoidance of in-ternal strife and defense against alien invasion.

In advocating a dictatorship or oligarchy to save us from ourselves, Hobbes is making an unjustified distinction between the oligarchs and citizens. The for-mer will act with wisdom and the long view, whereas the latter, when master-less, will dissolve society into warfare. As a philosopher, of course, he knows that there are no grounds for such class distinctions, so he resorts to what I will call a "political pipe dream." Somehow self-interest will prevent the dictator or oligarch from abusing the people. After all, he says, it is the people "in whose vigour consisteth their own strength and glory." It is as if the oligarchy will not, as easily any humans, fail to act in enlightened self-interest and begin to glut-tonously consume the well-being of the citizens. But the citizens, without a dic-tator, would definitely thus fail. The pipe dream of the inevitably benevolent dictator also includes the power of the dictator to magically know and to con-struct the material conditions of the well-being of the citizens. Hobbes neglects the massive web of activity by which, from each cottage to international sea lanes, humans feed, clothe, and house themselves, because he cares actively about only one aspect of that common good, the suppression of civil strife. The rest is left to the pipe dream, the benevolent omniscience of the dictator. And it

was not as if Hobbes did not know the history of certain English monarchs tax-
ing the citizens and the economy to the breaking point in the pursuit of foreign
wars, undoubtedly waged for "national security."

Locke considers the common good of citizens more amply than Hobbes, by
more prominently discussing their material needs and possessions. What is neglected is clearer in Locke: He starts by basing private property on human labor because that labor justifies a claim on a piece of the earth, that universal
gift of God to all humans in common. But almost immediately he makes "the
great and chief end" for forming the state the preservation of that private property, thereby de facto neglecting the many, and perhaps even in his day, the near
majority of citizens who never possess anything but their labor. Did it ever occur to Locke how many humans he thereby reduced to only incidental political
importance?

Although Locke does recognize that "laws ought to be designed for no
other end, ultimately, but the good of the people," he simply left unattended to
the manner in which economics can render meaningless the "equity before the
law," and with it can leave many of the citizens without the basic material
goods of life. The common good had not really been attended to. Once again a
kind of magic is left to fill in the details. His attention is focused on a single
class, one he hopes can form a majority in a democracy. Property and rights to
possess it being more sacred than life itself become the definition of the common good. Later writers will give the magical process whereby the unproper-
tied are supposed to obtain a full share of the common good a magical sounding
name: the "invisible hand."

Of course, the process did not happen, and when the nature of industrial
production made it difficult for workers, forbidden by law to form unions, to
protect the value of their labor, their only possession, their poverty and desperation made a mockery of the claim that government was attaining its end,
the common good. Only those who did not depend on the invisible hand were
happy with its magical role in justifying government's failure to attend to the
suffering of the people.

Marx, inflamed over this suffering and over the narrowness of the de facto
focus of government on the economically predominant classes, sought a solution. Marxism is just one of a group of efforts to bring back into the common
good the working-class segment of the true "common." Its failures have led
most "Marxist" states to incorporate much more freedom in their economies
until some, like Nicaragua, set the state-operated segment of the economy at
only 40 percent of the total. When one compares this to the U.S. economy,
which, including defense, is about 30 percent state-operated, one wonders what
the terms "Marxist" and "capitalist" mean. But when one sees the blood shed,
and the disastrous economic experiments involved in early efforts to install
"pure" Marxism, and the blood being shed today by right-wing governments
to prevent the refocusing of the government and the economy on the common
good, there is reason to be concerned about how such terms, and the vestiges
of ideology they represent, function in the attainment of the common good.

Like means themselves, ideologies about means must be subordinated to the end. The citizen and policymaker must think about the realistic capacity of the ideology to provide for the common good. For all the noble aspiration of Marx to do justice to the working class, ultimately a government and an economy have to be yoked together in a fashion that will provide enough of the material needs of humans, widely enough distributed, so that the rudiments of a human life are available to all. "Placing the means of production in the hands of the working class" is a slogan for placing them in the hands of a bureaucratic state. No justified hope that a state could successfully take over those economic functions existed. It was another pipe dream, another omniscient benefactor. But if one can condemn the right for not loving the common good or leaving it to the mercy of the invisible hand, the love of the common good in leftist ideologies is not much better if the *means* by which that common good will be served are left to untested fantasies, such as reeducation of mankind to be able to work long and hard without the incentive of betterment of one's condition. The Marxist appeal to this utopian selflessness is as dangerous a pipe dream as the appeal to an inevitable "trickle down" in a system that is allowed to use all the forces of government and economics to stem that trickle in order to "remain competitive."

While working in Congress, I had experience with very costly government programs aimed, at least by public proclamation, at the common good of other nations, namely, foreign agricultural development aid. Here repeated failures were tied to the pipe dreams of both the left and the right. On the left the pipe dream was that benevolent bureaucrats who did not know the poor, their needs, or their resources could construct projects that would help them. On the right the pipe dream was that massively expensive, energy/capital-intensive projects left in the hands of the rich and powerful would trickle down to the poor. And both types were affected by a shared pipe dream, that the poor would work to maintain a project, after outside aid was terminated, which did not benefit them.

Why would such pipe dreams be entertained? Because the centrally planned and/or massively energy-intensive projects were the only ones the foreign-aid institutions, like the Agency for International Development (AID), and their experts knew how to construct. So they were moved more by a desire to be active as instruments than by love of the end, that is, the common good of the poor. I gave a paper detailing proven development strategies in which the poor had a greater role and chance to benefit and which required a very responsive decentralized bureaucracy. An AID officer came to me after and said, "Those strategies assume that the agency field agents care about the poor. They are not there because they care about the poor. They are career foreign service officers and are simply climbing a career ladder. They will leave the country as soon as a better post opens up. We have to keep a tight bureaucratic control over them or they will really screw up."

I felt like saying, "Well, then, why don't you just get out of the business, since there is no way in Washington you can really know what the poor out there need." It should be noted that the failure is not traceable just to a faulty intention by our centralized bureaucracy (for example, the desire not to benefit the poor but to enlist the country on our side of some East-West struggle) but to the omniscient-leader (or bureaucracy) error of Hobbes and Marx.

I believe that Marx did not sense the implausibility of his project because his driving motivation was not love of the common good, but hatred, a desire to strike a blow against the enemy. And I believe the "abolition of private property" can be understood and criticized in just that way. It did not speak of the real end, nor refer to any constructive means to attain it.

But this is a danger every policymaker can face. A candidate for the Supreme Court confessed recently that his earlier writings opposing legally enforced equal access to public commercial establishments were based on a "libertarian pipe dream." Quite so. A hatred of government interference is not by itself constructive of the common good. Each act of government must be examined to see whether the tension between autonomy and legal restraints is respected. A debasing loss of autonomy for a trivial advance of some other good is as wrong as a serious harm to some good (say, self-esteem) to avoid a minor restraint on some group's autonomy. Remember, both personal autonomy and freedom from arbitrary public humiliation are elements of the common good. But the libertarian pipe dream, which would deprive the state of its ability to require contributions to the common good or so restrict the definition of that common good that it would not include protecting citizens against debasing public humiliation, or to imagine that commercial establishments which indulge in such humiliations will "automatically" eventually go out of business, is a heartless pipe dream.

Each new regulation or deregulation has to be realistically evaluated against its impact on the common good. And self-esteem, with its requirement that citizens not be publicly humiliated, must not be seen as part of the "good" only by those who do not expect to be so humiliated.

THE END MUST GOVERN THE MEANS

Human Sciences and Political Prudence

When I say, "Every deregulation must be evaluated against its impact on the common good," I am asking for a prediction. Such predictions, when reasonable, are based on historically experienced and tested general principles about human behavior both individual and collective. That is, we must have some "science" or knowledge of human nature; the most variable and resistant to prediction of any subject of study. The advantage is that we know this subject inside and out. We know our history and we see patterns. And, unlike in other sciences, we can understand those patterns as manifestations of reasons, motives, and impulses we ourselves feel. Political theory and action that does not draw upon this knowledge of human nature, or invents a fictitious nature, like an omniscient monarch or a selfless working class to fit prechosen political/economic structures, or chooses means to the common good of humans which debase the natural needs of humans, is sinning against the prime virtue of political life, after love of the common good, namely, prudence.

Prudence in the Shaping of Human Behavior

Prudence is the careful study of the available means to achieve some end; informed and unbiased comparison of those means with a view to selecting those with maximum ability to reach the end and with minimum costs or undesirable side-effects; and, finally, choice and firm application in action. In dealing with purely material sciences for creating material objects, prudence might be called technology policy. That term sounds a little harsh when applied to humans, but using the idea of technology policy helps us understand what political prudence requires, and to understand some of the more obvious mistakes in political action.

Prudence as a Source of Limits on Policy

To repair a mildly damaged new car, we do not use the hood as a work-bench to straighten out bent parts. We do not use means that damage the end. We try to find a place far from the car in which to apply heat, force, or acids, and we try to use tools and solvents which can absorb the damage of work and be stored away from the car or be discarded after the work is done. But in politics the materials we work with are humans and the workplace is the community. There is no way to physically separate production and finished product. Any means which badly damage humans, or which war against their own best and strongest natural tendencies, are imprudently chosen. Of course, government does involve "shaping" human behavior for the sake of the common good. But we know that reasonable humans are capable of accepting shaping which may require restraining or redirecting natural tendencies, but not utterly suppressing them. It is the function of reason in both personal and communal action not to suppress or deprive natural appetites of their objects but to direct them toward appropriate attainment of them. Hence the principal limitations of the means political prudence can recommend are derived from what sort of beings humans are and how they are likely to react both during and at the end of a time of policy change. Some limits are often enshrined as "sacred" human rights, but others are often ignored by political reformers. For example, prudence severely limits the resort to violence or civil war, because the cooperative work of a free society afterward would be nearly impossible due to abiding resentment and the desire to avenge the killing of friends and family. And since a reasonable autonomy is an important human good, you do not make slaves of the citizens whose common good you seek. You do not use the car's hood for a workbench.

Prudence as Opposed to Class Bias

The positive role is more constructive and more arduous. It is the requirement to be completely unbiased against any effective tools and to be equitable in their application. This is difficult for technical advisors and for political majorities to do, although for different reasons. Locke's elevation of property rights to a degree of sacredness, to be almost higher than that of life itself, can easily become a propertied-class bias against a tool, namely, limitations on property acquisition and use for the common good. It matters little if such a bias is shared by the majority, for majorities can be massively unjust. If property is so important for human dignity, especially to maintain autonomy against the state or against those who control access to basic human needs, then why should the resources of the state be used solely to protect those who already have it, rather than to help others get a share? The majority should know that when the sufferings of those deprived of a share are great enough, their efforts to escape their suffering will begin to damage the common good. Locke's confidence in democracy is permeated with the sense that the propertied classes, whom he favors, will recognize moral limits on their acquisition and use of property. We who enjoy that democracy and the state's defense of our property rights need to keep in mind that moral limits proceed from the damage to the common good done by excessive acquisition.

Prudence Opposed to Ideological Parity

The technical advisor has another problem. When his or her expertise is in politics, economics, agriculture, or engineering, there is a tendency to have a doctrine on what means are "right." If this doctrine excludes means which would work and do not otherwise violate the common good/human nature, why not at least consider them? Listening to a careful lecture on rangeland management, the speaker finally concluded that surrendering that land to short-term market interests would destroy its long-term potential for the common good. "Government restriction of the market uses seems desirable," he said, "but that would be socialism." Having been born and raised in a socialist city (Milwaukee), I wondered why the term "socialist" seemed to end the discussion. Nowadays, usually, city councils simply debate whether private or public ownership of some service will cost more or less or be more or less effective for the common good, hopefully including the service employees, and go with the best predictions they can get. That is what prudence dictates; the rest is ideology for its own sake, a sin against prudence. Prudence admits of, and often mandates, ideological inconsistency, because it is moved by love of mankind over any loyalty to theory.

Professional Imprudence as Bureaucratic Rationality

This kind of imprudence is characterized not by careless thinking but by too careful thinking, that is, the unwillingness to think about a broad enough range of policy options. This unwillingness can be found in almost any policy advisor in a centralized institution who works from a well-established base of expertise, whether scientific, economic, or administrative, to introduce new programs meant to serve the common good. It is an unwillingness that would never be called "ideological." It has a more insidious name: "rational." Let me describe it.

Policy tools of choice, for a new program or reform, must be those the government expert, either in Washington or in the field, can wield with confidence, based on a body of knowledge that is already grasped by the expert, and reliably applicable over time and in many places. Such tools must be plannable in advance and allow for budgetary and deadline estimates.

When I began my work in Washington, my background in the philosophy of science led me to take a special interest in applied science advisors in government policy. Science prides itself in its rationality, and the advisors tended to blame "politicians" for failures. Yet good arguments were given for the need to change the applied science tools themselves. Usually the advisors in power would resist, characterizing the innovators as irrational, soft-headed, and unscientific. Thus to solve international tensions, military weapons and massive "modern" agricultural projects rather than negotiations and village-scale low-tech farmer-operated projects are chosen respectively by the military and U.S. agricultural advisors. In health we get heart transplants for heavy smokers and high-tech cures rather than routine prenatal checks for the poor, which would be much cheaper and prevent more illness. What stunned me is the evidence that the "rationality" of the high-tech advisors is never shaken by evidence of repeated failure of their tools.

If this kind of rationality governs the choice of tools to improve the well-being of the poor or the lower economic classes, it is almost a guarantee of massive ineffectiveness, inefficiency, and failure. Since such failure cannot be admitted by the experts, it will lead to massive denials and ultimate abandonment of the effort to serve the common good by the bureaucracy. Why? Principally because the "body of knowledge" does not exist. Those parts of it that could exist because they are constant, such as the caloric and nutrient needs of the hungry, are rarely collected in usable form by centralized institutions or scholars. They might know how much humans need, but they don't know how much these humans, in this place, are getting already. The same is true with programs in health, housing, employment, and schooling. This has been recognized for a long time and led to a principle of political prudence called "subsidiarity." Subsidiarity states that any government action should be planned and carried out at the lowest level possible, that is, closest to the field of actual need and use, where the increase in the common good is to occur. I *believe that it has not been impressed on scientific advisors that they are professionally tempted to prefer models of technology that are antisubsidiary.* And this temptation leads them to join the resistance to political subsidiarity, which results in an antiprudential bias against whole genera of promising tools.

But the resistance to this principle is as massive as it is unconscious. Consider what subsidiarity would require if any federal support, even the most string-free, were to be given: Knowledge and ranking of local community needs and active community possession and maintenance of any changes will occur only if there is a community, that is, a cohesive and democratically governed group to integrate the benefits into an ongoing communal structure. The local agency will often have to help locate or even form such a community. Then this community, working with the local agency, will have to continually supply information and leadership to assist in the gradual adjustment, and frequent changes of plans, as the community itself begins to discover its needs. These latter can change overnight due, for example, to the closure of a large plant in the area.

It is important to remember that most good enjoyed by humans is enjoyed on the communal level, and the final end of destruction of the common good is dissolution of community. This means that the most serious wounds in the common good exist on the communal level and it is there the healing must start. But my sketch of communal development makes clear why the central bureaucracy expert will be biased against it. First of all, the expert becomes a passive receiver of information and initial plans. The expert cannot offer a single plan that is applicable to many areas over a large period of time. The expert will not be able to predict how long things will take, what the outcome will be in any detail, or how much a total project will cost. In short, the expert will no longer be an expert, will not be intellectually or administratively "in charge," will no longer have the image of "have expertise, will travel." The need to learn interactively with the client while "on the job" simply destroys the traditional image of the expert.

Subsidiarity and the facts of communal improvement are particularly difficult for "liberal" policymakers, because it so clearly limits what they can do with existing policy tools from research laboratories, policy think-tanks, and academic expertise. These institutions, although "spiritually" committed to the common good and to doing good where it is most needed, are no more accustomed to the role-reversal, "learn from the client" or "learn by doing" approach than those who have abandoned the effort to reach actual human communities.

After studying the nutritional needs of families of the growing numbers of unemployed in his heavily industrial district, the very liberal congressman I worked for finally had to say to his people, "You must plan and operate the marketbasket, gleaning, home/communal-canning, and nutritional-monitoring programs yourselves. I might be able to increase Department of Agriculture surplus food availability and to defend the Food Stamp program against more cuts, but I cannot even guarantee that." It might sound like the congressman took a very conservative "let-private-charitable-agencies-take-care-of-social-welfare" approach, but the fact was he could not find in the arsenal of tools at his disposal any which were not already biased in favor of top-down, hierarchical, centrally controlled, nonparticipatory scientific, technological, and administrative approaches. This bias reflects the character of the institutions that train and/or employ the wielders of these tools. These institutions rarely know anything about the communities they are placed in.

These comments will lead some to say, "That only proves what we have been saying. The government should get out of social welfare." But that amounts to saying that the goal of government is not the common good. And this will not return the government to a kind of neutral, equitable passivity. The supposition of such passivity is a delusional ignoring history and human nature. The state will remain active—and passive—depending on the needs and interests of those classes and groups with which the government agencies are in contact.

By now the painful dimensions of true political prudence will be clear. Not only will the policymaker have to guard against political and "expert" biases limiting the choice of means; he or she must fight for the development of more truly common-good-oriented tools in all government-supported institutions.

There will be many fine objections to the opinions just stated, most of which, I would predict, will be made by persons whose careers and expertise are formed and exercised in precisely the kinds of institutions I have criticized. In the face of this kind of debate, there are several arguments to underpin what I have said: One is from unexamined history—how often the best intentioned efforts at serving the true common good (as opposed to serving only the powerful) have failed. Why should we expect them to succeed now?

But since the sad history may be explained away as evidence of need of minor adjustments in current tools, the need for a wider ranging exercise of political prudence must be based on two further general claims: The first is about the affective powers of humans, their ability to love equitably. Without an explicit effort to reach the groups beyond the institutions and bring in the clients who will represent their communities and help develop the tools to construct missing elements of the common good, we will not see the desired improvement of political tools. Locke could not have made the general claim better, as he said in a slightly different context in your readings:

> . . . [F]or every one in that state [of nature] . . . passion and revenge is apt to carry them too far and with too much heat in their own cases, as well as negligence and unconcernedness to make them too remiss in other men's.

Therefore, political prudence requires that the planner reflect on his or her own affective limitations, and call into the prudential survey members of the beneficiary group, to democratize the planning because the beneficiaries are far more likely to provide the practical love of the good being sought, given that it is a good for themselves.

The second general claim, derived in part from the philosophy of technology, calls for the same democratization of political action by pointing out a pervasive limitation in the intellectual component of policy tools. These tools may seem to be based on "pure science," objective experience, and carefully evaluated practice. But when one realizes that the expertise one is habitually drawing on has not developed any of its science or practice in the communities it expects to assist, one should see that a blindness may exist which the most passionate love of common good cannot penetrate. To ignore these warnings of history and philosophy is to but repeat one of the underlying errors of both Hobbes and Marx, the ultimate reliance on the fantasy of an omniscient and benevolent few, and it matters little whether they be called oligarchs or technocrats.

In spite of my harsh judgment of Hobbes, one aspect of his writing should impress us, and that is the brutishness with which mankind can seem to be colored in times of increasing civic unrest. But Aristotle's warnings throughout the *Politics* on how that unrest is related to the condition of the poor and the size of the middle class should be heeded. We should be extremely concerned about the increasing numbers of lower-middle-class people falling into poverty, a statistic that is not revealed by "unemployment" figures. The remaining middle class will imperceptibly be led toward a choice between more economic justice for the poor and an authoritarian police state along Hobbesian lines, together with a handy and inconsistent philosophy of human nature that says the poor are naturally lawless, when it was, in fact, the middle class's own neglect that forced the poor to choose between self-preservation and social virtues.

PRACTICAL DEMOCRACY IN A GIANT REPUBLIC

The gravest danger of the active citizen is a kind of philosophic pessimism about weak human nature when the best candidate is not elected. Philosophers forget the importance of the nonintellectual component of citizenship, untiring participation. It is simply misguided to imagine that democracy can work with the election of good candidates. It is the nature of democracy and of the human nature of representatives within it that they will respond to the intelligent, persistent voices of their constituents who can demonstrate that they represent a considerable voting segment of their districts. There is no lobby more powerful than the citizens' lobby, especially of groups with long-term residential and communal/cultural roots, notably those connected with churches, schools, business, and labor in the district. Although there are grave dangers associated with the incredible sums of money flowing into election campaigns, it is ironic that unless citizens' lobbies make clear that they want campaign spending reform, only a rare candidate will be secure enough in his or her seat to dispense with such monies. Public interest lobbies which are not heavily represented by a local chapter with a permanent and large membership will never be able to match in dollars the contributions of groups who have high-volume financial affairs that can be affected by government action.

An example of this is the history of pesticide legislation which I covered. Originally the natural constituents of these laws were farmers, who stood to gain or lose the most by useless or dangerous pesticides. But eventually only the persistent constituents, chemical companies and environmentalists, were actively considered in the law and its administration. We saw the enforcers of the law resort to another "invisible hand" to care for the neglected constituents, the farmers. The Environmental Protection Agency (EPA) did not even require that the usefulness ("efficacy") of pesticides be reported! And young lawyers working for another neglected constituency were shocked when a liberal congressman's aide felt they were unreasonable in insisting that not even a small number of farmworker deaths be required before a chemical be restricted. Not even as few as six deaths? "Everyone has to compromise!" said the offended aide when the lawyers treated his suggestion as monstrous.

But, of course, money interests are persistent and they have the time to spend. In our office the chief legislative aide would sum up our need to allot our time justly with the admonition, "Remember, we are not here to help the rich get richer."

Yet is it not as desperate as it might seem, for all these monies have one object—competitive election campaigns in which the "price" of a vote goes up with each dollar added to the rival campaign chests. Remember, the campaign money does not buy votes directly but rather expensive media access to the voters. But the citizens' lobbies can offer the candidate favorable and informed access to their membership for only the price of doing the job of representation well. The lobby needs only to communicate regularly with the representative and his or her local and Washington staff by letter and phone, especially at the time of key committee and floor votes; to invite the representative to speak to the group several times each term; to discuss the representative's position intelligently in their local and national newsletters and form appropriate coalitions at election time; and, if the candidate of a specific party seems on the balance to be intent on the common good, to send members into the regular party apparatus to work as volunteers at election time. (I wish to discourage here "single-issue" campaigns, since they will rarely encompass the common good.)

It is notable that specific votes and committee work by representatives on legislation are what guide our republic, including foreign policy, which can cost the common-good treasury so many wasted dollars. When faced with policy decisions, everyone in a congressional office is far more impressed by informed constituent communications than by any special money interests. The former affirms them, rewards them, and augurs well for the continuation of their boss's and their own jobs. The latter bores them, since it is usually old stuff, and depresses them in the case that it tends to pull the representative away from the common good.

When we read with approval the rosy picture of democracy in Locke, we have to remind ourselves that there is no such thing as democracy that is not "grass-roots" democracy. The common good exists, grows, or dies at the grass roots and democracy's building or degrading of that common good occurs not at election time but during the legislative year. Hence the simple philosophic recommendations I and other philosophers make must offer intuitively clear constants and clear guidance for the actions of change at the grass-roots level. The rest ends up on the library shelf.

DISCUSSION QUESTIONS

1. What is democracy?
2. What is capitalism? In your estimation, is it compatible with democracy? Defend your answer.
3. What is communism? Is it compatible with democracy? Defend your answer.
4. Discuss Hobbes's view of human nature especially as it relates to the form of government he defends.
5. What does Hobbes mean by a "law of nature"? Cite and discuss three such laws as set forth by Hobbes.
6. What criticism(s) does Dundon make of Hobbes? Do you agree with Dundon? Defend your answer.
7. Discuss Locke's characterization of a state of nature. Contrast it with that given by Hobbes.
8. Discuss Locke's concept of private property.
9. According to Locke, what defects in a state of nature does a state with an organized government serve to remedy?
10. What reason(s) does Locke have for insisting upon rule by the majority?
11. What criticism(s) does Dundon make of Locke? Do you agree with him? Defend your answer.
12. Explain the connection which Marx and Engels claim exists between the development of modern industry within a capitalist society and the exploitation of the working class.
13. Discuss some of the ways in which Marx and Engels think capitalism exploits the working class and their families.
14. In what respects, if any, do you think Marx's and Engels's indictment of capitalism applies today? Defend your answer.
15. What criticism(s) does Dundon make of Marx? Do you agree with him? Defend your answer.
16. What is Dundon's main criticism of congressional politics?
17. Discuss some of Dundon's main recommendations for addressing this problem. In what respects, if any, do you agree with him? In what respects, if any, do you disagree with him? Defend your answers.
18. In the light of your studies in this chapter, what change(s), if any, would you make in government? Defend your answer.

III

LOGIC AND SCIENCE

7

LOGIC AND COMPUTER PROGRAMMING

Logic is a branch of philosophy that studies the rules and methods for correctly deriving (inferring) conclusions from sets of evidence called premises. As Wesley Salmon discusses in the first selection, logic studies two kinds of inference, those that are *inductive* and those that are *deductive*. The ancient Greek philosopher, Aristotle, can be rightfully considered the founder of deductive logic. For Aristotle, this type of logic, in the form of what he called *the categorical syllogism,* provided a necessary organ or tool for the acquisition of knowledge. The study of deductive logic was for him, "the science of sciences," which could be harnessed for the discovery of truth in all areas of scientific research and inquiry. Viewed in this light, it is easy to see why logic gets at the core of philosophy, for philosophers are, after all, first and foremost, seekers of wisdom and truth.

The study of deductive logic did not undergo much development beyond Aristotle's study until relatively recently. It was not until the nineteeth and twentieth centuries that substantial developments occurred. Among those who pioneered this expansion were Augustus DeMorgan (1806–1871), George Boole (1815–1864), John Venn (1834–1923), Gottlob Frege (1848–1925), and Bertrand Russell (1872–1970). Under the auspices of these and other philosophers and mathematicians, deductive logic became more "symbolic" in its approach. That is, through the development of a special technical language into which ordinary language could be translated, the statements and inferences of ordinary language could be handled with greater clarity and precision.

Perhaps nowhere are the contributions of deductive logic more evident than in the computer technology that we have come to rely upon in conducting the affairs of daily living. These contributions are at work when we go to the bank or ATM to withdraw from or add to our accounts, make a telephone call or send an e-mail or fax, travel by air or ground, surf the Net, check the electronic library indices or databases; prepare a paper on a word processor, play an electronic game, and sundry other commonplace activities. All such technology is driven by computer programs or software (as well as digital circuitry in its hardware) that represent applications, principles, methods, and techniques of deductive logic. By inspection of some elementary code, this can be grasped, even by a novice. Consider, for example, the following simple, linear program (written in QuickBasic), which assesses voter eligibility:

```
REM Asks following question and gets input
from user.
Print "Were you born in the United States?
(Answer 'Yes' or 'No')
    INPUT Answer$

REM Defines a variable x according to user's
response.
IF Answer$ = "Yes" THEN
    Let x = 1
    Go to Voter.Status
ELSE
    Let x = 0
END IF
REM Asks next question if and only if answer
to first question was no.
Print "Are you an American citizen? (Answer
'Yes' or 'No')
    INPUT Answer$

REM Defines a variable y according to user's
response.
IF Answer$ = "Yes" THEN
    Let y = 1
ELSE
    Let y = 0
END IF

REM Reports voter eligibility information
to user.
Voter.Status:
IF x = 1 or y = 1 THEN
    Print "You're eligible to vote in the
    United States"
ELSE
    Print "Sorry, you're ineligible to vote
    in the United States"
END IF
```

When this program is run, it asks users if they were born in the United States. If they say yes, then the program tells them that they are eligible to vote in the United States. Otherwise, the program asks a second question. It asks users if they are citizens of the United States. If they say yes, then the program tells them they are eligible to vote. Otherwise the computer tells them they are ineligible.

Notice the use of such logical concepts as *or, if . . . then . . .,* and *else* as well as variables (*x* and *y*) which are set to specific values under given truth conditions. All of these concepts are fundamental to the study of logic. Those who do not understand their meaning would find it difficult or impossible to create a working program.

The meanings of truth-functional connectives such as *or, and, if . . . then . . .,* and *not* can be precisely defined in terms of truth and falsehood. In calling these *truth-functional* connectives what is meant is that their truth values are functions of the truth values of the individual statements they connect. For example, the truth of the compound statement, "Aristotle invented syllogistic logic *and* Bertrand Russell invented truth tables" depends upon the truth values of each individual statement conjoined by *and.* If each is true (as is here the case), then their conjunction is true, and if at least one conjunction is false, then the whole conjunction is false.

In computer programming, although not necessarily in ordinary language, *else* statements are true if, and only if, at least one of the given alternatives is true but *not both* are true. In contrast, *or* statements are still true if both alternatives are true. Logicians sometimes make this same distinction by speaking about *inclusive* and *exclusive* senses of *or.* The distinction can be clarified by means of *truth tables.*

Truth tables provide a method for defining precisely the meaning of truth functional connectives. The method includes a *matrix* containing all possible combinations of truth values for all variables, and a *defining column* which specifies the value of the truth function for each combination. Where the letters *p* and *q* represent variables (placeholders for statements), and T = True and F = False, the respective truth tables for *or* and the computer language (exclusive) sense of *else* are as follows:

MATRIX	DEFINING COLUMN
p q	p or q
T T	T
T F	T
F T	T
F F	F

p q	p else q
T T	F
T F	T
F T	T
F F	F

Note that, in the first line of the truth table for *or,* the statement *p or q* is true when both *p* and *q* are true. In contrast, the first line of the *else* table shows that the statement *p else q* is false under the same truth value assignments.

For example, the *else* under Voter.Status in the code of our voter eligibility program causes the program to ignore one alternative when the other is true. Suppose the first alternative, $x = 1$ or $y = 1$, is true, say because $x = 1$. This causes the program to tell the user that he or she is eligible to vote. But since one cannot be *both* eligible and ineligible to vote, the *else* instructs the program to ignore the second alternative.

Look again under Voter.Status at the antecedent condition $x = 1$ or $y = 1$. As noted, if this statement is true, then the user is eligible to vote. But when is it true? Knowing that it is true when *at least one* (or both) of the two variables equals one (notice lines 1–3 of the truth table for *or*) makes it possible to set the program up so that it always skips the second question when the first is answered in the affirmative. Further, if the user were, by mistake, to put an "and" in place of the "or," then the program would malfunction because the "and" would require that both questions be answered in the affirmative whereas the second question would never be asked if the first were answered in the affirmative. In computer programming, a little bit of logic goes a long way!

In the second and third selections of this chapter, some basic logical concepts are introduced that have significant applications to computer programming. The second selection, by Howard Kahane, explores the logic of categorical syllogism, a form of class logic developed by Aristotle. The third selection, by Stephen Barker, explores further aspects of truth-functional logic.

The significance of the aforementioned logic is brought to light in the Practice section of this chapter by Greg Tropea, a professor of philosophy who also works as a computer software developer. As Tropea shows through discussion of actual projects, the training he received as a student of philosophy, especially logic, provided him with a useful foundation for doing computer programming. For example, he illustrates how knowledge of categorical logic helps in development of databases, and how truth-functional logic can help in creating code, troubleshooting, and organizing data.

It is significant that the skills acquired through training in philosophy in general, and logic in particular, may not only be instrumental in the production of code. According to Tropea, from the creation of databases to Web sites, these skills also play an important role in defining specific tasks that a contemplated program needs to perform, and in devising strategies for attacking the problem at hand. "There is," he states, "no substitute for following the logic of a problem in a way that is appropriate to the application one has in mind." Since the design stage of software production ultimately directs the production of code and accounts for the success of the application, the contributions of philosophical training to this stage cannot be underestimated.

It is noteworthy that Tropea's entry into computer programming was not a result of formal education in computer science. Rather, he began with his training in philosophy. As Tropea attests, there is a "natural" fit between computers and philosophy insofar as computers are tools for knowledge acquisition and philosophers are knowledge workers who are interested both in the acquisition of knowledge as well as the process of knowledge acquistion itself (epistemology). This natural fit has led some philosophers, typically ones who teach at major research institutions, to do work in artificial intelligence such as computer simulation of human thought processes (see chapter 12) and natural language processing. As Tropea also points out, there is also a current among philosophers who divide their time teaching philosophy (especially logic) and doing software development to focus on *educational* software. This focus has led to the development of a host of software products including ones that aid in the teaching of logic and critical thinking courses taught at colleges and universities. One example is afforded by programs that give students practice in working logic problems and that grade and administer tests and homework assignments (for example, the *Logic Works* developed by Rob Brady at Stetson University). Another is an interactive artificial intelligence technology that helps students locate fallacies in written documents (the *Belief-Scan Fallacy Finder* that I have developed).

Notwithstanding these and other contributions of philosophers to software development, Tropea addresses a still-popular conception that philosophical and technological questions are separate and that the former is not relevant to the latter. Against the view that technological questions are always *empirical* questions that exclude philosophical interpretation, he produces the following valid syllogism:

> All questions decided by rational application of subjective principles are philosophical questions.

> Some technological questions are decided by rational application of subjective principles.

> Therefore, some technological questions are philosophical questions.

As shall become apparent from Howard Kahane's discussion of syllogistic logic, this argument is valid, which means that if both premises are true, then so too is the conclusion. But are the premises true?

Tropea attempts to defend the second premise by providing examples of technological questions that are addressed by rationally applying "subjective principles." For example, he argues that choosing a style for naming variables, choosing a classification system for database design, and making decisions that affect the user's degree of comfort with the software—which may range from decisions about how to make the software user-friendly to ones about choosing a company to distribute it.

It might be argued, however, that the first premise is false and that the examples Tropea provides do not qualify as philosophical questions. For example, the type of variable nomenclature selected may involve a decision about what style would be most *expedient* for those charged with creating future revisions, but such decisions would be more empirical in character than philosophical.

Still, for those such as Tropea who appear to see software design as engendering artistic expression, the answer to the technological question may call for an aesthetic judgment that is inevitably anchored to a philosophical perspective about the nature and value of aesthetic objects.

Given Tropea's emphasis on imagination, insight, and creativity in computer programming, it is evident why he does not want to treat technological questions as narrow, empirical ones. For him, those who come to the fore of software development with a keen sense for the philosophical and logical are more likely to create something of superior value, for this is, he contends, precisely what is "needed to bridge the emptiness that lies between a bare, generically configured machine and a useful information-processing tool that falls readily to hand."

ISSUES

WESLEY C. SALMON

THE SCOPE OF LOGIC

When people make statements, they may offer evidence to support them or they may not. A statement that is supported by evidence is the conclusion of an argument, and logic provides tools for the analysis of arguments. Logical analysis is concerned with the relationship between a conclusion and the evidence given to support it.

When people reason, they make inferences. These inferences can be transformed into arguments, and the tools of logic can then be applied to the resulting arguments. In this way, the inferences from which they originate can be evaluated.

Logic deals with arguments and inferences. One of its main purposes is to provide methods for distinguishing those which are logically correct from those which are not.

ARGUMENT

In one of his celebrated adventures, Sherlock Holmes comes into possession of an old felt hat. Although Holmes is not acquainted with the owner of the hat, he tells Dr. Watson many things about the man—among them, that he is highly

---

SOURCE: Wesley C. Salmon, *Logic,* 2nd ed. pp. 1–5, 14–15, 18. © 1984. Reprinted by permission of Prentice-Hall, Inc., Upper Saddle River, NJ.

intellectual. This assertion, as it stands, is unsupported. Holmes may have evidence for his statement, but so far he has not given it.

Dr. Watson, as usual, fails to see any basis for Holmes's statement, so he asks for substantiation. "For answer Holmes clapped the hat upon his head. It came right over the forehead and settled upon the bridge of his nose. 'It is a question of cubic capacity,' said he; 'a man with so large a brain must have something in it.'" [1] Now, the statement that the owner of the hat is highly intellectual is no longer an unsupported assertion. Holmes has given the evidence, so his statement is supported. It is the conclusion of an argument. . . .

The term "argument" is a basic one in logic. We must explain its meaning. In ordinary usage, the term "argument" often signifies a dispute. In logic, it does not have this connotation. As we use the term, an argument can be given to justify a conclusion, whether or not anyone openly disagrees. Nevertheless, intelligent disputation—as opposed to the sort of thing that consists of loud shouting and namecalling—does involve argument in the logical sense. Disagreement is an occasion for summoning evidence if an intelligent resolution is sought.

Arguments are often designed to convince, and this is one of their important and legitimate functions; however, logic is not concerned with the persuasive power of arguments. Arguments which are logically incorrect often do convince, while logically impeccable arguments often fail to persuade. Logic is concerned with an objective relation between evidence and conclusion. An argument may be logically correct even if nobody recognizes it as such; or it may be logically incorrect even if everyone accepts it.

Roughly speaking, an argument is a conclusion standing in relation to its supporting evidence. More precisely, *an argument is a group of statements standing in relation to each other.*[2] An argument consists of one statement which is the conclusion and one or more statements of supporting evidence. The statements of evidence are called "premises." There is no set number of premises which every argument must have, but there must be at least one.

When Watson requested a justification for the statement about the owner of the hat, Holmes gave an indication of an argument. Although he did not spell out his argument in complete detail, he did say enough to show what it would be. We can reconstruct it as follows:

a]   1. This is a large hat.
       2. Someone is the owner of this hat.
       3. The owners of large hats are people with large heads.
       4. People with large heads have large brains.
       5. People with large brains are highly intellectual.
       6. The owner of this hat is highly intellectual.

This is an argument; it consists of six statements. The first five statements are the premises; the sixth statement is the conclusion.

The premises of an argument are supposed to present evidence for the conclusion. Presenting evidence in premises involves two aspects. First, the premises are statements of fact. Second, these facts are offered as *evidence for* the conclusion. There are, consequently, two ways in which the premises may fail to present evidence for the conclusion. First, one or more of the premises may be false. In this case, the *alleged* facts are not facts at all; the *alleged* evidence does not exist. Under these circumstances, we can hardly be said to have good grounds for accepting the conclusion. Second, even if the premises are all true—that is, even if the premises do accurately state the facts—they may not have an appropriate relation to the conclusion. In this case, the facts are as stated in the premises, but these facts are not *evidence for* the conclusion. In order for facts to be evidence for a conclusion they must be properly relevant to that conclusion. Obviously, it will not do merely to give any true statements to support a conclusion. The statements must have some bearing upon that conclusion.

If an argument is offered as a justification of its conclusion, two questions arise. First, are the premises true? Second, are the premises properly related to the conclusion? If either question has a negative answer, the justification is unsatisfactory. It is absolutely essential, however, to avoid confusing these two questions. In logic we are concerned with the second question only. When an argument is subjected to logical analysis, the question of relevance is at issue. *Logic deals with the relation between premises and conclusion, not with the truth of the premises.*

One of our basic purposes is to provide methods of distinguishing between logically correct and incorrect arguments. *The logical correctness or incorrectness of an argument depends solely upon the relation between premises and conclusion.* In a logically correct argument, the premises have the following relation to the conclusion: *If the premises were true, this fact would constitute good grounds for accepting the conclusion as true.* If the facts alleged by the premises of a logically correct argument are, indeed, facts, then they do constitute good evidence for the conclusion. That is what we shall mean by saying that the premises of a logically correct argument *support* the conclusion. The premises of an argument support the conclusion if the truth of the premises would constitute good reason for asserting that the conclusion is true. When we say that the premises of an argument support the conclusion, we are *not* saying that the premises are true; we are saying that there would be good evidence for the conclusion *if* the premises were true.

The premises of a logically incorrect argument may *seem* to support the conclusion, but actually they do not. Logically incorrect arguments are called "fallacious." Even if the premises of a logically incorrect argument were true, this would not constitute good grounds for accepting the conclusion. The premises of a logically incorrect argument do not have the proper relevance to the conclusion.

Since the logical correctness or incorrectness of an argument depends solely upon the relation between premises and conclusion, *logical correctness or incorrectness is completely independent of the truth of the premises.* In particular, it is wrong to call an argument "fallacious" just because it has one or more false premises. Consider the argument concerning the hat in example *a*. You may already have recognized that there is something wrong with the argument from the size of the hat to the intellectuality of the owner; you might have been inclined to reject it on the grounds of faulty logic. It would have been a mistake to do so. The argument is logically correct—it is not fallacious—but it does have at least one false premise. As a matter of fact, not everyone who has a large brain is highly intellectual. However, you should be able to see that the conclusion of this argument would have to be true if all of the premises were true. It is not the business of logic to find out whether people with large brains are intellectual; this matter can be decided only by scientific investigation. Logic *can* determine whether these premises support their conclusion.

As we have just seen, a logically correct argument may have one or more false premises. A logically incorrect or fallacious argument may have true premises; indeed, it may have a true conclusion as well.

> *b*]   *Premises:* All mammals are mortal.
>   All dogs are mortal.
>   *Conclusion:* All dogs are mammals.

This argument is obviously fallacious. The fact that the premises and the conclusion are all true statements does not mean that the premises support the conclusion. They do not. . . . For the present, we can indicate the fallacious character of *b* by pointing out that the premises would still be true even if dogs were reptiles (not mammals). The conclusion would then be false. It happens that the conclusion, "All dogs are mammals," is true, but there is nothing in the premises which provides any basis for it. . . .

DEDUCTIVE AND INDUCTIVE ARGUMENTS

What we have said so far applies to all types of arguments. The time has come to distinguish two major types: *deductive* and *inductive*. There are logically correct and incorrect forms of each. Here are correct examples.

> *a*]   *Deductive:* Every mammal has a heart.
>   All horses are mammals.
>   Every horse has a heart.

> *b*]   *Inductive:* Every horse that has ever been observed has had
>   a heart.
>   Every horse has a heart.

There are certain fundamental characteristics which distinguish between correct deductive and correct inductive arguments. We will mention two primary ones.

Deductive	*Inductive*
I. If all of the premises are true, the conclusion *must be true*.	I. If all of the premises are true, the conclusion is probably true but not necessarily true.
II. All of the information or factual content in the conclusion was already contained, at least implicitly, in the premises.	II. The conclusion contains information not present, even implicitly, in the premises.

It is not difficult to see that the two examples satisfy these conditions.

Characteristic I

The only way in which the conclusion of *a* could be false—that is, the only possible circumstance under which it could fail to be true that every horse has a heart—is that either not all horses are mammals or not all mammals have hearts. In other words, for the conclusion of *a* to be false, one or both of the premises must be false. If both premises are true, the conclusion must be true. On the other hand, in *b*, it is quite possible for the premise to be true and the conclusion false. This would happen if at some future time, a horse is observed which does not have a heart. The fact that no horse without a heart has yet been observed is some evidence that none ever will be. In this argument, the premise does not necessitate the conclusion, but it does lend some weight to it.

Characteristic II

When the conclusion of *a* says that all horses have hearts, it says something which has already been said, in effect, by the premises. The first premise says that all mammals have hearts, and that includes all horses according to the second premise. In this argument, as in all other correct deductive arguments, the conclusion states explicitly or reformulates information already given in the premises. It is for this reason that deductive arguments also have characteristic I. The conclusion must be true if the premises are true, because the conclusion says nothing which was not already stated by the premises. On the other hand, the premise of our inductive argument *b* refers only to horses that have been observed up to the present, while the conclusion refers to horses that have not yet been observed. Thus, the conclusion makes a statement which goes beyond the information given in the premise. It is because the conclusion says something not given in the premise that the conclusion might be false even though the premise is true. The additional content of the conclusion might be false, rendering the conclusion as a whole false. Deductive and inductive arguments fulfill different functions. The deductive argument is designed to make explicit the content of the premises; the inductive argument is designed to extend the range of our knowledge.

We may summarize by saying that the inductive argument expands the content of premises by sacrificing necessity, whereas the deductive argument achieves necessity by sacrificing any expansion of content.

It follows immediately from these characteristics that deductive correctness (known as *validity*. . . .) is an all or nothing affair. An argument either qualifies fully as a correct deduction or it fails completely; there are no degrees of deductive validity. The premises either completely necessitate the conclusion or they fail entirely to do so. Correct inductive arguments, in contrast, admit of degrees of strength, depending upon the amount of support the premises furnish for the conclusion. There are degrees of probability which the premises of an inductive argument can supply to a conclusion, but the logical necessity which relates premises to conclusion in a deductive argument is never a matter of degree. . . .

You may have noticed, quite correctly, that any inductive argument can be transformed into a deductive argument by the addition of one of more premises. It might, therefore, be tempting to regard inductive arguments as incomplete deductive arguments, rather than an important and distinct type. This would be a mistake. Even though every inductive argument can be made into a deductive argument by the addition of premises, the required premises are often statements whose truth is very doubtful. If we are trying to justify conclusions, it will not do to introduce highly dubious premises. Actually, the kind of argument which extends our knowledge is indispensable. For instance, if no such mode of argument were available, it would be impossible to establish any conclusions about the future on the basis of our experience of the past and present. Without some type of inductive reasoning, we would have no grounds for predicting that night will continue to follow day, that the seasons will continue to occur in their customary sequence, or that sugar will continue to taste sweet. All such knowledge of the future, and much else as well, depends upon the power of inductive arguments to support conclusions that go beyond the data presented in their premises.

NOTES

1. A. Conan Doyle, "The Adventure of the Blue Carbuncle," *Adventures of Sherlock Holmes* (New York and London: Harper & Row, n.d.), p. 157. Direct quotation and use of literary material from this story by permission of the Estate of Sir Arthur Conan Doyle.
2. The term "statement" is used to refer to components of arguments because it is philosophically more neutral than alternatives such as "sentence" or "proposition." No technical definition of "statement" is offered here, because any definition would raise controversies in the philosophy of language which need not trouble the beginner. More sophisticated readers may supply whatever technical definition seems most appropriate to them.

HOWARD KAHANE

ARISTOTELIAN LOGIC

The discipline of logic has existed for over two thousand years, since the first system was developed by Aristotle. It has become customary to apply the term "symbolic" to systems like sentential and predicate logic, and the terms *traditional, Aristotelian,* and *syllogistic* to the earlier systems.

In this part of the text, we present a fairly brief version of traditional logic starting with an account of syllogistic logic.

CATEGORICAL PROPOSITIONS

Syllogistic logic is primarily concerned with *categorical propositions. Categorical propositions* assert or deny relationships between terms or classes. For instance, the sentence "All humans are mortal" is a categorical proposition, and asserts (roughly) that all members of the class of humans are members of the class of mortals.

The term "humans," which designates the class of human beings, is said to be the *subject,* or *subject term,* and the term "mortal," which designates the class of mortals, is said to be the *predicate,* or *predicate term,* of the categorical proposition "All humans are mortal." Similarly, all categorical propositions contain a subject and a predicate, as well as some form of the verb "to be" ("is," "are," and so on) relating the subject and predicate.

There are four kinds of categorical propositions: (1) *universal affirmative,* having the general form "All S are P" (where S denotes some subject class and P some predicate class); (2) *universal negative,* having the general form "No S are P"; (3) *particular affirmative,* having the general form "Some S are P"; and (4) *particular negative,* having the general form "Some S are not P."

It is customary to use the capital letter A in symbolizing universal affirmative propositions. Thus, the universal affirmative "All humans are mortal" is symbolized as *HAM* (where H = "human" and M = "mortal"). Similarly, it is customary to use E for universal negatives, I for particular affirmatives, and O for particular negatives. Thus, the universal negative "No humans are mortal" is symbolized as *HEM*, the particular affirmative "Some humans are mortal" as *HIM,* and the particular negative "Some humans are not mortal" as *HOM.* It also is customary to refer to universal affirmative propositions as A propositions, universal negative propositions as E propositions, and so on.

SOURCE: Howard Kahane, *Logic and Philosophy,* 4th ed. © 1982. Reprinted by permission of Wadsworth Publishing, a division of Thomas Learning.

Notice that A, E, I, and O propositions differ with respect to two kinds of properties, namely, *quality* (being either affirmative or negative) and *quantity* (being either universal or particular). Thus, all I propositions are both *affirmative* (quality) and *particular* (quantity). For example, the I proposition "Some humans are mortal" is *affirmative* (quality), because it *affirms* that some humans are mortal, and *particular* (quantity), because it affirms that *some* (not necessarily all) humans are mortal. On the other hand, all E propositions are both *negative* (quality) and *universal* (quantity). For example, the E proposition "No humans are mortal" is *negative* (quality), because it *denies* that humans are mortal, and *universal* (quantity), because it denies of *all* humans that they are mortal.

The English language, like all natural languages, permits a great deal of variety in the expression of propositions. Take St. Augustine's interesting thesis that all sin is a kind of lying, which can be put into A form as "All sins are lies." We can also express this thesis in English as "Sins are lies," "He who sins, lies," "Sinning is lying," "To sin is to lie," "Anyone who sins, lies," "Whoever sins, lies," and so on. All of these therefore translate into A propositions. . . .

SYLLOGISMS

A *syllogism* is a particular kind of [deductive] argument containing three categorical propositions, two of them premises, one a conclusion.* One of the earliest syllogisms is the following:

> All humans are mortal.
> All Greeks are humans.
> _____
> ∴ All Greeks are mortal.

which can be symbolized as:

> MAP
> SAM
> _____
> ∴ SAP

The term P, the predicate of the conclusion, is said to be the *major term* of the syllogism; the term S, the subject of the conclusion, is said to be the *minor term;* and the term M, which occurs once in each premise but not in the conclusion, is said to be the middle term. Every syllogism has exactly three terms, each one repeated twice (but none repeated twice in the same proposition).

---

*The term "syllogism" can also be applied to other deductive arguments having two premises and a conclusion which, however, do *not* consist entirely of categorical propositions. These arguments are treated in this chapter in Stephen Barker's article, "The Logic of Truth Functions."—ED.

The *mood* of a syllogism is determined by the kind of propositions it contains. For instance, the above syllogism contains three A propositions, and so its mood is AAA. Similarly, the mood for the syllogism which is symbolized as

MAP
SIM
──────
∴ SIP

is AII.

The *figure* of a syllogism is determined by the positions of its major, minor, and middle terms in its premises. There are four figures, namely:

I. M___P   III. M___P
   S___M   M___S
   ∴ S___P   ∴ S___P

II. P___M   IV. P___M
    S___M   M___S
    ∴ S___P   ∴ S___P

Notice that the order of premises is important in determining the mood or the figure of a syllogism. The rule is that the predicate of the conclusion, the major term, must occur in the first premise. A syllogism with its premises in the proper order (and, of course, containing only three terms, each one appearing twice) is said to be in *standard form*.

The *form* of a syllogism is simply the combination of mood and figure. For instance, the two syllogisms discussed above have the forms AAA-I and AII-I respectively, and the syllogism

MAP
MES
──────
∴ SEP

has form AEE-III. (This syllogism happens to be invalid, but invalid syllogisms are still syllogisms.)

Examples:

Some other examples of syllogisms and their forms are:

1. IAO-III: 2. EOO-II:

   MIP   PEM
   MAS   SOM
   ──────   ──────
   ∴ SOP   ∴ SOP

3. AIE-I: 4. AEE-IV:

MAP	PAM
SIM	MES
∴ SEP	∴ SEP

5. EEE-III: 6. EIO-I:

MEP	MEP
MES	SIM
∴ SEP	∴ SOP

FIVE RULES FOR DETERMINING THE VALIDITY OR INVALIDITY OF SYLLOGISMS

[One] method for determining the validity or invalidity of syllogisms and syllogism forms is to use rules stating properties that all valid syllogisms must possess.

But before introducing a set of five rules of this kind, we must discuss the concept of *distribution*. In traditional logic texts, it is usually stated that a term in a proposition is *distributed* if (roughly) it says something about *all* members of the class designated by that term. For instance, the A proposition "All scientists are mathematicians" is said to distribute its subject term, since it says something about *all* scientists (namely that they are mathematicians), but not its predicate term, because it does not say something about *all* mathematicians. (It surely does not say, or imply, that all mathematicians are scientists.)

Traditional logic texts work out the distribution properties of all four kinds of categorical propositions. Letting S stand for subject terms and P for predicate terms, we can summarize the findings of the traditional logician as follows:

TABLE OF DISTRIBUTION

1. A propositions distribute S.
2. E propositions distribute S and P.
3. I propositions distribute neither S nor P.
4. O propositions distribute P.

Most students readily accept the results summarized in the first three lines of this table. But they find the idea expressed on the fourth line, that O propositions distribute their predicate terms, rather counterintuitive. And yet there is a certain plausibility to this idea. For instance, it seems plausible to say that the O proposition "Some scientists are not philosophers" distributes its predicate term, because it says of *all* philosophers that they are not some scientists (that is, that they are excluded from part of the class of scientists). In any event, we must say that O propositions distribute their predicates, or the six rules about to be presented will not function properly.

We now are ready to state a set of six rules for determining the validity of syllogisms. All valid syllogisms must have:

1. A middle term that is distributed at least once.
2. No term distributed in the conclusion that is not distributed in a premise.
3. At least one affirmative (nonnegative) premise.
4. A negative conclusion if and only if one of its premises is negative.
5. Exactly three terms, each one repeated twice.
6. At least one particular premise if the conclusion is particular (that is, at least one I or O premise if the conclusion is an I or O proposition).

Any syllogism that does not have all six of these properties is invalid.*

Examples:

1. The syllogism

All philosophers are mathematicians.	PAM
Some mathematicians are scientists.	MIS
∴ Some scientists are philosophers.	∴ SIP

violates the rule requiring that the middle term be distributed at least once, and hence is invalid.

2. The syllogism

All philosophers are mathematicians.	PAM
All mathematicians are scientists.	MAS
∴ All scientists are philosophers.	∴ SAP

violates the rule requiring that no term be distributed in the conclusion which is not distributed in a premise, and hence is invalid.

3. The syllogism

No mathematicians are philosophers.	MEP
Some scientists are not mathematicians.	SOM
∴ Some scientists are not philosophers.	∴ SOP

violates the rule requiring at least one affirmative premise, and hence is invalid.

---

*According to Kahane, the fifth rule cited above is included in the definition of a syllogism and is therefore unnecessary. It is, however, made explicit here.

4. The syllogism

Some scientists are not mathematicians.	SOM
All mathematicians are philosophers.	MAP
∴ Some scientists are philosophers.	∴ SIP

violates the rule requiring that the conclusion be negative, if a premise is negative, and hence is invalid. (This rule also requires that a premise be negative if the conclusion is negative.)

5. The syllogism

No scientists are mathematicians.
Some philosophers are metaphysicians.

∴ Some philosophers are not scientists.

violates the rule requiring that there be exactly three terms, each one repeated twice (since "mathematicians" and "metaphysicians" are different terms).

6. And the syllogism

No scientists are mathematicians.	PEM
All mathematicians are philosophers.	MAS
∴ Some philosophers are not scientists.	∴ SOP

violates the rule requiring that at least one premise be particular, if the conclusion is particular, and hence is invalid.*

---

*The fifth and sixth examples have been added by the editor—ED.

STEPHEN BARKER

THE LOGIC OF TRUTH FUNCTIONS

ARGUMENTS CONTAINING COMPOUND SENTENCES

We may think of an argument as having two parts. One part consists of those words which make up its logical skeleton, that is, its logical form or structure; the other part consists of those words which are the flesh with which the skeleton is filled out. For instance, (1) is an argument, and (2) is its logical skeleton:

1. All spiders are eight-legged.	2. All . . . are # # #
No wasps are eight-legged.	No * * * are # # #
Therefore no wasps are spiders.	∴ no * * * are . . .

In argument (1) the words "all," "no," and "are" make up the logical skeleton, while the words "spiders," "wasps," and "eight-legged" are the flesh with which the skeleton happens to be filled out. Notice that (1) is a valid argument; it is valid because (2) is a valid kind of skeleton. To say that (2) is a valid kind of skeleton or logical form is to say that *any* argument having this same form will have a true conclusion if its premises are true. That is, whatever word or phrase we insert for " . . .," whatever word or phrase we insert for " # # #," and whatever word or phrase we insert for " * * *," we never can turn (2) into an argument having true premises but a false conclusion.

All the arguments dealt with in the first part of this chapter had one important feature in common. They all were like (1) in that their logical skeletons had gaps that were to be filled by single words or phrases which we called general terms and symbolized by means of capital letters. However, not all arguments are like this. Consider argument (3) and its skeleton (4):

3. This is a wasp or this is a spider.	4. # # # or . . .
This is not a wasp.	Not # # #
Therefore this is a spider.	∴ . . .

Argument (3) is valid too, but notice the difference between (4) and (2). The gaps in skeleton (4) must be filled not by single words or phrases but by whole sentences. In argument (3) the sentences which happen to fill these gaps are the

SOURCE: Stephen Barker, *The Elements of Logic* 3rd ed. (New York: McGraw-Hill, 1980), pp. 87–93. Copyright © 1980 by the McGraw-Hill Book Company. Reproduced with permission of The McGraw-Hill Companies.

sentences "This is a wasp" and "This is a spider." Notice also that in analyzing this argument we must think of the first premise not as a categorical sentence but rather as a compound sentence; only by thinking of it in this way can we see what makes the argument valid. We shall now become acquainted with some of the main kinds of arguments that contain compound sentences like this, arguments whose fleshy parts are whole sentences.

Some of them are very simple, trivial forms of argument. You may think that they are pointless and silly. But remember that simple arguments can be combined to form chains of reasoning and a chain of reasoning may succeed in reaching an interesting conclusion that was not obvious, even if each step in it is trivial and obvious.

NEGATION

The simplest way of forming a compound sentence is by prefixing the words "It is not the case that." The sentence "It is not the case that wasps are spiders" is a compound sentence, for it contains within itself the simpler sentence "Wasps are spiders." * We say that the former sentence is the negation of the latter sentence. The single word "not" can be used instead: "Wasps are not spiders" is another way of expressing the negation of "Wasps are spiders." But notice that the word "not" is not as reliable in forming negations as is the phrase "It is not the case that." "Some wasps are not spiders" is *not* the negation of "Some wasps are spiders"; the negation of the latter sentence should be expressed "It is not the case that some wasps are spiders," and that is equivalent to "No wasps are spiders."

The negation of a given sentence should be its *contradictory;* that is, it should deny just what the sentence says, no less and no more. Therefore, the negation of the negation of a sentence will be equivalent to the original sentence itself. This provides us with one extremely simple form of argument that involves negation only.

DOUBLE NEGATION

Not (not p)	*e.g.,* It is not the case that wasps aren't insects.
∴ p	Therefore wasps are insects.
p	*e.g.,* Wasps are insects.
∴ not (not p)	Therefore it's not the case that wasps aren't insects.

---

*Such compound statements are called "truth functions" since their truth or falsehood is a *function* of the truth status of the simpler sentence(s) it contains. E.g., the sentence "It is not the case that wasps are spiders" is true (false) just in case its component sentence "wasps are spiders" is false (true)—ED.

Here, in representing the forms of compound sentences, we have stopped using cumbersome dots, dashes, and asterisks; instead, we use the letters "p," "q," and "r," which are to be thought of as doing just the same job, that is, marking places where sentences may be filled in.

DISJUNCTION

A compound sentence consisting of two simpler sentences linked together by "or" (or by "either . . . or . . .," which means just the same) is called a *disjunction* (or an *alternation*). A disjunction is symmetrical, in the sense that "p or q" always is equivalent to "q or p." We can rewrite our earlier skeleton (4) using letters:

DISJUNCTIVE ARGUMENT

p or q	*also:* p or q	*e.g.,* It will rain or it will snow.
Not p	not q	It will not rain.
∴ q	∴ p	Therefore it will snow.

These forms of disjunctive argument are valid because the first premise tells us that at least one component is true, while the second premise tells us that a certain component is not true; it follows that the other component must be true.

Sometimes there is an ambiguity about the word "or." When we say "p or q," sometimes we mean "p or q but not both." This is called the *exclusive* sense of "or." More often when we say "p or q," we mean "p or q or perhaps both." This is the *nonexclusive* sense of "or." In ordinary conversation, if a gentleman says to a lady in a tone of acquiescence, "I'll buy you a Cadillac or a mink coat," he is surely using "or" in the nonexclusive sense, since she cannot accuse him of having spoken untruthfully if he then gives her both. Cases of the exclusive sense of "or" occur, though more rarely. If a father says to his child in a tone of refusal "I'll take you to the zoo or to the beach," then the mother can accuse him of having spoken falsely if he takes the child both places.

Ordinarily, unless we have some reason to the contrary, we shall interpret the word "or" in the nonexclusive sense so that we can be sure of not taking too much for granted. Therefore, we regard the following two forms of argument as invalid:

INVALID DISJUNCTIVE ARGUMENTS

p or q	p or q	*e.g.,* He's guilty or she's guilty.
p	q	He's guilty.
∴ not q	∴ not p	Therefore she's not guilty.

These forms would be valid if "or" were understood in the exclusive sense, but they are invalid when "or" is understood in the commoner nonexclusive sense.

CONJUNCTION

A compound sentence consisting of two simpler sentences linked by the word "and" is called a *conjunction*. Sometimes, as in the sentence "They grew up and studied philosophy," the word "and" is used to mean "and then," indicating that one event occurred first and the other event occurred later. But other times, as in the sentence "I like cake and I like candy," the word "and" is simply used to join together two assertions, without indicating any temporal relationship. This latter sense of "and" is the more important one for logic. When "and" is used in this sense, conjunctions are symmetrical; that is, "p and q" is then equivalent to "q and p." In English, various other words, such as "but" and "although," often do essentially the same logical job as "and." One absurdly simple but perfectly valid form of conjunctive argument is this:

VALID CONJUNCTIVE ARGUMENT (SIMPLIFICATION)

p and q	*e.g.,* It will rain and snow.
∴ p	Therefore it will rain.

If we combine negation with conjunction, we can obtain a slightly less trivial kind of valid conjunctive argument.

VALID CONJUNCTIVE ARGUMENTS

| Not (p and q) | *e.g.,* She will not both fly and drive her car. |
p	She is flying.
∴ not q	Therefore she will not drive her car.

| Not (p and q) | *e.g.,* It will not both rain and snow. |
q	It will snow.
∴ not p	Therefore it will not rain.

The following forms, however, are invalid.

INVALID CONJUNCTIVE ARGUMENTS

| Not (p and q) | *e.g.,* Joe and Ted won't both come. |
Not p	Joe won't come.
∴ q	Therefore Ted will come.

| Not (p and q) | *e.g.,* He won't both buy and sell today. |
Not q	He won't sell today.
∴ p	Therefore he'll buy today.

CONDITIONALS

Another important kind of compound sentence involves the word "if." A sentence consisting of two simpler sentences linked by the word "if," or by the words "if . . . then # # # ," is called a *conditional,* or *hypothetical,* sentence. The part to which the word "if" is directly attached is called the *antecedent* of the conditional sentence, and the other part is called the *consequent.* To assert the conditional sentence is to say that the truth of the antecedent will ensure the truth of the consequent. For instance, someone who asserts "If tufa floats, then some rocks float" is saying that the truth of "Tufa floats" would be sufficient to ensure the truth of "Some rocks float."

Let us consider some (valid) forms of argument containing conditional sentences.

MODUS PONENS

If p then q   *e.g.,* If tufa floats, some rocks float.
p   Tufa does float.
_____   _____

∴ q   Therefore some rocks float.

MODUS TOLLENS

If p then q   *e.g.,* If pigs can fly, then dogs can fly.
Not q   Dogs cannot fly.
_____   _____

∴ not p   Therefore pigs can't fly.

Somewhat similar, but invalid,* are the following:

FALLACY OF AFFIRMING THE CONSEQUENT

If p then q   *e.g.,* If they want to come, they will send flowers.
q   They are sending flowers.
_____   _____

∴ p   Therefore they want to come.

FALLACY OF DENYING THE ANTECEDENT

If p then q   *e.g.,* If the car runs, it has gas.
Not p   The car does not run.
_____   _____

∴ not q   Therefore the car does not have gas.

_____

*We say that these arguments are invalid because, for the present, we are considering only deductive reasoning. However, such arguments are not always fallacious when they are intended as *inductive* arguments. In inductive reasoning the speaker claims only that his or her premises help to make the conclusion reasonable to believe; it sometimes is legitimate to make this weaker claim in connection with some arguments like these and others that are classified as deductively fallacious.

Another valid form has three conditional sentences, the consequent of the first being the same as the antecedent of the second:

CHAIN ARGUMENT (OR HYPOTHETICAL SYLLOGISM)

If p then q	*e.g.,* If the moon can be settled, then Mars can be settled.
If q then r	If Mars can be settled, then Jupiter can be settled.
∴ if p then r	Therefore if the moon can be settled, Jupiter can be settled.

PRACTICE

GREGORY TROPEA

THE PHILOSOPHER AS SOFTWARE DEVELOPER

FINDING A FOCUS IN COMPUTING

In the early days of microcomputers, when almost no one had them, a prospective client came over to the office to see the new technological wonders that so many newspaper stories were talking about. As he cautiously sat down at the keyboard, I turned my computer on and brought up the standard opening screen, which displayed in then-fashionable amber monochrome a ">" symbol, a blinking cursor, and an expanse of black. The man's response to his first up-close encounter with a computer was a surprise to me, though in retrospect not entirely unreasonable. "What does it do?" he asked. That was when I realized that computer users could be divided into two groups with contrary dispositions: those who are inclined to locate responsibility for what happens in the computer and those who are inclined to locate it in themselves.

Some people think it's bad form to answer a question with a question, but philosophers know that this can be a very good way to get at hidden assumptions that might be operating in a situation. In this case, while I could have accepted the prospective client's unintentionally loaded question as it had been framed and then exhausted both myself and the questioner by explaining the myriad incomprehensible possibilities opened up by the new machine, I didn't. "What do you *need* to do?" I responded. This was to focus attention away from the novelties of the technology and bring our thinking into that space of imagination in which some important aspects of the man's business could be identified and then formalized so that they could be represented and manipulated within the computer. Having a business need beyond the capabilities of

Gregory Tropea has worked with computers for nearly two decades. His writing on the subject ranges from short pieces about narrow, technical issues to extended discussions of existential questions raised by technology. He has been especially interested in applying the techniques of philosophical counseling to construction of information technology applications. Dr. Tropea has taught at Syracuse University, Chinese Culture University at Taipei, and is currently Critical Thinking Coordinator at California State University, Chico.

one's current staff is, after all, the most common reason for a businessperson to engage a computer consultant. A deeper reason for my response is that through an analysis of my own work that supplements everyday deduction with a little phenomenology, I long ago came to the conclusion that neither high technology nor clever logic (both of which are important in computing) should be thought of as the essence of successful business application programming; imagination is what truly opens up the possibilities in the first place. Think about it. If just about any business that wants to have a generically configured computer on every desk can do so, then there would not be any important business advantage in the mere possession of the standard machines; business advantages must trace to how the computers are configured and used to advance the mission of the enterprise.

Computers do enable us to do things that we have never done before, but nothing new happens in computing until someone imagines it. Once imagination has raised a possibility, however, it is important to evaluate it using all the tools of logic and critical thinking that we have at our disposal. Evaluation of possibilities is not just a matter of logic and critical thinking, of course, but also of intuition and interpretation of values. Juggling all of these elements successfully requires clarity of thinking and of purpose, which describes the traditional task of philosophy as I have understood it and enjoyed it. We might be inclined to think that this high-sounding phrase, "clarity of thinking and of purpose," only applies to the great issues in life, but what gives each existence its unique character occurs not just in the great general truths but also very much in the details. This brings me to my first general point about philosophy and computing, which is that in my experience as a computer user and programmer who must pay careful attention to details, philosophy has played an important role in building the crucial creative and analytical skills that are needed to bridge the emptiness that lies between a bare, generically configured machine and a useful information-processing tool that falls readily to hand. Let me explain further.

To most minds, philosophy and computer technology seem to have very little to do with each other, but I have discovered in over two decades of working with computers that philosophy and computing share several important points of intersection. Over this period the tools and insights of philosophy have proven themselves useful to many of my colleagues and me in such traditional computing tasks as general programming, database applications, and artificial intelligence, as well as larger issues of information system design. Philosophers working in the traditional ways have also been interested in social and personal issues related to technology since the very beginning of the industrial revolution more than two centuries ago, but the fact is that although philosophers have frequently addressed problems of everyday life, only rarely had they involved themselves directly with the technologies we use every day, until just recently. In its own way, though, each creative engagement of philosophically trained minds in one of these everyday tasks reveals some interesting things about philosophy that are not obvious if one thinks of philosophy only as an academic subject. When we focus on the larger intellectual challenges of computing instead of just the mechanical wizardry, philosophically significant issues and possibilities of computing can come into view. So, from my perspective, computing and philosophy have a dynamic and mutually beneficial relationship.

ARE TECHNOLOGICAL QUESTIONS EVER PHILOSOPHICAL ONES?

Many of the concerns of computer scientists and software application designers have turned out to be not only complex but also highly interesting to philosophers. But are these interesting phenomena truly philosophical concerns? Just deciding whether or not to become involved with computing on a professional level has caused some philosophers to reexamine what philosophy is to them, which is quite a radical impact in a field that has thousands of years of documented tradition. We would expect philosophers to be careful about the logic of such a decision. Of course, philosophy certainly is not the only field in which people make use of logic, and I've been challenged more than once by philosophers as to whether my work with computers is really philosophical.

Consider this syllogism (which, with minor rewriting resolves into standard form EAE-2, Cesare, for those who are interested):

> No philosophical questions are decided by empirical facts.
> All technological questions are decided by empirical facts.
> Therefore, no technological questions are philosophical questions.

The syllogism is a valid one, so if we accept its premises as stated in the first two sentences, we must accept the conclusion in the third sentence. But what if the premises seem to us to be true and the conclusion still doesn't feel quite right because, say, we suspect that there are larger issues in technology that might be better understood if they were clarified philosophically? In that sort of case, there are only a few options available: to make sure one's question about the conclusion is both relevant and precisely worded, to reexamine the premises to make sure each one is true in the sense it is being understood, and to make sure that any words or phrases that are used in the argument are understood in the same sense throughout.

In the argument above, both of the premises are somewhat controversial. The controversy in each case is primarily a matter of how the subject term is defined, which is always a tricky business when the thing being defined is an abstraction. As we step through this syllogism, it would be well to bear in mind that the sort of analysis just below is very similar to the kinds of considerations that can be quite helpful in making the categorical decisions that determine data structures in databases and spreadsheets. So, then, to consider the first sentence, the question is whether some interpretation of the predicate phrase "decided by empirical facts" really can never be one of the attributes of "philosophical questions." If we determine that these two concepts never apply to the same reality, then the sentence is true. Otherwise, for someone who holds to a more liberal definition of "philosophical questions" than the first premise above allows, it becomes plainly false, and there is no middle ground. So, while this syllogism is unquestionably valid according to the traditional rules of logic, there is still the possibility that it may be unsound.

With regard to the truth of the first premise, which sets out a live issue for working philosophers, the crucial challenge logically hangs on finding at least one actual case in which a philosophical question was or could be decided by empirical facts. Even if one expected such a case to exist, there would be no smooth road to this falsifying contradiction because a major logical obstacle has been created by the ways in which the issue has been analyzed. This obstacle is large, but it is also subtle for those coming to the issue for the first time. Among philosophers, those who readily accept the first premise (which is the major premise in this argument because it contains the predicate term of the conclusion) will want to use this proposition axiomatically as a test to *determine* whether a question is truly philosophical. These philosophers will not see the first premise as an arguable proposition that would be decided on the basis of a case that (1) concerned an empirical question and (2) was asserted to contain a philosophical question as well. (Recall that axioms are declared, and are not propositions that are either proved or disproved within a system of thought.) In other words, if one defines philosophy as a branch of knowledge in which only beliefs, definitions, and reason count for anything—as those who accept the first premise typically do—the sense experiences that we call empirical facts categorically have no place in philosophy, except as illustrations of things that have already been properly decided. And if one changes this specification just enough to allow perceptions of the world to count as facts about the world (and not just as facts of *perception* of the world), then the first premise very likely becomes false, but, for some people at least, the cost is far too high: the integrity of philosophy, which would then become a collection of mere opinions. The first premise of the syllogism, then, raises a highly charged issue in philosophy, where the assertion that an argued proposition is "just an opinion" is for some virtually a challenge to a duel and for others, who stress the interpretive character of all descriptions of reality, a comical irrelevancy.

When a question like this occurs in the course of setting up a database, the matter is often transformed into one about the most practical way of categorizing things. While it might seem that a quick decision to go with the most practical way of doing things would be simpler than following out the many implications of various possible definitions, the "quick decision" route actually becomes very complicated because the calculation of what is most practical must take into account many more factors than the typical definition. Constructing a good definition can save a tremendous amount of work if it clearly supplies the attributes that an information system needs to track and does not lead to the collection of unnecessary data. Moreover, definitions that are important to a project can be checked (admittedly, indirectly and imperfectly) by seeing if valid deductions that essentially contain them lead to conclusions that make sense in the world of actual experience.

With regard to the second premise in the syllogism above, the situation looks a little easier at first blush because virtually everyone agrees that the purpose of technology is to facilitate our interactions with the real world, whatever may be our sense of reality. Whether a technology works or does not work is simply an empirical question, as are most instances of the related question of whether one technological solution performs a task better than another according to some set of evaluation criteria. The important controversy hiding in this premise has to do with whether the empirical facts themselves decide technological questions or whether the ways in which the facts are evaluated and interpreted really determine the decisions. There was a time when some thinkers who called themselves "realists" could comfortably hold the view that things simply are what they generally appear to be and can be understood directly, without interpretation. This view has largely disappeared from philosophy as the complexities of understanding have become more evident, a change which has occurred in the twentieth century, at least partly due to the broad implications of such modern developments as Einstein's theories of relativity and the problems of creating artificial intelligence. Database architects are well aware of the interpretive conflicts that often attend the formalization of the business rules encoded into the database design. From a modern information technology perspective, the realist perspective tends to strangle the creative use of enterprise knowledge.

If one adopts the view that empirical facts are necessary to deciding any properly technological question (as contrasted with a philosophical question about technology, for example), then the composition of the sets of premises that are admissible as support for conclusions of properly *technological* arguments would always have to include at least one statement about an empirical fact. This circular-looking requirement would decide the truth of the second premise by invoking a definition in a way similar to the axiomatic approach to deciding the first premise. The only fly in the ointment here is that there are reasons to believe that some computer technology questions are best decided without decisive reference to empirical data of any sort, as our quick discussion of the second premise in the argument below suggests. So, the second premise of the syllogism above joins the first in making the conclusion of the syllogism a questionable one. Of course, any judgment about the soundness of an argument for a conclusion must be distinguished from the matter of whether the conclusion is factually correct, which can always be simply true independent of any particular argument. There are plenty of conclusions of invalid and unsound arguments that are still true statements; they simply are not sufficiently well supported by certain arguments in which they happen to appear as conclusions.

Since the first syllogism reveals some important issues for philosophers but ultimately gets us into muddy waters, let's leave it where it stands and try a different one to see if the participation of philosophers in computing can be more firmly established as philosophical activity or whether computing is just one of those things that philosophers might happen to be interested in as, say, a hobby which is useful enough that one can get paid to pursue it.

> All questions decided by rational application of subjective principles are philosophical questions.
> Some technological questions are decided by rational application of subjective principles.
> Therefore, some technological questions are philosophical questions.

Like our first syllogism, this one is also valid (AII-1, Darii). In this case, though, the premises are far less controversial. For starters, we want to make sure that the first premise is not mistaken for its converse, which would be that all philosophical questions are decided by rational application of subjective values. This second claim is neither logically equivalent to the first premise above (a common error in logic), nor is it as readily acceptable to all of philosophy's stakeholders. In this vein, we also would not want to interpret the argument as suggesting that every involvement of philosophers in computing is focused on rational application of subjective values, though this claim could accurately reflect the views of some philosophers. Taking this syllogism as given, though, we have at least established that some problems of technology call for philosophical attention.

We cannot leave this topic of the general involvement of philosophers in computing without clarifying one of the issues raised in the first premise of this second syllogism. It's about subjective principles. One could plausibly say that all principles are subjective, but there are some philosophers who intend some principles to be about objective reality, which they conceive basically as those conditions that exist whether or not anyone is thinking about them. We can sidestep this debate in the present case because computing is essentially about representation. Even when philosophers are dealing with the intentionally unambiguous certainties of deduction, the principles that apply are all mental inventions. So one thing philosophers will not be doing is using computers to adjudicate questions of objective and subjective truth.

As to the second premise, sufficient proof consists in presenting just one case in which a technological question is decided by rational application of subjective principles. This premise seems to me to be true in three different ways, corresponding to three different technological tasks. In programming, the first of the tasks I have in mind, there often are several ways to accomplish the same task that require about the same resources in time and computing power. The selection of one strategy over another in this situation seems to me to be a decision of a technological question. For example, a programmer could have an aesthetic preference for one way of naming memory variables over another. For someone charged with maintaining the program after the original programmer has departed the scene, the style of programming is not inconsequential and its ramifications for later development of the program are hard to predict. One could say that this sort of decision is aesthetic, not technological, but I would argue it is both. If we symbolize my idea as A & T, then by rule of simplification T is true. Individual memory variables will be named by the rational application of subjective principles, and it is not stretching language to say that programmers have philosophical views about such things as memory variables.

A second case that comes to mind is the selection of attributes that can become columns of a database table; this is especially interesting because it is customary for people to see the attributes of a thing as "really there" in the thing and miss entirely the absolute fictionality of all such schemes. If, for example, we have a boarding kennel and want to keep track of the dogs, our columns could be restricted just to the dog's name and breed. But we could also add other attributes, such as the owner's name, temperament of the dog, and others. In this case, the business rules that we have decided on will drive the technological implementation.

A third level at which the second premise could be true is the psychological. An example would be including a principle in the technology purchase calculus that those who will be using the technology should feel comfortable with it. Now feeling comfortable with a technology is not just a matter of keyboard and screen ergonomics. One might have strong feelings against a company one perceived as a monopoly or for a company that was active in social issues. Some would argue that proceeding on these grounds was bad reasoning because technological decisions were not being made strictly on the merits of the technology, but application of this common principle of critical thinking is itself open to dispute in ways that go beyond our discussion here.

There is much more that could be said about the second syllogism. That alone suggests that there are philosophical issues in computing, not the least of which is the separation of the philosophical issues from the nonphilosophical ones.

Philosophers in Computing

In this age dominated by practical technologies that are based on research in the natural sciences, it is easy to forget that the sciences originated as branches of philosophy. While philosophers have always been interested in how the world works, they have not favored the sort of interventionist experimentation that characterizes much of modern science; generally, philosophers have had a cautious and critical relationship with technology. In both East and West, philosophers have generally tried to understand things first in principle and have used naturalistic observation to illustrate and explain their thinking. Given this difference in style, the perception of philosophy as thoroughly nonscientific is understandable. But it is false.

As science has become increasingly technological, there has certainly been a widening gap between the practice of philosophy and the practices of science and technology, but it would be a mistake to overlook continuing connections. For example, the thought experiments of Einstein, Hawking, and other luminaries of modern physics clearly carry on the nontechnological tradition of philosophical analysis. Modern Darwinists develop careful explanations that have proven very important in keeping biological and ethical issues distinct, which not only contributes to ethical coherence, but also helps keep the field of biology focused on its own distinctive problems. The first requirement of any scientific theory is that it be deductively coherent, and this is established using the philosophically developed techniques of definition and inference. The experiments that test theories may be the most visible part of science, but they occur only after much abstract thinking that determines in advance what shall count as knowledge. Explaining the way things are and the way events happen—acquiring knowledge of objects and processes that comprise or cause the observable phenomena of the world—is most important to science, while the nature and organization of those explanations will be most interesting to philosophy. In humanity's efforts to understand the world and our place in it, scientists and philosophers have specialized in different kinds of knowing; scientists have concentrated on knowledge of phenomena, while philosophers have concentrated on knowledge of knowing.

Perhaps because of the close association of computers with knowledge work and their utility for knowledge workers, placing this particular technology among the interests of philosophy has a naturalness for philosophers that is often surprising to people long exposed to the false stereotype of the abstract thinker disengaged from particularities and the world of common concerns. My own doctoral work, which culminated in a dissertation grounded in Martin Heidegger's classic *Being and Time* and included a chapter based on his critique of technology, was intentionally constructed in accord with conventional academic priorities, but at the same time as I was completing a classical education, I was already using that education in ways utterly foreign to my more tradition-oriented professors. My decision to join the ever-growing number of philosophers in the twentieth century who have combined traditional work in philosophy with specialized skills in the practical details of the technologies that are used to accomplish various computing tasks was a conscious one. It involved coming to terms with some arguments about philosophy and computing whose conclusions are anything but agreed (as we shall see below), and I would be lying if I said that these issues were completely settled even in my own mind.

Philosophers are not generally trained to get involved with the technical side of computing, but they do for reasons that grow out of both formal study and personal, nonacademic interests. However philosophers happen to become involved in computing, though, the majority of those who take on problems of this technology still do most or all of their work in a university setting. Given the diversity of interests among philosophers, this similarity of employment conditions certainly doesn't mean that we all do the same kinds of things. Several major research universities have centers and institutes where philosophers are members of interdisciplinary teams that study and develop promising computing technologies, while at smaller liberal arts institutions and community colleges (where some of our best educational software originates), computing is usually far from the official mission of philosophy departments. But there is a rich professional life for philosophers interested in computing outside the academy also. A number of academically trained philosophers work as researchers and managers in high-technology enterprises that range in scale from major corporations to small start-ups, while yet others bring the considerable problem-solving skills of the professional philosopher to bear as information technology consultants. In addition to those who use the intellectual tools of philosophy to carry on or enhance specifically technological work, there are a number of philosophers who develop a sophisticated grasp of particular information technologies and then pursue inquiries into the social and ethical problems that arise in connection with these technologies, as well as larger questions of meaning and being that come into view as information technology changes the world. Meeting these people at conferences and trade shows, I am struck by both the breadth and depth of philosophers' involvements in computing.

Since the Internet became a prominent feature of academic life, philosophers have made good use of it to disseminate information, support discussions, and enhance teaching. As soon as I saw how the introduction of the Mosaic browser was speeding the evolution of this resource, I realized that a little thoughtful consideration was in order. Since I was the only person in my department who was familiar with the World Wide Web at the time, I became the department "webmaster" by default and began to set up a Web site. Instantaneous communication revealed to me that this story was being played out all over the world. The first question I encountered in the construction of the Web site was a practical one: What is the site for? This was something that had to be decided, but there was little guidance because almost no departmental sites existed at the time. My first Web page was a collection of links and graphics elements culled from whatever sites I had visited and liked. I could see that it served no purpose other than to prove that I was able to write some serviceable HTML (Hyper-Text Markup Language). It was at this point that the practical question needed to be answered. In the absence of policy, precedent, and other information that might bring order to this chaotic novelty, I gathered up a heap of impressions and theoretical ideas that essentially went like this:

> Browser technology provides simple, powerful, and inexpensive communication.
>
> An experiment making use of such a technology for education holds promise.
>
> The department has never had anything like a Web site.
>
> Setting up a departmental Web site would be experimental.
>
> This Web site will be identified as a philosophy department site.
>
> If it's a philosophy department site, it should be furthering the work of the department.
>
> There is no point in simply duplicating current work of instructors or staff.
>
> Conclusion 1: Setting up a Web site of our own holds promise.
>
> Conclusion 2: This Web site should be furthering the work of the department.
>
> Conclusion 3: It will not simply duplicate current work of instructors or staff.

My premises and conclusions were a mix of descriptive and prescriptive propositions. This is typical in setting up information projects. What was helpful about my incompletely specified deductions was not that they told me exactly what I should be doing, but that they reduced the bewildering field of possibility that existed when comparatively high-profile Web sites were devoted to everything from monitoring the contents of soda machines to extensive lists of just research links, while still providing direction for imagination of the site. This may not seem like a profound advance over intuition, but when one sits down to a blank screen with only vague intuitions of what is to be done, the need to deliver visible and operational realities becomes immediately apparent and exerts an uncompromising pressure. At this point in history, it's hard to imagine that there was ever a question about setting up a departmental Web site, but many saw the Internet as a transient frivolity. The difficulties of imagining basic Web site formats are also quite distant, now that so many alternative models have been put into place, but those questions were real and vexing, and those of us who created the first Web sites remember the almost daily appearance of questions that had not been posed before and of techniques we had not seen before. This anecdote symbolizes for me the general advantage that a philosophically informed outlook brings: namely, resources for dealing with novel and incompletely specified problems. Perhaps most important for understanding how philosophers work in computing, it also shows how deduction can be applied as a useful part of a practical reasoning process which is in some ways more complex than textbook illustrations that present purely deductive arguments for instructional purposes.

DATABASES AS A WAY INTO COMPUTING

Only a very few highly insulated people involved in computing can ignore the Web, which is not a monolithic specialty, but a composite of virtually all of the aspects of computing that have been important historically, and then some: communications, data entry and retrieval, graphics, several design disciplines, and others. Database application design has always been the most interesting area of computing to me, and it is even more so now that convenient access to vast resources through a browser can be fairly conveniently implemented. The general category of database design within computing includes not only the determination of how information is physically stored in a computer, but also the user interface for adding, viewing, and deleting data, all the decisions about what data the individual or enterprise needs to work with, and much about anticipating unknown future directions of the enterprise that the design will have to accommodate.

When I first became interested in databases in the early days of personal computers, I had the narrow interest of keeping track of the research notes for my doctoral dissertation. Until then, I had been a most casual computer user, mainly interested in using my computer (a converted industrial controller that was solid as a rock and just as fast) as a glorified typewriter that promised to save me hours of typing corrections. The first research note database I set up was a masterpiece of bad design, if I do say so myself. My project, as I have since realized, wasn't unusually ugly for its time because even among computer professionals, database design was practiced as a rather primitive science, mainly because the resources of categorical logic were not being fully exploited. My research into databases in the intervening years has turned up some sophisticated and influential discussions that had been appearing in the technical journals of the time, but these were expensive, limited-circulation publications heavy in math and logic that most people would generally have avoided even if they were given away free on street corners, and that in any case presupposed a level of "big iron" computing power that was unavailable to individuals and small businesses using primitive microcomputers, but, interestingly, now sits on many desktops. One implication of this increase in computing power is that developers of desktop database applications now must be much more sophisticated in logic to do state-of-the-art work than in the early days.

At that time, there was almost no academic preparation available that would prepare one for working with personal computers, so most of the people doing commercial work were amateurs like me who woke up one morning to find their hobbyist-level programming skills were in great demand by businesses around the world. The sudden appearance of a "ground-floor" opportunity out of nowhere largely explains why programmers and consultants developing desktop database applications for microcomputers in the early eighties typically paid little attention to theoretical issues, a situation not unlike the anarchic advent of the Internet in the early nineties. Also, in those early days of personal computing, both hardware and software were almost tragically unreliable when called upon to perform tasks of any complexity, and simply getting an application to work the same way twice was almost achievement enough. Almost. Generally speaking, early database designers treated computers as electronic filing cabinets that people would use very much as they had used hard-copy filing cabinets, and they did have to be reasonably reliable even if they weren't elegant. The common-sense approach that almost everyone was using at the time seemed like a fine application of analogical reasoning, but it led to very inefficient systems, as I immediately realized when I got involved with larger projects with unforgiving business requirements. Which brings up another general point, this time a parallel between computing and philosophy that philosophers have stated and experience has confirmed many times over: common-sense solutions to problems are not to be trusted uncritically.

This is an important principle that comes into play in just about every application I've been involved with. Its importance generally shows up in the most important stage of program creation: planning. There are actually several different planning stages in applications of any complexity, involving such different aspects of computing as interface design, program functionality, software technology choices, and hardware technology choices. These break down further still, but at every point there is a need to think the problems through carefully. One of the concepts in database design that remained obscure to many desktop application designers for a number of years is that of the normalized database. Basically, a normalized database is one in which a data element appears in only one place and in which data files contain elements that "belong together" in specific ways that generally make sense once you think about them in such a grouping. The logic of database normalization is obviously not intuitive because it took decades for the efficiencies of normalization to come into wide usage, and nonprofessionals still avoid using the technique. Let's consider an example that I have been working on to see how categorical deductions can be used to get beyond common sense.

One of the things I have wanted to do as an arts commissioner in the city where I live is help people who are interested in the artworks or services of local artists of all types to find them and to help artists get in touch with each other conveniently. The committee charged with making this service available also decided that arts-related businesses and behind-the-scenes people are an important part of the arts scene and ought to be in the loop. To this end, we initiated an ongoing compilation of a database of local artists and arts-related businesses by the city that anyone will be able to access over the Internet through the arts commission's Web pages. In its first realization, the city staffer who was assigned to implement our plan at the desktop created a monolithic data file that contained everything but the kitchen sink—artists' names, addresses, media in which they worked, kinds of services they could render, and the like. The database will never be so large as to tax the capabilities of even an average desktop computer, so we're not worried that continuing growth of this single data file would create performance problems, but once a database of this sort gets beyond just a few records, it starts to get messy for a number of reasons. Chief among these is inconsistent treatment of repeating data, which can be viewed as a problem that arises when items that arguably belong in a category used by the database are not always put into that category.

As an example, let's say that we are either entering data or searching our big "Artists" file and are concerned with a musician who plays the cello. If there's a field in the data file called "Instrument" that is part of a person's record along with name, address, and so on, either creation of a new record or a search for an existing record for someone who plays the cello will ordinarily involve typing the name of some musical instrument into a box. Of course, if our big file only has space for one instrument per musician, it will be pretty much useless because many musicians play more than one instrument, and we need to capture that fact. So in this design we would need to set the "Instrument" field up to hold the names of more than one instrument. Then we would want to call the field "Instruments" and let it contain lists of instruments. But then we'd have a lot of empty space in the database because of instances such as graphic artists who don't play instruments, theatre directors who don't have anything to do with instruments, and so on. And we'd also have to deal with people who are supposed to type in "cello" but who instead type "CELLO" or "cellist" or "cellists" or "celo" or "flute, guitarcello, piano" (containing the error of no space between "guitar" and "cello") or "strings" or "violoncello" or any of a number of other things that might not match up when someone is seeking a cello player. In all of these problem cases, the category is not being named consistently.

The standard ways of dealing with this sort of problem all take us into categorical thinking. By surveying our area of interest, we realize right away that not all artists are musicians, so maybe including an "Instrument" or "Instruments" field for each person adds needless bulk to the picture. We do know that all artists work in some medium, though. It might be watercolor or spoken word or cello, but there will always be something that manifests the work of art in the physical world. By reimagining the categories this way, we arrive at a more comprehensive way of classifying the entities in our database. So, to reflect this higher level of generality, our application might include a business rule that states something like this:

All artists are associated with at least one medium.

Another, logically equivalent, way of putting this rule is:

If an entity is an artist, it is associated with at least one medium.

When cast this way, a new problem shows up in the antecedent of the conditional: not every entity we are dealing with is an artist.

Since we have planned that there will be people or businesses in our database that are not artists themselves, we'll have to make sure they are not confused with the artists in the database. One way to do this would be to include a very economical feature called a "logical" field (designated "Artist" or something like that) for each person or business in the database; this field would have the value *True* if the entity is an artist and *False* if not. Or maybe it would be better to introduce more complexity and, instead of a simple logical "Artist" field, include a "Type" field that could tell us more specifically what the person or business does. But then what about someone who acts, plays an instrument, and sells stage makeup? Do we create a "Type" called "mixed" that doesn't really tell us anything? Do we make the "Type" field into a list? The list approach, at least, would allow a person to perform multiple functions and would save us from having to include a strange rule like the one just below, which obviously violates the Law of the Excluded Middle and yet, for purposes of certain searches (that need to find artists whose activities are not always in the capacity of artist), states an idea that somehow needs to be accounted for:

Some artists are not artists.

I can't imagine a computer that would be happy trying to deal with a business rule that looks anything like this proposition, though advanced applications of artificial intelligence need to be able to deal with such results. But somehow, without getting into advanced artificial intelligence, we want to allow all the things that people do professionally or semiprofessionally to show up in our database. This line of thinking opens up a new problem which is similar to the "medium" problem above. Specifically, there might be all kinds of things that would be useful to know about businesses that would not be part of anyone's concern about performing artists. Would we want to maintain fields for that information for everybody in one big file? Generally, no.

The solution that most database designers favor calls for, among other measures, creating separate files for each significant repeating category and then relating the items on a common key (such as a unique ID number) in these separate files back to a file of the sort that would contain the name and address information of our artists and arts-related businesses. So one solution to our artist/businessperson, medium problem could create a set of several files, three of which would be structured something like this:

PERSON/BUSINESS FILE	ART MEDIUM FILE	BUSINESS ACTIVITY FILE
ID	ID	ID
Name Fields	Medium	Activity
Address Fields		
Artist (logical type)		
Business (logical type)		

To explain this just briefly, the ID field is what ties these files together. In the Person/Business file, there would be only one instance of a particular ID, which would identify a unique individual or business. In that record, there would also be family name and given name fields, a street field, a city field, a zip field, and others for state, phone number, fax, Web site, and others. In this solution, the artist and business logical fields, if set to *True,* would tell the computer that there is something in the "Art Medium" file or the "Business Activity" file respectively. These latter two files could contain any number of entries for an entity in the "Person/Business" file, each of which would be a true predicate of the "Person/Business" it was linked to by the ID field. Note that the "Artist" and "Business" logical fields are actually logically unnecessary, because the programmer could always instruct the computer to look in the "Art Medium," and "Business" Activity files to see if there was anything in either of them for a particular ID. A programmer might make this sort of logical compromise in the interests of speed, since it might make for a sluggish program if it had to go hunting for files that might be located somewhere else on a network and look through them completely, only to report back to the screen that there wasn't anything there.

There are ways this three-file fragment of a database could be made more reliable. For example, we still haven't dealt with the CELLO, celo, cellist problem. One way to do this would be to create two files in place of the "Art Medium" file above. This is what they might look like:

COMPETENCE FILE	MEDIUM LIST FILE
ID	Medium code
Medium code	Medium name

In this approach, we can still have as many media for any artist as we want, but when the artist is credited with competence in a particular medium, that is done by picking a medium from a list on the screen instead of typing something in. Searches would also use that list. In this way, there would never be deviant spellings to contend with. But, one might object, there might be a medium that was not in the list. Certainly this could occur, and to handle it we should allow the addition of records to the "Medium List" file. The list could then grow as needed. In an actual business application, this sort of addition would be limited to operators who understood the naming conventions for the categories and there would be regular editing to make sure the list had retained its semantic integrity.

For most people, setting up a database along these lines is not the immediately obvious solution to their filing needs. It certainly wasn't for me. As I began doing commercial work, I discovered almost by accident that although I had no academic training in computer science and could not find anyplace to obtain training that was immediately relevant to the work that I was doing, my academically acquired skill in logic and expertise in phenomenology were extremely useful in defining specific tasks that my programs or those of my colleagues needed to perform and then making that performance happen. There is no substitute for following the logic of a problem in a way that is appropriate to the application one has in mind. Even now that computers have become commodity fixtures in homes and businesses, I find that people I introduce to new database techniques generally need a great deal of guidance in how to put information technology to use. What complicates the database application picture enormously is that computers are not just neutral tools in a business environment; they change the way business is done, which is a delicate matter to manage. And this leads deep into a very complex philosophical problem which is centered on the issue of how the kinds of observation of an enterprise or activity that are made possible by database technology affect both the observer and what is observed. This is especially difficult when the observer is part of what is observed, as in the case of someone who works in a business and is engaged in analyzing the performance of that business. Just by virtue of the ways information can flow and create dynamically changing situations, truth can become an elusively moving target.

The computing problems that first engaged skills I had developed through the study of philosophy were not anything so complex as the dynamics of interpretation or even the setting up of a set of related tables. They were, in fact, all the way over at the other end of the scale, but complexity develops quickly in computing. Anyone who attempts to program the step-by-step instructions that tell the machine exactly what to do next discovers just how much logic is encapsulated in even the simplest of our everyday interactions with the world. The necessary instructions to accomplish a given task can be given to the computer in lower-level languages, which offer relatively more control of the machine at the cost of issuing larger numbers of instructions in smaller steps, or in higher-level languages, which do not allow so much control of the functions of the machine but are closer to natural language (e.g., English). My preference has always been to work in higher-level languages because they offered faster, simpler, and more economical solutions to the problems I was dealing with and to use low-level language for very narrowly defined tasks such as controlling a printer or some other such thing (which I would prefer to avoid). But with a bewildering variety of technology choices always available, I have found it helpful to think each problem and solution option through on its own merits and to frame my technology issues first in terms of necessary and sufficient conditions.

I used this procedure a few years ago when a colleague at another university expressed interest in creating a piece of educational software similar to one I had written with another colleague at my own university that would use a shell program this second colleague and I had developed. The creation of one of these packages involves, among other things, keeping track of several thousand questions and answers, so it was natural for me to see the authoring task as a database problem. I had created a nifty little database application for this purpose that had supported the creation of several of these packages, but it only ran on the Macintosh. I was actually in the process of rewriting the program to add more capabilities and convenience at the time we began to think about creating this new package, but meeting a deadline was a necessity, and I could see there probably wouldn't be time to get a Windows version running to meet her schedule. What I had to determine to make this project happen on time was the set of sufficient conditions to deliver the package she wanted. Seeing the project requirements in terms of the simplest implication possible was useful. To do this, let C stand for the sufficient condition for satisfying her part of the requirements for getting one of these software packages together and let P stand for the package we would deliver. In other words, what was the minimum that she had to do? For her purposes, it looked like this:

`If C then P`

The challenge for me was to get out of the habitual ways of thinking about creating one of these packages and specify a bare minimum C, which would be her deliverable. By setting it up this way, my own habits and uncritically accepted assumptions retreated into the background and the project requirements took center stage. By tracing the process of producing the software, I realized that there was one intermediate phase of the multistep data-formatting process that we used in which the data elements existed as a formatted text file. So, all she really *needed* to do was create a text file that had everything in order down to the last line feed. This was certainly not as convenient for her or for me as having everything managed by a database program, but this rather tedious, low-tech approach did allow the project to be completed and delivered within the desired time frame.

The case above was something of an exception to the rule, because usually there is not so much flexibility in a situation that one can transfer a database task to a word processor without heroic efforts. Still, it is not at all uncommon in the desktop world for people to use relatively inefficient tools to accomplish some of their own work. Many times, for example, I have seen spreadsheet programs pressed into use as painfully inconvenient and error-prone database managers. There is one additional practical logic lesson hiding here, and that is about the careful specification of minimum sufficient conditions. In the example above, the minimum technological requirement for the authoring of the package was less than what we had been using, but one must be watchful about realistic technological minimums that (unlike our example) exceed what is expected. This is where the danger is, because the cost of appropriate technology can often engender wishful thinking to the effect that the task can be accomplished with less than what is really needed. We may employ valid logic in establishing the effects of what we specify as sufficient conditions, but it is important not to be blinded by validity; if the antecedent of the conditional (a sufficient condition) is not correctly specified in actual practice, the realization of the consequent may not match expectations.

Reliability is one of the key values in computing. Beyond the logic of the basic technology choices, any programmer learns quickly that for the accomplishment of specific tasks, there is no substitute for careful analysis of the logic of a program. The alternative is a program that is rich in what are often euphemistically referred to as "undocumented features." (This phrase was actually used by company in the eighties when confronted with evidence of what is normally called a bug.) A program that crashes or, worse, corrupts data without giving any notice that something is wrong can be just a minor inconvenience, but it can also threaten the existence of an enterprise. Recognition of this fact is behind much of the energy that has been devoted to the so-called "millennium" or "Y2K" bug, the inability of some programs to deal with time intervals that span the transition from one century to the next. Bugs are just about inevitable in first drafts of programs, but a good grasp of logic means that they can get found and fixed much more quickly.

This was brought home to me in a very elementary way when I was working on a large database project for a commercial client. In this case, the project involved queries that were run on an antiquated, idiosyncratic mainframe computer located in another state. The queries could become logically complex through use of an extensive set of attributes (columns in the database) and familiar Boolean operators (AND, OR, NOT) to specify the desired data set. A typical query might concatenate categories such as Product X, manufacture date A, manufacture date B, color Y, and color Z into a query like [Product X AND (color Y OR color Z) AND (manufacture date greater than date A AND manufacture date less than date B)], which translates a specification that might read like this: What I need is a list of all the Product X in color Y and color Z that we have, but I don't want any of the stuff that was made before date A. And the product that was made after date B doesn't matter to me right now either.

With many categories available, these queries could be both complex and expressive in ways that only emerge clearly after working with them for a while. In this project, the results of the queries were then downloaded to one of the client's computers, where they were further processed into a form that allowed for more efficient manipulation by the local database management program. Like many commercial data providers, the source of my project's raw data charged by the downloaded record. One night, I was working on a particularly complicated automated query-and-download routine and needed to bring in a few records to test my program, so I added a condition that was intended to filter out just about all records in the database. The query mistakenly asked for what I'll characterize as [attribute A OR attribute B] instead of [attribute A AND attribute B]. I expected the query and download to finish in less than a minute, so I just sat at the machine and waited as the downloaded data came in. And waited. And waited. And went to get a snack. And still it came. I figured I had just misjudged the size of the database or the speed of my connection, so I went home to sleep. When I came in the next morning, I had a hard disk crammed full of disorganized data and a crashed computer to deal with. When I got the mess cleaned up and went back to see what might have caused the unexpected volume returned by the query, that one Boolean operator turned out to be the whole problem. When I informed the database owner of the error, we had a good laugh at my expense, though the episode was far less expensive than it could have been, as the charges for the thousands of mistakenly downloaded records were graciously removed from the bill.

USING LOGIC TO GET ORGANIZED

One way of thinking of computers is as devices for keeping track of things. Even complex calculations occur as a large number of small operations, the results of which are stored and used in the succession of steps that carry out a command (which may be issued by a person or a program) to its conclusion. Of course, the goal in calculations as well as other computer operations that are not performed for the purpose of calculation is for the results to be perfectly reliable. We know we don't always get perfect reliability from computers because, for example, there logically has to be imprecision in the outcome of a calculation that uses results of division operations that do not reach completion within the number of decimal places that a computer can handle. (This imprecision was instrumental in the creation of chaos theory, often called complexity theory, which deals with irregular and unpredictable phenomena.) But even though there are limits to the precision of which any computer is capable, the majority of operations in a typical computing environment occur well within those limits. Importantly, it is possible to prove that when operations are restricted to the limits of precision of a computer, operations are or are not occurring reliably. The reliability of operations is due to the techniques of deductive logic, and selection of alternative operations within a program to accomplish specific tasks is a matter of logical consequence, especially since program capabilities may be used in ways the programmer did not originally intend. A program's range of logical possibilities may far exceed the original design requirements, but capabilities that are there, however imperfectly, will almost certainly be discovered and used by someone, so it is necessary to check for logical and practical "dead ends" with thoroughness.

Human beings use deductive logic regularly, but not quite in the same way as computers do. The most important difference is that application of deductive logic in computing begins at a far simpler level than the concepts that are meaningful to people. In a digital computer, the kind of machine in almost universal use at present, computation within the machine occurs through very simple magnetic manipulations in the computer's memory that may occur at the rate of millions, billions, or even trillions of operations per second. Each operation changes the state of the computer's memory. A computer's memory is very different from a human brain, but the logic that governs operations in a computer's memory uses exactly the same rules that philosophers have developed for logical operations generally. Programmers who need to manage these lower-level (less abstract) operations directly typically make use of the sort of two-valued logic that underlies all divisions of propositions into the categories of "True" and "False."

Direct manipulation of computer memory by application programmers is not necessary to accomplish most modern computing tasks because programming tools and high-level application programs (such as word processors or spreadsheets) generally take care of this low-level work by combining large numbers of small operations into larger ones. An example of an operation that occurs at a fairly high level of abstraction would be use of the backspace key to delete a space in the middle of a paragraph in a word processing document. This looks like a simple operation, but for it to occur correctly, the computer must know the point in the file that corresponds to the on-screen cursor, must relate the input from the keyboard to an electronic manipulation of the memory, must remove one and only one space character from the file at that point, must redraw a million individual pixels or so on the screen so that the display corresponds with the file, and so on. Most programmers never have to worry about the details of specifying individual pixels (and they'd never get any work done if they did), but that is because other programmers who created the programming tools have already organized the control of the details in a general way. To make sure that they are taking all the logical possibilities into account, programmers construct truth tables. Because a properly constructed truth table displays everything that could possibly occur within the range of the variables it handles, certain kinds of problems can easily be avoided. That's the good news. The bad news is that modern programs can easily become so complex that checking them would require infinitely large truth tables. The compromise is that programmers go as far as they can with deductive methods, which still covers a lot of ground.

The basic idea of how truth tables help programmers keep track of the results of operations in a computer's memory can be illustrated in principle without getting into complicated technical details. Let's say we are managing a consulting project and our computer is keeping track of whether work can be done on any day. Like many organizations, we will use a calendar program to keep track of who is able to show up at the customer's site. To be able to do our work, let's say we need a team of at least two people present at the customer's site, one of whom must be a programmer and one of whom must be a technician. One reason we need to do this bit of bookkeeping is that not everybody can be in town every day, and we cannot bill the customer if we don't have a functional team at the customer's site. Also, we want to be as efficient as possible in our scheduling, so as soon as we know we will not be able to get a functional team on site, we have our calendar program automatically send an e-mail to the other consultants so they can schedule themselves into other tasks. Let's say that Sally and Herb are programmers and Mike and Rose are technicians. The truth table below represents the essentials of the situation:

S	H	M	R	(S v H) & (M v R)
T	T	T	T	T
T	T	T	F	T
T	T	F	T	T
T	T	F	F	F
T	F	T	T	T
T	F	T	F	T
T	F	F	T	T
T	F	F	F	F
F	T	T	T	T
F	T	T	F	T
F	T	F	T	T
F	T	F	F	F
F	F	T	T	F
F	F	T	F	F
F	F	F	T	F
F	F	F	F	F

According to the business rule that says at least one programmer and one technician must be on site for work to proceed, which is what the right-most column represents (the "v" symbolizes a nonexclusive "or"), there are nine possible configurations of the four workers that are "legal" and seven that are not. We can know just from the unavailability on the same day of either the two programmers or the two technicians that we will not be able to schedule work at the client's site. We can also know from the availability of one of each, that we can schedule work, and it's still possible that either or both of the other two will show up. The truth table covers every eventuality that planning must deal with.

Or does it? Real-life situations may be a little more complicated than switching polarities in a memory bank. One way of interpreting cells in the rightmost column that have a value of "F" is that work cannot be scheduled. That's accurate, because it takes the availability of one programmer and one technician to trigger the scheduling of work. But what does an "F" in a cell in Rose's column actually mean? Does it mean she called in to say she's not available or that she hasn't called at all? Some programmers and analysts who work with database applications insist that two-valued logic can hide important business realities, and so should be replaced in some cases with a three-valued logic that includes a null value. In the illustration above, the truth table would have a null value in a cell until we knew one way or another what the programmer or technician would do. To cover all the logical possibilities would expand our truth table from sixteen rows to eighty-one rows (we'll spare you the details), so there's considerably more overhead in planning for all the possibilities that come with a three-valued logic. The applications recommended by proponents of three-valued logic typically do not require the building of truth tables, but this is one way of assessing the increase in logical complexity that results from a decision to move to three-valued logic.

Three-valued logic does appear to be more expressive than two-valued logic, but choosing to adopt it is not a simple matter. It turns out there are ways of dealing with whether a programmer or technician has confirmed availability status that are more economical in a three-valued system, and there are ways that are more economical in a two-valued system. How can this be? The answer lies in how the availability status confirmation fact is related to the status itself. If we set up an availability status confirmation column for each of the four people within the truth table above, that means each has two columns instead of one, and that accounting for every possible state of the system will take 256 rows. That is far less economical that the eighty-one rows that three-valued logic promises. If, however, we go outside our one truth table to set up a second that only deals with confirmation, we can do it in another sixteen row table with a fifth column for the expression H & S & R & M, which would be true when all had confirmed their availability or unavailability. In terms of storage requirements, the most economical two-valued solution requires 160 cells of data while the three-valued solution requires 405, but to get that economy we would have to deal with two files instead of one, which is considerably more complicated. These sorts of decisions are common in database work, and proponents of each approach can point to advantages. One interesting aspect of the debate about these two approaches is that it has often occurred more at the level of philosophy and mathematics than at the level of practical implementation issues. Perhaps not surprisingly, those writers with a more mathematical orientation—a clear majority—have tended to favor two-valued logic solutions, while philosophers have led the exploration of alternatives.

IN CONCLUSION

There is no doubt that computers could not do the things they do without the pioneering work of philosophers and that the continuing development of computing applications by individuals schooled in philosophy's techniques is a key factor in the dynamic growth of computing. There is much more that philosophers do in the world of computing; it would take a bookshelf to begin to cover the work in artificial intelligence, robotics, ergonomics, advanced logic, business rule formalization, game design, distributed computing architecture, and other areas. Computing has steadily moved from its early emphasis on bit- and byte-level manipulation of the machine to a focus on use of complex, prebuilt functions and objects. This shift has reduced the amount of machine technology one needs to program a machine to do useful work and turned most low-level operations into standardized elements. At the same time, as far less energy must be devoted to achieving basic functionality, the importance of program refinement increases. People are demanding more convenience and power as fast as the industry can deliver it. In my experience, the diverse skill sets of philosophers have been more fully utilized in computing with every passing year. I expect this trend to continue.

DISCUSSION QUESTIONS

1. Explain the following terms:
   (a) logic
   (b) induction
   (c) deduction
   (d) valid logical form
   (f) syllogism
2. Applying the six rules of categorical syllogisms introduced by Kahane, determine whether each of the following categorical syllogisms is valid or invalid. Indicate what rule is violated if the syllogism is invalid:
   a) All philosophy majors have taken at least one course in philosophy.
      Some computer scientists have not taken at least one course in philosophy.
      Therefore, some computer scientists are not philosophy majors.
   b) Some scientists are knowledgable about digital circuitry.
      All computer engineers who design hardware are scientists.
      Therefore, all computer engineers who design hardware are knowledgable about digital circuitry.
   c) No software developers are incapable of deductive reasoning.
      No logicians who despise high technology are software developers.
      Therefore, no logicians who despise high technology are incapable of deductive reasoning.
   d) All philosophy majors have skills that are useful in software design.
      Some very talented software developers are not philosophy majors.
      Therefore, some very talented software developers do not have skills useful in software design.
   e) Artificial intelligence systems that can think like humans have not yet been created.
      Programs that are self-aware and can reason deductively and inductively are artificial intelligence systems that can think like humans.
      Therefore, some programs that are self-aware and can reason deductively and inductively have not yet been created.
3. Suppose that you have created an inference engine (say in a computer language like Prolog) into which you have programmed all the *valid* inference rules of deductive logic that have been discussed in Stephen Barker's article in this chapter on "The Logic of Truth Functions." Whenever you "feed" the program information, it applies these rules and deduces conclusions. Suppose you feed the program the following information:
   (1) Herb is dating both Mary and Sally.
   (2) If Herb is dating both Mary and Sally, then Herb is dating two women.
   (3) It cannot both be true that Herb is dating two women and he is not playing the field.

(4) Either Herb is not playing the field or he is not ready to settle down and raise a family.

(5) If Herb is in love with Sally then he is ready to settle down and raise a family.

(6) If Herb is not in love with Sally then Sally will never get married.

(7) If Sally gets married then she will live happily ever after.

(8) If Mary gets married then she will have children.

(9) Mary will have children.

Your program will now assume that statements (1) through (9) are true, and will use them as premises from which to deduce conclusions. List all the *valid* conclusions that your program will deduce from these premises. For each conclusion you list be prepared to state (1) the premises from which the conclusion will be deduced and (2) the logical form or skeleton of the argument. Note: Once your program deduces a conclusion, that conclusion itself becomes one of the program's premises which it can use to deduce further conclusions.

4. Explain and illustrate the difference between an exclusive "or" and a nonexclusive (inclusive) "or." Why would this distinction be important to a computer programmer?

5. Explain the difference between "or" (in the nonexclusive sense) and "and." Recall Greg Tropea's anecdote of how his having mistakenly instructed a computer to download all data with attribute A OR B, when he really meant A *AND* B, caused the hard disk to fill and the computer to crash. Explain why this logical error caused so much more data to be downloaded.

6. Using your knowledge of the meaning of "or" and "and", determine whether each of the following arguments is valid. Be prepared to explain your answer:

    a) A
       ∴ A or B

    b) A or B
       ∴ A

    c) (A and not-A) or B
       ∴ B

    d) A
       ∴ A & (B or not-B)

    e) A & B
       ∴ A

7. Suppose that A is true, B is False, and C is False. What is the truth value of the following compound statement:

(A & B) or (not-B and not-C)

8. What reasons does Tropea give for thinking that philosophy (including but not restricted to logic) can be useful to a software developer? Do you agree with him? Defend your answer.

9. Tropea draws the conclusion that some technological questions are philosophical questions. State the premises from which he draw this conclusion: What is the mood and figure of this argument? Is it a valid argument? In your estimation, is each premise of this argument true? Defend your answer.

10. Digital circuitry, which controls computer output, depends upon truth functions. In the design of such circuitry, the values of *true* and *false* translate into *on* and *off*. A wire is *on* (= true) when current is passing through it; and a wire is *off* (= false) when no current is passing through it. The values of on and off are in turn represented mathematically as 1 and 0, respectively. (on = 1; off = 0). The following is a diagram of an "OR gate" (a digital "or" switch):

In order for the above digital switch to be turned on, it must have a value of 1.

a) What combination(s) of values for wire A and wire B would give the switch a value of 1? (Suggestion: Using the structure of a truth table, construct a table displaying all possible combinations.)

b) What combination(s) would give the switch a value of 0?

c) Answer questions a) and b) above for the "AND gate" diagramed below.

A ———⟩
B ———⟩———— AB

8

SCIENTIFIC METHOD: MEDICAL RESEARCH

In this chapter the focus will be on the use of *inductive* logic within the context of scientific inquiry. As was noted in the previous chapter, the mark of an inductive argument is that its conclusion follows from its premises with some degree of *probability* (in contrast to deductive arguments wherein the conclusion follows *necessarily* from the premises). Insofar as the scientific method rests upon inductive logic, its conclusions are thus also probabilistic. The quest for viable methods of scientific inquiry is, accordingly, tantamount to the quest for ways of achieving a greater likelihood that the conclusions proffered by science will be true.

In the first selection of this chapter, Irving Copi, employing a detective scenario from Sherlock Holmes, explores various stages of formulating and testing inductive hypotheses in order to solve scientific problems. First, the scientific process begins with the recognition of a *problem,* namely, a fact or set of facts which is so out of the ordinary that it calls for an explanation (for example, how did Enoch Drebber die?). Second, a *preliminary hypothesis* is formulated, specifically, a highly tentative explanation of the problem in question based upon previous knowledge (for instance, "Drebber was murdered at Brixton Road where the body was found"). Third, using the preliminary hypothesis as a guide, *additional facts* are gathered (for example, Drebber had poison on his lips). Fourth, *new hypotheses* are created in order to explain these other facts, as well as the earlier facts, and which, in turn, may lead to the discovery of still further facts and the creation of still further hypotheses to explain them, and so on (for example, "Drebber and his secretary—who was also later found dead—were both poisoned to death by the same man."). Fifth, *further consequences* are deduced from the hypotheses in question (the pills found at the scene of the murder of Drebber's secretary will contain poison, for example). Sixth, these consequences are then *tested.* If they turn out to be true, then the hypothesis is confirmed and its probability is increased; if they turn out to be false, then the probability of the hypothesis is diminished. The favorable hypothesis will then be the one with the greatest amount of predictive and explanatory power. Finally, the proffered hypothesis may be *applied* (that is, it is used to aid in apprehending Drebber's murderer).

In the Practice section of this chapter, Reidar K. Lie, a medical doctor (researcher in cardiology) who also holds a Ph.D. in the philosophy of science, shows how the inductive methodology outlined above is put to work in the context of medical problem solving in cardiology. Specifically, he discusses the problem of whether coronary bypass surgery is effective in terms of pain reduction and increased longevity for those afflicted with angina pectoris. In a lucid discussion, he shows how rival hypotheses or explanations to the effectiveness of this surgery, such as possible placebo effects of the surgery itself as well as built-in experimental biases, have made the case for the surgery far less convincing than may have at first appeared. Lie also discusses ways in which experiments can be designed in order to exclude such alternative explanations in testing hypotheses. In particular, he discusses the use of *randomized, controlled clinical trials* and *double blind clinical trials*.

Through these more refined methodologies for testing clinical hypotheses, he shows how the probability that a scientific conclusion is true may be significantly enhanced. Nevertheless, he ends by pointing to additional methodological problems, in particular, the problem of adequately testing preliminary hypotheses *before* clinical trials are undertaken. Indeed, since such trials involve risk of human life, this problem can hardly be underrated, especially from Lie's perspective as a physician.

ISSUES

IRVING M. COPI

SCIENCE AND HYPOTHESIS

The task of science, we all know, is to discover facts; but a haphazard collection of facts cannot be said to constitute a science. To be sure, some parts of science may focus on this or that particular fact. A geographer, for example, may be interested in the exact configuration of a particular coastline or a geologist in the rock strata in a particular locality. But in the more advanced sciences, bare descriptive knowledge of this or that particular fact is of little importance. The scientist is eager to search out more general truths, that particular facts illustrate and for which they are evidence. Isolated particular facts may be known—in a sense—by direct observation. That a particular released object falls, that this ball moves more slowly down an inclined plane than it did when

---

SOURCE: Irving M. Copi, *Introduction to Logic*, 7th ed. (New York: Macmillan, 1986), pp. 481–487, 492–301. Copyright © 1986 by the Macmillan Publishing Company. Reprinted by permission.

dropped directly downward, that the tides ebb and flow, all these are matters of fact open to direct inspection. But scientists seek more than a mere record of such phenomena: they strive to *understand* them. To this end they seek to formulate general laws that state the patterns of all such occurrences and the systematic relationships between them. The scientist searches for natural laws that govern particular events, and for the fundamental principles that underlie them.

This preliminary exposition of the theoretical aims of science can perhaps be made clearer by means of an example. By careful observation and the application of geometrical reasoning to the data thus collected, the Italian physicist and astronomer Galileo (1564–1642) succeeded in formulating the laws of falling bodies, which gave a very general description of the behavior of bodies near the surface of the earth. At about the same time the German astronomer Kepler (1571–1630), basing his reasonings very largely on the astronomical data collected by Denmark's Tycho Brahe (1546–1601), formulated the laws of planetary motion describing the elliptical orbits traveled by the planets around the sun. Each of these two great scientists succeeded in unifying the various phenomena in his own field of investigation by formulating the interrelations between them: Kepler in celestial mechanics, Galileo in terrestrial mechanics. Their discoveries were great achievements, but they were, after all, separate and isolated. Just as separate particular facts challenge the scientist to unify and explain them by discovering their lawful connections, so a plurality of general laws challenges the scientist to unify and explain *them* by discovering a still more general principle that subsumes the several laws as special cases. In the case of Kepler's and Galileo's laws, this challenge was met by one of the greatest scientific geniuses of all time, Sir Isaac Newton (1642–1727). By his Theory of Gravitation and his three Laws of Motion, Newton unified and explained celestial and terrestrial mechanics, showing them both to be deducible within the framework of a single more fundamental *theory*. Scientists seek not merely to know what the facts are, but to explain them, and to this end they devise "theories." To understand exactly what is involved here, we must consider the general nature of explanation itself.

In everyday life it is the unusual or startling for which we demand explanations. An office boy may arrive at work on time every morning and no curiosity will be aroused. But let him come an hour late one day, and his employer will demand an *explanation*. What is it that is wanted when an explanation for something is requested? An example will help to answer this question. The office boy might reply that he had taken the seven-thirty bus to work as usual, but the bus had been involved in a traffic accident which entailed considerable delay. In the absence of any other transportation, the boy had had to wait a full hour for the bus to be repaired. This account would probably be accepted as a satisfactory explanation. It can be so regarded because from the statements that constitute the explanation the fact to be explained follows logically and no longer appears puzzling. An explanation is a group of statements or a story from which the thing to be explained can logically be inferred and whose acceptance removes or diminishes its problematic or puzzling character. Of course the inference of the fact as conclusion from the explanation as premiss might have to be enthymematic, where the "understood" additional premisses may be generally accepted causal laws, or the conclusion may follow with probability rather than deductively. It thus appears that explanation and inference are very closely related. They are, in fact, the same process regarded from opposite points of view. Given certain premisses, any conclusion that can logically be inferred from them can be regarded as being explained by them. And given a fact to be explained, we say that we have found an explanation for it when we have found a set of premisses from which it can logically be inferred. . . .

Of course some proposed explanations are better than others. The chief criterion for evaluating explanations is *relevance*. If the tardy office boy had offered as explanation for his late arrival the fact that there is a war in Afghanistan or a famine in India, that would have been a very poor explanation, or "no explanation at all." Such a story would have had "nothing to do with the case"; it would have been *irrelevant*, because from it the fact to be explained *cannot* be inferred. The relevance of a proposed explanation, then, corresponds exactly to the cogency of the argument by which the fact to be explained is inferred from the proposed explanation. Any acceptable explanation must be relevant, but not all stories that are relevant in this sense are acceptable explanations. There are other criteria for deciding the worth or acceptability of proposed explanations.

The most obvious requirement to propose is that the explanation be *true*. In the example of the office boy's lateness, the crucial part of his explanation was a particular fact, the traffic accident, of which he claimed to be an eyewitness. But the explanations of science are for the most part *general* rather than particular. The keystone of Newtonian Mechanics is the Law of Universal Gravitation, whose statement is

> Every particle of matter in the universe attracts every other particle with a force which is directly proportional to the product of the masses of the particles and inversely proportional to the square of the distance between them.

Newton's law is not directly verifiable in the same way as a bus accident. There is simply no way in which we can inspect *all* particles of matter in the universe and observe that they do attract each other in precisely the way that Newton's Law asserts. Few propositions of science are *directly* verifiable as true. In fact, none of the important ones are. For the most part they concern *unobservable* entities, such as molecules and atoms, electrons and protons, chromosomes and genes. Hence the proposed requirement of truth is not *directly* applicable to most scientific explanations. Before considering more useful criteria for evaluating scientific theories, it will be helpful to compare scientific with unscientific explanations.

Science is supposed to be concerned with facts, and yet in its further reaches we find it apparently committed to highly speculative notions far removed from the possibility of direct experience. How then are scientific explanations to be distinguished from those that are frankly mythological or superstitious? An unscientific "explanation" of the regular motions of the planets was the doctrine that each heavenly body was the abode of an "Intelligence" or "Spirit" that controlled its movement. A certain humorous currency was achieved during World War II by the unscientific explanation of certain aircraft failures as being due to "gremlins," invisible but mischievous little men who played pranks on aviators. The point to note here is that from the point of view of observability and direct verifiability, there is no great difference between modern scientific theories and the unscientific doctrines of mythology or theology. One can no more see or touch a Newtonian "particle," an atom, or electron than an "intelligence" or a "gremlin." What, then, are the differences between scientific and unscientific explanations?

There are two important and closely related differences between the kind of explanation sought by science and the kind provided by superstitions of various sorts. The first significant difference lies in the attitudes taken toward the explanations in question. The typical attitude of one who really *accepts* an unscientific explanation is *dogmatic*. The unscientific explanation is regarded as being absolutely true and beyond all possibility of improvement or correction. During the Middle Ages and the early modern period, the word of Aristotle was the ultimate authority to which scholars appealed for deciding questions of fact. However empirically and open mindedly Aristotle himself may have arrived at his views, they were accepted by some schoolmen in a completely different and unscientific spirit. One of the schoolmen to whom Galileo offered his telescope to view the newly discovered moons of Jupiter declined to look, being convinced that none could possibly be seen because no mention of them could be found in Aristotle's treatise on astronomy! Because unscientific beliefs are absolute, ultimate, and final, within the framework of any such doctrine or dogma there can be no rational method of ever considering the question of its truth. The scientist's attitude toward his explanations is altogether different. Every explanation in science is put forward tentatively and provisionally. Any proposed explanation is regarded as a mere hypothesis, more or less probable on the basis of the available facts or relevant evidence. It must be admitted that the scientist's vocabulary is a little misleading on this point. When what was first suggested as a "hypothesis" becomes well confirmed, it is frequently elevated to the position of a "theory." And when, on the basis of a great mass of evidence, it achieves well-nigh universal acceptance, it is promoted to the lofty status of a "law." This terminology is not always strictly adhered to: Newton's discovery is still called the "Law of Gravitation," whereas Einstein's contribution, which supersedes or at least improves on Newton's, is referred to as the "Theory of Relativity." The vocabulary of "hypothesis," "theory," and "law" is unfortunate, since it obscures the important fact that *all* of the general propositions of science are regarded as hypotheses, never as dogmas.

Closely allied with the difference in the way they are regarded is the second and more fundamental difference between scientific and unscientific explanations or theories. This second difference lies in the basis for accepting or rejecting the view in question. Many unscientific views are mere prejudices that

their adherents could scarcely give any reason for holding. Since they are regarded as "certain," however, any challenge or question is likely to be regarded
as an affront and met with abuse. If those who accept an unscientific explanation *can* be persuaded to discuss the basis for its acceptance, there are only a
few grounds on which they will attempt to "defend" it. It is true because "we've
always believed it" or because "everyone knows it." These all too familiar
phrases express appeals to tradition or popularity rather than evidence. Or a
questioned dogma may be defended on the grounds of revelation or authority.
The absolute truth of their religious creeds and the absolute falsehood of all
others have been revealed from on high, at various times, to Moses, to Paul, to
Mohammed, to Joseph Smith, and to many others. That there are rival traditions, conflicting authorities, and revelations that contradict one another does
not seem disturbing to those who have embraced an absolute creed. In general,
unscientific beliefs are held independently of anything we should regard as *evidence* in their favor. Because they are *absolute,* questions of *evidence* for them
are regarded as having little or no importance.

The case is quite different in the realm of science. Since every scientific explanation is regarded as a hypothesis, it is regarded as worthy of acceptance
only to the extent that there is evidence for it. As a hypothesis, the question of
its truth or falsehood is open, and there is continual search for more and more
evidence to decide that question. The term "evidence" as used here refers ultimately to experience; *sensible* evidence is the ultimate court of appeal in verifying scientific propositions. Science is *empirical* in holding that sense experience
is the *test of truth* for all its pronouncements. Consequently, it is of the essence
of a scientific proposition that it be capable of being tested by observation.

Some propositions can be tested directly. To decide the truth or falsehood
of the proposition that it is now raining outside, we need only glance out the
window. To tell whether a traffic light shows green or red, all we have to do is
look at it. But the propositions offered by scientists as explanatory hypotheses
are not of this type. Such general propositions as Newton's Laws or Einstein's
Theory are not directly testable in this fashion. They can, however, be tested indirectly. The indirect method of testing the truth of a proposition is familiar to
all of us, though we may not be familiar with this name for it. For example, if
his employer had been suspicious of the office boy's explanation of his tardiness,
she might have checked up on it by telephoning the bus company to find out
whether an accident had really happened to the seven-thirty bus. If the bus
company's report checked with the boy's story, this would serve to dispel the
employer's suspicions; whereas if the bus company denied that an accident
had occurred, it would probably convince the employer that her office boy's
story was false. This inquiry would constitute an indirect test of the office boy's
explanation.

The pattern of indirect testing or indirect verification consists of two parts.
First, one deduces from the proposition to be tested one or more other propositions capable of being tested directly. Then, these conclusions are tested and
are found to be either true or false. If the conclusions are false, any proposition

that implies them must be false also. On the other hand, if the conclusions are true, that provides evidence for the truth of the proposition being tested, which is thus confirmed indirectly.

It should be noted that indirect testing is never demonstrative or certain. To deduce directly testable conclusions from a proposition usually requires additional premises. The conclusion that the bus company will confirm that its seven-thirty bus had an accident does not follow validly from the proposition that the seven-thirty bus did have an accident. Additional premises are needed, for example, that all accidents get reported to the company's office, that the reports are not mislaid or forgotten, and that the company does not make a policy of denying (or "covering up") its accidents. So the bus company's denying that an accident occurred would not prove the office boy's story to be false, for the discrepancy might be due to the falsehood of one of the other premises mentioned. Those others, however, ordinarily have such a high degree of probability that a negative reply on the part of the bus company would render the office boy's story very doubtful indeed.

Similarly, establishing the truth of a conclusion does not demonstrate the truth of the premises from which it was deduced. We know very well that a valid argument may have a true conclusion even though its premises are not all true. In the present example, the bus company might confirm that an accident happened to the seven-thirty bus because of some mistake in their records, even though no accident had occurred. So the inferred conclusion might be true even though the premises from which it was deduced were not. In the usual case, though, that is highly unlikely; so a successful or affirmative testing of a conclusion serves to corroborate the premises from which it was deduced.

It must be admitted that every proposition, scientific or unscientific, that is a relevant explanation for any observable fact has *some* evidence in its favor, namely, the fact to which it is relevant. Thus the regular motions of the planets must be conceded to constitute evidence for the (unscientific) theory that the planets are inhabited by "intelligences" that cause them to move in just the orbits that are observed. The motions themselves are as much evidence for that myth as they are for Newton's or Einstein's theories. The difference lies in the fact that that is the *only* evidence for the unscientific hypothesis. Absolutely no other directly testable propositions can be deduced from the myth. On the other hand, a very large number of directly testable propositions can be deduced from the scientific explanations mentioned. Here, then, is *the* difference between scientific and unscientific explanations. A scientific explanation for a given fact will have directly testable propositions deducible from it, other than the one stating the fact to be explained. But an unscientific explanation will have no other directly testable propositions deducible from it. It is of the essence of a scientific proposition to be empirically verifiable.

It is clear that we have been using the term "scientific explanation" in a quite general sense. As here defined, an explanation may be scientific even though it is not a part of one of the various special sciences like physics or psychology. Thus the office boy's explanation of his tardiness would be classified as a scientific one, for it is testable, even if only indirectly. But had he offered as explanation the proposition that "God willed him to be late that morning, and God is omnipotent," the explanation would have been unscientific. For although his being late that morning is deducible from the proffered explanation, no other directly testable proposition is, and so the explanation is not even indirectly testable and hence is unscientific.

Now . . . we are in a position to describe the general pattern of scientific research. It will be helpful to begin by examining an illustration of that method. A perennial favorite in this connection is the detective, whose problem is not quite the same as that of the pure scientist, but whose approach and technique illustrate the method of science very clearly. The classical example of the astute detective who can solve even the most baffling mystery is A. Conan Doyle's immortal creation, Sherlock Holmes. Holmes, his stature undiminished by the passage of time, will be our hero in the following account.

1. The Problem

Some of our most vivid pictures of Holmes are those in which he is busy with magnifying glass and tape measure, searching out and finding essential clues that had escaped the attention of those stupid bunglers, the "experts" of Scotland Yard. Or those of us who are by temperament less vigorous may think back more fondly on Holmes the thinker,

> . . . who, when he had an unsolved problem upon his mind, would go for days, and even for a week, without rest, turning it over, rearranging his facts, looking at it from every point of view until he had either fathomed it or convinced himself that his data were insufficient.[1]

But such memories are incomplete. Holmes was not always searching for clues or pondering over solutions. We all remember those dark periods—especially in the earlier stories—when, much to the good Watson's annoyance, Holmes would drug himself with morphine or cocaine. That would happen, of course, between cases. For when there is no mystery to be unraveled, nobody in his right mind would go out to look for clues. Clues, after all, must be clues *for* something. Nor could Holmes, or anyone else, for that matter, engage in profound thought unless he had something to think about. Sherlock Holmes was a genius at solving problems, but even a genius must have a problem before he can solve it. All reflective thinking, and this term includes criminal investigation as well as scientific research, is a problem-solving activity, as John Dewey and other pragmatists have rightly insisted. There must be a problem felt before either the detective or the scientist can go to work.

Of course, the active mind sees problems where the dullard sees only familiar objects. One Christmas season Dr. Watson visited Holmes to find that the latter had been using a lens and forceps to examine "a very seedy and disreputable hard-felt hat, much the worse for wear, and cracked in several places."[2] After they had greeted each other, Holmes said of it to Watson, "I beg that you will look upon it not as a battered billycock but as an intellectual problem."[3] It so happened that the hat led them into one of their most interesting adventures, but it could not have done so had Holmes not seen a problem in it from the start. A problem may be characterized as a fact or group of facts for which we have no acceptable explanation, that seem unusual, or that fail to fit in with our expectations or preconceptions. It should be obvious that *some* prior beliefs are required if anything is to appear problematic. If there are no expectations, there can be no surprises.

Sometimes, of course, problems came to Holmes already labeled. The very first adventure recounted by Dr. Watson began with the following message from Gregson of Scotland Yard:

> My Dear Mr. Sherlock Holmes:
> There has been a bad business during the night at 3, Lauriston Gardens, off the Brixton Road. Our man on the beat saw a light there about two in the morning, and as the house was an empty one, suspected that something was amiss. He found the door open, and in the front room, which is bare of furniture, discovered the body of a gentleman, well dressed, and having cards in his pocket bearing the name of "Enoch J. Drebber, Cleveland, Ohio, USA." There had been no robbery, nor is there any evidence as to how the man met his death. There are marks of blood in the room, but there is no wound upon his person. We are at a loss as to how he came into the empty house; indeed, the whole affair is a puzzler. If you can come round to the house any time before twelve, you will find me there. I have left everything in status quo until I hear from you. If you are unable to come, I shall give you fuller details, and would esteem it a great kindness if you would favour me with your opinion.
>
> Your faithfully,
> TOBIAS GREGSON[4]

Here was a problem indeed. A few minutes after receiving the message, Sherlock Holmes and Dr. Watson "were both in a hansom, driving furiously for the Brixton Road."

2. PRELIMINARY HYPOTHESES

On their ride out Brixton way, Holmes "prattled away about Cremona fiddles and the difference between a Stradivarius and an Amati." Dr. Watson chided Holmes for not giving much thought to the matter at hand, and Holmes replied: "No data yet. . . . It is a capital mistake to theorize before you have all the evidence. It biases the judgment."[5] This point of view was expressed by Holmes again and again. On one occasion he admonished a younger detective that "The temptation to form premature theories upon insufficient data is the bane of our profession."[6] Yet for all of his confidence about the matter, on this one issue Holmes was completely mistaken. Of course one should not reach a *final judgment* until a great deal of evidence has been considered, but this procedure is quite different from *not theorizing*. As a matter of fact, it is strictly impossible to make any serious attempt to collect evidence unless one *has* theorized beforehand. As Charles Darwin, the great biologist and author of the modern theory of evolution, observed,

> ... all observation must be for or against some view, if it is to be of any service.

The point is that there are too many particular facts, too many data in the world, for anyone to try to become acquainted with them all. Everyone, even the most patient and thorough investigator, must pick and choose, deciding which facts to study and which to pass over. One must have some working hypothesis for or against which to collect relevant data. It need not be a *complete* theory, but at least the rough outline must be there. Otherwise how could one decide what facts to select for consideration out of the totality of all facts, which is too vast even to begin to sift?

Holmes's actions were wiser than his words in this connection. After all, the words were spoken in a hansom speeding toward the scene of the crime. If Holmes really had no theory about the matter, why go to Brixton Road? If facts and data were all that he wanted, any old facts and any old data, with no hypotheses to guide him in their selection, why should he have left Baker Street at all? There were plenty of facts in the rooms at 221-B Baker Street. Holmes might just as well have spent his time counting all the words on all the pages of all the books there, or perhaps making very accurate measurements of the distances between each separate pair of articles of furniture in the house. He could have gathered data to his heart's content and saved himself cab fare into the bargain!

It may be objected that the facts to be gathered at Baker Street have nothing to do with the case, whereas those awaiting Holmes at the scene of the crime were valuable clues for solving the problem. It was, of course, just this consideration that led Holmes to ignore the "data" at Baker Street and hurry away to collect those off Brixton Road. It must be insisted, however, that the greater relevance of the latter could not be *known* beforehand but only conjectured on the basis of previous experience with crimes and clues. In fact, a *hypothesis* led Holmes to look in one place rather than another for his facts, the hypothesis that there was a murder, that the crime was committed at the place where the body was found, and that the perpetrator had left some trace or clue. Some such hypothesis is always needed to guide an investigator in the search for relevant data, for in the absence of any preliminary hypothesis, there are simply too many facts in this world to examine. The preliminary hypothesis ought to be highly tentative, and it must be based on previous knowledge. But a preliminary hypothesis is as necessary as the existence of a problem for any serious inquiry to begin.

It must be emphasized that a preliminary hypothesis, as here conceived, need not be a complete solution to the problem. The hypothesis that the man was murdered by someone who had left some clues to his identity on or near the body of the victim was what led Holmes to Brixton Road. This hypothesis is clearly incomplete: it does not say who committed the crime, or how it was done, or why. Such a preliminary hypothesis may be very different from the final solution to the problem. It will never be complete: it may be a tentative explanation of only part of the problem. But however partial and however tentative, a preliminary hypothesis is required for any investigation to proceed.

3. COLLECTING ADDITIONAL FACTS

Every serious investigation begins with some fact or group of facts that strike the investigator as problematic and thus initiate the whole process of inquiry. The initial facts that constitute the problem are usually too meager to suggest a wholly satisfactory explanation for themselves, but they will suggest—to the competent investigator—some preliminary hypotheses that lead to the search for additional facts. These additional facts, it is hoped, will serve as clues to the final solution. The inexperienced or bungling investigator will overlook or ignore all but the most obvious of them; but the careful worker will aim at completeness in the examination of those additional facts to which the preliminary hypotheses had led. Holmes, of course, was the most careful and painstaking of investigators.

Holmes insisted on dismounting from the hansom a hundred yards or so from their destination and approached the house on foot, looking carefully at its surroundings and especially at the pathway leading up to it. When Holmes and Watson entered the house, they were shown the body by the two Scotland Yard operatives, Gregson and Lestrade. ("There is no clue," said Gregson. "None at all," chimed in Lestrade.) But Holmes had already started his own search for additional facts, looking first at the body:

> . . . his nimble fingers were flying here, there, and everywhere, feeling, pressing, unbuttoning, examining. . . . So swiftly was the examination made, that one would hardly have guessed the minuteness with which it was conducted. Finally, he sniffed the dead man's lips, and then glanced at the soles of his patent leather boots.[7]

Then, turning his attention to the room itself,

> . . . he whipped a tape measure and a large round magnifying glass from his pocket. With these two implements he trotted noiselessly about the room, sometimes stopping, occasionally kneeling, and once lying flat upon his face. So engrossed was he with his occupation that he appeared to have forgotten our presence, for he chattered away to himself under his breath the whole time, keeping up a running fire of exclamations, groans, whistles and little cries suggestive of encouragement and hope. As I watched him I was irresistibly reminded of a pure-blooded, well-trained foxhound as it dashes backward and forward through the covert, whining in its eagerness, until it comes across the lost scent. For twenty minutes or more he continued his researches, measuring with the most exact care the distance between marks which were entirely invisible to me, and occasionally applying his tape to the walls in an equally incomprehensible manner. In one place he gathered up very carefully a little pile of gray dust from the floor and packed it away in an envelope. Finally he examined with his glass the word upon the wall, going over every letter of it, with the most minute exactness. This done, he appeared to be satisfied, for he replaced his tape and his glass in his pocket.

"They say that genius is an infinite capacity for taking pains," he remarked with a smile. "It's a very bad definition, but it does apply to detective work."[8] One matter deserves to be emphasized very strongly.

Steps 2 and 3 are not completely separable but are usually very intimately connected and interdependent. True enough, we require a preliminary hypothesis to begin any intelligent examination of facts, but the additional facts may themselves suggest new hypotheses, which may lead to new facts, which suggest still other hypotheses, which lead to still other additional facts, and so on. Thus having made his careful examination of the facts available in the house off Brixton Road, Holmes was led to formulate a further hypothesis that required the taking of testimony from the constable who found the body. The man was off duty at the moment, and Lestrade gave Holmes the constable's name and address.

Holmes took a note of the address.

> "Come along, Doctor," he said: "We shall go and look him up. I'll tell you one thing which may help you in the case," he continued, turning to the two detectives. "There has been murder done, and the murderer was a man. He was more than six feet high, was in the prime of life, had small feet for his height, wore coarse, square-toed boots and smoked a Trichinopoly cigar. He came here with his victim in a four-wheeled cab, which was drawn by a horse with three old shoes and one new one on his off fore-leg. In all probability the murderer had a florid face, and the fingernails of his right hand were remarkably long. These are only a few indications, but they may assist you."
>
> Lestrade and Gregson glanced at each other with an incredulous smile.
>
> "If this man was murdered, how was it done?" asked the former.
>
> "Poison," said Sherlock Holmes curtly, and strode off.[9]

4. FORMULATING THE HYPOTHESIS

In an investigation the stage will be reached, sooner or later, at which the investigator—whether detective, scientist, or ordinary mortal—will begin to feel that all the facts needed for solving the problem are at hand. The investigator has the "2 and 2," so to speak, but the task still remains of "putting them together." At such a time Sherlock Holmes might sit up all night, consuming pipe after pipe of tobacco, trying to think things through. The result or end product of such thinking, if it is successful, is a hypothesis that accounts for all the data, both the original set of facts constituting the problem and the additional facts to which the preliminary hypotheses pointed. The actual discovery of such an exploratory hypothesis is a process of creation, in which imagination as well as knowledge is involved. Holmes, who was a genius at inventing hypotheses, described the process as reasoning "backward." As he put it,

> Most people if you describe a train of events to them, will tell you what the result would be. They can put those events together in their minds, and argue from them that something will come to pass. There are few people, however, who, if you told them a result, would be able to evolve from their own inner consciousness what the steps were which led up to that result.[10]

Here is Holmes's description of the process of formulating an exploratory hypothesis. . . .

5. Deducing Further Consequences

A really fruitful hypothesis will explain not only the facts that originally inspired it, but will explain many others in addition. A good hypothesis will point beyond the initial facts in the direction of new ones whose existence might otherwise not have been suspected. And, of course, the verification of those further consequences will tend to confirm the hypothesis that led to them. Holmes's hypothesis that the murdered man had been poisoned was soon put to such a test. A few days later the murdered man's secretary and traveling companion was also found murdered. Holmes asked Lestrade, who had discovered the second body, whether he had found anything in the room that could furnish a clue to the murderer. Lestrade answered, "Nothing," and went on to mention a few quite ordinary effects. Holmes was not satisfied and pressed him, asking, "And was there nothing else?" Lestrade answered, "Nothing of any importance," and named a few more details, the last of which was "a small chip ointment box containing a couple of pills." At this information,

> Sherlock Holmes sprang from his chair with an exclamation of delight.
> "The last link," he cried, exultantly. "My case is complete."
> The two detectives stared at him in amazement.
> "I have now in my hands," my companion said, confidently, "all the threads which have formed such a tangle. . . . I will give you a proof of my knowledge. Could you lay your hands upon those pills?"
> "I have them," said Lestrade, producing a small white box.[11]

On the basis of his hypothesis about the original crime, Holmes was able to predict that the pills found at the scene of the second crime must contain poison. Here deduction has an essential role in the process of any scientific or inductive inquiry. The ultimate value of any hypothesis lies in its predictive or explanatory power, which means that additional facts must be deducible from an adequate hypothesis. From his theory that the first man was poisoned and that the second victim met his death at the hands of the same murderer, Holmes inferred that the pills found by Lestrade must be poison. His theory, however sure he may have felt about it, was only a theory and needed further confirmation. He obtained that confirmation by testing the consequences deduced from the hypothesis and finding them to be true. Having used deduction to make a prediction, his next step was to test it.

6. Testing the Consequences

The consequences of a hypothesis, that is, the predictions made on the basis of that hypothesis, may require various means for their testing. Some require only observation. In some cases, Holmes needed only to watch and wait—for the bank robbers to break into the vault, in the *Adventure of the Red-Headed League,* or for Dr. Roylott to slip a venomous snake through a dummy ventilator, in the *Adventure of the Speckled Band.* In the present case, however, an experiment had to be performed.

Holmes asked Dr. Watson to fetch the landlady's old and ailing terrier, which she had asked to have put out of its misery the day before. Holmes then cut one of the pills in two, dissolved it in a wineglass of water, added some milk, and

> . . . turned the contents of the wineglass into a saucer and placed it in front of the terrier, who speedily licked it dry. Sherlock Holmes's earnest demeanor had so far convinced us that we all sat in silence, watching the animal intently, and expecting some startling effect. None such appeared, however. The dog continued to lie stretched upon the cushion, breathing in a laboured way, but apparently neither the better nor the worse for its draught.
>
> Holmes had taken out his watch, and as minute followed minute without result, an expression of the utmost chagrin and disappointment appeared upon his features. He gnawed his lip, drummed his fingers upon the table, and showed every other symptom of acute impatience. So great was his emotion that I felt sincerely sorry for him, while the two detectives smiled derisively, by no means displeased at this check which he had met.
>
> "It can't be a coincidence," he cried, at last springing from his chair and pacing wildly up and down the room: "it is impossible that it should be a mere coincidence. The very pills which I suspected in the case of Drebber are actually found after the death of Stangerson. And yet they are inert. What can it mean? Surely my whole chain of reasoning cannot have been false. It is impossible! And yet this wretched dog is none the worse. Ah, I have it! I have it!" With a perfect shriek of delight he rushed to the box, cut the other pill in two, dissolved it, adding milk, and presented it to the terrier. The unfortunate creature's tongue seemed hardly to have been moistened in it before it gave a convulsive shiver in every limb, and lay as rigid and lifeless as if it had been struck by lightning.
>
> Sherlock Holmes drew a long breath, and wiped the perspiration from his forehead.[12]

By the favorable outcome of his experiment, Holmes's hypothesis had received dramatic and convincing confirmation.

7. APPLICATION

The detective's concern, after all, is a practical one. Given a crime to solve, he has not merely to explain the facts but to apprehend and arrest the criminal. The latter involves making application of his theory, using it to predict where the criminal can be found and how he may be caught. He must deduce still further consequences from the hypothesis, not for the sake of additional confirmation but for practical use. From his general hypothesis Holmes was able to infer that the murderer was acting the role of a cabman. We have already seen that

Holmes had formed a pretty clear description of the man's appearance. He sent out his army of "Baker Street Irregulars," street urchins of the neighborhood, to search out and summon the cab driven by just that man. The successful "application" of this hypothesis can be described again in Dr. Watson's words. A few minutes after the terrier's death,

> . . . there was a tap at the door, and the spokesman of the street Arabs, young Wiggins, introduced his insignificant and unsavoury person.
>
> "Please, sir," he said touching his forelock, "I have the cab downstairs."
>
> "Good boy," said Holmes, blandly. "Why don't you introduce this pattern at Scotland Yard?" he continued, taking a pair of steel handcuffs from a drawer. "See how beautifully the spring works. They fasten in an instant."
>
> "The old pattern is good enough," remarked Lestrade, "if we can only find the man to put them on."
>
> "Very good, very good," said Holmes, smiling. "The cabman may as well help me with my boxes. Just ask him to step in, Wiggins."
>
> I was surprised to find my companion speaking as though he were about to set out on a journey, since he had not said anything to me about it. There was a small portmanteau in the room, and this he pulled out and began to strap. He was busily engaged at it when the cabman entered the room.
>
> "Just give me a help with this buckle, cabman," he said, kneeling over his task, and never turning his head.
>
> The fellow came forward with a somewhat sullen, defiant air, and put down his hands to assist. At that instant there was a sharp click, the jangling of metal, and Sherlock Holmes sprang to his feet again.
>
> "Gentleman," he cried, with flashing eyes, "let me introduce you to Mr. Jefferson Hope, the murderer of Enoch Drebber and of Joseph Stangerson." [13]

Here we have a picture of the detective as scientist, reasoning from observed facts to a testable hypothesis that not only explains the facts but also permits a practical application.

NOTES

1. A. Conan Doyle, *The Man with the Twisted Lip.*
2. A. Conan Doyle, *The Adventure of the Blue Carbuncle.*
3. Ibid.
4. A. Conan Doyle, *A Study in Scarlet.*
5. Ibid.
6. A. Conan Doyle, *The Valley of Fear.*
7. Doyle, *A Study in Scarlet.*
8. Ibid.
9. Ibid.
10. Ibid.
11. Ibid.
12. Ibid.
13. Ibid.

PRACTICE

REIDAR K. LIE

THE PHILOSOPHER AS PHYSICIAN:
TESTING CLINICAL HYPOTHESES

HOW CAN WE KNOW THAT A TREATMENT
FOR A PARTICULAR DISEASE IS BENEFICIAL?

Any physician who treats patients is daily confronted by the following question: What therapeutic choice is best in a particular patient? In order to answer that question, the physician needs to know both what the *effects* of the various treatment options are and how *desirable* these effects are in terms of the patient's preferences. For example, in a patient with angina pectoris (chest pain as a result of narrowing of the coronary arteries, which supply blood to the heart), one acceptable treatment is coronary bypass surgery. When a physician deliberates about whether she should recommend or not recommend that particular treatment to her patient, she needs, among other things, to know what the chance is that the patient will die as a result of the operation, and also what the chance is that the pain will disappear after the operation. She also needs to know how *desirable,* from the patient's point of view, pain relief is in relation to the small chance of death as a result of the operation. In this essay, I shall not discuss the value choices involved in medical decision making, but mainly concentrate on how a physician can *know* that a particular treatment option really is effective. As a physician who is also interested in the philosophy of science, I have during the past several years tried to systematically examine this problem. In the following I will not be able to touch on all the difficulties one may encounter in an attempt to address this issue, but I will illustrate that some of the general strategies pointed out by Copi can very effectively be used to illuminate how we should go about finding out whether or not a particular treatment is effective. I shall use coronary artery bypass surgery as an example, since I myself have been interested mainly in how to apply the philosophy of science to cardiology. This particular case, however, also illustrates how difficult it sometimes can be to find out exactly what the effects of a particular treatment procedure are.

Coronary artery bypass surgery was introduced during the mid-1960s. Before that time nobody had tried the operation on any patients. The question at that time was, therefore, how can we know that the pain of angina pectoris will disappear after coronary bypass surgery? This question is the point of departure, the *problem,* or the hypothesis. Physicians would want to know the answer to this question in the same way Sherlock Holmes in Copi's example wants an answer to the question of who murdered Enoch Drebber. Let me, before I

Reidar K. Lie received his medical degree from the University of Bergen, Norway, in 1983 and his Ph.D. in philosophy from the University of Minnesota, Minneapolis, in 1987. He has taught in the Department of Medical Humanities, School of Medicine, at East Carolina University, and has done research in basic cardiology (ultrastructural changes in the heart after various pharmacological interventions). Dr. Lie has held a special interest in how recent work in the philosophy of science can illuminate theory changes in cardiology from around 1880 until today. Presently, Dr. Lie is a professor of philosophy at the University of Bergen, Norway, where, in addition to teaching regular philosophy courses, he teaches interdisciplinary courses in "Ethics and Health Policy" and "Research Ethics."

examine how we should test this hypothesis, first say a few words about why the question was formulated in this particular way. There is nothing strange about wanting a remedy for pain, but why did anybody suggest bypass surgery? Why not suggest herbal teas, or taking a train ride? It is clear that there are lots of possible treatment options, all of which *may* be helpful for patients with angina pectoris. Most of us would, however, dismiss many of these as not relevant to the problem of angina pectoris. As discussed by Copi, we form *preliminary* hypotheses, based on the knowledge we already possess, about which therapies will most probably be effective. With regard to angina pectoris, it is generally accepted that the pain is caused by narrowing of the coronary arteries, which leads to a diminished supply of blood to the heart muscle, which then again leads to pain. It is therefore natural to suggest that if one *bypassed* the narrowed segment of the coronary artery, one would again be able to establish a sufficient supply of blood to the heart, and thereby cause the pain to disappear. One may even be able to increase the life expectancy of these patients by reestablishing the blood supply to the heart muscle in this manner. In contrast, there is no evidence suggesting that train rides may be beneficial. The hypothesis that coronary artery bypass surgery is beneficial in patients with angina pectoris is therefore worthy of serious investigation.

EXCLUDING ALTERNATIVE EXPLANATIONS: THE PLACEBO EFFECT OF SURGERY

The next thing we need to do is to *test* this particular hypothesis. As discussed by Copi, we then deduce a consequence, or a prediction, from the hypothesis, and check to see whether the prediction turns out to be true. In this case, we predict that if we perform a coronary artery bypass operation on a patient, the pain will disappear. Let us assume that we have done so, and we have found that the pain does indeed disappear. Can we now accept the hypothesis that this particular operation is successful at alleviating pain? Not necessarily. As argued by Copi, "indirect testing is never demonstrative or certain." If we have observed the event we predicted from the hypothesis (in Copi's example, the confirmation by the bus company that the seven-thirty bus had an accident), we still have to rule out other possible explanations for the event observed. In Copi's example, we have to exclude the possibility that a bus accident was recorded by mistake. If alternative explanations for the event observed are implausible, as they are in the bus accident case, there is no problem. But if it is reasonable to accept an alternative explanation for the event we observed, then we cannot argue that the observed event represents a confirmation of the hypothesis. In order to see how this can be applied to the problem of coronary bypass surgery, let us more carefully formulate the hypothesis we want to have tested. We want to know whether the fact that we have *bypassed* a narrowed segment of a coronary artery is the cause of the disappearance of the pain. It is clear that when we do this operation, we simultaneously do a lot of other things which are necessary in order to get to the diseased artery: We have to give anaesthesia to the patient, we have to make an incision in the chest, we cut a lot of structures around the vessel, and so on. Strictly speaking, therefore, when we observe that the pain has disappeared after surgery, we cannot be sure that it is not any one of these other actions which has caused the pain to disappear. If we want to conclude that it is the bypassing of the narrowed segment of the artery that causes the pain to disappear, we have to argue that it is unlikely that all of the other things we do at the same time are capable of causing the pain to disappear. This, it turns out, is not the case, as the following example illustrates.

During the 1950s a popular treatment for coronary heart disease was to ligate (stop the flow of blood by tying a thread around it) an artery called the internal mammary artery. The therapy was regarded as highly effective, as the

pain disappeared in the vast majority of patients after this operation. Proponents of the therapy not only based their confidence in its effectiveness on such
a favorable clinical outcome, but also pointed to experimental evidence which
showed that the ligation resulted in an increased blood supply to the heart
muscle through the formation of an additional blood supply to the heart. The
procedure was thus justified by an appeal to an apparently well-established
pathophysiological theory. Many people, however, remained skeptical, and in
1959 two studies were published which showed that the operation was without
value. The patients were divided into two groups. In one group, an incision was
made in the chest, but the artery was not ligated. In the other group the artery
was ligated. The patients themselves did not know which procedure had been
performed on them.[1] After the operation, there was no difference between the
groups in terms of pain relief. The pain relief which had been observed earlier
was therefore caused by the placebo effect of the surgery itself, and not by the
ligation of the artery.[2]

What this example shows is that everything that is done to a patient before
and during surgery is capable of causing the pain to disappear. One does not
necessarily have to do anything to the patient that will improve the circulation
to the heart, but the fact that a patient thinks that something dramatic is going
to be done about his pain may itself be sufficient to cause the pain to disappear.
Therefore, when we observe that the pain disappears after coronary bypass surgery, we cannot be certain that it is the *bypassing* of the narrowed segment
which results in pain relief; it may just be a placebo effect of the surgery itself.

As discussed by Copi, we test a hypothesis by deducing a consequence which
we then either confirm or disconfirm. If it turns out that we do observe what
we predicted, this may show that it is reasonable to accept the hypothesis. This
is not always the case, however, as we have just illustrated. Whenever there is
an alternative by which we can also deduce the observed consequence, we cannot be sure which one of the two hypotheses we should accept. In the present
case, we cannot know, from this test alone, whether it is the bypassing of the
narrowed segment of the artery or the psychological effects of surgery that resulted in pain relief. It is beyond the scope of this essay to fully examine what
the cause of pain relief may be in this case. Let me only mention here that there
are certain things which indicate that the pain relief may be caused by the surgical procedure itself. For example, the relief of pain lasts longer, and occurs in
more patients, than one would expect by a placebo effect.

THE PROBLEM OF PATIENT SELECTION

Instead of pain relief, we may be interested in the effect of bypass surgery on
survival. Since patients with angina pectoris have narrowed coronary arteries,
resulting in some damage to their heart muscle, their life expectancy is lower
than that of the general population. If we improve the blood supply to the heart
muscle, it would be reasonable to expect that doing so would also result in a

longer life expectancy. Again, this is a preliminary hypothesis based on the pathophysiological knowledge we have about angina pectoris. We could also test this hypothesis by doing the operation, and then observing whether the patients who have had the operation live longer than those who have not had the operation. What we then do, in a sense, is to divide the population of angina pectoris patients into two groups, one which receives no treatment, or conventional treatment, and another which receives surgical treatment. Such a procedure is natural if we want to test a hypothesis which says that one procedure is better, or worse, than another. We do one of the procedures in one group, and the alternative in the other, and then observe whether we can discover any difference between the two groups. It would obviously take a number of years for us to be able to confirm or disconfirm this particular prediction based on the hypothesis. Let us assume that we have done this. (Again, these studies have already been done.) Could we now, if we observed an increased life expectancy in the bypass group (which is in fact what has been found), argue that this is also caused by a psychological effect of the surgery itself?

In this case, it is quite unlikely that the observed increased life expectancy is due to a placebo effect of the surgery rather than the surgical procedure itself. We do already possess quite a body of knowledge concerning the possibility of *pain relief* as a result of the treatment process itself, rather than the specific treatment given. In contrast, there is little knowledge which suggests that "psychological factors" surrounding treatment are capable of significantly influencing survival. It may of course be that we will someday discover such knowledge, but until we do, we have to conclude that an explanation in terms of the placebo effect for the increased life expectancy is not very plausible.[3]

Before we can accept that the result of such a study justifies the belief the surgery increases life expectancy in angina patients, we still have to exclude other possible alternative explanations. What we have done is to test the hypothesis in a number of patients, and we have observed that those who undergo surgery do indeed live longer than those who do not. We have also excluded the possibility that this can be explained by a placebo effect of the surgery itself. Let us also assume that we have excluded the possibility that other things we may have done to the patients, in addition to the bypassing of the narrowed segment, can explain the observed differences between the two groups. Is it nevertheless possible for there to be another explanation for the increased life expectancy we have observed?

What we have not said anything about is *how* the initial group of angina patients was divided into two groups. Let us envisage the following possibility: As we have already mentioned, it is plausible to expect that patients who get their blood supply to the heart muscle restored will live longer than those who do not. But initially, such a procedure has not been tried out in any patients. One would naturally want to try this procedure out, but since heart surgery is associated with many risks, one would want at least the patients in the initial trial group to be as healthy as possible—apart from their angina pectoris, of course. In this way, we would minimize the risks to the patients involved in such a trial. Considering this to be a good idea, we start our experiment. Whenever a patient with angina pectoris comes to us, we evaluate him and then decide whether he should receive surgical treatment or conventional medical treatment. We assign to surgery all those patients for whom we think the surgical procedure will not pose a significant risk. All the others receive standard medical therapy. After we have done this with a number of patients, we wait and see which group has the higher life expectancy. As we have already noticed, we find that those patients who received surgery live longer.

If this is what we have done, can we then conclude that coronary bypass surgery results in a higher survival rate compared with conventional treatment? Again, there is an obvious alternative explanation. Since we have carefully selected the patients in such a way that the more healthy patients received surgical treatment, it may be the case that we have observed a higher survival rate in this group of patients simply because they initially have a better prognosis. Surgical treatment may not have contributed anything at all to their higher survival rate, or may even have shortened their life expectancy, despite the fact that we observed that these patients lived longer.

Again, the above is similar to what actually happened. During the early 1970s, many studies showed that coronary bypass surgery prolonged life in angina patients. These studies, however, used so-called *historical controls*. This means that the patients who received surgery were compared with the known survival rate of patients who previously had received medical therapy. There are two possible sources of error in such an experiment. One we have already mentioned: the investigators may have, without being aware of it themselves, chosen patients who had a better prognosis regardless of the therapy they would receive. The second possibility is the fact that medical therapy has improved. If we want to argue that surgical treatment is better than *current* medical therapy, we cannot simply compare surgical patients with medically treated patients a few years ago, if medical therapy has changed. During the time when coronary artery bypass surgery was introduced, new drugs were developed which were probably beneficial in terms of increased life expectancy. If that is the case, we simply do not know whether surgery is better than the best current medical therapy.[4]

This again illustrates what we found in our discussion of pain relief. We wanted to know whether surgical treatment really has a beneficial effect in angina patients. We then tested the hypothesis, by comparing the results in those patients who have received surgery with those who have received standard medical therapy. Initially, it looked as if we had achieved a confirmation of our hypothesis. However, careful examination in both cases revealed that we can point to a plausible alternative explanation for the event we have observed: pain relief could have been caused by the placebo effect of surgery, and the increased survival could have been caused by the biased selection of patients. If we are ever going to be able to adequately test our hypothesis, we need some method by which we can exclude such alternative explanations for the observed event. One possibility is to carry out a *randomized, controlled clinical trial*. Let us now examine the characteristics of such a trial.[5]

THE METHODOLOGY OF RANDOMIZED, CONTROLLED CLINICAL TRIALS

Randomized, controlled clinical trials have two important characteristics. First, the kinds of patients one wants to include in the trial are carefully defined. For example, one may want to include all patients between the ages of thirty-five and fifty-five with angina pectoris who come to a particular clinic during a certain time period. Second, all of these patients are then divided into two groups by some random procedure. For example, every time a new patient enters the clinic one may throw a coin and assign the patient to one of the two treatment groups depending on whether the result was heads or tails. Both of these procedures ensure that there is no systematic difference in therapy. By requiring that all patients who come to a clinic be included in the trial, we avoid the possibility that patients with a particularly bad, or good, prognosis are excluded from the trial. By insisting that the group be divided into two treatment groups independently of the wishes of the physicians, we ensure that the physicians taking part in the trial will not, consciously or subconsciously, decide to place certain patients in one of the groups. Let us now assume that we have done this. If we observe that there is a difference between the two groups, can we then conclude that it was caused by the difference in treatment?[6]

It is now indeed implausible to argue that the effect observed is due to differences between the patient characteristics in the two groups, because we made a good effort to ensure that the two groups were the same, except in the treatment received. If that is the case, it is unlikely that any difference in outcome is caused by the difference in treatment. There is one remaining problem, however. We have not said anything about which part of the treatment should be regarded as causing the observed effect. Above we pointed out that it is possible for pain relief to be caused by the placebo effect of surgery. Similarly, if we compared two drug treatments, it is possible that a belief that one of the drugs is superior could cause the observed effect. If the physicians strongly suggested to those patients receiving the experimental drug that it is highly promising, whereas they told the patients receiving the standard therapy that it would probably not be very effective, it is indeed possible that this difference can explain different observed outcomes. Again, we have a plausible alternative explanation, which we have to rule out if we are going to have confidence in the result. This is easily done if we are comparing two different drugs by demanding that the trial be *double blind*. In a double blind clinical trial, neither the patient nor the treating physician knows who has received the standard treatment and who has received the experimental treatment. This is known only by a research coordinator not directly involved in patient care. Also, the two drugs are dispensed in exactly the same form (identical tablets, for example). Now we can, finally, rule out alternative explanations? We have made every effort to ensure that the two treatment groups are exactly alike, except in the drug treatment received. Any difference we now observe can, with a high degree of plausibility, be attributed to the drug received, and not to the particular characteristics of the patients, or to some of the other things we do to patients at the same time we administer the drugs.

It should also be evident that it is difficult, or impossible, to perform double blind trials for surgical treatments. This means that we cannot exclude the possibility that a treatment effect is caused by something other than the particular surgical procedure itself. As we mentioned, however, sometimes such an alternative explanation is plausible, and sometimes it is not. In the case of pain relief, it is indeed possible that it is caused by a placebo effect of the surgery itself, but in the case of an increase in life expectancy it becomes much harder to argue that it is due to something other than the surgical procedure.

IS CORONARY ARTERY BYPASS SURGERY BENEFICIAL?

I have discussed some of the problems involved in deciding what treatment we should suggest for a particular patient. We have seen how we can apply some of the general issues raised by Copi to this medical example. We start out with a problem, formulate preliminary hypotheses, test the hypotheses in a clinical trial, and exclude alternative explanations by the design of the trial. We have also seen how we can legitimately doubt the results of a scientific investigation if we have not followed certain procedures. Specifically, we have examined how difficult it has been to find out whether coronary surgery really is beneficial in patients with angina pectoris. Because many of the studies done until about the late 1970s had many deficiencies of the kind we have mentioned above, coronary artery bypass surgery was very controversial at that time. One should also mention that this surgical procedure was widely introduced then for large groups of angina patients, even though its beneficial effects had not been carefully documented. Beginning in the late 1970s, a number of randomized, controlled clinical trials were done, which documented that coronary artery bypass surgery did indeed prolong life in certain specific subgroups of patients with angina, whereas it was without effect on survival in the majority of the patients. Therefore, bypass surgery is at least beneficial in terms of increased life expectancy for *some* patients with angina pectoris. However, it has been consistently observed that the pain disappears after surgery in the vast majority of patients, even in those patients whose pain could not be controlled with medical therapy alone.

In conclusion, let me point out some remaining problems I am particularly interested in. Several times in this essay I mentioned that before we do a clinical trial on patients, we form preliminary hypotheses on the basis of the knowledge we already possess about a particular disease. It is clear of the knowledge we already possess about a particular disease. It is clear that we need to have some indication, before we introduce a new procedure even in a research project, that the procedure may benefit the patients. What we do not know is exactly how we should adequately test this preliminary hypothesis before we do a clinical trial. Also, when we have obtained the results from a clinical trial, there are usually remaining uncertainties. One example we mentioned concerned the cause of pain relief after coronary bypass surgery. When arguing for or against the plausibility of a particular hypothesis in these situations, we again refer to knowledge we already possess about the disease process. Again, it is uncertain exactly how we should do this. My belief is that an examination of these problems from the perspective of recent work in the philosophy of science will contribute to a solution.

NOTES

1. One should note that these patients were not asked whether they wanted to take part in this experiment. All of them believed that their internal mammary artery had been ligated. Thus a fundamental principle of research ethics, that patients give their *informed consent* to participate in a research project, was violated in this case.

2. The studies mentioned are L. A. Cobb, G. I. Thomas, D. H. Dillard, K. A. Merendino, and R. A. Bruce. An evaluation of internal-mammary-artery ligation by a double-blind technique. *New England Journal of Medicine* 260(1959): 1115–1118; and E. G. Dimond, C. F. Kittle, and J. E. Crockett. Comparison of internal mammary and artery ligation and sham operation for angina pectoris. *American Journal of Cardiology* 5(1960): 483–486. For a discussion in general about the placebo effect of surgery, see H. Benson and D. P. McCallie. Angina pectoris and the placebo effect. *New England Journal of Medicine* 300(1979): 1424–1429.

3. Although there *are* indications that psychological characteristics of patients are important in survival. For example, patients who conscientiously take their medication, even if the medication, unknown to the patient, does not contain an active drug, live longer. For a recent discussion in cancer research, see B. R. Cassileth, E. J. Lusk, D. S. Miller, L. L. Brown, and C. Miller. Psychosocial correlates of survival in advanced malignant disease. *New England Journal of Medicine* 312(1985): 1551–1555.

4. For a discussion, see S. H. Rahimtoola. Coronary bypass surgery for chronic angina — 1981: A perspective. *Circulation* 65(1982): 225–241.

5. A good introduction to the methodology of clinical trials can be found in S. J. Pocock. *Clinical trials. A practical approach*. New York: Wiley, 1983. It should also be emphasized that it is not suitable to test all clinical hypotheses by randomized, clinical trials. In some cases, other types of clinical trials may be more appropriate.

6. There are still some remaining problems, of a statistical nature, which we will not discuss here. Briefly, we would do a statistical test to make sure that we can be confident that the observed test could not have happened by chance. We shall here assume that this has been done.

DISCUSSION QUESTIONS

1. What is an explanation? What are some differences between scientific explanations and unscientific ones?
2. What is a hypothesis?
3. List and briefly explain the seven steps of scientific method as discussed by Copi.
4. What is angina pectoris? What is coronary bypass surgery? Why, according to Lie, was coronary bypass surgery proposed in the first place as a way of relieving the pain of angina pectoris?
5. Discuss the manner in which the hypothesis that coronary bypass surgery effectively reduces the pain of angina pectoris has been tested. What problems, according to Lie, have arisen in the testing of this hypothesis?
6. Discuss the manner in which the hypothesis that coronary bypass surgery effectively prolongs the life of angina pectoris patients has been tested. What problems, according to Lie, have arisen in the testing of *this* hypothesis?
7. Discuss the meaning and significance of the "randomized, controlled clinical trial" especially as it applies to the problems raised in question 6 above.
8. Discuss the meaning and significance of a "double blind" methodology. Can this methodology easily be applied to the testing of surgical treatments such as coronary bypass surgery? Explain your answer.
9. Can you think of any further constructive methodologies a medical researcher might employ in testing clinical hypotheses?
10. Can a medical researcher ever be certain that his or her clinical hypothesis is correct? Defend your answer.

IV

TRUTH AND KNOWLEDGE

9

PERSPECTIVES ON TRUTH: ART, HUMANITIES, AND SOCIAL SCIENCE

One fundamental question of *epistemology* (the theory of knowledge, from the Greek *episteme,* meaning "knowledge") is the nature of truth. In the first part of this chapter, three historically significant and sharply contrasting responses to this question are discussed: (1) Platonism, (2) logical positivism, and (3) pragmatism. In the second part, four practitioners—Maxine R. Morphis, Alfred L. Castle, Victor Guarino, and Deni Elliott—discuss the relevance of these traditions to their work areas—dance, historiography, psychology, and journalism, respectively.

The first selection contains excerpts from *The Republic,* a principal work of the ancient Greek philosopher Plato. Included in this selection is his famous "Allegory of the Cave," an allegorical presentation of his view that the beliefs we arrive at through *sense experience* do not constitute knowledge, but are rather mere opinions (*doxa*). For Plato, genuine knowledge (*episteme*) consists in the grasping of standards of reality that transcend our sense experience. These standards Plato calls the *Forms* or *Essences,* and they are, for him, eternal and immutable principles.

For instance, to grasp what justice really is, we must transcend what different people or societies claim to be just, for this is only opinion. To capture the *Essence of Justice* we must employ *abstract thinking or reasoning*—what Plato called "dialectic"—which gets us clear of sense experience.

A simple example of the kind of thinking process Plato had in mind may help here. When one is presented with a diagram of a triangle, or a triangular object, one visually experiences (via the optic nerve) the appearance of a particular (space-time) object. Our belief, at this point, that "Here is a triangle" is, as such, mere opinion and does not qualify as knowledge. However, insofar as this particular triangle is an instance of the Concept (or Form) of Triangularity (Plato would say that the particular object "participates" in this form by virtue of being an "imperfect copy" of it), one can be led "upward" from this particular instance of triangularity to consideration of the *Form* or *Essence of Triangularity* itself. Thereby, one can come to "see" (this time with the "mind's eye") that *triangularity* necessarily entails *threesidedness*. And, indeed, it is just such a rational apprehension (as distinct from the sense perception) that would, for Plato, qualify as knowledge, that is, it would be to grasp the *Form* or *Essence of Triangularity* and not merely some fleeting appearance of it.

Furthermore, to grasp such essences by means of this sort of abstract thinking is the *Essence of Philosophy* itself, and the philosopher is one who is an expert in this sort of inquiry. He or she has a kind of "privileged access" to knowledge which sets him or her apart from ordinary people—most of whom, Plato thought, remained in "the cave."

In short, Plato believes that objective standards of reality exist, and that it is through the power of *reason,* undiluted by sense experience, that such principles can be *discovered.* At most, sense experience provides us with an occasion to *begin to* think about what really is, but it is only through the "upward journey of the soul into the region of the intelligible" that true knowledge can be obtained.

Plato also presents his theory of Forms in terms of a "divided line" in which four *levels of reality* are represented in proportion to their measure of reality. These levels (from lesser to greater reality) are images, particular objects, mathematical objects, and Forms. The first is the level depicted in Plato's Allegory of the Cave by prisoners in an underground cave who take passing shadows cast upon the cave wall as reality. For Plato, it is a level of reality about which artists are conversant when they create likenesses of the objects in nature. It is a level with an inherent propensity to mislead, and to distort, higher reality.

The next level is that of *particular objects.* These may be considered prior in reality to images since they are that which images copy. This is the level of reality those who study human artifacts and events would address, for example, historians and anthropologists. On this level are changing and mutable space-time objects and events. These objects support belief or opinion, but not knowledge.

The next level (which takes us from the "sensible" to the "intelligible" world) is that of *mathematical objects,* which includes diagrams, blueprints, and other concrete representations of abstract mathematical ideas. This level is addressed by the applied mathematicians like geometricians. Today, it would include engineers, computer scientists, and applied philosophers. These studies, for Plato, would yield thinking or understanding which is "something between intelligence and mere acceptance of appearances."

The highest level, that of *Forms,* is addressed by pure philosophers or mathematicians. It is the level reached through dialectical reasoning, and yields knowledge (*episteme*). Alas, for Plato, pure philosophers would have a higher standing than applied philosophers!

In sharp contrast to the Platonic position is that of *logical positivism.* According to this approach to the problem of truth, the Platonist has, in effect, gotten things backward. For the logical positivist, sense experience is the (only) *correct* standard of truth, and any attempts to transcend this criterion ultimately terminate in meaningless assertions. Thus, in the selection from *Language, Truth and Logic,* Alfred Jules Ayer argues that "no statement which refers to a 'reality' transcending the limits of all possible sense experience can possibly have any literal significance; from which it must follow that the labours of those who have striven to describe such a reality [Plato, for one] have all been devoted to the production of nonsense."

For Ayer, ethics, along with much of traditional metaphysics, is nonsense insofar as its principles and judgments are not even *in principle* verifiable—that is, we cannot even imagine any sense experience that would verify them. Rather, according to Ayer, ethical judgments (such as "stealing money is wrong") are merely expressions of emotion that may also be calculated to arouse similar emotions in its audience. Thus, there is no branch of *knowledge* called ethics to which ethicists may lay claim as experts or authorities. The poet is, for Ayer, in a somewhat better epistemic situation than the metaphysician and the ethicist since "in the vast majority of cases the sentences which are produced by poets do have literal meaning." On the other hand, Ayer contends that poets and other literary artists aim at achieving certain effects or emotions in their audience, and not at truth, so that "literary works are largely composed of falsehoods."

The scientist, however, enjoys a higher epistemic status than any of the above since his or her sentences are not only literally meaningful; scientists (unlike poets) aim at truth, so that their sentences are subject to verification. The philosopher, for Ayer, serves the role of a kind of assistant to the scientist; for his or her job, roughly put, is one of analyzing and clarifying scientific hypotheses and everyday assumptions in order to guide the scientist in the pursuit of truth.

What is common to both positivists and Platonists is their quest for some reality to which truth must "correspond," and both present reality hierarchies (albeit opposing ones) for purveyors of truth such as artists and philosophers. For the Platonist, ultimate reality is the transcendent forms; for the positivists it is empirically verifiable fact. Both view truth as a static relationship of ideas to external reality.

In the next selection in this chapter excerpted from his essay on "Pragmatism's Conception of Truth," William James introduces a perspective that abandons the traditional concept of correspondence and instead views truth in terms of its *practical consequences.*

According to James, while it can be said that true ideas correspond or "agree" with reality, and can be verified, these concepts can (and should) be interpreted pragmatically. Asks James, what concrete difference will an idea's being true (or false) make in anyone's actual life? "What, in short, is the truth's cash value in experiential terms?" A true thought, he says, is one that "agrees with reality" in the sense that it "helps us to *deal,* whether practically or intellectually, with either the reality or its belongings, that doesn't entangle our progress in frustrations, that *fits,* in fact, and adapts our life to the reality's whole setting . . ." A true thought is "true because it is useful," or "it is useful because it is true."

In focusing attention on the utility of truth and away from the quest for an objective reality upon which to anchor it, James opens the door to the possibility of there being more than one valid description of reality, for, on this pragmatic conception, any manner of depicting reality will qualify as true if it *works* for the purposes at hand. Thus, scientists have their special ways of describing reality for scientific purposes, the poets have theirs, the metaphysicians theirs, and the ethicists theirs. Whereas none of these ways can claim to be "truer" or "better," each yields alternatives for "dealing" with reality. In contrast to Ayer and Plato, there is, on this conception, no epistemological "pecking order" among the different ways of dealing with reality. Instead, each is measured according to its usefulness.

One central problem with traditional correspondence theories of truth (for example, Plato's) is that it is difficult to see how we can ever *know* that our thoughts "correspond" with reality if reality is itself *outside* the sphere of our thoughts. Indeed, we cannot somehow venture outside our own mental states to check things out. One virtue of pragmatism is that, by focusing on the practical value of belief, it avoids the murky discussion of correspondence to external reality.

Still, it is sometimes argued that truth is one thing and its consequences another. Thus, it is said, even a belief that one would be better off not having may still be true. Truth may not *always* work.

This objection may derive at least some of its force as a result of applying the pragmatic conception to individual beliefs considered apart from a system of beliefs. For example, the (true) thought that one's income taxes are due next week may be highly unsatisfying, but it fits in with (supports and is supported by) a system that includes a penalty for not paying on time. True (false) ideas may thus be ones that fit in (conflict) with a set of coherent ideas; and the practical value of individual ideas may depend on their coherence, or lack thereof. Thus, James states that true ideas "lead to consistency" and to "stability," and false ones to "frustration" and "contradiction," and "Truth in science is what gives us the maximum possible sum of satisfactions, taste included, but consistency both with previous truth and with novel fact is always the most imperious claimant."

It is sometimes pointed out that a true idea that is not useful is not self-contradictory, and that therefore truth cannot be *defined* in terms of usefulness (say, in like manner that triangularity can be defined in terms of threesideness). Nevertheless, as James reminds us, the true would never have acquired a name suggestive of value had it not been useful from the start. Further, true ideas always have at least a *potential* to be useful. Thus, we store "extra truths away in our memories, and with the overflow we fill our books of reference. Whenever such an extra truth becomes practically relevant, it passes from cold-storage to do work in the world and our belief in it grows active."

All of the aforementioned theories—Platonism, positivism, and pragmatism—have practical applications, or at least present challenges, to any human activity engaged in the pursuit, employment, communication, or expression of knowledge. In this chapter, the concept of truth within four such areas will be explored: art, history, psychology, and journalism.

In the first Practice selection of this chapter, Maxine Morphis, a philosopher who has been a professional folk dancer as well as an instructor of folk dance, specializing in Middle Eastern and Greek dances, discusses Plato's theory of truth as it applies to the arts in general and to dance in particular. Although Morphis takes issue with much of what Plato says about art, she does see some "truth" in his view that at least some art can embody universal truths. More exactly, in light of her own dance experience, she argues that dance may express universal truths through its exploration of "abstract movement of the human body in space in a manner that can be interpreted as an exploration of the universal patterns of dance." Moreover, she also argues that dance can explore "universal themes of life by presenting an abstraction of experience that appears to transcend particular events." For example, she points to the "abdominal dance" as embodying certain dance movements frequently found cross-culturally, in women's dances—namely, "the use of the pelvic roll and abdominal muscles accompanied by hip motions and undulatory motions," and as embodying such "universal" themes as that of "fertility and child bearing." However, she makes plain that such cross-cultural movements and themes as embodied in dance merely reflect a "commonality of shared human experience" that does not entail a metaphysical commitment to a transcendent reality—the Platonic Forms. Nor, therefore, does Morphis accept the Platonic view that all art is but an imitation of this underlying reality (being "thrice removed" from it since art imitates perceptual objects which are themselves imitations of ultimate reality). Against Plato, she argues that the view of art as imitation seriously fails to "do justice to the dance experience." Finally, she argues that, although it may be desirable for artists to seek to embody universal truths (in the said fashion) in their art works—she herself has an "inclination to demand this kind of awareness in an artist"—this should not, contrary to Plato, be viewed as an essential aspect of art. The Platonic demand that artists also be philosophers who instance, albeit imperfectly, eternal truth in their works is, for Morphis, an unreasonable demand and would exclude many of our great artists.

In the second Practice selection, historian Alfred L. Castle discusses the role of the correspondence theory of truth in his work in historiography. In contrast to the pragmatist's approach, Castle sees historical fact claims as more than useful expedients to human ends. On the other hand, he is not a Platonist who subscribes to a realm of "directly accessible" and "absolute" facts to which historical claims must correspond. Rather, historical-fact claims can be tested for their veracity by comparing a "subjective concept" with a "set of sensations," and "if they match to some acceptable degree," the concept is true; otherwise it is false. In emphasizing the role of sense experience in verifying historical-fact claims, he thus adopts a form of correspondence theory which has affinities with that standard proffered by positivists. As such, truth is provisional—future experience can always disconfirm an accepted historical-fact claim; and it is probabilistic—the correspondence is always "imperfect" and evidence is never "complete."

Castle also considers the so-called *coherence* theory of truth as an alternative to the correspondence and pragmatist approaches. According to this theory (as it is applied to history), an historical-fact claim will be true just in case it "harmonizes" or "coheres" with other historical- fact claims that have been accepted as true. However, says Castle, although it has been a common practice to "compose history from the point of view of some comprehensive ideology which provides the basis for selecting, interpreting, and rearranging facts," the resulting system may, nevertheless, bear "little resemblance to reality." What is needed, according to Castle, is that such systems of historical-fact claims be anchored to the plane of sense experience, and this is where correspondence comes in.

Still, a serious problem arises for the historian who wishes to accept a correpondence theory of truth rather than the coherence account. Since historical-fact claims are about the past, there do not seem to be any accessible "facts" against which they may be tested. From the perspective of correspondence theory, it thus becomes questionable whether there can ever be any such thing as "objective knowledge" in history. In addressing this general issue, Castle considers a number of more specific criticisms such as that historical investigations are colored by the historian's own personal and social biases and values which, in effect, substitute for a lack of "hard" evidence.

In responding to these challenges, he attempts to clear the way for a discussion of some "simple values for conducting sound investigations" in history which he believes follow from the acceptance of the correspondence theory of truth as he has interpreted it. For example, he argues that, by supposing that there are specific verifiable object events to which historical-fact claims must correspond, the historian is better able to focus his or her inquiry on *relevant* evidence. Furthermore, he argues that the commitment to the correspondence theory provides a standard of "the best relevant evidence," which is evidence that is as closely related as possible to the event itself—the so-called "rule of immediacy."

Castle maintains that by accepting the basic assumptions of the correspondence theory of truth, historians are better able to conduct "sound investigations." It may thus appear that, in the end, Castle's own choice of a theoretical perspective on truth is itself conditioned by his pragmatic concerns, and accepting the correspondence theory of truth may be the most effective way he, as an historian, has of "dealing with reality."

In the third selection, Victor Guarino discusses his psychology practice with schizophrenic patients in a mental hospital. Examining several actual cases, Guarino employs three theories of truth-correspondence, coherence, and pragmatic—to address the reality status of the delusions and hallucinations that are part of the clinical definition of schizophrenia.

Guarino argues that these hallucinations and delusions—including auditory, visual, and ideational ones—are not sense perceptions in the ordinary sense of the word, nor are they rooted in sense perception. They do not *correspond* to any perceived reality, nor are they accessible to either psychologist or patient in the sense that they can be empirically verified.

Nevertheless, these mental states, claims Guarino, are "real" and "accessible" for the patient in the sense that they are out of the patient's control and the patient must cope with them. Indeed, they are "lived," even if not "perceived," realities for the patient, and they "fit in" or cohere with the patient's life, not in terms of what they are about, but in being potential threats to the patient's life.

These hallucinations and delusions are also, says Guarino, accessible to the psychologist in the sense that the psychologist must accept them as *lived* patient realities if he or she is to help the patient. These mental states also may correspond to reality for the psychologist in the sense that they match learned, clinical descriptions of hallucinations and delusions. From a pragmatic perspective, the true ideas for both psychologist and patient are antipsychotic medication and counseling to control these mental states, which are maladaptive and detrimental to the patient's welfare.

It might be argued against Guarino that hallucinations and delusions need not be maladaptive. For example, the victim of persistent sexual abuse who dissociates into two distinct individuals may be "dealing with reality" in the most worthwhile way possible given the circumstances. Indeed, it is reasonable to try to escape such victimization, and the split may be the closest thing to an escape. Similarly, the prisoner in the Nazi concentration camp who "identified" with his or her captor was acting rationally under the circumstances. What is maladaptive in ordinary situations may thus be adaptive in other extreme cases.

Nevertheless, a delusion may not serve a protective purpose when it persists even after the circumstances that created the need to escape no longer exist, or when there are new conditions that permit better options. So, from a pragmatic perspective, the persistent delusion used as a defense mechanism against "unbearable" living conditions may have long-term, negative utility value far outweighing its positive value.

In any event, Guarino thinks that it is "movie-land psychology" to try to explain hallucinations and delusions in schizophrenia in terms of stressful living conditions. The causal etiology of the disease, he says, is yet unknown, and such factors as socioeconomic and environmental conditions are "stressors, not causes."

One may still wonder whether there is a point at which a stressor can become a cause. As an analogy, being tired may be a stressor, but there is a point at which sleep deprivation can cause hallucinations! Further, the fact that the cause of schizophrenia is unknown does not mean that environmental conditions or motivational factors do not play any causal role. Even if we have not established that they do, this does not mean they don't.

In the end, Guarino falls back on the need of the psychologist to accept and understand that the patient's distress is part of the patient's lived reality. The psychologist must use those means—antipsychotic medication and counseling—that have proven *to work*. In this regard, the treatment of schizophrenia (the treatment of all mental illness?) is pragmatic. True ideas are those that work for both patient and psychologist.

In the third Practice selection of this chapter, journalist and philosophy professor Deni Elliott talks about the concept of journalistic truth. As Elliott suggests, there is a disparity between the manner in which journalistic codes of ethics describe truth and the manner in which it actually enters into a news story. While the codes (such as the Associated Press Managing Editors' *Statement of Ethical Principles*) assume truth to be a static principle that guides journalistic practice (truth is the good newspaper's "guiding principle"), Elliott argues that truth in journalism is an evolving process shaped by a progressive series of news perspectives. These news perspectives arise as a result of a selection process in which only certain data are chosen to report. In the process, "editorial judgment rather than external reality serves as the basis for what gets reported as news." News is, in this sense, created rather than discovered. Yet, if external reality is not "the basis" for journalistic truth, what guides editorial judgment?

Implicit in Elliott's response to this question is the journalist's tacit acceptance of a pragmatist approach to truth. Journalism serves an important purpose in a democratic society. Its primary purpose is to keep citizens informed about matters that have, or can have, bearing on their self-governance. Is a consumer product being recalled? Is the government possibly guilty of a breach of trust with its citizens? The truth for journalism is (or should be) primarily that which serves this utilitarian purpose. In James's terms, journalism is supposed to provide us with ideas that "lead us toward other moments which it will be worthwhile to have been led to," and by keeping us informed about what we would otherwise not have known, it saves us from the frustrations and dissatisfactions of not having had the truth.

As Elliott points out, the manner in which journalism carries out its purpose is a function of the specific journalistic medium. While print media such as newspapers have greater facility to deliver a more detailed coverage of a news item, broadcast media have less facility for in-depth coverage, although greater facility for providing perceptual insight. "Members of the audience," says Elliott, "if they are to make informed decisions about their self-governance, need both kinds of knowledge."

The pragmatic basis of journalistic truth appears also to be consistent with a *coherence* account of truth. As James himself insisted, in a true account, "the connexions and transitions come to us from point to point as being progressive, harmonious, satisfactory." A truthful journalistic account will not contradict a wider system of truths of which it is a component.

The problem of painting a coherent account of an event can be a challenge for both print and broadcast media. In presenting a videotape of an event, the editor must decide what part of the event to show. For example, showing a cop hitting a citizen paints a picture of police brutality. Also showing the citizen's prior attack upon the cop paints a much different picture. The larger picture is to be preferred from both coherence and pragmatic standpoints because it is more likely to deliver an account that fits in with other moments prior to, leading up to, and following the incident, and that therefore "comes to us from point to point as being progressive, harmonious, and satisfactory." Journalism that intentionally zeros in on one aspect of reality, without regard for its context, in order to sell newspapers or attract a wider audience, fails to perform its primary function. Such reports should, as Elliott frames it, "carry the disclaimer used in newspaper hoaxes from the nineteenth century, 'interesting if true'."

Perhaps all theories of truth entertained here have something important to say about the way reality is to be assessed. In any event, the four Practice selections in this chapter should provide a sense that outlooks on truth such as Platonism, positivism, and pragmatism do not simply represent theoretical excursions. They can and do affect the ways people work and, indeed, the ways they live.

ISSUES

PLATO

TRUTH AS EXTRA-SENSIBLE REALITY

THE ALLEGORY OF THE CAVE

Next, said I (Socrates), here is a parable to illustrate the degree in which our nature may be enlightened or unenlightened. Imagine the condition of men living in a sort of cavernous chamber underground, with an entrance open to the light and a long passage all down the cave. Here they have been from childhood, chained by the leg and also by the neck, so that they cannot move and can see only what is in front of them, because the chains will not let them turn their heads. At some distance higher up is the light of a fire burning behind them; and between the prisoners and the fire is a track with a parapet built along it, like the screen at a puppet-show, which hides the performers while they show their puppets over the top.

I see, said he.

SOURCE: *The Republic of Plato*, trans. F. M. Cornford (Oxford: Oxford University Press, 1941), pp. 227–232. Reprinted by permission of Oxford University Press.

Now behind this parapet imagine persons carrying along various artificial objects, including figures of men and animals in wood or stone or other materials, which project above the parapet. Naturally, some of these persons will be talking, others, silent.

It is a strange picture, he said, and a strange sort of prisoners.

Like ourselves, I replied; for in the first place prisoners so confined would have seen nothing of themselves or of one another, except the shadows thrown by the fire-light on the wall of the Cave facing them, would they?

Not if all their lives they had been prevented from moving their heads.

And they would have seen as little of the objects carried past.

Of course.

Now, if they could talk to one another, would they not suppose that their words referred only to those passing shadows which they saw?

Necessarily.

And suppose their prison had an echo from the wall facing them? When one of the people crossing behind them spoke, they could only suppose that the sound came from the shadows passing before their eyes.

No doubt.

In every way, then, such prisoners would recognize as reality nothing but the shadows of those artificial objects.

Inevitably.

Now consider what would happen if their release from the chains and the healing of their unwisdom should come about in this way. Suppose one of them was set free and forced suddenly to stand up, turn his head, and walk with eyes lifted to the light; all these movements would be painful, and he would be too dazzled to make out the objects whose shadows he had been used to seeing. What do you think he would say, if someone told him that what he had formerly seen was meaningless illusion, but now, being somewhat nearer to reality and turned towards more real objects, he was getting a truer view? Suppose further that he were shown the various objects being carried by and were made to say, in reply to questions, what each of them was. Would he not be perplexed and believe the objects now shown him to be not so real as what he formerly saw?

Yes, not nearly so real.

And if he were forced to took at the fire-light itself, would not his eyes ache, so that he would try to escape and turn back to the things which he could see distinctly, convinced that they really were clearer than these other objects now being shown to him?

Yes.

And suppose someone were to drag him away forcibly up the steep and rugged ascent and not let him go until he had hauled him out into the sunlight, would he not suffer pain and vexation at such treatment, and when he had come out into the light, find his eyes so full of its radiance that he could not see a single one of the things that he was now told were real?

Certainly he would not see them all at once.

He would need, then, to grow accustomed before he could see things in that upper world. At first it would be easiest to make out shadows, and then the images of men and things reflected in water, and later on the things themselves. After that, it would be easier to watch the heavenly bodies and the sky itself by night, looking at the light of the moon and stars rather than the Sun and the Sun's light in the day-time.

Yes, surely.

Last of all, he would be able to look at the Sun and contemplate its nature, not as it appears when reflected in water or any alien medium, but as it is in itself in its own domain. . . .

No doubt.

And now he would begin to draw the conclusions that it is the Sun that produces the seasons and the course of the year and controls everything in the visible world, and moreover is in a way the cause of all that he and his companions used to see.

Clearly he would come at last to that conclusion.

Then if he called to mind his fellow prisoners and what passed for wisdom in his former dwelling-place, he would surely think himself happy in the change and be sorry for them. They may have had a practice of honouring and commending one another, with prizes for the man who had the keenest eye for the passing shadows and the best memory for the order in which they followed or accompanied one another, so that he could make a good guess as to which was going to come next. Would our released prisoner be likely to covet those prizes or to envy the men exalted to honour and power in the Cave? Would he not feel like Homer's Achilles, that he would far sooner "be on earth as a hired servant in the house of a landless man" or endure anything rather than go back to his old beliefs and live in the old way?

Yes, he would prefer any fate to such a life.

Now imagine what would happen if he went down again to take his former seat in the Cave. Coming suddenly out of the sunlight, his eye would be filled with darkness. He might be required once more to deliver his opinion on those shadows, in competition with the prisoners who had never been released, while his eyesight was still dim and unsteady; and it might take some time to become used to the darkness. They would laugh at him and say that he had gone up only to come back with his sight ruined; it was worth no one's while even to attempt the ascent. If they could lay hands on the man who was trying to set them free and lead them up, they would kill him.

Yes, they would.

Every feature in this parable, my dear Glaucon, is meant to fit our earlier analysis. The prison dwelling corresponds to the region revealed to us through the sense of sight, and the fire-light within it to the power of the Sun. The ascent to see the things in the upper world you may take as standing for the upward journey of the soul into the region of the intelligible; then you will be in possession of what I surmise, since that is what you wish to be told. Heaven knows whether it is true; but this, at any rate, is how it appears to me. In the world of knowledge, the last thing to be perceived and only with great difficulty is the essential Form of Goodness. Once it is perceived, the conclusion must follow that, for all things, this is the cause of whatever is right and good; in the visible world it gives birth to light and to the lord of light, while it is itself sovereign in the intelligible world and the parent of intelligence and truth. Without having had a vision of this Form no one can act with wisdom in his own life or in matters of state.

So far as I can understand, I share your belief.

Then you may also agree that it is no wonder if those who have reached this height are reluctant to manage the affairs of men. Their souls long to spend all their time in that upper world—naturally enough, if here once more our parable holds true. Nor, again, is it at all strange that one who comes from the contemplation of divine things to the miseries of human life should appear awkward and ridiculous when, with eyes still dazed and not yet accustomed to the darkness, he is compelled, in a law-court or elsewhere, to dispute about the shadows of justice or the images that cast those shadows, and to wrangle over the notions of what is right in the minds of men who have never beheld justice itself.

It is not at all strange.

No; a sensible man will remember that the eyes may be confused in two ways—by a change from light to darkness or from darkness to light; and he will recognize that the same thing happens to the soul. When he sees it troubled and unable to discern anything clearly, instead of laughing thoughtlessly, he will ask whether, coming from a brighter existence, its unaccustomed vision is obscured by the darkness, in which case he will think its condition enviable and its life a happy one; or whether, emerging from the depths of ignorance, it is dazzled by excess of light. If so, he will rather feel sorry for it; or, if he were inclined to laugh, that would be less ridiculous than to laugh at the soul which has come down from the light.

That is a fair statement.

If this is true, then, we must conclude that education is not what it is said to be by some, who profess to put knowledge into a soul which does not possess it, as if they could put sight into blind eyes. On the contrary, our own account signifies that the soul of every man does possess the power of learning the truth and the organ to see it with, and that, just as one might have to turn the whole body round in order that the eye should see light instead of darkness, so the entire soul must be turned away from this changing world, until its eye can bear to contemplate reality and that supreme splendour which we have called the Good. Hence there may well be an art whose aim would be to effect this very thing, the conversion of the soul, in the readiest way; not to put the power of sight into the soul's eye, which already has it, but to ensure that, instead of looking in the wrong direction, it is turned the way it ought to be.

THE DIVIDED LINE

Conceive, then, that there are these two powers I speak of, the Good reigning over the domain of all that is intelligible, the Sun over the visible world—or the heaven as I might call it; only you would think I was showing off my skill in etymology.[1] At any rate you have these two orders of things clearly before your mind: the visible and the intelligible?

I have.

Now take a line divided into two unequal parts, one to represent the visible order, the other the intelligible; and divide each part again in the same proportion, symbolizing degrees of comparative clearness or obscurity. Then (A) one of the two sections in the visible world will stand for images. By images I mean first shadows, and then reflections in water or in close-grained, polished surfaces, and everything of that kind, if you understand.

Yes, I understand.

Let the second section (B) stand for the actual things of which the first are likenesses, the living creatures about us and all the works of nature or of human hands.

So be it.

Will you also take the proportion in which the visible world has been divided as corresponding to degrees of reality and truth, so that the likeness shall stand to the original in the same ratio as the sphere of appearances and belief to the sphere of knowledge?

Certainly.

Now consider how we are to divide the part which stands for the intelligible world. There are two sections. In the first (C) the mind uses as images those actual things which themselves had images in the visible world; and it is compelled to pursue its inquiry by starting from assumptions and travelling, not up to a principle, but down to a conclusion. In the second (D) the mind moves in the other direction, from an assumption up towards a principle which is not hypothetical; and it makes no use of the images employed in the other section, but only of Forms, and conducts its inquiry solely by their means.

I don't quite understand what you mean.

Then we will try again; what I have just said will help you to understand. (C) You know, of course, how students of subjects like geometry and arithmetic begin by postulating odd and even numbers, or the various figures and the three kinds of angle, and other such data in each subject. These data they take as known; and, having adopted them as assumptions, they do not feel called upon to give any account of them to themselves or to anyone else, but treat them as self-evident. Then, starting from these assumptions, they go on until they arrive, by a series of consistent steps, at all the conclusions they set out to investigate.

Yes, I know that.

You also know how they make use of visible figures and discourse about them, though what they really have in mind is the originals of which these figures are images: they are not reasoning, for instance, about this particular square and diagonal which they have drawn, but about *the* Square and *the* Diagonal;

---

[1] Some connected the word for heaven (οὐρανός) with ὁρᾶν 'to see' (*Cratylus,* 396 B). It is sometimes used for the whole of the visible universe.

and so in all cases. The diagrams they draw and the models they make are actual things, which may have their shadows or images in water; but now they serve in their turn as images, while the student is seeking to behold those realities which only thought can apprehend.[2]

True.

This, then, is the class of things that I spoke of as intelligible, but with two qualifications: first, that the mind, in studying them, is compelled to employ assumptions, and, because it cannot rise above these, does not travel upwards to a first principle; and second, that it uses as images those actual things which have images of their own in the section below them and which, in comparison with those shadows and reflections, are reputed to be more palpable and valued accordingly.

I understand: you mean the subject-matter of geometry and of the kindred arts.

(D) Then by the second section of the intelligible world you may understand me to mean all that unaided reasoning apprehends by the power of dialectic, when it treats its assumptions, not as first principles, but as *hypotheses* in the literal sense, things 'laid down' like a flight of steps up which it may mount all the way to something that is not hypothetical, the first principle of all; and having grasped this, may turn back and, holding on to the consequences which depend upon it, descend at last to a conclusion, never making use of any sensible object, but only of Forms, moving through Forms from one to another, and ending with Forms.

I understand, he said, though not perfectly; for the procedure you describe sounds like an enormous undertaking. But I see that you mean to distinguish the field of intelligible reality studied by dialectic as having a greater certainty and truth than the subject matter of the 'arts,' as they are called, which treat their assumptions as first principles. The students of these arts are, it is true, compelled to exercise thought in contemplating objects which the senses cannot perceive; but because they start from assumptions without going back to a first principle, you do not regard them as gaining true understanding about those objects, although the objects themselves, when connected with a first principle, are intelligible. And I think you would call the state of mind of the students of geometry and other such arts, not intelligence, but thinking, as being something between intelligence and mere acceptance of appearances.

You have understood me quite well enough, I replied. And now you may take, as corresponding to the four sections, these four states of mind: *intelligence* for the highest, *thinking* for the second, *belief* for the third, and for the last *imagining*.[3] These you may arrange as the terms in a proportion, assigning

---

[2] Conversely, the fact that the mathematician can use visible objects as illustrations indicates that the realities and truths of mathematics are embodied, though imperfectly, in the world of visible and tangible things; whereas the counterparts of the moral Forms can only be beheld by thought.

[3] Plato never uses hard and fast technical terms. The four here proposed are not defined or strictly employed in the sequel.

to each a degree of clearness and certainty corresponding to the measure in which their objects possess truth and reality.

I understand and agree with you. I will arrange them as you say.

ALFRED JULES AYER

SENSE-EXPERIENCE AS THE STANDARD OF TRUTH

The traditional disputes of philosophers are, for the most part, as unwarranted as they are unfruitful. The surest way to end them is to establish beyond question what should be the purpose and method of a philosophical enquiry. And this is by no means so difficult a task as the history of philosophy would lead one to suppose. For if there are any questions which science leaves to philosophy to answer, a straightforward process of elimination must lead to their discovery.

We may begin my criticising the metaphysical thesis that philosophy affords us knowledge of a reality transcending the world of science and common sense. Later on, when we come to define metaphysics and account for its existence, we shall find that it is possible to be a metaphysician without believing in a transcendent reality; for we shall see that many metaphysical utterances are due to the commission of logical errors, rather than to a conscious desire on the part of their authors to go beyond the limits of experience. But it is convenient for us to take the case of those who believe that it is possible to have knowledge of a transcendent reality as a starting-point for our discussion. The arguments which we use to refute them will subsequently be found to apply to the whole of metaphysics.

One way of attacking a metaphysician who claimed to have knowledge of a reality which transcended the phenomenal world would be to enquire from what premises his propositions were deduced. Must he not begin, as other men do, with the evidence of his senses? And if so, what valid process of reasoning can possibly lead him to the conception of a transcendent reality? Surely from empirical premises nothing whatsoever concerning the properties, or even the existence, of anything super-empirical can legitimately be inferred. But this objection would be met by a denial on the part of the metaphysician that his assertions were ultimately based on the evidence of his senses. He would say that he was endowed with a faculty of intellectual intuition which enabled him to know facts that could not be known through sense-experience. And even if it

SOURCE: Alfred Jules Ayer, *Language, Truth and Logic* (Boston: Dover, 1982), pp. 33–45. Copyright 1952 by Dover Publications, Inc. Reprinted by permission of the publisher.

could be shown that he was relying on empirical premises, and that his venture into a non-empirical world was therefore logically unjustified, it would not follow that the assertions which he made concerning this non-empirical world could not be true. For the fact that a conclusion does not follow from its putative premise is not sufficient to show that it is false. Consequently one cannot overthrow a system of transcendent metaphysics merely by criticising the way in which it comes into being. What is required is rather a criticism of the nature of the actual statements which comprise it. And this is the line of argument which we shall, in fact, pursue. For we shall maintain that no statement which refers to a "reality" transcending the limits of all possible sense-experience can possibly have any literal significance; from which it must follow that the labours of those who have striven to describe such a reality have all been devoted to the production of nonsense. . . .

The criterion which we use to test the genuineness of apparent statements of fact is the *criterion of verifiability*. We say that a sentence is factually significant to any given person, if and only if, he knows how to verify the proposition which it purports to express—that is, if he knows what observations would lead him, under certain conditions, to accept the proposition as being true, or reject it as being false. If, on the other hand, the supposed putative proposition is of such a character that the assumption of its truth, or falsehood, is consistent with any assumption whatsoever concerning the nature of his future experience, then, as far as he is concerned, it is, if not a tautology, a mere pseudo-proposition. The sentence expressing it may be emotionally significant to him; but it is not literally significant. And with regard to questions the procedure is the same. We enquire in every case what observations would lead us to answer the question, one way or the other; and, if none can be discovered, we must conclude that the sentence under consideration does not, as far as we are concerned, express a genuine question, however strongly its grammatical appearance may suggest that it does.

As the adoption of this procedure is an essential factor in the argument of this book, it needs to be examined in detail.

In the first place, it is necessary to draw a *distinction between practical verifiability, and verifiability in principle.* Plainly we all understand, in many cases believe, propositions which we have not in fact taken steps to verify. Many of these are propositions which we could verify if we took enough trouble. But there remain a number of significant propositions, concerning matters of fact, which we could not verify even if we chose; simply because we lack the practical means of placing ourselves in the situation where the relevant observations could be made. A simple and familiar example of such a proposition is the proposition that there are mountains on the farther side of the moon.[1] No rocket has yet been invented which would enable me to go and look at the farther side of the moon, so that I am unable to decide the matter by actual observation. But I do know what observations would decide it for me, if, as is theoretically conceivable, I were once in a position to make them. And therefore I say that the proposition is verifiable in principle, if not in practice, and is accordingly significant. On the other hand, such a metaphysical pseudo-proposition as "the Absolute enters into, but is itself incapable of, evolution and progress," [2] is not even in principle verifiable. For one cannot conceive of an observation which would enable one to determine whether the Absolute did, or did not, enter into evolution and progress. Of course it is possible that the author of such a remark is using English words in a way in which they are not commonly used by English-speaking people, and that he does, in fact, intend to assert something which could be empirically verified. But until he makes us understand how the proposition that he wishes to express would be verified, he fails to communicate anything to us. And if he admits, as I think the author of the remark in question would have admitted, that his words were not intended to express either a tautology or a proposition which was capable, at least in principle, of being verified, then it follows that he has made an utterance which has no literal significance even for himself.

A further distinction which we must make is the distinction between the "strong" and the "weak" sense of the term "verifiable." A proposition is said to be verifiable, in the strong sense of the term, if, and only if, its truth could be conclusively established in experience. But it is verifiable, in the weak sense, if it is possible for experience to render it *probable*. In which sense are we using the term when we say that a putative proposition is genuine only if it is verifiable?

It seems to me that if we adopt conclusive verifiability as our criterion of significance, as some positivists have proposed,[3] our argument will prove too much. Consider, for example, the case of general propositions of law—such propositions, namely, as "arsenic is poisonous"; "all men are mortal"; "a body tends to expand when it is heated." It is of the very nature of these propositions that their truth cannot be established with certainty by any finite series of observations. But if it is recognized that such general propositions of law are designed to cover an infinite number of cases, then it must be admitted that they cannot, even in principle, be verified conclusively. And then, if we adopt conclusive verifiability as our criterion of significance, we are logically obliged to treat these general propositions of law in the same fashion as we treat the statements of the metaphysician.

In face of this difficulty, some positivists[4] have adopted the heroic course of saying that these general propositions are indeed pieces of nonsense, albeit an essentially important type of nonsense. But here the introduction of the term "important" is simply an attempt to hedge. It serves only to mark the authors' recognition that their view is somewhat too paradoxical, without in any way removing the paradox. Besides, the difficulty is not confined to the case of general propositions of law, though it is there revealed most plainly. It is hardly less obvious in the case of propositions about the remote past. For it must surely be admitted that, however strong the evidence in favour of historical statements may be, their truth can never become more than highly probable. And to maintain that they also constitute an important, or unimportant, type of nonsense would be unplausible, to say the very least. Indeed, it will be our contention that no proposition, other than a tautology, can possibly be anything more than a probable hypothesis. And if this is correct, the principle that a sentence can be factually significant only if it expresses what is conclusively verifiable is self-stultifying as a criterion of significance. For it leads to the conclusion that it is impossible to make a significant statement of fact at all.

Nor can we accept the suggestion that a sentence should be allowed to be factually significant if, and only if, it expresses something which is definitely confutable by experience.[5] Those who adopt this course assume that, although no finite series of observations is ever sufficient to establish the truth of a hypothesis beyond all possibility of doubt, there are crucial cases in which a single observation, or series of observations, can definitely confute it. But, as we shall show later on, this assumption is false. A hypothesis cannot be conclusively confuted any more than it can be conclusively verified. For when we take the occurrence of certain observations as proof that a given hypothesis is false, we presuppose the existence of certain conditions. And though, in any given case, it may be extremely improbable that this assumption is false, it is not logically impossible. We shall see that there need be no self-contradiction in holding that some of the relevant circumstances are other than we have taken them to be, and consequently that the hypothesis has not really broken down. And if it is not the case that any hypothesis can be definitely confuted, we cannot hold that the genuineness of a proposition depends on the possibility of its definite confutation.

Accordingly, we fall back on the *weaker sense of verification.* We say that the question that must be asked about any putative statement of fact is not, Would any observations make its truth or falsehood *logically* certain? but simply, Would any observations be relevant to the determination of its *truth or falsehood?* And it is only if a negative answer is given to this second question that we conclude that the statement under consideration is nonsensical. . . .

This criterion seems liberal enough: In contrast to the principle of conclusive verifiability, it clearly does not deny significance to general propositions or to propositions about the past. Let us see what kinds of assertion it rules out.

A good example of the kind of utterance that is condemned by our criterion as being not even false but nonsensical would be the assertion that the world of sense-experience was altogether unreal. It must, of course, be admitted that our senses do sometimes deceive us. We may, as the result of having certain sensations, expect certain other sensations to be obtainable which are, in fact, not obtainable. But, in all such cases, it is further sense-experience that informs us of the mistakes that arise out of sense-experience. We say that the senses sometimes deceive us, just because the expectations to which our sense-experiences give rise do not always accord with what we subsequently experience. That is, we rely on our senses to substantiate or confute the judgements which are based on our sensations. And therefore the fact that our perceptual judgements are sometimes found to be erroneous has not the slightest tendency to show that the world of sense-experience is unreal. And, indeed, it is plain that no conceivable observation, or series of observations, could have any tendency to show that the world revealed to us by sense-experience was unreal.

Consequently, anyone who condemns the sensible world as a world of mere appearance, as opposed to reality, is saying something which, according to our criterion of significance, is literally nonsensical. . . .

Among those who recognize that if philosophy is to be accounted a genuine branch of knowledge it must be defined in such a way as to distinguish it from metaphysics, it is fashionable to speak of the metaphysician as a kind of misplaced poet. As his statements have no literal meaning, they are not subject to any criteria of truth or falsehood: but they may still serve to express, or arouse, emotion, and thus be subject to ethical or aesthetic standards. And it is suggested that they may have considerable value, as means of moral inspiration, or even as works of art. In this way, an attempt is made to compensate the metaphysician for his extrusion from philosophy.[6]

I am afraid that this compensation is hardly in accordance with his deserts. The view that the metaphysician is to be reckoned among the poets appears to rest on the assumption that both talk nonsense. But this assumption is false. In the vast majority of cases the sentences which are produced by poets do have literal meaning. The difference between the man who uses language scientifically and the man who uses it emotively is not that the one produces sentences which are incapable of arousing emotion, and the other sentences which have no sense, but that the one is primarily concerned with the expression of true propositions, the other with the creation of a work of art. Thus, if a work of science contains true and important propositions, its value as a work of science will hardly be diminished by the fact that they are inelegantly expressed. And similarly, a work of art is not necessarily the worse for the fact that all the propositions comprising it are literally false. But to say that many literary works are largely composed of falsehoods is not to say that they are composed of pseudo-propositions. It is, in fact, very rare for a literary artist to produce sentences which have no literal meaning. And where this does occur, the sentences are carefully chosen for their rhythm and balance. If the author writes nonsense, it is because he considers it most suitable for bringing about the effects for which his writing is designed.

The metaphysician, on the other hand, does not intend to write nonsense. He lapses into it through being deceived by grammar, or through committing errors of reasoning, such as that which leads to the view that the sensible world is unreal. But it is not the mark of a poet simply to make mistakes of this sort. There are some, indeed, who would see in the fact that the metaphysician's utterances are senseless a reason against the view that they have aesthetic value. And, without going so far as this, we may safely say that it does not constitute a reason for it.

It is true, however, that although the greater part of metaphysics is merely the embodiment of humdrum errors, there remains a number of metaphysical passages which are the work of genuine mystical feeling; and they may more plausibly be held to have moral or aesthetic value. But, as far as we are concerned, the distinction between the kind of metaphysics that is produced by a philosopher who has been duped by grammar, and the kind that is produced by a mystic who is trying to express the inexpressible, is of no great importance: what is important to us is to realize that even the utterances of the metaphysician who is attempting to expound a vision are literally senseless; so that henceforth we may pursue our philosophical researches with as little regard for them as for the more inglorious kind of *metaphysics which comes from a failure to understand the workings of our language.*

NOTES

1. This example has been used by Professor Schlick to illustrate the same point.
2. A remark taken at random from *Appearance and Reality,* by F. H. Bradley.
3. E.g., M. Schlick, "Positivismus and Realismus," *Erkenntnis,* Vol. I, 1930. F. Waismann, "Logische Analyse des Warscheinlichkeitsbegriffs," *Erkenntnis,* Vol. I, 1930.
4. E.g., M. Schlick, "Die Kausalitat in der gegenwartigen Physik," *Naturwissenschaft,* Vol. 19, 1931.
5. This has been proposed by Karl Popper in his *Logik der Forschung.*
6. For a discussion of this point, see also C. A. Mace, "Representation and Expression," *Analysis,* Vol. 1, No. 3; and "Metaphysics and Emotive Language," *Analysis,* Vol. II, Nos. 1 and 2.

WILLIAM JAMES

THE PRAGMATIST'S APPROACH TO TRUTH

Truth, as any dictionary will tell you, is a property of certain of our ideas. It means their "agreement," as falsity means their "disagreement," with "reality." Pragmatists and intellectualists both accept this definition as a matter of course. They begin to quarrel only after the question is raised as to what may precisely be meant by the term "agreement," and what by the term "reality," when reality is taken as something for our ideas to agree with.

In answering these questions the pragmatists are more analytic and painstaking, the intellectualists more offhand and irreflective. The popular notion is that a true idea must copy its reality. Like other popular views, this one follows the analogy of the most usual experience. Our true ideas of sensible things do indeed copy them. Shut your eyes and think of yonder clock on the wall, and you get just such a true picture or copy of its dial. But your idea of its "works" (unless you are a clockmaker) is much less of a copy, yet it passes muster, for it in no way clashes with the reality. Even though it should shrink to the mere word "works," that word still serves you truly; and when you speak of the "time-keeping function" of the clock, or of its spring's "elasticity," it is hard to see exactly what your ideas can copy.

You perceive that there is a problem here. Where our ideas cannot copy definitely their object, what does agreement with that object mean? Some idealists seem to say that they are true whenever they are what God means that we ought to think about that subject. Others hold the copy-view all through, and speak as if our ideas possessed truth just in proportion as they approach to being copies of the Absolute's eternal way of thinking.

These views, you see, invite pragmatistic discussion. But the great assumption of the intellectualists is that truth means essentially an inert static relation. When you've got your true idea of anything, there's an end of the matter. You're in possession; you *know*; you have fulfilled your thinking destiny. You are where you ought to be mentally; you have obeyed your categorical imperative; and nothing more need follow on that climax of your rational destiny. Epistemologically you are in stable equilibrium.

Pragmatism, on the other hand, asks its usual question. "Grant an idea or belief to be true," it says, "what concrete difference will its being true make in any one's actual life? How will the truth be realized? What experiences will be different from those which would obtain if the belief were false? What, in short, is the truth's cash-value in experiential terms?"

The moment pragmatism asks this question, it sees the answer: *True ideas are those that we can assimilate, validate, corroborate and verify. False ideas are those that we cannot.* That is the practical difference it makes to us to have true ideas; that, therefore, is the meaning of truth, for it is all that truth is known-as.

This thesis is what I have to defend. The truth of an idea is not a stagnant property inherent in it. Truth *happens* to an idea. It *becomes* true, is *made* true by events. Its verity *is* in fact an event, a process: the process namely of its verifying itself, its veri-*fication*. Its validity is the process of its valid-*ation*.

But what do the words verification and validation themselves pragmatically mean? They again signify certain practical consequences of the verified and validated idea. It is hard to find any one phrase that characterizes these consequences better than the ordinary agreement-formula—just such consequences being what we have in mind whenever we say that our ideas "agree" with reality. They lead us, namely, through the acts and other ideas which they instigate, into or up to, or towards, other parts of experience with which we feel all the while—such feeling being among our potentialities—that the original ideas remain in agreement. The connexions and transitions come to us from point to point as being progressive, harmonious, satisfactory. This function of agreeable leading is what we mean by an idea's verification. Such an account is vague and it sounds at first quite trivial, but it has results which it will take the rest of my hour to explain.

Let me begin by reminding you of the fact that the possession of true thoughts means everywhere the possession of invaluable instruments of action; and that our duty to gain truth, so far from being a blank command from out of the blue, or a "stunt" self-imposed by our intellect, can account for itself by excellent practical reasons.

The importance to human life of having true beliefs about matters of fact is a thing too notorious. We live in a world of realities that can be infinitely useful or infinitely harmful. Ideas that tell us which of them to expect count as the true ideas in all this primary sphere of verification, and the pursuit of such ideas is a primary human duty. The possession of truth, so far from being here an end in itself, is only a preliminary means towards other vital satisfactions. If I am lost in the woods and starved, and find what looks like a cow-path, it is of the utmost importance that I should think of a human habitation at the end of it, for if I do so and follow it, I save myself. The true thought is useful here because the house which is its object is useful. The practical value of true ideas is thus primarily derived from the practical importance of their objects to us. Their objects are, indeed, not important at all times. I may on another occasion have no use for the house; and then my idea of it, however verifiable, will be practically irrelevant, and had better remain latent. Yet since almost any object may some day become temporarily important, the advantage of having a general stock of *extra* truths, of ideas that shall be true of merely possible situations, is obvious. We store such extra truths away in our memories, and with the overflow we fill our books of reference. Whenever such an extra truth becomes practically relevant to one of our emergencies, it passes from cold-storage to do work in the world and our belief in it grows active. You can say of it then either that "it is useful because it is true" or that "it is true because it is useful." Both these phrases mean exactly the same thing, namely that here is an idea that gets fulfilled and can be verified. True is the name for whatever idea starts the verification-process, useful is the name for its completed function in experience. True ideas would never have been singled out as such, would never have acquired a class-name, least of all a name suggesting value, unless they had been useful from the outset in this way.

From this simple cue pragmatism gets her general notion of truth as something essentially bound up with the way in which one moment in our experience may lead us towards other moments which it will be worth while to have been led to. Primarily, and on the common-sense level, the truth of a state of mind means this function of *a leading that is worth while*. When a moment in our experience, of any kind whatever, inspires us with a thought that is true, that means that sooner or later we dip by that thought's guidance into the particulars of experience again and make advantageous connexion with them. This is a vague enough statement, but I beg you to retain it, for it is essential.

Our experience meanwhile is all shot through with regularities. One bit of it can warn us to get ready for another bit, can "intend" or be "significant of" that remoter object. The object's advent is the significance's verification. Truth, in these cases, meaning nothing but eventual verification, is manifestly incompatible with waywardness on our part. Woe to him whose beliefs play fast and loose with the order which realities follow in his experience; they will lead him nowhere or else make false connexions.

By "realities" or "objects" here, we mean either things of common sense, sensibly present, or else common-sense relations, such as dates, places, distances, kinds, activities. Following our mental image of a house along the cow-path, we actually come to see the house; we get the image's full verification. *Such simply and fully verified leadings are certainly the originals and prototypes of the truth-process.* Experience offers indeed other forms of truth-process, but they are all conceivable as being primary verifications arrested, multiplied or substituted one for another.

Take, for instance, yonder object on the wall. You and I consider it to be a "clock," altho no one of us has seen the hidden works that make it one. We let our notion pass for true without attempting to verify. If truths mean verification-process essentially, ought we then to call such unverified truths as this abortive? No, for they form the overwhelmingly large number of the truths we live by. Indirect as well as direct verifications pass muster. Where circumstantial evidence is sufficient, we can go without eye-witnessing. Just as we here assume Japan to exist without ever having been there, because it *works* to do so, everything we know conspiring with the belief, and nothing interfering, so we assume that thing to be a clock. We *use* it as a clock, regulating the length of our lecture by it. The verification of the assumption here means its leading to no frustration or contradiction. Verifi*ability* of wheels and weights and pendulum is as good as verification. For one truth-process completed there are a million in our lives that function in this state of nascency. They turn us *towards* direct verification; lead us into the *surroundings* of the objects they envisage; and then, if everything runs on harmoniously, we are so sure that verification is possible that we omit it, and are usually justified by all that happens.

Truth lives, in fact, for the most part on a credit system. Our thoughts and beliefs "pass," so long as nothing challenges them, just as bank-notes pass so long as nobody refuses them. But this all points to direct face-to-face verifications somewhere, without which the fabric of truth collapses like a financial system with no cash-basis whatever. You accept my verification of one thing, I yours of another. We trade on each other's truth. But beliefs verified concretely by *somebody* are the posts of the whole superstructure.

Another great reason—beside economy of time—for waiving complete verification in the usual business of life is that all things exist in kinds and not singly. Our world is found once for all to have that peculiarity. So that when we have once directly verified our ideas about one specimen of a kind, we consider ourselves free to apply them to other specimens without verification. A mind that habitually discerns the kind of thing before it, and acts by the law of the kind immediately, without pausing to verify, will be a "true" mind in ninety-nine out of a hundred emergencies, proved so by its conduct fitting everything it meets, and getting no refutation.

Indirectly or only potentially verifying processes may thus be true as well as full verification-processes. They work as true processes would work, give us the same advantages, and claim our recognition for the same reasons. All this on the common-sense level of matters of fact, which we are alone considering.

But matters of fact are not our only stock in trade. *Relations among purely mental ideas* form another sphere where true and false beliefs obtain, and here the beliefs are absolute, or unconditional. When they are true they bear the name either of definitions or of principles. It is either a principle or a definition that 1 and 1 make 2, that 2 and 1 make 3, and so on; that white differs less from gray than it does from black; that when the cause begins to act the effect also commences. Such propositions hold of all possible "ones," of all conceivable "whites" and "grays" and "causes." The objects here are mental objects. Their relations are perceptually obvious at a glance, and no sense-verification is necessary. Moreover, once true, always true, of those same mental objects. Truth here has an "eternal" character. If you can find a concrete thing anywhere that is "one" or "white" or "gray" or an "effect," then your principles will everlastingly apply to it. It is but a case of ascertaining the kind, and then applying the law of its kind to the particular object. You are sure to get truth if you can but name the kind rightly, for your mental relations hold good of everything of that kind without exception. If you then, nevertheless, failed to get truth concretely, you would say that you had classed your real objects wrongly. . . .

Between the coercions of the sensible order and those of the ideal order, our mind is thus wedged tightly. Our ideas must agree with realities, be such realities concrete or abstract, be they facts or be they principles, under penalty of endless inconsistency and frustration. . . .

To "agree" in the widest sense with a reality *can only mean to be guided either straight up to it or into its surroundings, or to be put into such working touch with it as to handle either it or something connected with it better than if we disagreed.* Better either intellectually or practically! And often agreement will only mean the negative fact that nothing contradictory from the quarter of that reality comes to interfere with the way in which our ideas guide us elsewhere. To copy a reality is, indeed, one very important way of agreeing with it, but it is far from being essential. The essential thing is the process of being guided. Any idea that helps us to *deal,* whether practically or intellectually, with either the reality or its belongings, that doesn't entangle our progress in frustrations, that *fits,* in fact, and adapts our life to the reality's whole setting, will agree sufficiently to meet the requirement. It will hold true of that reality. . . .

The overwhelming majority of our true ideas admit of no direct or face-to-face verification—those of past history, for example, as of Cain and Abel. The stream of time can be remounted only verbally, or verified indirectly by the present prolongations or effects of what the past harbored. Yet if they agree with these verbalities and effects, we can know that our ideas of the past are true. *As true as past time itself was,* so true was Julius Caesar, so true were antediluvian monsters all in their proper dates and settings. That past time itself was, is guaranteed by its coherence with everything that's present. True as the present *is,* the past *was* also.

Agreement thus turns out to be essentially an affair of leading—leading that is useful because it is into quarters that contain objects that are important. True ideas lead us into useful verbal and conceptual quarters as well as directly up to useful sensible termini. They lead to consistency, stability and flowing human intercourse. They lead away from excentricity and isolation, from foiled and barren thinking. The untrammelled flowing of the leading-process, its general freedom from clash and contradiction, passes for its indirect verification; but all roads lead to Rome, and in the end and eventually, all true processes must lead to the face of directly verifying sensible experiences *somewhere,* which somebody's ideas have copied.

Such is the large loose way in which the pragmatist interprets the word agreement. He treats it altogether practically. He lets it cover any process of conduction from a present idea to a future terminus, provided only it run prosperously. It is only thus that, "scientific" ideas, flying as they do beyond common sense, can be said to agree with their realities. It is, as I have already said, *as if* reality were made of ether, atoms or electrons, but we mustn't think so literally. The term "energy" doesn't even pretend to stand for anything "objective." It is only a way of measuring the surface of phenomena so as to string their changes on a simple formula.

Yet in the choice of these man-made formulas we cannot be capricious with impunity any more than we can be capricious on the common-sense practical level. We must find a theory that will *work;* and that means something extremely difficult; for our theory must mediate between all previous truths and certain new experiences. It must derange common sense and previous belief as little as possible, and it must lead to some sensible terminus or other that can be verified exactly. To "work" means both these things; and the squeeze is so tight that there is little loose play for any hypothesis. Our theories are wedged and controlled as nothing else is. Yet sometimes alternative theoretic formulas are equally compatible with all the truths we know, and then we choose between them for subjective reasons. We choose the kind of theory to which we are already partial; we follow "elegance" or "economy." . . . Truth in science is what gives us the maximum possible sum of satisfactions, taste included, but consistency both with previous truth and with novel fact is always the most imperious claimant. . . .

"*The true,*" to put it very briefly, *is only the expedient in the way of our thinking, just as "the right" is only the expedient in the way of our behaving.* Expedient in almost any fashion; and expedient in the long run and on the whole of course; for what meets expediently all the experience in sight won't necessarily meet all further experiences equally satisfactorily. Experience, as we know, has ways of *boiling over,* and making us correct our present formulas.

The "absolutely" true, meaning what no further experience will ever alter, is that ideal vanishing-point towards which we imagine that all our temporary truths will some day converge. It runs on all fours with the perfectly wise man, and with the absolutely complete experience; and, if these ideals are ever realized, they will all be realized together. Meanwhile we have to live today by what truth we can get today, and be ready tomorrow to call it falsehood. Ptolemaic astronomy, Euclidean space, Aristotelian logic, Scholastic metaphysics, were expedient for centuries, but human experience has boiled over those limits, and we now call these things only relatively true, or true within those borders of experience. "Absolutely" they are false; for we know that those limits were casual, and might have been transcended by past theorists just as they are by present thinkers. . . .

The most fateful point of difference between being a rationalist and being a pragmatist is now fully in sight. Experience is in mutation, and our psychological ascertainments of truth are in mutation—so much rationalism will allow; but never that either reality itself or truth itself is mutable. Reality stands complete and ready-made from all eternity, rationalism insists, and the agreement of our ideas with it is that unique unanalyzable virtue in them of which she has already told us. As that intrinsic excellence, their truth has nothing to do with our experiences. It adds nothing to the content of experience. It makes no difference to reality itself; it is supervenient, inert, static, a reflexion merely. It doesn't *exist,* it *holds* or *obtains,* it belongs to another dimension from that of either facts or fact-relations, belongs, in short, to the epistemological dimension—and with that big word rationalism closes the discussion.

PRACTICE

MAXINE MORPHIS

THE PHILOSOPHER AS DANCER: IN CONSIDERATION OF PLATO'S THEORY OF TRUTH

When discussing representative excerpts from Plato's works, such as "The Allegory of the Cave," we often examine his ideas in various contexts. Plato's views on art can give us great insight into his epistemology and ontology, as well as his views of proper social order. Plato maintains that art must go beyond mere imitation in order to represent ultimate truth. Although the idea that art should represent some form of universal truth is appealing in many ways, Plato goes on to advocate ideas that are much more difficult to accept: the censorship of art, and the claim that the best artists are artist-philosophers. I would like to examine Plato's approach to art and pinpoint some of the difficulties with his theory.

Plato's views of truth in art are of particular interest to me, since I have practiced professionally in both art and philosophy. It is a special skill of the individual trained in philosophy that she can stand back and look at her life and examine its meaning. As I teach Plato to my students, I reflect on the ways in which study of his work expanded my own views during my years as a professional folk dancer specializing in Middle Eastern and Greek dances. Because of my wider interests in dance, I have regarded myself as a dancer, not as a folk dancer. Within my personal dance experience there lies a consciousness of higher

Maxine Morphis received her Ph.D. from Brandeis University. Her academic experience has included teaching positions at Ball State University, University of Hartford, Connecticut College, and most recently Oakton Community College in Des Plaines, Illinois. Although Dr. Morphis has a wide background in aesthetics, her most recent concentration has been in business ethics and women's studies.

Currently, she serves as an information management and training consultant to a variety of clients, with a focus on international investment banking. Dr. Morphis has been fascinated by the art of dance since childhood, an interest heavily influenced by her mother's own experiences in the theater. A native of Brooklyn, New York, she believes that growing up in the midst of that city's varied ethnic population afforded invaluable exposure to the music and folk dance arts of many regions. She performed and taught Middle Eastern dance for ten years in Connecticut as owner of Riva's Middle Eastern Dance Studios and as a dance instructor for various recreation departments in that area. Her continued studies in dance have included contra dancing, flamenco (whose historical roots lie partially in the Middle East), and various Latin American dance styles.

aims for the dance. The goal is not just to enjoy movement, or to learn new steps from another country, but to express some of the essential human feelings and universality of human experience embodied in these dances. Could Plato's views support this kind of approach, or did the masterful Greek teach in a way that did not allow for some significant part of what I regard as the vitality of the human spirit?

Given that Plato does not think that humans can or should live without the arts, it may be surprising that there is some controversy about whether he held a cohesive theory of art. Some scholars hold that minimally Plato did not have an organized and well-developed theory of art, while others argue that he had a theory of art, but a poor one.[1] Whether Plato's views of art hold together as a theory or not is not my topic here. My own sense is that Plato had a direction in mind for the perfect society toward which all aspects of life should work, and that in the process he may have cast aside as harmful some of the essential purposes of art.

PLATO'S VIEWS OF ART

What is the proper goal or purpose for art? Plato views art as having the same goal that all human endeavors have: knowing the ultimate truths of the World of Being. Only by realization of this goal can the proper society and the good life for the individual be obtained. Therefore, in order to be praised, or indeed even to be allowed in Plato's Republic, the artist must be artist-philosopher as well. Art that does not meet Plato's standards of seeking and presenting the ultimate truths of the World of Being is to be censured.

How does Plato arrive at these views? He is a system builder, and as such, his work is unique and can be difficult to understand, because no part stands in isolation from the other parts. Central to Plato's system is his Theory of Ideas (Forms). This theory is tremendously complex and is integral to Plato's epistemology, ontology, linguistics, value theory, and theory of education. The eternal World of Being is reality, while the changing, everyday world of our senses and experience, the World of Becoming, is in a significant sense less real. The individuals or particulars of the World of Becoming participate in the Ideas (Forms). To know truth, we must know the World of Being, and the relationship of things in our experience to that world. For example, beautiful things participate in the Form of Beauty and are measured as they approximate the perfect Beauty.

Anyone who finds the Theory of Ideas to be vague and difficult to understand is not alone. After all, some of Aristotle's main disagreements with Plato center around this undefined notion of "participation" in the Ideas. For example, Plato says that Man should not live without beauty. However, even though we strive to know the Forms, Beauty is difficult to understand. It is related to the Good, and is a genuine characteristic of objects or ideas. Beauty is friendly, and the friendly is soft and smooth and slips through one's fingers (*Lysis* 216c–d). We "know" what beauty is, but are incapable of describing it. Certainly, this kind of vagueness makes it difficult to know the ultimate truth about beauty, or anything else. Yet it is our task to know the Ideas, and the task of good art is to represent them correctly.

At this point, it is necessary to keep in mind that Plato's language concerning the arts reflects a view of art that differs from our own. For example, the Greeks did not distinguish between what we generally term the fine arts, the finer crafts, and the work of craftsmen. The Greek word *poiesis* means "making," and is applicable to all arts and crafts. The term *mousike* included the elements of poetry as well as music, and was even extended to rhythm in general, as in gymnastics. *Mousike* is even applied to the higher forms of philosophy as well as to spiritual harmony.[2] In part because of this wider application of terms, it is fair to say that when Plato's general commentary centers on any one of the arts, such as poetry, the basic ideas can be generalized to all the arts.

For the sake of clarity, a more detailed look at Plato's view of art is best presented in two sections: the role of art as imitator of truth, and the role of art in society.

Art as Imitation

Mimesis is the Greek term for imitation, and Plato speaks about *mimesis* as being a common feature of all the arts. *Mimesis,* or copying of reality, is a concept that was applied to the theater prior to Plato, but expanded by Plato to be applied to poetry.[3] Although what is meant by "copying" is not always clear, copying is a significant concept in Plato's ontology, as we clearly see in "The Allegory of the Cave." Copies have lower value, and indeed the whole World of Becoming is but a copy of the true realities in the World of Being. For Plato, arts that are merely imitative, especially poetry, present copies of human activities in the World of Becoming and are, therefore, copies of copies. Plato gives us the example of a couch. God produces the couch that "really in itself is" (that is, the Idea). The cabinetmaker "does not make the idea or form which we say is the real couch, the couch in itself, but only some particular couch" (*Republic* 597C). The painter imitates the couch made by the carpenter, and thus his work is at a third level removed from reality. Painting only imitates the appearance of an object which itself is less than the Idea.

Song is constituted of words, tune, and rhythm (*Republic* 398c). Plato views music and rhythm as imitative of speech. Accordingly, he views various musical modes in terms of the human state of affairs with which they are associated: "rhythms and music generally are a reproduction expressing the moods of better and worse men" (*Laws* 798d). Some musical modes are associated with drunkenness, softness, and sloth; other modes are gentle and convivial; still other modes are suited for warriors. For example, the modes "that would fittingly imitate the utterances and accents of a brave man" (*Republic* 399c) would be suited for soldiers or others who must face difficult tests of fortitude. The best rhythms would be the rhythms of a life that is orderly and brave and "require the foot and the air to conform to that kind of man's speech and not the speech to the foot and the time" (*Republic* 400a).

The dance is mimetic in the same way. Dance is seen as representation of the spoken word through body motion and gestures which arise from the fact that no one keeps perfectly still when speaking. Thus body motion elaborates the spoken idea (*Laws* 816). Dance is not performed without music or rhythms of some sort, and these have already been linked to the behavior of persons. "A well educated man can both sing and dance as well" (*Laws* 654b). Plato is against the confusion of truth and verisimilitude,[4] and all of the imitative arts are open to this problem.

Art and Society

Notice that from the concept of art as imitation, Plato has quickly moved to the idea that mere imitation is a poor thing, thrice distanced from reality. But distance from Truth is not the only difficulty with mere imitation. The more significant problem is that both the artist and his audience (both young and old) can be deceived into thinking that this poor imitation *is* reality. For example, if the painter makes a picture of a carpenter, "by exhibiting at a distance his picture of a carpenter he would deceive children and foolish men, and make them believe it to be a real carpenter" (*Republic* 598c). Plato is concerned not only that others will be deceived but that the individual creator himself will be unable to distinguish knowledge, ignorance, and imitation (*Republic* 598d). The imitative artist is without knowledge or even correct belief about that which is represented, and cannot evaluate his own work properly in terms of its beauty or badness (*Republic* 602a). This artist would not know whether he had represented truly or not. "But, I take it, if he had genuine knowledge of the things he imitates he would far rather devote himself to real things than to the imitation of them" (*Republic* 599b). Tragic poets are typical of these ignorant imitators who will then present their work to the vulnerable multitude. Homer himself falls into this difficulty (*Republic* 599d).

To make matters worse, once an artist realizes that he can fool the crowd, he may also choose to indulge in the lowest forms of imitation: those which knowingly seek to please the crowd and are lucrative at the expense of true art.[5] No doubt, Plato's times were not exempt from examples of potentially good artists settling for crowd appeal.[6]

Clearly his view of *mimesis* has led us directly to Plato's view of the role that art plays in society. The swiftness of the transition of this discussion from the nature of art to its role in society reveals again the way in which it is impossible to separate Plato's view of art in the *Republic* from his vision of the nature of man, of the perfect society, and his Theory of Ideas.

We might ask Plato, "What's wrong with a little crowd appeal? The audience goes home satisfied, and the artist can make a living." Plato's campaign against both witting and unwitting deception rests on his realizition that the arts have tremendous powers to influence how we think and feel. They can stir our emotions and feelings of empathy. When we leave a performance, we carry the message of that performance deep within us.

Moreover, art is central to man's life and education. Proper education is a key issue in the development of the Republic. Without proper education there can be no proper citizens, proper leaders, and thus a proper society. Traditional education in Greece includes *gymnastike* for the body and *mousike* for the soul (*Republic* 376e).[7] At this point it is easy to see the source of Plato's fears concerning the arts. He fears that the misleading forms of imitation are potentially too influential, and are capable of leaving an indelible mark on the hearers at an early age (*Republic* 378d–e). He specifically worries about the skill in discourse that will fool the young into thinking that they are listening to the truth (*Sophist* 234c).

Plato's view springs in part from the tradition of his times that poets, such as Homer, were touched by divine inspiration, and were to be taken as educators worthy of study, holders of the keys to ultimate truths (*Republic* 598e); *Ion* 533e, 534b–e; and *Phaedrus* 245a). Such divinely inspired art has its place in the enjoyment of our lives, as long as it is properly understood and kept in its correct place. Art is not a good educator, though, since poets are not philosophers, and poetry is the result of fevered inspiration rather than knowledge.[8] In their delivery, the arts appeal to the passions of the soul rather than reason. Poetry and drama in particular can seduce an audience into sympathy with the characters, even if these characters exhibit morally dubious behavior. Indeed, to the extent that the Greek theater achieves greatness in exploring the behavior of Medea or Phaedra, equally does it increase its power to draw tolerance and even defense of these tortured souls.[9] The audience will imaginatively identify with the immoral characters, and the public will be misled into taking these half-truths for truths (*Republic* 602b–d).

Moreover, as discussed above, the *mimesis* of art is thrice removed from the realities of the World of Being. For these reasons, even the teachings contained in the works of great poets such is Homer are not clear, despite the possibility of their divine origin. Indeed, Homer becomes the paradigm of the poet who should not be taken as educator (*Republic* 599–600e).

Because of this view, Plato enters his famous argument for censorship, arguing that in the ideal state, art must be censored so that its possible immoral effects can be avoided. Poetry, as a vehicle for education, should he censored (*Republic* 377b–c). Objectionable stories must not be admitted into the city, and neither young nor old must listen to them in prose or verse. The Republic will allow only that which praises the gods and good men (*Republic* 378b–d, 380b, 395c–d, 605b and 607a; *Laws* 800). He discards most of the stories now in use, for example, those of Homer and Hesiod, which are false, ugly, and misrepresent the nature of gods and heroes, or which show heroes in the throes of personal lamentations (*Republic* 377c–d, 605d). Visual arts are supervised for the same reasons (*Republic* 522a–b, 536d). These criticisms apply to performers as well.

Although music is "imitative" in a completely different sense than is poetry, music is not exempt from this general criticism and censorship of the arts:

> As for other movement of the body as a whole—in the main it may properly be
> called dancing—we must bear in mind that it has two species, one reproducing

motions of comely bodies with a dignified effect, the other those of uncomely bodies with a ludicrous, and that, further, the comic and the serious kinds have each two subspecies. One species of the serious sort represents the movements of the comely body and its valiant soul in battle and in the toils of enforced endurance, the other the bearing of the continent soul in a state of prosperity and duly measured pleasure; an appropriate name for the latter would be the *dance of peace*. The war dance has a different character, and may properly be called the *Pyrrhic;* it depicts the motions of eluding blows and shots of every kind. . . . In these dances the upright, well-braced posture which represents the good body and good mind, and in which the bodily members are in the main kept straight, is the kind of attitude we pronounce right, that which depicts their contrary, wrong. In the case of the dance of peace, the question to be raised in every case is whether the performer succeeds or fails in maintaining throughout his performance a graceful style of dancing in a way becoming to the law-abiding man. So we have, in the first place, to draw a distinction between questionable dances and those which are above question. What then is the distinction, and where should the line be drawn? (*Laws* 814d–815b)

Dances that imitate those who are drunk, dances which are involved in bacchanals or the like, are "unfit for a citizen" (*Laws* 815d, 816d).

In sum, then, we see Plato promoting the idea of censorship to avoid seduction of the citizenry to morally reprehensible ways. The incredibly powerful and captivating influence of the arts could, in effect, harm the Republic in a way almost unavailable to other forms of human endeavor, so the arts must be kept and cultivated for the benefit of the society only.

We can admit no poetry into our city save only hymns to the gods and the praises of good men. For if you grant admission to the honeyed Muse in lyric or epic, pleasure and pain will be lords of your city instead of law and that which shall from time to time have approved itself to the general reason as best. (*Republic* 607a)

If the poets can defend their art properly and show their appropriateness and usefulness in a well-governed state, they will be admitted (*Republic* 607b–c).

The good artist (poet) becomes one who is poet-philosopher. He has the basis for knowing the universal truths and is not imitative in the lower sense. Moreover, he will know which themes are proper to present to the public.

Then, by heaven, am I not right in saying that . . . we shall never be true musicians—neither we nor the guardians that we have undertaken to educate—until we are able to recognize the forms of soberness, courage, liberality, and high-mindedness, and all their kindred and their opposites, too." (*Republic* 402c)

PLATO'S VIEW OF ART: DOES IT WORK?

In Plato's system, the ultimate task is to know truth through knowledge of the World of Being, so it is perfectly reasonable for him to envision the task of the artist as seeking to represent these truths. Even though contemporary thought does not accept Plato's Theory of Ideas, there is still opportunity to discuss the framework of what he was saying. I will focus on three issues: (1) Is the goal of art to express universal truths? (2) Are there "legitimate themes" for art in society? (3) Is it the function of the "true" artist to be consciously striving toward these goals?

1. **Can we think of art as attempting to express universal truths?** Plato's discussion of the goal of art is hampered by several factors: the lack of understanding of the various aspects of the arts, the absence of a theory of *techne,*[10] and the lack of recognition of essential differences between the arts. If we grant Plato's idea that what is needed is an enlightened form of *mimesis*—one that sheds light on ultimate truth—we are still left with the fact that the dance will not and cannot do what a concert violinist, a novelist, or a poet can do. If Plato has a deep understanding of the dance, it is not reflected in the *Dialogues*. Although it is probably not within Plato's cultural experience to understand the abstractness of motion presented in certain modern dances, he has certainly not examined the many facets of dance with which we could expect him to be aware. First, there is the moment of dance in which the dancer's body as a fine-tuned instrument expresses both idea and elegance in its motion through space and time. Within this performance, there is the dancer's own experience of dance, which is imitative of no theme. The issue of theme arises when the dance functions either within a play, for a ritual, or according to the interests of the choreographer. Choreography stands as its own aspect of dance; Plato has focused only on *mimesis*. Morover, he speaks of dance as imitative of the spoken word, not of emotions. He can't have been ignorant of the extent to which Greek dance celebrated the emotions. Ancient Greek culture is renowned for the dances with which it marked war and peace as well as religious functions. These dances ranged from the sedate to the highly demonstrative, with the latter coming to full fruition in the Dionysian tradition. We can assume that Plato includes the emotional aspect of dance under the association of dance with music and rhythms which imitate the moods of better or worse men.

In short, Plato's focus on *mimesis* simply does not do justice to the dance experience. However, aspects of his thought on this subject warrant consideration. Certainly there is a note of sympathy in all of us toward the idea that art is imitative of life and that art should express common human truths. However, we must define our terms, and the terms here are too vague to be useful. Once we begin to seek rigor in these terms, many of us will shrink from seeking ultimate truths in the ontologically independent Ideas, preferring instead a concept grounded in a more contemporary psychological or anthropological approach.

Plato is seeking to cast light upon the problem of universals, and there are at least two ways in which this issue is reflected in dance. First, dance explores the abstract movement of the human body in space in a manner that can be interpreted is an exploration of the universal patterns of dance. Second, dance explores universal themes of life by presenting an abstraction of experience that appears to transcend particular events. The description of the dancer as expressing ultimate truth is a familiar one. For example, it was said of Ruth St. Denis in her dance, "The Incense":

> At one moment, she stands utterly still except that the hand bearing the tray moves slowly upward, almost hugging the body and head, until the dancer herself seems to have become a holy stele, a column of truth, or, perhaps, a stilled human receptable for divine illumination.[11]

In my own dance experience, I have discovered that folk dance expresses universality in both movement and themes. Folk dances reflect a cross-cultural commonality of movement in both the overall patterns of the dances and the steps of the dancers within the dance. For example, it is common to classify folk dances into groups such as rounds, open rounds, serpentine rounds, open couple, closed couple, and sitting dances. Many steps and rhythms are also found around the world. For example, the folk dance teacher can instruct experienced dancers by calling for a "grape vine" step or a schottische step. All dancers respond to the descriptions of jumping movements, hopping movements, or wild ecstatic movements as categories. Although no one wishes to deny the uniqueness of each culture, it is amazing to discover the extent of shared movements among them.

Although most folk dances involve both sexes, my dance studio focused on women dancing women's dances, for themselves, their psyches, and their figures. In these dances, as well as in the costumes and music, we found the commonality of experience of all women. A good example of universality in movememt is found in the use of the pelvic roll and abdominal muscles accompanied by hip motions and undulatory motions, as frequently found in women's dances. Often grouped as "danse du ventre," or "abdominal dance," these dances are found in northern Africa, and are traditionally ascribed to Egypt, although the details of their origins are shrouded by time. In Celebes, the dance is called *messeri,* a form of the Arabian word *másri,* meaning Egyptian.[12] This type of movement is found throughout the Middle East, as well as in the Caroline Islands, New Guinea, and Polynesia among other areas. Although often seen by misguided observers as "obscene" (and often used toward that end in the carnivals and midways of the United States), these movements are certainly mimetic in nature and linked to the theme of fertility and child-bearing. Although sometimes used by women to attract men, or sometimes to instruct the supposedly innocent bride and groom, this type of dance is often not done in the presence of men. Middle Eastern and Asian traditions often dictate that women of "proper" upbringing dance only within their homes and in all-female groups. The traditions of the Yemenite as well as the Hasidic Jews reflect this segregation of women. For this reason, the dance is used by women among women as a method of instruction in an incredibly healthy form of body movement for the child-bearing years, as a way to hand down wisdom from one woman to another, and as a pleasant way to raise the consciousness of the child-bearer.

Traditional themes tie directly to commonality of movements. In this way, international folk dance is particularly good for exposing the universality of human experience through both movements and themes. Dances are easily grouped as wedding, harvest, funeral, weapon, animal, occupational, initiation, and fertility dances, to name a few. Another good example of the link between movement and theme is the *Kolo*. The Balkan *Kolo* is a "wheel." (The wheel image is a very common one, as exemplified by the names of the Salzburg *Rädel,* and the Spanish *Reda,* as well as in the American "wheel" and "wheel around" steps.) The *Kolo* may have originated in Serbia, where the closed circle of dancers moved around an object of worship seeking magic from within the ring. An open circle symbolizes an open door through which evil can escape and good can enter.[13] *Kolos* come in a wide variety, but the *Kolo* in rural areas retains remnants of fertility rites when led by a girl carrying a snake or garland in her hands or around her neck.[14] Still another example is the *Horos* (chain dances), which are also found in many countries wearing slightly varied guises.

The reappearance of themes leads the dancer to explore the cultures from which the dances spring. For example, the woman's adornment may reflect her dowry or her family's wealth, and the flowing clothes her modesty. Is the role of women in that society different from our own? Are there surprising—even shocking—similarities of experience among all women? The ubiquitous Greek handkerchief is often decorative or useful for movement in the dance, but it can also express the social moods of flirtation, passion, or a promise given. What adornments in our own social history have served the same purposes? Differences in cultural practices are underscored, to be sure, but more importantly the similarities in our social needs and experiences are found.

If this is what we mean by the truths of universal experience—in form, rhythm, and themes—if commonality of shared human experience stands as a type of universal truth, then I can be sympathetic to Plato's direction. However, the two most common categories of interpretation of these facts both fall short of Plato's theory. One interpretation argues that since the roots of human dance can be found in the "dances" of higher animals, there is a governing necessity in human nature that dictates certain types of movement and even certain types of social involvement.[15] Various versions of this argument propose necessity as biologically or psychologically based, while others reach for the concept of "human spirit." The opposing interpretation is that the patterns of history reflected by invasions, movement of trade, and other interactions between peoples can by themselves account for the mixing and mingling of dance forms. The Moorish invasion of Spain and the endless trade routes through Africa are good examples. The conflict between these interpretations leads us back to the closely related "nature/nurture" controversy that haunts so many questions about human activities. The first interpretation makes a metaphysical claim, the exact nature of which varies from thinker to thinker, while the second interpretation attempts to be empirical in nature. Yet even the former view, which comes closest to Plato's approach, by and large avoids the metaphysical claim that there are universal truths (Forms) that have an objective, eternal existence and which are to be mirrored as standards for achievement. Plato's direction of thought leads us to questions of interest, but not necessarily to adoption of his solutions.

2. Are there proper themes for the arts? Even after understanding Plato's systematic view of the *Republic,* it is difficult to be sympathetic with his recommendations for censorship. In placing these restrictions on creativity, Plato limits the understanding of universal themes which art can present.

My topic here is truth, not censorship, but it is important to keep in mind that Plato's metaphysics of truth does not require censorship. Rather, it is his beliefs about human nature that lead him here. In spite of the fact that Socrates was falsely accused of misleading the youth, Plato apparently thinks that youth, as well as the general public, can indeed be misled.

He is certainly not alone in history, or in our own times, in these concerns. Television has often been accused of being systematically misleading in its fuzzy distinctions between documentary and "docu-drama." We cannot help but wonder what Plato would say about contemporary American youth taking what they see in movies and on television for reality, or of the court case in which a young defendant claimed that his violent acts were imitations of what he saw on television!

It would seem that while Plato stands opposed to art that is reduced to crowd pleasing, he sees no contradiction in art that is required to "please" the authorities of the state. Perhaps this results from his belief that the artists who are capable of enlightened thought would see the correctness of this path and would willingly present only the types of art that reflect truth couched in suitable subject matter.

It is unfortunate that Plato is alienated from the main forms of Greek dance, especially dances associated with the "lower" emotions and with the Chorus involved in unacceptable dramas. To adopt his views would be to eliminate from acceptability much of what has descended to us as Greek folk dance, particularly that which comes from Dionysian roots.

Plato's outlook would also cause us to cast aside some of the greatest efforts in dance to express universal truths. Part of the revolution presented by modern dance is the breaking away from the lightweight themes of nineteenth-century ballet in favor of themes of greater depth and insight. Isadora Duncan showed that dance could be about the soul and emotions, while Ruth St. Denis and Ted Shawn utilized religious experience and ritual, among other new subject matters. Martha Graham's "American Provincials" explored the relationship between the piety of Puritanism and the Dionysian ritual of pagan religious observance.[16] Graham later did dances of social comment and history, such as "American Document." [17] This small number of examples alone shows the great loss to dance that would be incurred by limitation on theme. Plato's censorship would only serve to bar our access to truth, and the public would be misled in yet another way.

3. Must the artist be philosopher-artist? In all forms of dance, folk dance as well as ballet and musical theater, there is something that I instinctively seek from the dancer beyond an effort to move the limbs beautifully and to express one's self. For me, the title "artist," as distinct from "great performer," implies a conscious effort to go beyond an imitation of life toward an enlightenment about life, toward something that might even defy the concepts of beauty.

There are many examples of dancers historically considered to be artists who embody universal truths in their art. In the dance, when we think along these lines, we think of the grandeur and elevated status of a Nijinski or Pavlova in the ballet, or of St. Denis or Graham in modern dance. Why? Is it the years of training? Is it cultural snobbery? Or is it the belief that the rigor of the dancer's training must also impart a vision that goes beyond the immediate performance? This may be why folk dance, by its nature, occupies an odd position in the arts. Folk dance is done by individuals as part of their traditions, not as a conscious seeking of truth, but as a cultural expression of truths on various occasions. Thus, folk dance is not intellectualized, nor is it often done professionally, and the practitioners fail miserably on Plato's standards no matter how well they dance. Folk art begins to satisfy those standards only as we begin to study it.

Yet, despite my inclination to demand this kind of awareness of an artist, I must argue that once we examine this line of thought, we can see that it is impossible to expect all artists, especially performers, to be actively and consciously seeking ultimate truths. In fact, the demands of performance may preclude being a philosopher-artist, and we are often disappointed to discover that the much lauded dancer does not also possess the expertise in the philosophy of her art for which we had hoped.

Moving to the opposite extreme, the accusation of lack of awareness has been launched at many great dancers: "The person drawn to dance as a profession is notoriously unintellectual. He thinks with his muscles, delights in expression with body not words, finds analysis painful and boring, and is a creature of physical ebullience." [18] This view reflects a stereotype similar to that of the jazz musician who can play brilliantly but can't explain why or how. It does not serve any good purpose to cling to stereotypes of either extreme. However, we must question whether it is fair to ask of any one person that she achieve excellence in both performance and the philosophy of her art as well. Certainly this requirement would rob the title "artist" from many great figures in all of the arts.

Isadora Duncan is just one example of an artist who approximates Plato's ideals in many ways, but who still fails in others. She is a seeker of universal truths, influenced by philosophers such as Schopenhauer and Whitman; but despite her years of study, she could not be deemed an artist-philosopher. Moreover, her choice of themes goes to the passionate rather than being restricted to the "behavior of good men." Duncan held that speech and rational thinking were born of the brain, and dancing "is the Dionysian ecstasy which carries away all. It is impossible to mix in any way, one with the other." [19] She is enraptured with the Greek chorus and tries to capture it in her dance, [20] but she stresses the soul of the dance and its unity with poetry, music, and dramaturgy. [21] In spite of her differences in view, it is fascinating to see how her words occasionally echo Plato:

> It must always be kept in mind that there are two classes of dancing: the sacred and the profane. By profane, I do not mean sinful, but simply that dancing which expresses the physical being and the joy of the senses, whereas sacred dancing expresses the aspirations of the spirit to transform itself into a higher sphere than the terrestrial.[22]

She sees the dichotomy, but will not qualify by his standards.

> It is possible to dance in two ways: One can throw oneself into the spirit of the dance, and dance the thing itself: *Dionysus*. Or one can *contemplate* the spirit of the dance—and dance as one who relates a story: *Apollo*.[23]

Plato would probably applaud Duncan for her efforts, but criticize her for being confused about the importance of the human passions.

In the final analysis, I doubt that Plato would be satisfied by many of our great artists. The ways in which the artist seeks out and demonstrates ultimate truth are, by their very nature, different from the ways that the philosopher approaches the same task. Few are the number of individuals who can combine both approaches, and even fewer are those who would satisfy Plato once his standards of propriety are imposed.

CONCLUSION

In short, Plato's view of art is incomplete and cannot work. We can share his leaning toward a concept of universal truths, if these truths can be interpreted as commonalities of human experience. We can share the belief that these truths transcend what is convenient or functional for us to understand about the nature of Man. Art, through the kind of imitation of life that abstracts greater realities from the immediate moment, can point out these truths in ways that are unique to art. However, this view of universal truth is a far cry from Plato's World of Being. Further, Plato limits the ability of art to search for truth, because of his beliefs about the need for censorship.

It is an old saying that to know darkness, one must know light. To know truth, we must seek all truths and have confidence that a proper education will allow us to avoid the seductive pitfalls of misrepresentation. We need to educate youth to the ways of the vendors of cheap imitations of life, while being able to retain a position for both light entertainment and art in society. In this way, the artist can be mistress of her own domain and be allowed the unbridled creative freedom to express truth as she finds it.

NOTES

1. John Fisher, "Did Plato Have a Theory of Art?," *Pacific Philosophical Quarterly*, 63 (1982): 93; and Whitney J. Oates, *Plato's View of Art* (New York: Scribner's, 1972), p. 3.
2. Julius A. Elias, *Plato's Defence of Poetry* (London: Macmillan, 1984), p. 2.
3. Fisher, op. cit., p. 97.
4. Evanghelos A. Moutsopoulos, "Truth in Art," *Diogenes*, 132 (Winter 1985): 108.

5. Ibid., pp. 107–108.
6. Ibid., p. 108.
7. J. M. Beil Waugh, "Art and Morality: The End of an Ancient Rivalry?," *Journal of Aesthetic Education,* 20 (Spring 1986): 5.
8. Oates, op. cit., pp. 33–36.
9. Waugh, op. cit. P. 14.
10. Fisher, op. cit., p. 97.
11. Walter Terry, quoted by Joseph H. Mazo, *Prime Movers: The Makers of Modern Dance in America* (New York: Morrow, 1977), p. 74.
12. Curt Sachs, *World History of Dance,* trans. Bessie Schönberg (New York: Norton, 1937), pp. 23–24.
13. Jane A. Harris, Anne Pittmen, and Marlys S. Waller, *Dance a While* (Burgess, 1968), p. 176.
14. Lois Ellfeldt, *Folk Dance* (Wm. C. Brown, 1969), p. 47.
15. Sachs, op. cit., pp. 1–12.
16. Mazo, op. cit., p. 168.
17. Ibid., pp. 170–171.
18. Doris Humphrey, *The Art of Making Dances,* ed. Barbara Pollack (New York: Holt, Rinehart and Winston, 1959), p. 17.
19. Mazo, op. cit., p. 47.
20. Ibid., p. 46.
21. Isadora Duncan, "The Dance of the Greeks," in Sheldon Cheney, ed., *The Art of the Dance* (New York: Theatre Arts Books, 1969), pp. 92–96.
22. Isadora Duncan, "Dancing in Relation to Religion and Love," ibid., p. 122.
23. Isadora Duncan, "Fragments and Thoughts," ibid., p. 140.

ALFRED L. CASTLE

THE PHILOSOPHER AS HISTORIAN:
THE CORRESPONDENCE
APPROACH TO TRUTH

Historians, in league with their colleagues in all other disciplines, aspire to recognize truth. Although the special province of historians is the past, they pride themselves on discovering causes for human action which can survive the scrutiny of rational analysis. As with other disciplines, furthermore, the philosophy of truth which historians adopt has profound consequences for their craft and for their claims to objectivity.

Philosophers recognize the existence of three primary theories of truth. These three, which have been subject to considerable debate and analysis, are the *coherence, pragmatic,* and *correspondence* theories. Each provides guidelines for checking fact-claims.

Alfred L. Castle received his Ph.D. from the University of New Mexico/International University in 1978 and did postdoctoral studies at Columbia University (1979–1980). He was a National Endowment for the Humanities fellow (1978, 1981, 1985) and a Hoover fellow (1983, 1985, 1988). Formerly the vice president for development and executive director of the New Mexico Military Institute Foundation, Dr. Castle served as the director of development and as an associate professor at Hawaii Pacific College.

According to the coherence position, a fact-claim or proposition is true if it harmonizes—that is, coheres—with other facts that one has already accepted as true. The historian, for example, can reject the proposition that the Civil War was caused by Woodrow Wilson's intransigence on the slavery issue because the fact-claim made by such a proposition does not harmonize with other known facts. For the coherence theorist, a proposition can only be true if it is both self-consistent and coherently connected with our system of judgments as a whole.

The coherence test for truth is helpful to aspects of knowledge not directly verifiable by personal observation. The past, for example, is not available to direct observation. In addition, most of the claims about contemporary events that we do not witness are "tested" by making them cohere with the facts we already accept as true.

Philosophers have long recognized that the coherence test for truth has a most serious drawback. The reason for this is that a fact-claim may fit coherently with a large number of previously accepted "facts," all of which are themselves false. Moreover, a fact that is true may be rejected simply because it does not harmonize with a previously accepted set of false fact-claims. Thus, it is easy to construct a complex coherent system that is, nonetheless, false. Unless previously accepted data is well supported by evidence, the truth of a new proposition is doubtful despite its harmony with other propositions.

For historians, this point is significant. System-building has been a tradition of political theorists, theologians, sociologists, philosophers, and others. It has been a common practice to compose history from the point of view of some comprehensive ideology which provides the basis for selecting, interpreting, and rearranging facts. The resulting systems may provide coherent frameworks for judging fact-claims while bearing little resemblance to reality.

Another fact test is the pragmatic test for truth. Developed originally by the nineteenth-century logician Charles S. Peirce, who found ideas meaningful only if they made some difference in our experience, pragmatism was elaborated by the American philosopher William James. For James, the truth-value of any idea is to be determined by the results; that is, a true idea brings about desired effects. We have come to be familiar with the statement that "if an idea works, then it is true."

Conceived in an era notable for philosophical doubt, pragmatism urges us to see criteria for truth-claims as temporary resting places constructed for useful and temporary ends. In other words, all criteria for judging the truth of a proposition are no more than transitory solutions, constructed by a community to facilitate its inquiries. Pragmatism, for example, views the truth-claims of physics as being useful in our coping with certain parts of the universe, while biology deals with other parts. Our different inquiries in facing different parts of the universe lead to different and equally "true" sets of provisional truth-tests. Thus, history, art, literature, and chemistry, in addition to all disciplines, possess their claims to truth. As James points out, no final claim to a static truth can be made for those who adopt pragmatism as a guide.

Historians and others have noted, however, that pragmatism possesses a disturbing paradox. In order for an idea to work pragmatically, one must believe that it is true on other than pragmatic criteria. In order for an idea to work pragmatically, we must believe it in terms of *correspondence*. For example, in order for the belief in Christ to work, one must accept that Christ exists as a real person; one must believe that there is an objective person separate from our wishes which corresponds to concepts of Him. Even though we may not be able to verify the belief through direct observation, if it is not held on a *correspondence* basis, then the belief can have no *pragmatic* results.

For example, the philosopher Friedrich Nietzsche believed that the falseness of an opinion is not any objection to it. Rather, the question for him was how far the opinion was life-furthering, life-preserving, species-preserving, and, perhaps, species-creating. For Nietzsche to hold this position, he had to believe the criterion on nonpragmatic grounds. For even this would-be pragmatist, Life was an absolute truth and good that sat in judgment of propositions which would direct our lives.

Historians, unconvinced by the temptations of the coherence and pragmatic persuasions, have generally accepted a third great test for truth. The correspondence test, initially articulated in Plato's *Sophist* and later developed in modern times by George Edward Moore and Bertrand Russell, requires one to verify a mental concept against a real object/event; and if the subjective concept "corresponds to" the real object/event, then the concept is considered true.

Quite simply, if you are told that it is raining outside, you can go outside and look to see if it is. If there is a correspondence between the proposition "it is raining outside" and actual weather conditions, then the fact-claim, a proposition, is true and factual. This, as Alfred Jules Ayer has pointed out, is practical verifiability. Other propositions, such as "there are mountains on the farthest side of Pluto," defy practical observation. Nonetheless, such a proposition is verifiable in principle as we would, given the opportunity, know what observations would decide its truth for us if we were in a position to make them.

For modern correspondence theorists, however, truth is still problematic and precautions must be taken when checking to see if subjective mental concepts and propositions do correspond with a real object/event.

Philosophers are aware, however, of the human mind's imaginative operations and the way it creates concepts. No created concept is ever an exact reproduction of any external object/event. The mind is selective in its translation of physical events in the external world. Since no mental concept can ever correspond exactly to real object/events, we may only enjoy a degree of correspondence between the two. If the degree of correspondence is high, we hold the fact-claim to be true; if it is not, we decide it is false. Contrary to Platonism, modern philosophers allow for truth's reticence in disclosing itself. Further, unlike Platonism, modern adherents of the correspondence theory of truth realize that we are limited to our own subjective "experiencing world" and that verifying a subjective concept (which we can experience) with a real object/event (which we cannot directly experience) is not possible. What we can do in employing the test is to compare a concept with a set of sensations. We check, therefore, subjective concepts with a subjective set of sensations. If they match to some acceptable degree, we call the concept true; if not, we call it false. Even for the contemporary correspondence adherent, truth is often uncertain and provisional. Pontius Pilate's desperate inquiry about truth, found in the *New Testament*, remains the poignant question of the ages that Nietzsche thought it was.

As an active historian, I am sensitive to the limitations of my craft and its conscious dependence on the correspondence theory of truth for its appeal to acceptable levels of accuracy and objectivity. Research in history, as in other areas of science, selects and abstracts from the concrete occurrences studied; no matter how detailed my historical study of a period may be, it is never an exhaustive account of what actually happened.

My colleagues in the sciences, and positivists in general, often impugn my discipline's claim that objective knowledge of the past is possible. Their concerns seem to lie in the following:

1. Historical inquiry is selective in its starting point. My current research in 1930s U.S. diplomatic history, for example, may be conditioned by my education, family history, the availability of research grants in this field, or a sense of political mission related to current foreign issues. Perhaps it is something else.

This granted, however, I maintain, with Morris Cohen, that there is no *prima facie* reason to believe that, because an historical inquiry begins with a specific problem, or because there are causal determinants for my choice, I am in principle prevented any more than is a natural scientist from rendering an adequate account of my subjects.

A corollary objection of many positivists to my claim for correspondence-driven objectivity is that the selectivity of my craft is unique in that I am ineluctably concerned with "value-impregnated" subject matter. History, this argument goes, embodies some universally accepted cultural value or is instrumental to the actualization of such a value. Consequently, we are told that the historian, unlike the physical scientist, is hopelessly intwined in value-impregnated occurrences in which humans are the primary subject of study.

However, some "historical studies," such as astronomy, geology, and biology, exclude humans from their primary object. More importantly, even when the object of the historical study is humans and their values, it by no means follows that we must share or even judge those values. It is quite enough for us to describe them and perhaps assign causes for these values. For example, in my writing on President Herbert Hoover, I find that my professional obligation is to describe his opposition to Roosevelt's foreign policy and to analyze the causes for his noninterventionist values. I need not share them.

2. Skepticism concerning the possibility of objective explanations in human history is based on the presumption that personal and social biases have preconditioned my study. Sociologists of knowledge contend that most or all thought is influenced and controlled by the "existential situation" in which it occurs. This is especially the case, it is argued, when thinking involves human affairs, the interpretation of observed facts, the selection of historical problems to address, and the judging of standards for validity in measuring evidence. Every historical claim about human behavior is said to be valid only within a particular social setting; the belief that explanations which are true for everyone are possible in historical inquiry is viewed as a kind of self-deception (or "ideology") of a culture.

Indeed, no study of mine nor any of my colleagues has taken place in a vacuum. I chose my interest in 1930s foreign policy because my great-uncle, the former under secretary of state for President Hoover, was an active spokesman for noninterventionist positions at this time. In addition, I had been educated in an environment that valued outright pacifism. But it does not follow from my personal circumstance that the conscious and unconscious value commitments associated with my status as an historian inevitably caused my conclusion that Roosevelt made some provocative foreign policy choices that helped lead Japan to attack Pearl Harbor in 1941 (see "William R. Castle and Opposition to U.S. Involvement in an Asian War, 1939–1941" in *Pacific Historical Review,* October 1985). The preconceptions I brought to my analysis of the causes for U.S. involvement in Asia were neutral to differences in social value. The fact that my conclusions are shared by many investigators with different educational and social backgrounds (many of my conclusions are held by Marxist historians) is not an uncommon occurrence in my field.

3. Critics of historiographic claims to objectivity also aver that standards of validity—or methods of determining whether a fact is true or false—are causally related to other cultural traits, and that class, natural bias, worldview, and social status frequently influence what conclusions we accept. For example, the conclusions reached by Northern and Southern historians about the efficacy of Reconstruction after the Civil War clearly reflect their respective biases. Yet, the fact that biased thinking may be detected and its sources investigated shows that the case for objective, correspondence-based explanations in history is possible. Indeed, the very assertion that a historian exhibits identifiable bias assumes that there is a valid distinction between biased and unbiased thinking and that an "external" standard exists by which we can judge sound from unsound reasoning. Consequently, it is possible, even if difficult, to correct the bias and impose better evidential standards on our writing. Accurate historical explanation may be difficult; it is, however, a difficulty that all disciplines share to one degree or another.

4. Finally, historians are told that because every historical event possesses seemingly unlimited relations to other historical events, no explanation can ever disclose (correspond to) the full reality of what actually happened. For example, my account of Roosevelt's foreign-policy decisions with respect to Japan covers only a few aspects of these occurrences and stops short of revealing all antecedents of his decisions. This fact leads some critics to claim that my rendering of Roosevelt's foreign-policy actions is incomplete and, hence, not totally accurate.

This assertion of necessary incompleteness and arbitrariness is, however, inaccurate. It is never the task of any investigation initiated by a specific problem or question to reproduce its entire subject matter. Not only is the simple fact that inquiry is selective no grounds for doubting the objective character of historical conclusions; if an inquiry were not selective, it would never resolve the specific question that generated it. For example, in posing the question of how much Sanford Dole's first constitution for the Republic of Hawaii was influenced by his correspondence with the Columbia University political theorist John W. Burgess, I ignored many details of the history of both Hawaii and the United States (see "Advice for Hawaii: The Dole-Burgess Letters" in *The Hawaiian Journal of History,* 1981, pp. 24–30). My concentration was solely on their seminal correspondence and its actual influence on Dole's thinking. This selective investigation ignored much that was interesting in their personal histories and the histories of their nations. Still, using accepted standards of validity and causation, I was able to find a "selected" link to Dole's intellectual development.

A related objection stems from another misconception; in effect, it assumes that since every causal condition for an event has its own causal conditions, the event is never fully explained unless the entire regressive series of the latter conditions is also explained. If I were investigating President Reagan's decision to invade Grenada, I would offer his anticommunism as a partial cause; an immediate question would be what caused his anticommunism, and I might suggest his relation to the political Right in the 1980s. This in turn would generate a question about what caused his relationship to the political Right in the 1980s. This analytical regression could continue indefinitely, with the historical process paralyzed as a result. Those who criticize historians for the inability to study the "whole story" forget that, as Ernest Nagel reminded us, B is a cause of A even if C is a cause of B. When some future position of a planet is predicted with the help of gravitational theory and initial information about the initial condition of the solar system at some given time, there is not ground for skepticism simply because the assumed initial conditions are in turn the outcome of previous ones.

We historians respond to specific questions knowing that a good answer for one of them is not a good or even relevant solution for the others. In responding to the question of what caused Reagan's invasion of Grenada, I am responsible only if I clarify and qualify the question so that my historical study is both limited in scope and historically accurate. The fact that one question may suggest yet another and initiate several new investigations invites admiration for the progressive nature of the entire scientific enterprise while also guaranteeing a healthy historical humility.

Historical relativism, the most common expressions of the above concerns, became particularly powerful in the United States in the 1930s. Unpersuaded that history had made the same kind of progress as the natural sciences had, and perhaps appalled at the absurd historical claims made in World War I and pre-World War II years, some historians themselves came to doubt the objective efficacy of their profession. Such historians as Charles Beard, Karl Mannheim, and Carl Becker joined other respectable historians in expressing their doubts about the possibility of obtaining access to historical truths, a doubt that continues in many positivist and pragmatic corners.

Relativists, quite routinely, confuse the way knowledge is acquired with the validity of that knowledge. I might, for example, out of patriotic fervor, indicate that Japan led sneak attacks on Pearl Harbor and be able to prove that the statement is true, no matter what my motives for making it might have been. Second, as I discussed above, relativists wrongly argue that because all historical accounts must be partial in the sense of being incomplete, they must be partial in the sense of being false. An incomplete account of an event can be an objectively true account though not the whole truth. Third, relativists all argue, in ignorance of the paradox, that they and their friends are exempt from relativism in some degree. As indicted above, this is due to their appeal to trans-relativist appeals to absolute standards of verification which can stand in judgment of historical inadequacies. In their further assertion that history is "merely subjective," they forget that "subjective" is a correlative term which cannot be meaningful unless its opposite, "objective," is also meaningful. No knowledge can be subjective unless some knowlege is objective.

Clio, the muse of history, is indeed reticent to reveal her truths. Yet, if we accept the basic assumptions of the correspondence theory of truth, that truth consists of agreement between subjective concepts and propositions and external, objective, verifiable objects/events, we can discern simple rules for conducting sound investigation. If specific concerns of historical proof are not widely taught, or even agreed upon, it is a fault of our entire profession.

As a historian who, despite its imperfections, accepts the correspondence theory for measuring truth, I have attempted in my writing to follow these guidelines as the key logical consequences of the theory:

1. Sound evidence, as analytic historians such as Arthur C. Danto have pointed out, must consist in the establishment of a satisfactory relationship between the *factum probandum* (the proposition to be proved) and the *factum probans* (the material that is proffered as proof). Every fact in history is an answer to a question. Moreover, evidence which is useful and true and sufficient to answer one question may be false in relation to another. Quite simply put, we historians must not simply get the facts right, we must get the right facts—that is, relevant facts—right. For example, in asking the question of what contributions the historian Maurice Garland Fulton made to the historiography of the Lincoln County Wars, I sought factual material to answer only that question. The many facts I discovered regarding his relationship to the emerging understanding of Southern Reconstruction poetry in the 1930s had to be largely ignored (see "Maurice Garland Fulton: Historian of New Mexico and the Southwest," *New Mexico Historical Review,* April 1980, pp. 121–138). Through posing a specific question, and assuming that there is an objective object or event to which our true propositions correspond, historians are able to proceed cautiously to answer the question.

2. Historians must not only provide relevant and good evidence, they must also search for the best relevant evidence. This latter sort of evidence is usually evidence that is most nearly immediate to the event itself. This rule of immediacy, as the historian David H. Fischer has called it, means that the best evidence is the event itself. Less cogent evidence would include the remains of the event, direct observation of it, secondhand reports of it, and so on.

Intellectual historians, for example, often analyze the influence of the thought of one thinker on the thought of another. They are fortunate in being able, in most cases, to analyze direct expressions of the thoughts of both thinkers through their speeches and published writing. When I asked the extent, if any, of Karl Jaspers' influence on the thought of Flannery O'Connor, I spent most of my time seeking answers through an examination of her letters, her essays, and her short stories. I then compared her ideas regarding existentialism and redemption with Jaspers' ideas as they were expressed in his many philosophical works. This type of intellectual history, called the internal history of ideas, focuses less on the consequence of ideas for human action than on intellectual parallels and possible causal relations between two or more thinkers. The objective reality to which my propositions must correspond to be acceptable is the written work itself. The rule of immediacy holds here as the written work of a thinker is generally accepted as the closest expression of his or her formal thought that we have (see "Karl Jaspers and Flannery O'Connor: The Hermeneutic Of Being," *Southwest Philosophical Studies,* April 1981, pp. 128–141).

3. Proper evidence must always be affirmative. So-called "negative evidence" proves nothing. The nonexistence of an event or object is established not by no evidence but by affirmative evidence that it did not exist. This simple rule of affirmation avoids the intellectual muddle which occurs when we assume that because there is no evidence for event X's existence, not-X is a proven proposition. For example, in my inquiry into the U.S. foreign policy which led up to Pearl Harbor, I could not conclude that because there is no known evidence for Roosevelt's plotting to cause the attack, it has been proven that he did not.

4. As suggested earlier, all inferences from empirical evidence are probabilistic. Moreover, this rule of probability recognizes the limitations of the correspondence theory of truth. Historians are required to demonstrate more than that X was probably the case. They must determine the probability of X in relation to the probability of alternatives. They cannot disprove X by demonstrating that not-X was possible, but only by showing that not-X was more probable than X. For example, in my examination of the origins of Isaac Singer's notion of the relationship between play, freedom, and beauty, I had to demonstrate not only that it was possible that he drew his ideas from Friedrich Schiller, but that, based on evidence, it was more probable that he did than did not. Since direct evidence was lacking, my obligation was to establish the proposition that Singer drew from the aesthetics of Schiller with a high degree of probability based on imperfect evidence (see "Gimpel's Will to Believe: Friedrich Schiller's Aesthetic in Isaac Singer's 'Gimpel the Fool,'" *Southwest Philosophy Studies,* Spring 1983, pp. 123–129).

5. The meaning of any statement depends upon the context from which it is taken. No historical statement used in evidence can transcend time and space, and none may apply in a universal fashion. When searching for evidence that the Japanese were willing to negotiate arms reduction in 1930, I had to be careful that statements by various Japanese diplomats about the matter are not understood in exactly the same way Americans in 1986 would understand the term "partial disarmament." When Japanese diplomats prepared to negotiate

the London Naval Disarmament Conference, their pronouncements about the need to reduce international tension through naval reductions must be understood in the context of Japanese history, politics, and culture in the early twentieth century, not American history, politics, and culture in the 1980s. To confuse these two would be to arrive at erroneous conclusions (see "Ambassador Castle in Japan: The London Naval Conference of 1930," *Naval History*, 1988).

6. Finally, in seeking accuracy, historians must not make statements which are precise beyond what the evidence warrants. Degrees of precision do vary greatly from one piece of evidence to another. With the advent of "quantifiable history," we have seen some significant advances in our understanding of social, political, and economic history. Still, nuances of language will continue to suffice for the articulation of evidence which defies quantification.

Historians have much to gain from unearthing our assumptions about what constitutes truth and our procedures for testing for it. My own work has proceeded on the conscious assumption that there are objective events and objects which sound rules of empirical and logical investigation can ascertain. If my education and historiographical experience make it difficult to adopt Platonism's contention that absolute truth is directly accessible, I, nonetheless, also believe that historical truths are not merely pragmatic. Well-established historical truths, though difficult to arrive at, are as immortal as the logical rules for accessing them. As the philosopher Brand Blanshard concluded, "truth is the approximation of thought to reality. It is thought on its way home. Its measure is the distance thought has traveled—toward that intelligible system which unites its ultimate object with its ultimate end." With humility, but with confidence, we may proceed to trust sound evidence, objectivity, correspondence, logic, and an accessible past.

DENI ELLIOTT

THE PHILOSOPHER AS JOURNALIST: A PRAGMATIC APPROACH TO TRUTH

The sequence of stories evolved with a karmic sense of perfect timing. I was preparing a newsroom seminar for reporters and editors at the *Louisville* (KY) *Courier-Journal*, where I worked for a three-month stint as reporter and ethics coach. The seminar topic: Truth.

The first in the unplanned series was a front-page story. A couple of dozen 14–20-year-olds were arrested on various charges related to the production of false IDs. These were middle-class suburban kids intent on buying alcohol who

Deni Elliott is the University Professor of Ethics and Director of the Practical Ethics Center at The University of Montana-Missoula. She is a professor in the Department of Philosophy and adjunct professor at the School of Journalism. She came to Montana in 1992 after serving for six years as the founding director for the Dartmouth College Ethics Institute. Deni was the Mansfield Professor of Ethics in Public Affairs 1992–96. She has a B.A. in Communication from the University of Maryland, M.A. in Philosophy from Wayne State University and an interdisciplinary doctoral degree from Harvard University involving work at the Kennedy School of Government, Department of Philosophy, Graduate School of Education, and Harvard Law School.

supported a counterfeit production system to do it. Principals, parents, and arrested youth were quoted in the story that detailed the law enforcement sting operation. No underage person was identified.

A few days later, again a front-page story. This report told the story of the consequences for the arrested teens. With a reporter and parents following, they spent a day at the county jail and got a stern lecture from the judge. The judge let them off easy this time; he counseled, and there would be no record. He certainly hoped that the day's experience had them "Scared Straight." A photograph caught the teens in the courtroom, shot from behind to avoid identification. A couple of them told reporters that the experience was awful and the jail was worse than they expected.

The next day, a new wrinkle appeared. Inner-city leaders complained that if it had been *their* kids arrested rather than the white suburban kids, there surely would have been charges and records. And, on top of it, these leaders complained, everyone knew that the "Scared Straight" techniques were controversial at best. It was not likely that they did any good. And the reporter found national experts on juvenile crime who backed up these claims. Inner-city and suburban teens are treated differently when suspected of criminal activity. And, there seemed to be little evidence that the tactics used with the Louisville youth would do any good.

The next day, the final story in this sequence, the paper delivered a story of a teen arrested at a local rock concert for buying beer with a fake ID. The girl, identified this time, was part of the original group arrested and put through the "Scared Straight" routine. She cautioned the reporter against drawing conclusions regarding the success of the program based on her personal failure.

With the eager cooperation of the reporter who wrote this series of stories, we dissected the published accounts and discussed questions of truth. The journalists treated the series as a philosophical puzzle. Each story seemed accurate, but somehow, the truth that was told kept changing. Was this a story of suburban kids who got caught doing what suburban kids do everywhere? Well, yes. But it was also a story of privilege that comes with class and color. And it was a story about a popular but ineffective technique for keeping kids out of trouble. And it was a story of recidivism as well. The reporters and editors agreed that not one of those different renditions of the emerging story could have been told sooner.

The epistemology of journalism is different from the development of more static scientific knowledge. Rather than producing reproducible results as does the scientist, the journalist publishes a snapshot in a series of evolving narratives, each having some slice of the truth. Journalistic practice implicitly rejects idealist or rationalist ideas of the search for knowledge as bound to a solid, objective foundation. It rejects the notion of the learner or reporter as that of nonintrusive observer. Yet the function of journalism, as reflected in accepted codes of ethics and standards for practice, according to all but the most philosophically inclined, is the search for and the telling of the truth.

Here I will explicate the notion of truth implicit in print and broadcast news reporting and clarify the journalistic responsibility to choose the stories to be told under the guise of news and to choose the perspective of the telling.

The American Society of Newspaper Editors devotes one article in its "Statement of Principles" to truth and accuracy. Article IV tells us:

> Good faith with the reader is the foundation of good journalism. Every effort must be made to assure that the news content is accurate, free from bias and in context, and that all sides are presented fairly. Editorials, analytical articles and commentary should be held to the same standards of accuracy with respect to the facts as news reports. Significant errors of fact, as well as errors of omission, should be corrected promptly and prominently.[1]

The Associated Press Managing Editors states the truth-related responsibility of news organizations more succinctly: "The good newspaper is fair, accurate, honest, responsible, independent and decent. Truth is its guiding principle."[2] The Society of Professional Journalists says that journalists should "Seek Truth and Report It."[3] The Radio-Television News Directors Association explains, "The responsibility of radio and television journalists is to gather and report information of importance and interest to the public accurately, honestly and impartially."[4]

The notions of reporting accurately and reporting the truth described in the codes and taught in journalism schools rest on the assumption that news is external, existing as a flower might in a meadow, waiting to be noticed and picked. But, as the *Courier-Journal* stories illustrate, the truths of the news story are rather created by the combined perspectives of the reporter, the photographer, the editors, and other gatekeepers who fashion the published story. While news as creation is seemingly obvious, journalists and consumers alike seem uncomfortable that editorial judgment rather than external reality serves as the basis for what gets reported as news. Rather than view the journalist as an objective spectator and conduit, I describe the reporting process as one of professional perspective with the resulting story as the product of that perspective.

The methods that go into determining which truths get reported and which do not are methods rooted in conventional practice. They are methods that evolved for the most pragmatic of reasons: They are the ones that work.

Journalists begin the assessment of a potential story by wondering if the story would be meaningful or important to a significant share of the audience. If the answer is affirmative, research begins.

As little is often known about the specifics at this stage, whether the story is worth researching will depend on how closely it seems to match conventional genre. Is it a story about how well government is doing its job? Is it a story that informs the audience about some occurrence that may affect their lives or the lives of others? Is it a story about a brave individual in conflict with forces of nature or illness? Is it a story of an individual's bad deeds and the community's response? Is it a story with unexpected characters, context, or turn of events? These are the basic categories of events and issues that become the news.

Journalistic research includes examination of documents and search for historical connection, but it turns on the use of human sources. Journalists report what people say. The people who are used as the vehicles for development of the story include those involved with the experience and credible experts who can provide perspective for the event or issue under examination. Who is chosen, which voices are ignored, have a clear affect on the journalist's perspective and the resulting published report.

Then, from the combination of interviews and gathered bits of data, journalists weave a coherent narrative, all from the perspective of what the audience needs or most wants to know. Journalism educators John Merrill and Jack Odell describe the final selection process this way:

The reporter never selects all the potential truth; he or she leaves much of it, or most of it, unselected and thus unreported, but does get some of it. And it is this "some" that we are referring to as . . . the selected truth. This is what forms the core of the journalistic news story. It is this selected portion of the truth that the reporter weaves into subjective patterns, calling the final product "news." At this level of truth the journalist selects from the potential truth certain things which may actually be used in the story. The journalist never really does use all of this selected truth in the story, but theoretically all of it could be used.[5]

When working as a reporter/ethics coach at *The Philadelphia Inquirer* in the mid-1980s, I was given the not-exciting assignment of writing a story about Temple University's third heart transplant. The news element that appealed to my editors was clear. The procedure was still unusual. An individual, a man in his early thirties in this case, was saved from death by a medical miracle. The sources were equally obvious: the patient and his family, the doctors or hospital spokesperson, and a few paragraphs full of information about how heart transplants were giving the promise of full life spans to those who would otherwise die young.

I chose not to work this story within the expected categories. I searched for an angle that might make this story a vehicle for helping the audience and policy makers understand a context larger than this particular event.

I asked the patient, family, and friends where the money came from to fund the procedure. Answer: bake sales and other community fund-raising events.

I asked health care workers and hospital administrators why the cost for the transplant was so high. Answer: The technology and personnel required to perform these delicate operations were very expensive. The procedures cost several tens of thousands of dollars or hundreds of thousands of dollars because the hospital had to be paid back for its costs.

I asked insurance companies that didn't cover these procedures why they didn't. Answer: They considered the surgery still experimental.

I asked transplant coordinators and donor bank administrators what happened to the otherwise qualified patients who couldn't raise enough money. Answer: They died.

Looking at a story likely to become a small report on an inside page from a perspective different from what was expected created a major front-page story on de facto rationing. Both approaches would have revealed "truths." But, it is journalistic perspective that determines which truths are most important.

Delighted as I was with the story's play and the positive comments of my colleagues, I found that I had underestimated the nature of public response. The transplant story generated far less comment than a story I had written less than half its size that told of the birth of an Indian rhino at the local zoo.

My foray into broadcast news convinced me that television reporting is meant to provide truths different in kind from those reported in the daily newspaper.

When I was writing for newspapers, I found myself wondering, "What do my readers need to know to make this particular event or issue meaningful to them? How can I make this relevant to the largest possible audience?" Now, reporting a story for the evening news, I found myself wondering, "If my viewers were here, what would they notice visually? If they had a chance to ask one or two quick questions, what would they most want to know?"

The conventional limitations of the usual local news program include short story packages (between one minute, thirty seconds and two minutes, fifteen seconds in length) and depend on strong visuals to move the story along. Conventional wisdom dictates that the reporter do the final stand-up, the concluding comment at the end of the story, at the scene of the event. Because visuals and taped interviews are gathered at the beginning of the research process, these concluding comments are often taped hours before the story is actually put together in broadcast form. The result is that the broadcast reporter's concluding comment, which should correspond to the print reporter's "nut graph" (a paragraph at the beginning of the story that sums it up for the reader), is usually vague and contains only that information that is patently obvious.

The kind of knowledge offered by television news is thus importantly different from that offered by a newspaper. Television news offers vicarious experience through its reporters; print news offers contextual meaning. Both products require journalistic perspective, but the intended end products are not the same. Some suggest that the divergence is narrowing as print news seeks to provide more experiential details and television news provides sound bites long enough to include argument rather than simple observations. While it is possible for newspapers to be livelier and still provide their kind of truth, and while it is possible for television news programs to be deeper and more thoughtful and still provide their kind of truth, one need not substitute for the other. Members of the audience, if they are to make informed decisions regarding their self-governance, need both kinds of knowledge. Seeing and hearing events and interviews provides something like first-hand experience; receiving context for specific events and issues provides a rationalistic background for understanding.

The epistemic choices are important to notice because of their differences from those that produce the more common static, objective notion of truth. These journalistic choices have ethical importance as well. Choosing to focus on one element of a story at the expense of another determines how the audience will understand the story and how the story subject will be portrayed.

C. Delores Tucker, a sixty-eight-year-old former secretary of state for Pennsylvania, provides a case in point for how journalistic choices can cloud the truth to the detriment of a story and its subject. Ms. Tucker, beginning in 1993, became an outspoken critic of the pornographic and drug-oriented misogynistic lyrics found in "gangsta rap." She brought to her leadership a trail of awards and recognitions for more than thirty years of work on behalf of black youth and African Americans. Tucker received support for her efforts to stop production and distribution of gangsta rap music, including support from William

Bennett, former U.S. secretary of education, U.S. Senator Joseph Lieberman, presidential candidate Robert Dole, and General Colin Powell.

In 1996, the now-deceased gangsta rap vocalist Tupac Shakur released an album, *All Eyez on Me,* with the song, "How Do You Want It," that included the following: Delores Tucker, you's a muthaf-----, instead of tryin' to help a nigga, you destroy a brotha." In another song on the same album, a track, "Wonda Why they Call B" included the following: "Got your legs up trying to get rich. Keep your head up and legs closed Dear Ms. Delores Tucker."

Following the release of the album and other events that Ms. Tucker found threatening, she filed suit July 21, 1997, for intentional infliction of emotional distress, slander, and invasion of privacy. In what is considered by lawyers to be a usual addition to suits claiming emotional distress, Mr. Tucker, who is 70 years old, claimed that he "as a result of his wife's injuries, suffered a loss of advice, companionship and consortium."

Reports of that complaint over the next month included many that included the erroneous claim that Ms. Tucker had sued because the lyrics ruined her sex life. A headline on the front page of the *Philadelphia News* read, "Suit vs. Shakur estate says 'vile' lyrics ruined her rep—and her sex life."

The *Los Angeles Times* reported in the second paragraph of its story, "Among other things, the lawsuit says, the anguish caused by those lyrics cut down on her sex life with her husband."

The Associated Press sent out on its wire a story with the following lead, "One of America's most outspoken foes of gangsta rap says Tupac Shakur's crude lyrics about her have wrecked her sex life."

From Grapevine in *Rolling Stone Magazine,* "The last and perhaps most inane complaint is from anti-rap activist C. Delores Tucker, who is suing for $10 million. Tucker claims that she and her husband haven't been able to have sex in more than two years because of derogatory references to her on Shakur's 1995 album, *All Eyez on Me.*"

While "lack of consortium" can mean loss of sexual relations, sex and consortium are not synonymous. No claim is made regarding the Tuckers' sex life. Yet, the idea that Tucker was claiming that the lyrics damaged her sex life took on a life of its own, resulting in the publication of this claim by more than 100 news organizations.

Sometimes news organizations cause harm that is justified by the careful use of journalistic perspective to present important snapshots of truth to an audience that needs that information for self-governance. Too often, stories like these regarding Delores Tucker sacrifice the truth for the sensational. Rather than news, such reports should carry the disclaimer used in newspaper hoaxes from the nineteenth century, "Interesting if true."

NOTES

1. American Society of Newspaper Editors, 1975
2. Associated Press Managing Editors, 1994
3. Society of Professional Journalists, 1996

4. Radio-Television News Directors, 1986
5. John C. Merrill and S. Jack Odell, *Philosophy and Journalism* (New York: Longman, 1983), 173.

VICTOR GUARINO

THE PHILOSOPHER AS PSYCHOLOGIST: TRUTH AND THE SCHIZOPHRENIC PATIENT

As a philosopher, my interest in psychology was inspired by its focus upon psychic acts from the viewpoint of their subjective and objective contents. Inasmuch as human behavior is largely a manifestation of mental processes, it may be regarded as their expression. Hence, a scientific study of behavior, which is psychology, can illuminate how and why an individual interprets and relates to the real world, which is philosophy. Many psychological difficulties and attitudes are basically philosophical, and both disciplines converge in treatment practice. I hope to illustrate this relationship by referring to specific cases I have treated as a psychologist in the intensive care ward of a mental hospital. Although I had already practiced as a psychologist in state, federal, and private clinics, this was my first experience in a mental hospital outside of my internship training, and it presented a challenge for me. The ward administered to an average of twenty-five seriously mentally ill patients for whom there remained the hope of release to the community. About half of them were schizophrenic. An average stay was six months for many of them, some of whom returned more than once, either voluntarily or by court order. I devised the treatment programs for each patient and functioned as a consult to the psychiatrist and staff, conducted staff training workshops and support groups, administered tests, assisted in planning for aftercare upon release, visited and assessed group homes and treatment programs, and provided individual counseling.

The Diagnostic and Statistical Manual of Mental Disorders, 4th ed. (DSMV-IV) of the American Psychiatric Association basically requires delusions (e.g. thought broadcasting, being controlled by a dead person) and auditory hallucinations in the diagnosis of schizophrenia. A common conception of mentally ill people is that they are wildly aggressive. Actually, they are inhibited and withdrawn. These people are coping the best way they know in order to survive. They are trying to adapt, to conform to and assimilate reality just as the rest of us must do. The difficulty is that their coping is maladaptive in the context of reality as it is defined in their cultures or subcultures. Further, it is not a matter of choice for them, for it is beyond their control. Questions immediately arise:

Victor Guarino commenced his philosophical studies at New York University and completed them at the Universities of Louvain and Paris, where he obtained his doctoral degree under the tutelage of Paul Ricoeur. His major interest in phenomenological psychology prompted further studies in graduate psychology at St. John's and Nova Universities, and prepared him for work as a psychologist and therapist, which he regards as applied philosophy. He has been employed as a psychologist with the youth service center in Idaho, Montana State Hospital, the Naval Family Service Center, community clinics, and in a supervisory clinical capacity for IHS. He has taught as an adjunct instructor wherever he has worked, and continues as such at Indian River Community College in Florida.

Are their hallucinations and delusions real for them? Are they useful as adaptative measures for their survival? If so, then how? Do they somehow "fit" them into the everyday world? Can I as a professional employ them in treatment? If so, then how? Will their voices stop if I tell them they don't really exist? Will their delusions stop if I tell them they aren't real? In other words, what is the truth value, the reality of these experiences? I will briefly discuss three theories of truth, and then try to answer these questions in the light of these theories with examples of individual cases I have treated.

THEORIES OF TRUTH

Logically, truth is a quality of a judgment, which is a simple proposition containing a subject and a predicate that are joined (or separated) by a form of the verb "to be." Objects, such as trees, dogs, stars, colors are not "true." Rather, something we say about them may or may not be true. The truth or falsity of statements we make about reality, our beliefs or judgments about reality, may not be universally shared. To defend them, we seek to reduce them to verifiable, or experienceable facts. Not all of them can be verified in this way. Nevertheless, we may still reasonably believe them to be true, employing three different though interrelated theories of truth: the correspondence theory, the coherence theory, and the pragmatic theory.

The Correspondence Theory

According to the correspondence theory, truth is the conformity of the mind to facts. "This paper is white." You observe the paper, you see the color . . . you connect them. The resulting statement is true because it coincides with the fact of the paper's whiteness. It is true because the paper is white. The difficulty with this theory is that there are many truths that do not require facts to be true, such as mathematical or geometrical truths: $2 + 2 = 4$ is true whether we mean trees, dreams, oceans, or universes; the circumference of any circle is $2\pi R$, including the one in my mind, yours, or anyone's. Furthermore, there are truths we rely upon in everyday life that are not immediately verifiable in simple sense experiences. The four seasons, for instance, result from the earth's orbiting around the sun; day and night result from the earth's rotation on its axis, but no telescope in the world will be able to spot an "orbit" in the sky or an "axis" passing through the earth. These are true because of the law of gravity which we can verify by dropping a pencil. However, there are many intervening truths between the falling pencil and the orbiting and rotating planets.

The Coherence Theory

The coherence theory of truth attempts to overcome the difficulties of the correspondence theory. According to this theory, we accept the truth of a statement because it is consistent with, coheres, or fits into the pattern of truths with which we are already comfortable. We believe in the existence of subatomic particles as quarks and leptons because they explain, "fit" in with, make sense of truths already accepted. A difficulty with the coherence theory is that one's system of reality may include talking horses, or aliens from outer space seeking to destroy earth. The controversy over unidentified flying objects peopled with extraterrestrials involves a clash of different coherent systems of belief.

The Pragmatic Theory

The pragmatic theory of truth is based upon the conviction that true knowledge is action, to know is to do, productively and profitably. It is concerned more with the usefulness or value of truth. Although the pragmatic movement in America was really originated by Charles S. Peirce, its chief proponent and defender was William James. In describing this theory, James employed such imaginative metaphors as "truth is the cash value of an idea," causing his detractors to accuse him of reducing truth to the subject alone, thereby negating any objectivity. James countered that such a criticism was absurd, as there would simply be no consciousness at all without an object to be conscious of. His response was cited by none other than Edmund Husserl, the originator of phenomenology, as one of its foundational precepts. James also described pragmatism as an "open door" theory, a theory of discovery, profitable and productive in that it "opens the door" to other truths that we would not otherwise have known. Some of these beliefs may remain in what James calls "cold storage" until they can be useful. Democritus's atomic theory, for instance, finally became "useful" in the nineteenth century.

APPLICATIONS OF THEORIES OF TRUTH TO ACTUAL CASES

Cases Involving the Counseling of Patients with Schizophrenia

In contrast to more severe psychoses (such as those discussed in the next section), the patients in the following cases did not exhibit a complete and total break with reality as culturally defined. These patients were able to meaningfully express themselves, and comprehend others, during their psychotic episodes. This made it possible to do counseling with them during such periods:

*

Francine was a twenty-two-year-old young lady who hallucinated the voices of three young men, Bobby, Jerry, and Marty. The voices could occur at any time, and were frequently overwhelming. They insisted that she kill herself, employing every persuasive argument at their command. These "boys" seemed to have been acquaintances in her early teenage years. She did once date a boy named Bobby (the prominent voice) who was killed in a motorcycle accident, but her reaction to his death was appropriate.

I could tell when these voices occurred, for Francine would become withdrawn and self-absorbed. I would ask if she were hearing them, and whether she was all right. My aim was to teach her how to confront these voices by herself. Francine was a perfect patient. She cooperated and complied in every way possible. She did not want these voices because they could bring her to the edge and generally exhausted her both physically and mentally. Most times she was able to deal with them. When they were overwhelming, she would become careless in her usually immaculate appearance, her appetite would wane and she just wanted to be alone. At these times I would sit with her and we would talk. Our conversation might proceed as follows:

PSYCHOLOGIST: Are the voices back?
FRANCINE: Yes.
PSYCHOLOGIST: Who is it?
FRANCINE: Bobby.
PSYCHOLOGIST: What's he saying?
FRANCINE: It's better where he is what am I waiting for?

PSYCHOLOGIST: Tell him you're happy where you are and to leave you alone. You have too much to live for. You have friends and parents who love you and care for you.

FRANCINE: (With some conviction) Yeah.

(Pause.)

PSYCHOLOGIST: What's he saying now?

FRANCINE: He's laughing at me. He doesn't believe me. Marty's there too. They're both laughing.

PSYCHOLOGIST: Why don't you tell them if they're so happy where they are they'd leave you alone. They're lying. They're miserable and they want you to be miserable too. They're jealous of you.

FRANCINE: That's true.

I would let her be and watch her until her condition improved, or I would repeat the process of debating with the "voices" to reinforce her conviction to stay alive. Her medication would also be reassessed.

What is the truth value of Francine's hallucination? Was it a sensory perception? No, and she knew that. She didn't turn to some imaginary person and repeat my suggestions aloud. She did not hear the voices in the general sense of the word. Were they real for her? They were an event to her. Was there a world we had to enter if we were to help her? No, there was not, because the voices were directly accessible to Francine alone, the only person capable of relating to them. Insofar as they were apparently out of her control and autonomous, Francine had to accept them as part of her world and therefore she was forced to deal with them. They were accessible to her in the sense that her responses to them might result in a desired change: their cessation and her peace of mind. They "fit" in her world as potential threats to her existence. How to stop them? Her death was one sure way, but that would be counter-productive and not at all pragmatic. More productive and life-preserving means were medication and reasoning to stave them off. These were pragmatic beliefs that served as a protective force in her belief system as well as in mine. She relied upon them to survive; I relied upon them to help her.

My own world had to expand to include the possibility of a person hearing voices coming from outside her head, voices of people who were not real. This phenomenon already fit into my system of beliefs from my own training. The correspondence theory also applied for me, as here was the victim of auditory hallucinations just as my studies described. Francine made her hallucinations accessible to me, and I helped her to deal with them effectively. Their possibility had to become part of my belief system if I were to help her at all, even though we both realized they were not real in the ordinary sense. I had to accept the fact that, for Francine, the hallucinations had the value of reality, and in that sense they were her reality. She was not perceiving them in the ordinary meaning of the word. She was living them. Only by accepting this truth as part of my belief system could I even begin to try to help her in her struggle against them, and the means I and the psychiatrist employed were the very pragmatic truths Francine accepted as part of her belief system: antipsychotic medication and therapy. My object was to stop them from happening. If not that, then to help her to cope with them without harming herself. Psychoanalysis could not help. Knowledge of how they related to past events in her life would not stop them from happening. In fact, they might reinforce them. Actually, the hallucinations tended to increase in frequency and intensity over time despite our efforts. Francine would request discharge when she felt stable enough to live in the community, but she was wise enough to recommit herself when the hallucinations dangerously impaired her functioning. However, her prognosis was poor.

*

Twenty-two-year-old Joseph believed that the CIA was in league with the FBI against him. His delusion involved auditory hallucinations: messages directed at him through loudspeakers such as radio and television. He accused the staff of trying to poison him in the guise of medications, suspecting us all of being undercover agents. The delusion was easily disprovable, for it was a disorganized, patchwork affair whose elements Joe pulled out of the air to overcome objections. His desperation at making coherent sense of it was sufficient indication of its tenuous connection to reality. I suspected that even he might have realized this. Why, then, did he continue to have it? What end did it serve?

Joe's natural mother abandoned him and his father when he was a toddler. His father made his living as a truckdriver and was always on the road, and Joe was placed in foster care until his father eventually remarried, when Joe came to live with him and his stepmother. She did not want him around, making this clear with numerous beatings and deprivations. Joe reported that he told his father about her mistreatment. His father was sympathetic but seemed helpless. Besides, his stepmother was careful not to abuse him when his father was home. His schooling was never consistent. Hungry much of the time, ashamed to attend school, he ran away.

Joe hoboed for some years and fell in with a crowd of runaways who committed petty crimes for their livelihood. Finally apprehended, he was placed in a correctional institution and became physically violent. Apparently, this was when his delusion surfaced, coupled with his auditory hallucinations. He was eventually diagnosed as a paranoid schizophrenic and committed to the hospital for intensive care. He was docile and asocial, with very little interest in anything. He slept much of the time and blamed his fatigue on the medication, which was continually reassessed. The medication was strong, but Joe had been and could still be dangerous. We established a rapport, and I tried to encourage him to learn something so he could eventually live independently. Despite his listlessness and short attention span, and although he was necessarily under medication, I tested him to determine if he could take some classes anyway. He sat through the test for forty-five minutes and tried to keep alert, which seemed enough to build some hope on, even though he was far from G.E.D. potential.

Out of the blue, his father, after two years of silence, phoned to say he would visit and take Joe out for dinner. Joe's eyes shone with hope for the first time. The visit was successful. His father had divorced and was trying to make arrangements to take Joe along with him in his travels. This wasn't possible, but perhaps eventually Joe could learn to live independently in the community. His father's promises dwindled. He would phone to say he would visit and then cancel so many times that the seesaw effect upon Joe's emotions was very damaging. I told the father either to visit or stay away . . . no more promises. Joe's life continued as before . . . sleeping most of the time, disregarding others and his surroundings, unapproachable in group. Once he vaguely acknowledged to me that he may have been schizophrenic. This was "our" secret, for he vehemently denied it to all the other professionals in progress interviews, and in the special conference with his lawyer, the psychiatrist, hospital officials, the nurse, social worker and myself for the purpose of administering medication to him without his consent. He would say: "Nobody believes me," referring to the the FBI-CIA plot against him. I think what he meant was: "Nobody understands me," for that is what we had to do. The fact of Joe's having a delusion had to fit into our belief system. We had to accept it if we were to help him at all. The only productive assistance was medication to keep the psychosis in remission and try through support therapy to help him cope with it and enjoy some control of his life. Whatever worked to this end was worth trying. This was my pragmatic belief.

Joe's delusion was a living reality for him. The "plot" against him could not be disproved, for he alone held the key to it; it was accessible to us only through him. I often wondered whether he, as its "gatekeeper", found a source of control that gave him some support in an illness over which he feared he had no control whatsoever.

The messages from radio and television were not sensory in the ordinary meaning of the word. In fact, Joe would have been surprised if I ever told him that I heard them also. I think he would have begun to lose faith in me. However, the misfortunes in his life could account for them. He could make them fit in some way to fashion a coherent meaning for what he considered to be his victimization. Still, he would constantly need to reconcile discontinuities between the real world common to all of us, himself included, and his lived reality. He knew that in the real world nobody wanted to threaten him. Staff and other patients were friendly and helpful. He shared his room with another with no difficulties, ate with others, recreated with others. The worst censures he ever received were those of technicians such as: "Joe, clean your room. It's a mess!" Besides, many individuals lived through harrowing life situations without becoming seriously mentally ill. Certainly, the circumstances of his life were severe stressors. Joe might have employed them in trying to make some sense of the reality of his delusion, but that does not mean they were the cause. Emotional disturbances could be expected as normal reactions to them, but not a serious thought disorder. We might also ask whether his mistreatment by his stepmother and the inaction of his father were the result of an already developing psychosis that neither of them could understand. Perhaps they unwittingly implemented its course while thinking they were trying to correct his "misbehavior."

*

Jeanmarie was an unmarried, thirty-five-year-old mother of three teenage girls, each by multiracially different fathers. Raised as the daughter of a diplomat, she had lived with her parents in several countries, boasting of having been enrolled in twenty-four different schools, often for one month at a time. She was bright and highly manipulative, able to survive in the community and to send her daughters to public schools. Further, she had managed to obtain her antipsychotic medication without cost and never signed a release of information by anyone to anyone. Her parents did not think she was a fit mother. She reported that her father molested one of her daughters, but extracted the promise not to talk to the girl about it, nor would she allow her parents to be consulted, which of course they couldn't be as no release of information would be signed. Jeanmarie reported visual and auditory hallucinations of a beautiful, luminescent, angelic boy, Star, who foretold future events. She claimed that the predicted events really happened, that she sometimes wished she wasn't told, though her sincerity was doubtful. She talked incessantly, exhausting the listener with pressurized speech consisting of both tangential ideas and strings of loose associations. She medicated herself faithfully, though there were times when, in order to experience Star, she disrupted the schedule. However, this could be dangerous, because she would lose control. Her religious practices were ecstatic. She patronized churches with her daughters that promised rapturous experiences, in fact shopped around for them, and believed she was a special child of God.

Jeanmarie befriended a wide variety of unusual people, and life at home was somewhat hectic and always tense, if not bizarre. Her daughters were precocious, and all were extroverts. She had them diagnosed as bipolar, ensuring their welfare, a self-fulfilling prophecy, it seemed, and she reported their behaviors with an apparently uncanny knowledge of bipolar disorder. Jeanmarie presented herself as schizophrenic. Actually, she was schizoaffective. As lived experiences, her hallucinations were real to her. She accepted the fact that they were hallucinatory, and agreed to her diagnosis. When Star first appeared to her, she "lost it for weeks, I was in another world. People thought I was staring into space, but it was Star." The psychotic episode was not drug-induced. Her children were placed in foster care and she was committed to a mental hospital.

Jeanmarie was on welfare and strictly managed her finances to remain within that category. She dreamed of becoming a publisher and had many ideas which she never pursued, so utterly disorganized was her mind. She presented a pathological need to rigidly control everything and everyone in her environment. It seemed to me that this was because she feared losing control of herself. She could be too strict with her children, almost abusive, and therapeutic sessions included child-rearing issues which were helpful to her. She really loved her children despite their codependent relationship. They were the one, stabilizing focus in her chaotic mental life. Jeanmarie used her hallucinations as some kind of a horoscope and she interpreted actual events to conform to their messages, or vice versa. However, she never admitted to having changed a course of action based upon Star's predictions. Still, the hallucinations could have had the pragmatic value of qualifying her as someone special. Perhaps she was making the most of their persistent intrusion in that way.

*

Elle was an attractive, sophisticated, twenty-six-year-old lady from a small, rural town, the daughter of a wealthy professional man. Her doting father sent her to a school in London where she studied ballet. When she was nineteen, Elle's father died suddenly. A more austere economy became necessary. The ballet career was at least stalled. It was uncertain whether the shock of her father's death was a major factor in the onset of her illness. Certainly the loss of a significant person in her life and the ensuing change in lifestyle could be considered severely stressful.

Elle would walk about the house performing ballet steps totally naked. These behaviors escalated to where she would perform them in the public park across the street from her home, in broad daylight. She began to wander about at all hours. Finally, scantily dressed, on a wintry day she boarded a bus at the local bus terminal and demanded to be taken to the airport. She seemed to be on her way to London. She was admitted to the mental hospital.

Elle was very proper, ladylike, and articulate. She tiptoed through life like a ballet dancer, and clung to the now unrealistic hope of becoming one. She would often perform a pirouette or a pas de deux, to the female staff's consternation as being a "flaunt." One morning she excitedly mentioned to me that she was called by some London ballet school the night before. They were going to send her a plane ticket to start the new semester. I rejoiced with her. It obviously never happened in our perceptual world, but it made sense to her because, intentionally, she was a ballet dancer. The incident was soon forgotten, and life went on as usual. Elle also believed she had a special relationship with God. Magical thinking and superstitious beliefs are included among characteristics of schizophrenia, and one might mistakenly attribute Elle's concern as stereotypical. I found her concern to be intelligent and insightful. It was a search for meaning. She was too intelligent to believe in any apparitions or visions.

Elle exhibited to me the profound disorganization of the illness. She would sit forever were there no external prompt to perform daily living skills, as showering, or caring for her clothes. Consequently, although she spent a small fortune on cosmetics, jewelry, and clothing, she often smelled and had to be forced into the shower by glowering female staff members who really liked her but thought she was spoiled. I tried behavior modification. She was enthusiastic about the idea, but could not adhere to even the simplest schedule on her own.

A new miracle drug, Clozaril, appeared on the scene. Apparently, it worked by a different mechanism from other antipsychotics, and was a new hope for schizophrenia. Manufactured in Switzerland, it was relatively cheap on the continent, but not in the United States. We wanted to try it on Elle. Despite its cost, we argued that it would actually save the state money for she could be returned to the community. To our surprise, we had great difficulty trying to convince her to try it. Why would anyone in her situation hesitate for a moment to get out of this place? The answer is simple: fear of the unknown. A downside of mental hospitals is the dependence (and if staff is not careful, the codependence) such a situation may foster. For those stricken with the real possibility of loss of reason and control, predictability is a luxury. Elle was fearful of the possible freedom this medication promised because of the responsibility it imposed. She had already been sent home on visits, even discharged, but with no success. Finally, with the assurance that she was free to return if any need arose, she agreed to try it. A few days after the first ministration, at our group meeting, I announced Elle's plans for departure. She politely thanked everyone for having put up with "my illness," for their help and support, at last recognizing and appreciating their existence. This was indeed a hopeful sign, perhaps a real breakthrough. Finally, Elle was sent home, but in only one month she was back. It was reported that she did not remain faithful to her medication schedule and started drinking and resuming former inappropriate behaviors.

Elle tried to live in her delusive ballet world. She comported herself as a danseuse. The realities of her age, weight, and mental instability were starkly real, however. She recognized her "illness," but balked at being labeled schizophrenic due to its stigmatizing effect. Was her disorganization a reflection of her frustration at being unable to incorporate her lived, intentional world into the real, perceptual world common to all? Curiously, in my own belief system, she was a ballerina by temperament and she had a certain grace, and that is how I treated her. However, she was not the premiere danseuse of her intentional world. Here was a clash between a belief system and fact. It was the mind/body problem at its worst: a perpetual separation between her intentional world, her lived reality, and the real world. It almost seemed an identity crisis.

Cases Involving More Severe Pyschoses

There were cases in which no attempt was made by the patient to try to fit delusions or hallucinations into a coherent belief system. There appeared to be two entirely separate worlds: the sudden intrusion of the delusion seemed to displace the real world. It seemed I was observing another person entirely:

*

Richard was a patient in his seventies, diagnosed with paranoid schizophrenia. Capable of extremely violent and destructive behavior, he had grown mellow with age. Transferred from a high security ward to ours with less restrictions, he endeared himself to everyone because of his wit and heart. Periodically, he suffered sudden, unpredictable episodes of violent temper. His language became scatalogical. With a blank stare, focused upon no real object, he cast every imaginable curse and threat. At these times, I found that by simply letting him be, he would return to normal. There was no way to analyze this behavior, for during the episode he was entirely unreachable by anyone, and referring to it would needlessly distress him.

*

Angela, a widow in her fifties and a mother of grown children, lived in the community. When her delusions and hallucinations began to recur, she would commit herself to the hospital for readjustment of medication and stabilization.

She would then request discharge, which would be granted. Angela was a kind and lovely lady who knitted clothing and made linens for a livelihood. Many on the staff were her customers. Her psychosis became more frequent and intense with each episode. At her last visit, she hallucinated for three sleepless nights and two days, ranting constantly, seemingly referring to situations and talking to imaginary people in an endless series of loose associations that made no sense at all. It seemed as though she was trying to explain herself. Her language was scatalogical, totally out of keeping with her regular self. She was greatly agitated, flinging her arms about, ranting, as though trying to convince somebody of something. She was watched night and day and all her vital signs periodically checked. When the episode passed, she became her sweet, normal self, and remembered nothing. She would never have forgiven herself if she knew the language she had used. Was she trying to reconcile her delusional world with the real one? There was no way of knowing.

I believe both Richard and Angela portrayed the incurable nature of schizophrenia which, for them, was deteriorating into degenerative dementia and gradual dissociation into an entirely delusive world.

CONCLUSIONS

Of all the patients mentioned, none of them had a choice as to the occurrence of the hallucinations or delusions he or she experienced, for they were completely intrusive. Elements may have been borrowed from the perceptual world that is common to all of us, which is natural, for it is their perceptual world as well. For instance, a real paranoid person living in a culture in which distrust and suspicion are socially acceptable would be distrustful and suspicious about the wrong things and not by choice. Psychotic people are out of the context of reality in all cultures, and this is characterized by non-conformity to the acceptable norms of their cultures. Jeanmarie's hallucinations may appear contrived for she seemed to use them to her advantage, but this suspicion dissolves when we realize that they did not improve, but rather aggravated and increasingly impaired her mental functioning. She didn't experience them in order to profit from them. She simply tried to make the most of what she could not control. Joe's delusion may give meaning to the misfortunes of his life, but it wasn't his free decision to experience it. To say they caused it is simply movie-land psychology, an attempt to fit it into some acceptable belief system that we could understand. Besides, many people in similar and even worse circumstances do not become mentally ill. Francine's therapy was in part based upon the coherence theory: she had a suicide wish, thus she had to be convinced that her life had value. Still, her hallucinations continued and grew more intense. Elle's sole focus in life was the delusion of being a ballerina. Ordinarily, one might convince a person with such an unfulfilled dream that she could find life satisfaction in teaching ballet or in somehow being actively involved in it. The profound disorganization resulting from her illness precluded any progress in that direction.

The point is, we cannot presume there are motivations for the delusions and hallucinations in schizophrenia, as that implies that we can enter someone's lived world to fix them, when no "entry" is possible. None of the hallucinations or delusions was directly accessible to me. It was only through my patients that I could have had any experience of them. I had to make the possibility and the fact of their experiences a part of my belief system in order to help them. The only way to help was to find pragmatic means to make these phenomena stop, and if that were not possible, to help these people find a way to cope with them and to live as independently as they possibly could. However we try to explain them as the result of socioeconomic and environmental "conditions," these factors are stressors, not causes. The cause of schizophrenia is still unknown. There is no cure as yet. Perhaps it is incurable. All of us have to live with some limitations and most of us successfully learn to cope with them. Why not a schizophrenic person?

It might be tempting to liken the situation to that of a novelist or an artist imagining a fictional world. However, that world does have a basis in the common perceptual world and does involve a chain of possible perceptions back and forth between both worlds, the real and the ideal. All the theories of truth can apply. *Alice through the Looking Glass* is really a logical exercise based upon the common perceptual world and derives all of its whimsy from the possibility of perceiving it backwards. She can also finally toss up the inhabitants of her Wonderland as only being a pack of cards and walk off. The victim of delusions and hallucinations cannot do that. Mental illness is like being painted into a corner with no way out. Still, all the theories apply in different ways. The patient's life is a search for meaning and satisfying adjustment just as it is for the rest of us. The psychologist must accept and understand the patient's distress as a part of his or her world in order to alleviate it. Each must trust the other in the belief that both desire and aim for the same end: the patient's welfare. Finally, the underlying truth that remains operative throughout this entire process for doctor, patient and anyone else concerned is that mental illness is a real fact perceiveable to all that must be somehow dealt with in the interest and preservation of human dignity.

REFERENCES

American Psychiatric Association, *Diagnostic and Statistical Manual Of Mental Disorders*, 4th ed. (DSMV-IV). Washington, D.C., American Psychiatric Association, 1994.

Kendell, Robert E. "Schizophrenia: Clinical Features." In Helzer, John E., M.D., and Samuel B. Guze, M.D., (eds.) *Psychoses, Affective Disorders, and Dementia*, Vol. Two. Philadelphia, J. B. Lippincott Company, 1986.

Merleau-Ponty, M. *Phenomenology Of Perception*. London, Routledge & Kegan Paul, 1962.

Shea, Shawn C., M.D. *Psychiatric Interviewing, the Art of Understanding*. Philadelphia, W.B. Saunders Company, Harcourt Brace Jovanovich, Inc., 1988.

DISCUSSION QUESTIONS

1. Discuss the primary symbolism employed by Plato in his "Allegory of the Cave" as he uses it to approach the question of what is truth.

2. In Plato's Allegory, Socrates remarks that "if they [the cave dwellers] could lay hands on the man who was trying to set them free and lead them up, they would kill him." What do you think is the significance of this remark?

3. Describe each of the four levels of reality on Plato's "divided line." Do you agree with Plato's view that reality can be divided into levels? Explain and defend your view.

4. What do you think Plato might have said about technology that creates "virtual reality" if he were alive today? What, in your estimation, is the difference between "virtual reality" and "true reality"? Could the former ever become indistinguishable from the latter? If not, why not? If so, what implications (if any) would this have for our understanding of truth?

5. Discuss Ayer's approach to the question of what is truth. What criticisms would Platonists have of this approach?

6. Discuss William James's approach to the question of what truth is. What criticisms would Platonists have of this approach? What might a positivist like Ayer say?

7. Both Ayer and James believe that true ideas or beliefs must be "verifiable." Discuss, compare, and contrast what each means by this.

8. Compare and contrast Plato and Ayer on the role of the philosopher. Do you agree with either of these views? Defend your answer.

9. How would Plato have assessed *applied* philosophy in comparison to *pure* philosophy? Would he have considered one to be "better" than the other? Explain. Do you agree with him?

10. Describe Plato's theory of art, especially as it relates to his theory of truth. What are some of Morphis's criticisms of his view?

11. How, according to Morphis, can art, specifically folk dance, express universal truths? In what way(s) does her view agree with Plato's? In what way(s) does it differ?

12. In your opinion, does good art always have to express truth? What other possible standards of good art can you think of?

13. What reason(s) does Plato have for wanting to censor a lot of art of his time? What criticisms does Morphis make of Plato's reasons for censoring art?

14. In your opinion, should art (including movies, television shows, magazines) ever be censored? Explain and defend your answer. What similarities (if any) and differences (if any) are there between the reasons you have just given and those entertained by Plato himself?

15. What is the "coherence" theory of truth? What criticism does Castle make of this theory especially as it is used as a test of historical fact claims?

16. Is there a relationship between a coherence test for truth and a pragmatic test? Explain.

17. According to Castle, the pragmatic test for truth engenders a "disturbing para-
    dox." What is this paradox? Do you agree with Castle? How do you think James
    would respond to Castle? Defend your answer.

18. Briefly explain Castle's "correspondence" theory of truth as he applies it to
    historical-fact claims. As between positivists and Platonists, which view does
    Castle's view most closely resemble?

19. Do you agree with Castle's claim that there can be "objective" knowledge of his-
    tory? In addressing this question, consider some of the objections to Castle's view
    as discussed in his article.

20. Castle proposes five "guidelines" that he follows in his historical investigations
    and which, he argues, arise out of applying the correspondence theory of truth to
    historiography. Briefly list and discuss the merit of each of these guidelines.

21. Discuss some of the ways in which each of the three theories of truth—correspon-
    dence, coherence, and pragmatic—are relevant to Victor Guarino's work with
    schizophrenic patients.

22. What is the difference between a delusion and an hallucination? Illustrate each
    using some of Guarino's case examples. What is the difference between a halluci-
    nation and a "true" perception?

23. According to Guarino, in what sense were his patients' delusions and hallucina-
    tions "real for them"? In your view, were these mental states any less real for these
    patients than any other mental state is for the one having it? Defend your view.

24. Guarino says that he had to accept his patients' "truths" as part of his *own* belief
    system in order to help them. What does he mean by accepting them as part of his
    own belief system? Use some of Guarino's cases to illustrate your response.

25. Guarino thinks that the delusions and hallucinations in schizophrenia are always
    maladaptive? What exactly does this mean? Do you agree with him? Defend your
    position.

26. At the end of his article, Guarino contrasts an artist's imagination of a fictional
    world with the world inhabited by a person with schizophrenia. What differences
    does he see with each? What do you think Plato might say about the reality of
    such delusions and hallucinations?

27. Referring to the difference between the fictional world of the artist and that of the
    person with schizophrenia, Guarino says that the latter is "like being painted into
    a comer with no way out." What does he mean? Do you agree with him?

28. Discuss Deni Elliott's concept of journalistic truth. Discuss the relevance of corre-
    spondence, coherence, and pragmatic theories of truth to this concept.

29. What is the difference between the manner in which codes of journalism treat
    truth and the manner in which Elliott approaches it?

30. Codes of ethics as well as journalists often stress the need to provide a "balanced"
    account of the news. What does "balanced" mean, and, in your estimation, should
    journalists as purveyors of truth take it seriously?

31. What criticisms might Platonists have of the way in which Deni Elliott approaches
    the topic of truth in journalism? What do you suppose a positivist like Ayer
    might say?

32. What difference(s) is there in the way broadcast journalism and print journalism present the truth? What problem(s) does each confront in presenting truth? In your opinion, is one of these media any more efficient than the other in delivering truth? Defend your answer.

33. Suppose you were employed as a journalist and your assigmnent was to write a story on teenage crime in the United States. How would you approach this task? What "angle" would you take? What facts would you include? What facts would you exclude? How would you determine whether information was worthy of in-cluding? What standard(s) would you employ for determining whether informa-tion you decided to include was "true" or "accurate"? Defend your approach.

34. In the light of your readings in this chapter, how do you think the question of what is truth should be answered? Defend your view.

10

THEORIES OF KNOWLEDGE AND ELEMENTARY SCHOOL EDUCATION

The selections in this chapter offer contrasting perspectives on the concept of knowledge. The first four are excerpted from classical works in epistemology which attempt to provide accounts of how human beings come to their knowledge of things. In the Practice section, these perspectives are then related to elementary school education.

The first selection "Rationalism," is taken from *Meditations* I and II of René Descartes (1596–1650), a French philosopher recognized as the father of modern philosophy. Generally speaking, *rationalism* emphasizes the mind's power to discover truths about the world by thought alone, without the aid of the senses. (As you will recall from chapter 7, Plato is an example of such a philosopher.) In the spirit of rationalism, Descartes sets out to see if, by thought alone, he can discover some truth(s) about the world, about which he can be absolutely certain and upon which he can anchor all other knowledge.

Descartes begins by doubting everything he can possibly find any reason to doubt. To help him in this *methodic* doubting, he supposes that, instead of a benevolent God, there is a very powerful and evil demon out to deceive him in any way possible. Descartes's question is then whether there can be anything about which even such an evil demon could not possibly deceive him. Descartes is prepared to admit the possibility that the existence of his own body and even arithmetical truths like "$2 + 3 = 5$" are illusions set in his mind by the evil demon. However, there is one thing that even such an evil demon could not dissuade him of; that is his own existence. So long as he thinks he exists, he must really exist; for how could there be such thought without something—some ego—to do that thinking? Descartes just cannot doubt his own existence. Indeed, the more he tries to doubt this proposition, the more certain he is of its truth. (Try telling yourself that you do not exist and see what happens!) Through thought alone Descartes thus believes he is able to discover the certainty of his own existence.

Descartes is not, however, content with knowing that he exists. He also wants to know *what* he is. To use an ancient term, he is looking for the "essence" of himself, that is, that which belongs to him necessarily and so cannot be sub-tracted from himself without, in effect, subtracting himself. Descartes arrives at the conclusion that "I am not more than a thing which thinks . . . a thing which doubts, understands, affirms, denies, wills, refuses, which also imagines and feels."

In a similar fashion, using as his illustration a piece of wax, Descartes in-vestigates the "essence" of "the bodies we touch and see" (physical objects) and arrives at the conclusion that they are things which are *extended* in space. This, argues Descartes, is another "intuition of the mind" and not "an act of vision, nor of touch, nor of imagination."

In further *Meditations* (not included herein), Descartes goes on to try to prove the existence of God and of the external world, resting all of this knowl-edge on the foundational truth of his own existence. Although most philoso-phers today do not agree that Descartes had succeeded in his endeavor of constructing a rational proof of all human knowledge from one indubitable starting point, his insistence upon applying rigorous and systematic standards to epistemological problems has left its mark on epistemology today. More-over, he provides us with a clear example of how a rationalist may attempt to arrive at certain knowledge of our world without relying on the senses.

The second selection of this chapter is taken from *An Essay Concerning Human Understanding* by John Locke (1632–1704), a British philosopher. Broadly speaking, empiricism is the view that all of our ideas are ultimately de-rived from experience. According to Locke's empiricism, all of our "simple ideas" out of which we build up our entire stock of "complex ideas" come to us either through *sensation* (seeing, hearing, touching, tasting, smelling) or by *reflection* upon the operations of our own minds (perception, thinking, doubt-ing, believing, reasoning).

For example, my complex idea of a dog is made up of further complex ideas such as "tail," "head," "legs," "fur," and so on, which are, in turn, made up of further complex ideas. Ultimately, however, such further ideas are re-ducible to certain empirical ideas (colors, textures, shapes, and the like), which, being "simple," cannot themselves be further divided.

Once we are furnished by experience with such a stock of ideas, the mind is capable of relating them as cognizable propositions (for example, "My dog has fleas"). However, whereas the ideas which constituted such propositions were, for Locke, derived from experience, he did not hold that our knowledge of the propositions themselves necessarily depended upon experience. Locke was enough of a rationalist to endow the mind with the power to discern at least some relations between ideas without the aid of experience. For example, for Locke, the proposition that "the external angle of all triangles is bigger than either of the opposite internal angles" is a necessary or certain proposition dis-covered by thought and not by sense perception. (Compare the proposition "My dog has fleas," which is, indeed, discovered by sense perception.)[1]

According to Locke, all simple ideas of sensation are produced in us by objects existing *outside our minds.* Such external objects are composed of particles of *matter.* All particles of matter, or aggregates thereof, are characterized by certain *objective* properties, namely, extension, figure, number, and motion. These properties which "really exist in the bodies themselves" Locke calls *primary qualities.*

When a person comes in perceptual range of an external object, it acts, by means of the particular arrangement of primary qualities of its "insensible parts," to produce certain ideas or sensations in the person. Ideas produced of the primary qualities themselves are, according to Locke, "resemblances" or "copies" of patterns actually existing in the material substance. For example, the perceived shape of an external object resembles its *actual* shape. On the other hand, some ideas produced in us by such objects are not resemblances of them. For example, the sweet taste of sugar is subjective, on the palate, so to speak. There is nothing like it in the sugar itself. What *is* in the sugar is just a certain arrangement of primary qualities (a certain atomic configuration) which gives it the power to produce a sweet sensation in one who tastes it. Such qualities which are "nothing in the objects themselves, but powers to produce various sensations in us by their primary qualities . . . as colors, sounds, tastes, etc." Locke terms *secondary qualities.*

Locke's causal theory of perception, as sketched above, was challenged by a theory known as "epistemological idealism." In the third selection of this chapter, George Berkeley (1685–1753), an Irish philosopher, develops this rival perspective largely by means of criticism of Locke's theory. Specifically, by forcefully arguing that Locke's concept of matter and the related distinction between primary and secondary qualities involved a logical contradiction, Berkeley came to the conclusion that the existence of physical objects depends entirely upon their *being perceived* and not upon any material substances existing outside our minds. Indeed, since all we can ever perceive are our ideas, a material substance which is not itself an idea is entirely unknowable and devoid of any practical significance. For Berkeley, physical objects are simply collections of ideas. For example, an apple is just "a certain color, taste, smell, figure, and consistence which having been observed to go together, are accounted one distinct thing, signified by the name 'apple.'" If all these apple-sensations were subtracted, there would remain nothing of the apple. There is no material apple behind the sensible apple, as Locke had argued. To suppose so is just to multiply entities unnecessarily.

Berkeley's epistemological idealism, as described above, however, faces its own difficulty. If objects exist only when perceived, then they must go out of existence when they are not being perceived by anyone. If I leave the room and nobody else is left in the room, then all the furniture in the room must accordingly cease to exist. Reality then comes and goes with a turn of the head or a blink of the eye, which is absurd. Locke, of course, has an answer to this problem. When we are not perceiving the furniture, the material objects still remain along with their powers to produce certain ideas in us. Berkeley, however, also had an answer. Even when we humans are not looking, God is still there to perceive things, keeping reality constant. Whereas Locke employed matter as the grounds of reality, Berkeley substituted God.

Berkeley's appeal to God, however, encounters its own problem. If the doctrine of matter is objectionable because matter lies outside our phenomenal world, does not that also apply to God? Historically, it was just such a criticism of Berkeley that led David Hume (1711–1776), a Scottish philosopher, to his skeptical rejection of the doctrine that souls exist (including God) as well as the doctrine that matter exists. For Hume, the only meaningful concepts were ones derived from experience. Since immaterial substances as well as material ones were outside our sense experience, they were equally meaningless. (You should note that Hume's empiricism set the stage for logical positivism of the sort defended by A. J. Ayer in chapter 7.)

In the fourth selection of this chapter, David Hume applies his thoroughgoing empiricism to the problem of causation. Hume's basic problem is to find the experiences which give rise to the idea of causation. He locates such empirical bases in three relations: we designate A to be the cause of B if and only if (1) A and B are *contiguous* with one another (in close spatial proximity), (2) A occurs (temporally) *prior* to B, and (3) there is a *constant conjunction* between A and B (events like A are always followed by ones like B). When these three relations are experienced, we are led by "custom" or force of habit to infer B from A. For example, we expect the motion of one billiard ball to generate motion in another billiard ball which it strikes. There is nothing in the first motion *per se* to allow us to demonstrate that motion will occur in the second. We can only do so after we have experienced a constant conjunction between similar events in the past. And there is, Hume argues, no demonstration or sure proof that "the future must be conformable to the past."

Hume's account of causation may, however, be challenged. First, it is not clear that contiguity is a necessary condition of the causal relation, for it could be argued that there can be causation at a distance as in, for instance, the gravitational effects of one heavenly body on another. Second, it is not clear that the (temporal) priority of the cause is a necessary condition of the causal relation; for it is arguable that *simultaneous* causation is possible. For example, according to Newton's Third Law of Motion, to every action there is an equal and opposite reaction. Thus, for instance, in pressing my hand against the wall, I might be said to cause, simultaneously, an opposite reaction. Third, two events may be constantly conjoined without being causally related. To use an example of John Stuart Mill, night might be regularly followed by day (and conversely) but that hardly means that night causes day, or that day causes night. Notwithstanding these points of criticism, however, Hume's emphasis on the empirical and contingent status of the causal relation has, indeed, proven to be an important contribution to our understanding of the natural sciences.

The epistemological theories outlined above raise some troublesome questions about knowledge: What can be known outside of our own thoughts and feelings? Is there anything about which we can be certain? How can we distinguish between appearance and reality? Mightn't all of our conscious existence be, in reality, a coherent dream? Do physical objects exist when nobody is there to perceive them? Can we be certain that the future will resemble the past?

Many adults may feel somewhat uncomfortable about raising such questions, perhaps because they have grown accustomed to *assuming* some answer to them (for example, that there just *is* a world outside of my thoughts). To even raise such questions may threaten the foundations of everything else they may have long accepted. (Indeed, Descartes himself admits that he had to wait until a mature age when he had "delivered [his] mind from every care" and was "happily agitated by no passions" before he could "at last seriously and freely address [himself] to the general upheaval of all [his] former opinions.")

However, although adults may tend to shy away from such questions (some may even call them silly or a waste of time), *children* appear to have a natural curiosity about such things. Indeed, it is not infrequent that a parent is embarrassed by a child's "How do you know" interrogative. (Moreover, the old parental standby "Because I say so" is, philosophically speaking, crude.)

In the Practice section of this chapter, Matthew Lipman, director of the Institute for the Advancement of Philosophy of Children at Montclair State College in New Jersey, shows how he has incorporated epistemological issues such as those raised by Descartes, Locke, Berkeley, and Hume into elementary school education. Lipman's strategy has been to write and publish a number of philosophical novels for children (among them, *Pixie* and *Harry Stottlemeier's Discovery*) which present fictional children's encounters wherein philosophical issues are addressed. Accompanied by exercise manuals, these books have been successfully employed in the classrooms of elementary schools throughout the world to stimulate philosophical thinking in children. The ultimate goal of Lipman's endeavor is, as such, providing children with "the philosophical tools to become critically reflective about their own education, thereby helping them to become more reasonable beings."

In the essay contained in this chapter, Lipman describes, through a log he had kept, some of his firsthand experience teaching *Pixie* to a class of fourth graders in a New York City elementary school in Manhattan. (Only those parts of his log that are relevant to the epistemological issues raised in this chapter have been included.) He also includes relevant exercises he employed in the course of his teaching. Moreover, throughout he suggests interesting parallels between the issues discussed by Descartes, Locke, Berkeley, and Hume and those that were raised in the classroom—at the same time, leaving the reader room to discover other possible parallels. For example, at one point Lipman asked the class if "thinkers make thoughts as shoemakers make shoes"; to which a little girl responded "Sure—out of other thoughts." Here the reader cannot fail to see some similarity to Locke's claim that "complex ideas" are composed of "simple ones."

To what extent are the children's conversations, as described by Lipman, representative of what takes place in traditional philosophical discussions? Are the conceptual problems similar? Are the logical moves similar? Lipman's response to such questions as these is that, in the end, "readers will have to judge these matters for themselves."

NOTE

1. An extended discussion of the senses in which Locke may be regarded as a rationalist and those in which he may be regarded as an empiricist is contained in Elliot D. Cohen, "Reason and Experience in Locke's Epistemology, " *Philosophy and Phenomenological Research,* Vol. 45, No. 1 (1984): 71–85.

ISSUES

RENÉ DESCARTES

RATIONALISM

MEDITATION I: OF THE THINGS WHICH MAY BE BROUGHT WITHIN THE SPHERE OF THE DOUBTFUL

It is now some years since I detected how many were the false beliefs that I had from my earliest youth admitted as true, and how doubtful was everything I had since constructed on this basis; and from that time I was convinced that I must once for all seriously undertake to rid myself of all the opinions which I had formerly accepted, and commence to build anew from the foundation, if I wanted to establish any firm and permanent structure in the sciences. But as this enterprise appeared to be a very great one, I waited until I had attained an age so mature that I could not hope that at any later date I should be better fitted to execute my design. . . . To-day, then, since very opportunely for the plan I have in view I have delivered my mind from every care [and am happily agitated by no passions] and since I have procured for myself an assured leisure in a peaceable retirement, I shall at last seriously and freely address myself to the general upheaval of all my former opinions.

Now for this object it is not necessary that I should show that all of these are false—I shall perhaps never arrive at this end. But inasmuch as reason already persuades me that I ought no less carefully to withhold my assent from matters which are not entirely certain and indubitable than from those which

SOURCE: René Descartes, *Meditations* (I and II), in *The Philosophical Works of Descartes,* trans. Elizabeth S. Haldane and G. R. T. Ross (New York: Cambridge University Press, 1955), pp. 145–157. Copyright 1955 by Cambridge University Press. Reprinted with the permission of Cambridge University Press.

appear to me manifestly to be false, if I am able to find in each one some reason to doubt, this will suffice to justify my rejecting the whole. And for that end it will not be requisite that I should examine each in particular, which would be an endless undertaking; for owing to the fact that the destruction of the foundations of necessity brings with it the downfall of the rest of the edifice, I shall only in the first place attack those principles upon which all my former opinions rested.

All that up to the present time I have accepted as most true and certain I have learned either from the senses or through the senses; but it is sometimes proved to me that these senses are deceptive, and it is wiser not to trust entirely to anything by which we have once been deceived.

But it may be that although the senses sometimes deceive us concerning things which are hardly perceptible, or very far away, there are yet many others to be met with as to which we cannot reasonably have any doubt, although we recognise them by their means. For example, there is the fact that I am here, seated by the fire, attired in a dressing gown, having this paper in my hands and other similar matters. And how could I deny that these hands and this body are mine, were it not perhaps that I compare myself to certain persons, devoid of sense, whose cerebella are so troubled and clouded by the violent vapours of black bile, that they constantly assure us that they think they are kings when they are really quite poor, or that they are clothed in purple when they are really without covering, or who imagine that they have an earthenware head or are nothing but pumpkins or are made of glass. But they are mad, and I should not be any the less insane were I to follow examples so extravagant.

At the same time I must remember that I am a man, and that consequently I am in the habit of sleeping, and in my dreams representing to myself the same things or sometimes even less probable things, than do those who are insane in their waking moments. How often has it happened to me that in the night I dreamt that I found myself in this particular place, that I was dressed and seated near the fire, whilst in reality I was lying undressed in bed! At this moment it does indeed seem to me that it is with eyes awake that I am looking at this paper; that this head which I move is not asleep; that it is deliberately and of set purpose that I extend my hand and perceive it; what happens in sleep does not appear so clear nor so distinct as does all this. But in thinking over this I remind myself that on many occasions I have in sleep been deceived by similar illusions, and in dwelling carefully on this reflection I see so manifestly that there are no certain indications by which we may clearly distinguish wakefulness from sleep that I am lost in astonishment. And my astonishment is such that it is almost capable of persuading me that I now dream.

. . . Physics, Astronomy, Medicine and all other sciences which have as their end the consideration of composite things are very dubious and uncertain; but that Arithmetic, Geometry and other sciences of that kind which only treat of things that are very simple and very general, without taking great trouble to ascertain whether they are actually existent or not, contain some measure of certainty and an element of the indubitable. For whether I am awake or asleep, two and three together always form five, and the square can never have more than four sides, and it does not seem possible that truths so clear and apparent can be suspected of any falsity [or uncertainty].

Nevertheless I have long had fixed in my mind the belief that an all powerful God existed by whom I have been created such as I am. But how do I know that He has not brought it to pass that there is no earth, no heaven, no extended body, no magnitude, no place, and that nevertheless they seem to me to exist just exactly as I now see them? And, besides, as I sometimes imagine that others deceive themselves in the things which they think they know best, how do I know that I am not deceived every time that I add two and three, or count the sides of a square, or judge of things yet simpler, if anything simpler can be imagined? . . .

I shall then suppose, not that God who is supremely good and the fountain of truth, but some evil genius not less powerful than deceitful, has employed his whole energies in deceiving me; I shall consider that the heavens, the earth, colours, figures, sound, and all other external things are nought but the illusions and dreams of which this genius has availed himself in order to lay traps for my credulity; I shall consider myself as having no hands, no eyes, no flesh, no blood, nor any senses, yet falsely believing myself to possess all these things; I shall remain obstinately attached to this idea, and if by this means it is not in my power to arrive at the knowledge of any truth, I may at least do what is in my power [i.e., suspend my judgment], and with firm purpose avoid giving credence to any false thing, or being imposed upon by this arch deceiver, however powerful and deceptive he may be. . . .

MEDITATION II: OF THE NATURE OF THE HUMAN MIND; AND THAT IT IS MORE EASILY KNOWN THAN THE BODY

The Meditation of yesterday filled my mind with so many doubts that it is no longer in my power to forget them. And yet I do not see in what manner I can resolve them; and, just as if I had all of a sudden fallen into very deep water, I am so disconcerted that I can neither make certain of setting my feet on the bottom, nor can I swim and so support myself on the surface. I shall nevertheless make an effort and follow anew the same path as that on which I yesterday entered, i.e., I shall proceed by setting aside all that in which the least doubt could be supposed to exist, just as if I had discovered that it was absolutely false; and I shall ever follow in this road until I have met with something which is certain, or at least, if I can do nothing else, until I have learned for certain that there is nothing in the world that is certain. Archimedes, in order that he might draw the terrestrial globe out of its place, and transport it elsewhere, demanded only that one point should be fixed and immoveable; in the same way I shall have the right to conceive high hopes if I am happy enough to discover one thing only which is certain and indubitable.

I suppose, then, that all the things that I see are false; I persuade myself that nothing has ever existed of all that my fallacious memory represents to me. I consider that I possess no senses; I imagine that body, figure, extension, move-ment, and place are but the fictions of my mind. What, then, can be esteemed as true? Perhaps nothing at all, unless that there is nothing in the world that is certain.

But how can I know there is not something different from those things that I have just considered, of which one cannot have the slightest doubt? Is there not some God, or some other being by whatever name we call it, who puts these reflections into my mind? That is not necessary, for is it not possible that I am capable of producing them myself? I myself, am I not at least something? But I have already denied that I had senses and body. Yet I hesitate, for what follow from that? Am I so dependent on body and senses that I cannot exist without these? But I was persuaded that there was nothing in all the world, that there was no heaven, no earth, that there were no minds, nor any bodies: was I not then likewise persuaded that I did not exist? Not at all; of a surety I myself did exist since I persuaded myself of something [or merely because I thought of something]. But there is some deceiver or other, very powerful and very cun-ning, who ever employs his ingenuity in deceiving me. Then without doubt I ex-ist also if he deceives me, and let him deceive me as much as he will, he can never cause me to be nothing so long as I think that I am something. So that af-ter having reflected well and carefully examined all things, we must come to the definite conclusion that this proposition: I am, I exist, is necessarily true each time that I pronounce it, or that I mentally conceive it.

But I do not yet know clearly enough what I am, I who am certain that I am; and hence I must be careful to see that I do not imprudently take some other object in place of myself, and thus that I do not go astray in respect of this knowledge that I hold to be the most certain and most evident of all that I have formerly learned. . . .

What am I, now that I suppose that there is a certain genius which is ex-tremely powerful, and, if I may say so, malicious, who employs all his powers in deceiving me? Can I affirm that I possess the least of all those things which pertain to the nature of body? I pause to consider, I resolve all these things in my mind, and find none of which I can say that it pertains to me. It would be tedious to stop to enumerate them. Let us pass to the attributes of soul and see if there is any one which is in me? What of nutrition or walking [the first men-tioned]? But if it is so that I have no body it is also true that I can neither walk nor take nourishment. Another attribute is sensation. But one cannot feel with-out body, and besides I have thought I perceived many things during sleep that I recognised in my waking moment as not having been experienced at all. What of thinking? I find here that thought is an attribute that belongs to me; it alone cannot be separated from me. I am, I exist, that is certain. But how often? Just when I think; for it might possibly be the case if I ceased entirely to think, that I should likewise cease altogether to exist. I do not now admit anything which is not necessarily true: to speak accurately I am not more than a thing which thinks, that is to say a mind or a soul, or an understanding, or a reason, which are terms whose significance was formerly unknown to me. I am, however, a real thing and really exist; but what thing? I have answered: a thing which thinks. . . .

What is a thing which thinks? It is a thing which doubts, understands, [conceives], affirms, denies, wills, refuses, which also imagines and feels.

Certainly it is no small matter if all these things pertain to my nature. But why should they not so pertain? Am I not that being who now doubts nearly everything, who nevertheless understands certain things, who affirms that one only is true, who denies all the others, who desires to know more who is averse to being deceived, who imagines many things, sometimes indeed despite his will, and who perceives many likewise, as by the intervention of the bodily organs? Is there nothing in all this which is as true as it is certain that I exist, even though I should always sleep and though he who has given me being employed all his ingenuity in deceiving me? Is there likewise any one of these attributes which can be distinguished from my thought, or which might be said to be separated from myself? For it is so evident of itself that it is I who doubts, who understands, and who desires, that there is no reason here to add anything to explain it. And I have certainly the power of imagining likewise; for although it may happen (as I formerly supposed) that none of the things which I imagine are true, nevertheless this power of imagining does not cease to be really in use, and it forms part of my thought. Finally, I am the same who feels, that is to say, who perceives certain things, as by the organs of sense, since in truth I see light, I hear noise, I feel heat. But it will be said that these phenomena are false and that I am dreaming. Let it be so; still it is at least quite certain that it seems to me that I see light, that I hear noise and that I feel heat. That cannot be false; properly speaking it is what is in me called feeling; and used in this precise sense that is no other thing than thinking.

From this time I begin to know what I am with a little more clearness and distinction than before; but nevertheless it still seems to me, and I cannot prevent myself from thinking, that corporeal things, whose images are framed by thought, which are tested by the senses, are much more distinctly known than that obscure part of me which does not come under the imagination. Although really it is very strange to say that I know and understand more distinctly these things whose existence seems to me dubious, which are unknown to me, and which do not belong to me, than others of the truth of which I am convinced, which are known to me and which pertain to my real nature, in a word, than myself. But I see clearly how the case stands: my mind loves to wander, and cannot yet suffer itself to be retained within the just limits of truth. Very good, let us once more give it the freest rein, so that, when afterwards we seize the proper occasion for pulling up, it may the more easily be regulated and controlled.

Let us begin by considering the commonest matters, those which we believe to be the most distinctly comprehended, to wit, the bodies which we touch and see; not indeed bodies in general, for these general ideas are usually a little more confused, but let us consider one body in particular. Let us take for example, this piece of wax: it has been taken quite freshly from the hive, and it has not yet lost the sweetness of the honey which it contains; it still retains somewhat of the odour of the flowers from which it has been culled; its colour, its figure, its size are apparent; it is hard, cold, easily handled, and if you strike it with the finger, it will emit a sound. Finally all the things which are requisite to cause us distinctly to recognize a body, are met within it. But notice that while I speak and approach the fire what remained of the taste is exhaled, the smell evaporates, the colour alters, the figure is destroyed, the size increases, it becomes liquid, it heats, scarcely can one handle it, and when one strikes it, no sound is emitted. Does the same wax remain after this change? We must confess that it remains; none would judge otherwise. What then did I know so distinctly in this piece of wax? It could certainly be nothing of all that the senses brought to my notice, since all these things which fall under taste, smell, sight, touch, and hearing, are found to be changed, and yet the same wax remains.

Perhaps it was what I now think, viz. that this wax was not that sweetness of honey, nor that agreeable scent of flowers, nor that particular whiteness, nor that figure, nor that sound, but simply a body which a little before appeared to me as perceptible under these forms, and which is now perceptible under others. But what, precisely, is it that I imagine when I form such conceptions? Let us attentively consider this, and abstracting from all that does not belong to the wax, let us see what remains. Certainly nothing removeable. But what is the meaning of flexible and movable? Is it not that I imagine that this piece of wax being round is capable of becoming square and of passing from a square to a triangular figure? No, certainly it is not that, since I imagine it admits of an infinitude of similar changes, and I nevertheless do not know how to compass the infinitude by my imagination, and consequently this conception which I have of the wax is not brought about by the faculty of imagination. What now is this extension? Is it not also unknown? For it becomes greater when the wax is melted, greater when it is boiled, and greater still when the heat increases; and I should not conceive (clearly) according to truth what wax is, if I did not think that even this piece that we are considering is capable of receiving more variations in extension than I have ever imagined. We must then grant that I could not even understand through the imagination what this piece of wax is, and that it is my mind alone which perceives it. I say this piece of wax in particular, for as to wax in general it is yet clearer. But what is this piece of wax which cannot be understood excepting by the mind? It is certainly the same that I see, touch, imagine, and finally it is the same which I have always believed it to be from the beginning. But what must particularly be observed is that its perception is neither an act of vision, nor of touch, nor of imagination, and has never been such although it may have appeared formerly to be so, but only an intuition of the mind, which may be imperfect and confused as it was formerly, or clear and distinct as it is at present, as my attention is more or less directed to the elements which are found in it, and of which it is composed.

Yet in the meantime I am greatly astonished when I consider [the great feebleness of mind] and its proneness to fall [insensibly] into error; for although without giving expression to my thoughts I consider all this in my own mind, words often impede me and I am almost deceived by the terms of ordinary language. For we say that we see the same wax, if it is present, and not that we simply judge that it is the same from its having the same colour and figure. From this I should conclude that I knew the wax by means of vision and not simply by the intuition of the mind; unless by chance I remember that, when looking from a window and saying I see men who pass in the street, I really do not see them, but infer that what I see is men, just as I say that I see wax. And yet what do I see from the window but hats and coats which may cover automatic machines? Yet I judge these to be men. And similarly solely by the faculty of judgment which rests in my mind, I comprehend that which I believed I saw with my eyes. . . .

But finally here I am, having insensibly reverted to the point I desired, for, since it is now manifest to me that even bodies are not properly speaking known by the senses or by the faculty of imagination, but by the understanding only, and since they are not known from the fact that they are seen or touched, but only because they are understood, I see clearly that there is nothing which is easier for me to know than my mind. But because it is difficult to rid oneself so promptly of an opinion to which one was accustomed for so long, it will be well that I should halt a little at this point, so that by the length of my meditation I may more deeply imprint on my memory this new knowledge.

JOHN LOCKE

EMPIRICISM

INTRODUCTION

. . . I must here in the entrance beg pardon of my reader for the frequent use of the word *idea,* which he will find in the following treatise. It being that term which, I think, serves best to stand for whatsoever is the object of the understanding when a man thinks, I have used it to express whatever is meant by *phantasm, notion, species,* or whatever it is which the mind can be employed about in thinking; and I could not avoid frequently using it.

I presume it will be easily granted me that there are such *ideas* in men's minds: everyone is conscious of them in himself, and men's words and actions will satisfy him that they are in others. . . .

SOURCE: John Locke, *An Essay Concerning Human Understanding,* ed. John W. Yolton (London: Everyman's Library/Dent, 1961), pp. 9, 77–79, 90–91, 104–106, 129–132. Reprinted by permission of the publisher, J. M. Dent & Sons Ltd.

OF IDEAS IN GENERAL, AND THEIR ORIGINAL

Every man being conscious to himself that he thinks, and that which his mind is applied about whilst thinking being the *ideas* that are there, it is past doubt that men have in their minds several *ideas* such as are those expressed by the words *whiteness, hardness, sweetness, thinking, motion, man, elephant, army, drunkenness* and others: it is in the first place then to be inquired, how he comes by them? . . .

Let us then suppose the mind to be, as we say, white paper void of all characters, without any *ideas*. How comes it to be furnished? Whence comes it by that vast store which the busy and boundless fancy of man has painted on it with an almost endless variety? Whence has it all the materials of reason and knowledge? To this I answer, in one word, from *experience;* in that all our knowledge is founded, and from that it ultimately derives itself. Our observation, employed either about *external sensible objects, or about the internal operations of our minds perceived and reflected on by ourselves, is that which supplies our understandings with all the materials of thinking.* These two are the fountains of knowledge, from whence all the *ideas* we have, or can naturally have, do spring.

First, *our senses,* conversant about particular sensible objects, do *convey into the mind* several distinct *perceptions* of things, according to those various ways wherein those objects do affect them. And thus we come by those *ideas* we have of *yellow, white, heat, cold, soft, hard, bitter, sweet,* and all those which we call sensible qualities; which when I say the senses convey into the mind, I mean, they from external objects convey into the mind what produces there those *perceptions.* This great source of most of the *ideas* we have, depending wholly upon our senses, and derived by them to the understanding, I call SENSATION.

Secondly, the other fountain from which experience furnisheth the understanding with *ideas* is the *perception of the operations of our own minds* within us, as it is employed about the *ideas* it has got; which operations, when the soul comes to reflect on and consider, do furnish the understanding with another set of *ideas,* which could not be had from things without. And such are *perception, thinking, doubting, believing, reasoning, knowing, willing,* and all the different actings of our own minds; which we, being conscious of and observing in ourselves, do from these receive into our understandings as distinct *ideas* as we do from bodies affecting our senses. This source of *ideas* every man has wholly in himself; and though it be not sense, as having nothing to do with external objects, yet it is very like it, and might properly enough be called internal sense. But as I call the other *sensation,* so I call this REFLECTION, the *ideas* it affords being such only as the mind gets by reflecting on its own operations within itself. By REFLECTION then, in the following part of this discourse, I would be understood to mean that notice which the mind takes of its own operations, and the manner of them, by reason whereof there come to be *ideas* of these operations in the understanding. These two, I say, viz. external material things as the objects of SENSATION, and the operations of our own minds within, as the objects of REFLECTION, are to me the only originals from whence all our *ideas* take their beginnings. . . .

These, when we have taken a full survey of them and their several modes, combinations, and relations, we shall find to contain all our whole stock of *ideas,* and that we have nothing in our minds which did not come in one of these two ways. Let anyone examine his own thoughts and thoroughly search into his understanding and then let him tell me whether all the original *ideas* he has there are any other than of the objects of his *senses,* or of the operations of his mind, considered as objects of his *reflection.* And how great a mass of knowledge soever he imagines to be lodged there, he will, upon taking a strict view, see that he has *not any* idea *in his mind but what one of these two have imprinted,* though perhaps, with infinite variety compounded and enlarged by the understanding, as we shall see hereafter. . . .

I pretend not to teach, but to inquire; and therefore cannot but confess here again that external and internal sensation are the only passages that I can find of knowledge to the understanding. These alone, as far as I can discover, are the windows by which light is let into this *dark room.* For, methinks, the *understanding* is not much unlike a closet wholly shut from light, with only some little opening left, to let in external visible resemblances, or *ideas* of things without: would the pictures coming into such a dark room but stay there, and lie so orderly as to be found upon occasion, it would very much resemble the understanding of a man in reference to all objects of sight and the *ideas* of them. . . .

OF SIMPLE IDEAS

The better to understand the nature, manner, and extent of our knowledge, one thing is carefully to be observed concerning the *ideas* we have, and that is that *some* of them are *simple* and *some complex.*

Though the qualities that affect our senses are, in the things themselves, so united and blended that there is no separation, no distance between them, yet it is plain the *ideas* they produce in the mind enter by the senses simple and unmixed. For, though the sight and touch often take in from the same object, at the same time, different *ideas,* as a man sees at once motion and colour, the hand feels softness and warmth in the same piece of wax: yet the simple *ideas* thus united in the same subject are as perfectly distinct as those that come in by different senses. The coldness and hardness which a man feels in a piece of *ice* being as distinct *ideas* in the mind as the smell and whiteness of a lily, or as the taste of sugar, and smell of a rose; and there is nothing can be plainer to a man than the clear and distinct perception he has of those simple *ideas;* which, being each in itself uncompounded, contains in it nothing but *one uniform appearance* or conception in the mind, and is not distinguishable into different *ideas.*

These simple *ideas,* the materials of all our knowledge, are suggested and furnished to the mind only by those two ways above mentioned, viz. *sensation* and *reflection.* When the understanding is once stored with these simple *ideas,* it has the power to repeat, compare, and unite them, even to an almost infinite variety, and so can make at pleasure new complex *ideas*. But it is not in the power of the most exalted wit or enlarged understanding, by any quickness or variety of thought, to *invent or frame one new simple* idea in the mind, not taken in by the ways before mentioned; nor can any force of the understanding *destroy* those that are there, the dominion of man in this little world of his own understanding being much what the same as it is in the great world of visible things; wherein his power, however managed by art and skill, reaches no further than to compound and divide the materials that are made to his hand, but can do nothing towards the making the least particle of new matter, or destroying one atom of what is already in being. The same inability will everyone find in himself, who shall go about to fashion in his understanding any simple *idea*, not received in by his senses from external objects, or by reflection from the operations of his own mind about them. I would have anyone try to fancy any taste which had never affected his palate, or frame the *idea* of a scent he had never smelt; and when he can do this, I will also conclude that a blind man hath *ideas* of colours and a deaf man true distinct notions of sounds. . . .

PRIMARY AND SECONDARY QUALITIES

Whatsoever the mind perceives in itself, or is the immediate object of perception, thought, or understanding, that I call *idea;* and the power to produce any *idea* in our mind, I call *quality* of the subject wherein that power is. Thus a snowball having the power to produce in us the *ideas* of *white, cold,* and *round,* the power to produce those *ideas* in us as they are in the snowball I call *qualities;* and as they are sensations or perceptions in our understandings, I call them *ideas;* which *ideas,* if I speak of sometimes as in the things themselves, I would be understood to mean those qualities in the objects which produce them in us.

Qualities thus considered in bodies are:

First, such as are utterly inseparable from the body, in what state soever it be; such as in all the alterations and changes it suffers, all the force can be used upon it, it constantly keeps; and such as sense constantly finds in every particle of matter which has bulk enough to be perceived; and the mind finds inseparable from every particle of matter, though less than to make itself singly be perceived by our senses. V.g., take a grain of wheat, divide it into two parts, each part has still *solidity, extension, figure,* and *mobility;* divide it again, and it retains still the same qualities; and so divide it on, till the parts become insensible: they must retain still each of them all those qualities. For division (which is all that a mill or pestle or any other body does upon another in reducing it to insensible parts) can never take away either solidity, extension, figure, or mobility from any body, but only makes two or more distinct separate masses of matter, of that which was but one before; all which distinct masses, reckoned as so many distinct bodies, after division make a certain number. These I call *original* or *primary qualities* of body; which I think we may observe to produce simple *ideas* in us, viz. solidity, extension, figure, motion or rest, and number.

Secondly, such *qualities* which in truth are nothing in the objects them-selves but powers to produce various sensations in us by their *primary quali-ties,* i.e. by the bulk, figure, texture, and motion of their insensible parts, as colours, sounds, tastes, etc. These I call *secondary qualities.* To these might be added a third sort, which are allowed to be barely powers, though they are as much real qualities in the subject as those which I, to comply with the common way of speaking, call *qualities,* but for distinction, *secondary qualities.* For the power in fire to produce a new colour, or consistency in wax or clay, by its pri-mary qualities, is as much a quality in fire as the power it has to produce in me a new *idea* or sensation of warmth or burning, which I felt not before, by the same primary qualities, viz. the bulk, texture, and motion of its insensible parts.

The next thing to be considered is how *bodies* produce *ideas* in us; and that is manifestly *by impulse,* the only way which we can conceive bodies operate in.

If then external objects be not united to our minds when they produce *ideas* in it and yet we perceive *these original qualities* in such of them as singly fall under our senses, it is evident that some motion must be thence continued by our nerves or animal spirits, by some parts of our bodies, to the brains or the seat of sensation, there to *produce in our minds the particular* ideas *we have of them.* And since the extension, figure, number, and motion of bodies of an observable bigness may be perceived at a distance *by* the sight, it is evident some singly imperceptible bodies must come from them to the eyes, and thereby convey to the brain some *motion,* which produces these *ideas* which we have of them in us.

After the same manner that the *ideas* of these original qualities are pro-duced in us, we may conceive that the *ideas of secondary qualities* are also *produced,* viz. *by the operation of insensible particles on our senses.* For it be-ing manifest that there are bodies and good store of bodies, each whereof are so small that we cannot by any of our senses discover either their bulk, figure, or motion, as is evident in the particles of the air and water and others ex-tremely smaller than those, perhaps as much smaller than the particles of air or water as the particles of air or water are smaller than peas or hail-stones: let us suppose at present that the different motions and figures, bulk and number, of such particles, affecting the several organs of our senses, produce in us those different sensations which we have from the colours and smells of bodies: v.g. that a violet, by the impulse of such insensible particles of matter, of peculiar figures and bulks, and in different degrees and modifications of their motions, causes the *ideas* of the blue colour and sweet scent of that flower to be produced in our minds. It being no more impossible to conceive that God should annex such *ideas* to such motions, with which they have no similitude, than that he should annex the *idea* of pain to the motion of a piece of steel dividing our flesh, with which that *idea* hath no resemblance.

What I have said concerning *colours* and *smells* may be understood also of *tastes* and *sounds, and other the like sensible qualities;* which, whatever reality we by mistake attribute to them, are in truth nothing in the objects themselves but powers to produce various sensations in us, and depend *on those primary qualities,* viz. bulk, figure, texture, and motion of parts, as I have said.

From whence I think it is easy to draw this observation: that the *ideas of primary qualities* of bodies *are resemblances* of them, and their patterns do really exist in the bodies themselves; but the *ideas produced* in us *by* these *secondary qualities have no resemblance* of them at all. There is nothing like our *ideas* existing in the bodies themselves. They are, in the bodies we denominate from them, only a power to produce those sensations in us; and what is sweet, blue, or warm in *idea* is but the certain bulk, figure, and motion of the insensible parts in the bodies themselves, which we call so. . . .

OF COMPLEX IDEAS

We have hitherto considered those ideas in the reception whereof the mind is only passive, which are those simple ones received from *sensation* and *reflection* before mentioned, whereof the mind cannot make one to itself, nor have any *idea* which does not wholly consist of them. But as the mind is wholly passive in the reception of all its simple *ideas,* so it exerts several acts of its own whereby out of its simple *ideas,* as the materials and foundations of the rest, the others are framed. The acts of the mind, wherein it exerts its power over its simple *ideas,* are chiefly these three: (1) Combining several simple *ideas* into one compound one; and thus all complex *ideas* are made. (2) The second is bringing two *ideas,* whether simple or complex, together, and setting them by one another, so as to take a view of them at once, without uniting them into one; by which way it gets all its *ideas* of relations. (3) The third is separating them from all other *ideas* that accompany them in their real existence: this is called *abstraction;* and thus all its general *ideas* are made. This shows man's power, and its way of operation, to be much the same in the material and intellectual world. For the materials in both being such as he has no power over either to make or destroy, all that man can do is either to unite them together, or to set them by one another, or wholly separate them, I shall here begin with the first of these in the consideration of complex *ideas,* and come to the other two in their due places. As simple *ideas* are observed to exist in several combinations united together, so the mind has a power to consider several of them united together as one *idea,* and that not only as they are united in external objects, but as itself has joined them. *Ideas* thus made up of several simple ones put together, I call *complex,* such as are *beauty, gratitude, a man, an army, the universe;* which, though complicated of various simple *ideas,* or *complex ideas* made up of simple ones, yet are, when the mind pleases, considered each by itself as one entire thing, and signified by the one name. . . .

Complex ideas, however compounded and decompounded, though their number be infinite and the variety endless wherewith they fill and entertain the thoughts of men, yet I think they may be all reduced under these three heads:

1. Modes.
2. Substances.
3. Relations.

First, *Modes* I call such complex *ideas* which, however compounded, contain not in them the supposition of subsisting by themselves, but are considered as dependences on, or affections of substances; such as the *ideas* signified by the words *triangle, gratitude, murder,* etc. And if in this I use the word *mode* in somewhat a different sense from its ordinary signification, I beg pardon: it being unavoidable in discourses differing from the ordinary received notions either to make new words or to use old words in somewhat a new signification, the latter whereof in our present case is perhaps the more tolerable of the two. . . .

Secondly, the *ideas* of *substances* are such combinations of simple *ideas* are taken to represent distinct particular things subsisting by themselves, in which the supposed or confused *idea* of substance, such as it is, is always the first and chief. Thus if to substance be joined the simple *idea* of a certain dull whitish colour, with certain degrees of weight, hardness, ductility, and fusibility, we have the *idea* of *lead;* and a combination of the *ideas* of a certain sort of figure, with the powers of motion, thought, and reasoning, joined to substance, make the ordinary *idea* of *a man.* Now of substances also, there are two sorts of *ideas:* one of single substances, as they exist separately, as of *a man* or *a sheep;* the other of several of those put together, as an *army* of men, or *flock* of sheep; which *collective* ideas *of* several *substances* thus put together are as much each of them one single *idea* as that of a man or an unit.

Thirdly, the last sort of complex *ideas* is that we call *relation,* which consists in the consideration and comparing one *idea* with another. . . .

GEORGE BERKELEY

EPISTEMOLOGICAL IDEALISM

It is evident to anyone who takes a survey of the objects of human knowledge, that they are either ideas actually imprinted on the senses, or else such as are perceived by attending to the passions and operations of the mind, or lastly ideas formed by help of memory and imagination, either compounding, dividing, or barely representing those originally perceived in the aforesaid ways. By sight I have the ideas of light and colours with their several degrees and variations. By touch I perceive, for example, hard and soft, heat and cold, motion and resistance, and of all these more and less either as to quantity or degree. Smelling furnishes me with odours, the palate with tastes, and hearing conveys sounds to the mind in all their variety of tone and composition. And as several of these are observed to accompany each other, they come to be marked by one

SOURCE: George Berkeley, *A Treatise Concerning the Principles of Human Knowledge* (New York: Doubleday, 1974), pp. 151–165. Reprinted from *The Empiricists.*

name, and so to be reputed as one thing. Thus, for example, a certain color, taste, smell, figure and consistence having been observed to go together, are accounted one distinct thing, signified by the name 'apple'. Other collections of ideas constitute a stone, a tree, a book, and the like sensible things: which, as they are pleasing or disagreeable, excite the passions of love, hatred, joy, grief, and so forth.

But besides all that endless variety of ideas or objects of knowledge, there is likewise something which knows or perceives them, and exercises divers operations, as willing, imagining, remembering about them. This perceiving, active being is what I call *mind, spirit, soul, or my self*. By which words I do not denote any of my ideas, but a thing entirely distinct from them, wherein they exist, or, which is the same thing, whereby they are perceived; for the existence of an idea consists in being perceived.

That neither our thoughts, nor passions, nor ideas formed by the imagination, exist without the mind, is what everybody will allow. And it seems no less evident that the various sensations or ideas imprinted on the sense, however blended or combined together (that is, whatever objects they compose), cannot exist otherwise than in a mind perceiving them. I think an intuitive knowledge may be obtained of this by anyone that shall attend to what is meant by the term *exist* when applied to sensible things. The table I write on, I say, exists, that is, I see and feel it; and if I were out of my study I should say it existed, meaning thereby that if I was in my study I might perceive it, or that some other spirit actually does perceive it. There was an odour, that is, it was smelled; there was a sound, that is to say, it was heard; a colour or figure, and it was perceived by sight or touch. This is all that I can understand by these and the like expressions. For as to what is said of the absolute existence of unthinking things without any relation to their being perceived, that seems perfectly unintelligible. Their *esse is percepi*, nor is it possible they should have any existence out of the mind or thinking things which perceive them. . . .

But, say you, though the ideas themselves do not exist without the mind, yet there may be things *like* them whereof they are copies or resemblances, which things exist without the mind, in an unthinking substance. I answer, an idea can be like nothing but an idea; a colour or figure can be like nothing but another colour or figure. If we look but ever so little into our thoughts, we shall find it impossible for us to conceive a likeness except only between our ideas. Again, I ask whether those supposed originals or external things, of which our ideas are the pictures or representations, be themselves perceivable or no? If they are, they are ideas, and we have gained our point; but if you say they are not, I appeal to anyone whether it be sense to assert a colour is like something which is invisible; hard or soft, like something which is intangible; and so of the rest.

Some there are who make a distinction betwixt *primary and secondary* qualities: by the former, they mean extension, figure, motion, rest, solidity or impenetrability, and number: by the latter they denote all other sensible qualities, as colours, sounds, tastes, and so forth. The ideas we have of these they acknowledge not to be the resemblances of anything existing without the mind or unperceived; but they will have our ideas of the primary qualities to be patterns or images of things which exist without the mind, in an unthinking substance which they call *matter*. By *matter* therefore we are to understand an inert, senseless substance, in which extension, figure, and motion do actually subsist. But it is evident from what we have already shown, that extension, figure, and motion are only ideas existing in the mind, and that an idea can be like nothing but another idea, and that consequently neither they nor their archetypes can exist in an unperceiving substance. Hence it is plain that the very notion of what is called *matter* or *corporeal substance* involves a contradiction in it.

They who assert that figure, motion, and the rest of the primary or original qualities do exist without the mind, in unthinking substances, do at the same time acknowledge that colours, sounds, heat, cold, and suchlike secondary qualities, do not, which they tell us are sensations existing in the mind alone, that depend on and are occasioned by the different size, texture, and motion of the minute particles of matter. This they take for an undoubted truth, which they can demonstrate beyond all exception. Now if it be certain, that those original qualities are inseparably united with the other sensible qualities, and not even in thought capable of being abstracted from them, it plainly follows that they exist only in the mind. But I desire any one to reflect and try, whether he can by any abstraction of thought conceive the extension and motion of a body without all other sensible qualities. For my own part, I see evidently that it is not in my power to frame an idea of a body extended and moved, but I must withal give it some colour or other sensible quality which is acknowledged to exist only in the mind. In short, extension, figure, and motion, abstracted from all other qualities, are inconceivable. Where therefore the other sensible qualities are, there must these be also, to wit, in the mind and nowhere else. . . .

I shall farther add, that after the same manner as modern philosophers prove certain sensible qualities to have no existence in matter, or without the mind, the same thing may be likewise proved of all other sensible qualities whatsoever. Thus, for instance, it is said that heat and cold are affections only of the mind, and not at all patterns of real beings existing in the corporeal substances which excite them, for that the same body which appears cold to one hand seems warm to another. Now why may we not as well argue that figure and extension are not patterns or resemblances of qualities existing in matter, because to the same eye at different stations, or eyes of a different texture at the same station, they appear various, and cannot therefore be the images of anything settled and determinate without the mind? Again, it is proved that sweetness is not really in the sapid thing, because the thing remaining unaltered the sweetness is changed into bitter, as in case of a fever or otherwise vitiated palate. Is it not as reasonable to say, that motion is not without the mind, since if the succession of ideas in the mind become swifter, the motion, it is acknowledged, shall appear slower without any alteration in any external object?

In short, let anyone consider those arguments, which are thought manifestly to prove that colours and tastes exist only in the mind, and he shall find they may with equal force be brought to prove the same thing of extension, figure, and motion. . . .

But though it were possible that solid, figured, movable substances may exist without the mind, corresponding to the ideas we have of bodies, yet how is it possible for us to know this? Either we must know it by sense, or by reason. As for our senses, by them we have the knowledge only of our sensations, ideas, or those things that are immediately perceived by sense, call them what you will: but they do not inform us that things exist without the mind, or unperceived, like to those which are perceived. This the materialists themselves acknowledge. It remains therefore that if we have any knowledge at all of external things, it must be by reason, inferring their existence from what is immediately perceived by sense. But what reason can induce us to believe the existence of bodies without the mind, from what we perceive, since the very patrons of matter themselves do not pretend there is any necessary connexion betwixt them and our ideas? I say it is granted on all hands (and what happens in dreams, frenzies, and the like, puts it beyond dispute) that *it is possible we might be affected with all the ideas we have now, though no bodies existed without, resembling them.* Hence it is evident the supposition of external bodies is not necessary for producing our ideas, since it is granted they are produced sometimes, and might possibly be produced always in the same order we see them in at present, without their concurrence. . . .

In short, if there were external bodies, it is impossible we should ever come to know it; and if there were not, we might have the very same reasons to think there were that we have now. Suppose, what no one can deny possible, an intelligence, without the help of external bodies, to be affected with the same train of sensations or ideas that you are, imprinted in the same order and with like vividness in his mind. I ask whether that intelligence hath not all the reason to believe the existence of corporeal substances, represented by his ideas, and exciting them in his mind, that you can possibly have for believing the same thing? Of this there can be no question; which one consideration is enough to make any reasonable person suspect the strength of whatever arguments he may think himself to have for the existence of bodies without the mind. . . .

But say you, surely there is nothing easier than to imagine trees, for instance, in a park, or books existing in a closet, and nobody by to perceive them. I answer, you may so, there is no difficulty in it: but what is all this, I beseech you, more than framing in your mind certain ideas which you call books and trees, and at the same time omitting to frame the idea of anyone that may perceive them. But do not you yourself perceive or think of them all the while? This therefore is nothing to the purpose: it only shows you have the power of imagining or forming ideas in your mind; but it doth not show that you can conceive it possible the objects of your thought may exist without the mind: to make out this, it is necessary that you conceive them existing unconceived or unthought of, which is a manifest repugnancy. When we do our utmost to conceive the existence of external bodies, we are all the while only contemplating our own ideas. But the mind taking no notice of itself is deluded to think it can and doth conceive bodies existing unthought of or without the mind; though at the same time they are apprehended by or exist in itself. . . .

I find I can excite ideas in my mind at pleasure, and vary and shift the scene as oft as I think fit. It is no more than willing, and straightway this or that idea arises in my fancy: and by the same power it is obliterated, and makes way for another. This making and unmaking of ideas doth very properly denominate the mind active. Thus much is certain, and grounded on experience: but when we talk of unthinking agents, or of exciting ideas exclusive of volition, we only amuse ourselves with words.

But whatever power I may have over my own thoughts, I find the ideas actually perceived by sense have not a like dependence on my will. When in broad daylight I open my eyes, it is not in my power to choose whether I shall see or no, or to determine what particular objects shall present themselves to my view; and so likewise as to the hearing and other senses, the ideas imprinted on them are not creatures of my will. There is therefore some other will or spirit that produces them.

The ideas of sense are more strong, lively, and distinct than those of the imagination; they have likewise a steadiness, order, and coherence, and are not excited at random, as those which are the effects of human wills often are, but in a regular train or series, the admirable connexion whereof sufficiently testifies the wisdom and benevolence of its Author. Now the set rules or established methods, wherein the mind we depend on excites in us the ideas of sense, are called the *Laws of Nature:* and these we learn by experience, which teaches us that such and such ideas are attended with such and such other ideas, in the ordinary course of things. . . .

The ideas imprinted on the senses by the Author of Nature are called *real things:* and those excited in the imagination, being less regular, vivid, and constant, are more properly termed *ideas,* or *images of things,* which they copy and represent. But then our sensations, be they never so vivid and distinct, are nevertheless *ideas,* that is, they exist in the mind, or are perceived by it, as truly as the ideas of its own framing. The ideas of sense are allowed to have more reality in them, that is, to be more strong, orderly, and coherent than the creatures of the mind; but this is no argument that they exist without the mind. They are also less dependent on the spirit or thinking substance which perceives them, in that they are excited by the will of another and more powerful spirit: yet still they are *ideas,* and certainly no idea, whether faint or strong, can exist otherwise than in a mind perceiving it. . . .

If any man thinks this detracts from the existence or reality of things, he is very far from understanding what hath been premised in the plainest terms I could think of. Take here an abstract of what has been said. There are spiritual substances, minds or human souls, which will or excite ideas in themselves at pleasure: but these are faint, weak, and unsteady in respect of others they perceive by sense, which being impressed upon them according to certain Rules or Laws of Nature, speak themselves the effects of a mind more powerful and wise than human spirits. These latter are said to have more *reality* in them than the former: by which is meant that they are more affecting, orderly, and distinct, and that they are not fictions of the mind perceiving them. And in this sense, the sun that I see by day is the real sun, and that which I imagine by night is the idea of the former. In the sense here given of 'reality,' it is evident that every vegetable, star, mineral, and in general each part of the mundane system, is as much a real being by our principles as by any other. Whether others mean anything by the term 'reality' different from what I do, I entreat them to look into their own thoughts and see.

It will be urged that thus much at least is true, to wit, that we take away all corporeal substances. To this my answer is, that if the word 'substance' be taken in the vulgar sense, for a combination of sensible qualities, such as extension, solidity, weight, and the like: this we cannot be accused of taking away. But if it be taken in a philosophic sense, for the support of accidents or qualities without the mind: then indeed I acknowledge that we take it away, if one may be said to take away that which never had any existence, not even in the imagination.

DAVID HUME

THE EMPIRICAL GROUNDS
OF CAUSAL REASONING

It is evident that all reasonings concerning *matter of fact* are founded on the relation of cause and effect, and that we can never infer the existence of one object from another unless they be connected together, either mediately or immediately. In order, therefore, to understand these reasonings we must be perfectly acquainted with the idea of a cause; and in order to do that, we must look about us to find something that is the cause of another.

Here is a billiard ball lying on the table, and another ball moving toward it with rapidity. They strike; and the ball which was formerly at rest now acquires a motion. This is as perfect an instance of the relation of cause and effect as any which we know either by sensation or reflection. Let us therefore examine it. It is evident that the two balls touched one another before the motion was communicated, and that there was no interval betwixt the shock and the motion. *Contiguity* in time and place is therefore a requisite circumstance to the operation of all causes. It is evident, likewise, that the motion which was the cause

SOURCE: An *Inquiry Concerning Human Understanding* by David Hume, © 1955. Reprinted by permission of Prentice-Hall, Inc., Upper Saddle River, NJ.

is prior to the motion which was the effect. *Priority* in time is, therefore, another requisite circumstance in every cause. But this is not all. Let us try any other balls of the same kind in a like situation, and we shall always find that the impulse of the one produces motion in the other. Here, therefore, is a *third* circumstance, viz., that of a *constant conjunction* betwixt the cause and effect. Every object like the cause produces always some object like the effect. Beyond these three circumstances of contiguity, priority, and constant conjunction I can discover nothing in this cause. The first ball is in motion, touches the second, immediately the second is in motion and when I try the experiment with the same or like balls, in the same or like circumstances, I find that upon the motion and touch of the one ball motion always follows in the other. In whatever shape I turn this matter, and however I examine it, I can find nothing further.

This is the case when both the cause and effect are present to the senses. Let us now see upon what our inference is founded when we conclude from the one that the other has existed or will exist. Suppose I see a ball moving in a straight line toward another—I immediately conclude that they will shock, and that the second will be in motion. This is the inference from cause to effect, and of this nature are all our reasonings in the conduct of life; on this is founded all our belief in history, and from hence is derived all philosophy excepting only geometry and arithmetic. If we can explain the inference from the shock of the two balls we shall be able to account for this operation of the mind in all instances.

Were a man such as Adam created in the full vigor of understanding, without experience, he would never be able to infer motion in the second ball from the motion and impulse of the first. It is not anything that reason sees in the cause which makes us *infer* the effect. Such an inference, were it possible, would amount to a demonstration, as being founded merely on the comparison of ideas. But no inference from cause to effect amounts to a demonstration. Of which there is this evident proof. The mind can always *conceive* any effect to follow from any cause, and indeed any event to follow upon another; whatever we *conceive* is possible, at least in a metaphysical sense; but wherever a demonstration takes place the contrary is impossible and implies a contradiction. There is no demonstration, therefore, for any conjunction of cause and effect. And this is a principle which is generally allowed by philosophers.

It would have been necessary, therefore, for Adam (if he was not inspired) to have had *experience* of the effect which followed upon the impulse of these two balls. He must have seen in several instances that when the one ball struck upon the other, the second always acquired motion. If he had seen a sufficient number of instances of this kind, whenever he saw the one ball moving toward the other, he would always conclude without hesitation that the second would acquire motion. His understanding would anticipate his sight and form a conclusion suitable to his past experience.

It follows, then, that all reasonings concerning cause and effect are founded on experience, and that all reasonings from experience are founded on the supposition that the course of nature will continue uniformly the same. We conclude that like causes, in like circumstances, will always produce like effects. It may now be worth while to consider what determines us to form a conclusion of such infinite consequence.

It is evident that Adam, with all his science, would never have been able to *demonstrate* that the course of nature must continue uniformly the same, and that the future must be conformable to the past. What is possible can never be demonstrated to be false; and it is possible the course of nature may change, since we can conceive such a change. Nay, I will go further and assert that he could not so much as prove by any *probable* arguments that the future must be conformable to the past. All probable arguments are built on the supposition that there is this conformity betwixt the future and the past, and therefore [he] can never prove it. This conformity is a *matter of fact,* and if it must be proved will admit of no proof but from experience. But our experience in the past can be a proof of nothing for the future but upon a supposition that there is a resemblance betwixt them. This, therefore, is a point which can admit of no proof at all, and which we take for granted without any proof.

We are determined by *custom* alone to suppose the future conformable to the past. When I see a billiard ball moving toward another, my mind is immediately carried by habit to the usual effect, and anticipates my sight by conceiving the second ball in motion. There is nothing in these objects—abstractly considered, and independent of experience—which leads me to form any such conclusion: and even after I have had experience of many repeated effects of this kind, there is no argument which determines me to suppose that the effect will be conformable to past experience. The powers by which bodies operate are entirely unknown. We perceive only their sensible qualities—and what *reason* have we to think that the same powers will always be conjoined with the same sensible qualities?

It is not, therefore, reason which is the guide of life, but custom. That alone determines the mind in all instances to suppose the future conformable to the past. However easy this step may seem, reason would never, to all eternity, be able to make it.

PRACTICE

MATTHEW LIPMAN

THE PHILOSOPHER AS ELEMENTARY SCHOOL TEACHER: EPISTEMOLOGY APPLIED TO FOURTH-GRADE EDUCATION

My first experience in the teaching of philosophy occurred at Brooklyn College in 1953. The following year I began doing the same thing at Columbia University. I was to remain at Columbia for eighteen years, and at the City University of New York for twenty-two years. During the greater portion of that time, I taught philosophy pretty much the way it had been taught to me when I was a college student. I took the conditions of education for granted. It was only very gradually that I began to question the appropriateness of what I was doing.

The 1960s was a decade of unrest, and the rate at which doubts began to seep in soon accelerated. By the time of the Columbia riots in 1968, I had begun to suspect that much of what I was trying to teach my students either already knew or couldn't make relevant to their lives. The remainder that I had to offer them was simply too little and too late.

The aftermath of the riots was highly instructive. The university had shown itself to be a marvelous institution of maximum internal diversity within a framework of minimal adaptability. What was lacking was a process of internal self-correction that would keep it flexible, and neither the administration nor the faculty nor the students were able to contrive ways of introducing such flexibility. There was no hope for reform from within, I concluded. We all shared the same unquestioned assumptions, and, by and large, we all thought too much alike. Something was needed to change our thinking—to open it up and free it—but this would have to start much, much earlier, perhaps in elementary school.

On the few occasions on which I had happened to discuss philosophical ideas with young acquaintances—my own children and their friends—I found them eager and inquisitive, especially the ten- to twelve-year-olds. I began to wonder if such an age level might not be the best at which to start. It was only much later that I realized how much earlier it was necessary to begin.

Portions of this paper are reprinted with permission of Temple University Press from Matthew Lipman, *Philosophy Goes to School*. Philadelphia: Temple University Press, 1988. Portions are also reprinted with permission of the publisher from Matthew Lipman, "Sessions with Pixie in P.S. 87: A Classroom Log," *Analytic Teaching*, Vol. 3, No. 1 (November–December 1982).

Matthew Lipman attended Stanford and Columbia universities and was then professor of philosophy at Columbia for eighteen years. Since 1972 he has been professor of philosophy at Montclair State University, where he also directs the Institute for the Advancement of Philosophy for Children. He has been a Fulbright scholar to the Sorbonne and recipient of a three-year study grant from the Rockefeller Foundation. He is the author of eleven books and the coauthor of six others. His books have been translated and published in ten languages.

My first thought was to write a story portraying a group of children discovering logic. In this way, I told myself, a child reading the story might learn some of the principles of logic and become a better reasoner. After I had written a few pages, however, I saw that it would take a book containing a number of chapters in order to present, in the unpretentious language of children, the logic contained in my introductory course for college students.

Another alarming thought was that children would be bored by a book dealing only with reasoning. They would want something to reason about, something of intellectual substance that they could "get their teeth into." For this purpose, I concluded, nothing could be better than philosophy. After all, the ideas contained in the vast philosophical heritage were all contestable ideas, inviting controversy and argument. At the same time, they were of the greatest importance, including all the ideals to which human beings had ever aspired. Good! I would write *Harry Stottlemeier's Discovery,* and I would include in it the discovery by fictional children of ethical notions, epistemological notions, metaphysical and aesthetic notions—all of which interested children, I suspected, but about which they were afraid—or simply too uninformed—to ask.

And so the first children's philosophical novel was written, and it was followed, over the next decade or so, by five others for children of various ages. Accompanying each of these books was a huge manual for teachers, crammed with discussion plans, activities, and games that would strengthen the reasoning and conceptual skills of the students. The philosophical substance of the novels was derived largely from the classroom discussions I had had with college students. The children were invited to discuss questions similar to those philosophers had always discussed: Can we trust our senses? Is our knowledge of the world reliable? Are relationships real? What are qualities?

Questions such as these have to do with the nature of human knowledge. As such, they belong to that branch of philosophy known as *epistemology*. Now, there is no branch of philosophy which I believe to be necessarily beyond the reach of children, but epistemology would seem to be particularly useful to them. Their intense curiosity about the world is often accompanied by an intense scepticism about their own ability to know. They are quite aware of the frequency with which they must admit to not knowing. This in turn suggests that a greater familiarity on their part with epistemology might have important consequences for their education.

Such, at any rate, was my reasoning. My hypothesis was that the application of epistemology to education could be a very beneficial step. In one sense, there was nothing new in the idea: for many years, philosophers of education had routinely included epistemology in the philosophical preparation of teachers. What was new in what I was advocating was the utilization of philosophy by the children themselves in the furtherance of their own education.

Applied philosophy is an enterprise in which philosophy is used to solve "practical problems." If my understanding of the phrase "practical problems" was correct, it meant "problems of practice," and this included educational practice. In this sense I could recognize in what I was doing—providing children with the philosophical tools to become critically reflective about their own education and thereby helping them become more reasonable beings—a clear instance of applied philosophy.

The first of the philosophical children's novels, *Harry Stottlemeier's Discovery,* was written in 1969; the fifth, *Pixie,* for children of about nine years of age, was written in 1980. Pixie is a complex little girl—inquisitive, naive, pushy, manipulative, reflective, and analytical. The book is, as she carefully observes, not her story itself, but the story of how her story came to be. It is the history of her writing a story she never reveals to us.

Early in 1982 I decided I needed to get some firsthand experience in the teaching of *Pixie. Pixie* had been published the previous year and was already in use in a number of school districts. Since I wasn't getting much feedback from the teachers, I decided to offer an abbreviated course in *Pixie* to some fourth graders. The school I selected was P.S. 87, in Manhattan. The principal, Naomi Hill, was hospitable to the idea, and the classroom teacher, Gloria Goldberg, made me feel quite welcome. I promised to arrive at nine o'clock every Thursday, and to stay for thirty or forty minutes. I knew I could hardly accomplish much in so short a time: *Pixie* would normally be offered for three forty-five-minute sessions a week for the entire school year. In all, I was able to manage only twelve sessions, during which time we read the first six chapters and the last episode in the seventh.

The fourth graders, being from the West Side of Manhattan, were a highly diversified group. A few struggled with the reading, while others read with the pacing and expression of adults. Several were just becoming familiar with English. Some were bold and outspoken, while others were timorous or silent. Indeed, on one occasion in which we were "going around the room" with a series of questions, one frail, anxious little girl burst into tears when it was finally her turn to answer. But generally there were lots of hands up during discussions, and I felt satisfied that they understood the material in *Pixie,* and that most of them seemed to enjoy it.

The accounts of each session were written from memory after each session, and since no audiotapes were made, it would be difficult to check their accuracy. But this is of little importance: what matters is whether regular classroom teachers succeed in using *Pixie* to cultivate the thinking skills of their pupils and generally to enhance their students' powers of reflection. Having tested the waters a bit, I concluded the experiment feeling encouraged.

I would like to offer some relevant parts of my log from that period as descriptive evidence of what it can be like to do philosophy with children. Since the classroom discussion often revolved about topics originally stimulated by the children's reading of *Pixie* but then developed by means of exercises from the instructional manual, I think it may be useful to intersperse the reading of the log with consideration of a few of these exercises.

The philosophy that takes place in this classroom makes use of ordinary language and avoids as much as possible the technical terminology of traditional academic philosophy. But the question that is bound to be asked is this: to what extent are these children doing *real* philosophy? That is, to what extent are the children's conversations representative of what takes place in traditional philosophical discussions? Are the conceptual problems similar? Are the logical moves similar? If philosophical dialogue among adults generally results in some matters becoming clarified while others turn out to be murkier than previously suspected, does the same thing happen when children engage in dialogue? Readers will have to judge these matters for themselves, but such judgments require the presentation of alleged similarities or correspondences between professional philosophy and philosophy done with children. To facilitate this kind of inquiry on the reader's part, I have some classic texts (by René Descartes, John Locke, George Berkeley, and David Hume) at the beginning of this chapter, as well as some explanatory remarks interspersed at relevant points. I should like to add that the *sequence* of ideas encountered as Pixie unfolds her story cannot be expected to correspond to the historical sequence of philosophical developments that took place when Locke responded to Descartes' philosophy and Berkeley and Hume responded to Locke's; however, many of Pixie's ideas themselves are derived from these philosophers.

Here, then, are epistemological parts of the journal I kept, together with some of the exercises I made use of with the class. In addition to the explications of the foregoing readings from Descartes, Locke, Berkeley, and Hume I have occasionally referred the reader to the works of other philosophers whose ideas more closely match Pixie's own.

January 28, 1982

Class read Chapter 2 from beginning to end. We then discussed it a page at a time. I would ask, "What interests you on this page?" "Is there anything written on this page that you'd like to talk about?" In either case, the comment was put on the board.

The exercises matched the conversation very well. The first problem raised was that of possibility, and they were interested in noting that everything was not possible, but that it was possible to think about things that were not possible—at least some things.

EXERCISE: Is everything possible?

1. Is it possible to think your best friend's thoughts?
2. Is it possible to think of a river that runs uphill?
3. Is it possible to think of a circle that's really a square?
4. Is it possible for a cat to give birth to puppies?
5. Is it possible for there to be a sound without anyone to hear it?
6. Is it possible for Monday to be the day after Tuesday?
7. Is it possible for there to be a thought without someone to think it?
8. Is it possible that you are now dreaming that you are awake?
9. Is it possible that you are now on the moon?
10. Is everything possible?

The passage about Pixie's foot falling asleep was cited. Conversation went like this:

—Can your foot be asleep but you remain awake?
—Yes.
—Can both your feet be asleep but you remain awake?
—Yes.
—Can both your feet and both your arms be asleep but you remain awake?
—Yes.
—Can your whole body be asleep but your head be awake?
—Yes.
—How about the other way around? Can your head be asleep and your whole body awake?
—(boy in back row) Sure, when a person is sleepwalking.

The class is here beginning to explore what we mean when we say we are "awake" and "asleep." It is a distinction which ancient philosophers were aware could have important consequences for human knowledge. (Thus Heraclitus remarks, "Those awake have one ordered universe in common, but in sleep every man turns away to one of his own.") Nor can we fail to note that this is precisely where Descartes starts, just a few paragraphs after the beginning of his *First Meditation.*

Descartes wants to know what we as human beings are capable of knowing. To accomplish this, he deliberately engages in systematically doubting everything he had learned, everything reported to him by his senses, everything produced by his own mental processes. He is not just being negative. He is trying to find out if there is anything at all that can resist this corrosive scepticism. If it should turn out that there is something that cannot be doubted—or, more precisely, something whose existence does not become problematical just because we question it—then that something may be able to serve as the foundation for all our knowledge.

As we go through the first two *Meditations,* we learn that Descartes did indeed discover something which he took to be beyond all doubt—namely, his own thinking. No matter how badly mistaken our thinking may be, it is still thinking—of this he felt totally assured. He also felt secure in the next step he took, which was to infer, from the fact that thinking was taking place, that he existed. (Many a philosopher since Descartes has questioned whether "I think" can be inferred from the fact that thinking is occurring, or that "I exist" follows necessarily from "I think.")

Having determined to his own satisfaction that he is a "thing that thinks," and that a thing that thinks is a thing "which doubts, understands, conceives, affirms, denies, wills, refuses" as well as imagines and feels, Descartes turns his attention to what may lie outside himself. He examines a piece of wax, virtually all of whose properties change once it is warmed by the fire. Yet it remains "extended" and must therefore be an extended thing, as he must be a thinking thing. What is more, it is his *mind,* specifically his judgment, which enables him to ascertain that the wax of a few moments ago and the wax of this present moment, so different in appearance, are in reality one and the same piece of wax.

These then are the indubitable foundations of human knowledge, Descartes tells us. By methodically engaging in scepticism, he believes that he has succeeded in refuting scepticism. Our knowledge, when founded on what the mind itself is certain of, is therefore founded on bedrock, Descartes claims, and we can be confident of its reliability.

Before we leave Descartes, there is another of his contentions that we may want to consider. He has suggested that his body is an extended thing, like the piece of wax. Bodies are extended in space and do not think. Only minds think. He therefore identifies himself with his mind. But what then is the relationship between the mind and the body? This is the vexatious question which Descartes bequeathed to succeeding generations of philosophers.

Another conversation proceeded in this fashion:

On page 2, line 4, Miranda sees the cat chasing its tail. When you look at yourself in the mirror, is that like a cat chasing its tail?

No, the cat's chasing its body, but when I look in the mirror, I see the *appearance* of my body. (Natasha?)

Well, okay. But how about this? Is a cat chasing its tail like a kite flying in circles?

The kite has a tail, just like the cat (girl in middle).

They're not the same, because the cat chases its tail *intentionally* (boy at front table).

It is obvious that the boy at the front table has at this point made a claim of considerable importance. He notes that both the cat and the kite move in circles, but says that the cat does so *intentionally* while the kite does not. While it is tempting to pause and dwell on this distinction, momentous as it is for distinguishing persons from things (compare Descartes' description of minds and bodies), it is necessary to note something else in the discussion: the reference to *appearance.* The girl who makes the remark evidently wants her classmates to recognize that what is seen in the mirror is not the body, but only its appearance, as distinguishable from the palpable reality of the body itself.

Now this distinction between Appearance and Reality again had ancient roots, and the reader of Plato's *Republic* will find a very concise statement of it in chapter 24, where Plato distinguishes between the merely apparent, perceivable world revealed by our senses, and the reality of Forms grasped by the mind. When Locke constructs his own theory of knowledge, some fifty years after Descartes, he concedes that our senses do not reveal the world as it "really" is: our senses can merely fill the mind with copies that *represent* the external, material universe. Locke ends his *Essay* sceptical about our ever achieving knowledge of reality, although he had started out with high hopes of showing how sound our knowledge was.

Let's go back to the question Descartes raised having to do with the trustworthiness of our knowledge. Is what the mind knows real, Descartes asks, and even if it is, does the mind really know it? Now, what is it the mind knows? One group of philosophers, those known as *empiricists,* contended that the mind could know only what the senses reported to it, because the senses are the only channels through which we are in touch with the outside world. In contrast, those called *rationalists* (of which Descartes was one) maintained that the senses were unreliable, and that the foundations of knowledge had to be formed by the mind.

As he proceeded with the writing of the *Essay,* Locke ran into a number of stumbling-blocks which he was unable to bypass. He saw them as permanent limitations upon our knowledge of the external world. And yet, Locke felt, they are only of minor consequence: our knowledge may not be perfect, but it is good enough for all our purposes.

One of the chief difficulties Locke encountered was the result of his attempting to formulate a representational theory of knowledge. Such a theory would explain, he felt, how the ideas in the mind were accurate copies of the things in the world. Thus we each have in our minds a little world of ideas that more or less faithfully represents the external world of material things.

When you observe a tree, what actually occurs, Locke maintains, is that the tree causes your eyes to transmit a tree-like image which is flashed within the mind. What you really observe, then, is not the tree itself, but the representation or copy of the tree. The mind is not in touch with the world in any direct sense; it can only entertain and examine the representations of the world transmitted to it by the senses. The tree is the cause, the copy of the tree in our minds is the effect. Yet we observe only the effect, we do not observe the cause; we observe only the copy, we can never observe the original. Hence we can never be absolutely sure that our copies are true copies, and this is a primary reason why a shade of doubt is cast upon all our knowledge, if we accept the copy theory Locke proposes.

There is another problem that must be mentioned here, stemming from Locke's distinction between "primary and secondary qualities." By primary qualities, Locke says he means solidity, extension, figure, motion or rest, and number—qualities he considers inseparable from material bodies. Secondary qualities, he says are powers in objects themselves "to produce various sensations in us by their primary qualities," sensations such as colors, sounds, and tastes. But while primary qualities produce ideas that resemble their original causes, secondary qualities do not. The ideas of color, sound, odor, and taste do not resemble anything in objects themselves. They are solely in our minds. Thus the real world, according to Locke, consists of matter in motion; it consists of solid, extended, measureable shapes, but it is devoid of colors, sounds, and odors. We delude ourselves when we think the rose is really red and has a lovely scent: it has the power to arouse these ideas in us, but the redness our mind contemplates corresponds to nothing in the rose itself.

If the material objects in the world are the causes of nonmaterial ideas in our minds, what assurance do we have that the ideas resemble those objects? Do effects generally resemble their causes? It would not appear to be the case, with the result that we have no basis for believing that the ideas of things necessarily resemble those things. We are left with having to take that resemblance on faith, or disbelieving in it completely.

> *February 4, 1982*
>
> Class read whole of chapter 3. Good discussion of first half of chapter. We talked about "reading faces." They claimed that you could read someone's face and tell what that person was feeling. I asked if what the person *said* was ever different from what could be read in that person's face. Yes, they agreed. In that case, I asked, what do you do? One girl answered, "In that case, I always trust what I read in the face."
>
> Another discussion dealt with falsity, the occasion being Pixie's father's proposal to give her false teeth. I asked if a mask was a false face. Someone said, a false face yes, but a real mask.

One of the major aims of epistemology, of course, is to distinguish *truth* from *falsity.* You will also recall, having read Descartes' *Meditations,* that he is intensely disturbed by the possibility that the images aroused in him by his senses, like those in dreams, may be simply false. This leads him to doubt methodically and to doubt everything. But then he discovers that the more he doubts, the more undeniable it is that doubting is going on. Since doubt exists, then thinking *must* exist, and if there is thinking going on, then he *must* exist as its thinker. It is at this point that Descartes abandons his sceptical stance and affirms that, while we may not know everything, what we know we know for certain.

The children in my classroom had arrived at no stage of their inquiry in which their knowledge was beyond dispute. Indeed, they were just beginning to consider the variety of circumstances under which statements might be called *true* or *false*. Here is one of the exercises used at this point:

DISCUSSION PLAN: When is something false?

1. If a person has an artificial eye, do we call it a "false" eye?
2. If a person has artificial teeth, do we say he has "false" teeth?
3. Can you think of any circumstances under which you might call the front of a building false?
4. Can you think of any circumstances under which you might call a vegetable false?
5. Can words be false?
6. Can questions be false?
7. Can exclamations be false?
8. Can sentences be false?
9. Is there any difference between being false and being wrong?
10. Is there any difference between being false and being incorrect?
11. Is a false friend an unfaithful friend?
12. Is there anything false about wearing eyeglasses?
13. Is there anything false about wearing a wig?
14. Is a mask a false face?
15. If a person is carrying a stolen driver's license, does that make it a false driver's license?

February 11, 1982

We talked about relationships that could be observed and those that could not be observed. They were clear about family relationships (that being a cousin or a nephew was not observable) but less clear about the perceivability of "being taller than" or "far from."

We did an exercise on family relationships. One child was taken in by the question, "If two brothers each have a sister, does that mean they have two sisters?" However, other members of the class explained the correct answer to her.

Finally I asked, "if your parents had no children, does that mean you probably won't have any?" One student said (with agreement from several others), "if your parents had no children, you wouldn't exist." To which one student responded, "You could if you had been adopted." Shows their ability to examine a question carefully, see what it presupposes, and to give counter-examples.

February 24, 1982

Today students returned their homework (writing the beginnings to a story whose ending had been given to them). We then read pp. 29–31, and discussed p. 29.

Many theories of what happens to the light when you turn off the switch. Does the light "go out?" If not, what happens to it? I asked if dark was the absence of light. Puzzlement. I asked if cold was the absence of heat. More puzzlement. I asked if dark was to light as cold was to heat. Some tentative assent. I contrasted that sentence (written on board) with "hands are like feet." I asked how hands were like feet (they said fingers, toes, etc.). I asked them to complete the sentence "Hands are like feet as _____." Here a flock of hands went up:

"as one nostril is to the other nostril"
"as elbows are to knees"
"as your upper lip is to your lower lip"
"as your left hand is to your right hand"

(Notice that most of them are similarities of appearance; the elbow-knees comparison is a similarity of *function*. This one came from James.)

I didn't identify "simile" and "analogy" as the names of the two types of comparisons, but we contrasted them, and they seemed to understand the difference. Molly said that the analogy was a statement that said one *relationship* was like another.

With Mollie's introduction of the word "relationship," as well as her acute perception that analogies state the similarity of one relationship to another, we find ourselves at a new stage of epistemological investigation, both in the class I was conducting and in the development of modern theories of knowledge. Both rationalists and empiricists find *relationships* an indispensable notion. For empiricists, what is of critical importance is the relationship of *correspondence* between ideas in the mind and things in the world. For rationalists, what is critical is the relationship of *consistency* among ideas. Rationalists maintain that one-to-one correspondence of things and ideas cannot assure that the resultant knowledge will be *coherent;* it could instead be chaotic.

Although rationalists may concede that we are put in touch with things by means of our senses, they would still argue that our knowledge is not of things but of the relationships among things. They prefer to see every intellectual discipline as a study of relationships: geometry of geometrical relationships, physics of physical relationships, chemistry of chemical relationships, and so on. To all of this, hard-core empiricists would reply with a snort, "Relationships! They aren't real and objective! They're only in the mind!" And so rationalists and empiricists, while agreeing that relationships are important, often disagree about their subjectivity or objectivity.

When Molly proposed that an analogy was a relationship between two relationships, she moved the level of class discussion to a higher level. Now we could talk about distinguishing not merely between things but between relationships as well. After all, to be able to approach analogical reasoning critically, students would have to be able to perceive differences among relationships as well as similarities. I wish I could say that I recognized this opportunity immediately and capitalized upon it by introducing a variety of exercises relevant to Molly's suggestion. But I must have realized that most of the class was still unsure about relationships, to say nothing of relationships among relationships. I therefore had the class do a few comparison exercises. Fortunately, some weeks later, the whole question of analogies erupted again, and I was able to get into the topic in much greater detail.

As we notice toward the close of the Locke selection, Locke distinguishes between simple and complex ideas (complex ideas being composed by the mind out of simple ones), and he distinguishes three kinds of complex ideas: modes, substances, and relationships (or "relations," as he calls them). As he puts it, "*relation* . . . consists in the consideration and comparing one idea with another." In order to give the students some practice in recognizing relationships as well as types of relationships, we did some of this exercise:

EXERCISE: Relationships in the form of comparisons

Whenever we compare two things, we are saying that the two things have a certain relationship to one another. If we say that France is older than the United States, we are comparing the two countries with respect to age.

Comparisons can be classified in many different ways, such as comparisons of weight, of color, of feelings, of value, and so on. A number of such classes are given below, with examples of each kind. See how many more examples of each kind you can think up.

FAMILY	TIME	VALUE	SPACE
is a cousin of	is later than	is better than	is farther away than
is a sister of	is earlier than	is superior to	is closer than
is the father of	is the day before	is worth more than	is larger than
is the aunt of	is the day after	is cheaper than	is rounder than
is the wife of	is slower than	is no better than	is more angular than

TOUCH	TASTE	SOUND	COLOR
is softer than	is more bitter than	is louder than	is bluer than
is rougher than	is sweeter than	is softer than	is redder than
is fluffier than	is saltier than	is more shrill than	is more purple than
is smoother than	is tastier than	is more harsh than	is lighter than
is greasier than	is more sour than	is more on key than	is darker than

WEIGHT	FEELINGS	ACTIONS	CHARACTER
is heavier than	is happier than	is clumsier than	is more stubborn than
is lighter than	is angrier than	is more restless than	is more courageous than

CAUSE-EFFECT	MEANS-END	PART-WHOLE	CLASS-MEMBERS
is the cause of	is designed to	is part of	is a member of
is the result of	is intended to	participated in	belongs to the class of
brings about	is meant to	is involved in	is a
makes	is made so that	belong to	is one of

March 18, 1982

The class read the last episode of chapter 5. "Is there anything on page 33 that interests you?" Yes. "*Far* and *near* are space relationships." This launched a lengthy discussion of the way a relational term might stand for a relationship in the way that a noun might stand for a thing. It seemed to be a good time to introduce the "cat" exercise on words and things.

EXERCISE: Words and things

1. Is "word" a word?
2. Is the word "cat" a cat?
3. Are cats words?
4. Is "cats" a word?
5. Does the word "cat" have fur?
6. Is this a cat—or a picture of a cat?
7. Is this a cat—or a picture of a cat?
8. Is "cat" a word—or a picture of a word?
9. Is a word—or a picture of the word "word" ?
10. Is this a picture of a cat—or a picture of a picture of a cat?
11. This is a cat from the other side. What does a word look like from the other side?
12. What is the relationship between cats and the word "cat"?
13. What is the relationship between words and the word "word?"

I asked, writing the word "cat" on the board, "What is this?" "A cat." "A cat? Does it have fur and claws and does it purr?" "No, it's the *word* for cat," they said. I drew a cat on the board. "What's this?" "A cat." "Is it?" I asked. This time they're more cautious. Someone says, "It's a *picture* of a cat!" "Oh," I said, and drew a frame around the illustration. "So what's this?" "That's a picture of a picture of a cat," they said.

We then discussed whether names *describe* the things they *stand for* or *refer to* or *mean*. We took up classification relationships, ranging from animals through cats through (their suggestions) calico cats and so on down to individually named cats. We discussed "being a kind of" as a relationship.

The session ended with a consideration of a comparison of relationships (Puppies are to dogs as kittens are to cats) contrasted with a comparison of things (puppies are like kittens), and with my identifying the two kinds of things as respectively *analogies* and *similes*.

The foregoing discussion had reached a critical juncture when the students disagreed as to whether the drawing on the board was a cat or a picture of a cat. The direction which the conversation actually took was toward further exploration of the notion of relationships. But a little reflection on the children's disagreement would be sufficient to show that the class was, in effect, dividing into two groups, one of whom identified the drawing as a representation of a cat, and the other of whom called it a cat. To the philosophical descendants of the rationalists, known as *idealists,* the copy or representational theory of knowledge that Locke advocated was totally wrong. The ideas in our minds are not copies of anything at all. Since we can know only what is in our minds, and our minds contain only ideas, then what we call things are nothing but combinations of ideas. Hence things exist in the mind, not outside the mind. In fact, the idealists argued, Locke himself had opened the door to this epistemological approach when he said that primary qualities alone were copies; secondary qualities were not copies of anything.

So Locke had asserted the existence of a material world existing outside the mind, and had claimed that primary qualities, like figure, size, and shape, were copies of material things. It was precisely upon these two of Locke's claims that George Berkeley was to fasten some twenty years later, in 1710. Berkeley denied the existence of a material world existing outside the mind, and if this were so, then there were no material things of which ideas could be copies. The only things we can say really exist, Berkeley insists, are the things we perceive. Now what is it we perceive? We can perceive nothing but our own ideas, Berkeley insists. What we mean by *perception* is not a process by which the senses observe the images presented it by the senses. The mind is like a prisoner who has spent all his life in a room equipped with a variety of television sets. He may fantasize that the images he sees on the various screens correspond to material objects existing in an outside world, but there is absolutely no way he can be sure of this. The names applied to things would in fact apply only to the images he observes, not to unobserved things that allegedly correspond to those images. Hence Berkeley's conclusion that there is no such thing as matter, and everything is made of ideas.

Berkeley believes his formulation of the knowledge process is more simple and economical than Locke's account. He thinks that the notion of matter is superfluous, because matter has never been observed, and therefore cannot be shown to exist. By focusing on just what the senses report to us and by abandoning the presupposition of a material, external world, Berkeley believes he has devised a presentational rather than a representational theory of knowledge, founded on a consistent and thoroughgoing empiricism.

March 25, 1982

[Among other things] we talked about Pixie's question (asked of her sleeping mother, whose eyelid Pixie has lifted up), "Momma, are you in there?" "A person isn't *inside* her body, she *is* her body," said Natasha. I asked whether their friend is in the room with them when their friend's voice comes into the room through the telephone. They said yes; one said that we go as far as our senses. I asked, "Do we go as far as our drawings and paintings? Are they part of us too?" "Yes," they said. But Saskia proceeded to remark, "There are two things here. There's the you that's your body and there are the things you make or do." This is the discussion plan I used in the course of this conversation:

DISCUSSION PLAN: *Where are we?*

Pixie says, "Momma, are you in there?"

1. Is Pixie's mother inside her body?
2. If Pixie were to look in her mother's eyes when her mother is awake, would Pixie then see her mother?
3. Would it be a good analogy to say, "A person lives in his body the way people live in their houses?"
4. When we wake up in the morning, would it make sense for us to say, as we open our eyes, "World, are you out there?"
5. Would it be sensible for Pixie to call out, when she hears a knock on the door, "Isabel, are you out there?"
6. Is it possible that a person is *neither* inside his body nor outside his body?
7. Is it possible that a person is *both* inside and outside his body?
8. When you talk to your friend, and you listen to your friend's voice on the telephone, is your friend's voice in your room?
9. If your friend's voice is in your room, is your friend in your room?
10. Think of your room at home. Is it now in your mind? If so, is it now in school?

May 6, 1982

We script-read pp. 40–42, and after some discussion of the individual examples of analogies given in the chapter, we proceeded to the "Review Exercise" called "Evaluating analogies."

REVIEW EXERCISE: Evaluating analogies

In this exercise, you are to give grades to the analogies, based on the following scale:

A = very good
B = good
C = okay, neither bad nor good
D = poor
E = unacceptable

Be prepared to give a reason for the grade you assign.

1. Thoughts are to thinkers as shoes are to shoemakers.
2. Giggling is to laughing as whimpering is to crying.
3. Pins are to pinning as needles are to needling.
4. Pins are to pinheads as needles are to needle eyes.
5. Bread is to puddles as butter is to rain.
6. Words are to stories as seeds are to flowerbeds.
7. Ideas are to children as memories are to adults.
8. Trying to get someone else to think is like walking a dog.
9. Taking home a report card is like removing a Bandaid from an open wound.
10. Trying to listen to two different conversations at the same time is like trying to boil water in the refrigerator.
11. Trying to learn something from TV is like trying to learn something from skywriting.

12. Putting sauerkraut over your pizza is like putting chow mein in your milkshake.
13. Trying to reach someone by means of a test is like trying to put in a bicycle tire by means of a pressure gauge.
14. Chalk is to blackboard as pencil is to paper.
15. Older people are different from younger people in the same way that Americans are different from foreigners.

I asked the members of the class what they thought of "Thoughts are to thinkers as shoes are to shoemakers." Most of them thought it is a good analogy. Thinking to play devil's advocate, I asked what shoemakers made shoes out of. Leather, rubber, and glue, they said. And do thinkers make thoughts as shoemakers make shoes, I asked. Mollie said, Sure—out of other thoughts. I told her that her answer was wonderful.

What intrigued me about Mollie's answer was its similarity with Locke's contention that our "complex ideas" are composed of "simple ideas." Locke's notion of simple ideas was the counterpart of the simple and indivisible atoms of seventeenth-century physics. From there it must have seemed a plausible and obvious step for Locke to suppose that complex ideas (like beauty, gratitude, and the universe) were composed of simple ideas like the coldness of ice, the smell of a lily, and the taste of sugar, just as physical things are composed of irreducible tiny atoms. There is an enchanting purity to the claim made by Locke that complex wholes are composed of simple parts, and while it may be so, it need not be. Logicians warn us not to assume that what is true of the part must be true of the whole, or that what is true of the whole is also true of the part. And yet, as I turned the matter over in my mind, I couldn't help wondering if I was being fair to Mollie. After all, she hadn't introduced the notion of "simple and complex"—Locke did. Mollie had merely suggested that thoughts are *made of* (not the same as *comprised of*) other thoughts, and this presented the possibility that the mind is not finite but infinite, for every thought would need to have been made of other thoughts, and so on ad infinitum. Her hypothesis preoccupied me for some days afterward.

Our little class in philosophy was beginning to wind down, but I hoped that today we would at least be able to read through chapter 7 of *Pixie,* with the episode about Adam at the conclusion of it. Let me say something about this episode. It is drawn from some remarks by the Scottish philosopher David Hume. Though much impressed with Berkeley's reasoning, Hume remained unconvinced by it. Knowledge cannot be derived from thinking alone, Hume maintained. Something else is needed, and that something is *experience.* Given a variety of possible accounts of an event, we can decide only by experience which account is true. If a being such as Adam were to be suddenly created, fully rational but totally lacking in experience, he would be unable to distinguish between two explanations of an event, no matter how fantastic or preposterous we ourselves might consider them.

In like manner, the children in *Pixie* are led to invent a hypothetical Adam accompanying them on their bus trip to the zoo. They present Adam with two possible explanations of the origin of children: that they were once as big as mountains, but have been steadily shrinking, or that they were once extremely tiny, but have been steadily growing. On their face, these two hypotheses may seem equally bizarre and preposterous or, as the children put it, equally "unbelievable." It is experience alone which enables us to call the one hypothesis false and the other true.

Hume goes on, as the reader will note in the selection, to assert that reason alone can never establish the necessity of any causal explanation. The relationship between cause and effect is psychological and subjective. We are accustomed to note that a certain event is followed by another, and we infer that one is cause and the other effect. But we do not discover causality in nature: we come to believe in it due to our having observed certain pairs of events to be constantly conjoined. It is here that we must leave our brief glimpse of seventeenth- and eighteenth-century epistemology, with its brilliant but inconclusive forays into the nature of knowledge by Descartes, Locke, Berkeley, and Hume, just as we can now take a last look at the philosophy class in P.S. 87.

> We then script-read the last episode in chapter 7 (about Adam). They said they were interested in the notion of "the unbelievable." I asked if they could give me an example of something unbelievable. The little wisp of a girl in the front with straw-colored hair, Nora, replied, "War." This fairly staggered me, so I asked her to explain. "It's just so horrible," she replied, "it's just more than we can—" Is what she was trying to formulate this: that war is *unthinkable?* I failed to follow it up, because this interpretation didn't occur to me at the time.
>
> It's worthwhile pointing out, in passing, how often the first comment from the children is the most dramatic. The other comments so often take the lead of the first, but in a less original way; the first often has a breathtakingly original quality about it.
>
> We worked some more on whether unbelievable stories could be true ("fictional" was their word). One student brought in the notion of "tall tales" and we talked about Baron Munchausen a bit. At first, one or two students insisted that Adam would find the theory that we have grown *more* plausible than the one that we have shrunk. But we discussed the difficulty of this, considering such examples of the possible truth of implausible ideas as that "the sun doesn't rise." What I found difficult to elicit from the class was the notion that one doesn't select among ideas on the basis of their plausibility or implausibility, but on other grounds. What other grounds? It was not until the end of the hour, the very end, that Sara proposed "evidence." I figured that was close enough.
>
> *June 24, 1982*
>
> Returned today to pick up the post-tests. Since it was only 8:30, most of the students hadn't yet arrived. But as I passed the playground behind the school, I saw a baseball game in progress, and there was the indomitable Ashaki, wearing a bright-colored headband, on first base. As I turned away it came over me once again, but more powerfully and affectingly than ever, how little we know of children's intellectual capabilities, and how sure we are of their limitations.

DISCUSSION QUESTIONS

1. Why does Descartes believe that the senses are untrustworthy but the mind is reliable?

2. In what sense does Locke hold that the contents of the mind are representative of the world?

3. Why does Berkeley argue that, since the mind knows only ideas, the existence of matter cannot be proven?

4. What is Hume's basis for contending that, given several contrasting stories or accounts of an event, it is only our experience, and not our minds, which can distinguish the accounts that are true from those that are false?

5. It has been said that Descartes and Locke believe the world is made of two substances, but Berkeley believes it is made of only one. Do you agree with this statement? Explain.

6. Contrast Descartes and Hume with regard to the ability of the mind to judge the evidence received from the senses.

7. On what grounds does Berkeley claim that things are nothing but combinations of ideas?

8. Is it possible that neither the mind alone nor the senses alone can guarantee the reliability of human knowledge? Explain.

9. Since Berkeley is able to argue that the mind exists but not matter, how might someone argue that matter exists but not mind?

10. Comment on the following statement: "The material and the mental are distinguished *in* our experience; they therefore cannot be presumed to exist *prior to* our experience."

11. Comment on the following statement: "The objectivity of human knowledge is not a function of the mind *or* the senses, but of the method of inquiry."

12. What similarities, if any, do you notice between professional epistemology (such as that of Descartes, Locke, Berkeley, and Hume) and that of Lipman's fourth graders? What differences, if any, do you notice?

13. Can you point to anything in particular the children said which raises an epistemological issue? (Try to find examples not explicitly pointed out by Lipman.)

14. Do you think that children are more apt to be interested in epistemological issues than adults, or vice versa? Justify your answer.

15. After completing his work with the fourth graders, Lipman was struck "more powerfully and affectingly than ever, how little we know of children's intellectual capabilities, and how sure we are of their limitations." What exactly do you think Lipman is getting at here? What implications, if any, does what Lipman is saying have for elementary school education?

16. In your opinion, are there any good reasons for teaching epistemology to children? Defend your answer.

17. If you were able to make any changes in public education, what changes, if any, would you make? Defend your answer.

18. How would you define "education"?

V

MINDS AND MATTER

11

FREE WILL, DETERMINISM, AND PHILOSOPHICAL COUNSELING

In this chapter the philosophical problem of free will versus determinism will be addressed and related to the dynamics of psychotherapy. In the Practice section, these concepts will in turn be applied to a logic-based variant of philosophical counseling.

By "determinism" is meant the doctrine that every event in the universe, including human behavior, can at least in principle be explained and predicted according to causal laws. In this view, there is no such thing as "free will" or "autonomous action," if what is intended by these are spontaneous or uncaused events. The entire universe is lawful.

Few of us would question such lawfulness at the level of ordinary physical events. For example, when lighting a match under certain conditions (such as the presence of oxygen, the dryness of the match, the sufficient application of fiction) we suppose that a flame will occur. If the match fails to ignite, then we infer that something has gone wrong, that some condition necessary for its igniting was absent; and if the match does ignite, we suppose a sufficient causal basis. According to the determinist, the same is true of all human behavior, which always has a sufficient causal explanation and represents no gap in the lawfulness of the universe. When a human being "chooses" to do X rather than Y, the ensuing behavior is not the result of some spontaneous or uncaused volition that places the behavior outside the range of scientific explanation. If the volitional act exists at all, or is relevant to the outcome, it too can be accounted for by some causal law.

In the first selection of this chapter, excerpted from *Beyond Freedom and Dignity,* B. F. Skinner defends a particular brand of determinism called *behaviorism*. For Skinner, this is a methodological approach to psychology that emphasizes scientific control of behavior and that views mental events (volitions, desires, feelings, and the like) as causally inefficacious and therefore irrelevant to the scientific control of behavior. Behavior is not viewed as a mere "symptom" or effect of some private psychic state but rather as itself the primary data of psychology—data that can be scientifically studied, explained, and predicted.

According to Skinner, this science of behavior seeks to explain human behavior in terms of *environmental* conditions that lawfully determine it. For example, he tells us that young people drop out of school or refuse to get jobs
because of "defective social environments in homes, schools, factories, and elsewhere." By discovering the laws whereby human organisms interact with their
environments, a science of behavior can help to solve such social problems.

As Skinner himself acknowledges, a science that seeks to control the environment for purposes of solving social ills raises the problem of "who is to construct the controlling environment and to what end." The obvious danger here
is that such a science can fall into the hands of those who would use it for self-
serving ends. And what indeed would be the *correct* values to program? Moreover, those who recognize a right of self-determination, a right to make one's
own free choices without being manipulated or coerced by others, the attempt
to program particular values—even the "correct" ones—would be wholly unacceptable, even if such a program did solve social problems. Nonetheless, the
determinist would take this rejection to be based upon the false assumption
that human behavior can ever be self-determined in the first place.

A chief obstacle in the way of the advance of a science of behavior, argues
Skinner, has been our persistence in explaining human behavior in terms of
inner psychic life rather than in terms of external environmental conditions. If
human behavior emanates from a psychic life that is "free" or "autonomous"
(in the sense of being uncaused), a science of behavior is not possible. It is only
by relinquishing our belief in "autonomous man" that such a science can hope
to proceed.

Still, our belief in autonomous man is not so easily shaken since it is bound
up with other fundamental concepts and practices. According to Skinner, in the
traditional view, persons are "free" or "autonomous," and can therefore be
held *responsible* for their behavior—in the sense that they may be both justly
blamed as well as praised for it. But a science of behavior denies human responsibility altogether by denying that human beings ever act freely. Rather, it
"shifts the credit as well as the blame to the environment," and, thereby it requires some "sweeping changes" in traditional theories and practices, ones that
adherents "naturally resist."

Skinner's rejection of the traditional view may be represented in the following argument:

> (1) Necessarily, if we are responsible for our actions then we possess free will.
> (2) Our wills are never free.
> Therefore, we are never responsible for our actions.

Premise (1) appears to be true if "responsible" is taken in its *moral* sense.
According to this understanding, Premise (1) says that a person can meaningfully be morally blamed or given credit for an action only if the person could
have acted differently under the given circumstances. Moral culpability and
credit assume that the subject was not incapable of acting otherwise. The excuse that "I couldn't have done otherwise" is, on this understanding, always a

morally acceptable excuse. This excuse has also been applied in assessing *legal* responsibility in criminal proceedings. For example, lawyers have successfully defended clients by showing that their criminal actions were a result of causal forces beyond their control, including the subtle conditioning of having been exposed to TV violence, or the mind-altering effects of an abnormal physiological condition.

It is noteworthy that when Skinner says that a science of behavior "shifts the credit as well as the blame to the environment" he does not mean the moral sense of these terms. The environment is no more a proper bearer of moral responsibility than are human beings who lack free will. What he appears to be saying is that the environment is *causally* responsible for human behavior.

In the next selection of this chapter, Jean-Paul Sartre, a contemporary French philosopher, challenges Premise (2) of Skinner's argument by coming to the defense of autonomous man. According to Sartre, "atheistic existentialism," the view he represents, starts with the proposition that "existence precedes essence," which means that human beings *define themselves* through their own freely chosen actions. Human beings are not, as Skinner maintains, creatures whose behavior is fashioned by environmental conditions lying outside their control. To the contrary, for Sartre, "there is no determinism—man is free, man is freedom." Nor, as Skinner maintains, is the psychic life of a human being to be discounted. "Man is, indeed, a project which possesses a subjective life, instead of being a kind of moss, or a fungus, or a cauliflower." Moreover, whereas a science of behavior—by Skinner's own admission—questions the "dignity" or "worth" of human beings, existentialism "alone is compatible with the dignity of man, it is the only one which does not make man into an object."

Finally, contrary to Skinner, Sartre maintains that human beings are responsible for their behavior and "any man who takes refuge . . . , by inventing some deterministic doctrine, is a self-deceiver." Sartre, in effect, turns Skinner's argument on its head. His response to Skinner may be represented as follows:

(1) Necessarily, if we possess free will, then we are responsible for our actions.
(2) We do possess free will.
Therefore, we are responsible for our actions.

The sense of "responsible" here is still a moral one. However, in Sartre's view, our moral responsiblity looms wide. It is, he states, "much greater than we might have supposed, because it involves all mankind." Thus, in choosing for oneself, Sartre believes one must accept the choice as valid for all other persons. If I get married, then I embrace monogamy, not just for myself, but for all others. If I enlist in a war, then the war is one that is valid for all others. Sartre suggests that whatever results from an institution one supports is also one's responsibility. Thus, all the casualties of a war that I accept are also my casualities, even if they do not die at my hand. For Sartre, the old saw "I only work here" only hides one's responsibility. Even the custodian who chooses to work in a factory that is manufacturing a dangerous product assumes the risk and all untoward results thereof.

Sartre's concept of responsibility depends upon his view that human reality is rooted in human subjectivity ("Man is at the start a plan which is aware of itself".) Being responsible here does not mean *causally* responsible. The soldier is not responsible for every casualty of a war in this sense. Responsibility here is the subjective sense of having made a conscious, self-aware choice to embrace a given institution or "plan."

It is often easier for one to hide behind an excuse ("The devil made me do it," "It's my job," "It's God's will," "I was ordered to do it") than to take full responsibility in this subjective sense. Nevertheless, for Sartre, those who make excuses for their choices live in "bad faith"; they are lying to themselves. For Sartre, taking responsibility means that there are no excuses. It means that "in the bright realm of values we have no excuse behind us nor justification before us. We are alone with no excuses." While we are free to believe in God or in capitalism or in communism or in any other ideology, these values are correct only because we have chosen them. We are the authors of these values and whatever follows from them. Our freedom to choose is not circumscribed by any value other than the ones we have ourselves freely chosen. For Sartre, this is a source of much human forlornness because "neither within him nor without does he find anything to cling to. He can't start making excuses for himself."

It should be noted that, in insisting on free will and responsibility, Sartre is not naively claiming that human beings are capable of doing whatever they will to do. Obviously, human beings are not free to defy physical laws; they are born into particular social environments, and they all confront the inevitability of death. Nevertheless, human beings may freely determine their relations to such "human conditions." For example, even a person born into slavery can refuse to participate in that social practice, preferring death to such denigration, or he or she can choose to acquiesce in the practice. Either way, he or she chooses and is responsible. While Skinner views human beings as merely causal products of their environments, Sartre views them as freely and responsibly determining themselves in relation to their environments.

Sartre and Skinner may both be viewed as representing sharply contrasting perspectives regarding the problem of free will and determinism. Whereas Skinner strongly denies free will, the significance of our psychic life, and the existence of human responsibility, Sartre insists on these and carries them to their limits. Between such polar opposites, however, other views are possible.

For example, some determinists, sometimes called "soft determinists," have attempted to preserve a sense of freedom while insisting on a wholly deterministic universe. For instance, Moritz Schlick argues that "a man is free when he does not act under compulsion; and he is compelled or unfree when he is hindered from without in the realization of his natural desires." [1] Thus, a person is unfree when "he is locked up, or chained, or when someone for at the point of a gun to do what otherwise he would not do." In either case, however—free or unfree—a person's behavior is causally determined in this view. (This perspective is at least hinted at by Skinner himself when he remarks that "the distinction between 'being free' and 'being compelled' is tenable only so long as a word like 'compel' suggests a particularly conspicuous and forcible mode of control.") However, for philosophers like Sartre who view free acts as spontaneous and uncaused—as not explainable in terms of causal laws—such a perspective would not be acceptable.

In contrast to Skinner's view, which takes environment to be the primary causal factor in affecting behavior, determinist positions are also possible that take *unconscious, psychological motivation* to be the primary underlying causal factor. As John Hospers puts it, "the unconscious is the master of every fate and the captain of every soul." Borrowing from Freud, Hospers argues that unconscious pyschological causes that are intact as young children can provide a complete causal account of our actions, for example, a women who, after suffering through several abusive marriages, chooses another man who will carry on this chain of abuse. On a conscious level, it appears to her that she has freely chosen to marry these men, but, in fact, "her super-ego, always out to maximize the torment in the situation seeing what dazzling possibilities for self-damaging behavior are promised . . . compels her to make the choice she does, and even to conceal the real basis of the choice behind an elaborate facade of rationalizations."[2]

A central question confronting this view is whether we are ever able *consciously* to transcend such unconscious determinism to make changes in our lives. As we will see, some psychologists, such as Eric Berne, argue that we can redirect our behavior by consciously adopting new "life scripts." If so, then the unconscious need not be "master of every fate."

Free will positions are also possible which take *some* human behavior to be causally determined. Indeed, from the premise that some human behavior is determined it does not follow that no human behavior is ever free or uncaused. For example, the craving of a heroin addict for heroin may be said to be causally determined without admitting that all desires are equally determined. From the perspective of determinists like Skinner, however, *all* human behavior is causally determined.

What evidence is there to suggest that all (not just some) of our behavior is causally determined? Skinner argues that determinism slowly gains confirmation "as new evidences of the predictability of human behavior are discovered." However, it can be argued that actuarial or statistical evidence does not necessarily tell against the existence of free will. For instance, we may be able to predict with considerable accuracy how many people will die on the highways on a holiday weekend, but such predictability is not inconsistent with the existence of free will. What appears requisite to foreclose the possibility of free will are universal laws, not merely statistical ones, although these are not as readily adducible by determinists.

Free willists also encounter the problem of evidence. For example, it is sometimes argued that the evidence for free will can be discovered by anyone who cares to introspect while making a choice. When you choose X rather than Y, it may well appear from your inside perspective that you could have chosen Y instead. Still, appearances, much like statistics, can be mistaken.

In the third selection of this chapter, Gale Spieler Cohen, a mental health counselor and professor of human services, provides a lucid discussion of three theories of psychological counseling—person-centered therapy, rational-emotive behavior therapy, and transactional analysis. Relating these three theories to the perspectives of Sartre and Skinner, she attempts to expose the philosophical foundations of these theories regarding the free will versus determinism issue.

Gale Cohen's discussion of the relationships between philosophy and counseling gives credibility to a burgeoning movement in the United States and other nations, that of *philosophical counseling*. The concept of taking philosophy to the marketplace instead of keeping it in the academy is not a new idea. Indeed, it is one with which the ancient Greek philosopher Socrates has often been credited. Nevertheless, with the growth of applied philosophy has come renewed and increasing awareness of the power of philosophy to solve everyday problems of living. The Practice section of this chapter discusses a philosophical counseling project I had undertaken in the mid-eighties when the movement in this country was virtually nonexistent.

The project was undertaken with the aim of developing a systematic approach to using logic and critical thinking in helping people to solve problems of living.[3] The project involved counseling with married couples who were experiencing dysfunction in their marriages. One of the cases I encountered, which is discussed here, concerned two clients, dubbed Bob and Janet, in which the presenting problem was a "lack of communication." As this case dramatically unfolds, the issues raised by Sartre and Skinner regarding the question of free will, and the relevance of counseling theories such as those examined by Gale Cohen, are brought into sharp focus in a practical context. In the end, I suggest that the fate of both Bob and Janet depended largely upon whether they were able to transcend their individual socializations and assert their autonomy.

In 1989 I cofounded the American Society for Philosophy, Counseling, and Psychotherapy (ASPCP), which is currently the main professional association for philosophical counseling in the United States. In drafting the *Standards of Ethical Practice* for the Society, we sought a clear expression of the importance of client autonomy in philosophical counseling. The second principle of this code received the following formulation:

> Philosophical practitioners should facilitate maximum client participation in philosophical explorations. They should avoid dictating "correct" answers to client queries and issues, but should actively encourage the client's own engagement of reflective powers and rational determinations. In cases in which a client is seeking assistance for purposes of resolving a specific problem such as an ethical problem or other practical matter, philosophical practitioners may, in the light of philosophical exploration of the matter, suggest possible courses of action. However, they should make clear to the client that the final decision rests with the client.

As the case of Bob and Janet suggests, adoption of "existence precedes essence" as a counseling philosophy may prove more useful than its converse.

Clients often come to counseling (psychological as well as philosophical) because problems in their lives seem "outside their control." They feel like cogs in a rigid determinism which, to their frustration, decides their unhappy destinies. Clients who learn to depend on their counselors for "advice" may merely substitute one dependency for another. It is therefore fitting that, in counseling, "the final decision rests with the client."

Does my logic-based approach to philosophical counseling effectively preserve client autonomy?

It is my contention that logic can be used both *methodologically* and *didactically* in philosophical counseling. For example, in the case of Janet, I used syllogistic logic as a *method* for uncovering and exploring suppressed premises in her belief system, thereby helping her to examine her socialization. But I also used logic didactically when I tried to *teach* Bob about the problems inherent in generalizing from insufficient samples.

Perhaps my didactic use of logic runs the greatest risk of impeding client autonomy, for the charge might be made that I am "telling the client how to think." Still there are two distinct senses to the phrase "telling the client how to think." One can tell clients what *thoughts or ideas* to have, or one can tell them what sort of *thinking processes* to use in deciding for themselves what to think. While the line between these two senses may not always be clear, client autonomy is more likely preserved if counselors avoid the former sense but seek to apply the latter. This latter sense seems most consonant with the ASPCP *Ethical Standards*.

Nevertheless, even if facilitating a client's *sense* of autonomy is essential to successful counseling, one can still question whether such freedom is real or merely a useful appearance, a subjectivity belied by a universe tightly woven together by cause and effect. If so, then the subjective appearance of freedom may itself be but another effect in a rigid determinism.

NOTES

1. Moritz Schlick, "When Is a Man Responsible?" in *Free Will and Determinism*, ed. Bernard Berofsky (New York: Harper and Row, 1966), p. 59.
2. John Hospers, "Meaning and Free Will," *Philosophy and Phenomenological Research*, vol. 10, no. 3 (March 1950), pp. 17–26.
3. For an example of more recent work see Elliot D. Cohen, "Syllogizing RET: Applying Formal Logic in Rational-Emotive Therapy," *Journal of Rational-Emotive and Cognitive-Behavior Therapy*, vol. 10, no. 4 (winter 1992); Elliot D. Cohen, *Caution: Faulty Thinking Can Be Harmful to Your Happiness: Logic for Everyday Living*, Second ed., Fort Pierce: Fla.: Trace-WilCo, 1994; Elliot D. Cohen, "Philosophical Counseling: Some Roles of Critical Thinking." In *Essays on Philosophical Counseling*, ed. Ran Lahav and Maria Da Venza Tillmanns. New York: University Press of America, 1995.

ISSUES

B. F. SKINNER

BEHAVIORISM

. . . The world of the mind steals the show. Behavior is not recognized as a subject in its own right. In psychotherapy, for example, the disturbing things a person does or says are almost always regarded merely as symptoms, and compared with the fascinating dramas which are staged in the depths of the mind, behavior itself seems superficial indeed. In linguistics and literary criticism, what a man says is almost always treated as the expression of ideas or feelings. In political science, theology, and economics, behavior is usually regarded as the material from which one infers attitudes, intentions, needs, and so on. For more than twenty-five hundred years close attention has been paid to mental life, but only recently has any effort been made to study human behavior as something more than a mere by-product.

The conditions of which behavior is a function are also neglected. The mental explanation brings curiosity to an end. We see the effect in causal discourse. If we ask someone, "Why did you go to the theater," and he says, "Because I felt like going," we are apt to take his reply as a kind of explanation. It would be much more to the point to know what has happened when he has gone to the theater in the past, what he heard or read about the play he went to see, and what other things in his past or present environments might have induced him to go (as opposed to doing something else), but we accept "I felt like going" as a sort of summary of all this and are not likely to ask for details. . . .

Unable to understand how or why the person we see behaves as he does, we attribute his behavior to a person we cannot see, whose behavior we cannot explain either but about whom we are not inclined to ask questions. We probably adopt this strategy not so much because of any lack of interest or power but because of a longstanding conviction that for much of human behavior there *are* no relevant antecedents. The function of the inner man is to provide an explanation which will not be explained in turn. Explanation stops with him. He is not a mediator between past history and current behavior, he is a *center* from which behavior emanates. He initiates, originates, and creates, and in doing so he remains, as he was for the Greeks, divine. We say that he is autonomous—and, so far as a science of behavior is concerned, that means miraculous.

SOURCE: B. F. Skinner, *Beyond Freedom and Dignity* (New York: Knopf, 1971), pp. 12–15, 19–22, 24–25. Copyright 1971 by B. F. Skinner. Reprinted by permission of Alfred A. Knopf, Inc.

The position is, of course, vulnerable. Autonomous man serves to explain only the things we are not yet able to explain in other ways. His existence depends upon our ignorance, and he naturally loses status as we come to know more about behavior. The task of a scientific analysis is to explain how the behavior of a person as a physical system is related to the conditions under which the human species evolved and the conditions under which the individual lives. Unless there is indeed some capricious or creative intervention, these events must be related, and no intervention is in fact needed. The contingencies of survival responsible for man's genetic endowment would produce tendencies to *act* aggressively, not feelings of aggression. The punishment of sexual behavior changes sexual *behavior,* and any feelings which may arise are at best by-products. Our age is not suffering from anxiety but from the accidents, crimes, wars, and other dangerous and painful things to which people are so often exposed. Young people drop out of school, refuse to get jobs, and associate only with others of their own age not because they feel alienated but because of defective social environments in homes, schools, factories, and elsewhere.

We can follow the path taken by physics and biology by turning directly to the relation between behavior and the environment and neglecting supposed mediating states of mind. Physics did not advance by looking more closely at the jubilance of a falling body, or biology by looking at the nature of vital spirits, and we do not need to try to discover what personalities, states of mind, feelings, traits of character, plans, purposes, intentions, or the other prerequisites of autonomous man really are in order to get on with a scientific analysis of behavior. . . .

We have moved forward by dispossessing autonomous man, but he has not departed gracefully. He is conducting a sort of rear-guard action in which, unfortunately, he can marshal formidable support. He is still an important figure in political science, law, religion, economics, anthropology, sociology, psychotherapy, philosophy, ethics, history, education, child care, linguistics, architecture, city planning, and family life. These fields have their specialists, and every specialist has a theory, and in almost every theory the autonomy of the individual is unquestioned. The inner man is not seriously threatened by data obtained through casual observation or from studies of the structure of behavior, and many of these fields deal only with groups of people, where statistical or actuarial data impose few restraints upon the individual. The result is a tremendous weight of traditional "knowledge," which must be corrected or displaced by a scientific analysis.

Two features of autonomous man are particularly troublesome. In the traditional view, a person is free. He is autonomous in the sense that his behavior is uncaused. He can therefore be held responsible for what he does and justly punished if he offends. That view, together with its associated practices, must be re-examined when a scientific analysis reveals unsuspected controlling relations between behavior and environment. A certain amount of external control can be tolerated. Theologians have accepted the fact that man must be predestined to do what an omniscient God knows he will do, and the Greek dramatist took inexorable fate as his favorite theme. Soothsayers and astrologers often claim to predict what men will do, and they have always been in demand. Biographers and historians have searched for "influences" in the lives of individuals and people. Folk wisdom and the insights of essayists like Montaigne and Bacon imply some kind of predictability in human conduct, and the statistical and actuarial evidences of the social sciences point in the same direction.

Autonomous man survives in the face of all this because he is the happy exception. Theologians have reconciled predestination with free will and the Greek audience, moved by the portrayal of an inescapable destiny, walked out of the theater free men. The course of history has been turned by the death of a leader or a storm at sea, as a life has been changed by a teacher or a love affair, but these things do not happen to everyone, and they do not affect everyone in the same way. Some historians have made a virtue of the unpredictability of history. Actuarial evidence is easily ignored; we read that hundreds of people will be killed in traffic accidents on a holiday weekend and take to the road as if personally exempt. Very little behavioral science raises "the spector of predictable man." On the contrary, many anthropologists, sociologists, and psychologists have used their expert knowledge to prove that man is free, purposeful, and responsible. Freud was a determinist—on faith, if not on the evidence—but many Freudians have no hesitation in assuring their patients that they are free to choose among different courses of action and are in the long run the architects of their own destinies.

This escape route is slowly closed as new evidences of the predictability of human behavior are discovered. Personal exemption from a complete determinism is revoked as a scientific analysis progresses, particularly in accounting for the behavior of the individual. Joseph Wood Krutch has acknowledged the actuarial facts while insisting on personal freedom: "We can predict with a considerable degree of accuracy how many people will go to the seashore on a day when the temperature reaches a certain point, even how many will jump off a bridge . . . although I am not, nor are you, compelled to do either." But he can scarcely mean that those who go to the seashore do not go for good reason, or that circumstances in the life of a suicide do not have some bearing on the fact that he jumps off a bridge. The distinction is tenable only so long as a word like "compel" suggests a particularly conspicuous and forcible mode of control. A scientific analysis naturally moves in the direction of clarifying all kinds of controlling relations.

By questioning the control exercised by autonomous man and demonstrating the control exercised by the environment, a science of behavior also seems to question dignity or worth. A person is responsible for his behavior, not only in the sense that he may be justly blamed or punished when he behaves badly, but also in the sense that he is to be given credit and admired for his achievements. A scientific analysis shifts the credit as well as the blame to the environment, and traditional practices can then no longer be justified. These are sweeping changes, and those who are committed to traditional theories and practices naturally resist them.

There is a third source of trouble. As the emphasis shifts to the environment, the individual seems to be exposed to a new kind of danger. Who is to construct the controlling environment and to what end? Autonomous man presumably controls himself in accordance with a built-in set of values; he works for what he finds good. But what will the putative controller find good, and will it be good for those he controls? Answers to questions of this sort are said, of course, to call for value judgments.

Freedom, dignity, and value are major issues, and unfortunately they become more crucial as the power of a technology of behavior becomes more nearly commensurate with the problems to be solved. The very change which has brought some hope of a solution is responsible for a growing opposition to the kind of solution proposed. This conflict is itself a problem in human behavior and may be approached as such. A sciece of behavior is by no means as far advanced as physics or biology, but it has an advantage in that it may throw some light on its own difficulties. Science is human behavior, and so is the opposition to science. What has happened in man's struggle for freedom and dignity, and what problems arise when scientific knowledge begins to be relevant in that struggle? Answers to these questions may help to clear the way for the technology we so badly need. . . .

Almost all our major problems involve human behavior, and they cannot be solved by physical and biological technology alone. What is needed is a technology of behavior, but we have been slow to develop the science from which such a technology might be drawn. One difficulty is that almost all of what is called behavioral science continues to trace behavior to states of mind, feelings, traits of character, human nature, and so on. Physics and biology once followed similar practices and advanced only when they discredited them. The behavioral sciences have been slow to change partly because the explanatory entities often seem to be directly observed and partly because other kinds of explanations have been hard to find. The environment is obviously important, but its role has remained obscure. It does not push or pull, it *selects,* and this function is difficult to discover and analyze. The role of natural selection in evolution was formulated only a little more than a hundred years ago, and the selective role of the environment in shaping and maintaining the behavior of the individual is only beginning to be recognized and studied. As the interaction between organism and environment has come to be understood, however, effects once assigned to states of mind, feelings, and traits are beginning to be traced to accessible conditions, and a technology of behavior may therefore become available. It will not solve our problems, however, until it replaces traditional prescientific views, and these are strongly entrenched. Freedom and dignity illustrate the difficulty. They are the possessions of the autonomous man of traditional theory, and they are essential to practices in which a person is held responsible for his conduct and given credit for his achievements. A scientific analysis shifts both the responsibility and the achievement to the environment. It also raises questions concerning "values." Who will use a technology and to what ends? Until these issues are resolved, a technology of behavior will continue to be rejected, and with it possibly the only way to solve our problems.

JEAN-PAUL SARTRE

EXISTENTIALISM

What is meant by the term *existentialism?*

... What complicates matters is that there are two kinds of existentialist; first, those who are Christian, among whom I would include Jaspers and Gabriel Marcel, both Catholic; and on the other hand the atheistic existentialists, among whom I class Heidegger, and then the French existentialists and myself. What they have in common is that they think that existence precedes essence, or, if you prefer, that subjectivity must be the starting point.

Just what does that mean? Let us consider some object that is manufactured, for example, a book or a paper-cutter: here is an object which has been made by an artisan whose inspiration came from a concept. He referred to the concept of what a paper-cutter is and likewise to a known method of production, which is part of the concept, something which is, by and large, a routine. Thus, the paper-cutter is at once an object produced in a certain way and, on the other hand, one having a specific use; and one can not postulate a man who produces a paper-cutter but does not know what it is used for. Therefore, let us say that, for the paper-cutter, essence—that is, the ensemble of both the production routines and the properties which enable it to be both produced and defined—precedes existence. Thus, the presence of the paper-cutter or book in front of me is determined. Therefore, we have here a technical view of the world whereby it can be said that production precedes existence.

When we conceive God as the Creator, He is generally thought of as a superior sort of artisan. Whatever doctrine we may be considering, whether one like that of Descartes or that of Leibnitz, we always grant that will more or less follows understanding or, at the very least, accompanies it, and that when God creates He knows exactly what He is creating. Thus, the concept of man in the mind of God is comparable to the concept of paper-cutter in the mind of the manufacturer, and, following certain techniques and a conception, God produces man, just as the artisan, following a definition and a technique, makes a

SOURCE: Jean-Paul Sartre, "Existentialism," tr. Bernard Frechtman, in *Existentialism and Human Emotions* (Andover, UK: Routledge [Methuen], 1985) Reprinted by permission of the publisher.

paper-cutter. Thus, the individual man is the realization of a certain concept in the divine intelligence.

In the eighteenth century, the atheism of the *philosophes* discarded the idea of God, but not so much for the notion that essence precedes existence. To a certain extent, this idea is found everywhere; we find it in Diderot, in Voltaire, and even in Kant. Man has a human nature; this human nature, which is the concept of the human, is found in all men, which means that each man is a particular example of a universal concept, man. In Kant, the result of this universality is that the wild-man, the natural man, as well as the bourgeois, are circumscribed by the same definition and have the same basic qualities. Thus, here too the essence of man precedes the historical existence that we find in nature.

Atheistic existentialism, which I represent, is more coherent. It states that if God does not exist, there is at least one being in whom existence precedes essence, a being who exists before he can be defined by any concept, and that this being is man, or, as Heidegger says, human reality. What is meant here by saying that existence precedes essence? It means that, first of all, man exists, turns up, appears on the scene, and, only afterwards, defines himself. If man, as the existentialist conceives him, is indefinable, it is because at first he is nothing. Only afterward will he be something, and he himself will have made what he will be. Thus, there is no human nature, since there is no God to conceive it. Not only is man what he conceives himself to be, but he is also only what he wills himself to be after this thrust toward existence.

Man is nothing else but what he makes of himself. Such is the first principle of existentialism. It is also what is called subjectivity, the name we are labeled with when charges are brought against us. But what do we mean by this, if not that man has a greater dignity than a stone or table? For we mean that man first exists, that is, man first of all is the being who hurls himself toward a future and who is conscious of imagining himself as being in the future. Man is at the start a plan which is aware of itself, rather than a patch of moss, a piece of garbage, or a cauliflower; nothing exists prior to this plan; there is nothing in heaven; man will be what he will have planned to be. . . . But if existence really does precede essence, man is responsible for what he is. Thus, existentialism's first move is to make every man aware of what he is and to make the full responsibility of his existence rest on him. And when we say that a man is responsible for himself, we do not only mean that he is responsible for his own individuality, but that he is responsible for all men.

The word subjectivism has two meanings, and our opponents play on the two. Subjectivism means, on the one hand, that an individual chooses and makes himself; and, on the other, that it is impossible for man to transcend human subjectivity. The second of these is the essential meaning of existentialisin. When we say that man chooses his own self, we mean that every one of us does likewise; but we also mean by that that in making this choice he also chooses all men. In fact, in creating the man that we want to be, there is not a single one of our acts which does not at the same time create an image of man as we think he ought to be. To choose to be this or that is to affirm at the same time the value of what we choose, because we can never choose evil. We always choose the good, and nothing can be good for us without being good for all.

If, on the other hand, existence precedes essence, and if we grant that we exist and fashion our image at one and the same time, the image is valid for everybody and for our whole age. Thus, our responsibility is much greater than we might have supposed, because it involves all mankind. If I am a working-man and choose to join a Christian trade-union rather than be a communist, and if by being a member I want to show that the best thing for man is resignation, that the kingdom of man is not of this world, I am not only involving my own case—I want to be resigned for everyone. As a result, my action has involved all humanity. To take a more individual matter, if I want to marry, to have children; even if this marriage depends solely on my own circumstances or passion or wish, I am involving all humanity in monogamy and not merely myself. Therefore, I am responsible for myself and for everyone else. I am creating a certain image of man of my own choosing. In choosing myself, I choose man.

. . . Dostoievsky said, "If God didn't exist, everything would be possible." That is the very starting point of existentialism. Indeed, everything is permissible if God does not exist, and as a result man is forlorn, because neither within him nor without does he find anything to cling to. He can't start making excuses for himself.

If existence really does precede essence, there is no explaining things away by reference to a fixed and given human nature. In other words, there is no determinism, man is free, man is freedom. On the other hand, if God does not exist, we find no values or commands to turn to which legitimize our conduct. So, in the bright realm of values, we have no excuse behind us, nor justification before us. We are alone, with no excuses.

That is the idea I shall try to convey when I say that man is condemned to be free. Condemned, because he did not create himself, yet, in other respects is free; because, once thrown into the world, he is responsible for everything he does. The existentialist does not believe in the power of passion. He will never agree that a sweeping passion is a ravaging torrent which fatally leads a man to certain acts and is therefore an excuse. He thinks that man is responsible for his passion.

The existentialist does not think that man is going to help himself by finding in the world some omen by which to orient himself. Because he thinks that man will interpret the omen to suit himself. Therefore, he thinks that man, with no support and no aid, is condemned every moment to invent man. Ponge, in a very fine article, has said, "Man is the future of man." That's exactly it. But if it is taken to mean that this future is recorded in heaven, that God sees it, then it is false, because it would really no longer be a future. If it is taken to mean that, whatever a man may be, there is a future to be forged, a virgin future before him, then this remark is sound. But then we are forlorn.

. . . Quietism is the attitude of people who say, "Let others do what I can't do." The doctrine I am presenting is the very opposite of quietism, since it declares, "There is no reality except in action." Moreover, it goes further, since it adds, "Man is nothing else than his plan; he exists only to the extent that he fulfills himself; he is therefore nothing else than the ensemble of his acts, nothing else than his life."

According to this, we can understand why our doctrine horrifies certain people. Because often the only way they can bear their wretchedness is to think, "Circumstances have been against me. What I've been and done doesn't show my true worth. To be sure, I've had no great love, no great friendship, but that's because I haven't met a man or woman who was worthy. The books I've written haven't been very good because I haven't had the proper leisure. I haven't had children to devote myself to because I didn't find a man with whom I could have spent my life. So there remains within me, unused and quite viable, a host of propensities, inclinations, possibilities, that one wouldn't guess from the mere series of things I've done."

Now, for the existentialist there is really no love other than one which manifests itself in a person's being in love. There is no genius other than one which is expressed in works of art; the genius of Proust is the sum of Proust's works; the genius of Racine is his series of tragedies. Outside of that, there is nothing. Why say that Racine could have written another tragedy, when he didn't write it? A man is involved in life, leaves his impress on it, and outside of that there is nothing. To be sure, this may seem a harsh thought to someone whose life hasn't been a success. But, on the other hand, it prompts people to understand that reality alone is what counts, that dreams, expectations, and hopes warrant no more than to define a man as a disappointed dream, as miscarried hopes, as vain expectations. In other words, to define him negatively and not positively. However, when we say, "You are nothing else than your life," that does not imply that the artist will be judged solely on the basis of his works of art; a thousand other things will contribute toward summing him up. What we mean is that a man is nothing else than a series of undertakings, that he is the sum, the organization, the ensemble of the relationships which make up these undertakings.

. . . [T]his theory is the only one which gives man dignity, the only one which does not reduce him to an object. The effect of all materialism is to treat all men, including the one philosophizing, as objects, that is, as an ensemble of determined reactions in no way distinguished from the ensemble of qualities and phenomena which constitute a table or a chair or a stone. We definitely wish to establish the human realm as an ensemble of values distinct from the material realm . . . .

Besides, if it is impossible to find in every man some universal essence which would be human nature, yet there does exist a universal human condition. It's not by chance that today's thinkers speak more readily of man's condition than of his nature. By condition they mean, more of less definitely, the *a priori* limits which outline man's fundamental situation in the universe. Historical situations vary; a man may be born a slave in a pagan society or a feudal lord or a proletarian. What does not vary is the necessity for him to exist in the world, to be at work there, to be there in the midst of other people, and to be mortal there. The limits are neither subjective nor objective, or, rather, they have an objective and a subjective side. Objective because they are to be found everywhere and are recognizable everywhere; subjective because they are *lived* and are nothing if man does not live them, that is, freely determine his existence with reference to them. And though the configurations may differ, at least none of them are completely strange to me, because they all appear as attempts either to pass beyond these limits or recede from them or deny them or adapt to them. Consequently, every configuration, however individual it may be, has a universal value.

. . . If we have defined man's situation as a free choice, with no excuses and no recourse, every man who takes refuge behind the excuse of his passions, every man who sets up a determinism, is a dishonest man.

The objection may be raised, "But why mayn't he choose himself dishonestly?" I reply that I am not obliged to pass moral judgment on him, but that I do define his dishonesty as an error. One can not help considering the truth of the matter. Dishonesty is obviously a falsehood because it belies the complete freedom of involvement. On the same grounds, I maintain that there is also dishonesty if I choose to state that certain values exist prior to me; it is self-contradictory for me to want them and at the same state that they are imposed on me. Suppose someone says to me, "What if I want to be dishonest?" I'll answer, "There's no reason for you not to be, but I'm saying that that's what you are, and that the strictly coherent attitude is that of honesty."

Besides, I can bring moral judgment to bear. When I declare that freedom in every concrete circumstance can have no other aim than to want itself, if man has once become aware that in his forlornness he imposes values, he can no longer want but one thing, and that is freedom, as the basis of all values. That doesn't mean that he wants it in the abstract. It means simply that the ultimate meaning of the acts of honest men is the quest for freedom as such. A man who belongs to a communist or revolutionary union wants concrete goals; these goals imply an abstract desire for freedom; but this freedom is wanted in something concrete. We want freedom for freedom's sake and in every particular circumstance. And in wanting freedom we discover that it depends entirely on the freedom of others, and that the freedom of others depends on ours. Of course, freedom as the definition of man does not depend on others, but as soon as there is involvement, I am obliged to want others to have freedom at the same time that I want my own freedom. I can take freedom as my goal only if I take that of others as a goal as well. Consequently, when, in all honesty, I've recognized that man is a being in whom existence precedes essence, that he is a free being who, in various circumstances, can want only his freedom, I have at the same time recognized that I can want only the freedom of others.

Therefore, in the name of this will for freedom, which freedom itself implies, I may pass judgment on those who seek to hide from themselves the complete arbitrariness and the complete freedom of their existence. Those who hide their complete freedom from themselves out of a spirit of seriousness or by means of deterministic excuses, I shall call cowards; those who try to show that their existence was necessary, when it is the very contingency of man's appearance on earth, I shall call stinkers.

. . . Existentialism is nothing else than an attempt to draw all the consequences of a coherent atheistic position. . . . Existentialism isn't so atheistic that it wears itself out showing that God doesn't exist. Rather, it declares that even if God did exist, that would change nothing. There you've got our point of view. Not that we believe that God exists, but we think that the problem of His existence is not the issue.

GALE SPIELER COHEN

THEORIES OF COUNSELING AND THE FREE WILL–DETERMINISM ISSUE

The diverse theories of counseling and psychotherapy encompass a wide array of approaches to the actual counseling situation. Three such approaches discussed herein are the person-centered approach,* as exemplified by Carl Rogers, Rational-Emotive Behavior Therapy (REBT), as practiced by Albert Ellis, and Transactional Analysis (TA), as espoused by Eric Berne. This paper seeks to explain the basic assumptions behind the three counseling approaches and to describe the counseling process at work in each. Additionally, these approaches will be presented within the context of the issue of free will and determinism. We do not intend here to represent a comprehensive elucidation of the numerous counseling methodologies used by today's practitioners.

THE PERSON-CENTERED APPROACH

The person-centered approach asserts that the quality of the relationship between therapist and client is the factor responsible for growth and change in the counseling situation. If the counselor possesses certain basic qualities, and if such qualities are recognized by the client, constructive progress will occur.

The well-functioning person-centered therapist, of necessity, has the following attributes. He or she must be a congruent individual who expresses

---

Gale Spieler Cohen is a licensed mental health counselor and coordinator of the Human Services Program at Indian River Community College. She is also co-author of *The Virtuous Therapist* (Wadsworth, 1999).
*Formerly referred to as the client-centered approach.

unconditional positive regard for the client, and is able to experience empathetic understanding of the client's phenomenal world.

Congruence, as defined by Rogers, is realized when the therapist is fully aware of his or her own feelings and attitudes, and acts in accordance with those feelings. He or she does not hide behind a public facade.

Unconditional positive regard is explained as a warm, but nonpossessive caring for the client. This includes acceptance of the client's feelings and/or experiences irrespective of their nature. Rogers contends that such unconditional positive regard enables a client to discover meaning for oneself.

Empathetic understanding is another basic quality the Rogerian counselor should exhibit. This enables the counselor to "sense the client's private world as if it were your own, but without ever losing the 'as if' quality. . . ."[1]

Since Rogers views persons as possessing a forward-moving nature, he asserts that clients who seek therapy will be able to help themselves when the therapist exemplifies the conditions of congruence, empathetic understanding, and unconditional positive regard, and when the client recognizes these qualities in the therapist.

As Rogers places emphasis on the counseling relationship itself, he does not rely on the use of therapeutic "technique" to effect change. Rather, he approaches the counseling situation by placing emphasis on the client's subjective world. This occurs when the counselor perceives the true meaning of what the client is communicating, which often involves looking beyond the face value of what the client is actually saying. It is also important that a counselor look for nonverbal cues with which a client might be communicating.

The therapist, as empathetic listener, is able to then reflect back to the client the essence of what the client is feeling. By demonstrating that he or she understands the client's subjective world, the therapist is able to help to facilitate change on the part of the client.[2]

RATIONAL-EMOTIVE BEHAVIOR THERAPY

Rational-Emotive Behavior Therapy (REBT), as practiced by Albert Ellis, is a didactic, directive, cognitive, and behavioral approach to counseling. It is based on Ellis' contention that people have a tendency to embrace irrational beliefs and thus to "disturb themselves" because of these beliefs. Such beliefs are based on ideas that are acquired early in life. Ellis asserts, however, that people are capable of changing these irrational beliefs and that change can be accomplished by detecting irrational beliefs and by attacking and challenging them.

The central theory in REBT is the ABC theory, in which A indicates an Activating Event, B one's Belief System, and C the emotional Consequences. It is Ellis' contention that people do not directly experience emotional Consequences from an Activating Event *per se,* but instead arrive at certain Consequences by the way they perceive the Activating Event, that is, by the Belief System they embrace.

Consider the following example:

(**A**) John has flunked out of college.
(**B**) John believes that it is terrible for one to flunk out of college.
(**C**) John feels worthless and ashamed.

Ellis would assert that John's Belief System (B), which holds that it is terrible to flunk out of college, caused the emotional Consequence (C), that is, John's feelings of worthlessness and shame, and not the Activating Event (A) by itself.

Ellis holds that one's irrational beliefs usually are of four basic types:

1. You think that someone or something *should, ought,* or *must* be different from the way it actually does exist.
2. You find it *awful, terrible,* or *horrible* when it is this way.
3. You think that you *can't bear* . . . this person or thing that you concluded *should* not have been as it is.
4. You think that you or some other person (or people) have made or keep making horrible errors and that because you or they must not act the way they clearly do act, you or they deserve nothing good in life . . . and can . . . receive the label of louse. . . .[3]

As therapist, Ellis sets out to identify and challenge a client's irrational beliefs, and does so by using a highly directive approach which includes behavioral homework assignments, shame-attacking exercises, and the restructuring of the client's belief system in accordance with what Ellis would term a "logical belief system."

Thus, in the previously illustrated case of John, John's new Belief System would affect his emotional Consequence in the following way:

(**A**) I flunked out of college.
(**B**) I wish this hadn't happened, but I will either enroll elsewhere, or seek another type of training and/or employment.
(**C**) I feel disappointed, but I will take constructive action.[4]

Rational-Emotive Behavior Therapy, unlike Carl Rogers' person-centered aproach, is a directive approach to counseling; its ample use of techniques is also in contrast to Rogers' approach in which the counseling relationship itself is seen as the vehicle of change. While Ellis emphasizes an objective, rational mode of thinking, Rogers emphasizes the client's subjective world. As practitioner, Ellis' highly didactic posture differs sharply from that of Rogers, who views himself as a facilitator helping the client to realize change for himself or herself.

TRANSACTIONAL ANALYSIS

Transactional Analysis (TA) is a cognitive and behavioral approach to counseling originated by Eric Berne. TA takes as its central premise the belief that the present-day decisions people make about their lives are based on childhood influences and decisions. Berne asserts that these childhood beliefs form "life-scripts" which the adult usually tenaciously follows. However, it is Berne's conviction that life-scripts can be altered if the client comes to understand that such decisions are often no longer viable in adult life.

According to Berne, persons act in ways they believe will enable them to receive "strokes" from others. "Strokes" may be defined as "any act implying recognition of another's presence."[5] They can be either of a positive or a negative nature, although positive strokes are preferred, and they may take the form of verbal utterances, physical intimacy, or other nonverbal signs of approval. In Berne's view, the stroke is the basic element of interaction among people. An exchange of strokes is called a "transaction."

The TA practitioner holds that every person has three basic ego states: the Parent, the Adult, and the Child. When we are in the Parent ego state, we behave in ways we believe our parents would have acted. Our Adult ego state is exemplified when we act rationally and autonomously, while our Child ego state serves to reenact the behavior and beliefs that were inculcated in childhood. TA clients will have, among their goals, the task of acquainting themselves with their three ego states and learning to become aware of which of the states they are in at any particular point in time.

Berne contends that each of the three ego states has its place, and it is only when the Child and/or Parent ego state(s) intrude(s) on the Adult ego state (contamination), or when one or two of the ego states are not truly functioning (exclusion), that pathology arises. An example of the former is the individual whose Child ego state prevents him or her from functioning appropriately as an adult. An instance of the latter case is exemplified by the person who functions almost entirely in his or her Parent ego state, behaving as he or she believes his or her parent(s) acted or would have acted.

The process by which one learns of the functioning of one's ego states is called "structural analysis." Some clients participate in structural analysis and end their therapy there.

For those who continue with therapy, transactional analysis may be initiated. (The reader will note that transactional analysis here signifies one stage of the total counseling process also entitled Transactional Analysis.) The stage of transactional analysis involves the messages, both verbal and nonverbal, that people send to one another. Messages are between the various ego states of individuals and these "transactions" between ego states may take various forms.

In a complementary transaction, the response to a stimulus is "appropriate and expected and follows the natural order of healthy human relationships."[6] Such transactions can be between two Parent ego states, two Adult ego states, two Child ego states, or a Parent ego state and a Child ego state.

Crossed transactions occur when a message from one of a person's three ego states is sent to the appropriate ego state of another person, but is instead answered by one of the respondent's other ego states. An example of this would be the Adult of one individual suggesting to the Adult of another individual that they should together repair the house on the weekend. If the respondent answers, "You just don't want me to play tennis!" we can see that he or she has changed the pattern of the response into one between the Child and Parent ego states.

Transactions are means by which persons acquire strokes and may take the form of what Berne calls procedures, rituals, pastimes, and games. For the purposes of brevity, we will discuss only games.

Berne describes a game as a series of transactions involving a hidden message and leading to a predictable outcome. It is Berne's contention that games are basically dishonest, but are used by most people as a means of securing the "stroking" that they need. Thus, game playing can be seen as a substitute for the more preferable form of human relating, that is, intimate relationships. Persons engage in games that allow them to adhere to their early decisions or life-scripts.

The following is an example of an early decision leading up to a particular type of game playing.[7] A young girl constantly receives conflicting messages from her alcoholic father. Unsure as to whether he will be loving or hostile at any particular time, the child attempts to alternate between staying away from him and acting affectionately toward him. Her father's responses, though, are so unpredictable that the child becomes confused. Finally, after her father creates a highly unpleasant confrontation with her mother, the young girl decides that she will never love a man, for they are all no good. This early childhood decision forms the basis of the child's life-script, to be carried into her adult life.

As a woman, this individual appears, on the surface, to seek out and establish viable encounters and/or relationships with men. However, on a closer look, it can be seen that she deliberately creates situations in which men mistreat her.

One such example of this type of behavior is evident in an instance in which she makes an apparent attempt to seduce a man. He responds with romantic overtures, and the woman then slaps him and berates him for such advances. When the man retaliates, the woman can then affirm her original position that men are no good. This game supports the woman's life-script, which she decided upon as a young girl, and enables her to continue to maintain that men are no good, and that therefore she will never love a man.

Although game-free intimacy is viewed by Berne as the preferable mode of living, he contends that games offer some people intimacy that is desperately needed. If involved in game playing, an individual, Berne believes, should play the games which offer him or her the best payoff (outcome). Game analysis allows the client to recognize the games he or she plays and gives him or her the freedom to decide what games to play and how to play them (if at all).

According to Berne, a client can regain the autonomy of early infancy by rediscovering one's own awareness, spontaneity, and intimacy.[8]

Although the relationship between TA therapist and client is considered to be one of equals, the TA practictioner, like the REBT therapist, assumes a didactic role in the counseling process. In this way, both approaches differ from the Rogerian approach.

Another assumption shared by both TA and REBT adherents is that one's behaviors and feelings are largely learned, and can be consciously altered. While TA and REBT depend, to a significant extent, upon a cognitive element in the counseling situation, person-centered counseling proceeds by concentrating on the client's affective realm.

SKINNER AND SARTRE

Analysis of some of the basic assumptions inherent in the three theories of psychotherapy we have discussed will enable the reader to discern some fundamental similarities and differences between these theories and the philosophical views espoused by Skinner and Sartre.

Skinner's position with regard to human behavior is a "deterministic" one. Determinism upholds the doctrine that *every* event has a particular cause and that people do not possess free will. Skinner states that people can be neither praised nor blamed for their actions because the environment, not individuals themselves, shape human behavior. Behavior, for Skinner, is shaped by the giving and withholding of reinforcements and therefore, persons cannot be held responsible for their deeds. As well, he deems feelings and one's "mental life" as mere "by-products" of one's behavior.

Sartre, quite unlike Skinner, embraces an existential position and is a free willist. He holds that "existence precedes essence," or that persons create themselves by the things they do in life. Consistent with this tenet is Sartre's belief that because individuals create their own essence, there can be no specific human nature.

Determinism, for Sartre, is nonexistent. Rather, he emphasizes that "man is freedom."[9] Such emphasis on the free will of persons leads Sartre to the inevitable conclusion that persons are responsible for their actions as well as for their passions. It is Sartre's contention that people are "the sum of their actions."[10] Thus, for Sartre, we cannot speak of our potentialities of our inclinations, but should concentrate instead on our deeds.

PERSPECTIVES ON FREE WILL AND DETERMINISM: ELLIS, ROGERS, AND BERNE

Like Sartre, Ellis believes that persons control their own destinies and denies the assumption that they are completely or almost competely conditioned. Ellis' supposition that free will exists is incorporated into his counseling process. As clients come to recognize the irrationality of their various belief systems, they can choose to replace such belief systems with new and more viable ones.

However, unlike Sartre, Ellis allows for biological or innate tendencies which may partly influence human behavior. Sartre, on the other hand, dismisses temperaments as being unimportant because a person is capable of acting the way he or she wills himself or herself to act.

Although Ellis' stance as a free willist can be recognized, his therapeutic style incorporates many behavioristic techniques. Like Skinner, Ellis holds that practice and reinforcement do, indeed, create learned behavior. The point of departure between the two theorists appears to be the extent to which this belief is carried. Skinner, wholly deterministic in his views, leaves no room for free will. Ellis sees man as possessing free will, but capable of various types of conditioned behavior. The assumption that some of our behavior is causally linked and not always a result of free will does not negate Ellis' conviction that we largely control our own destinies.

Despite the fact, however, that Ellis believes that we are self-directed he does not appear to emphasize responsibility. This differs from Sartre's firmly vocalized conviction that when one acts, one assumes responsibility not only for oneself but for humanity as well.

Another point of departure between Ellis and Sartre lies in the fact that Ellis points out universalizable fallacies of thinking to his clients. Sartre, in contrast, places ultimate primacy on each person's individuality. Ellis' emphasis on the sameness of people with regard to illogical belief systems is also at odds with Sartre's view that there is no "human nature."

Rogers, on the other hand, believes in human nature, one which is forward-moving and rational. In the Rogerian counseling situation, the client is regarded "as if" he or she had the freedom to change his or her own behaviors. Rogers, as we have seen, espouses the belief that specific characteristics on the part of the counselor are necessary, and sufficient conditions which allow the client to constructively change his or her own behavior. One such characteristic is that of congruence, which, as mentioned earlier, is the state in which one functions without pretense or facades. The description of congruence appears to be similar to the "authenticity" which Sartre describes as behaving in good faith or being true to oneself.

With regard to moral standards, Sartre takes a relativist stance. Though he contends that when one acts, one is taking responsibility for all of humanity, he holds that all that is expected from us is that we choose freely. Sartre rejects any absolute standards of morality.

Rogers' therapeutic posture also seems consistent with a relativist perspective. The unconditional positive regard the therapist exhibits toward the client is given irrespective of a client's feelings or actions. Rogers does not attempt to suggest or indoctrinate his clients with any particular set of beliefs.

Although Rogers, at first glance, appears to embrace a free willist postion, this is not so. He treats his clients "as if" they have freedom; however, this feeling of freedom is, for the client, simply a subjective reality. Objectively, Rogers holds that he is "a scientist, committed to a complete determinism."[11] This theoretical stance is not inconsistent with his phenomenological framework, as he believes that each person has his or her own subjective reality.

Rogers, like Skinner, sees himself as setting up conditions that predict and influence behaviors. Unlike Skinner, however, Rogers believes that each person is responsible for his or her own decisions.[12]

Although any notion of determinism is at striking odds with a position such as that of Sartre, we must remember that while in the counseling relationship, Rogers proceeds "as if" his clients are truly free. As we have also seen, Rogers, like Sartre, maintains that we are responsible for our own actions.

Berne, in his Transactional Analysis approach to counseling, states that persons are "scripted" or conditioned early in life to adopt their particular life modes and styles. They are also driven by basic biological needs, for example, stimulus hunger, in order to survive. As we have seen, social stimulus hunger, for human beings, is satisfied by strokes. Such an emphasis on conditioning and biological mandates reminds one of Skinner's determinism. However, although Berne contends that much, if not most, of human behavior is determined, he allows for the possibility that some of us may be able to assert true free will. In referring to the TA client who has, to some degree, learned to control his free energy, Berne asserts "at first he relies heavily on external stimuli . . . but he learns more and more to affect the [shifts of one's real self between ego states] through autonomous acts of volition." [13]

Game playing, as interpreted by Berne, is a means by which persons avoid intimacy. It is his assertion that a game-free relationship is the most desirable form of interaction between persons. In this respect, Berne is in accordance with Sartre's view of the authentic individual. Unlike Sartre though, he believes that game-free relationships are the ideal and may be unattainable for many persons. Thus, Berne asserts that games are permissible if the individuals playing them exercise care in choosing the games they play and the persons with whom they can play. If such precautions are followed, Berne contends that a person can still maintain his or her authenticity. [14]

In attempting to draw both comparisons as well as contrasts between counseling approaches and philosophical stances, one also recognizes that such comparisons and contrasts can be made among the three counseling approaches themselves.

Both Ellis, in his REBT, and Berne, in his TA, give credence to the role of biology in determining human behavior. Ellis' theory appears to afford free will a stronger foothold than does Berne's.

Rogers, as we have seen, does not speak of biological determinants of human nature, and proceeds, in the therapeutic relationship, "as if" persons were free. It has been shown, however, that Rogers, "as a scientist," upholds the doctrine that actions and events are determined.

Deemphasis on the importance of feelings, as embraced by Skinner can be seen in Ellis' conviction that "feeling proves nothing except that you feel." [15] This lies in sharp contrast to Rogers' emphasis on a client's phenomenal world.

Both REBT and TA are didactic in their counseling approaches, as opposed to the person-centered approach in which the therapist acts as a facilitator of change, rather than as a director of it. This may stem, in part, from both Ellis' and Berne's similar convictions that individuals engage in universalizable types of behavior.

As representative counseling approaches, the person-centered approach,

REBT, and TA lend themselves to both comparisons and contrasts with Sartre's as well as with Skinner's perspective on the free will and determinism issue. The reader can ascertain that philosophical speculation and theorizing are incorporated into the formulation of the various approaches to the counseling encounter.

Notes

1. Carl R. Rogers, *On Becoming a Person* (Boston: Houghton Mifflin, 1961), p. 284.
2. Regarding the above discussion of Rogers, see generally ibid.
3. Albert Ellis, "The Basic Clinical Theory of Rational-Emotive Therapy," in *Handbook of Rational-Emotive Therapy*, ed. Albert Ellis and R. Greiger (New York: Springer, 1977), pp. 9–10.
4. Regarding the above discussion of Ellis, see generally ibid.
5. Eric Berne, *Games People Play* (New York: Ballantine, 1964), p. 15.
6. Ibid, p. 29.
7. Eric Berne, *Group Treatment* (New York: Grove Press, 1966), pp. 264–266.
8. Regarding the above discussion of Berne, see generally ibid.
9. Jean-Paul Sartre, "Existentialism Is a Humanism," in *Existentialism from Dostoevsky to Sartre*, ed. Walter Kaufmann (New York: New American Library, 1975), p. 353.
10. Ibid, p. 358.
11. Rogers, *On Becoming a Person*, p. 192.
12. Carl R. Rogers, "Some Issues Concerning the Control of Human Behavior: A Symposium," in *Carl Rogers: The Man and His Ideas*, ed. Richard I. Evans (New York: Dutton, 1975), pp. ixxvii—ixxix.
13. Berne, *Group Treatment*, p. 307.
14. Ibid., p. 308.
15. Ellis, p. 24.

PRACTICE

ELLIOT D. COHEN

The Philosopher as Counselor

In this chapter, you have so far examined contrasting perspectives on free will and determinism (Sartre and Skinner, respectively) and have seen how these perspectives bear upon specific counseling or psychotherapeutic approaches such as person-centered therapy, Rational-Emotive Behavior Therapy (REBT), and Transactional Analysis (TA). It should therefore be apparent that philosophical perspectives can and do color and fashion the practice of counselors. It is not

Elliot D. Cohen (Ph.D., Brown University) is professor of philosophy at Indian River Community College and editor in chief and founder (1981) of the *International Journal of Applied Philosophy*. His books include *The Virtuous Therapist: Ethical Practice of Counseling and Psychotherapy* with Gale Spieler Cohen (Brooks Cole, 1998), *AIDS: Crisis in Professional Ethics*, with Michael Davis (Temple University Press, 1994) and *Philosophical Issues in Journalism* (Oxford University Press, 1993). He is cofounder of the American Society for Philosophy, Counseling, and Psychotherapy (ASPCP), the North American chapter for philosophical counseling. As the society's ethics committee chair, he drafted its *Principles of Ethical Practice* (1995). A version of his proposed "contagious, fatal diseases" rule (addressing notification of sex partners of HIV-seropositive clients) was adopted by the American Counseling Association in its revised Code of Ethics (1995). Professor Cohen is inventor and U.S. patent holder of computerized belief scanning technology that detects logical fallacies in people's thinking. He is the director of the Institute of Critical Thinking in Fort Pierce, Florida where he has conducted clinical research in logical-based modes of philosophical counseling.

simply that philosophical stances influence the theoretical understanding of psychotherapy. It is also that they directly influence the ways counselors treat their clients and, conversely, the ways their clients treat them.

It was this very natural wedding of philosophy and counseling that first attracted me to this area of *praxis*. As an applied philosopher, I sought a worthwhile practical outlet for my philosophical training; the longer I studied theories of counseling, the stronger became my conviction that philosophy could be fruitfully put to work in this area.

One remark by Ellis especially stuck in my mind: "Since my youth I have made the in-depth study of philosophy a hobby of mine and by incorporating these principles into my therapeutic approach, I discovered that my clients could achieve more effective results in far less time than I hoped for while using the other approaches." [1] It was this particular remark that led me to study Ellis quite vigorously and resulted in what appeared to be a modified version of REBT that incorporated aspects of other theories such as TA, person-centered therapy, and existentialism. After about a year of study, I decided to put theory into practice.

Fortunately, I was able to find a local counseling agency under the direction of a clinical psychologist who was receptive to the sort of thing I wanted to do—which was, very generally stated, to apply philosophy to counseling. Since I had some interest in marriage counseling as a possible outlet for my research, the psychologist agreed to give me some clients whom I could counsel under his direction. There was no fee charged for the sessions, and the clients were informed from the beginning that they would be part of a research project.

Since my approach was a modified REBT approach, it included, as I will explain, a large cognitive element. My director pointed out that it was not the sort of approach that would be likely to work on clients functioning at low intellectual levels. My clients were thus initially screened. Of course, this itself raised some serious questions about the significance of any "success ratio" I might achieve.

In what follows, I will discuss one of my cases which, I think, well shows some of the ways philosophical considerations, specifically those of free will and determinism, can and do impact upon problems arising in the context of counseling.

The case I will describe concerns a white middle-class couple who had been married for three years. I will call the husband Bob and the wife Janet. Both were in their late forties. Bob had been married once before and, after a marriage of nineteen years, his wife had divorced him. He had three grown children, was a manager in a large firm, and held a graduate degree in business management and an undergraduate degree in theology. Raised in a very "strict religious" home, he had been "expected" to become a clergyman. And although he had practiced as a minister and pastoral counselor for some time, he later gave it up for a career in business.

Janet had been married twice before and had one daughter from her first marriage which ended, after seventeen years, with the death of her husband.

Her first marriage had been a rather traditional one; Janet was a mother and homemaker and her husband "wore the pants." Her second husband, whom she described as a "con artist," clandestinely had seven wives (simultaneously!). During the time he had been married to Janet, he had beaten and mentally abused her and had also succeeded in swindling her out of a considerable amount of money.

The past histories of Bob and Janet had suggested a good deal to me. As you have seen, behaviorists like Skinner emphasize environmental factors as paramount in shaping a person's character. In this case it seemed reasonable to suppose, at the start, that the strict religious socialization (conditioning)? Bob received and the subjection Janet had undergone could have had a significant bearing on their present marital relationship. As this case unfolded, I was to discover just how correct these suppositions were.

My first session was a joint meeting with both Janet and Bob present. It had been Janet's idea to seek counseling. As she saw it, her marriage was suffering from a "lack of communication." Bob, on the other hand, displayed a good deal of resistance to counseling, and was just going along with it because "this was what she wanted." As time went on, Bob became more amenable to the idea of counseling and began to "open up" more. However, for reasons that will become clearer later on, we never did fully overcome the obstacle of his resistance.

I did not enter into the counseling relationship with the idea that I was going to serve as an "expert" advice-giver who would lecture my clients on the principles of a good marriage. Rather, I saw my clients as *autonomous* beings who had some questions to answer for themselves. I viewed the sessions as occasions upon which clients could express and clarify their *own* beliefs and feelings. I tried to understand and empathize with these expressions, and I tended to listen a good deal more than I spoke. But as I listened, I was also drawing some inferences of my own, putting pieces of their lives together logically much like an intricate jigsaw puzzle. Sometimes the pieces seemed to fit; other times there were gaps which seemed inexplicable.

I cannot say, however, that my attitude was, like Rogers, one of "unconditional positive regard" for whatever the client expressed; for there were, it seemed to me, some limits to a counselor's "positive regard" for what a client might express.

As you have already seen, it is a basic tenet of REBT theory that people's troublesome emotions or behavior can often be traced to certain "irrational" or "unjustified" beliefs they harbor about events in their lives. Moreover, by giving up such beliefs, it is also possible, according to this theory, for people to get rid of these troublesome emotions or behavior. This approach is of particular significance from the perspective of autonomy since it views people as having considerable control over the ways they act and feel. People are not mere puppets whose emotional and behavioral responses to events in their lives are completely determined by forces lying outside their control. At the same time, however, REBT is a view that sets limits upon the "positive regard" counselors can have for what their clients may think or feel. Counselors, in this view, also serve a didactic, directive function in helping clients to think more "rationally."

Now, in applying REBT, I had been particularly concerned that I might end up short-circuiting the clients' own free choices by indoctrinating them according to my own values and beliefs. At the same time, though, I was not convinced that there were no "objective" standards of "rational" belief.

My solution to the above problem was to stick as closely as possible to the *principles of logic* when functioning in a directive capacity. That is, I was prepared to show clients where they had reasoned fallaciously in coming to their beliefs about events. What I wished to avoid, however, was telling clients *what* specifically to believe or disbelieve. Ultimately they had to make their own decisions, but it was my job to tell them when they had logical flaws in their arguments. (In retrospect, there were times when I probably went beyond these logical strictures in my directiveness; but they did, for the most part, mark the limits of my directive activities.)

It seemed to me that by using logic to set limits on "positive regard," I would be the least likely to stifle individual freedom of autonomy. In fact, like Kant, it was my conviction that an autonomous or free being is, by definition, a *rational* being,[2] and that by helping my clients to think more logically about their concerns, I would, *ipso facto*, be helping them to be more autonomous or freer. As you shall soon see, it was my clients' capacity to think logically about their own socialized attitudes which presented the only hope they had of liberating themselves from the social conditioning that enslaved them.

The following is a dialogue between Bob and me which illustrates some logical limits to the idea of "positive regard":

B: My wife has a New England mentality.
C: Does your wife come from New England?
B: Yes.
C: What do you mean by a "New England mentality"?
B: People from New England are crude; they just say whatever is on their minds without first thinking about what they are saying.
C: Have you known many people from New England?
B: No. But the ones I've known have been like that.
C: How can you say, then, that *all* people from New England are like that on the basis of such a small sampling?
B: All right, maybe not all of them are like that; but Janet is one of the ones who *is* like that.

In the above conversation, what I had tried to do was to deflate a generalization which had led Bob to a stereotyping of his wife. As I later explained to him, it is difficult to see Janet as an *individual* when she is seen instead as a "New Englander" with a "New England mentality." Rather than seeing each other as instances of some general class, each spouse had to come to see the other as an individual in his or her own right. As Sartre would put it, each had to realize that the "existence" of the other did indeed "precede" his or her "essence."

One way in which I tried to get the couple to view each other as distinct individuals was to give them a "homework assignment" that consisted of listing five things each liked about the other as well as five things each disliked about the other. The lists were prepared independently and I then met separately with each of them to discuss the items on the lists. For example, Janet typically concentrated on negative aspects of Bob's character such as his "temper," "black moods," "put downs," and "lack of respect for belongings." However, in preparing her lists, she was given an opportunity to reflect upon Bob's *positive* features (as she then perceived them) such as his "intelligence," "looks," "love-making," "morals," "willingness to work hard," and "ability to function in business." One virtue of preparing and discussing such lists is that it can discourage unwarranted inferences from some negative aspect of a spouse's character to "damning" conclusions about the *whole* person—a logical mistake which Ellis has appropriately called "damnation."

In my approach I relied a good deal on syllogistic logic.[3] Here is an example of my use of such logic in the case in point.

During one private session (that is, Bob was not present), Janet told me that, although she should be able to offer her husband advice, it is her husband who should have the final say in family matters. When I asked her why she felt this way, she said that it is *the man* who should "wear the pants." I quite naturally saw Janet's reasoning in the form of a simple *syllogism* which went as follows:

> The man should wear the pants (that is, make the final decisions).
> My husband is the man.
> ∴ My husband should wear the pants.

Seeing Janet's reasoning as such a syllogism enabled me to better focus upon the *premises* of her reasoning. My next move was to question her "major premise," so I asked her why she thought "the man should wear the pants." She responded that men are better than women at making decisions. Janet had, as I saw it, generated a *further* syllogism as follows:

> Those best at making decisions should wear the pants.
> Men are best at making decisions.
> ∴ Men should wear the pants.

As you might suspect, my next move was to ask Janet why she thought men were best at making decisions. It was at this juncture that Janet's argument broke down: she simply did not have any response which she herself could finally accept. As the session went on, she admitted having knowledge in some areas (specifically, real estate and investment) which made her better qualified than her husband to make decisions in those areas.

As I reflect back upon this session, something quite intriguing, from the perspective of exploring the problem of free will, had happened. Janet's initial insistence that "the man should wear the pants" was undoubtedly a result of the socialization she had received as a female in a male-dominated society. Janet's belief about the inferior status of women in marriage was not one she had ever *critically* accepted. With regard to this belief, she was not Sartre's Autonomous Man, but rather, as Skinner would see it, a product of a thoroughgoing determinism. Yet, in this session, Janet was able, perhaps for the first time, to transcend that socialization, to look critically upon it, and to see its manifest absurdity. I am not saying that she was thereby liberated, but I do think that such a rational scrutiny of her own socialization was an important first step.

In later sessions I continued to talk with Janet about her thoughts on a woman's status in marriage. She explained how Bob enjoyed telling jokes at functions and how she herself tried not to say anything humorous for fear that she might overshadow him. She tried her best to "stay in the background" so that he would not resent her. As time went on, however, she became more aware of the self-defeating nature of such behavior. She observed that when she was submissive, Bob was less respectful of her (he was sarcastic, criticized her) than when she asserted her autonomy.

I also continued to meet with Bob, sometimes privately, sometimes with Janet present. In private sessions, Bob spoke more openly about his feelings and was less defensive. In joint sessions, there was the clear aura of a wall he had erected between himself and his wife.

At times it looked as though relations were improving between the two. In retrospect, however, I realize that this was just an illusion. Gradually, the situation worsened. Bob began to drink heavily and the wall began to thicken.

By the time of the last session I was to have with Bob (this was a joint session), he was displaying the greatest amount of resistance ever. He denied having any drinking problem and rationalized his drinking as his way of "getting back" at his wife for smoking—a feature of Janet that he strongly disliked.

It seemed evident at this juncture that there was an important piece missing from the jigsaw puzzle of Bob's life, a piece that was needed to satisfactorily explain his present marital problems. There was something important Bob was not telling anybody. Realizing the hopelessness of the situation so long as Bob's resistance persisted, I decided to confront him—knowing full well that I might alienate him further. I indicated to him that the excuse he gave for his excessive drinking (to "get back" at his wife for smoking) was probably just a smokescreen for some more important underlying concern of his.

I had suspected, from the start, that socialization had played a substantial part in the problems this couple had experienced. On the one hand, Janet had been socialized into a submissive role; on the other hand, Bob had been brought up to believe that the man "wears the pants." Neither spouse, however, seemed comfortable with his or her indoctrination. At the close of this session I tried something quite experimental: I gave an edited excerpt of John Stuart Mill's

Subjection of Women[4] to each client. I asked each to read it and then to discuss it with the other. My hope was that this might generate some useful ideas and discussions between them about the ways men and women are socialized.

Although Bob refused further counseling (on the grounds that he really did not need any), I continued to meet with Janet. At the next session I talked with her about her response to Mill's essay. She told me that she was particularly struck by Mill's point that women are socialized into becoming "willing slaves," and that what Mill had said applied to her own case. As she left my office that day, she turned toward me, looked me squarely in the eyes, and said, "No more willing slave." It was then indeed difficult for me to escape the sense that the Autonomous Man whom Skinner had tried to bury was still alive in her!

During that same session I also had learned from Janet of another breakthrough. Although Bob did not identify the problem, he had revealed to Janet, in a letter, that he had a "problem," that it was a "bad" one, and that she would not remain married to him if she knew what it was. (Since Bob revealed this information to Janet the day after my last session with him, I wondered if he had been inspired by what had transpired at that session. I can, of course, only speculate.)

One week later, the "problem" surfaced: Bob was a homosexual! He explained to Janet that he had been having homosexual relations since the age of ten. When he married Janet, he thought he could leave this life behind him, but he had been mistaken.

The circumstances were further compounded by Janet's fear of AIDS. She had had sex for the past three years with a homosexual who had had multiple sex partners, and who had not, so far as she could determine, taken any precautions. In helping her explore her options, I suggested that she and Bob might consider getting AIDS-tested. Both eventually did. Whereas Janet tested "negative," Bob's results were conflicting; upon more extensive testing, however, the results were classified as "nonreactive."

Janet's initial response to her finding out about Bob's homosexuality was one of self-pity, particularly over what she perceived to be the "deceit" he had perpetrated on her. In spite of these very deep hurtful feelings, however, she still had a desire to remain with him. She expressed fear about supporting herself financially without Bob's help; she proclaimed that she "loved" him even though she "hated" him; she still held out hope that he might be able to leave his homosexual past behind him; and she expressed bewilderment about how he could favor another man over her.

It seemed evident that Janet had not gotten clear of her "willing slavery." Her socialized belief in her own inferiority had once again surfaced. If Bob had done this to her, then she must have done something to deserve it, and she was prepared to carry the guilt if only he would accept her back into his life.

I talked with Janet about her desire to "reform" Bob. One way in which I approached this issue was to ask her to imagine how she herself might feel if she inhabited a lesbian world in which she had a heterosexual preference. My point was to help Janet increase her empathetic understanding of Bob's circumstances and, perhaps, to help her relieve some of her own guilty feelings.

At this time, Bob and Janet had been living under the same roof, but this arrangement came to an end when one night he got drunk and beat her. (She suffered bruises, scratches, and a torn ligament in her foot.) Although she called the police, she could not "bring herself" to press charges. As with her second marriage, she was once again the "victim" of wife abuse. But this was not any mere coincidence. Janet's socialization as a "willing slave" had probably played a significant part.

In the weeks that followed, I continued to talk with Janet about the need not to be a "willing slave" and the importance of taking control of her own life. I emphasized that what she needed to do was to take constructive action; that she had decisions to make and things to do about her circumstances; that her life would change only if she did something about it. Although I did not tell her *what* to do, I did explore some of her options such as getting a job. I did not presume to know what would be best for her to do. *She* had to decide this. What I did presume to know was that she needed to be autonomous, to take control of her own life, and to do this by taking constructive action. As Sartre has urged, a person is *no* more than the sum of his or her actions. The Autonomous Man does not exist without action, for the only way one can ever *define oneself* is through one's actions. If Janet were to be autonomous, then she would, indeed, have to *do* things about her circumstances.

Fortunately, Janet did do some things about her circumstances: She enrolled in a college course, got a job, prepared her house for sale, and filed for a legal separation. The last time I spoke to her, she told me that although she "has her moments," she "feels good"; she feels like she is "in control of things." She also told me that she keeps her copy of Mill's *Subjection of Women* handy, and is still underlining things in it.

As for Bob, I do not presume to know what his fate will be, but I am convinced that, unless he is able to assert his autonomy, to become a self-determining agent rather than a pawn of society, the prognosis for his future does not appear to be very encouraging.

From early childhood, Bob was indoctrinated with the "musts" of being a man. Since his own sexual preferences were at odds with these "musts," he had attempted to conceal his desires in the hope that they might go away or at least not be found out. The result of such "musturbation" (Ellis) or "bad faith" (Sartre) had been a heavy burden of guilt and frustration which undoubtedly expressed itself in his abusive treatment of Janet, and in his drinking. Bob's only hope now was to come to grips with his true feelings, and to break down the social wall which had for so long divided him from himself.

In discussing this case, I have attempted to show the significance of the concepts of free will and determinism as they apply to counseling. I do not claim that anything I have said, strictly speaking, *proves* the existence of free will in Skinner's sense of an "Inner Man" whose function it is to "provide an explanation which will not be explained in turn." In the metaphysical sense, determinism has not been ruled out. Nevertheless, I hope I have shown that counseling cannot do without the *assumption* that there is free will. More specifically, counselors should promote an atmosphere in which clients can openly express themselves; logically examine their own feelings, beliefs, and behavior; and explore the range of possible actions which could help them to deal constructively with their problems. But all this can be understood only if it is assumed, in the first place, that clients have the power of free will, that they can indeed function as autonomous or *self*-determining agents.

The famous American pragmatist philosopher William James maintained that "from any strict theoretical point of view, the question [of whether there is free will or determinism] is insoluble. To deepen our theoretical sense of the *difference* between a world with a chance in it and a deterministic world is the most I can hope to do."[5] Now, a world in which determinism were accepted would be a world in which clients would inevitably come to see themselves as sorts of automata, and their counselors as sorts of technicians whose job it was to "overhaul" or "recondition" them. However, it was in fact this kind of inert mode of confronting the world which, in the first place, made a "willing slave" out of Janet and which led Bob into an "inauthentic" form of existence filled with frustrations. Moreover, an unavoidable manner of dealing with these problems was, as we have seen, the assertion of autonomy, *not* its further surrender. If people were to view their thoughts, feelings, and deeds as mere conditioned responses, or mere responses to causal stimuli, then they would inevitably lose the zest and vitality for solving their own problems. It has, however, been my contention that people *can* actually solve their own problems by "transcending" the world of conditioned responses, or stimulus-response relations, by functioning as *rational* agents, not as cogs in a machine. Counselors should, accordingly, help foster this sense of rational self-determination in their clients. Even if it cannot be proven from a "strict theoretical point of view," the assumption of free will is crucial in counseling. At the same time, however, counselors must recognize the forces of environment which can mold and shape people's thoughts, feelings, and deeds; and which can also destroy that sense of autonomy.

NOTES

1. Albert Ellis, *How to Live with—and without—Anger* (New York: Readers Digest Press, 1977), p. 8.
2. Immanuel Kant, *Groundwork of the Metaphysics of Morals*, tr. H. J. Paton (New York: Harper & Row, 1964), 98–99.
3. See Howard Kahane's discussion of the syllogism in "Aristotelian Logic," in chapter 5 of this text. See also Elliot D. Cohen, "The Use of the Syllogism in RET," *Journal of Counseling and Development*, September 1987.
4. See the Issues section of chapter 3 of this text.
5. William James, "The Dilemma of Determinism," in *William James: Essays in Pragmatism*, ed. Alburey Castell (New York: Hafner, 1969), p. 47.

DISCUSSION QUESTIONS

1. What is meant by the doctrine of "determinism"? By "behaviorism"?
2. Is it possible to accept determinism while consistently believing in free will? Explain your answer.
3. What does Sartre mean by "existence precedes essence"? How does Sartre's atheism (his belief that God does not exist) relate to this doctrine? What implications does this doctrine have for the belief in a human nature?
4. What is your position on the free will–determinism issue? Defend your position.
5. Discuss Sartre's perspective on human responsibility and compare it to Skinner's perspective. Is the existence of human responsibility compatible with determinism? Explain your answer.
6. Describe Carl Rogers's person-centered approach to psychotherapy. Define briefly each of the following concepts as they function in this approach: (a) empathetic understanding, (b) unconditional positive regard, (c) congruence.
7. Describe Albert Ellis's Rational-Emotive Behavior approach to psychotherapy. Discuss his "ABC theory" as it functions in this approach.
8. Discuss Eric Berne's Transactional Analysis approach to psychotherapy. Define briefly each of the following terms as they function in this approach: (a) life-script, (b) game, (c) ego states, (d) transaction.
9. Discuss some of the ways each of the three above-mentioned psychotherapeutic approaches (Rogers, Ellis, and Berne) deals with the free will–determinism issue.
10. Recall the case described by Cohen in the Practice section of this chapter. In what ways might Beme's concepts of "life-script" and "game" pertain to the lives of Bob and Janet?
11. In your opinion, did Janet, at any time in the counseling process, exercise free will? Did Bob? Defend your answers.
12. Discuss the merit of Cohen's application of Sartre's doctrine of "existence precedes essence" in counseling Janet and Bob.
13. According to Sartre, "Man is . . . nothing else than the ensemble of his acts . . ." What does Sartre mean by this? How did Cohen apply this doctrine in counseling Janet?
14. Discuss the merit of Cohen's use of John Stuart Mill's *Subjection of Women* as a counseling tool.
15. What is Cohen's view about employing Rogers's idea of "unconditional positive regard" as a counseling position? What function do the principles of logic play in Cohen's approach to counseling? In your opinion, was there any time in the counseling process where Cohen tried to impose his own values on Janet or Bob? In your opinion, should counselors ever attempt to instill their own values in clients? Defend your answers.
16. Describe and discuss the merits of Cohen's use of the logic of syllogism as a tool for helping Janet to explore her own belief system.
17. If you were a counselor, how, in general, would you approach the issue of free will and determinism in dealing with your clients? Defend your answer.

12

MINDS, BODIES, AND ARTIFICIAL INTELLIGENCE

This chapter will explore the ancient metaphysical problem popularly called "the mind-body problem" and its relations to the field of Artificial Intelligence (AI), a branch of computer science that investigates and devises methods for building expert systems and simulating human intelligence.

The mind-body problem is the problem of specifying the relation between mind and body—or, alternatively put, between mental and physical states. Generally speaking, approaches to this problem may be divided into two categories: *dualistic* theories and *monistic* theories. According to dualistic approaches, there exist *two* distinct entities, namely a mind *and* a body; according to monistic approaches, there is just *one* entity, either a mind *or* a body.

One historically significant variant of dualism is the *interactionist theory,* which is examined by Baruch Brody in the first selection of this chapter. This theory received its most elaborate development in the work of the seventeenth-century French philosopher Rene Descartes. (See also chapter 10.) According to Descartes, minds are distinct from bodies. Whereas minds are *res cogitans* ("thinking things"), bodies are *res extensa* ("spatially extended things"). Although distinct substances, each is causally bound up with the other: one's mind causes changes in one's body and, conversely, one's body causes changes in one's mind.

A further example of a dualistic conception is *epiphenomenalism.* According to this theory, bodies cause changes in minds although, contrary to Descartes's two-way interactionism, minds are not capable of affecting bodies. Rather, mental states are causally inefficacious by-products ("epiphenomena") of physical processes. All changes in the universe can thus be accounted for by appealing to physical processes.

On the monistic side of metaphysical theory are *idealist* and *materialist* theories. According to idealism, the only entities are minds; physical objects, including one's body, are actually "collections of sense data." This view receives its most elaborate development in the work of George Berkeley. (See also chapter 10.)

Materialist theories hold just the opposite of idealist theories; that is, that the only real entities are physical ones. An example of such a theory is so-called *metaphysical behaviorism* (in contradistinction to the methodological sort defended by B. F. Skinner in chapter 11). According to this kind of materialism, mental states are actually *definable* in terms of sets of behavior. For example, the term "anger" is, on this view, a kind of shorthand for a set of associated behaviors, such as shouting and stamping, accompanied by certain physiological changes such as increased pulse rate and adrenalin flow. One common objection to this theory, however, is that it would seem possible to manifest such behavioral states without being in the mental state presumed by the behavior. For example, an actor may pretend to be angry without actually *being* angry. Conversely, it also appears possible for one to be in a certain mental state—say, that of being angry—without behaviorally showing it.

Another materialist theory is the so-called *identity theory,* which Jerome A. Shaffer examines in the second selection of this chapter. According to this theory, our mental states are, as a matter of fact, "identical" with (although not definable in terms of) our brain states. On this view, the mind and the brain are thus one and the same thing. As a materialist theory, this theory is inconsistent with religious conceptions such as belief in life after death of the body and the concept of God as an immaterial being.

In the third selection excerpted from *Minds, Brains, and Science,* John R. Searle, starting with a particular philosophical view about the mind-body problem, examines the question of whether machines can think. According to Searle, brains (neurological brain processes) *cause* minds (mental processes such as thoughts and sensations). In addition, minds are *features* of brains, that is, mental processes are just properties of systems of neurological brain processes. Likening the case to that of other physical properties such as liquidity, he points out that we may sensibly say that the liquidity of water is caused by its molecular structure (that of H_2O) while at the the same time agreeing that liquidity is a property of H_2O. In a similar vein, he claims that a system of neurons can both cause thoughts as well as have them as properties.

In contrast to the above view—which he considers a "minority view"—Searle examines "the prevailing view" in philosophy, psychology, and AI. This is, instead, the view that the brain is essentially a digital computer (the hardware) while the mind is a computer program (the software). Against this view, Searle argues that computer programs merely manipulate uninterpreted strings of symbols without understanding them. These programs are defined by their syntactical (formal) structure, but they have no semantical contents (the symbols do not mean anything to the computer).

To illustrate this point, Searle invokes his well-known "Chinese room" analogy in which he asks you to imagine that you are locked in a room with a rule book for exchanging Chinese symbols as they are passed in and out of the room. While you may provide answers in Chinese to questions being passed into the room, you may nevertheless not speak a word of Chinese or, for that matter, even know that you are answering questions posed in Chinese. Analogously, according to Searle, so too would any digital computer fail to understand its subject's contents when it goes through a process of manipulating symbols.

On the other hand, argues Searle, the symbols that minds manipulate have semantical contents, they mean something to the individual mind. A computer program, with its lack of semantical import, is therefore not sufficient to give a system a mind. Thus the way in which brains cause minds cannot be explained solely in terms of the syntactical functions of computer programs.

According to Searle, the difference between computer programs and brains is that the latter is biological; "their biology," he states, "matters." It is not "an irrelevant fact about the mind that it happens to be realized in human brains." Nevertheless, even if it is assumed that computer programs do not presently understand the symbols they manipulate, it does not follow that the explanation for this is inextricably linked to the fact that they are nonbiological, for it is still possible that the solution lies in some other technical deficiency of the program. All that Searle appears justified in concluding is that the biological nature of the brain *may* be relevant.

Searle does comes to the conclusion that "Anything else that caused minds would have to have causal powers at least equivalent to those of the brain," but he explicates this conclusion in terms of the possibility of there being other (nonhuman) *biological* life forms that possess minds. The conclusion, however, does not rule out the possibility of nonbiological entities having minds such as ones composed of silicon chips.

In the Practice section, Herbert Simon challenges Searle's claim that computers cannot think. Drawing from his own vast experience in cognitive psychology and in building computer programs that model human intelligence, Simon sets out to demonstrate how computer programs can simulate such thinking activities as intuition, insight, and creativity. Simon's *modus operandi* is, first, to operationally define what it means for a human to engage in the thought activity in question, and, second, to check this definition against the computer program. If the two match, then he concludes that the computer, like the human, has also performed the thinking activity. Simon asserts:

> to answer the question of whether an appropriately programmed computer can think, we establish a task and a set of criteria to determine whether a human being is thinking when performing that task. If the computer, given the same task, not only produces the same result but also matches the behavior of the human in all observable respects, and in particular, matches the processes the human is observably using during performance of the task, then we conclude that the computer is also thinking. . . .

For example, Simon operationally defines intuition in terms of a "rapid solution and inability to report a sequence of steps leading up to the solution." Insofar as a computer program simulates the process and result (problem solution) of intuition, the computer has an intuition.

Still, as Searle reminds us, *simulation* is not necessarily the same thing as *duplication*. While Searle may agree that a computer program can simulate thought processes like intuition, his contention is that the computer program cannot *understand* anything, and therefore cannot think.

Simon's response to Searle is a denial that computers cannot understand the symbols they manipulate. Referring to Searle's Chinese room argument, he maintains that Searle needed to give his room windows so the translators could see into the real world and associate the Chinese symbols with the situations they denote. According to Simon, computer programs have existed for a quarter of a century with the capability to discriminate between symbols on the basis of the situations they denote. If so, then perhaps Searle's claim that thought must always be imbedded in biological systems should also be rejected.

Nonetheless, it is noteworthy that Simon's definitions of thought processes are *operational* ones, that is, they are coached in terms of observable behavior. This leaves out phenomenological criteria such as the conscious awareness of oneself as the subject of an intuition or insight. Are computers ever self-aware?

From a Cartesian perspective, it might be argued that both Searle and Simon have it wrong. Mental processes are activities of immaterial souls. While they are causally integrated with physical systems, they are not ultimately dependent upon them for their existence. Thus, minds are neither caused by brains nor are they computer programs that require brains or other hardware to run them. Further, it is not their corporeal nature, biological or otherwise, that accounts for their ability to think. To the contrary, it is their immateriality. Such are the substrata of consciousness and self-awareness.

Clearly, this Cartesian view is not likely to impress those who seek scientific explanations of thought. Nor is it clear that postulating immaterial souls is the best hypothesis to explain all the facts. Indeed, such an explanation only brings us back to Descartes's problem of explaining how distinct substances as the mental and the physical interact with one another.

On Simon's view, the mind-body problem is more efficiently dealt with by empirical science than by such philosophical speculation. Indeed, on his view, it is philosophy that stands to learn from science, and what it stands to learn is that minds and brains are two interdependent components of physical systems. The mind (thought processes) is supported by the brain (the hardware). The mind needs the brain for it to work, but the brain is itself useless without the mind.

ISSUES

BARUCH A. BRODY

MIND-BODY DUALISM: THE INTERACTIONIST THEORY

The dualist position advances the following claims about human beings:

1. They are composed out of two entities, a body which is a physical object located in space, and a soul which is nonphysical and not located in space.
2. It is the soul that thinks, feels emotions, has perceptions, and makes decisions.
3. The soul and the body interact, so that the thoughts and decisions of the soul cause the body to move and act in certain ways, while the physical stimuli impinging upon the body cause certain perceptions in the soul.
4. The purely physical characteristics of human beings are characteristics of the body.

We find a well-known presentation of this view in the writings of René Descartes:

> All that we experience as being in us, and that to observation may exist in wholly inanimate bodies, must be attributed to our body alone; and, on the other hand, all that which is in us and which we cannot in any way conceive as possibly pertaining to a body, must be attributed to our soul. Thus because we have no conception of the body as thinking in any way, we have reason to believe that every kind of thought which exists in us belongs to the soul. . . . Those [thoughts] which we relate to the things which are without us, to wit the objects of our senses, are caused, at least when our opinion is not false, by these objects which, exciting certain movements in the organs of the external senses, excite them also in the brain by the intermission of the nerves, which cause the soul to perceive them. . . . The whole action of the soul consists in this, that solely because it desires something, it causes the little gland [in the body] to which it is closely united to move in the way requisite to produce the effect which relates to this desire. (*Passions of the Soul,* Part I)

Some dualists have gone even further. They have claimed that a human being is really just a soul, that the body is simply a physical object to which the soul is attached. They have sometimes even claimed that the body is best compared to a prison or a trap for the soul. The desires and perceptions that it causes in the soul interfere with the proper activities of the soul, so the best thing for us to do is to ignore them (especially, the desires) as much as possible. This extreme dualism, which is very widely spread in certain religious writings, was expressed by Socrates in Plato's *Phaedo:*

> And purification, as we saw sometime ago in our discussion, consists in separating the soul as much as possible from the body, and accustoming it to withdraw from all contact with the body and concentrate itself by itself, and to have its dwelling, so far as it can, both now and in the future, alone by itself, freed from the shackles of the body.

Not all dualists, however, have held these additional views, and we shall put them aside to concentrate on the more central themes of dualism that are outlined above.

Why are people dualists? We have already seen a number of factors that explain the attractiveness of dualism. Dualism clearly offers a straightforward explanation of certain undeniable dualities in human nature. In particular, it tells why human beings, physical themselves, are capable of performing a wide variety of activities that cannot be performed by ordinary physical objects. According to the dualist explanation, human beings can perform these activities only because they have a soul as well as a body, for these activities are activities of the soul.

This factor immediately raises the question of whether aninials also have souls. After all, they are also capable of performing many activities that cannot be performed by ordinary physical objects. This issue was hotly debated in the seventeenth and eighteenth centuries. At that time, there were dualists who were fully prepared to accept the view that animals have souls (a view which had been held, in a different way, by Aristotle and many medieval thinkers). . . . However, most thinkers at the time, like Descartes, felt that the activities of animals could be completely explained by special facts about their bodies. Naturally, this raised the question as to whether the same thing couldn't be said about human beings. Perhaps our special capacities are explainable by the special and complex structure of our bodies.

This leads us to another point. The fact that human beings perform activities which ordinary objects do not is obviously going to fail as an argument for dualism unless the dualist can show that the materialist explanation is inadequate . . .

A second factor which attracts people to dualism is that it leaves open the possibility of survival after death. One fact that we are all aware of—though many of us try to avoid thinking about it—is that we will die. Each of us knows that his body will to a large extent be destroyed in a relatively short period after death. Is that the end of us, or do we continue to exist anyway? This is the question of personal survival. Dualism suggests that we may, for there is a major part of us, the soul, that might survive the destruction of the body. (Believers in psychic phenomena, in fact, often feel that it offers evidence for dualism.)

Regarding this factor we should note, to begin with, that a dualist need not be committed to belief in personal survival. Dualism itself is neutral on that issue. All that can legitmately be said is that dualism leaves open the possibility that a major part of us will survive the destruction of the body after death. Secondly, the fact that dualism leaves open this possibility is not an argument for its truth. For that, we would have to know that we actually do survive our death. All that can be said is that this factor is responsible for much of the popularity of dualism.

Traditional materialism offers two sorts of objections to dualism. One (the interaction objection) is directed towards the claims of the dualist, and the other (the other-minds objection) is concerned with the question of knowledge and the implications of dualism in this realm. Let us look at each of these objections and at the responses that dualists have made to them.

The interaction objection. This objection addresses itself to claim 3 of dualism, the claim that the body and the soul interact. It is not surprising that the dualist makes this claim, for it certainly appears as if our thoughts and feelings influence our actions, and as if physical stimuli influence our perceptions and thoughts. But this objection asks how this interaction can take place if the dualist is right about the soul and body being of such different natures? As David Hume put it:

> Is there any principle in all nature more mysterious than the union of soul with body, by which a supposed spiritual substance acquires such an influence over a material one that the most refined thought is able to actuate the grossest matter? Were we empowered by a secret wish to remove mountains or control the planets in their orbit, this extensive authority would not be more extraordinary, nor more beyond our comprehension. (*Inquiry Concerning Human Understanding*, section 7.)

The basic strategy for meeting this objection has traditionally been put as follows. We clearly need to concede that there is a relation between the mental and the physical. After all, our thoughts and feelings are clearly related to the bodily motions which follow them in time. And the physical stimuli impinging upon our sensory organs are clearly related to the perceptions and thoughts which follow them in time. There is no reason, however, to concede that the relation in question is a causal relation. And if we can find some other account of the relation, the interaction problem will be solved. But what is that other relation?

It is the relation of *correlation.* Our subsequent bodily motions are correlated with earlier thoughts and feelings but the latter do not cause the former. The physical stimuli impinging upon our sensory organs are correlated with subsequent perceptions and thoughts, but they do not cause them. Another question arises here, however, for what is the cause of these correlations? Why, for example, are our decisions to act in certain ways normally correlated with our subsequently acting that way if the former do not cause the latter? In response to these obvious and overwhelming objections, the seventeenth and eighteenth century dualists invoked the deity. They did so, however, in two different ways. Some, like Malebranche, held a view called *occasionalism.* This said that the correlation is maintained by the constant intervention of God. Others, like Leibniz, felt there was a *pre-established harmony,* that is, that the correlation was established for all time by God when he created the universe. One can get a sense of the nature of this dispute by reading the following passage from a letter of Leibniz:

> I say that God created the universe in such a way that the soul and the body, each acting according to its laws, agree in their phenomena. You think, M., that this coincides with the hypothesis of occasional causes. . . . My opinion is different. . . . Everything happens to each substance in consequence of the first state which God gave to it in creating it, and putting aside extraordinary interventions the originary agreement consists only in the conservation of the substance itself conformably to its preceding state and to the changes which it carries in itself. (*Letter to Arnauld,* April 30, 1687)

Despite their ingeniousness, these theories of correlation have been rejected by most dualists. They have felt that the use of God in this sort of way is a form of intellectual cheating; one cannot just invoke him as a solution to any unresolved problem. Moreover, this whole approach may be based on a nonexistent distinction because it is not clear that there is a difference between the causal relation and the correlation invoked as a substitute.

In recent years, dualists have claimed that the whole interaction problem is a pseudoproblem based upon the unwarranted and mistaken assumption that two substances must be sufficiently like each other to interact causally. With what justification, they have asked, can we rule out the possibility of two substances interacting just because they are different? . . .

The other-minds objection. This objection cannot be dismissed that easily. It begins by observing that, according to dualism, the soul is a nonphysical object which has no spatial location. It cannot, then, be perceived by external senses. Now, as a matter of fact, dualists feel that we have a power of introspection, an ability to perceive what is going on in our own souls. In this way, we are able to immediately know that we have a soul and which thoughts and emotions it has and which decisions it makes. But what about the soul (the mind) of others? How can we know that they have one? And even if we can, how do we know what is going on in it? Doesn't dualism really commit us to a terrible ignorance about other people? And isn't it therefore in error?

Dualism, then, must deal with this problem of how we can know about the minds of others. How do we know that someone else is in pain? How do we know when someone else loves us (or doesn't)? How can we find out what anyone believes? These can be practical as well as philosophical problems, and the truth of the matter is that we often don't know. But, in many cases, we can figure out what other people think or feel. How do we do that? Presumably, we figure it out on a basis of their behavior. For example, if we see someone writhing on the ground we infer on the basis of their behavior that they are in pain. Again, we conclude that someone loves us on the basis of the way that person behaves toward us.

It is just this that gives rise to problems for the dualist. According to the dualist, pain is a sensation that we feel in our soul. How then can we infer that it is occurring in someone else's soul when all that we can observe is the writhing of that person's body? According to the dualist, love is an emotion that takes place in our soul. How then can we infer that it is occurring in someone else's soul when all that we can observe are certain ways of behaving? In short, the dualist has to explain how we can infer what is going on in the soul when all that we can observe is the behavior of the body.

Obviously, dualists will insist that that inference is legitimate. But they have to offer an explanation of its legitimacy. There are two major dualist accounts, the *analogy-account* and the *explanation-account*.

According to the analogy-account, we first learn about the connection between what goes on in the soul and how bodies behave by observing it in our own case. We see, for example, the way that the love in our soul leads us to behave in certain ways. Then, we infer that the other people behave analogously. They must be feeling love when they behave similarly towards us. John Stuart Mill wrote:

> I conclude that other human beings have feelings like me, because, first, they have bodies like me, which I know, in my own case, to be the antecedent condition of feelings; and because, secondly, they exhibit the acts, and other outward signs, which in my own case, I know by experience to be caused by feelings. (*Examination of Sir William Hamilton's Philosophy*, chapter 12)

This account seems incomplete. What is the justification for assuming that other people behaved analogously? If we know only about the connection between the mental and the physical from our own case, how can we be sure that the same connection holds for other people? Perhaps, for example, they feel a different emotion and not love? Perhaps they don't feel any emotion at all? Somehow, the analogy of our own case seems too weak a foundation for the whole of our knowledge about other minds. It would be different, of course, if we could at least sometimes directly check to see that other people have analogous feelings and thoughts. But we never can. . . .

Not all philosophers find this objection to the analogical approach conclusive. There are philosophers who claim that there is no significance to the fact that I cannot directly check whether someone else has feelings and thoughts. The analogy is valid so long as there are no features distinguishing us that might provide the basis for my having thoughts and feelings while you don't. . . .

Despite this attempt to defend the analogy-account, many philosophers have concluded that it would be preferable to find a different, more satisfactory account. They have proposed the explanation-account of our knowledge of other minds.

In order to understand the explanation-account, we should understand the basis for inferences made from what has been observed to what has not been observed. Suppose, for example, that you are a detective trying to figure out who the murderer is. You collect a number of observations (the clues) and you infer from them something that you have not observed (that x is the murderer). What is the justification for such an inference? Well, suppose that the clues are that the butler's fingerprints were found on the murder weapon, that the missing $10,000 was found in his Swiss bank account, etc. The conclusion that is inferred, that the butler is the murderer, is justified because it seems to be the best explanation of the clues. If the butler didn't kill the victim, what are his fingerprints doing on the murder weapon, what is the money doing in his Swiss bank account, etc.? And if there is a better explanation, if these questions can be answered, then the inference is not justified.

This seems to be a very common pattern of inferences from the observed to the unobserved. Consider, as a more substantial example, the inferences that lead scientists to accept the theory that all material objects are composed of atoms. No one has seen these atoms that are supposed to make up all matter, and yet we all believe that they exist. Why? Well, the atomic theory of matter does, in fact, seem to be the best explanation of a whole variety of observed phenomena (e.g., the ways in which chemical elements combine to form compounds). It is this that justifies the inference to its truth.

According to the explanation-account, then, the very same type of inference underlies our knowledge of the thoughts and feelings of other people. When we see someone's body writhing, we infer that he is in pain because his being in pain is the best account of why his body is moving in the ways that it is moving. When we see a man behaving in certain ways towards a woman, we infer that he loves her because his being in love is the best explanation of his behavior. In general, we believe in the thoughts and feelings of others because that belief is the best explanation of their behavior. To quote H. H. Price:

> But the argument is not only analogical. The hypothesis which it seeks to establish may also be considered in another way. It provides a simple explanation of an otherwise mysterious set of occurrences [intelligent speech acts]. . . . If there is another mind which uses the same symbols as I do and combines them according to the same principles, and if this mind has produced these noises in the course of an act of spontaneous thinking: then I can account for the occurrence of these noises. ("Our Evidence for the Existence of Other Minds," *Philosophy*, 1938)

We have seen then that the dualists have ways of responding both to the interaction objection and the other-minds objection. Nevertheless, there are many philosophers who would prefer a materialist account of human beings. Some of them do so because they do not find that the dualists have satisfactorily explained away their problems. But others have a different reason, one that needs to be explored more fully.

There are many different conceptions of the nature and function of philosophy. One of these conceptions is particularly important for understanding this last basis for a materialist approach. According to this conception, the purpose of philosophy is to present a comprehensive way of thinking about the nature of the world. In other words, this conception would ask philosophy to present a unified picture of the nature of things. Arguing from such a conception of philosophy, some philosophers have concluded that dualism is unacceptable. One such philosopher, J. J. C. Smart, presented that argument in the following fashion:

> Presumably a comprehensive way of thought would be one that brought all intellectual disciplines into a harmonious relationship with one another. It may turn out that there are some realms of discourse, such as theology, which cannot be brought into a harmonious relationship with the various sciences. Any attempt to do so would result in violence to logic or to scientific facts, or may involve arbitrariness and implausibility. (Consider, for example, the implausibility of a theory which asserts that the mechanistic account of evolution by natural selection and mutation is broadly true, but that there is a special discontinuity in the case of man, to whom was superadded an immortal soul.) If this is so, such anomalous branches of discourse will have to be rejected and will not form part of the reconstruction of our total conceptual scheme. (*Philosophy and Scientific Realism,* chapter 1)

In order to properly evaluate this argument, we must first review the sorts of scientific facts that Smart and philosophers like him feel are important in putting forward a unified view of man. There are two main sets of such facts, those having to do with the origin of life and those having to do with the origin of man.

The question of the origin of life has perplexed mankind for a long time. There is, of course, the religious view that life was created by God in a special act of creation. But could one offer a nonreligious account of the origin of life? Pasteur, of course, in a series of famous experiments, had attacked the old view that living organisms can be generated spontaneously from inorganic matter. As a result, important nineteenth-century scientists like Lord Kelvin and Helmholtz concluded that life on earth must have been transmitted to the earth from other places in the universe. This view, is of course extremely implausible, since the conditions in outer space (extreme cold, intense radiation, etc.) make it highly unlikely that any living things could survive the trip.

As a matter of fact, the great Russian scientist, A. I. Oparin, was the first to put forward a reasonable, scientific account of the origin of life. On Oparin's view, life emerged from the nonliving as intense radiation caused the formation of more and more complex organic compounds until the simplest living things appeared. In his fundamental work, *The Origin of Life* (first published in Russian in 1936), Oparin worked out the main outlines of this process and showed how the whole process was chemically possible.

Suppose then that we have a world in which there are simple living organisms. How does that serve as the foundation for explaining the origin of the more complex organisms that we encounter in the world today? To answer this question, scientifically minded philosophers turn to the theory of evolution (which was first put forward in the nineteenth century by Charles Darwin and developed extensively since then).

Briefly, this theory contains two elements. One is devoted to explaining the way in which new forms of life emerge from earlier forms. The other explains the mechanisms by which these new forms persevere once they have developed. In the modern theory of evolution, the process of mutation is used to explain the origin of the new forms while that of natural selection is used to explain the perseverance of certain new forms (the ones that are favorably adapted to the ecological niche in which they first emerge).

But how is all of this related to the dispute between materialism and dualism? Smart and others would presumably argue as follows: In trying to put forward a unified picture of man, we must take into account these factors about the origin of man. Looking at scientific theories, we see an earth which at one time contained only inorganic chemical elements. Over a long period of time, organic compounds developed, eventually of such complexity that we can justifiably talk of them as being alive. Then, through the process of evolution, even more complex forms of life emerged. Finally, man appears. At what point in this whole process did the soul appear? Phrased, perhaps, in a more sophisticated way, doesn't a materialistic conception of man fit more naturally into this process than a dualistic conception? And if so, doesn't that provide us with at least some reason for adopting materialism?

Those who offer this argument do not think of it as a conclusive refutation of dualism. It is good that they do not because (1) while the evidence for this account of the origin of man is quite strong, it would certainly, be incorrect to call it absolutely conclusive, and (2) the dualist can claim that his thesis is, nevertheless, compatible with this scientific view of the origin of man. (Religious dualists have sometimes said, for example, that God united the soul with the body only when a certain complexity of life had been achieved.) Nevertheless, these considerations certainly are sufficient to make us look more closely at materialism. . . .

JEROME A. SHAFFER

MATERIALISM:
THE IDENTITY THEORY

Materialism is one of the very oldest theories. It was a familiar doctrine to the ancient Greeks of the fourth and fifth centuries B.C. The spokesman for this

SOURCE: Jerome A Shaffer, *Philosophy of Mind* Copyright 1994. Reprinted by permission of Prentice-Hall, Inc., Upper Saddle River, NJ.

view, Democritus, held that nothing exists but material atoms and the void and that everything in the world is nothing but the interactions of these atoms as they move through the void. Even the most complex behavior of human beings can be resolved into interactions between the atoms. A modern materialist would allow a more complicated picture than "atoms and the void." He would bring in subatomic particles and antiparticles, electromagnetic waves, a relativized view of "the void," various kinds of forces and energies, and the rest of the conceptual apparatus of contemporary physics. But he would still hold that nothing exists but such physical phenomena; if such terms as "thought," "feeling," "wish," etc., have any meaning at all, they must refer in the last analysis to physical phenomena. So-called mental events are really nothing but physical events occurring to physical objects.

We should, at the outset, distinguish materialism as characterized here from another doctrine which has already been mentioned, epiphenomenalism. . . . The latter is a dualistic theory which allows that the mind is separate and distinct from the body but also insists that the mind is utterly dependent causally upon the body, that everything which happens in the mind is a result of events in the body, and that the mind is utterly powerless to affect the body in any way. Such a view is often called materialistic, since it places the highest *importance* on the material side of things. It is in the sense that Karl Marx was materialistic, for he held that "conceiving, thinking, the mental intercourse of men, appear at [the earliest] stage as the direct efflux of their material behavior." Notice that Marx is not saying men's conceiving, thinking, and mental intercourse *are nothing but* their material behavior. That would be materialism as here characterized. He is saying that they are the "efflux," i.e., a *separate, nonmaterial* outflow which originates and derives from material behavior. Such a view is not materialistic in our sense.

The materialist holds that nothing but the physical exists—matter, energy, and the void. But then what are thoughts, feelings, wishes, and the other so-called mental phenomena? . . .

[One] version of materialism we shall consider, and currently the most seriously discussed, is known as the identity theory. It is the theory that thoughts, feelings, wishes, and the rest of so-called mental phenomena are identical with, one and the same thing as, states and processes of the *body* (and, perhaps, more specifically, states and processes of the nervous system, or even of the brain alone). Thus the having of a thought is identical with having such and such bodily cells in such and such states, other cells in other states.

The sense of "identity" relevant here is that in which we say, for example, that the morning star is "identical" with the evening star. It is not that the expression "morning star" means the same as the expression "evening star"; on the contrary, these expressions mean something different. But the object referred to by the two expressions is one and the same; there is just one heavenly body, namely, Venus, which when seen in the morning is called the morning star and when seen in the evening is called the evening star. The morning star is identical with the evening star; they are one and the same object.

Of course, the identity of the mental with the physical is not exactly of this sort, since it is held to be simultaneous identity rather than the identity of a thing at one time with the same thing at a later time. To take a closer example, one can say that lightning is a particularly massive electrical discharge from one cloud to another or to the earth. Not that the word "lightning" *means* "a particularly massive electrical discharge . . ."; when Benjamin Franklin discovered that lightning was electrical, he did not make a discovery about the meaning of words. Nor when it was discovered that water was H_2O was a discovery made about the meanings of words; yet water is identical with H_2O.

In a similar fashion, the identity theorist can hold that thoughts, feelings, wishes, and the like are identical with physical states. Not "identical" in the sense that mentalistic terms are synonymous in meaning with physicalistic terms but "identical" in the sense that the actual events picked out by mentalistic terms are one and the same events as those picked out by physicalistic terms.

It is important to note that the identity theory does not have a chance of being true unless a particular sort of correspondence obtains between mental events and physical events, namely, that whenever a mental event occurs, a physical event of a particular sort (or at least one of a number of particular sorts) occurs, and vice versa. If it turned out to be the case that when a particular mental event occurred it seemed a matter of chance what physical events occurred or even whether any physical event at all occurred, or vice versa, then the identity theory would not be true. So far as our state of knowledge at the present time is concerned, it is still too early to say what the empirical facts are, although it must be said that many scientists do believe that there exists the kind of correspondences needed by identity theorists. But even if these correspondences turn out to exist, that does not mean that the identity theory will be true. For identity theorists do not hold merely that mental and physical events are correlated in any particular way but that they are one and the same events, i.e., not like lightning and thunder (which are correlated in lawful ways but not identical) but like lightning and electrical discharges (which always go together because they are one and the same).

What are the advantages of the identity theory? As a form of materialism, it does not have to cope with a world which has in it both mental phenomena and physical phenomena, and it does not have to ponder how they might be related. There exist only the physical phenomena, although there do exist two different ways of talking about such phenomena: physicalistic terminology and, in at least some situations, mentalistic terminology. We have here a dualism of language, but not a dualism of entities, events, or properties.

But do we have merely a dualism of languages and no other sort of dualism? In the case of Venus, we do indeed have only one object, but the expression "morning star" picks out one phase of that object's history, where it is in the mornings, and the expression "evening star" picks out another phase of that object's history, where it is in the evenings. If that object did not have these two distinct aspects, it would not have been a *discovery* that the morning star and the evening star were indeed one and the same body, and, further, there would be no point to the different ways of referring to it.

Now it would be admitted by identity theorists that physicalistic and mentalistic terms do not refer to different phases in the history of one and the same object. What sort of identity is intended? Let us turn to an allegedly closer analogy, that of the identity of lightning and a particular sort of electrical phenomenon. Yet here again we have two distinguishable aspects, the appearance to the naked eye on the one hand and the physical composition on the other. And this is also not the kind of identity which is plausible for mental and physical events. The appearance *to the naked eye* of a neurological event is utterly different from the experience of having a thought or a pain.

It is sometimes suggested that the physical aspect results from looking at a particular event "from the outside," whereas the mental results from looking at the same event "from the inside." When the brain surgeon observes my brain he is looking at it from the outside, whereas when I experience a mental event I am "looking" at my brain "from the inside."

Such an account gives us only a misleading analogy, rather than an accurate characterization of the relationship between the mental and the physical. The analogy suggests the difference between a man who knows his own house from the inside, in that he is free to move about within, seeing objects from different perspectives, touching them, etc., but can never get outside to see how it looks from there, and a man who cannot get inside and therefore knows only the outside appearance of the house, and perhaps what he can glimpse through the windows. But what does this have to do with the brain? Am I free to roam about inside my brain, observing what the brain surgeon may never see? Is not the "inner" aspect of my brain far more accessible to the brain surgeon than to me? He has the X rays, probes, electrodes, scalpels, and scissors for getting at the inside of my brain. If it is replied that this is only an analogy, not to be taken literally, then the question still remains how the mental and the physical are related.

Usually identity theorists at this point flee to even vaguer accounts of relationship. They talk of different "levels of analysis," or of different "perspectives," or of different "conceptual schemes," or of different "language games." The point of such suggestions is that the difference between the mental and the physical is not a basic, fundamental, or intrinsic one, but rather a difference which is merely relative to different human purposes or standpoints. The difference is supposed to exist not in the thing itself but in the eye of the beholder.

But these are only hints. They do not tell us in precise and literal terms how the mental and the physical differ and are related. They only try to assure us that the difference does not matter to the real nature of things. But until we are given a theory to consider, we cannot accept the identity theorist's assurance that some theory will do, only he does not know what it is.

One of the leading identity theorists, J. J. C. Smart, holds that mentalistic discourse is simply a vaguer, more indefinite way of talking about what could be talked about more precisely by using physiological terms. If I report a red afterimage, I mean (roughly) that something is going on which is like what goes on when I really see a red patch. I do not actually *mean* that a particular sort of brain process is occurring, but when I say something is going on I refer (very vaguely, to be sure) to just that brain process. Thus the thing referred to in my report of an afterimage is a brain process. Hence there is no need to bring in any nonphysical features. Thus even the taint of dualism is avoided.

Does this ingenious attempt to evade dualistic implications stand up under philosophical scrutiny? I am inclined to think it will not. Let us return to the man reporting the red afterimage. He was aware of the occurrence of something or other, of some feature or other. Now it seems to me obvious that he was not necessarily aware of the state of his brain at that time (I doubt that most of us are ever aware of the state of our brain) nor, in general, necessarily aware of any physical features of his body at that time. He might, of course, have been incidentally aware of some physical feature but not insofar as he was aware of the red afterimage as such. Yet he was definitely aware of something, or else how could he have made that report? So he must have been aware of some nonphysical feature. That is the only way of explaining how he was aware of anything at all.

Of course, the thing that our reporter of the afterimage was aware of might well have had further features which he was *not* aware of, particularly, in this connection, physical features. I may be aware of certain features of an object without being aware of others. So it is not ruled out that the event our reporter is aware of might be an event with predominantly physical features—he just does not notice those. But he must be aware of some of its features, or else it would not be proper to say he was aware of *that* event. And if he is not aware of any physical features, he must be aware of something else. And that shows that we cannot get rid of those nonphysical features in the way that Smart suggests.

One would not wish to be dogmatic in saying that identity theorists will never work out this part of their theory. Much work is being done on this problem at the present time, for it arises in other areas of philosophy as well as in the philosophy of mind. In particular philosophers of science are concerned with the problem. We saw that the identity theory used such analogies as the identity of lightning with electrical phenomena and the identity of water with molecules consisting of hydrogen and oxygen. But the question to be raised is what kind of identity we are dealing with in such cases. Do we have mere duality of terms in these cases, duality of features, properties, or aspects, or even duality of substances? Very similar issues arise. So it is quite possible that further work on this problem of identity will be useful in clarifying the identity theory of the mental and the physical. But at the present the matter is by no means as clear as it should be.

Even if the identity theorist could clarify the sense of "identity" to be used in his theory, he would still face two other problems. These concern coexistence in time and space. Coexistence in time and space are conditions that must be met if there is to be identity. That is to say, for two apparently different things to turn out to be one and the same, they must exist at the same time and in the same location. If we could show that Mr. A existed at a time when Mr. B did not, or that Mr. A existed in it place where Mr. B did not, then this would show that Mr. A and Mr. B were different men. It is by virtue of these facts about identity that an alibi can exonerate a suspect: if Mr. A was not in Chicago at the time, then he could not be one and the same with the man who stole the diamonds in Chicago.

So if mental events are to be identical with physical events, then they must fulfill the conditions of coexistence in time and space. The question is, Do they?

So far as coexistence in time is concerned, very little is known. The most relevant work consists in direct stimulation of an exposed part of the brain during surgery. Since only a local anesthetic is necessary in many such cases the patient may well be fully conscious. Then, as the surgeon stimulates different parts of his brain, the patient may report the occurrence of mental events—memories, thoughts, sensations. Do the physical events in the brain and the mental events occur at precisely the same time? It is impossible to say. All that would be required is a very small time gap to prove that the physical events were not identical with the mental events. But it is very difficult to see how the existence of so small a time gap could be established. And even if it were, what would it prove? Only that the mental event was not identical with just that physical event; it would not prove it was nonidentical with any physical event. So it could well be that coexistence in time is present or is not. I do not think that we shall get much decisive information from empirical work of the sort here described. The identity theorist, then, does not have to fear refutation from this quarter, at least not for a long time.

How about coexistence in space? Do mental events occur in the same place the corresponding physical events occur? This is also a very difficult question to answer, for two reasons. First our present ignorance of neurophysiology, especially concerning the brain and how it functions, allows us to say very little about the location of the relevant physical events. This much does seem likely: they are located in the brain. Much more than that we do not at present know, although as the time passes, we should learn much more. The second reason for our difficulty in telling if there is coexistence in space has to do with the location of mental events. Where do thoughts, feelings, and wishes occur? Do they occur in the brain? Suppose you suddenly have the thought that it is almost suppertime; where does that occur? The most sensible answer would be that it occurs wherever you are when you have that thought. If you are in the library when you have that thought, then the thought occurs in the library. But it would he utterly unnatural to ask where inside your body the thought occurred; in your foot, or your liver, or your heart, or your head? It is not that any one of these places is more likely than another. They are all wrong. Not because thoughts occur somewhere *else* within your body than your foot, liver, heart, or head—but because it *makes no sense at all* to locate the occurrence of a thought at some place within your body. We would not understand someone who pointed to a place in his body and claimed that it was *there* that his entertaining of a thought was located. Certainly, if one *looked* at that place, one would not *see* anything resembling a thought. If it were replied to this that points can be located in the body without being seen there, then it should be pointed out that one *feels* the pain there but one hardly feels a thought in the body.

The fact that it makes no sense at all to speak of mental events as occurring at some point within the body has the result that the identity theory cannot be true. This is because the corresponding physical events do occur at some point within the body, and if those physical events are identical with mental events, then those mental events must occur at the same point within the body. But those mental events do not occur at any point within the body, because any statement to the effect that they occurred here, or there, would be senseless. Hence the mental events cannot meet the condition of coexistence in space, and therefore cannot be identical with physical events.

Our inability to give the location within the body of mental events is different from our inability to give the location of the corresponding physical events within the body. In the latter case, it is that we do not know enough about the body, particularly the brain. Some day, presumably, we will know enough to pin down pretty exactly the location of the relevant physical events. But in the case of mental events it is not simply that at present we are ignorant but that someday we may well know. What would it be like to discover the location of a thought in the brain? What kind of information would we need to be able to say that the thought occurred exactly *here?* If by X rays or some other means we were able to see every event which occurred in the brain, we would never get a glimpse of a thought. If, to resort to fantasy, we could so enlarge a brain or so shrink ourselves that we could wander freely through the brain, we would still never observe a thought. All we could ever observe in the brain would be the *physical* events which occur in it. If mental events had location in the brain, there should be some means of detecting them there. But of course there is none. The very idea of it is senseless.

Some identity theorists believe this objection can be met. One approach is to reply that this objection begs the question: if the identity theory is true, and mental events are identical with brain events, then, paradoxical as it may sound, mental events do indeed have location, and are located precisely where the physical events are located. Another approach is to reply that the relevant physical events should be construed as events which happen to the body as a whole, and therefore occur where the body as a whole is located; then it is not so paradoxical to give location to the mental events, for they would be located where the body is located but would not be located in any particular part of the body.

We have carried our discussion of the identity theory to the very frontier of present philosophical thinking. We can only leave it to the reader to decide how well it can meet the objections which are raised to it.

JOHN SEARLE

MINDS, BODIES, AND COMPUTERS

. . . Though we do not know in detail how the brain functions, we do know enough to have an idea of the general relationships between brain processes and mental processes. Mental processes are caused by the behaviour of elements of the brain. At the same time, they are realised in the structure that is made up of those elements. I think this answer is consistent with the standard biological approaches to biological phenomena. Indeed, it is a kind of commonsense answer to the question, given what we know about how the world works. However, it is very much a minority point or view. The prevailing view in philosophy, psychology, and artificial intelligence is one which emphasises the analogies between the functioning of the human brain and the functioning of digital computers. According to the most extreme version of this view, the brain is just a digital computer and the mind is just a computer program. One could summarise this view—I call it 'strong artificial intelligence', or 'strong AI'—by saying that the mind is to the brain, as the program is to the computer hardware.

This view has the consequence that there is nothing essentially biological about the human mind. The brain just happens to be one of an indefinitely large number of different kinds of hardware computers that could sustain the programs which make up human intelligence. On this view, any physical system whatever that had the right program with the right inputs and outputs would have a mind in exactly the same sense that you and I have minds. So, for example, if you made a computer out of old beer cans powered by windmills; if it had the right program, it would have to have a mind. And the point is not that for all we know it might have thoughts and feelings, but rather that it must have thoughts and feelings, because that is all there is to having thoughts and feelings: implementing the right program.

Most people who hold this view think we have not yet designed programs which are minds. But there is pretty much general agreement among them that it's only a matter of time until computer scientists and workers in artificial intelligence design the appropriate hardware and programs which will be the equivalent of human brains and minds. These will be artificial brains and minds which are in every way the equivalent of human brains and minds.

Many people outside of the field of artificial intelligence are quite amazed to discover that anybody could believe such a view as this. So, before criticising it, let me give you a few examples of the things that people in this field have actually said. Herbert Simon of Carnegie-Mellon University says that we already have machines that can literally think. There is no question of waiting for some future machine, because existing digital computers already have thoughts in exactly the same sense that you and I do. Well, fancy that! Philosophers have

SOURCE: Reprinted by permission of the publisher from *Minds, Brains and Science* by John Searle, Cambridge, MA: Harvard University Press, Copyright © 1984 by John R. Searle.

been worried for centuries about whether or not a machine could think, and now we discover that they already have such machines at Carnegie-Mellon. Simon's colleague Alan Newell claims that we have now discovered (and notice that Newell says 'discovered' and not 'hypothesised' or 'considered the possibility', but we have *discovered*) that intelligence is just a matter of physical symbol manipulation; it has no essential connection with any specific kind of biological or physical wetware or hardware. Rather, any system whatever that is capable of manipulating physical symbols in the right way is capable of intelligence in the same literal sense as human intelligence of human beings. Both Simon and Newell, to their credit, emphasise that there is nothing metaphorical about these claims; they mean them quite literally. Freeman Dyson is quoted as having said that computers have an advantage over the rest of us when it comes to evolution. Since consciousness is just a matter of formal processes, in computers these formal processes can go on in substances that are much better able to survive in a universe that is cooling off than beings like ourselves made of our wet and messy materials. Marvin Minsky of MIT says that the next generation of computers will be so intelligent that we will 'be lucky if they are willing to keep us around the house as household pets'. My all-time favourite in the literature of exaggerated claims on behalf of the digital computer is from John McCarthy, the inventor of the term 'artificial intelligence'. McCarthy says even 'machines as simple as thermostats can be said to have beliefs'. And indeed, according to him, almost any machine capable of problem-solving can be said to have beliefs. I admire McCarthy's courage. I once asked him: 'What beliefs does your thermostat have?' And he said: 'My thermostat has three beliefs—it's too hot in here, it's too cold in here, and it's just right in here.' As a philosopher, I like all these claims for a simple reason. Unlike most philosophical theses, they are reasonably clear, and they admit of a simple and decisive refutation. It is this refutation that I am going to undertake in this chapter.

The nature of the refutation has nothing whatever to do with any particular stage of computer technology. It is important to emphasise this point because the temptation is always to think that the solution to our problems must wait on some as yet uncreated technological wonder. But in fact, the nature of the refutation is completely independent of any state of technology. It has to do with the very definition of a digital computer, with what a digital computer is.

It is essential to our conception or a digital computer that its operations can be specified purely formally; that is, we specify the steps in the operation of the computer in terms of abstract symbols—sequences of zeroes and ones printed on a tape, for example. A typical computer 'rule' will determine that when a machine is in a certain state and it has a certain symbol on its tape, then it will perform a certain operation such as erasing the symbol or printing another symbol and then enter another state such as moving the tape one square to the left. But the symbols have no meaning; they have no semantic content; they are not about anything. They have to be specified purely in terms of their formal or syntactical structure. The zeroes and ones, for example, are just numerals; they don't even stand for numbers. Indeed, it is this feature of digital computers that makes them so powerful. One and the same type of hardware, if it is appropriately designed, can be used to run an indefinite range of different programs. And one and the same program can be run on an indefinite range of different types of hardwares.

But this feature of programs, that they are defined purely formally or syntactically, is fatal to the view that mental processes and program processes are identical. And the reason can be stated quite simply. There is more to having a mind than having formal or syntactical processes. Our internal mental states, by definition, have certain sorts of contents. If I am thinking about Kansas City or wishing that I had a cold beer to drink or wondering if there will be a fall in interest rates, in each case my mental state has a certain mental content in addition to whatever formal features it might have. That is, even if my thoughts occur to me in strings or symbols, there must be more to the thought than the abstract strings, because strings by themselves can't have any meaning. If my thoughts are to be *about* anything, then the strings must have a *meaning* which makes the thoughts about those things. In a word, the mind has more than a syntax, it has a semantics. The reason that no computer program can ever be a mind is simply that a computer program is only syntactical, and minds are more than syntactical. Minds are semantical, in the sense that they have more than a formal structure, they have a content.

To illustrate this point I have designed a certain thought-experiment. Imagine that a bunch of computer programmers have written a program that will enable a computer to simulate the understanding of Chinese. So, for example, if the computer is given a question in Chinese, it will match the question against its memory, or data base, and produce appropriate answers to the questions in Chinese. Suppose for the sake of argument that the computer's answers are as good as those of a native Chinese speaker. Now then, does the computer, on the basis of this, understand Chinese, does it literally understand Chinese, in the way that Chinese speakers understand Chinese? Well, imagine that you are locked in a room, and in this room are several baskets full of Chinese symbols. Imagine that you (like me) do not understand a word of Chinese, but that you are given a rule book in English for manipulating these Chinese symbols. The rules specify the manipulations of the symbols purely formally, in terms of their syntax, not their semantics. So the rule might say: 'Take a squiggle-squiggle sign out of basket number one and put it next to a squoggle-squoggle sign from basket number two.' Now suppose that some other Chinese symbols are passed into the room, and that you are given further rules for passing back Chinese symbols out of the room. Suppose that unknown to you the symbols passed into the room are called 'questions' by the people outside the room, and the symbols you pass back out of the room are called 'answers to the questions'. Suppose, furthermore, that the programmers are so good at designing the programs and that you are so good at manipulating the symbols, that very soon your answers are indistinguishable from those of a native Chinese speaker. There you are locked in your room shuffling your Chinese symbols and passing out Chinese symbols in response to incoming Chinese symbols. On the basis of the situation as I have described it, there is no way you could learn any Chinese simply by manipulating these formal symbols.

Now the point of the story is simply this: by virtue of implementing a formal computer program from the point of view of an outside observer, you behave exactly as if you understood Chinese, but all the same you don't understand a word of Chinese. But if going through the appropriate computer program for understanding Chinese is not enough to give *you* an understanding of Chinese, then it is not enough to give *any other digital computer* an understanding of Chinese. And again, the reason for this can be stated quite simply. If you don't understand Chinese, then no other computer could understand Chinese because no digital computer, just by virtue of running a program, has anything that you don't have. All that the computer has, as you have, is a formal program for manipulating uninterpreted Chinese symbols. To repeat, a computer has a syntax, but no semantics. The whole point of the parable of the Chinese room is to remind us of a fact that we knew all along. Understanding a language, or indeed, having mental states at all, involves more than just having a bunch of formal symbols. It involves having an interpretation, or a meaning attached to those symbols. And a digital computer, as defined, cannot have more than just formal symbols because the operation of the computer, as I said earlier, is defined in terms of its ability to implement programs. And these programs are purely formally specifiable—that is, they have no semantic content.

We can see the force of this argument if we contrast what it is like to be asked and to answer questions in English, and to be asked and to answer questions in some language where we have no knowledge of any of the meanings of the words. Imagine that in the Chinese room you are also given questions in English about such things as your age or your life history, and that you answer these questions. What is the difference between the Chinese case and the English case? Well again, if like me you understand no Chinese and you do understand English, then the difference is obvious. You understand the questions in English because they are expressed in symbols whose meanings are known to you. Similarly, when you give the answers in English you are producing symbols which are meaningful to you. But in the case of the Chinese, you have none of that. In the case of the Chinese, you simply manipulate formal symbols according to a computer program, and you attach no meaning to any of the elements.

Various replies have been suggested to this argument by workers in artificial intelligence and in psychology, as well as philosophy. They all have something in common; they are all inadequate. And there is an obvious reason why they have to be inadequate, since the argument rests on a very simple logical truth, namely, syntax alone is not sufficient for semantics, and digital computers insofar as they are computers have, by definition, a syntax alone.

I want to make this clear by considering a couple of the arguments that are often presented against me.

Some people attempt to answer the Chinese room example by saying that the whole system understands Chinese. The idea here is that though I, the person in the room manipulating the symbols do not understand Chinese, I am just the central processing unit of the computer system. They argue that it is the whole system, including the room, the baskets full of symbols and the ledgers containing the programs and perhaps other items as well, taken as a totality, that understands Chinese. But this is subject to exactly the same objection I made before. There is no way that the system can get from the syntax to the semantics. I, as the central processing unit have no way of figuring out what any of these symbols means; but then neither does the whole system.

Another common response is to imagine that we put the Chinese understanding program inside a robot. If the robot moved around and interacted causally with the world, wouldn't that be enough to guarantee that it understood Chinese? Once again the inexorability of the semantics-syntax distinction overcomes this manoeuvre. As long as we suppose that the robot has only a computer for a brain then, even though it might behave exactly as if it understood Chinese, it would still have no way of getting from the syntax to the semantics of Chinese. You can see this if you imagine that I am the computer. Inside a room in the robot's skull I shuffle symbols without knowing that some of them come in to me from television cameras attached to the robot's head and others go out to move the robot's arms and legs. As long as all I have is a formal computer program, I have no way of attaching any meaning to any of the symbols. And the fact that the robot is engaged in causal interactions with the outside world won't help me to attach any meaning to the symbols unless I have some way of finding out about that fact. Suppose the robot picks up a hamburger and this triggers the symbol for hamburger to come into the room. As long as all I have is the symbol with no knowledge of its causes or how it got there, I have no way of knowing what it means. The causal interactions between the robot and the rest of the world are irrelevant unless those causal interactions are represented in some mind or other. But there is no way they can be if all that the so-called mind consists of is a set of purely formal, syntactical operations.

It is important to see exactly what is claimed and what is not claimed by my argument. Suppose we ask the question that I mentioned at the beginning: 'Could a machine think?' Well, in one sense, of course, we are all machines. We can construe the stuff inside our heads as a meat machine. And of course, we can all think. So, in one sense of 'machine', namely that sense in which a machine is just a physical system which is capable of performing certain kinds of operations, in that sense, we are all machines, and we can think. So, trivially, there are machines that can think. But that wasn't the question that bothered us. So let's try a different formulation of it. Could an artefact think? Could a man-made machine think? Well, once again, it depends on the kind of artefact. Suppose we designed a machine that was molecule-for-molecule indistinguishable from a human being. Well then, if you can duplicate the causes, you can presumably duplicate the effects. So once again, the answer to that question is, in principle at least, trivially yes. If you could build a machine that had the same structure as a human being, then presumably that machine would be able to think. Indeed, it would be a surrogate human being. Well, let's try again.

The question isn't: 'Can a machine think?' or: 'Can an artefact think?' The question is: 'Can a digital computer think?' But once again we have to be very careful in how we interpret the question. From a mathematical point of view, anything whatever can be described *as if* it were a digital computer. And that's because it can be described as instantiating or implementing a computer program. In an utterly trivial sense, the pen that is on the desk in front of me can be described as a digital computer. It just happens to have a very boring computer program. The program says: 'Stay there.' Now since in this sense, anything whatever is a digital computer, because anything whatever can be described as implementing a computer program, then once again, our question gets a trivial answer. Of course our brains are digital computers, since they implement any number of computer programs. And of course our brains can think. So once again, there is a trivial answer to the question. But that wasn't really the question we were trying to ask. The question we wanted to ask is this: 'Can a digital computer, as defined, think?' That is to say: 'Is instantiating or implementing the right computer program with the right inputs and outputs, sufficient for, or constitutive of, thinking?' And to this question, unlike its predecessors, the answer is clearly 'no'. And it is 'no' for the reason that we have spelled out, namely, the computer program is defined purely syntactically. But thinking is more than just a matter of manipulating meaningless symbols, it involves meaningful semantic contents. These semantic contents are what we mean by 'meaning'.

It is important to emphasise again that we are not talking about a particular stage of computer technology. The argument has nothing to do with the forthcoming, amazing advances in computer science. It has nothing to do with the distinction between serial and parallel processes, or with the size of programs, or the speed of computer operations, or with computers that can interact causally with their environment, or even with the invention of robots. Technological progress is always grossly exaggerated, but even subtracting the exaggeration, the development of computers has been quite remarkable, and we can reasonably expect that even more remarkable progress will be made in the future. No doubt we will be much better able to simulate human behaviour on computers than we can at present, and certainly much better than we have been able to in the past. The point I am making is that if we are talking about having mental states, having a mind, all of these simulations are simply irrelevant. It doesn't matter how good the technology is, or how rapid the calculations made by the computer are. If it really is a computer, its operations have to be defined syntactically, whereas consciousness, thoughts, feelings, emotions, and all the rest of it involve more than a syntax. Those features, by definition, the computer is unable to *duplicate* however powerful may be its ability to *simulate*. The key distinction here is between duplication and simulation. And no simulation by itself ever constitutes duplication.

What I have done so far is give a basis to the sense that those citations I began this talk with are really as preposterous as they seem. There is a puzzling question in this discussion though, and that is: 'Why would anybody ever have thought that computers could think or have feelings and emotions and all the rest of it?' After all, we can do computer simulations of any process whatever that can be given a formal description. So, we can do a computer simulation of the flow of money in the British economy, or the pattern of power distribution in the Labour party. We can do computer simulation of rain storms in the home counties, or warehouse fires in East London. Now, in each of these cases, nobody supposes that the computer simulation is actually the real thing; no one supposes that a computer simulation of a storm will leave us all wet, or a computer simulation of a fire is likely to burn the house down. Why on earth would anyone in his right mind suppose a computer simulation of mental processes actually had mental processes? I don't really know the answer to that, since the idea seems to me, to put it frankly, quite crazy from the start. But I can make a couple of speculations.

First of all, where the mind is concerned, a lot of people are still tempted to some sort of behaviourism. They think if a system behaves as if it understood Chinese, then it really must understand Chinese. But we have already refuted this form of behaviourism with the Chinese room argument. Another assumption made by many people is that the mind is not a part of the biological world, it is not a part of the world of nature. The strong artificial intelligence view relies on that in its conception that the mind is purely formal; that somehow or other, it cannot be treated as a concrete product of biological processes like any other biological product. There is in these discussions, in short, a kind of residual dualism. AI partisans believe that the mind is more than a part of the natural biological world; they believe that the mind is purely formally specifiable. The paradox of this is that the AI literature is filled with fulminations against some view called 'dualism', but in fact, the whole thesis of strong AI rests on a kind of dualism. It rests on a rejection of the idea that the mind is just a natural biological phenomenon in the world like any other.

I want to conclude this chapter by putting together the thesis of the last chapter and the thesis of this one. Both of these theses can be stated very simply. And indeed, I am going to state them with perhaps excessive crudeness. But if we put them together I think we get a quite powerful conception of the relations of minds, brains and computers. And the argument has a very simple logical structure, so you can see whether it is valid or invalid. The first premise is:

1. *Brains cause minds.*

Now, of course, that is really too crude. What we mean by that is that mental processes that we consider to constitute a mind are caused, entirely caused, by processes going on inside the brain. But let's be crude, let's just abbreviate that as three words—brains cause minds. And that is just a fact about how the world works. Now let's write proposition number two:

2. *Syntax is not sufficient for semantics.*

That proposition is a conceptual truth. It just articulates our distinction between the notion of what is purely formal and what has content. Now, to these two propositions—that brains cause minds and that syntax is not sufficient for semantics—let's add a third and a fourth:

3. *Computer programs are entirely defined by their formal, or syntactical structure.*

That proposition, I take it, is true by definition; it is part of what we mean by the notion of a computer program.

4. *Minds have mental contents; specifically they have semantic contents.*

And that, I take it, is just an obvious fact about how our minds work. My thoughts, and beliefs, and desires are about something, or they refer to something, or they concern states of affairs in the world; and they do that because their content directs them at these states of affairs in the world. Now, from these four premises, we can draw our first conclusion; and it follows obviously from premises 2, 3 and 4:

CONCLUSION 1. *No computer program by itself is sufficient to give a system a mind. Programs, in short, are not minds, and they are not by themselves sufficient for having minds.*

Now, that is a very powerful conclusion, because it means that the project of trying to create minds solely by designing programs is doomed from the start. And it is important to re-emphasise that this has nothing to do with any particular state of technology or any particular state of the complexity of the program. This is a purely formal, or logical, result from a set of axioms which are agreed to by all (or nearly all) of the disputants concerned. That is, even most of the hardcore enthusiasts for artificial intelligence agree that in fact, as a matter of biology, brain processes cause mental states, and they agree that programs are defined purely formally. But if you put these conclusions together with certain other things that we know, then it follows immediately that the project of strong AI is incapable of fulfilment.

However, once we have got these axioms, let's see what else we can derive. Here is a second conclusion:

CONCLUSION 2. *The way that brain functions cause minds cannot be solely in virtue of running a computer program.*

And this second conclusion follows from conjoining the first premise together with our first conclusion. That is, from the fact that brains cause minds and that programs are not enough to do the job, it follows that the way that brains cause minds can't be solely by running a computer program. Now that also I think is an important result, because it has the consequence that the brain is not, or at least is not just, a digital computer. We saw earlier that anything can trivially be described as if it were a digital computer, and brains are no exception. But the importance of this conclusion is that the computational properties of the brain are simply not enough to explain its functioning to produce mental states. And indeed, that ought to seem a commonsense scientific conclusion to us anyway because all it does is remind us of the fact that brains are biological engines; their biology matters. It is not, as several people in artificial intelligence have claimed, just an irrelevant fact about the mind that it happens to be realised in human brains.

Now, from our first premise, we can also derive a third conclusion:

CONCLUSION 3. *Anything else that caused minds would have to have causal powers at least equivalent to those of the brain.*

Ann this third conclusion is a trivial consequence of our first premise. It is a bit like saying that if my petrol engine drives my car at seventy-five miles an hour, then any diesel engine that was capable of doing that would have to have a power output at least equivalent to that of my petrol engine. Of course, some other system might cause mental processes using entirely different chemical or biochemical features from those the brain in fact uses. It might turn out that there are beings on other planets, or in other solar systems, that have mental states and use an entirely different biochemistry from ours. Suppose that Martians arrived on earth and we concluded that they had mental states. But suppose that when their heads were opened up, it was discovered that all they had inside was green slime. Well still, the green slime, if it functioned to produce consciousness and all the rest of their mental life, would have to have causal powers equal to those of the human brain. But now, from our first conclusion, that programs are not enough, and our third conclusion, that any other system would have to have causal powers equal to the brain, conclusion four follows immediately:

CONCLUSION 4. *For any artefact that we might build which had mental states equivalent to human mental states, the implementation of a computer program would not by itself be sufficient. Rather the artefact would have to have powers equivalent to the powers of the human brain.*

The upshot of this discussion I believe is to remind us of something that we have known all along: namely, mental states are biological phenomena. Consciousness, intentionality, subjectivity and mental causation are all a part of our biological life history, along with growth, reproduction, the secretion of bile, and digestion.

PRACTICE

HERBERT A. SIMON

SIMULATING HUMAN THINKING: AN EMPIRICAL APPROACH TO THE MIND-BODY PROBLEM

COMPUTER PROGRAMS AS THEORIES

During the 1930s and '40s, and into the early '50s, I carried my Diogenes' lantern through many fields of mathematics seeking the right tools for studying human thought, but neither analysis nor finite math seemed to fill the bill. To

Herbert A. Simon, educated in political science at the University of Chicago (Ph.D., 1943), studied there also with Rudolf Carnap. At Carnegie Mellon University since 1949, he is currently Richard King Mellon University Professor of Computer Science and Psychology. In 1978, he received the Nobel Prize in Economics, and in 1986 the National Medal of Science.

Following an old suggestion of Carnap, that it is easier to examine the internal operations of a computer than those of the brain, Simon simulates human thinking by programming computers to think and thereby explores the relations of mind with matter.

use these mathematical tools, one had to force the phenomena into the Procrustean bed of real numbers or algebraic and topological abstractions that seemed to leave much of the content behind. Computer languages, with their ability to handle symbols of every kind, changed all that by permitting one to implement a very literal representation of human symbol processing in the machine's memories and processes.

Computer programs written in whatever languages are, at the most abstract level, simply systems of difference equations, with all of the power of such equations to describe the states and temporal paths of complex symbol systems.

To be sure, these equation systems can almost never be solved in closed form; but the computer itself, in providing the powerful tool of simulation, offers a solution to that problem too.[2]

As you are well aware, the requirements of simulating the behavior of physical symbol systems called for symbol-manipulating languages quite different from the algebraic languages used in numerical computing and led to the invention of list processing languages like the IPLs and then LISP, and still later to production-system languages like OPS-5 and logic-programming languages like PROLOG. With these languages the computer simulation can produce symbolic outputs that can be compared directly, and with very little translation, with human outputs, especially verbal protocols.

ARTIFICIAL INTELLIGENCE AND COGNITIVE PSYCHOLOGY

My interest in AI has been, from the beginning, primarily an interest in its application to psychology. Equally exciting opportunities emerged at the same time for designing computer programs that, without necessarily imitating human methods, could perform difficult tasks at expert professional levels. As the construction of expert systems has played second fiddle to human simulation in my own research program, I shall have little to say about it here. My focus will not be on computer *achievement* of humanoid skills, but on computer *imitation* of the processes people use to manifest such skills.

In this research, the computer program is not a "metaphor" but a precise language of theory for cognitive psychology in the same sense that differential equations are a language of theory for physics. Theories written in AI list-processing languages are tested in exactly the same way as theories written in differential equations. We use the theories to make predictions, which are then tested against behavior captured in the laboratory or observed in the field.[3]

Psychology is an empirical science. It is the study of how human beings behave and of the processes occurring in their minds (that is, their brains) that bring this behavior about. The science of psychology proceeds by observing the phenomena of thinking, by building theories to describe and explain the phenomena, and by laying phenomena and theory side by side to see how closely they match. The preceding three sentences would be no more and no less true if for "psychology" we substituted "physics" or "geology" or "biology," with

---

[2] Simulation is increasingly employed within traditional mathematics as well, for the increasingly complex systems under study there also defy closed solution.

[3] The theories of physics consist not only of the differential equations, but also certain properties of these equations that can be deduced from them (e.g., the principle of conservation of energy in mechanics). Theories defined by difference equations (programs) may also possess deducible properties, which then become part of the theory. For example, from the short-term memory structure embodied in recent versions of EPAM, the short-term memory capacity can be deduced from the structure and parameters of the program.

corresponding changes in the names of the phenomena studied. We will later describe the comparison process in more detail.

The fact that psychology is studied by scientists who themselves are human beings is of no more account than the fact that physics is studied by scientists who consist of atoms or that biology is studied by scientists who eat, breathe and procreate. What we are interested in, in all of these cases, are not the scientists but the phenomena and the theories that describe and explain the phenomena. At the general level, good methodology in physics or chemistry is good methodology in psychology. At more specific levels, each field has to invent methods and instruments for observing and theorizing that are appropriate to the phenomena of interest. The methods are to be judged by the same standards in every case.

I feel obliged to repeat these rather obvious sentiments here because books, written in armchair comfort, continue to be published from time to time that try to evaluate by philosophical means psychological theories written in computer languages. Let me explain why I regard such books as misguided. In fact, instead of trying to use philosophical analysis to settle psychological questions, which are empirical matters, I propose to reverse directions and to suggest that, with recent advances in psychology, we are now in a position to use psychological theories, and the empirical evidence on which they are founded, to settle some issues that have been important, historically, in philosophy.

Cognitive Psychology's Empirical Base

As psychology is an empirical science, we can only judge whether and to what extent particular theoretical proposals are valid by comparing them with data. In the face of such comparisons, philosophical speculation is superfluous; in the absence of such comparisons, it is helpless. Therefore, if we wish to evaluate the claims of theories of thinking (whether these theories take the form of computer programs or some other form), we would do well to spend most of our time studying the empirical evidence and making the explicit comparisons with the computer traces.

By now, such evidence is voluminous. This is not the place to review it, but I'll cite just one very specialized example. In the book, *Protocol Analysis* (1993), which Anders Ericsson and I have written, treating the methodology for testing cognitive theories by comparing human think-aloud protocols with computer traces, there are forty-two pages of references. It is not unreasonable to ask anyone who proposes to evaluate the validity of verbal reports as data either to become acquainted with a substantial portion of this literature or to announce clearly his or her amateur status. Similarly, it is not unreasonable to ask anyone proposing to pronounce on memory capacity or the acquisition and response speeds of human memory to become acquainted with that large literature.

There are, of course, comparably large literatures on problem solving, reasoning, perceiving, and many other topics. Any serious assessment of our knowledge of human thought processes or of the veridicality of theories that purport to describe or explain these processes must rest on the data reported in this literature.

What theories are available for testing, and what kinds of phenomena do they address? Again, I can only cite a few examples, some from my own work and some from the work of others. An early example is the General Problem Solver (GPS), whose central mechanism, means-ends analysis, has been shown empirically, in numerous studies, to be a much-used heuristic in human problem solving. (A small fraction of these empirical tests are discussed in Newell & Simon, 1972; you will find others in the two volumes of my *Models of Thought,* 1979, 1989.) Contemporary with GPS is EPAM, a model of human perceptual and memory processes due originally to Feigenbaum, which has been tested successfully against empirical data from experiments on verbal learning, expert memory performances in several domains of expertise (including expertise in mnemonics), and concept attainment. (For some of the empirical tests see Feigenbaum & Simon, 1984; and Richman, Staszewski and Simon, 1995.)

A somewhat later system is John Anderson's ACT* (1983), which focuses especially on semantic memory and the explanation of contextual effects through spreading activation. A very different and still newer theory, or set of theories, are "neural" networks of the connectionist variety that have shown capacities to learn in a variety of tasks (McClelland & Rumelhart, 1986). Quite recently, Allen Newell, in collaboration with John Laird, Paul Rosenbloom and others, has produced Soar, a vigorous push from GPS into a far more general and unified architecture, which demonstrates the relevance of multiple problem spaces and learning by chunking (Newell, 1990). Still closer to the topics I shall address in the remainder of this paper is the BACON system (see Langley, et al., 1987) and its close relatives, GLAUBER, STAHL, KEKADA (Kulkarni & Simon, 1988), LIVE (Shen, 1994) and others that simulate many of the discovery processes that are discernible in the activities of scientists. Some of the models I have mentioned are complementary, some are competitive, as theories are in any science.

To understand these systems, not just as interesting examples of artificial intelligence but as theories of human thinking, and to adjudicate among them when they conflict, we must devote just as much attention to the experimental and other empirical evidence about the phenomena they model as to the structures and behaviors of the programs themselves. Errors in the evaluation of these programs as psychological theories are caused less often by lack of knowledge or inaccurate knowledge about the programs than by lack of knowledge or inaccurate knowledge about how human subjects behave when they are confronted with the same tasks as the programs were tested on.

For one example, the brittleness of computer programs when they wander outside the task domain for which they are programmed is often mentioned as a defect of these programs, viewed as psychological theories, without noticing the extraordinary brittleness of human behavior when it wanders outside the arena of the actor's experiences. (Inexperienced urbanites lost in a wilderness frequently freeze or starve to death in circumstances where experienced savages survive. Novices playing their first bridge hand bid and discard almost randomly.) Theories cannot be compared with facts unless the theories are specified precisely and the facts known thoroughly.

Limits of Explanation?

In the remainder of this paper I shall put the information processing explanation of thinking to what is usually regarded as a severe test. The idea that the processes humans use in everyday, relatively routine and well-structured tasks can be modeled accurately by computers has gained, over the years, a considerable amount of acceptance—more among experimental psychologists than among people who are more distant from the data. The idea that these models can be extended to ill-structured tasks of the kinds that require ingenuity, perhaps even creativity, when performed by humans is less widely accepted. This is no more a philosophical question than the questions that I have discussed previously. It is a question about certain kinds of human behavior and whether these kinds of behavior can be modeled by computers. It is to be settled by comparing the records of human behavior with the output of computer models, just as we settle questions in physics by comparing the laboratory behavior of physical systems with the differential equations of physical theory.

I shall focus on three terms that appear frequently in the literature and in popularized psychology (not always with the same meanings) and which have been used to label behaviors that are often claimed to be beyond explanation by programmable mechanisms. The three terms are "intuition," "insight," and "inspiration." In addressing the cognitive phenomena associated with each of these terms, I shall first define the term so that we can determine when the corresponding phenomena are being exhibited. Without clear tests that enable us to identify the occasions of "intuition," "insight," and "inspiration," there are no phenomena to explain.

I cannot claim that the definitions I shall propose represent the only ways in which these terms are, or can be, used. I will claim that they correspond to the usual meanings, and that the operational tests on which they are based are the operational tests that are commonly used to determine when people are being "intuitive," "insightful," or "inspired." These are the properties the definitions should possess if they are to be used in theories of intuition, insight, and inspiration.

Having established operational tests for the phenomena, we shall look at the evidence as to whether people and computers exhibit the processes in question, and if so, under what circumstances. What I shall show is, first, that the presence or absence of phenomena like these, sometimes claimed to be ineffable, can be determined objectively, and second, that certain computer programs are mechanisms that exhibit these phenomena and thereby provide explanations for them.

INTUITION

Let me start with the process of human thinking that is usually called "intuition." Before we can do research on intuition, we have to know what it is; in particular, we must have some operational definition that tells us when intuition is being exhibited by a human being and when it is not. It is not too difficult to construct such a definition.

The marks that are usually used to attribute an intelligent act (say, a problem solution) to intuition are that: (1) the solution was reached rather rapidly after the problem was posed, and (2) the problem solver could not give a veridical account of the steps that were taken in order to reach it. Typically, the problem solver will assert that the solution came "suddenly" or "instantly." In the few instances where these events have been timed, "suddenly" and "instantly" turn out to mean "in a second or two," or even "in a minute or two."

That's essentially the way my dictionary defines intuition, too: "the power or facility of knowing things without conscious reasoning." Let us take the criteria of rapid solution and inability to report a sequence of steps leading up to the solution as the indications that people are using intuition. These are the criteria we actually use to judge when intuition is being exhibited. Applying these criteria, we now have some clearly designated phenomena to be explained; we can try to construct some difference equations (computer programs) that behave intuitively.

Intuitive thinking is frequently contrasted with "logical" thinking. Logical thinking is recognized by being planful and proceeding by steps, each of which (even if it fails to reach its goal) has its reasons. Intuitive thinking, as we have seen, proceeds by a jump to its conclusions, with no conscious deliberateness in the process. But intuitive and logical thinking can be intermingled. The expert, faced with a difficult problem, may have to search planfully and deliberately, but is aided, at each stage of the search, by intermediate leaps of intuition of which the novice is incapable. Using what appear to be (in systems programming terms) "macros," frequent intuitive jumps, the expert takes long strides in search, the novice numerous tiny steps.

A Theory (Computer Model) of Intuition

Having specified how we will recognize intuition when it occurs, the next task in building a theory of it is to design a computer program (or find one already built) that will solve some problems intuitively—as determined by exactly the same criteria as we employ to determine when people are using intuition. The program will solve these problems, if they are easy, in a (simulated) second or two and will be unable to provide a (simulated) verbal report of the solution process. Fortunately, at least one such program already exists: the EPAM program (Richman, Staszewski & Simon, 1995), which first became operative about 1960. It was not designed with intuition in mind, but rather to simulate human rote verbal learning, for which there already existed at that time a large body of empirical data from experiments run over the previous seventy years. EPAM accounted for the main phenomena found in these data.

The core of EPAM is a tree-like discrimination net that grows in response to the stimuli presented to it and among which it learns to discriminate, and a short-term memory that will hold a few familiar symbols (7 ± 2?), but will retain them more than two seconds only if it has time to rehearse them. EPAM's discrimination net is somewhat similar to the Rete nets that are used to index production systems. EPAM learns the correct discriminations by experience, with only feedback of right" or "wrong" to its responses. EPAM nets have been taught to discriminate among more than 3×10^5 different stimuli, and there is nothing final about that number.

These learned patterns, once acquired, can now be recognized when presented to EPAM because it sorts them through its net, the recognition time being logarithmic in the total number of stimuli in the net. If the net has a branching factor of four, then recognition of a net discriminating among a million stimuli could be achieved by performing about ten tests ($4^{10} = 1,048,576$). The EPAM model, its parameters calibrated from data in verbal learning experiments, can accomplish such a recognition in a tenth to a fifth of a second. If we add additional time for utterance of a response, the act of recognition takes a second or less.

Now suppose we confront EPAM with a situation that is recognizable from its previous experience (a collection of medical symptoms, say). It can now access, in less than a second, information about a disease that is presumably responsible for these symptoms. As EPAM is able to report symbols that reach its short-term memory (where the result of an act of recognition is stored), it can report the name of the disease. As it cannot report the results of the individual tests performed on the symptoms along the path, it cannot describe how it reached its conclusions. Even if it can report the symptoms that were given it (because it stored some of them in memory during the presentation), it cannot give a veridical account of which of these were actually used to make the diagnosis or how they were considered and weighed during the recognition process.[4] We might add, "even as you and I," for these are also the characteristics of human diagnosis: the physician can report what disease he or she has recognized, but cannot give a veridical report of which symptoms were taken into account, or what weights were assigned to them.

To simulate the diagnostic process in more complex cases, we need a system that contains, in addition to EPAM's discrimination net and the long-term

---

[4] This does not mean that EPAM cannot be programmed to trace its steps, but that the simulation of its verbal processes will report only symbols that are stored, at the time of reporting, in short-term memory. The trace of nonreportable processes must be distinguished from the simulation of processes the theory claims to be reportable.

memory it indexes and accesses, some capabilities for solving problems by heuristic search—a combination of EPAM with a sort of General Problem Solver (GPS) or Soar. Then we will observe this combined system not only recognizing familiar symptoms and their causes, but also reasoning to infer what additional tests might discriminate among alternative diagnoses that have been recognized as possible causes of the initial symptoms.

Automatic medical diagnosis systems now exist that perform diagnostic tasks far more accurately than EPAM alone could, for they take into account alternative diagnoses, do some simple reasoning about relations among symptoms, and are able to request additional tests on the patient to achieve greater discriminatory power and accuracy. These systems, of course, are using a combination of intuition, as usually defined, and "logical" thought (including means-ends analysis in some form). Our current interest is not in machine competence in medical diagnosis but in models of intuition. EPAM, as described, is exhibiting intuition, as defined operationally, and modeling at least the first stage of thought (the recognition stage) of an experienced physician confronted with a set of symptoms.

Testing the Model of Intuition as Recognition

What grounds do we have for regarding this basic recognition mechanism, which lies at the core of EPAM, as a valid theory of the process that causes people to have intuitions? Simply that it has the same manifestations as human intuition: it occurs on the same time scale accompanied with the same inability to explain the process. Nor was it explicitly "cooked up" to exhibit these properties: they are basic to a system that was designed with quite other simulation tasks in mind. This is exactly the test we apply in validating any theory: we look at the match between the theory and the phenomena and at the ratio of amount of data explained to number of parameters available for fitting.

We can extend the tests of this theory of intuition further. It is well known that human intuitions that turn out to be valid problem solutions rarely occur to humans who are not well informed about the problem domain. For example, an expert solving a simple problem in physics takes a few computational steps without any preplanning and reports the answer. The recorded verbal protocol shows the steps, but no evidence of why they were taken (no mention of the goals, operators, or the algebraic expressions in which numbers were substituted). A novice solving the same problem works backwards from the variable to be evaluated, explicitly stating goals, the equations used and the substitutions in the equations. In one experiment, the novice's protocol was approximately four times as long as the expert's (Simon & Simon, 1978) and exhibited no intuition—only patient search. Novices who replace this search by guessing seldom guess correct answers. This is exactly what EPAM predicts: that there is no recognition without previous knowledge, and no intuition without recognition. Notice that intuition can be as fallible as the recognition cues on which it is based.

There are a number of experimental paradigms for carrying out tests on this theory that intuition is simply a form of recognition. The expert/novice paradigm has already been mentioned: experts should frequently report correct intuitive solutions of problems in their domain, while novices should seldom report intuitions, and if they report any, a large proportion should be incorrect. Experts who are able to report intuitions in their domains should be unable to do so in domains where they are not expert. By making cues more or less obvious, it should be possible to increase or decrease the frequency of correct intuitions; misleading cues should induce false intuitions. Hints of various kinds should draw attention to cues, hence facilitate intuition. These are only the most obvious possibilities, all of which have been tested with positive outcomes for the theory.

Experiments on intuition are best carried out on tasks where the correctness of answers can be verified, at least after the fact. We would want to identify "false intuition" to explain the cases (probably very frequent but hard to pinpoint in domains where objective criteria of correctness are lacking) where the presence of certain features in a situation leads subjects to announce a sudden solution although the connection between the cue and the inferences drawn from it is invalid. Determining the circumstances that encourage or discourage false intuition would involve research on the characteristics of situations that subjects attend to, and the beliefs they hold that lead them to the erroneous solutions. Some of the research that has been done on the psychology of so-called "naive physics" fits this general paradigm, as does some of the research on "garden paths" (spontaneous but erroneous interpretations) in syntactic analysis of sentences.

We see that intuition, far from being a mysterious and inexplicable phenomenon, is a well known process: the process of recognizing something on the basis of previous experience with it, and as a result of that recognition, securing access in long-term memory to the things we know about it. What subjects can report about the origins of their intuitions, and what they can't report, are exactly what we would predict from a theory that explained the phenomena associated with recognition. As a matter of fact, we could simplify our vocabulary in psychology if we just abandoned the word "intuition," and used the term "recognition" instead.

INSIGHT

Another process of thought that has sometimes been declared to be inexplicable by mechanical means is insight. My dictionary, this time, associates insight closely with intuition. In fact, its second definition of "intuition" is: "quick and ready insight." Its explicit definition of "insight" is not much more helpful: "the power or act of seeing into a situation: understanding, penetration." Again, we gain an impression of suddenness, but in this case accompanied by depth. Perhaps we shall want to regard any instance of insight as also an instance of intuition, in which case our work is already done, for we have just proposed a theory of intuition. Let's see, however, if there is an alternative—some other phenomenon that needs explanation and to which we can attach the word "insight."

Consider the "aha" phenomenon. Someone is trying to solve a problem, without success. At some point, a new idea comes suddenly to mind—a new way of viewing the problem. With this new idea comes a conviction that the problem is solved, or will be solved almost immediately. Moreover, the conviction is accompanied by an understanding of why the solution works. At this point we hear the "aha," soon followed by the solution—or occasionally by a disappointed realization that the insight was illusory. In some cases, after a problem has been worked on for some time without progress, it is put out of mind for a while, and the "aha" comes unexpectedly, at a moment when the mind was presumably attending to something else.

In both scenarios, with and without the interruption, the phenomenon shares the characteristics of intuitive solution: suddenness of solution (or at least of the realization that the solution is on its way), and inability to account for its appearance. The process differs from intuition in that: (1) the insight is preceded by a period of unsuccessful work, often accompanied by frustration, (2) what appears suddenly is not necessarily the solution, but the conviction of its imminence, (3) the insight involves a new way of looking at the problem (the appearance of a new problem representation accompanied by a feeling of seeing how the problem works) and (4) sometimes (not always), the insight is preceded by a period of "incubation," during which the problem is not attended to consciously, and occurs at a moment when the mind has been otherwise occupied. The third of these features is the source of the feeling of "understanding" and "depth" that accompanies the experience of insight. Again, these are the phenomena we use to identify instances of insight in human beings (ourselves or others). We can take the presence of these four features as our operational definition of insight, and using it, we now have some definite phenomena that we can study and seek to explain.

A Theory (Computer Program) of Insight

Let me now describe a computer program that can experience insight, defined in the manner just indicated. I shall present this theory a little more tentatively than the theory of intuition proposed earlier because, while it demonstrates that a computer program can have insights, the evidence is a little less solid than for intuition that it matches all aspects of the human experience of insight.

Again, a program that combines the capabilities of EPAM and the General Problem Solver constitutes the core of the theory. (1) We suppose that a GPS-like or Soar-like problem solver is conducting, unsuccessfully so far, a heuristic (selective) search for a problem solution. (2) It holds in long-term memory some body of information about the problem and knowledge of methods for attacking it. (3) Unfortunately, it is following a path that will not lead to a solution (although of course it is unaware of this). (4) We assume that the search is serial, its direction controlled by attentional mechanisms that are represented by the flow of control in the program. (5) Much of this control information, especially information about the local situation, is held in short-term memory, and is continually changing. (6) At the same time, some of the more permanent features of the problem situation are being noticed, learned, and stored in long-term memory, so that the information available for problem solution is changing, and usually improving. (7) The control structure includes an interrupt mechanism which will pause in search after some period without success or evidence of progress, and shift activity to another problem space where the search is not for the problem solution but for a different problem representation and/or a different search control structure. (8) When search is interrupted, the control information held in short-term memory will be lost, so that if search is later resumed, the direction of attention will be governed by the new representation and control structure, hence may lead the search in new directions. (9) As the nonlocal information that has been acquired in long-term memory through the previous search will participate in determining the search direction, the new direction is likely to be more productive than the previous one.

Empirical Tests of the Theory of Insight

Now we have introduced nine assumptions to explain the insight that may occur when the search is resumed, which hardly looks like a parsimonious theory. But these assumptions were not introduced into the composite EPAM-GPS to solve this particular problem. All are integral properties of these systems, whose presence is revealed by many different kinds of evidence obtained in other tasks.

One body of evidence supporting this model of insight comes from an experimental investigation of the Mutilated Checkerboard problem that Craig Kaplan and I conducted a few years ago (Kaplan & Simon, 1990). We begin with a chessboard (sixty-four squares) and thirty-two dominos, each of which can cover exactly two squares. Obviously, we can cover the chessboard with the dominos, with neither squares nor dominos left over. Now, we mutilate the chessboard by removing the upper-left and lower-right corner squares leaving a board of sixty-two squares. We ask subjects to cover it with thirty-one dominos or to prove it can't be done.

This is a difficult problem. Most people fail to solve it even after several hours effort. Their usual approach is to attempt various coverings as systematically as possible. As there are tens of thousands of ways to try to cover the board, after some number of failures they become frustrated, their efforts flag and they begin to wonder whether a covering exists. Increasingly they feel a need to look at the problem in a new way, but people seem not to have systematic methods for generating new problem representations. Some subjects simplify by replacing the 8 × 8 board with a 4 × 4 board, but this does not help.

Hints do help. Although few subjects solve the problem without a hint, many do with a hint, usually in a few minutes after the hint is provided. For example, the experimenter may call attention to the fact that the two squares left uncovered after an unsuccessful attempt are always the same color, opposite to the color of the excised corner squares. Attending to this fact, subjects begin to consider the number of squares of each color as relevant, and soon note that each domino covers a square of each color. This leads quickly to the inference that a set of dominos must always cover the same number of squares of each color, but that the mutilated board has more squares of the one color than of the other: Therefore, a covering is impossible.

Subjects who discover this solution, with or without a hint, exhibit behaviors that satisfy our definition of insight. The solution is preceded by unsuccessful work and frustration; it appears suddenly; it involves a new representation of the problem that makes the problem structure evident. The subjects come to the solution quite quickly once they attend to the critical property (equality of the numbers of squares of each color that are covered). This is also true of the few subjects who solve the problem without being given a hint. These subjects have their "aha!" when they attend to the fact that the uncovered squares are always the same color, and that the mutilated board has more squares of that color than of the other. Aided by cues or not, successful subjects often (literally) say "aha!" at the moment of recognizing the relevance of the parity of squares of the two colors.

Moreover, the mechanisms that bring about the solution are those postulated in our computer theory of insight, as can be seen by examining the list given above. Steps six through nine are the critical ones. In the case of hints, attention is directed to the crucial information by the hint, this information is stored in memory, and the search resumes from a new point and with a new direction of attention that makes the previous attempts to cover the board irrelevant. In the case of subjects who solve without a hint, the direction of attention to the invariant color of the uncovered squares may derive from a heuristic to attend to *invariant* properties of a situation—the properties that do not change, no matter what paths are searched in solution attempts.

There are probably several such heuristics (surprise is another one) that shift people's attention to particular aspects of a problem situation, thereby enabling the learning of key structural features and redirecting search. The evidence for such heuristics is not limited to laboratory situations; the role of the surprise heuristic in scientific discovery has been frequently noted. I shall return to it later.

The role of attention in insight receives further verification from a variant on the experiment. Different groups of subjects are provided with different chessboards: (1) a standard board, (2) a ruled 8 × 8 matrix without colors, and (3) an uncolored matrix with the words "bread" and "butter" ("pepper" and "salt" will do as well) printed on alternate squares. More subjects find the solution in condition 3 than in condition 1; and more in condition 1 than in condition 2. The reason for the latter difference is obvious: presence of the alternating colors provides a cue to which a subject's attention may be directed. What is the reason for the superiority of "bread" and "butter" over red and black? Subjects are familiar with standard chessboards and have no reason to think that the color has any relevance for this problem, hence don't attend to it. In the case of "bread" and "butter," the subjects' attention is attracted to this unusual feature of the situation; they wonder why "those crazy psychologists put those labels on the squares." Here we obtain direct support for the hypothesis that direction of attention to the key features of the situation provides the basis for solution. Noticeability of a feature is essential, whether it is provided by an explicit clue or some other means.

INSPIRATION (ALIAS CREATIVITY)

The term "inspiration" is surrounded by an aura of the miraculous. Interpreted literally, it refers to an idea that is not generated by the problem solver, but is breathed in from some external, perhaps heavenly, source. To inspire, says my faithful dictionary, is to "influence, move, or guide by divine or supernatural inspiration." A bit circular, but quite explicit about the exogenous, nonmaterial source. A Greek phrase for it was more vivid: to be inspired (e.g., at Delphi) was to be "seized by the god."

The notion that creativity requires inspiration derives from puzzlement about how a mechanism (even a biological mechanism like the brain), if it proceeds in its lawful, mechanistic way, can ever produce novelty. The problem is at the center of Plato's central question in the *Meno*: How can an untutored slave boy be led through a geometric argument until he understands the proof? The answer Plato provides, which hardly satisfies our modern ears, is that the boy knew it all the time; his new understanding was simply a recollection of a prior understanding buried deep in his memory (a recognition or intuition?). What bothers us about the answer is that Plato does not explain where the buried knowledge came from.

Combinatorially Generated Novelty

Let's leave the *Meno* . . . and go directly to the question of how a mechanism creates novelty, for novelty is at the core of creativity. In fact, we shall define *creativity* operationally, in full accordance with general usage, as novelty that is regarded as having interest or value (economic, esthetic, moral, scientific or other value).

I shall start with an example. There are about ninety-two stable elements in nature, composed of protons and neutrons (and these, in turn, of component particles). There are innumerable molecules, chemical species, almost none of which existed just after the Big Bang or just after the ninety-two elements first appeared in the universe.

Here is novelty on a mind-boggling scale; how did it come about? The answer is "combinatorics." Novelty can be created, and is created, by combinations and recombinations of existing primitive components. The twenty-six letters of the alphabet (or, if you prefer the seventy-odd phonemes of English) provide the primitives out of which a denumerable infinity of words can be created. New numbers, new words, new molecules, new species, new theorems, new ideas all can be generated without limit by recursion from small finite sets of primitives.

The traditional name in AI for this basic novelty-producing mechanism is *generate and test*. One uses a combinatorial process to generate new elements, then tests to see if they meet desired criteria. A good example of a generate-and-test system that can create novelty valuable for science is the BACON program (Langley, Simon, Bradshaw and Zytkow, 1987). BACON takes as inputs uninterpreted numerical data and, when successful, produces as outputs scientific laws (also uninterpreted) that fit the data.[5]

Selective Search as Inspiration

The law-generating process that BACON uses to find laws that describe data is not a random search process. The space of "possible functions" is not finite, and even if we limited search to some finite portion of it, any useful domain would be too large to yield often to random search. Basically, BACON's law generator embodies three heuristics for searching selectively: First, it starts with simple functions, then goes on (by combinatorial means) to more complex ones. We don't have to pause long to define "simple" or "complex." The simple functions are just those primitive functions that BACON starts with (in fact, the linear function); the compound functions are formed by multiplying or dividing pairs of functions by each other. A function is "simple" if it is generated early in the sequence, "complex" if generated later.

Second, BACON is guided by the data in choosing the next function to try. In particular, it notices if one variable increases or decreases monotonically with respect to another, testing whether ratios of the variables are invariant in the first case, products in the second, and shaping the next function it generates accordingly. This simple operation generates a wide class of algebraic functions, and by enlarging a bit the set of primitive functions (e.g., adding the exponential, logarithmic and sine functions), the class of generatable functions could be greatly broadened. The main point is that BACON's choice of the next function to test depends on what kind of fit with the data the previously tried functions exhibited.

Third, in problems involving data about more than two variables, BACON follows the venerable experimental procedure of changing one independent variable at a time. Having found conditional dependencies among small sets of variables, it explores the effects of altering other variables.

---

[5] I hasten to add that BACON has discovered no new scientific laws (although other programs built on the same generate-and-test principle have); but it has *rediscovered*, starting with only the same data that the original discoverer had, a number of the most important laws of eighteenth- and nineteenth-century physics and chemistry.

That is essentially all there is to it. With these simple means, and provided with the actual data that the original discoverers used, BACON rediscovers Kepler's Third Law (It finds $P = D^{3/2}$ on the third or fourth try), Ohm's Law of current and resistance, Black's Law of temperature equilibrium for mixtures of liquids and a great many others. There are many other laws it *doesn't* discover, which is an essential fact if it is to be regarded as a valid theory of human performance. Humans also *don't* discover laws more often than they do discover them.

To validate BACON as a theory of human discovery, we would like to have as detailed historical data as possible on how the human discoveries were actually made, but sometimes the data are quite scanty. About all we know about Kepler's discovery of his Third Law is that he initially made a mistake, declaring that the period of revolution of the planets varied as the square of their distance from the sun. Some years later, he decided the fit of law to data was poor and went on to find the correct law. Interestingly enough, BACON first arrives at Kepler's erroneous square law, rejects it as not fitting the data well enough, and goes on to the correct law almost immediately. With a looser parameter to test whether a law fits the data, BACON would make Kepler's mistake.

Sometimes the processes of BACON can be tested directly against human processes. Yulin Qin and I (1990) gave students the data (from the *World Almanac*) on the periods and distances of the planets—labeling the variables simply x and y, without interpretation. In less than an hour, four of fourteen students found and fitted the 3/2-power law to the data. The students who succeeded used a function generator that responded to the nature of the misfits of the incorrect functions. The students who failed either were unable to generate more than linear functions or generated functions whose form was independent of previous fits and misfits.

I spell out this example to show that theories of inspiration are constructed and tested in exactly the same manner as other scientific theories. Once the phenomena have been defined, we can look for other phenomena that accompany them and for mechanisms that exhibit the same behavior in the same situations. In historical cases more favorable than Kepler's, we may have voluminous data on the steps toward discovery. In the case of both Faraday and Krebs, for example, laboratory notebooks are available, as well as the published articles and autobiographical accounts. In these cases, we have many data points for matching the scientist's behavior with the model's predictions.

Discovery of New Concepts

I have now cited a few pieces of evidence—many more exist—that scientists do not have to be "seized by the god" to discover new laws; such laws, even laws of first magnitude, can be arrived at by quite understandable and simulatable psychological processes. But what about new concepts? Where do they come from?

BACON is provided with one heuristic that I have not yet mentioned. When it discovers that there is an invariant relation in the interaction between two or more elements in a situation, it assigns a new property to the elements, measuring its magnitude by the relative strength of each element's action (one of the elements is assigned a unit value, becoming the standard). For example, BACON notices that when pairs of bodies collide, the ratio of accelerations of any given pair is always the same. BACON defines a new property (let's call it "obstinance"), and assigns an obstinance of 1 to body A, and an obstinance to each other body inversely proportional to the magnitude of its acceleration in collisions with A. Of course, *we* know that "obstinance" is what we usually call "inertial mass," and that BACON has reinvented that latter concept on the basis of this simple experiment.

This procedure turns out to be a quite general heuristic for discovering new concepts. BACON has used it to reinvent the concepts of specific heat, of refractive index, of voltage, of molecular weight and atomic weight (and to distinguish them) and others. Here again, inspiration turns out to be a by-product of ordinary heuristic search.

All of these results are available in the psychological and cognitive science literature (Langley, Simon, Bradshaw and Zytkow, 1987). They will not be improved by philosophical debate, but rather by careful empirical study to determine the range of their validity and the goodness with which they approximate the observed phenomena. Debate, philosophical or otherwise, is pointless without familiarity with the evidence.

Other Dimensions of Discovery

Scientists do many things besides discovering laws and concepts. They plan and carry out experiments and interpret the findings, invent new instruments, find new problems, invent new problem representations. There are other dimensions to discovery, but these are perhaps the most important. I shall say no more about experiments (see Kulkarni and Simon, 1988) or instruments or problem-finding here. Some processes for finding new representations have already been examined in our discussion of insight. There is still plenty of work to be done, but so far, no evidence of which I am aware that the explanation of the phenomena of intuition, insight, and inspiration will require the introduction of mechanisms or processes unlike those that have been widely employed in simulating human thinking. That, of course, is an empirical claim—actually, not so much a claim as an invitation to join in the exciting task of explaining how machines like people and computers can think, and sometimes think creatively.

NEUROPHYSIOLOGICAL FOUNDATIONS

It will not have passed without notice that I have said almost nothing about the brain as a physiological organ. My silence should not be interpreted as doubt that the mind is in the brain, or a suggestion that processes beyond the physiological are required for its operation. The reason for my omission of the physiology of the brain is quite different. As I have pointed out in other contexts, sciences generally progress most effectively if they focus upon phenomena at particular levels in the scheme of things. Hunters of the quark do not, fortunately, need to have theories about molecules, or vice versa. The phenomena of nature arrange themselves in levels (Simon, 1981) and scientists specialize in explaining phenomena at each level (high energy physics, nuclear physics, analytic chemistry, biochemistry, molecular biology . . . neurophysiology, symbolic information processing, and so on), and *then,* in showing (at least in principle) how the phenomena at each level can be explained (reduced) to the terms and mechanisms of the theory at the next level below.

At the present moment in cognitive science, our understanding of thinking at the information processing level has progressed far beyond our knowledge of the physiological mechanisms that implement the symbolic processes of thought. (Fortunately, on the computer side, we know full well how the symbolic processes are implemented by electronic processes in silicon.) Our ignorance of neurology is regrettable but not alarming for progress at the information-processing level, for this same skyhook picture of science is visible in every scientific field during some period—usually a long period—in the course of its development. Nineteenth-century chemistry had little or no base in physics, and biology had only a little more in chemistry.

There is no reason why research in cognition should not continue to develop vigorously at both physiological and information processing levels (as it is now doing) watching carefully for the indications, of which there already are a few, that we can begin to build the links between them—starting perhaps with explanations of the nature of the physiological mechanisms (the "chips" and "integrated circuits") that constitute the basic repositories of symbolic memory in the brain. While we await this happy event, there is plenty of work for all of us, and no lack of knowledge of cognitive mechanisms at the symbolic level I have been considering in this paper.

SOME PHILOSOPHICAL IMPLICATIONS

Several questions of major interest to philosophy that are closely connected with cognition are empirical questions that cannot be solved by fact-free speculation, no matter how sophisticated it may be. A major difficulty with these questions is that finding empirical data to answer them appears to require us to look inside the human head, which is not easy to do, especially if introspection is ruled out as an incorrigibly solipsistic process. This presents a difficulty, but not an insuperable difficulty. The view that we cannot build testable theories of the processes within the head, including the processes of thought, is no more tenable than the view that biochemical theory cannot capture the laws of life. With the coming of computers and the demonstration that they can model not only the products but also the processes of thought, this mental vitalism is no longer defensible.

Testability of Theories of Mental Phenomena

To say that there are many variables within the head that are not directly observable is simply to say that a theory of mental phenomena will contain theoretical terms, not a novelty for any of the sciences. In such situations we need
to ensure that there is a sufficiently high ratio of observables to unknowns in
our theories so that the values of the theoretical terms are overdetermined,
hence ascertainable by convergent methods and testable. (Simon, 1970, 1983,
1985; Shen and Simon, 1993). When we construct a theory of mental phenomena in the form of a computer simulation, we test it by observing human
subjects and a computer program performing exactly the same tasks, with identical inputs of stimuli. Then we compare the trace of the computer, at an appropriate level of detail, with observations of the human behavior (including
verbal behavior) over the same interval of time. The examples provided in this
paper have illustrated how this strategy has been employed to validate computer models of intuition, insight, and creativity.

Specifically, to answer the question of whether an appropriately programmed computer can think, we establish a task and a set of criteria to determine whether a human being is thinking when performing that task. If the
computer, given the same task, not only produces the same result but also
matches the behavior of the human in all observable respects, and in particular
matches the processes the human is observably using during performance of the
task, then we conclude that the computer is also thinking—i.e., that the processes that produce the result for the computer can be mapped on the processes
that produced the same result for the human.

Thus, to determine whether the theoretical term "thinking" applies to the
computer, we use the same test that we use to determine whether it applies to
the human subject. Of course, we do not in this way find any magic that solves
the problem of Hume—we do not *prove* that our theory of thinking is correct:
but merely that it is compatible with the available empirical evidence. Again,
this does not distinguish methods of theory verification in psychology from
those in any other science. In no science does research *prove* the correctness of
a theory; at best it shows that it has not been falsified and provides a reasonable fit to some body of facts.

The Mind-Body Problem

Suppose, now, that we have constructed a computer program that passes this
test of thinking, for some range of tasks. We can now ask what solution, if any,
it offers to the mind-body problem. It was Carnap, in 1955, who first explicitly
proposed this use of the computer as a tool in epistemology.[6] This is the way he
put his proposal:

---

[6] Carnap (1955) reprinted in Carnap (1956).

In order to make the method of structure analysis applicable, let us now consider the pragmatic investigation of the language of a robot rather than that of a human being. In this case we may assume that we possess much more detailed knowledge of the internal structure. . . . Just as the linguist [e.g., Quine's linguist in *Word and Object*], . . . begins with pointing to objects, but later, after having determined the interpretation of some words, asks questions formulated by these words, the investigator of [the robot's] language . . . begins with presenting objects . . . but later, on the basis of tentative results concerning the intensions of some signs . . . proceeds to present predicate expressions . . . which use only those interpreted signs. . . .

Instead of using this behavioristic method, the investigator may here use the method of structure analysis. On the basis of the given blueprint of [the robot], he may be able to calculate the responses which [it] would make to various possible inputs. In particular, he may be able to derive from the given blueprint . . . fairly precise boundaries for the intensions of certain concepts. . . .

It is clear that the method of structure analysis, if applicable, is more powerful than the behavioristic method, because it can supply a general answer and, under favorable circumstances, even a complete answer to the question of the intension of a given predicate. . . .

The intension of a predicate can be determined for a robot just as well as for a human speaker, and even more completely if the internal structure of the robot is sufficiently known to predict how it will function under various conditions.

With the advance of computers and programming languages in the years since Carnap made his proposal, we can now describe, in detail, computer programs that, by using a physical symbol system to carry out thought, embody a clear answer to the mind-body problem. Just as a brain uses neurons and associated tissues to store information (in ways that we do not understand in detail), so a computer uses physical devices (of quite diverse mechanical, electrical, and electronic varieties) to store information (in ways that we do understand in detail). What is required in both cases is a system built of components that can be maintained, with some stability, in one or another of two or more states, and that can input and output information by signaling the current states of these components. The specific substances of which these memories are built, and the physical or biological processes they use to maintain and alter memory contents are relevant only in fixing the capacity, stability, and speed of the system, and do not limit its basic qualitative capabilities. . . .

[A] demonstrably mechanistic system (a "body" in the form of a physical symbol system) is capable of thinking (using "mind" processes), where the operational definition of "thinking" is identical with the definition used to determine when people are thinking. It cannot be emphasized too strongly that the operational test of thinking involves comparison of both product and process. With this definition and empirical findings, the research in cognitive science has shown that a mind is simply a brain at work.

If we wish to preserve the two terms, "mind" and "brain," in our language, then we can use the former for the processes of thought, and the latter for the structure that supports the processes. There is no more mystery in the relation between these two components than in the relation of the cardboard of which an old IBM punchcard is fabricated, and the punching of a pattern of holes in it. The former is the memory, a part of the brain; the latter is the process of storing knowledge in the brain. To describe any dynamic system—the planets revolving about the sun, or an electric generator—we must describe both the physical parts as organized, and the processes they undergo: organized substance and process. The brain and mind are a dynamic system; hence their description takes this same form. There is nothing epiphenomenal about mind, for without process, the brain does not think. As one component of the system is substance, the other process, they are not identical.

The Chinese Room

Searle has rejected this solution of the mind-body problem on the grounds that the wrong definition of thinking has been applied. Thinking, he argues, requires *understanding* the object of thought; and computers, he claims, cannot understand. He provides as an example the parable of a room in which translation from English to Chinese (or vice versa) is going forward, but simply by means of a lexicon that finds the proper Chinese translation for each English word (or phrase, or sentence) without reference to the word's intension. Hence, the translation can be done without understanding of either language.

The answer to Searle is that he has described the wrong room. If the room had windows, so that the translators could see in the real world instantiations of the situations described by the text, then they (assumed to know English) could acquire Chinese meanings, building up their lexicon in the form of a huge discrimination net that sorts both situations and linguistic expressions according to their sensed properties (the intensions), and associates expressions with the situations they denote. Now the Chinese text is associated with its intensions, and these are used to associate to English text corresponding to these intensions. A computer system, ZBIE, that carries out these processes was constructed and described a quarter century ago by Siklóssy (1972). It could also be used to construct a Chinese-English lexicon (or vice versa), using the associations of both languages with their intensions to link the former.

Siklóssy's demonstration that a computer can learn the intensions of words, phrases, and sentences shows empirically that computers are capable of thinking even if the "thinking" is so defined as to require knowledge of the intensions of the symbols the mind is manipulating in the process of thought. Hence, our solution of the mind-body problem remains valid even if we use this stricter definition of thinking and mind.

CONCLUSION

Artificial intelligence is an empirical science with two major branches. One branch is concerned with building computer programs (and sometimes robots) to perform tasks that are regarded as requiring intelligence when they are performed by human beings. The other is concerned with building computer programs that simulate, and thereby serve as theories of, the thought processes of human beings engaged in these same tasks. I have directed my remarks to the outer edge of AI research belonging to the latter branch, where it is concerned with phenomena that are often regarded as ineffable, and not explainable by machine models. I have shown that, on the contrary, we have already had substantial success in designing and implementing empirically tested information-processing theories that account for the phenomena of intuition, insight, and inspiration. I have no immediate urge to predict how much further we shall go in the future or how fast. The continual progress on the journey over the past forty years has been speedy enough for me. . . .

Traditional philosophy has much more to learn today from AI than AI has to learn from philosophy, for it is the human mind we must understand—and understand as a physical symbol system—in order to advance our understanding of the classical questions that philosophers have labeled "epistemology" and "ontology" and the "mind-body problem" (Simon, 1992).

My argument stands on a solid body of fact. I have mentioned a considerable number of these facts, drawn from papers in refereed journals or similarly credible sources. I may perhaps be pardoned for drawing a large portion of the facts I have cited from work in which I have been involved. I could have made an even stronger case if I had broadened the base, but I would have been familiar with fewer of the details. If you want to calibrate my base of evidence, you can multiply it by several orders of magnitude to take account of the work of all the other members of the AI and cognitive science communities who have been engaged in simulation of human thinking. In my account, I have tried not to talk about "future hopes of understanding or modeling human thinking," but to confine myself to documented, easily replicable, present realities about our present capabilities for modeling and thereby explaining human thinking, even thinking of those kinds that require the processes we admiringly label "intuitive," "insightful," and "inspired."

I have used the mind-body problem to illustrate how cognitive science, using computer simulation as a tool of theory, can bring light to bear on important epistemological problems. The conclusion reached from a large and consistent body of empirical evidence is that brain and mind are simply the essential substance and process that define any system, computer or human, capable of thinking.

If I have challenged some dimensions of human uniqueness, I hope I will not be thought scornful of human beings, or of our capacity to think. To explain a phenomenon is not to demean it. An astrophysical theory of the Big Bang or a three-dimensional chemical model of DNA do not lessen the fascination of the heavens at night or the beauty of the unfolding of a flower. Knowing how we think will not make us less admiring of good thinking. It may even make us better able to teach it.

REFERENCES

Anderson, J. R. (1983). *The Architecture of Cognition*. Cambridge, MA: Harvard University Press.

Anzai, Y., & Simon, H. A. (1979). The theory of learning by doing. *Psychological Review, 86*, 124–140.

Carnap, R. (1955). Meaning and synonymy in natural languages. In Carnap (1956).

Carnap, R. (1956). *Meaning and Necessity* (2nd ed). Chicago, IL: University of Chicago Press.

Ericsson, K. A. & Simon, H. A. (1993). *Protocol analysis: Verbal Reports as Data* (rev. ed.). Cambridge, MA: The MIT Press.

Feigenbaum, E. A. & Simon, H. A. (1984). EPAM-like models of recognition and learning. *Cognitive Science, 8*, 305–336.

Kaplan, C. A. (1989). *Hatching a theory of incubation*. Unpublished doctoral dissertation, Department of Psychology, Carnegie Mellon University, Pittsburgh, PA.

Kaplan, C. A. & Simon, H. A. (1990). In search of insight. *Cognitive Psychology, 22*, 374–419.

Kulkarni, D. & Simon, H. A. (1988). The processes of scientific discovery: The strategy of experimentation. *Cognitive Science, 12*, 139–176.

Langley, P., Simon, H. A., Bradshaw, G. L. & Zytkow, J. M. (1987). *Scientific discovery: Computational explorations of the creative process*. Cambridge, MA: The MIT Press.

McClelland, J. L. & Rumelhart, D. E. (1986). *Parallel distributed processing* (volumes 1 and 2). Cambridge, MA: The MIT Press.

Newell, A. (1990). *Unified theories of cognition*. Cambridge, MA: Harvard University Press.

Newell, A. & Simon, H. A. (1972). *Human problem solving*. Englewood Cliffs, NJ: Prentice-Hall.

Plato, *The Meno*

Quillian, R. (1967). *Semantic memory*. Unpublished doctoral dissertation, Department of Psychology, Carnegie Institute of Technology.

Qin Y. & Simon, H. A. (1990). Laboratory replication of scientific discovery processes. *Cognitive Science, 14*, 281–312.

Richman, H. B., Staszewski, J. J. & Simon, H. A., (1995). Simulation of expert memory using EPAM IV. *Psychological Review, 102*, 305–330.

Shen, W. (1994). *Autonomous learning from the environment*. New York, NY: W. H. Freeman.

Shen, W., & Simon, H. A. (1993). Fitness requirements for scientific theories containing recursive theoretical terms. *British Journal for the Philosophy of Science, 44*, 641–652.

Siklóssy, L. (1972). Natural language learning by computer. In H. A. Simon & L. Siklóssy, (eds.), *Representation and Meaning*. Englewood Cliffs, NJ: Prentice-Hall.

Simon, D. P., & Simon, H. A. (1978). Individual differences in solving physics problems. In R. S. Siegler (ed.), *Childrens's thinking: What develops?* Hillsdale, NJ: Lawrence Erlbaum.

Simon, H. A. (1970). The axiomatization of physical theories. *Philosophy of Science, 39*, 16–26.

Simon, H. A. (1975). The functional equivalence of problem solving skills. *Cognitive Psychology, 7*, 268–288.

Simon, H. A. (1983) Fitness Requirements for scientific theories. *British Journal for the Philosophy of Science, 34,* 355–365.

Simon, H. A. (1985) Quantification of theoretical terms and the falsifiability of theories. *British Journal for the Philosophy of Science, 36,* 291–298.

Simon, H. A. (1976). Bradie on Polanyi on the Meno paradox. *Philosophy of Science, 43,* 147–151.

Simon, H. A. (1979, 1989). *Models of Thought.* New Haven, CT: Yale University Press.

Simon, H. A. (1996). *The sciences of the artificial,* (3rd ed.). Cambridge, MA: The MIT Press.

Simon, H. A. (1992). The computer as a laboratory for epistemology. In L. Burkholder (ed.), *Philosophy and the computer.* Boulder, CO: The Westview Press.

DISCUSSION QUESTIONS

1. What is the difference between mind-body dualism and mind-body monism?
2. What does the interactionist theory (Cartesian dualism) assert? What properties does Descartes ascribe to mind? What properties does he ascribe to matter?
3. What objection(s) might be raised against the interactionist theory? Do you find such criticism convincing? Defend your answer.
4. What does epiphenomenalism assert? Do you find this theory convincing? Defend your answer.
5. Discuss the difference between materialism and idealism.
6. What does the identity theory assert? What objection(s) might be raised against this theory? Do you find such criticism convincing? Defend your answer.
7. It is sometimes argued that mental states are always "intentional" or "purposeful-ness," that is they *refer to* or are *about* objects or states of affairs existing outside the mind in the world. For example, a desire is always for something; a belief is about something; a sensation is with respect to a certain part of the body (an itch on one's nose, for example). Would you say that a thermostat or a heat-seeking rocket is purposeful or intentional in a similar way? Are software programs intentional or purposeful in a similar way? In other words, can physical systems be intentional like mental states or is this at least part of what distinguishes the latter from the former? Defend your answer.
8. John Searle argues that mental states are caused by brains and are, at the same time, features or properties of them. However, some have challenged Searle's view on the grounds that his claim implies that the mind would be a cause of itself, and that this is not possible. In your view, is it possible for mental processes to be caused by brains and still be properties of them? Defend your answer.
9. Explain Searle's position on whether digital computers can think. What is his "Chinese room argument? What is Herbert Simon's response to Searle's "Chinese room argument"? Did you find this argument convincing? Do you think Simon has successfully refuted Searle's position? Defend all answers.
10. Discuss Simon's view about the mind and its relationship to the brain, and compare his position on the mid-brain relationship to that of Searle.
11. Describe and illustrate Simon's method for determining whether a computer can think? In your view, is Simon's method a sound one? Defend your answer.
12. Discuss at least two of Simon's examples of thought simulation which he thinks show that computers can think. Do you find any of Simon's examples convincing? Defend your position.
13. Describe Simon's view of the following theories about the relationship between mind and body: (1) the identity theory; (2) epiphenomenalism.
14. Simon believes that science has solved the philosophical problem about the relationship between mind and body. Why does he say this?
15. Do you think that any artificial intelligence research aiming at simulating human thinking could ever, now or in the future, *conclusively* solve the mind-body problem? Defend your answer.

VI

RELIGION AND
MYSTICISM

13

THEISM, ATHEISM, AND THE CLERGY

In this chapter, the question of God's existence and its bearing on human existence and the problem of evil will be explored.

One traditional approach to the question of God's existence has been that of attempting to construct rational proofs or *demonstrations*. Such proofs are, generally speaking, divisible into two kinds: (1) a priori proofs and (2) a posteriori proofs. Whereas the former attempt to prove God's existence by *thought* alone, the latter begin with sense experience of ordinary objects in nature.

In the first selection of this chapter, taken from The Proslogium, St. Anselm (1033–1109), a Benedictine monk, presents an example of an a priori proof. Beginning with the definition of God as "that than which nothing greater can be conceived," he attempts to demonstrate that God must exist—for a being which does not exist cannot be "that than which nothing greater can be conceived" inasmuch as a being, which does exist—in reality as well as in thought—will be greater. Roughly put, since God is perfect, by definition, He must exist; otherwise He would not be perfect. Hence the proposition that "God exists" is necessarily true and its denial is self-contradictory.

Although it is left to the reader to consider the merit of the ontological proof, it should be noted, at this point, that this proof has historically, even in Anselm's own time,[1] encountered philosophical objections. One major objection came in the eighteenth century from Immanuel Kant, who argued that the proof engendered a logical confusion. "Existence, " Kant argued, is not a predicate that can embellish the description of a thing. Rather, "existence" relates a description of a thing to the world; it is not itself part of that description. For example, in predicating "yellow" of a thing (say a dog), I do indeed add to its description. But in saying that it exists, I do not change its description: I simply assert that something in the world fits that description. Whereas "yellow" is a predicate, "existence" is not. If so, then the description of a thing cannot be perfected by adding existence to it, yet this is just what the ontological proof demands.

In the second selection, excerpted from the *Summa Theologica*, St. Thomas Aquinas (1225–1274), the great Scholastic theologian and philosopher, advances five a posteriori proofs of God's existence. Beginning with different sense observations of what is found in nature, he attempts, in five ways, to logically prove God's existence. For example, in the first proof he begins by noting that "it is certain, and evident to our senses, that some things are in motion." But since such motion can only be generated by something else that is in motion, the observed motion requires the existence of something else in motion; which motion must, in turn, be explained by some further motion, and so on. Therefore, unless there is to be generated an infinite regress of motions (and, therefore, no motion to start any of the subsequent motions), there must be a first mover that moves without itself being moved: which mover "everyone understands to be God."

Although Aquinas himself rejected the ontological argument, there is an interesting relation between that argument and the "cosmological" argument mentioned above. If God is a necessarily existing being (as the ontological argument maintains), then there is no point in explaining God's existence in terms of any other existence. Indeed, the question "Why does God exist?" would be much like asking "Why are triangles three-sided?" That, of course, follows from the very definition of a triangle. And, similarly, God's existence would follow from His definition. Consequently, any regress of motions (or "efficient causes," as discussed in Aquinas's second proof) will terminate with God's existence.

In the third selection, excerpted from *Philosophical Fragments,* Soren Kierkegaard (1813–1855) calls into question the whole business of constructing rational proofs of God's existence. He argues that the process of proof merely begs the question by assuming God's existence at the very outset. For Kierkegaard, reason cannot prove God's existence. What is always required, as regards belief in God, is a "leap" of faith. Moreover, human reason is circumscribed by its own limitations and cannot comprehend what is beyond its own comprehension: "it cannot absolutely transcend itself."

In the fourth selection, from *I and Thou,* Martin Buber (1878–1965) also takes the stand that God's existence cannot be proven rationally. Moreover, he maintains that God "by its nature . . . cannot be understood as a sum of qualities, not even as an infinite sum of qualities raised to a transcendental level." God is thus absolutely indefinable. Nevertheless, human beings are capable of entering into a relation with God, with their "eternal Thou."

Buber distinguishes between two relationships into which human beings can enter: *I-It* and *I-Thou*. In the *I-It* relation, human beings relate to a being (for example, a tree or another person) as a space-time object, as some analyzable thing, as an "It." For example, I can relate to a tree by classifying it into a species and "study it as a type in its structure and mode of life." A person may similarly relate to another person by looking upon that being in terms of some limited function or purpose (for example, as my spouse, my physician, and the like). Alternatively, one can relate to another as I and Thou. In such a relation, the relata are fused with the totality of reality. There are no divisions of parts or space-time partitions, no attempt to analyze. In taking another human being as ones *Thou,* the "human being is not *He* or *She,* bounded from every other *He* and *She,* a specific point in space and time within the net of the world; nor is he a nature able to be experienced and described, a loose bundle of named qualities. . . . [H]e is Thou and fills the heavens."

According to Buber, it is through entering such particular I-Thou relations that we may enter into relation with our eternal Thou. For Buber, then, God speaks to us, and is spoken to, through the manner in which we relate to others in our lives. Those who seek God through more traditional routes, including the attempt to prove His existence, are apt to be eluded.

In the fifth selection of this chapter, excerpted from *Thus Spake Zarathustra*, German philosopher Friedrich Nietzsche (1844–1900) exemplifies an atheistic perspective. Employing a literary approach, Nietzsche, through the mouthpiece of Zarathustra, a fictitious Persian philosopher and teacher, preaches the "overcoming of man," that is, the demise of traditional moral and religious values. Says Zarathustra, "Once the sin against God was the greatest sin; but God died, and these sinners died with him. To sin against the earth is now the most dreadful thing, and to esteem the entrails of the unknowable higher than the meaning of the earth." Proffering his nihilistic premise, Nietzsche raises a question about the meaningfulness of human existence amidst a godless earthbound universe. As put by the mortally injured tightrope walker a moment before his death, "If you speak the truth . . . I lose nothing when I lose my life. I am not much more than a beast that has been taught to dance by blows and a few meager morsels." Nietzsche, however, has substituted *aesthetic* values for religious ones. In response to the dying man's words, Zarathustra answers, "By no means. . . . You have made danger your vocation; there is nothing contemptible in that. Now you perish of your vocation."

On Nietzsche's view, there is no meaning to one's life prior to that which one fashions for oneself. As Jean-Paul Sartre says, for human reality, "existence precedes essence." Nature is not already infused with order, purpose, and meaning. Nor does nature bear the mark of a kind and benevolent God. Good and evil are the creations of human beings, not of God. In Nietzsche's view, there is, therefore, no problem of why evil things can happen in the face of an all-good, omnipotent (all-powerful) God.

The latter problem, sometimes dubbed "the problem of evil," is the topic of the next two selections of this chapter. In the sixth selection, John H. Hick presents two related "theodicies" (justifications of God's goodness in the face of evil). The first theodicy attempts to reconcile God's goodness with the existence of *moral* evil or human wickedness by appealing to personal freedom. (Such attempts at justification are called "theodicies.") In Hick's view, such evil is a consequence of permitting human beings free will. While it would have been possible for God to create beings who were predetermined to always do what was morally right, such beings would not be free *in relation to* God. They would have rather resembled puppets, incapable of entering into a meaningful personal relationship with their Creator as His children.

The second theodicy Hick presents attempts to account for the existence of *nonmoral* evil—natural disasters and other evils that occur by no human fault or misdeed—by arguing that a world devoid of such evil would exclude the possibility of human beings becoming "children of God" through their freely confronting such impediments. If the world were a hedonic paradise, then there would be no place for "soul building," that is the free development of virtue.

For example, courage and fortitude would be impossible in a world without danger or problems to overcome.

It may nevertheless be questioned whether at least certain past evils have been *excessive* and pointless even for the divine purposes of allowing human freedom and virtue. While God need not have eliminated all dangers, was it necessary to permit pandemics and natural disasters in which millions of people, including innocent children suffer and lose their lives? Where was God during the extermination of six million Jews?

In the seventh selection, on "Evil and the Limits of God: Jewish Perspectives," Neil Gillman discusses the problem of evil in the aftermath of the Holocaust. While Hick embraces God's status as omnipotent even in the face of enormous evil, some Jewish thinkers have found such an approach untenable and have settled upon a view in which God's powers are intrinsically limited.

According to Mordecai Kaplan, God is "the power (within nature) that makes for salvation, where salvation means the actualization of all values." As for Buber, there is no duality between God and His creation. God is not a metaphysical being set apart from nature but is rather what is good in nature. These good qualities of nature—such as justice, morality, and creativity—tend to destroy evil. Nevertheless, since evil is a persistent fact that can never be completely eradicated, God's power is limited.

A more extreme version of the God-in-nature perspective is held by Richard Rubenstein. According to the latter, while God is to be identified with nature, God is not simply the good aspects of nature but rather the powers of nature as such. Nature in itself is indifferent about good and evil. Rubenstein employs Nietzsche's metaphor that "God is dead" to drive home the fact that, in the aftermath of the Holocaust, the traditional Jewish concept of God as infinitely good and powerful is no longer feasible.

Changing the metaphor, Buber attempts to account for the absence of God in the face of great evil, by speaking of the "eclipse of God." This metaphor represents the temporary fluctuation from I-Thou to I-It in God's relationship with human beings. One may wonder, however, whether such a metaphor only begs the question, for one may still want to know why six million Jews became It to their eternal Thou at a time when they so desperately needed Him. For Rubenstein, there was just one acceptable explanation: such an "eternal Thou" was "dead."

In the first Practice selection, Father Robert R. Gerl, a Roman Catholic priest, discusses the practical implications of the theistic stances espoused in this chapter. Describing his experience of ministering to a terminally ill cancer patient, he attempts to exemplify the ways in which reason, faith, and the I-Thou relation can all have their respective contributions to human existence, especially in the context of the dying process in which a person comes face to face with the awesome question of the meaning of human existence.

In the second Practice selection of this chapter, Rabbi Allan I. Freehling speaks candidly about his active involvement in advancing just social treatment of those afflicted with HIV/AIDS (Human Immunodeficiency Virus/Acquired

Immune Deficiency Syndrome). As founding chair of the Los Angeles Commission on AIDS, a founder of the AIDS Interfaith Counsel, and chair of the Reform Movements Committee on AIDS (among other socially proactive groups), Rabbi Freehling recounts a story about community efforts to help, often met with opposition from traditionalists who viewed AIDS as God's just punishment of the many homosexuals afflicted with the disease for their sinful sexual activity. Drawing out the consistent implications of Judaism, which stresses the priority of saving human life above all other religious interests, Rabbi Freehling has made it a main mission of his life to work toward religious values that teach we are "bonded to all of God's creatures," and that "there is no way that a person can justify condemnation of another individual."

In this regard, Rabbi Freehling relies on Buber's concept of finding the eternal Thou through the particular I-Thou relationships we develop with others. Quoting Buber, he reminds us that "He who loves brings God and the World together."

This world, however, also includes an AIDS pandemic. To those afflicted with this disease who queried the Rabbi as to why God would "permit good people to die such horrible deaths," his response was not like that of John Hick, to assure these patients that there was a larger divine purpose for their suffering. Instead, he conveyed the idea that God is not omnipotent and responsible for everything. He shared with them Mordecai Kaplan's idea of God as what is good in the world and that faith involves the wisdom and strength of will to explore and promote that good. Such ideas, says the Rabbi, were "liberating" and gave some of these patients a new perspective upon which to view their relationship with God.

This new perspective, which views God and salvation in terms of nature, does not appear to offer the AIDS patients hope for eternal life. It is thus consistent with the Old Testament, which views death as final. "His [moral man's] breath departs; he returns to the dust; on that day his plans come to naught." (Psalm 146:3–4). We are here reminded of Zarathustra's response to the tightrope walker who feared that his life would be without meaning if there were no afterlife. Said Zarathustra, "You have made danger your vocation; there is nothing contemptible in that. Now you perish of your vocation." This new way of viewing things brought consolation to the dying tightroper walker. In a similar vein, for at least some AIDS patients, the limited concept of God gave meaning and purpose to living and perishing as a person of faith. However, as will become apparent, this is at odds with Father Gerl's view that "to the theistic thinker, this life and its finiteness never seem to give a sense of fulfillment."

NOTE

1. For example, Gaunilo, a contemporary of Anselm, argued that by parity of reasoning it would be possible to prove the existence of the perfect island. See Gaunilo's "On Behalf of the Fool" in *St. Anselm: Basic Writings*, tr. S. N. Deane, 1903.

ISSUES

ST. ANSELM

THE ONTOLOGICAL PROOF OF GOD'S EXISTENCE: THE *A PRIORI* APPROACH

And so, Lord, do thou, who dost give understanding to faith, give me, so far as thou knowest it to be profitable, to understand that thou art as we believe; and that thou art that which we believe. And, indeed, we believe that thou art a being than which nothing greater can be conceived. Or is there no such nature, since the fool hath said in his heart, there is no God? (Psalms xiv. i). But, at any rate, this very fool, when he hears of this being of which I speak—a being than which nothing greater can be conceived—understands what he hears, and what he understands is in his understanding; although he does not understand it to exist.

For it is one thing for an object to be in the understanding, and another to understand that the object exists. When a painter first conceives of what he will afterwards perform, he has it in his understanding, but he does not yet understand it to be, because he has not yet performed it. But after he has made the painting, he both has it in his understanding, and he understands that it exists, because he has made it.

Hence, even the fool is convinced that something exists in the understanding, at least, than which nothing greater can be conceived. For, when he hears of this, he understands it. And whatever is understood, exists in the understanding. And assuredly that, than which nothing greater can he conceived, cannot exist in the understanding alone. For, suppose it exists in the understanding alone: then it can be conceived to exist in reality; which is greater.

Therefore, if that, than which nothing greater can be conceived, exists in the understanding alone, the very being, than which nothing greater can be conceived, is one, than which a greater can be conceived. But obviously this is impossible. Hence, there is no doubt that there exists a being, than which nothing greater can be conceived, and it exists both in the understanding and in reality.

And it assuredly exists so truly, that it cannot even be conceived not to exist. For, it is possible to conceive of a being which cannot be conceived not to exist; and this is greater than one which can be conceived not to exist. Hence, if that, than which nothing greater can be conceived, can be conceived not to

SOURCE: *St. Anselm: Basic Writings*, 2nd ed., trans. S. N. Deane, pp. 7–10. Copyright 1962 by the Open Court Publishing Company, a division of Carus Publishing Company, Peru, IL. Reprinted by permission.

exist, it is not that, than which nothing greater can be conceived. But this is an irreconcilable contradiction. There is, then, so truly a being than which nothing greater can be conceived to exist, that it cannot even be conceived not to exist; and this being thou art, O Lord, our God.

So truly, therefore, dost thou exist, O Lord, my God, that thou canst not be conceived not to exist; and rightly. For if a mind could conceive of a being better than thee, the creature would rise above the Creator; and this is most absurd. And, indeed, whatever else there is, except thee alone, can be conceived not to exist. To thee alone, therefore, it belongs to exist more truly than all other beings, and hence in a higher degree than all others. For, whatever else exists does not exist so truly, and hence in a less degree it belongs to it to exist. Why, then, has the fool said in his heart, there is no God (Psalms xiv. 1), since it is so evident, to a rational mind, that thou dost exist in the highest degree of all? Why, except that he is dull and a fool?

But how has the fool said in his heart what he could not conceive; or how is it that he could not conceive what he said in his heart? since it is the same to say in the heart, and to conceive.

But, if really, nay, since really, he both conceived, because he said in his heart; and did not say in his heart, because he could not conceive; there is more than one way in which a thing is said in the heart or conceived. For, in one sense, an object is conceived when the word signifying it is conceived; and in another, when the very entity, which the object is, is understood.

In the former sense, then, God can be conceived not to exist; but in the latter, not at all. For no one who understands what fire and water are can conceive fire to be water, in accordance with the nature of the facts themselves, although this is possible according to the words. So, then, no one who understands what God is can conceive that God does not exist; although he says these words in his heart, either without any, or with some foreign, signification. For, God is that than which a greater cannot even be conceived. And he who thoroughly understands this, assuredly understands that this being so truly exists, that not even in concept can it be nonexistent. Therefore, he who understands that God so exists, cannot conceive that he does not exist.

I thank thee, gracious Lord, I thank thee; because what I formerly believed by thy bounty, I now so understand by thine illumination, that if I were unwilling to believe that thou dost exist, I should not be able not to understand this to be true.

ST. THOMAS AQUINAS
_____

FIVE WAYS OF PROVING GOD'S EXISTENCE: THE *A POSTERIORI* APPROACH

We proceed thus to the Third Article:

Objection 1. It seems that God does not exist; because if one or two contraries be infinite, the other would be altogether destroyed. But the name *God* means that He is infinite goodness. If, therefore, God existed, there would be no evil discoverable; but there is evil in the world. Therefore God does not exist.

Objection 2. Further, it is superfluous to suppose that what can be accounted for by a few principles has been produced by many. But it seems that everything we see in the world can be accounted for by other principles, supposing God did not exist. For all natural things can be reduced to one principle, which is nature; and all voluntary things can be reduced to one principle, which is human reason, or will. Therefore there is no need to suppose God's existence.

On the contrary, it is said in the person of God: *I am Who am* (Exodus 3:14). . . .

The Existence of God can be proved in five ways.

The first and more manifest way is the argument from motion. It is certain, and evident to our senses, that in the world some things are in motion. Now whatever is moved is moved by another, for nothing can be moved except it is in potentiality to that towards which it is moved; whereas a thing moves inasmuch as it is in act. For motion is nothing else than the reduction of something from potentiality to actuality. But nothing can be reduced from potentiality to actuality, except by something in a state of actuality. Thus that which is actually hot, as fire, makes wood, which is potentially hot, to be actually hot, and thereby moves and changes it. Now it is not possible that the same thing should be at once in actuality and potentiality in the same respect, but only in different respects. For what is actually hot cannot simultaneously be potentially hot; but it is simultaneously potentially cold. It is therefore impossible that in the same respect and in the same way a thing should be both mover and moved, i.e., that it should move itself. Therefore, whatever is moved must be moved by another. If that by which it is moved be itself moved, then this also must needs be moved by another, and that by another again. But this cannot go on to

_____

SOURCE: Anton C. Pegis, ed., *Introduction to St. Thomas Aquinas* (1948), pp. 24–27. Reprinted by permission of the A. C. Pegis Estate.

infinity, because then there would be no first mover, and consequently, no other mover, seeing that subsequent movers move only inasmuch as they are moved by the first mover; as the staff moves only because it is moved by the hand. Therefore it is necessary to arrive at a first mover, moved by no other; and this everyone understands to be God.

The second way is from the nature of efficient cause. In the world of sensible things we find there is an order of efficient causes. There is no case known (neither is it, indeed, possible) in which a thing is found to be the efficient cause of itself, for so it would be prior to itself, which is impossible. Now in efficient causes it is not possible to go on to infinity, because in all efficient causes following in order, the first is the cause of the intermediate cause, and the intermediate is the cause of the ultimate cause, whether the intermediate cause be several, or one only. Now to take away the cause is to take away the effect. Therefore, if there be no first cause among efficient causes, there will be no ultimate, nor any intermediate, cause. But if in efficient causes it is possible to go on to infinity, there will be no first efficient cause, neither will there be an ultimate effect, nor any intermediate efficient causes; all of which is plainly false. Therefore it is necessary to admit a first efficient cause, to which everyone gives the name of God.

The third way is taken from possibility and necessity, and runs thus. We find in nature things that are possible to be and not to be, since they are found to be generated, and to be corrupted, and consequently, it is possible for them to be and not to be. But it is impossible for these always to exist, for that which can not-be at some time is not. Therefore, if everything can not-be, then at one time there was nothing in existence. Now if this were true, even now there would be nothing in existence, because that which does not exist begins to exist only through something already existing. Therefore, if at one time nothing was in existence, it would have been impossible for anything to have begun to exist; and thus even now nothing would be in existence—which is absurd. Therefore, not all beings are merely possible, but there must exist something the existence of which is necessary. But every necessary thing either has its necessity caused by another, or not. Now it is impossible to go on to infinity in necessary things which have their necessity caused by another, as has been already proved in regard to efficient causes. Therefore we cannot but admit the existence of some being having of itself its own necessity, and not receiving it from another, but rather causing in others their necessity. This all men speak of as God.

The fourth way is taken from the gradation to be found in things. Among beings there are some more and some less good, true, noble, and the like. But *more* and *less* are predicated of different things according as they resemble in their different ways something which is the maximum, as a thing is said to be hotter according as it more nearly resembles that which is hottest; so that there is something which is truest, something best, something noblest, and, consequently, something which is most being, for those things that are greatest in truth are greatest in being. . . . Now the maximum in any genus is the cause of all in that genus, as fire, which is the maximum of heat, is the cause of all hot things. . . . Therefore there must also be something which is to all beings the cause of their being, goodness, and every other perfection; and this we call God.

The fifth way is taken from the governance of the world. We see that things which lack knowledge, such as natural bodies, act for an end, and this is evident from their acting always, or nearly always, in the same way, so as to obtain the best result. Hence it is plain that they achieve their end, not fortuitously, but designedly. Now whatever lacks knowledge cannot move towards an end, unless it be directed by some being endowed with knowledge and intelligence; as the arrow is directed by the archer. Therefore some intelligent being exists by whom all natural things are directed to their end; and this being we call God.

Reply Objection 1. As Augustine says: Since God is the highest good, He would not allow any evil to exist in His works, unless His omnipotence and goodness were such as to bring good men even out of evil. This is part of the infinite goodness of God, that He should allow evil to exist, and out of it produce good.

Reply Objection 2. Since nature works for a determinate end under the direction of a higher agent, whatever is done by nature must be traced back to God as to its first cause. So likewise whatever is done voluntarily must be traced back to some higher cause other than human reason and will, since these can change and fail; for all things that are changeable and capable of defect must be traced back to an immovable and self-necessary first principle, as has been shown.

SØREN KIERKEGAARD

WHY GOD'S EXISTENCE CANNOT BE PROVEN

But what is this unknown something with which the Reason collides when inspired by its paradoxical passion, with the result of unsettling even man's knowledge of himself? It is the Unknown. It is not a human being, insofar as we know what man is; nor is it any other known thing. So let us call this unknown something: God. It is nothing more than a name we assign to it. The idea of demonstrating that this unknown something (God) exists could scarcely suggest itself to the Reason. For if God does not exist it would of course be im-

SOURCE: Søren Kierkegaard, *Philosophical Fragments*, trans. David Swenson. Copyright © 1985 by Princeton University Press. Reprinted with permission of Princeton University Press.

possible to prove it; and if he does exist it would be folly to attempt it. For at the very outset, in beginning my proof, I will have presupposed it, not as doubtful but as certain (a presupposition is never doubtful, for the very reason that it is a presupposition), since otherwise I would not begin, readily understanding that the whole would be impossible if he did not exist. But if when I speak of proving God's existence I mean that I propose to prove that the Unknown, which exists, is God, then I express myself unfortunately. For in that case I do not prove anything, least of all an existence, but merely develop the content of a conception. Generally speaking, it is a difficult matter to prove that anything exists; and what is still worse for the intrepid souls who undertake the venture, the difficulty is such that fame scarcely awaits those who concern themselves with it. The entire demonstration always turns into something very different from what it assumes to be, and becomes an additional development of the consequences that flow from [our] having assumed that the object in question exists. Thus I always reason from existence, not toward existence, whether I move in the sphere of palpable sensible fact or in the realm of thought. I do not, for example, prove that a stone exists, but that some existing thing is a stone. The procedure in a court of justice does not prove that a criminal exists, but that the accused, whose existence is given, is a criminal. Whether we call existence an *accessorium* or the external *prius*, it is never subject to demonstration . . .

If it were proposed to prove Napoleon's existence from Napoleon's deeds, would it not be a most curious proceeding? His existence does indeed explain his deeds, but the deeds do not prove his existence, unless I have already understood the word "his" so as thereby to have assumed his existence. But Napoleon is only an individual, and insofar there exists no absolute relationship between him and his deeds; some other person might have performed the same deeds. Perhaps this is the reason why I cannot pass from the deeds to existence. If I call these deeds the deeds of Napoleon, the proof becomes superfluous, since I have already named him; if I ignore this, I can never prove from the deeds that they are Napoleon's, but only in a purely ideal manner that such deeds are the deeds of a great general, and so forth. But between God and his works there exists an absolute relationship; God is not a name but a concept. Is this perhaps the reason for his *essentia involvit existentiam* [essence involves existence]? The works of God are such that only God can perform them. Just so, but where then are the works of God? The works from which I would deduce his existence are not immediately given. The wisdom of God in nature, his goodness, his wisdom in the governance of the world—are all these manifest, perhaps, upon the very face of things? Are we not here confronted with the most terrible temptations to doubt, and is it not impossible finally to dispose of all these doubts? But from such an order of things I will surely not attempt to prove God's existence; and even if I began I would never finish, and would in addition have to live constantly in suspense, lest something so terrible should suddenly happen that my bit of proof would be demolished. From what works then do I propose to derive the proof? From the works as apprehended through an ideal interpretation, i.e., such as they do not immediately reveal themselves. But in that case it is not from the works that I prove God's existence. I merely develop the ideality I have presupposed, and because of my confidence in *this* I make so bold as to defy all objections, even those that have not yet been made. In beginning my proof I presuppose the ideal interpretation, and also that I will be successful in carrying it through; but what else is this but to presuppose that God exists, so that I really begin by virtue of confidence in him?

And how does God's existence emerge from the proof? Does it follow straightway, without any breach of continuity? Or have we not here an analogy to the behaviour of these toys, the little Cartesian dolls? As soon as I let go of the doll it stands on its head. As soon as I let it go—I must therefore let it go. So also with the proof for God's existence. As long as I keep my hold on the proof, i.e., continue to demonstrate, the existence does not come out, if for no other reason than that I am engaged in proving it; but when I let the proof go, the existence is there. But this act of letting go is surely also something; it is indeed a contribution of mine. Must not this also be taken into the account, this little moment, brief as it may be—it need not be long, for it is a leap. . . .

Whoever therefore attempts to demonstrate the existence of God (except in the sense of clarifying the concept, and without the *reservatio finalis* noted above, that the existence emerges from the demonstration by a leap) proves in lieu thereof something else, something which at times perhaps does not need a proof, and in any case needs none better; for the fool says in his heart that there is no God, but whoever says in his heart or to men: "Wait just a little and I will prove it"—what a rare man of wisdom is he! If in the moment of beginning his proof it is not absolutely undetermined whether God exists or not, he does not prove it; and if it is thus undetermined in the beginning he will never come to begin, partly from fear of failure, since God perhaps does not exist, and partly because he has nothing with which to begin. A project of this kind would scarcely have been undertaken by the ancients. Socrates at least, who is credited with having put forth the physico-teleological proof for God's existence, did not go about it in any such manner. He always presupposes God's existence, and under this presupposition seeks to interpenetrate nature with the idea of purpose. Had he been asked why he pursued this method, he would doubtless have explained that he lacked the courage to venture out upon so perilous a voyage of discovery without having made sure of God's existence behind him. At the word of God he casts his net as if to catch the idea of purpose; for nature herself finds many means of frightening the inquirer, and distracts him by many a digression. . . .

What then is the Unknown? It is the limit to which the Reason repeatedly comes, and insofar, substituting a static form of conception for the dynamic, it is the different, the absolutely different. But because it is absolutely different, there is no mark by which it could be distinguished. When qualified as absolutely different it seems on the verge of disclosure, but this is not the case; for the Reason cannot even conceive an absolute unlikeness. The Reason cannot negate itself absolutely, but uses itself for the purpose, and thus conceives only such an unlikeness within itself as it can conceive by means of itself; it cannot absolutely transcend itself, and hence conceives only such a superiority over itself as it can conceive by means of itself.

MARTIN BUBER

I AND THOU

To man the world is twofold, in accordance with his twofold attitude.

The attitude of man is twofold, in accordance with the twofold nature of the primary words which he speaks.

The primary words are not isolated words, but combined words.

The one primary word is the combination *I-Thou*.

The other primary word is the combination *I-It;* wherein, without a change in the primary word, one of the words *He* and *She* can replace *It*.

Hence the *I* of man is also twofold.

For the *I* of the primary word *I-Thou* is a different *I* from that of the primary word *I-It*.

Primary words do not signify things, but they intimate relations.

Primary words do not describe something that might exist independently of them, but being spoken they bring about existence.

Primary words are spoken from the being.

If *Thou* is said, the *I* of the combination *I-Thou* is said along with it.

If *It* is said, the *I* of the combination *I-It* is said along with it.

The primary word *I-Thou* can only be spoken with the whole being.

The primary word *I-It* can never be spoken with the whole being.

There is no *I* taken in itself, but only the *I* of the primary word *I-Thou* and the *I* of the primary word *I-It*.

When a man says *I* he refers to one or other of these. The *I* to which he refers is present when he says *I*. Further, when he says *Thou* or *It,* the *I* of one of the two primary words is present.

The existence of *I* and the speaking of *I* are one and the same thing.

When a primary word is spoken the speaker enters the word and takes his stand in it. . . .

SOURCE: Reprinted with the permission of Scribner, a Division of Simon & Schuster, Inc. from *I and Thou* by Martin Buber, tr. by Ronald Gregor Smith. Translation copyright © 1958 by Charles Scribner's Sons.

I consider a tree.

I can look on it as a picture: stiff column in a shock of light, or splash of green shot with the delicate blue and silver of the background.

I can perceive it as movement: flowing veins on clinging, pressing pith, suck of the roots, breathing of the leaves, ceaseless commerce with earth and air—and the obscure growth itself.

I can classify it in a species and study it as a type in its structure and mode of life.

I can subdue its actual presence and form so sternly that I recognize it only as an expression of law—of the laws in accordance with which a constant opposition of forces is continually adjusted, or of those in accordance with which the component substances mingle and separate.

I can dissipate it and perpetuate it in number, in pure numerical relation.

In all this the tree remains my object, occupies space and time, and has its nature and constitution.

It can, however, also come about, if I have both will and grace, that in considering the tree I become bound up in relation to it. The tree is now no longer *It*. I have been seized by the power of exclusiveness.

To effect this it is not necessary for me to give up any of the ways in which I consider the tree. There is nothing from which I would have to turn my eyes away in order to see, and no knowledge that I would have to forget. Rather is everything, picture and movement, species and type, law and number, indivisibly united in this event.

Everything belonging to the tree is in this: its form and structure, its colours and chemical composition, its intercourse with the elements and with the stars, are all present in a single whole.

The tree is no impression, no play of my imagination, no value depending on my mood; but it is bodied over against me and has to do with me, as I with it—only in a different way.

Let no attempt be made to sap the strength from the meaning of the relation: relation is mutual.

The tree will have a consciousness, then, similar to our own? Of that I have no experience. But do you wish, through seeming to succeed in it with yourself, once again to disintegrate that which cannot be disintegrated? I encounter no soul or dryad of the tree, but the tree itself.

If I face a human being as my *Thou*, and say the primary word *I-Thou* to him, he is not a thing among things, and does not consist of things.

Thus human being is not *He* or *She*, bounded from every other *He* and *She*, a specific point in space and time within the net of the world; nor is he a nature able to be experienced and described, a loose bundle of named qualities. But with no neighbour, and whole in himself, he is *Thou* and fills the heavens. This does not mean that nothing exists except himself. But all else lives in *his* light.

Just as the melody is not made up of notes nor the verse of words nor the statue of lines, but they must be tugged and dragged till their unity has been scattered into these many pieces, so with the man to whom I say *Thou*. I can take out from him the colour of his hair, or of his speech, or of his goodness. I must continually do this. But each time I do it he ceases to be *Thou*.

And just as prayer is not in time but time in prayer, sacrifice not in space but space in sacrifice, and to reverse the relation is to abolish the reality, so with the man to whom I say *Thou*. I do not meet with him at some time and place or other. I can set him in a particular time and place; I must continually do it: but I set only a *He* or a *She*, that is an *it*, no longer my *Thou*.

So long as the heaven of *Thou* is spread out over me the weeds of causality cower at my heels, and the whirlpool of fate stays its course.

I do not experience the man to whom I say *Thou*. But I take my stand in relation to him, in the sanctity of the primary word. Only when I step out of it do I experience him once more. In the act of experience *Thou* is far away.

Even if the man to whom I say *Thou* is not aware of it in the midst of his experience, yet relation may exist. For *Thou* is more than *It* realises. No deception penetrates here; here is the cradle of the Real Life. . . .

The *Thou* meets me through grace—it is not found by seeking. But my speaking of the primary word to it is an act of my being, is indeed *the* act of my being.

The *Thou* meets me. But I step into direct relation with it. Hence the relation means being chosen and choosing, suffering and action in one; just as any action of the whole being, which means the suspension of all partial actions and consequently of all sensations of actions grounded only in their particular limitation, is bound to resemble suffering.

The primary word *I-Thou* can be spoken only with the whole being. Concentration and fusion into the whole being can never take place through my agency, nor can it ever take place without me. I become through my relation to the *Thou*; as I become *I*, I say *Thou*.

All real living is meeting. . . .

The extended lines of relations meet in the eternal *Thou*.

Every particular *Thou* is a glimpse through to the eternal *Thou*; by means of every particular *Thou* the primary word addresses the eternal *Thou*. Through this mediation of the *Thou* of all beings fulfilment, and nonfulfillment, of relations comes to them: the inborn *Thou* is realised in each relation and consummated in none. It is consummated only in the direct relation with the *Thou* that by its nature cannot become *It*.

Men have addressed their eternal *Thou* with many names. In singing of Him who was thus named they always had the *Thou* in mind: the first myths were hymns of praise. Then the names took refuge in the language of *It*; men were more and more strongly moved to think of and to address their eternal *Thou* as an *It*. But all God's names are hallowed, for in them He is not merely spoken about, but also spoken to.

Many men wish to reject the word God as a legitimate usage, because it is so misused. It is indeed the most heavily laden of all the words used by men. For that very reason it is the most imperishable and most indispensable. What does all mistaken talk about God's being and works (though there has been, and can be, no other talk about these) matter in comparison with the one truth that all men who have addressed God had God Himself in mind? For he who speaks the word God and really has *Thou* in mind (whatever the illusion by which he is held), addresses the true *Thou* of his life, which cannot be limited by another *Thou,* and to which he stands in a relation that gathers up and includes all others.

But when he, too, who abhors the name, and believes himself to be godless, gives his whole being to addressing the *Thou* of his life, as a *Thou* that cannot be limited by another, he addresses God. . . .

Every real relation with a being or life in this world is exclusive. Its *Thou* is freed, steps forth, is single, and confronts you, it fills the heavens. This does not mean that nothing else exists; but all else lives in *its* light. As long as the presence of the relation continues, this its cosmic range is inviolable. But as soon as a *Thou* becomes *It,* the cosmic range of the relation appears as an offence to the world, its exclusiveness as an exclusion of the universe.

In the relation with God unconditional exclusiveness and unconditional inclusiveness are one. He who enters on the absolute relation is concerned with nothing isolated any more, neither things nor beings, neither earth nor heaven; but everything is gathered up in the relation. For to step into pure relation is not to disregard everything but to see everything in the *Thou,* not to renounce the world but to establish it on its true basis. To look away from the world, or to stare at it, does not help a man to reach God; but he who sees the world in Him stands in His presence. "Here world, there God" is the language of *It;* "God in the world" is another language of *It;* but to eliminate or leave behind nothing at all, to include the whole world in the *Thou,* to give the world its due and its truth, to include nothing beside God but everything in him—this is full and complete relation.

Men do not find God if they stay in the world. They do not find Him if they leave the world. He who goes out with his whole being to meet his *Thou* and carries to it all being that is in the world, finds Him who cannot be sought. . . .

The eternal *Thou* can by its nature not become *It;* for by its nature it cannot be established in measure and bounds, not even in the measure of the immeasurable, or the bounds of boundless being; for by its nature it cannot be understood as a sum of qualities, not even as an infinite sum of qualities raised to a transcendental level; for it can be found neither in nor out of the world; for it cannot he experienced, or thought; for we miss Him, Him who is, if we say "I believe that He is"—"He" is also a metaphor, but "*Thou*" is not. . . .

The description of God as a Person is indispensable for everyone who like myself means by "God" not a principle (although mystics like Eckhart sometimes identify him with "Being") and like myself means by "God" not an idea (although philosophers like Plato at times could hold that he was this): but who rather means by "God," as I do, him who—whatever else he may be—enters into a direct relation with us men in creative, revealing and redeeming acts, and it thus makes it possible for us to enter into a direct relation with him. This ground and meaning of our existence constitutes a mutuality, arising again and again, such as can subsist only between persons. The concept of personal being is indeed completely incapable of declaring what God's essential being is, but it is both permitted and necessary to say that God is *also* a person.

But now the contradiction appears in the appeal to the familiar content of the concept person. This says that it is indeed the property of a person that its independence should consist in itself, but that it is limited in its total being by the plurality of other independent entities; and this can of course not be true of God. This contradiction is countered by the paradoxical description of God as the absolute Person, i.e. the Person who cannot be limited. It is as the absolute Person that God enters into direct relation with us. The contradiction yields to deeper insight.

As a Person God gives personal life, he makes us as persons become capable of meeting with him and with one another. But no limitation can come upon him as the absolute Person, either from us or from our relations with one another; in fact we can dedicate to him not merely our persons but also our relations to one another. The man who turns to him therefore need not turn away from any other *I-Thou* relation; but he properly brings them to him, and lets them be fulfilled "in the face of God."

One must, however, take care not to understand this conversation with God—the conversation of which I have to speak in this book and in almost all the works which followed—as something happening solely alongside or above the everyday. God's speech to men penetrates what happens in the life of each one of us, and all that happens in the world around us, biographical and historical, and makes it for you and me into instruction, message, demand. Happening upon happening, situation upon situation, are enabled and empowered by the personal speech of God to demand of the human person that he take his stand and make his decision. Often enough we think there is nothing to hear, but long before we have ourselves put wax in our ears.

The existence of mutuality between God and man cannot be proved, just as God's existence cannot be proved. Yet he who dares to speak of it, bears witness, and calls to witness him to whom he speaks—whether that witness is now or in the future.

FRIEDRICH NIETZSCHE

HUMAN EXISTENCE WITHOUT GOD

When Zarathustra came into the next town, which lies on the edge of the forest, he found many people gathered together in the market place; for it had been promised that there would be a tightrope walker. And Zarathustra spoke thus to the people:

"*I teach you the overman.* Man is something that shall be overcome. What have you done to overcome him?

"All beings so far have created something beyond themselves; and do you want to be the ebb of this great flood and even go back to the beasts rather than overcome man? What is the ape to man? A laughingstock or a painful embarrassment. And man shall be just that for the overman: a laughingstock or a painful embarrassment. You have made your way from worm to man, and much in you is still worm. Once you were apes, and even now, too, man is more ape than any ape.

"Whoever is the wisest among you is also a mere conflict and cross between plant and ghost. But do I bid you become ghosts or plants?

"Behold, I teach you the overman. The overman is the meaning of the earth. Let your will say: the overman *shall* be the meaning of the earth! I beseech you, my brothers, *remain faithful to the earth,* and do not believe those who speak to you of otherworldly hopes! Poison-mixers are they, whether they know it or not. Despisers of life are they, decaying and poisoned themselves, of whom the earth is weary: so let them go.

"Once the sin against God was the greatest sin; but God died, and these sinners died with him. To sin against the earth is now the most dreadful thing, and to esteem the entrails of the unknowable higher than the meaning of the earth.

"Once the soul looked contemptuously upon the body, and then this contempt was the highest: she wanted the body meager, ghastly, and starved. Thus she hoped to escape it and the earth. Oh, this soul herself was still meager, ghastly, and starved: and cruelty was the lust of this soul. But you, too, my brothers, tell me: what does your body proclaim of your soul? Is not your soul poverty and filth and wretched contentment?

"Verily, a polluted stream is man. One must be a sea to be able to receive a polluted stream without becoming unclean. Behold, I teach you the overman: he is this sea; in him your great contempt can go under.

SOURCE: Excerpted from "Thus Spake Zarathustra" in *The Portable Nietzsche*, ed. and trans. Walter Kaufmann. Translation copyright 1954 by The Viking Press, Inc. Copyright renewed 1982 by Viking Penguin, Inc. Used by permission of Viking Penguin, a division of Penguin Putnam, Inc.

"What is the greatest experience you can have? It is the hour of the great contempt. The hour in which your happiness, too, arouses your disgust, and even your reason and your virtue.

"The hour when you say, 'What matters my happiness? It is poverty and filth and wretched contentment. But my happiness ought to justify existence itself.'

"The hour when you say, 'What matters my reason? Does it crave knowledge as the lion his food? It is poverty and filth and wretched contentment.'

"The hour when you say, 'What matters my virtue? As yet it has not made me rage. How weary I am of my good and my evil! All that is poverty and filth and wretched contentment.'

"The hour when you say, 'What matters my justice? I do not see that I am flames and fuel. But the just are flames and fuel.'

"The hour when you say, 'What matters my pity? Is not pity the cross on which he is nailed who loves man? But my pity is no crucifixion.'

"Have you yet spoken thus? Have you yet cried thus? Oh, that I might have heard you cry thus?

"Not your sin but your thrift cries to heaven; your meanness even in your sin cries to heaven.

"Where is the lightning to lick you with its tongue? Where is the frenzy with which you should be inoculated?

Behold, I teach you the overman: He is this lightning, he is this frenzy. . . . "

Then something happened that made every mouth dumb and every eye rigid. For meanwhile the tightrope walker had begun his performance: he had stepped out of a small door and was walking over the rope, stretched between two towers and suspended over the market place and the people. When he had reached the exact middle of his course the small door opened once more and a fellow in motley clothes, looking like a jester, jumped out and followed the first one with quick steps.

"Forward, lamefoot!" he shouted in an awe-inspiring voice. "Forward, lazybones, smuggler, pale-face, or I shall tickle you with my heel! What are you doing here between towers? The tower is where you belong. You ought to be locked up; you block the way for one better than yourself." And with every word he came closer and closer; but when he was but one step behind, the dreadful thing happened which made every mouth dumb and every eye rigid: he uttered a devilish cry and jumped over the man who stood in his way. This man, however, seeing his rival win, lost his head and the rope, tossed away his pole, and plunged into the depth even faster, a whirlpool of arms and legs. The market place became as the sea when a tempest pierces it: the people rushed apart and over one another, especially at the place where the body must hit the ground.

Zarathustra, however, did not move; and it was right next to him that the body fell, badly maimed and disfigured, but not yet dead. After a while the shattered man recovered consciousness and saw Zarathustra kneeling beside him. "What are you doing here?" he asked at last. "I have long known that the devil would trip me. Now he will drag me to hell. Would you prevent him?"

"By my honor, friend," answered Zarathustra, "all that of which you speak does not exist: there is no devil and no hell. Your soul will be dead even before your body: fear nothing further."

The man looked up suspiciously. "If you speak the truth," he said, "I lose nothing when I lose my life. I am not much more than a beast that has been taught to dance by blows and a few meager morsels."

"By no means," said Zarathustra. "You have made danger your vocation; there is nothing contemptible in that. Now you perish of your vocation; for that I will bury you with my own hands."

When Zarathustra had said this, the dying man answered no more; but he moved his hand as if he sought Zarathustra's hand in thanks.

Meanwhile the evening came, and the market place hid in darkness. Then the people scattered, for even curiosity and terror grow weary. But Zarathustra sat on the ground near the dead man, and he was lost in thought, forgetting the time. At last night came, and a cold wind blew over the lonely one.

Then Zarathustra rose and said to his heart: "Verily, it is a beautiful catch of fish that Zarathustra has brought in today! Not a man has he caught but a corpse. Human existence is uncanny and still without meaning; a jester can become man's fatality. I will teach men the meaning of their existence—the overman, the lightning out of the dark cloud of man. . . ."

JOHN H. HICK

THE PROBLEM OF EVIL: THE FREE-WILL AND SOUL-BUILDING ARGUMENTS

To many, the most powerful positive objection to belief in God is the fact of evil. Probably for most agnostics it is the appalling depth and extent of human suffering, more than anything else, that makes the idea of a loving Creator seem so implausible and disposes them toward one or another of the various naturalistic theories of religion.

As a challenge to theism, the problem of evil has traditionally been posed in the form of a dilemma: if God is perfectly loving, he must wish to abolish evil; and if he is all-powerful, he must be able to abolish evil. But evil exists; therefore God cannot be both omnipotent and perfectly loving.

Certain solutions, which at once suggest themselves, have to be ruled out so far as the Judaic-Christian faith is concerned.

SOURCE: *Philosophy of Religion*, 2nd ed., by John Hick. Copyright © 1965. Reprinted by permission of Prentice-Hall, Inc., Upper Saddle River, NJ.

To say, for example (with contemporary Christian Science), that evil is an illusion of the human mind, is impossible within a religion based upon the stark realism of the Bible. Its pages faithfully reflect the characteristic mixture of good and evil in human experience. They record every kind of sorrow and suffering, every mode of man's inhumanity to man and of his painfully insecure existence in the world. There is no attempt to regard evil as anything but dark, menacingly ugly, heart-rending, and crushing. In the Christian scriptures, the climax of this history of evil is the crucifixion of Jesus, which is presented not only as a case of utterly unjust suffering, but as the violent and murderous rejection of God's Messiah. There can be no doubt, then, that for biblical faith evil is unambiguously evil and stands in direct opposition to God's will.

Again, to solve the problem of evil by means of the theory (sponsored, for example, by the Boston "Personalist" School)[1] of a finite deity who does the best he can with a material, intractable and coeternal with himself, is to have abandoned the basic premise of Hebrew-Christian monotheism; for the theory amounts to rejecting belief in the infinity and sovereignty of God.

Indeed, any theory that would avoid the problem of the origin of evil by depicting it as an ultimate constituent of the universe, co-ordinate with good, has been repudiated in advance by the classic Christian teaching, first developed by Augustine, that evil represents the going wrong of something that in itself is good.[2] Augustine holds firmly to the Hebrew-Christian conviction that the universe is *good*—that is to say, it is the creation of a good God for a good purpose. He completely rejects the ancient prejudice that matter is evil. There are, according to Augustine, higher and lower, greater and lesser goods in immense abundance and variety; but everything that has being is good in its own way and degree, except in so far as it may have become spoiled or corrupted. Evil—whether it be an evil will, an instance of pain, or some disorder or decay in nature—has not been set there by God, but represents the distortion of something that is inherently valuable. Whatever exists is, as such, and in its proper place, good; evil is essentially parasitic upon good, being disorder and perversion in a fundamentally good creation. This understanding of evil as something negative means that it is not willed and created by God; but it does not mean (as some have supposed) that evil is unreal and can be disregarded. On the contrary, the first effect of this doctrine is to accentuate even more the question of the origin of evil.

Theodicy,[3] as many modern Christian thinkers see it, is a modest enterprise, negative rather than positive in its conclusions. It does not claim to explain,

---

[1] Edgar Brightman's *A Philosophy of Religion* (Englewood Cliffs, N.J.: Prentice-Hall, Inc., 1940), chaps. 8–10, is a classic exposition of one form of this view.

[2] See Augustine's *Confessions*, Book VII, Chap. 12; *City of God*, Book XII, Chap. 3; *Enchiridion*, chap. 4.

[3] The word "theodicy," from the Greek *theos* (God) and *dike* (righteous), means the justification of God's goodness in the face of the fact of evil.

nor to explain away, every instance of evil in human experience, but only to point to certain considerations that prevent the fact of evil (largely incomprehensible though it remains) from constituting a final and insuperable bar to rational belief in God.

In indicating these considerations it will be useful to follow the traditional division of the subject. There is the problem of *moral evil* or wickedness: why does an all-good and all-powerful God permit this? And there is the problem of the *nonmoral evil* of suffering or pain, both physical and mental: why has an all-good and all-powerful God created a world in which this occurs?

[THE FREE-WILL ARGUMENT]

Christian thought has always considered moral evil in its relation to human freedom and responsibility. To be a person is to be a finite center of freedom, a (relatively) free and self-directing agent responsible for one's own decisions. This involves being free to act wrongly as well as to act rightly. The idea of a person who can be infallibly guaranteed always to act rightly is self-contradictory. There can be no certainty in advance that a genuinely free moral agent will never choose amiss. Consequently, the possibility of wrongdoing or sin is logically inseparable from the creation of finite persons, and to say that God should not have created beings who might sin amounts to saying that he should not have created people.

This thesis has been challenged in some recent philosophical discussions of the problem of evil, in which it is claimed that no contradiction is involved in saying that God might have made people who would be genuinely free but who could at the same time be guaranteed always to act rightly. A quote from one of these discussions follows:

> If there is no logical impossibility in a man's freely choosing the good on one, or on several occasions, there cannot be a logical impossibility in his freely choosing the good on every occasion. God was not, then, faced with a choice between making innocent automata and making beings who, in acting freely, would sometimes go wrong: there was open to him the obviously better possibility of making beings who would act freely but always go right. Clearly, his failure to avail himself of this possibility is inconsistent with his being both omnipotent and wholly good.[4]

A reply to this argument is indirectly suggested in another recent contribution to the discussion.[5] If by a free action we mean an action that is not ex-

---

[4] J. L. Mackie, "Evil and Omnipotence," *Mind* (April, 1955), p. 209. A similar point is made by Antony Flew in "Divine Omnipotence and Human Freedom," *New Essays in Philosophical Theology*. An important critical comment on these arguments is offered by Ninian Smart in "Omnipotence, Evil, and Supermen," *Philosophy* (April, 1961), with replies by Flew (January, 1962) and Mackie (April, 1962).

[5] Flew, in *New Essays in Philosophical Theology.*

ternally compelled but that flows from the nature of the agent as he reacts to the circumstances in which he finds himself, there is indeed no contradiction between our being free and our actions being "caused" (by our own nature) and therefore being in principle predictable. There is a contradiction, however, in saying that God is the cause of our acting as we do but that we are free be-ings *in relation to God.* There is, in other words, a contradiction in saying that God has made us so that we shall of necessity act in a certain way, and that we are genuinely independent persons in relation to him. If all our thoughts and actions are divinely predestined, however free and morally responsible we may seem to be to ourselves, we cannot be free and morally responsible in the sight of God, but must instead be his helpless puppets. Such "freedom" is like that of a patient acting out a series of posthypnotic suggestions: he appears, even to himself, to be free, but his volitions have actually been predetermined by another will, that of the hypnotist, in relation to whom the patient is not a free agent.

A different objector might raise the question of whether or not we deny God's omnipotence if we admit that he is unable to create persons who are free from the risks inherent in personal freedom. The answer that has always been given is that to create such beings is logically impossible. It is no limitation upon God's power that he cannot accomplish the logically impossible, since there is nothing here to accomplish, but only a meaningless conjunction of words[6]— in this case "person who is not a person." God is able to create beings of any and every conceivable kind; but creatures who lack moral freedom, however superior they might be to human beings in other respects, would not be what we mean by persons. They would constitute a different form of life that God might have brought into existence instead of persons. When we ask why God did not create such beings in place of persons the traditional answer is that only persons could, in any meaningful sense, become "children of God," capable of entering into a personal relationship with their Creator by a free and uncom-pelled response to his love. . . .

The necessary connection between moral freedom and the possibility, now actualized, of sin throws light upon a great deal of the suffering that afflicts mankind. For an enormous amount of human pain arises either from the inhu-manity or the culpable incompetence of mankind. This includes such major scourges as poverty, oppression and persecution, war, and all the injustice, in-dignity, and inequity that occur even in the most advanced societies. These evils are manifestations of human sin. Even disease is fostered to an extent, the limits of which have not yet been determined by psychosomatic medicine, by emo-tional and moral factors seated both in the individual and in his social envi-ronment. To the extent that all of these evils stem from human failures and wrong decisions, their possibility is inherent in the creation of free persons inhabiting a world that presents them with real choices followed by real consequences.

---

[6] As Aquinas said, ". . . nothing that implies a contradiction falls under the scope of God's om-nipotence." *Summa Theologica,* Part I, Question 25, Art. 4.

THE SOUL-BUILDING ARGUMENT

We may now turn more directly to the problem of suffering. Even though the major bulk of actual human pain is traceable to man's misused freedom as a sole or part cause, there remain other sources of pain that are entirely independent of the human will, for example, earthquake, hurricane, storm, flood, drought, and blight. In practice, it is often impossible to trace a boundary between the suffering that results from human wickedness and folly and that which falls upon mankind from without; both kinds of suffering are inextricably mingled together in human experience. For our present purpose, however, it is important to note that the latter category does exist and that it seems to be built into the very structure of our world. In response to it, theodicy, if it is wisely conducted, follows a negative path. It is not possible to show positively that each item of human pain serves a divine purpose of good; but, on the other hand, it does seem possible to show that the divine purpose as it is understood in Judaism and Christianity could not be forwarded in a world that was designed as a permanent hedonistic paradise.[7]

An essential premise of this argument concerns the nature of the divine purpose in creating the world. The sceptic's assumption is that man is to be viewed as a completed creation and that God's purpose in making the world was to provide a suitable dwelling-place for this fully formed creature. Since God is good and loving, the environment that he has created for human life to inhabit will naturally be as pleasant and comfortable as possible. The problem is essentially similar to that of a man who builds a cage for some pet animal. Since our world, in fact, contains sources of hardship, inconvenience and danger of innumerable kinds, the conclusion follows that this world cannot have been created by a perfectly benevolent and all-powerful deity.[8]

Christianity, however, has never supposed that God's purpose in the creation of the world was to construct a paradise whose inhabitants would experience a maximum of pleasure and a minimum of pain. The world is seen, instead, as a place of "soul making" or person making in which free beings, grappling with the tasks and challenges of their existence in a common environment, may become "children of God" and "heirs of eternal life." A way of thinking theologically of God's continuing creative purpose for man was suggested by some of the early Hellenistic Fathers of the Christian Church, especially Irenaeus. Following hints from Saint Paul, Irenaeus taught that man has been made as a person in the image of God but has not yet been brought as a free and responsible agent into the finite likeness of God, which is revealed in Christ.[9] Our world, with all its rough edges, is the sphere in which this second and harder stage of the creative process is taking place.

---

[7] From the Greek *hedone*, pleasure.

[8] This is essentially David Hume's argument in his discussion of the problem of evil in his *Dialogues*, Part XI.

[9] See Irenaeus's *Against Heresies*, Book IV, Chaps. 37 and 38.

This conception of the world (whether or not set in Irenaeus's theological framework) can be supported by the method of negative theodicy. Suppose, contrary to fact, that this world were a paradise from which all possibility of pain and suffering were excluded. The consequences would be very far-reaching. For example, no one could ever injure anyone else: the murderer's knife would turn to paper or his bullets to thin air; the bank safe, robbed of a million dollars, would miraculously become filled with another million dollars (without this device, on however large a scale, proving inflationary); fraud, deceit, conspiracy, and treason would somehow always leave the fabric of society undamaged. Again, no one would ever be injured by accident: the mountain climber, steeplejack, or playing child falling from a height would float unharmed to the ground; the reckless driver would never meet with disaster. There would be no need to work, since no harm could result from avoiding work; there would be no call to be concerned for others in time of need or danger, for in such a world there could be no real needs or dangers.

To make possible this continual series of individual adjustments, nature would have to work by "special providences" instead of running according to general laws that men must learn to respect on penalty of pain or death. The laws of nature would have to be extremely flexible: sometimes gravity would operate, sometimes not; sometimes an object would be hard and solid, sometimes soft. There could be no sciences, for there would be no enduring world structure to investigate. In eliminating the problems and hardships of an objective environment, with its own laws, life would become like a dream in which, delightfully but aimlessly, we would float and drift at ease.[10]

One can at least begin to imagine such a world. It is evident that our present ethical concepts would have no meaning in it. If, for example, the notion of harming someone is an essential element in the concept of a wrong action, in our hedonistic paradise there could be no wrong actions—nor any right actions in distinction from wrong. Courage and fortitude would have no point in an environment in which there is, by definition, no danger or difficulty. Generosity, kindness, the *agape* aspect of love, prudence, unselfishness, and all other ethical notions which presuppose life in an objective environment could not even be formed. Consequently, such a world, however well it might promote pleasure, would be very ill adapted for the development of the moral qualities of human personality. In relation to this purpose it might be the worst of all possible worlds!

It would seem, then, that an environment intended to make possible the growth in free beings of the finest characteristics of personal life must have a good deal in common with our present world. It must operate according to general and dependable laws; and it must involve real dangers, difficulties, problems, obstacles, and possibilities of pain, failure, sorrow, frustration, and defeat. If it did not contain the particular trials and perils that—subtracting man's own

---

[10] Tennyson's poem, *The Lotus-Eaters*, well expresses the desire (analyzed by Freud as a wish to return to the peace of the womb) for such "dreamful ease."

very considerable contribution—our world contains, it would have to contain others instead.

To realize this is not, by any means, to be in possession of a detailed theodicy. It is to understand that this world, with all its "heartaches and the thousand natural shocks that flesh is heir to," an environment so manifestly not designed for the maximization of human pleasure and the minimization of human pain, may nevertheless be rather well adapted to the quite different purpose of "soul making." . . . [11]

---

[11] This brief discussion has been confined to the problem of human suffering. The large and intractable problem of animal pain is not taken up here. For a discussion of it see, for example, Austin Farrer, *Love Almighty and Ills Unlimited* (Garden City, N.Y.: Doubleday & Company, Inc., 1961), chap. 5, and John Hick, *Evil and the God of Love* (London: Collins, The Fontana Library, 1968), pp. 345–53.

NEIL GILLMAN

EVIL AND THE LIMITS OF GOD: JEWISH PERSPECTIVES

THE MANY FACES OF EVIL

The most persistent challenge to faith in God comes from the cluster of issues that we call "the problem of evil." In its starkest form, the challenge is this: If God exists, if His will is sovereign, and if He is just and compassionate, why are pain, suffering, and evil so intractable a dimension of human living?

But we have to go beyond this formulation. First, we have to distinguish between the suffering caused by one human being to another (homicide, slander, theft), and suffering that his a natural cause, such as disease or an earthquake. The first type directs our attention to human nature. We want to know why people are capable of inflicting pain on other human beings, sometimes inadvertently, but often deliberately and consciously. We usually account for this by positing human freedom and making the case that, on the whole, the benefits of freedom outweigh its negatives. But when we confront as massive a trauma as the Holocaust, we are struck by the inadequacy of that explanation. It doesn't begin to explain the suffering.

The second kind of suffering directs our attention to the nature of things in the world at large. We want to know, for example, why, nature itself is so constructed that it can produce the AIDS virus—not how, but why? Why does a seven-year-old child suddenly develop cancer of the brain? Why are some babies born with congenital heart defects? Why are people killed in hurricanes, tidal waves, and tornadoes?

SOURCE: From *Sacred Fragments*. Copyright 1990 by The Jewish Publication Society. Used by permission.

Both kinds of suffering raise the existential question: "Why me?" Sometimes the answer is clear: I neglect my health so I get sick. My life situation is so stressful that I will abuse my children. But then a psychotic goes berserk and empties his rifle randomly into a crowd of people. Or a beam detaches itself from a building under construction, falls to the street, and kills a passerby. Or an airplane crash kills a group of people who happen to have chosen this particular flight. The sheer randomness of the event poses the existential question in its sharpest form.

Overarching all of these formulations is the frequent gap between the virtue of the sufferer and his pain. The traditional Jewish formulation of the problem is: "Why do the righteous suffer? Why do the evil prosper?" For the believer, the issue is God's alleged justice. Thus the name "theodicy" (Greek: *theos,* God; *dike* order, right, just) for that area of theology that attempts to "justify" or vindicate God, to maintain His justice in the face of random, apparently unjustified suffering. No other theological problem has proven to be so intractable. There simply are no totally adequate explanations for the death of an innocent child from leukemia, or the lightning bolt that kills an innocent young man. . . .

EVIL AND THE POWER OF GOD

The focus of all theological speculation about the place of evil in the world is its relationship to God. The dilemma is clear: If God is omnipotent, then He is in some way responsible for evil. If He is not responsible, then He is not omnipotent; then evil exists independently of God's will and God's sovereignty is severely impaired. The choice lies between an omnipotent God who is responsible for evil and a limited God who is not.

If these are the two options, then normative Jewish theology really had no choice. Monotheism was so deeply ingrained in Judaism and dualism so deeply abhorred that there was no way evil could be allowed an independent reality of its own. Isaiah 45:6–7 puts it unambiguously: "I am the Lord and there is none else, I form light and create darkness, I make weal (Hebrew: *shalom*) and create woe (Hebrew: *ra*)—I the Lord do all these things." But there is no discounting the palpable discomfort that accompanies this unambiguous attribution of evil to God. In fact, note that when this verse was inserted into the daily morning liturgy, the last phrase was softened to read "I make weal and create all things," instead of "and create woe." Of course, "all things" includes "woe," but who thinks of that meaning when we recite the daily liturgy?

Once we establish God's ultimate responsibility for evil, the problem then becomes reconciling evil with His justice and His benevolence, in short, with the personal character of the monotheistic God. That is the substance of all theodicies. The biblical doctrine of retribution is one way of accomplishing this reconciliation. The rabbinic doctrine of individual eschatology [eternal salvation for the righteous] is another. Still a third is a view of human freedom as evidence of God's self-willed limitation of His power. This last doctrine sees human beings as the proximate cause of much of the evil in the world but God as the ultimate cause, for it is He who created us free. That's why the efficacy of repentance as preempting punishment becomes so fundamental to Judaism. Because God created the possibility for humanly caused evil, He had to provide us with the means to escape its consequences. . . .

If the options are an omnipotent God who is responsible for evil or a limited God who is not, it wasn't until our own century that a Jewish thinker opted for the second of these choices. To be precise, the notion that God may, in His own freedom, *choose* to limit Himself and His power, is as old as the Bible; it is at the heart of Moses' claim that God must not destroy the Israelites after the golden calf episode (Exodus 32:11–14). He clearly has the power to do so and He may even be justified in doing so, but first, what will the Egyptians say? And second, what about His promise to the community's forebears that their progeny would be "as numerous as the stars of the sky"? Moses argues, here, that God should not exercise His power in this instance because of a commitment that He Himself freely entered into.

That God may *will* to limit His power, then, is familiar. But that He may be *intrinsically* limited is a startling contribution of a modern Jewish theologian. Not surprisingly, that thinker was Mordecai Kaplan. Recall Kaplan's definition of God as the power (within nature) that makes for salvation, where salvation means the actualization of all values. The actualization of all values means the elimination of all evil. The Kaplanian God, then, is the very drive, inherent throughout the natural order, to rid the world of evil. But that drive has not as yet won out; evil is still very much part of the natural fabric. Hence Kaplan's God as innately limited—not a self-willed limitation but an inherent one. Evil has not as yet been eliminated simply because God is incapable of eliminating it.

The purely theological dimension of Kaplan's work lies in his radical redefinition of how we conceive of God. The traditional approach begins with the fact of a personal God and then considers what kind of a Being He is and how He functions in nature and history. Kaplan proposes that we stand this approach on its head. Instead of beginning with a personal Being, we should begin with those of our experiences that reveal our set of values, then use these experiences to define God.

The tradition begins by postulating a being—God—who is good, compassionate, just, and the rest. Kaplan begins by seeing goodness, compassion, and justice in the world and then identifying these as "godly," in fact, as God Himself. We define God by His activity. God is what He does. To the extent that our experience of the world reveals goodness, compassion, morality, creativity, and the rest, the world reveals God—not a personal Being but a quality or dimension of the natural order.

A particularly poignant elaboration of Kaplan's position—and the problems it raises—lies in his response to a reader's question: "How would you answer the question of a child who I asked: 'Why did God make polio?'" Kaplan answers: "God did not make polio. God is always helping us humans to make this a better world, but the world can not at once become the kind of world He would like it to be." He continues by enumerating what God is doing: He gives us the intelligence to understand, prevent, and cure disease; He enables us to develop the technology to make polio more bearable; He gives us friends and families who care for us when we are ill. All of these are manifestations of God at work in the world. He is the sum total of all the good things we discover in our lives.

But the stubborn reality is that however much all of these manifestations of goodness are true and real, so is the child's polio. Both the good and the disease are part of the natural order. We wonder why Kaplan focuses on and unifies the ensemble of goodness in nature and calls them God, but refuses to unify the ensemble of evil qualities in nature and call these Evil. The dualistic implications of Kaplan's position are clear: If God is one of many processes in nature, there can be others, and these others can also be unified. Potentially then, we can have two Gods—a good God and an evil one—or even more.

Kaplan himself stubbornly refuses to go that route. But once we begin by defining God through our human experience of goodness, and once we admit that this human experience is ambiguous—that we experience evil as much as goodness—the dualistic conclusion seems entirely legitimate. That's why traditional Jewish thinking preferred to postulate God's omnipotence and deal with the problems that position raises, rather than accept a Kaplanian, inherently limited God and its implications.

A more recent formulation of Kaplan's position is spelled out in Harold Kushner's *When Bad Things Happen to Good People*. Kushner's book, written out of the deeply felt personal trauma of the death of his son at age 14 of progeria, is not primarily a theological treatise, even though he addresses the theological problems raised by his experience. Kushner writes to counter our intuitive—and the traditional—inclination to see God as responsible for human suffering. He sees the random instances that we encounter daily as manifestations of a leftover chaos that God's creative impulse is not able to control, what Milton Steinberg called "the still unremoved scaffolding of the edifice of God's creativity." Again, a limited God. God, does much for us; He has created a world where the good outweighs the evil. But He does not, He can not, eliminate evil from the world.

If there is a difference between Kaplan and Kushner, it reflects the fact that Kaplan wrote in the first part of our century and Kushner, some decades later. There is a pervasive optimism in Kaplan that is absent in Kushner. Kaplan seems to believe that evil is progressively being eliminated, that the drive for salvation is gaining ground. Kushner seems resigned to the inevitability of evil and suffering as an inherent part of nature.

But if Kushner's theology recalls Kaplan, the impulse behind his book brings to mind Job. Here again, a personal experience is pitted against a long-standing theological tradition, and here again, the tradition is asked to yield. It is simply inconceivable to Kushner that God could in any way be responsible for his son's illness. The more traditionalist of Jewish theologians may be offended by Kushner's radical redefinition of the Jewish God, but the immense popularity of the book testifies to the readiness of many believing Jews to accept his redefinition.

GOD AND AUSCHWITZ

With the Holocaust, the problem of evil acquires a new and terrifying urgency. Jewish theological responses to the Holocaust can be grouped into two broad classes.

The first sees the Holocaust as one more instance of human cruelty, perhaps more massive than ever but not intrinsically different and hence not posing significantly new theological or religious challenges. The death of six million Jews and countless other human beings is not necessarily more problematic than the death of one innocent child. The Jewish theological tradition, in this view, has developed resources to deal with the problem and these resources are applied to the Holocaust.

The other view sees the Holocaust as totally unprecedented. The sheer scope of the massacre, the malevolence with which it was perpetrated, the machinelike efficiency of the Nazi death camps, the active involvement and passive acquiescence of countless, ordinary human beings, the fact that the world of Auschwitz was conceived and carried out by the most cultured of European nations—any or all of these factors make the Holocaust totally unique. In this view, the resources that the tradition has evolved for dealing with suffering are simply inadequate. We can not write this trauma off as one more instance of human cruelty. The vexing theological question "Where was God?" will not go away by simply postulating human freedom. In fact, it is made all the more poignant by Judaism's cardinal claim that God and Israel share a unique intimacy. Indeed, then, where was He? Why did He let it happen?

One response that is almost universally rejected by all thinking segments of the community is that the Holocaust is God's punishment for Israel's sin. If the Holocaust accomplished anything, it effectively killed the doctrine of retribution as the key to Jewish theodicies. It may have worked for centuries, but today it is viewed as an obscenity. It has not been invoked by any but the most traditionalist wings of the Jewish community, by those who maintain the sanctity of the past, come what may. To everyone else, the sheer disparity between the "explanation" and the event is so wide that it just does not merit serious consideration. This is our paradigmatic instance of the death of a portion of the Jewish myth. It must be replaced—but by what?

RUBENSTEIN'S "DEATH OF GOD" THEOLOGY

The most radical answer to that question is Richard Rubenstein's striking claim that after the Holocaust "we live in the time of the death of God." Rubenstein's assumption is that the Holocaust represents a radically new phenomenon that demands an equally radical response. His use of the "death of God" imagery is but one of many radical positions that this imaginative theologian has proposed. It is typical of his readiness to stretch or even ignore the commonly accepted parameters of Jewish theological inquiry, even to the point of offending most of his contemporaries. But his thinking can not be ignored.

The "death of God" movement developed in the 1960s as a Christian theological response to that era's sense of social and religious alienation. It drew heavily on the thought of Friedrich Nietzsche and Jean-Paul Sartre and the theological idiom of Paul Tillich, in claiming that the traditional God of the Judaeo-Christian tradition had become irrelevant to the culture and social issues of the day. More specifically, it emerged as a response to the stubborn and persistent presence of evil in society and to God's seeming indifference to that evil.

The very phrase "the death of God" carries a powerful Christian resonance. The Christian God had to die in order to accomplish His preordained mission. His death symbolizes God's paradoxical identification with humanity and becomes the instrument for the vicarious remission of human sins. It is also but an interim step toward His ultimate resurrection. Rubenstein adopts this image, minus its specifically Christian connotations, because of his conviction that it is the only way Jews can deal with the issue of God in the era of the death camps.

Rubenstein is forthright in admitting that no human being can say that God "really" died. What *has* died is our conception of God, our theological and religious symbols and myths. The statement "God has died" is a statement about human beings; it is a cultural fact. It says that the way we have conceived of God and His relation to humanity and particularly to Israel no longer works. It has been decisively killed by our historical experience. "[T]he thread uniting God and man, heaven and earth, has been broken. We stand in a cold, silent, unfeeling cosmos, unaided by any purposeful power beyond our own resources. After Auschwitz, what else can a Jew say about God?"

Note the distinction between claiming that God has died and claiming that our myth has died. The first is considerably starker than the second. But, ultimately, if all we have is our myths about God—if no human being has access to what God is in Himself—then the two claims are functionally equivalent and equally final. After Auschwitz, we can no longer speak of a caring, compassionate, personal God. Radical events require a radical *midrash,* a radically new myth.

Paradoxically, Rubenstein proceeds to argue that in an age of the death of God, we need religion—its communities, traditions, rituals, norms, and institutional structures—more than ever. They provide us with the shared context that enables us to deal with the crises that are inherent in human existence.

As for God, the death of the traditional God of Judaism does not mean the death of all of our concepts of God. In its place, Rubenstein suggests we return to the God of the mystics, God as Holy Nothingness, the totally indeterminate and indeterminable God who is the source of all creation and to which all of creation returns. Rubenstein is aware of the heretical implications of this new image. Since the all-powerful, free, and personal God of traditional monotheism has failed us, we fall back on the God who is the embodiment of the implacable rhythms of nature. Rubenstein finds there the renewed sense of security and serenity that comes from knowing our place in the cosmic order of things—and that the traditional image of God is no longer able to provide. In fact, Rubenstein reverts to an image of God that is very close to that of the pagan religions in which everything in the world is ultimately subject to blind, implacable natural forces. Our salvation lies in resigning ourselves to their sway over our destiny as well. . . .

Rubenstein's God, like Kaplan's, is then very much within nature. Yet the two thinkers are far apart. Kaplan's God is the embodiment of a system of values that is closely tied to the liberal-progressive context of early-twentieth-century America. Rubenstein's God is much more the embodiment of the cycles of nature and hence totally neutral in regard to value. From Rubenstein's perspective, Kaplan's theology can't even begin to deal with the Holocaust. If nature does indeed manifest a quasi-biological drive toward salvation, how can we account for the kind of stubborn, radical impulse to evil that emerged during that period? It is simply not adequate to posit the fact of human freedom and our innate human reluctance to ally ourselves with the salvational impulse. But what else can Kaplan say, given his theological assumptions! Kaplan never wrote a systematic response to the Holocaust, we may surmise, not only because his creative period was well behind him by the time Jews became aware of the issues. . . .

It is significant . . . that Rubenstein's proposals have failed to strike deep roots even among the less traditional of contemporary Jewish thinkers. The issue is less the fact of his break with tradition—we have seen equally radical departures in the writings of many of his predecessors—than the point on which he breaks and the problematic nature of his alternative. To do away with the notion of a God who cares deeply for the fate of Israel is to reject the cornerstone of the Jewish myth; without this, the entire myth collapses. Further, however much Rubenstein stresses the need for religion in an age of the death of God, one can only wonder how that religious tradition can have any authority whatsoever. Finally, did Judaism successfully resist the inroads of paganism for four millennia only to return, at this stage, to a prebiblical, pagan way of viewing our place in nature?

BUBER'S "ECLIPSE OF GOD"

The alternative path is to return to the tradition and rework its own internal resources for dealing with human suffering on the assumption that, however massive this particular trauma, the tradition has had a long history in dealing with this type of experience.

Paradoxically, the most influential representative of this approach is Martin Buber—hardly the most traditionalist of contemporary Jewish thinkers. Buber's answer to the question "Where was God?" is to speak of an "eclipse of God," an image that evokes the familiar biblical "hiding of His face."

In the Bible itself, God's hiding of His face is most frequently a form of retribution—but not always. Sometimes—Psalm 13 is an excellent example—it represents a mysterious ebb in the divine-human relationship that the human being simply can not fathom but experiences as palpably real and terrifying. For Buber, the "eclipse" represents an inherent stage in the dynamic of the

I-Thou/I-It relationships. All relationships know both their moments of intimacy as well as their moments of withdrawal. I-Thou becomes I-It, which eventually can become I-Thou again. Only the partners in the relationship can testify to the presence or the absence of their partner, and only in the moment of each experience.

The term "eclipse," when applied to God, is as much a symbol as the term "death." The difference is that an eclipse is temporary but death is final. Rubenstein explicitly rejects Buber's image because it is too soft; for him, it does not capture the impact of the Holocaust. But for Buber, it does.

To use another idiom, if a *midrash* exists in a state of tension between past and present, between the claims of authenticity and of contemporaneity, Rubenstein is prepared to strain the pole of authenticity to capture what he feels is a radically unprecedented event. Buber takes the opposite path and works to integrate the event into the categories of classical Jewish theology. The decision between these two *midrashim* can not depend on any external criterion; each of us has to decide which of the two images speaks to us, moves us, captures our own sense of the meaning of the experience, and provides us with a renewed sense of purpose.

But we should not underestimate the terror that is inherent in the sense of God's eclipse. In Buber's existential framework, the leap of faith is filled with risk for it has no basis in reason or experience. Buber's disciple, Emil Fackenheim, poses the particularly devastating nature of our contemporary awareness of God's absence: IS it indeed temporary, or is it "the final exposure of an age-old delusion?" The believer can never know for sure, but in the meantime, must continue to trust. This is the subjective quality of existentialist faith. . . .

The Buberian response is also reflected in the thinking of a contemporary theologian, Irving Greenberg. Greenberg seizes on the dialectical tension between the Buberian I-Thou and I-It, on the alternating moments of presence and absence, affirmation and denial, faith and nonfaith. Both moments are an inherent part of the process; the error is to fix on either one of the polarities as exclusive and final. Neither classical theism nor atheism can do justice to the complex nature of our relationship with God. The tension itself, the very tenuous and indeterminate nature of religious faith, its fragmented quality is simply inevitable. God is a "moment God"; faith is a "moment faith."

The full implication of this position is that atheism is an integral part of the experience of faith. There is no faith without moments of despair, just as there is no despair without moments of affirmation. It is not at all clear who is the believer and who the atheist. They differ only in the frequency of their moments of despair or affirmation, not at all in the certainty or demonstrability of their positions. Applying this perspective to the Holocaust, Greenberg suggests that it reveals, with particular urgency, the full weight of the tension inherent in the life of religious faith.

Still a third discussion of these issues from a Buberian perspective is in Eliezer Berkovits' *Faith After the Holocaust*. To Berkovits too, Auschwitz does not stand alone. Jewish history is littered with Holocausts just as it is studded with expressions of God's love for Israel. Both are true, both part of the complex pattern of Jewish history. Berkovits takes the daring step of balancing Auschwitz with the reestablishment of the State of Israel. Both have to be integrated simultaneously into the larger pattern of Jewish history. To isolate either one is to misread that pattern.

In fact, Berkovits sees God's presence even in the throes of the Holocaust. He refers to the countless instances of courage, determination, and humanity that occurred even in the death camps. He reminds us that in fact, the Jewish people did survive the Holocaust, despite its powerlessness. The Holocaust, then, reveals both aspects of God's relationship to Israel—His presence as well as His absence.

On the issue of theodicy, Berkovits reaffirms the biblical notion of a God who withdraws from history so that human beings may exercise their freedom. God's tolerance of human cruelty becomes, paradoxically, an affirmation of His respect for humanity. This may lead to human suffering, but there is no escaping that outcome. If God exalts human freedom, He must tolerate evil, and if He tolerates evil, people will suffer. Yet God waits, even for the sinner and even despite the suffering of the victims. That's what makes Him God.

FOR FURTHER STUDY

Begin with Clifford Geertz' "Religion as a Cultural System" in his *The Interpretation of Cultures* (pb Basic Books, 1973). This seminal article in the anthropology of religion provides an indispensable background to understanding the impact of the problem of evil on religion. . . .

On the eschatological resolution of the problem of evil, Mordecai Kaplan's approach to the problem, pp. 115–120 of his *Questions Jews Ask: Reconstructionist Answers* (see ch. 4). Kaplan's response to the child who is suffering from polio is on pp. 117–120 of this volume. Harold Kushner's *When Bad Things Happen to Good People* (Schocken, 1981; pb Avon, 1983) is a restatement of an essentially Kaplanian position with emphasis on its pastoral implications. Harold M. Schulweis' *Evil and the Morality of God* (Hebrew Union College Press, 1984) deals with the more technical, theological assumptions of that approach.

On Holocaust theology, Richard Rubenstein's "death of God" theology is expressed concisely in his contribution to *The Condition of Jewish Belief* (see ch. 7), and more extensively in a number of papers collected in *After Auschwitz: Radical Theology and Contemporary Judaism* (pb Bobbs-Merrill, 1966). On the metaphor of God's "eclipse," see Emil Fackenheim's "On the Eclipse of God" in his *Quest for Past and Future* and the material on the Holocaust collected in *The Jewish Thought of Emil Fackenheim* (See ch. 7). Eliezer Berkovits' *Faith After the Holocaust* (pb Ktav, 1973) has been widely read, and Irving Greenberg's "Cloud of Smoke, Pillar of Fire: Judaism, Christianity, and Modernity after the Holocaust" in *Auschwitz: Beginning of a New Era?* edited by Eva Fleischner (pb Ktav, 1977) is a significant restatement of the Buberian position. Elie Wiesel, of course, has struggled with the implications of this event for Judaism. To this reader, his novel *Night* (pb Bantam,

1983) remains his starkest and most powerful statement. Relatively unknown and now out of print but incredibly suggestive is another novel, *The Third Pillar*, by Soma Morgenstern (Farrar, Straus and Cudahy, 1955), which uses themes from Jewish mysticism to deal with the impact of the Holocaust. Heschel's "The Meaning of This Hour" is included in his *Man's Quest for God* (Scribner's 1954; pb title, *Quest for God*, Crossroad, 1982).

Finally, Steven T. Katz' *Post-Holocaust Dialogues* (New York University Press, 1983; pb 1985) is a critical study of all of these responses.

PRACTICE

FR. ROBERT R. GERL

THE PHILOSOPHER AS PRIEST: APPLYING PROOFS OF GOD'S EXISTENCE TO THE CASE OF A DYING CANCER PATIENT

THE CASE

I have found from my experience in working in a parish that when people face a critical moment in life, they evaluate their lives and often discuss their values and philosophy of life.

I have often visited the local hospital to see parishioners who were confined. One time there was a sixty-one-year-old woman I visited who had just learned that she had cancer. She was active in the parish, and was a wife, mother, and grandmother. She attended Mass every day and was a Catholic all her life.

After the first visit in the hospital, I continued to minister to her over several months at home. She was terminal and often reviewed her life. We often spoke candidly. In the many conversations we shared, she told me how she came to believe in God. She spoke of her mother and father and the loving home she came from.

Belief in God was something that was passed on to her from her parents. She once said, "I never had reason not to trust my parents so I guess I never mistrusted what they taught me and told me about God. I wonder now as I face this final difficulty if I made a mistake in believing in God!" This woman was certainly calling her own meaning of her life into question as she faced the finiteness of life.

In the time we spent together, she spoke of how she marveled at the world and the many mysteries she experienced at the time she was growing up on the farm. The miracle of seeing a calf born, of watching the corn grow, of making

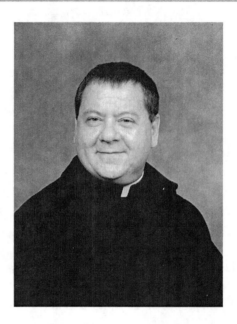

Fr. Robert R. Gerl has been a faculty member and Dean of Education and Human Services at Nazareth College in Kalamazoo (1986–1991) and afterwards served as Academic Vice President and Chief Operating officer of St. Catharine College in Springfield, Kentucky. Currently, he is in the Campus Ministry at St. Thomas More Student parish as well as at Western Michigan University, Kalamazoo Valley Community College, and Kalamazoo College, and teaches humanities, philosophy, and psychology, part time, at several institutions of higher education. The recipient of a post-doctoral award at University of Louisville in Curriculum Development (1994), Fr. Gerl holds several graduate degrees, including an MA in clinical/school psychology (Radford University, 1974), an MTS in pastoral studies and behavioral science (St. Francis Seminary, 1977), a D.Min. in pastoral counseling/theology (St. Mary's Seminary and University, 1986), and is currently completing a Ph.D. in Adult and Continuing Education at Michigan State University. Holder of Michigan state licenses in counseling, social work, marriage and family therapy, and addictions therapy, he is also presently Director of the BRIDGES program of Catholic Family Services in Kalamazoo, where he supervises clinical work in individual, couples, marriage, and group counseling.

milk ready for the dairy, and others; and on and on she marveled at the work of creation around her. "Somehow, as I was so deeply involved in this life on the farm and all of creation, I knew in my heart that there was an all-powerful God. I also used to watch my father. He was able to lift heavy bails of hay, fix tractors, and do jobs that seemed so impossible. My father seemed so all-knowing and all-powerful. I now look back and realize that when I was learning about God, I often was able to understand such abstract ideas as God was everywhere, God was all-knowing, God was love, God was almighty because God was presented as "Father," and these same things I believed about my own father. He was all-powerful, he could do anything, he was loving."

It would appear that what was experienced at first by the sixty-one-year-old woman facing death was that she realized that through her experience of nature she was able to come to an internalized acceptance of a God who does exist. It was from her life on the farm and her experience of her father that she was able to accept all that she was taught formally about God.

It was later when I returned to talk more with this woman that she began to tell me that, as she faced life's difficulties as she continued in life, she sometimes wondered about God. Did he abandon her? Was there really a God? "How come these things happened to me when I have accepted this all-powerful being and now I feel so powerless? Sometimes as I examine all that I have gone through in life, birth, death of family members, bankruptcy of our business, my husband's illness, my daughter's divorce, my mind cannot reconcile my belief in God. I have never really understood what was going on in my life. I knew I still believed in God but things were not the same and somehow what seemed so sure from my childhood and experience of nature on the farm seemed so distanced and unconnected to my experience now." I assured her that she never truly lost faith and that this is something that most people experience as a stage of their growing in faith in life.

I continued to visit this woman at home as she got closer to her final days. In the continued conversations she began to take another look at her life. She said, "Isn't it amazing that as I face this final turn in my life I have come to a deeper appreciation of God's love for me!" I asked, "What has led you onto this train of thinking now?" She proceeded to relate how everyone has been so good to her now in her illness that she has certainly come to see what the Gospels of Christianity have tried to tell her throughout life regarding serving God through our relationships with our brothers and sisters in this world. "I have noted that there is a certain quality of concern and love shown to me by my family that I didn't feel very often in life. I often felt taken for granted and used by family as they needed certain things. But now there seems to be a genuine concern for me and my needs, and in this care they have certainly made me realize again that I am loved. In this way I guess I feel loved and cared for by God too." Somehow these different ways of relating and experiencing God in her life seemed to confuse her. "I don't know why I feel different about God now and at different times in my life. Maybe I have just tried to understand something I cannot understand."

One of the final discussions I had with this woman was about the meaning of life. She indicated that "if I did not have my faith and my knowledge of God, then I would see this moment as a complete end. I would certainly feel that all I lived for was for nothing." For those who embrace the theistic philosophy, it certainly is meant to provide some sense of meaning to life and some sense of hope for the future. To the theistic thinker, this life and its finiteness never seem to give a sense of fulfillment. That certainly seemed to be the point of this dying woman when she felt her life would have been for nothing or without meaning if there was no supreme being.

AN ANALYSIS OF THE CASE: APPLYING THEOLOGICAL PERSPECTIVES

Consider St. Anselm's ontological proof of God's existence, which asserts that one can conceive of a Being which nothing greater can be conceived of. It also allows that if the word is conceived, the object is conceived as well. Anselm would state that at this level God could be conceived not to exist, but there is another aspect to Anselm's thought that has to do with understanding. He asserts that when the word and object are conceived and understood, then one cannot conceive that the object does not exist.

In the case presented, the sixty-one-year-old woman had a life that led her to believe that God existed as the Being beyond which nothing greater could be conceived. She came to this understanding through the examination of the earth and all creation which the life on the farm provided for her. This occurred at a very young age when she was in her formative years. Adding to this experience the woman had this understanding passed on and supported by her significant others such as parents and teachers.

These situations provided her with the ability not only to conceive of the word and the concept, as Anselm states, but these living situations also helped provide understanding of the concept, word, and entity. Once this has been established, it is hard or impossible to posit nonexistence for the theistic thinker. Even though this woman faced many traumas, crises, life events, and even doubt of God's existence, according to Anselm's ontological proof she could not have arrived at denying God's existence because she had this understanding of the entity of God.

Against this ontological perspective, Friedrich Nietzsche calls for a conceptualization of meaning tied to the earth and the nonexistence of God. Nietzsche calls us to a sense that human beings cannot transcend this earthbound reality. The conclusion that would be contrary to Anselm is that a human being cannot give meaning to the existence of God and therefore can conceive that God does not exist. This is a new way to conceptualize moral and religious values. It is a way of conceptualizing foreign to theistic thought.

The woman's experience would not allow her to abandon her meaning in a Greater Being. In her case it seemed impossible to reject the existence of God, thus verifying the truth of Anselm's position that once meaning has been ascribed to the concept, or entity, it cannot be denied to exist. This is seen in the fact that the woman does not give up her belief in God.

St. Thomas goes about trying to prove the existence of God. He outlines five cosmological proofs. The method he uses to arrive at the conclusion that God exists is through an examination of nature. It is through principles observed to be in operation in nature that St. Thomas infers logically the existence of God. The basic point of St. Thomas is that "Grace builds on nature."

St. Thomas' first proof is that God is the Prime Mover. His conclusion is that for something to move in a direction it must be put in motion by a mover. He bases this notion on what he observes in the world of nature or created things. For instance, if there was an accident that involved a five-car pile up, the first car in the back that hit the car in front of it and so on could lead a person to the conclusion that the person who made the first collision was the prime mover setting the other cars in motion. From examining such real events, Thomas deduced that God was, as creator, the Prime Mover for the world set in motion.

Motion, growth, development are sure signs of life. What started this? Obviously, the First Mover, God! In the case of the woman, all the life events certainly are the result of the Prime Mover who has set her life in motion. She believes that her life is directed by God. Since this woman believes that God exists, there is an implicit understanding that God is directing the movement of her life.

St. Thomas states that the efficient cause is another proof of God's existence. The woman understands the reality of efficient causation from her experience and life on the farm. It can be posited that from her farm life she would have come to this understanding by examining how she learned the way milk was produced. The efficient cause of milk would be observed to be the cow. There must be a cow that eats the grass, that digests the cud which produces the milk. In looking at this simple example, the woman, or any of us, can conclude that there must be a primary efficient cause which causes milk to be produced.

For one would realize that thought cannot go back indefinitely to cause after cause; it must stop with a prime cause. There must be a primary efficient cause. In applying this insight to a theistic view of life, the woman in this case sees each life change as the result of an efficient cause which leads her to the primary efficient cause of God as the cause/source of life and life's ongoing growth. This is probably how she sees the tragic life events; they are the result of the primary efficient cause that brings about growth and these events are the way growth will take place.

In his third proof of God, Aquinas addresses the issue of necessity. It is necessary, he argues, for God to exist. His argument posits that something that does exist, which had not existed, depends upon something already existing. This reasoning leads to recognizing that some being has in itself its own necessity to exist and causes in others their own necessity. Necessity is referring to that which must exist to create all else that exists.

The woman in this case under examination came to see the necessity of her existence and the existence of others who cared for her in her illness. From facing her terminal illness and impending death, this woman came to realize that she did not create her life and control it. "I have always lived believing in God but not realizing that I didn't control my life. I lived as though I had complete power over my destiny, but I see now that I don't. I even realize that I never thought that my beginning of my living was dependent upon something greater than my parents." She came to realize that her existence was dependent on a being that always existed and drew its necessity from itself.

For this woman there was a realization, at this time, that there was a God who needed to exist to create her and to give life meaning. She realized her powerlessness in this illness but realized that she was created to be in relationship with God. "It's at times like these that I realize that God created me to be with Him. This is what it's all about. It's really the only thing necessary for life."

Somehow, if God is necessary to be, then others are necessary to be for the same reason, which is to be for each other. "I have been married for thirty-two years. I now realize what marriage is about. It's for one to be there for the other. It's just how God is there for me and I'm there for God."

It was through this understanding that this woman came to see how God creates others' necessity. It is by making people for people, in the same way in which God made us for Him and in which God is for us. Others' necessity is relational and it is necessary for our survival, which is how this woman came to realize others' necessity as being created by God. As a matter of fact, she could only know this necessity of others for others by her situation in which others were needed to help her in living at this time of her life. Their help was a necessity which was created by the fact that this woman came to be.

The fourth way St. Thomas proves God's existence is through a gradation in things. There comes a hierarchy of being that one can sense and learn. This can be seen in the development of what was held as important to the woman throughout her life. Bankruptcy, divorce, illness, and death which occurred throughout her lifetime served to draw her to a deeper understanding of what is important in life. For instance, when she went bankrupt she found that money did not give her meaning or purpose, and the current illness has her find value in other people. These events are drawing her to a natural way of seeing value in higher levels of being, and this process can draw her to an acknowledgment of the prime value of the Ultimate Being called God.

The fifth way of coming to know God in the Thomistic method is through looking at the governance of the world. This proof is based upon knowledge. Beings without knowledge cannot work toward an end and thus must be directed toward an end by some intelligent being. In this woman's life certain things cannot direct themselves since they do not have knowledge in themselves. For instance, her illness does not have knowledge in itself. It must be directed to some end, and since it cannot direct itself to an end there must be some intelligent being directing it for some end. This seems to explain why the woman, who doesn't seem to have knowledge of the end of all the crises in her life, continues to believe. She appears to live off an implicit sense that there is an intelligent Being directing all these things and events to a meaningful end.

From a different theistic point of view Kierkegaard posits that proof of God is not something that can be done. Kierkegaard says that God is the Unknown. It is the limit that reason always comes to, for human reason is limited. Reason cannot always understand or prove everything in experience.

It was Kierkegaard's intent to show that reason, when it is separated from the "leap of faith," blurs the essence of one's relationship with God. He points out that to center in on proving the existence of a transcendent deity only reduces the idea of God to the human mind's own limited understanding. Kierkegaard wants the reader to realize that it is really hard to prove the existence of something greater than one's self. The limited mind cannot comprehend such an awesome being since it is greater than the created human mind. So the leap of faith is certainly essential in Kierkegaard's view.

This particular woman is unable to make sense out of apparently conflicting values. She gives birth but then must face death. Why? She admits she doesn't understand these events in her life. She continues to believe in God. This basically is the "leap of faith" Kierkegaard is speaking of. In the midst of her current terminal cancer, the woman wonders why this is even happening to her. She knows she has lived a good life. She believes in God and follows all the dictates this demands. So, why must I face this tragedy, she asks. No logical, reasoned conclusion surfaces. Reason is limited in this sense. Thus the woman continues to believe not on any proof, logic, or reason, but simply believes in that which is unknown.

One could ask why she should continue to believe. Why not stop believing? In part, one could suspect that she knows that all things have a purpose and will work out. Drawing from the Thomistic idea that grace builds on nature, she experienced tragedy on the farm and knew that it would work out in the course of nature as, she observed, did all the events of life on the farm. There could be a natural sense inside her that allows her to trust and therefore permits her leap of faith that God does exist and directs even that which a human being cannot comprehend.

I do suspect that, in addition, the woman has learned to follow a path based on understanding relationships and has an understanding of how God works, through understanding human relations. She is able to believe because she has a real sense of the whole, the interrelatedness of all creation. Her experience of being cared for in her illness verified that it is not just her illness that others are caring for. It is her, totally, everything she is, that is being cared for and in relation to the other. For Buber, when this happens one is experiencing the relation with the eternal *Thou*. That is, it is the relationship of one with God. It is possible that the woman maintains her faith because she has experienced the eternal *Thou* in the *I-Thou* relationship she has with those who are providing care for her in her sickness. Buber would say she has encountered the care of God in the care of others.

What seems to be going on here is a different approach to God. It is like the way of speaking of God's nature as Buber sees it. Buber's approach to the nature of God differs sharply from the traditional theological endeavor to define God in terms of Divine attributes, and it differs from the philosophical concern for finding a rational proof for the existence of God. What is at play here with this woman is similar to Buber's assertion that God cannot he encountered by making his existence the object of reflection. As you have seen, for Buber, God is found and known only in the relationship he calls *I-Thou.* This woman is finding the quality of the *I-Thou* relationship in the way all of the significant people in her life are now relating to her in her need. It seems to bring out those relational qualities that help one prepare for the quality of relationship that is hoped for with the Divine.

For Buber there are two primary attitudes a person might take: *I-Thou* and *I-It.* The primary difference between the two postures derives from the mode of relating rather than from the objects to which the *I* relates. In the *I-It* interchanges, the *I* attempts to control, use, or manipulate the other; whereas the *I-Thou* relation entails openness, mutuality, and a freeing of the other fully to be itself in its uniqueness. According to Buber, God, the eternal *Thou,* is somehow present whenever persons relate to each other in this way as *I-Thou.* Therefore, in Buber we find no description of God in terms of images but, rather, a God who can be heard and listened to. Therefore, as this sixty-one-year-old terminally ill patient related to her husband and family in a more open, caring, genuine fashion, she is experiencing a new sense of relationship with God and can listen to God and hear God in a real sense that lays a foundation for a deeper relationship with the Divine.

The atheistic philosophy is reflected in the work of Nietzsche. In his work is seen a real lack of acknowledgment of beings to transcend themselves. To look at otherworldly hopes is a poison. The earth is not seen as a reflection of a supreme being. The earth is the ultimate value, and human beings are to be subdued. This implies that people are not filled with otherworldly potential and possibility but are no better than other beasts that are to be tamed. For the theistic thinker there is a view of the world filled with a greater possibility; one does not have to live in a spirit of resignation. For the atheistic thinker the earth and life situations will become the "overman" that subdues the person. To the theistic person there is a deep sense that the person possesses the ability, relationship to the Ultimate Being, that will allow the person to subdue the situation.

The woman in the case believes that she can make sense out of her terminal illness due to the fact that she did bring some meaning to bear to the other crises she encountered in living. One gets a sense of possibility, a sense of life in the face of death from this theistic thinker.

For Nietzsche and the atheistic thinker there is no such potential or possibility. The only possibility is that life events will subdue the person. The world is not seen holistically and as interrelated in the atheistic view of things. Things are fragmented and not in union with each other. Subduing the fragments, and people are some of the fragments, is the way to make sense of the world and life.

In the case at hand, the woman has not been subdued. She has been open to see all the potential there is in life. This yields to a life of hope for there is more to come; whereas the atheistic view will yield only resignation to what is.

ALLEN I. FREEHLING

THE PHILOSOPHER AS RABBI: CONFRONTING EVIL IN THE FACE OF THE HIV/AIDS PANDEMIC

In Reform Judaism's High Holy Days prayer book, *Gates of Repentance,* we are reminded that "Birth is a beginning and death is a destination. And, life is a journey—a sacred pilgrimage—to life everlasting."

In the next few pages, I want to share with you that aspect of my life's journey which has been profoundly affected by the presence of HIV/AIDS in our society, and to indicate how the theological and practical challenges of this dreadful pandemic have caused my life to become more of a pilgrimage than ever before.

To place things in proper perspective, I need to put before you some instructions we that have received from Rabbi Hillel, a Talmudic sage who lived from 30 B.C.E. (Before the Common Era)–10 C.E. (Common Era); he taught his disciples: "What is hateful to you do not do to another person." (*Pirke Avot–Chapters/Sayings of the Fathers*)

Extending this idea, a mystic sage, Moses Cordovero, instructed his followers: "In everyone there is something of his fellow-man. Hence, when the *Torah* teaches, 'Love your neighbor,' we learn that he is really you yourself." (*Tomer Deborah*)

Thus, we are required to know ourselves very well, and to identify those words and actions that both please and harm us. Furthermore, Hillel and Cordovero would insist that we must rely upon empathy when we interact with others in ways which should always satisfy and never injure them.

So, each of us needs to maintain a delicate balance between selfishness and selflessness.

Furthermore, in developing my thesis, I also want to call to mind the teachings of the prophet Isaiah, who portrayed God as insisting that we "Unlock the shackles of injustice, undo the fetters of bondage, let the oppressed go free, break every cruel chain, share our bread with the hungry, bring the homeless into our houses, and clothe the naked." (58:1–14)

Finally, the message of Rabbi Abraham Joshua Heschel must be brought to mind, because his is the assertion that creation is an evolutionary process in which both God and humanity have a shared responsibility. He wrote: "God is in need of man for the attainment of His ends, and religion—as Jewish tradition understands it—is a way of serving these ends, of which we are in need, even though we may not be aware of them, ends which we must learn to feel the need of. Life is a partnership of God and man. . . . God is a partner and a partisan in man's struggle for justice, peace, and holiness. And, it is because of His being in need of man that He entered into a covenant with him for all time,

Rabbi Allan Freehling is Senior Rabbi at University Synagogue in Los Angeles where he has been since 1972. He holds a bachelor's degree from the University of Miami, a second bachelor's degree and a master's diploma from Hebrew Union College, a doctorate from Kensington College, and an honorary doctorate from Hebrew Union College. While responding to what he refers to as "our prophetic mandate to repair the tattered fabric of society," Rabbi Freehling has a long and distinguished record as a social justice proponent in Southern California, throughout the United States, and abroad. He leads a large number of religious and secular organizations, which concentrate on such diverse issues as poverty and homelessness, abuse and crime, HIV/AIDS prevention and patient care, interfaith and interracial relations, public education and mental health, environmental issues, the Israel/U.S. connection, and the cause of peace in the Middle East. He is father of three and has six grandchildren.

a mutual bond embracing God and man, a relationship to which God, and not just man, is committed." (Heschel, 1959)

This means that not only are *we* in search of God but "God is in search of man." From this we learn that God is a constant presence in our lives and that there is an ongoing covenantal relationship that links us not only to God but to one another, as well.

It is this covenant that allows us not only to make the most of our lives but also to magnify the lives of others. Ours is the mandate to celebrate life in all of its fullness. It is for this reason that Judaism's ancient sages permitted their adherents to abrogate any and all of the prohibitions imposed upon them—these are restrictions which cause traditionalists to demand that no labor is performed on the Sabbath day—if someone's life was in danger and that such a person had to be saved through the active intervention of others.

It's within this context that three Jewish concepts are of vital importance to what I want to comment on: The idea of *tikkun olam* tells us that we have a responsibility to help repair the tattered fabric of our society; the word *chesed* reminds us that we are to treat ourselves and all others with loving kindness; and, the notion that we are required to perform *mitzvot* exists to show us that each of us has worthy deeds to accomplish.

A few more words about God are necessary . . .

If a person is a religious traditionalist, that individual insists that God is the sole author of the *Torah*—the first five books of the Bible—as well as some other subsequent holy texts. So, here is a person who worships an imminent God portrayed as a micromanager who blesses or curses people depending upon their words and actions. For the traditionalist, the matter of "free will" is a questionable subject.

Those of us who are religious nontraditionalists argue that the Torah and other works were not divinely revealed at a single moment; rather, they are the writings of divinely inspired individuals, who wrote their messages over an extended period of time and in response to situations that they were experiencing. As a teacher of mine, Rabbi Sheldon Blank taught his rabbinic students, "A prophet and other sages were not famous and revered because of their foresight but because of their insight."

So, for us God is a transcendent macromanager dependent upon everyone to be involved in the evolutionary process of creation. Thus, when we read the first chapters of the Book of Genesis, we learn that everything created by God is good and orderly. It is humanity that erroneously causes evil and chaos to reign supreme.

On this subject, Louis Jacobs has written: "The problem of evil has always been a stumbling block to believers of a supremely beneficent Being, and the problem is acute when even one child is born hideously deformed or dies a horrible death. In this sense, the problem is as old as the belief in God. Yet, after the Holocaust, many Jewish thinkers have found themselves psychologically incapable of accepting the traditional solutions that evil is a means to a glorious end. . . . Many Jewish thinkers still declare that they do believe in God, though not in the God of traditional Jewish theism." (Jacobs, 1973)

Agreeing with those philosophers, it is my opinion that we—and not God!—are the source of every kind of disharmony; however, when we rely upon God to be our role model, we ultimately discover that ours is the ability to restore goodness and orderliness at all times and in every place.

Therefore, Hillel, Isaiah, and many other teachers of ours insist that we have no choice but to be continually attentive to our own needs, as well as that which is essentially required by every person with whom we share our lives.

Expanding upon this idea, whether one is a traditionalist or not, the teachings of Martin Buber bridge over what seems to be a huge theological gap. He wrote: "What a man does now and here with holy intent is no less important, no less true—being a link with divine being—than is life in the world to come. (Heschel, 1964)

In other words, while a belief in God is significant, of far greater importance is that which we do to sustain every person and every thing created by God.

It is upon this foundation that I have built my adult life and structured my years as a rabbi. My abiding purpose is to serve God as a teacher and practitioner of Jewish teachings, to be a community activist who is continually seeking ways to illuminate any dark places where people have been abandoned, betrayed, harmed and ignored, and to urge others to share with me the task of bettering the human condition in every way possible.

This then leads us to an understanding that "civil rights" guarantee freedom and liberty not only to peoples of color but to anyone whose life is at risk because of the existence of bias, hate and prejudice. You see, if Buber is correct when he suggests that we are in an "I-Thou" relationship with God, and that "He who loves brings God and the World together," (Buber, 1952) it follows that we are also unquestionably bonded to all of God's creatures. Thus, there is no way that a person can justify his condemnation of another individual.

Nevertheless, when researchers at the University of California-Los Angeles and at a few other medical centers first identified the AIDS virus, it was shown that—with very rare exception—the vast majority of those infected with HIV/AIDS were young, sexually active, gay white men. Immediately, a number of outspoken religious traditionalists launched their venomous, verbal attacks, citing passages in scripture and insisting that homosexuality was an "abomination" and that those individuals who were afflicted were being punished by God as a result of their "sinful" sexual behavior.

So, not only did the gay community have to contend with a seemingly unchecked epidemic that fast became an unrelenting global pandemic, but many of those adversely affected believed that they and God were at odds and that most of society was totally unsympathetic to their plight.

Here was the very moment when my theology and pragmatic community activism coalesced to motivate me to become actively involved—and to urge others to join me—in this worthy cause, because I am convinced that God is not punitive, that homosexuality is not a chosen lifestyle but it exists as a result of a genetic circumstance, that HIV/AIDS is not a God-inflicted "plague," and that those who are infected are not being victimized by a vengeful God, because of their "wrongdoing."

Instead, I agree with Marcus Herz, when he wrote: "Within a person innumerable forces are incessantly at work like so many instruments, so as to preserve in its entirety this beautiful house containing an individual immortal soul, and these forces act with all the order, concord and harmony imaginable. If weakness (or illness) disturb this harmony, these forces act against one another, and disease announces the approach of danger, and bids man to prepare to overcome them." (Herz)

Thankfully, as I began to plunge deeply into an effort to be of help, I found that there were many other men and women ready to act in a collaborative effort, as long as they were effectively led. This is the basis upon which my pilgrimage moved forward.

Within months of the identification of the virus being made public, the Los Angeles County Board of Supervisors established a commission on AIDS. Each of its five elected members appointed two people to serve on the commission. I was one of them, and then—at our first meeting—my colleagues asked me to be the founding chair. We were mandated to confer regularly with staff members of the Department of Health Services, as well as with leaders of an emerging number of AIDS health care and services providers; we granted them unconditional access to our monthly meetings.

In turn, it was our responsibility to bring carefully crafted recommendations to the supervisors for them to deliberate and to consider enacting. From the beginning, we urged action that would intensify the availability of medical treatment—especially for impoverished people with AIDS—and expand upon supportive services for them and for their relatives, lovers, and friends who were also caught up in the vortex of this epidemic that caused so many people to become desperately ill. When we made our presentations to the Supervisors, we found two members of the Board regularly allied with us, two who were opposed to almost everything that we suggested, and one "swing vote" who was resistant but at least willing to hear us out.

A county-funded study prepared by Price Waterhouse was released soon after we began our work. It contained a forecast: By the year 2000—unless there was a dramatic decrease in unprotected sexual activity—no fewer than 300,000 and as many as 400,000 people in Los Angeles would be HIV positive, and all of those individuals would eventually die of AIDS. It was also shown in this projection that the epidemic would soon cease to be the exclusive problem of gay white men—the lives of their counterparts in communities of color, as well as a huge number of women and children would be increasingly at risk.

It was under these circumstances that we urged the Board of Supervisors to be proactive, vis a vis providing open access to health care facilities, helping to fund hospices, funding candid and forthright HIV/AIDS education programs and articulate epidemic prevention campaigns, to authorize the free distribution of condoms throughout the community, to permit needle exchange programs (so as to curtail the spread of HIV among those who were abusing drugs), and to order the closing of bath houses, because they were places in which unprotected sexual activity was running rampant in the gay community.

There was fierce opposition to much of what we advocated among some religious traditionalists, but their zealous tirades at sessions of the Board of Supervisors were offset by well-documented presentations offered by both the AIDS

Commission and our advocates, plus accurate reports appearing in local news-papers and heard on radio and television, as well as an assortment of very re-sponsible editorials that were being published and broadcast on a regular basis.

Thus, there was a merger of philosophy and pragmatism, which met the challenge of HIV/AIDS. We were able to withstand attacks being launched by biased and prejudiced people who perverted religious doctrine for reasons of their own.

Elsewhere, theology and the teachings of diverse faith communities came to the fore as larger and larger numbers of men and women were aroused out of their slumber, so they could help wage a battle against the ravishes of HIV/AIDS. As a result, those who were infected soon realized that a vast support system was emerging to benefit them.

Let me cite some other situations in which I was involved . . .

Soon after the epidemic was acknowledged, AIDS Project Los Angeles came into being. Initially, it was an organization exclusively staffed and funded by members of the gay community. But, several of us, who were "straight" faith community leaders, indicated that we were interested in helping to fund and to thereby strengthen the health care facilities and social services which APLA was offering.

Two of us were invited to serve on the group's board, and—as an exten-sion—we organized the AIDS Interfaith Council, which I cochaired, as the president of the Board of Rabbis of Southern California, along with the Cath-olic community's archbishop and the then interim bishop of the Episcopal dio-cese. Of particular concern to us was the plight of people of color who were HIV positive—hostile attitudes regarding homosexuality, and so on, were resulting in families not taking advantage of accessible medical treatment and other sup-portive services that were theirs for the asking because of culture-induced shame and/or their ignoring reality, since they were in total denial.

While the Episcopal Church was constantly in the vanguard of finding cre-ative ways to cope with this epidemic—in terms of extending a helping hand to those who were infected and afflicted, and in furthering efforts to educate men, women and children so as to prevent the further spread of HIV/AIDS—other faith communities were initially less effective. But, over a period of time, many other mainstream denominations caught up and shared responsibility in this area of human concern.

Along the way, an alarming situation in the Jewish community resulted in our issuing a call for action. In the early days of the epidemic, blood was not being tested in hospitals, so there was no way to know if some donated pints were HIV/AIDS tainted before they were used for transfusions.

It was under these circumstances that twin children were born at a medical center, and one of the newborns required transfused blood in order that his life be saved. A few years later, the twins were enrolled at a synagogue's preschool, and the child, who had received a pint of virus-laden blood, developed HIV/AIDS. Even as he lay dying of this disease, hysterical parents of other children enrolled at the nursery school insisted his very healthy sibling be removed from the student body for fear that he would somehow infect their sons and daughters. The institution's embattled administration yielded to these demands; thus, a grievous situation became all the worse.

Hearing about this, I drafted a policy statement for our synagogue's Board of Trustees to consider and eventually adopt. It focused not only on how our congregation would positively respond to the needs of children and adult members who might be HIV positive, but it also spelled out how we would be supportive of any staff member who became infected. Eventually, our document was disseminated among reform congregations throughout the United States for their consideration. Many of them adapted it to meet their own needs.

Meanwhile, having been stimulated by my reports, when I spoke and wrote about my experiences, in an attempt to teach congregants about Judaism's attitude toward social responsibility in the midst of this pandemic, our synagogue's sisterhood decided to perform an extraordinary *mitzvah*. It was brought to their attention that a growing number of infected people were coming to the County/U.S.C. Medical Center for treatment at the HIV/AIDS Outpatient Unit. If any of these patients left the facility to have lunch, they would lose their place in line—besides, some were too destitute to bring or to purchase lunch for themselves, so their need for nourishment was not being addressed.

Soon thereafter and twice a month on Thursdays, women congregants began to gather in our Synagogue's kitchen early in the morning to prepare boxed meals, and then they took them to County/U.S.C. where they distributed more than 200 lunches at a time, while visiting with grateful recipients throughout the afternoon. Eventually, members of other temples and churches came on board. Now, the Outpatient Clinic's clients are never on site without their being assured that lunch will be served to them by a host of faith communities' volunteers, who are blessing them and being blessed by them in turn.

There are some vital lessons that I've learned along the way . . .

For instance, fear causes some people to react in inappropriate ways; for example, during the initial period of the HIV/AIDS epidemic, I was asked by several grieving survivors never to mention the cause of death even though they knew that their loved ones had died as a result of AIDS, and, when some families were informed that relatives were gay and infected, they expressed the misguided and uninformed hope that homosexuality could be "fixed" so that the disease would "go away."

While I encountered some very ill men and women, I found them to be people of faith. They never renounced God. Yet, a few of them were very angry at God for "allowing" them to become HIV/AIDS infected. When they asked me why God would permit good people to die such horrible deaths, I suggested that God is not omnipotent and responsible for everything—good and bad—that we encounter in our lives.

I often shared with them some of the ideas of Rabbi Mordecai M. Kaplan, who taught: "God denotes a relationship of supreme importance to a people or to mankind. The functional idea of God is derived not from metaphysical speculation or supernatural revelation but naturalistically from the process of discovering the meaning of human self-fulfillment or salvation. Whatever constitutes salvation for a religious community determines its idea of God. . . . That which brings order out of chaos and fosters world responsibility, love, and creativity manifests divinity and shapes the idea of God. . . . Faith is neither passive nor arbitrary but calls for wisdom to explore the real and potential good, and for the will to activate that good." (Kaplan, 1964)

These liberating ideas gave those with whom I met permission to rethink their beliefs, to articulate—in new ways—the relationship they had with God, and to reach deep within themselves to find an enduring faith in God that both comforted and strengthened them at a time when positive and helpful attitudes were desperately needed.

In our conversations, I found that for some God was perceived as a being that was omniscient—fully aware of everything that we say and do—and yet unwilling (or perhaps unable?) to direct all of our actions; that is a responsibility left in our hands.

Thus, the pandemic proved to be a transformative reality in their lives, because they had an opportunity to wrestle with their own concept of God and to deal with the matter of "free will" as they experienced it. There were those with whom I had these discussions who found themselves in agreement with Rabbi Heschel, who wrote: "Freedom is not a principal of uncertainty, the ability to act without motive, nor is it identical to an act of choice.

"Rather, it is the ability to react to the unique and the novel. It is liberation from tyranny of the self-centered ego, an event that occurs in rare creative moments of self-transcendence as an act of spiritual ecstasy. Its nature is a mystery, but without it there is no meaning to the moral life." (Heschel, 1955)

Simultaneously, the presence of HIV/AIDS and the death of so many young people caused a significant number of us to concentrate on issues related to death and dying, to acknowledge the fact that all of us are mortal, to wonder about the viability of a person's spirit/soul once the body ceases to function, and so on.

And, since this pandemic always endangers the lives of those who are engaged in unprotected sexual activity and/or the sharing of tainted needles when abusing drugs, and inasmuch as science has yet to discover a foolproof cure, our concerns and activities related to HIV/AIDS must remain on high alert.

As a member of the Board of Directors of the International Associations of Physicians in AIDS Care, I am well aware of the fact that we need to intensify worldwide education and prevention programs, including the widespread distribution of condoms—despite some churches' objections—and to dramatically decrease the cost of pharmaceutical "cocktails," which severely curb the devastating effects of the virus on the human immune system. Also, we must be assertive in wiping away lingering prejudice and shame whenever they stand in the way of infected people receiving compassionate treatment and support.

As I suggested earlier, Jewish theology insists that nothing is more important than is our saving a person's life. Yet, all too many lives are being taken because we are not being as vigilant as we should be in the midst of this pandemic.

Our faith in God demands that we be persistent and tireless; however, more often than not we seem to be excessively slothful and uncaring.

As the chair of the Reform Movement's Committee on AIDS, I'm concerned that far too many people still do not consider the epidemic to be a "Jewish issue," so they choose to ignore their responsibility to help—by means of education and doing whatever they should do—to ward off dangerously reckless attitudes and unwarranted behavior among both sexually active young people and adults, and to be responsive to those individuals who are HIV/AIDS infected and who require their assistance.

Perhaps it would be well for all of us to consider these words written by the illustrious philosopher-physician Maimonides: "It is clear that the perfection of man, which may truly be glorified in, is the one acquired by that person who has achieved, in a measure corresponding to his capacity, an apprehension of Him (may He be exalted) and who knows His providence extending over His creatures as manifested in the act of bringing them into being and in their governance as it is. The way of life of such an individual, after he has achieved this apprehension, will always have in view *loving kindness, righteousness* and *judgment* . . ."(Maimonides, 1963)

It is here that we learn how important it is that we strive for perfection, to overcome our weaknesses, and to find harmony with all of God's creation. To engage ourselves in that process, we need to echo the words of the Israelites who gathered at Mount Sinai to hear the message of God which was transmitted to them by Moses. Like them, we have no choice but to say: "*Naaseh v'nishma*— we shall do and we shall harken."

And, since I began this piece depicting life as a journey, which becomes a pilgrimage, I want to end by sharing with you a parable written by an eighteenth-century rabbi, Chayim of Tsanz: "A man, wandering lost in the forest for several days, finally encountered another. He called out, 'Brother, show me the way out of this forest!' The man replied, 'Brother, I too am lost. I can only tell you this—the ways I have tried lead nowhere; they have only led me astray. Take my hand, and let us search for the way together.'" Rabbi Chayim would add: "So it is with us. When we go our separate ways, we may go astray; let us join hands and look for the way together." (*Gates of Prayer*)

REFERENCES AND A SELECTED BIBLIOGRAPHY

Adler, Mortimer J. and Charles Van Doren, eds. 1977. *Great Treasury of Western Thought.* New York: R. R. Bowker Company.

Baron, Joseph I., ed. 1956. *A Treasury of Jewish Quotations.* South Brunswick, N.J.: A. S. Barnes and Co., Inc.

Buber, Martin. 1952. *At the Turning.* New York: Farrar, Strauss and Young.

Buber, Martin. 1958. *I and Thou.* New York: Charles Scribner's Sons.

Chavel, Charles, ed. 1980. *Encyclopedia of Torah Thoughts.* New York: Shilo Publishing House, Inc.

Cohen, Arthur A. and Paul Mendes-Flohr, eds. 1987. *Contemporary Jewish Religious Thought.* New York: Charles Scribner's Sons.

Gates of Prayer. 1975. New York: Central Conference of American Rabbis.

Gates of Repentance. 1978. New York: Central Conference of American Rabbis.

Heschel, Abraham Joshua. 1955. *God in Search of Man: A Philosophy of Judaism.* New York: Farrar, Strauss and Cudahy.

—. 1959. *Between God and Man: An Interpretation of Judaism.* New York: The Free Press.

—. 1961. *Man is Not Alone: A Philosophy of Religion.* New York: Farrar, Strauss, and Young.

—. 1964. *Between Man and Man.* New York: Macmillan Paperbacks.

—. 1965. *Who is Man?* Stanford, CA: Stanford University Press.

Herz, Marcus. *Physician's Prayer.*

Jacobs, Louis. 1973. *A Jewish Theology.* West Orange N.J.: Behrman House.

Kaplan, Mordecai. 1934. *Judaism as Civilization.* New York: Thomas Yoseloff.

—. 1964. *The Purpose and Meaning of Jewish Existence.* Philadelphia: Jewish Publication Society of America.

—. 1966. *The Knowledge of Man.* New York: Harper and Row.

Klagsbrum, Francine, ed. 1980. *Voices of Wisdom.* New York: Pantheon Books.

Maimonides, Moses. 1963. *The Guide of the Perplexed.* Chicago: The University of Chicago Press.

Monteflore, C. G. and H. Lowe, eds. 1974. *A Rabbinic Anthology.* New York: Schocken Books.

Novek, Simon, ed. 1963. *Great Jewish Thinkers of the Twentieth Century.* New York: The B'nai B'rith Department of Adult Jewish Education.

Pardes Rimonim. 1708. Amsterdam.

Philosophies of Judaism. 1964. Philadelphia: The Jewish Publication Society of America.

Rosten, Leo. 1972. *Leo Rosten's Treasury of Jewish Quotations.* Philadelphia: The Jewish Publication Society of America.

Schlipp, Paul Arthur and Maurice Friedman, eds. 1967. *The Philosophy of Martin Buber.* New York: The Library of Living Philosophers.

Tanakh: The Holy Scriptures. 1985. Philadelphia: The Jewish Publication Society of America.

Woods, Ralph L., ed. 1966. *The World Treasury of Religious Quotations.* New York: Hawthorn Books, Inc.

ADDENDUM VIS-À-VIS GOD AND THE PRESENCE OF EVIL

On the subject of God and the presence of evil in the world, I believe that Mordecai Kaplan's words, found in an essay entitled "The God of Our Salvation," are of great importance:

"The awareness of God implies that the potency of good is greater than that of evil. The sense of greater potency arises out of the fact that, whereas the evil is such by reason of its being fortuitous and aimless, the good is such by reason of its having purpose.

"We say: 'Where there is a will there is a way.' By that we record the experience that, despite the obstacles to a determined will presented by circumstances which are fortuitous, or which are less informed by purpose or plan, the determined will is bound to win out in the end.

"Likewise, when we experience Godhood, we experience it in the form of faith that, despite the obstacles to man's salvation, there are enough forces in the world which can be depended on to enable man to achieve it, provided, of course, that man is willing to avail himself of them. 'This much can be said with assurance,' writes a modern theologian, 'we live in a world where the triumph of evil can never be complete, since evil systems destroy themselves by their own greed and egotism.'

"When, however, we not only reify, or hypostatize, but also *absolutize* Godhood, we are confronted by a logical dilemma. That is to say, if we assume that God is *absolutely* omnipotent, we cannot possibly allow for the existence of anything that might even attempt to resist or oppose God. On the other hand, if we do not wish to delude ourselves, we cannot deny the existence of evil, which, by its very nature, is the antithesis of Godhood.

"Not a single one of the numerous theodicies, or attempts of thinkers to reconcile the goodness of God with the existence of evil has ever proved convincing.

"We might, perhaps, resolve the dilemma by assuming that God's omnipotence is not an actually realized fact at any point of time, but a potential fact. That is to say, if we take into account the indefinite duration of Godhood, it is possible to conceive that the evil, which now mars the cosmos, will ultimately be eliminated. Or, we might become resigned to the intrinsic inability of the human mind to resolve the dilemma, except by the practical effort to reduce the amount of evil in the world, so as to leave the world the better for our having lived in it."

Elaborating on this theory when considering
the tragic results of the Holocaust

As a follow-up to the teachings of Rabbi Kaplan, consider these words by Rabbi Richard Rubenstein:

"The religious problem of evil gained unprecedented urgency for Jewish religious thought in the aftermath of the worst communal disaster ever experienced in all of Jewish history, the extermination of the European Jews during World War II.

"From the perspective of the normative theology of covenant and election, the Holocaust could be understood only as God's just and righteous punishment of Israel for her failure to abide by her ancient and immutable covenant.

"Nevertheless, even among the most stringently Orthodox, few thinkers were able to interpret the Holocaust as Jeremiah had interpreted the first fall of Jerusalem (retribution as a result of Israel's not upholding the covenant) and Rabbi Johanan ben Zakkai had interpreted the second (God's punishment for the wrongdoing of His elect community).

"Once again, Jewish religious thinkers attempted to mitigate the harsh and uncompromising ethical rationalism of covenant theology. In general, the mitigations sought to reaffirm the abiding validity and credibility of God's relations to Israel (the Jewish people), while rejecting the punitive interpretation of the Holocaust.

"Thinkers, such as Arthur A. Cohen and Eliezer Berkovits, have limited God's role to that of a teacher of essentially free human agents and identified the Holocaust as the work of human beings who rejected the teachings of the teacher.

"Emil L. Fackenheim has adopted a different approach, rejecting the ethical rationalism of covenant theology when literally understood while metaphorically reaffirming God's presence in Jewish history.

"Still another strategy of mitigation has been advanced by Ignaz Maybaum, who reaffirmed the literal meaning of the covenant while identifying the Holocaust victims as vicarious sacrificial offerings for the redemption of humanity rather that the objects of divine punitive justice.

"This writer, alone among modern theologians, has insisted that, if the covenant as traditionally understood within the Jewish religious mainstream is to be reaffirmed in the aftermath of the Holocaust, none of the mitigating strategies will prove to be of enduring credibility. This writer further argued that, after Auschwitz, Jewish religious belief has been thrust on the horns of an exceedingly bitter dilemma:

One can affirm either the abiding validity of Israel's covenant with God or the nonpunitive character of the Holocaust—but not both.

"If God is taken to be the all-powerful author of the covenant, the biblical and rabbinic interpretation of the first and second destructions of Jerusalem must be seen as the model for the Jewish interpretation of the Holocaust. If it is no longer possible to interpret Israel's history in accordance with this model, the traditional view, that God acts justly in Israel's history, loses much of its residual credibility.

"Thus, in the aftermath of the Holocaust, the religious problem of evil raises questions that go to the very heart of Israel's perennial understanding of its relation to God and, indeed, the viability of Judaism as a religious tradition.

"It may be that the metaphor for the understanding of Israel's relationship with God, that arose out of the international politics of the ancient Near East in the fourteenth and fifteenth centuries B.C.E., must give way to an as yet unformulated new metaphor." (Cohen and Mendes-Flohr, 1987)

DISCUSSION QUESTIONS

1. What is the difference between an a priori proof of God's existence and an a posteriori one? What makes St. Anselm's proof an a priori proof? What makes St. Thomas's five proofs a posteriori?

2. Discuss the ontological argument. What objections can be made against it? Discuss the merit of these objections.

3. Discuss each of the "five ways" of St. Thomas. What objections can be raised against each? Discuss the merit of these objections.

4. Why does Kierkegaard deny that God's existence can be proven? Do you agree with him? Defend your answer.

5. Discuss Buber's distinction between the *I-Thou* and *I-It* relations.

6. What similarities are there between Kant's "categorical imperative" to treat humanity as an "end in itself" and never as a "means only" and Buber's distinction between *I-Thou* and *I-It?* What differences are there between Buber and Kant? (See chapter 2.)

7. How, according to Buber, can one converse with God? Do you find Buber convincing? Defend your answer.

8. What is Buber's objection to any attempt to *define* God? Is Buber's claim that God is a person subject to this objection? Defend your answer.

9. What do you think Nietzsche meant when he said that "God has died"?

10. Discuss the merit of the tightrope walker's statement that "if you [Zarathustra] speak the truth . . . I lose nothing when I lose my life. I am not much more than a beast that has been taught to dance by blows and a few meager morsels."

11. In your opinion, is it possible to believe in God without believing in Heaven or Hell? In Heaven or Hell without believing in God? Defend your answer.

12. In what ways did the cancer patient discussed by Father Gerl attempt to prove God a posteriori, from her experiences?

13. Why did this patient, at one point, encounter a problem in maintaining her belief in God? Do you think her doubts were justified? Defend your answer.

14. How did this patient manage to overcome her doubts about God's existence? Discuss the respective roles of reason and faith as they pertain to the patient's overcoming of these doubts.

15. At one point, Father Gerl states that the patient never really lost faith in God. In your view, is this consistent with the patient's doubts about God's existence? Explain.

16. Discuss the relevance of Buber's *I-Thou* and *I-It* relations to the patient's situation. In your opinion, did this patient truly enter into a relation with God? Defend your answer.

17. What is "the problem of evil"? What is a theodicy? Discuss and assess the merit of John Hick's free-will and soul-building theodicies.

18. Discuss Mordecai Kaplan's view of God and evil. Discuss Rubenstein's position and compare it to that of Kaplan. What difference(s), if any, do you see between

Rubenstein's view and that of Nietzsche? Discuss Buber's view of God and evil and compare and contrast it with that of Rubenstein.

19. In his quest to provide community support for persons with HIV/AIDS, Rabbi Freehling refers to the opposition he encountered from religious traditionalists who believed that AIDS was a just punishment of homosexuals for their sin against God. In response, he states, "I am convinced that God is not punitive, that homosexuality is not a chosen life-style but it exists as a result of a genetic circumstance, that HIV/AIDS is not a God-inflicted 'plague', and that those who are infected are not being victimized by a vengeful God, because of their 'wrongdoing.'" Discuss the merit of the latter statement.

20. Referring to a quoted passage from Rabbi Heschel, Rabbi Freehling remarks that, not only are human beings in search of God, but "God is in search of man." Discuss the meaning and significance of this statement.

21. Agreeing with Buber, Rabbi Freehling states that ". . . while a belief in God is significant, of far greater importance is that which we do to sustain every person and every thing created by God." Do you agree with Freehling? Defend your answer.

22. Freehling, Gerl, and Nietzsche's Zarathustra each counsel someone who is dying as a result of some evil or misfortune. Discuss, compare, and contrast each of these counsels as it relates to eternal salvation, God, and the meaning of mortal existence.

24. Louis Jacobs, as quoted in Freehling, writes:

"The problem of evil has always been a stumbling block to believers of a supremely beneficent Being, and the problem is acute when even one child is born hideously deformed or dies a horrible death. In this sense, the problem is as old as the belief in God. Yet, after the Holocaust, many Jewish thinkers have found themselves psychologically incapable of accepting the traditional solutions that evil is a means to a glorious end . . . Many Jewish thinkers still declare that they do believe in God, though not in the God of traditional Jewish theism."

In your view, can the traditional solutions satisfactorily account for such extreme evils as that of the Holocaust? Why, indeed, do bad things happen to good people? Compare and contrast your own view with the views held by the thinkers mentioned in questions 17 and 18 above.

25. In an essay entitled "Pragmatism and Religion," the American pragmatist philosopher William James writes,

"On pragmatic principles, we cannot reject any hypothesis if consequences useful to life flow from it. Universal conceptions, as things to take account of, may be as real for pragmatism as particular sensations are. They have, indeed, no meaning and no reality if they have no use. But if they have any use, they have that amount of meaning. And the meaning will be true if the use squares well with Life's other uses. Well, the use of the Absolute is proved by the whole course of men's religious history. The eternal arms are then beneath."

In your view, how is the "truth" of religious belief to be assessed? Is it to be assessed in terms of its usefulness as James suggests? Is there just one correct religious conception, for example, God as infinite Being versus God as a limited power of goodness in nature, or are there many? Are the "true" religious beliefs ones confirmed through religious experience? (See also the following chapter on "Mysticism and Cosmic Consciousness.")

14

MYSTICISM AND COSMIC CONSCIOUSNESS

A central focus in the previous chapter was on the possibility of establishing God's existence by constructing logical arguments or proofs. In this chapter, a primary focus will be on the possibility of a *direct* or *immediate* communion with the divine, that is, upon what has sometimes been called "mystical experience" or "cosmic consciousness."

In the first selection of this chapter, William James (1842–1910), a famous American pragmatist, argues for the metaphysical and epistemic respectability of some of these experiences. He begins by setting down two criteria which he thinks suffice for marking off mystical experience from other varieties of experience. First, he says, such experience is "ineffable"—like a state of feeling, "no adequate report of its content can be given in words." However, unlike states of feeling, the latter states are also "noetic" in character—that is, they are "states of insight into depths of truth unplumbed by the discursive intellect."

Experiences of the above sort have been, in James's words, "methodologically cultivated" by a number of religious groups including Hindus, Buddhists, Mohammedans, and Christians. Moreover, he argues that the order of mystical experiences shows the simple dichotomy between sense experience and reason to be unacceptable. "They open out the possibility of other orders of truth." Although, for James, not all mystical states are authoritative (since they, like other experiences, must be "sifted and tested and run the gauntlet of confrontation with the total context of experience"), the "higher ones" point to such important values as that of "the ideal, of vastness, of union, of safety, and of rest." For this reason, they may provide us with "the truest of insights into the meaning of this life."

The reader should keep in mind, however, that James is, after all, a pragmatist. For him, the "true" or the "authoritative" is intimately bound up with the "useful" and the "expedient." It is "only the expedient in the way of our thinking, just as 'the right' is only the expedient in the way of our behaving." [1] (See also the Issues section on pragmatism in chapter 7.) For those who are not sympathetic to this approach to truth, the metaphysical status of mystical experience may appear to be otherwise.

In the second selection of this chapter, excerpted from *Mysticism and Logic,* Bertrand Russell presents such a challenge. Although he believes, in agreement with James, that the values embodied in mysticism should be "commended as an attitude toward life," it is, as a "metaphysical creed," a "mistaken outcome of the emotion."

According to Russell, mysticism errs in its one-sided reliance on "intuition" (as distinct from sense, reason, and analysis) as sufficient grounds of knowledge. Similarly, its subscription to a reality distinct from what appears to the senses, along with its commitment to the perfect unity and goodness of this reality, does not square with the pronouncements of logic and science. While the mystic's vision makes fruitful contributions to an attitude toward life, its attempt to make out reality, as it would idealize it—dismissing logic and the evidence of the senses where these contradict this ideal—cannot, from an impartial standpoint, be validated.

In the Practice selection of this chapter, Alan Watts, a well-known interpreter of Eastern philosophies, especially Zen Buddhism, discusses his own "mystical" or "cosmic" experiences, exemplifying those aspects raised by James and Russell—ineffability, intuitiveness, unity, timelessness, goodness, the rejection of logic, and the like. He also attempts to show how his role as a writer and philosopher has itself been transformed by these experiences. According to Watts, it is not the main mission of a philosopher, who has been united with the divine, to assume the role of a moralist or reformer whose purpose it is to improve others. Rather, in the spirit of the "philosopher as artist," "out of simple exuberance or wonder he wants to tell others of the point of view from which the world is unimaginably good as it is, with people just as they are." Although Watts denies any purpose of improving others through his vision, still he does not deny the moral efficacy of the attitude that arises out of "cosmic consciousness." (On this matter, therefore, he does, after all, concur with both Russell and James.)

Of course, those who are skeptical about the metaphysical status of Watts's experience, particularly nonmystics, may ask for proof that his claimed vision is not merely the product of his imagination. We thus return to the problem raised earlier. And Watts's answer seems here to closely parallel James's. Watts tells us that the "attitude of faith must be basic." Correspondingly, "Faith State" and "Mystic State," says James, are "practically convertible terms." Unless we are to end in total doubt and total lack of "movement," we must repose such faith, beyond proof, in our senses or feelings. So viewed, however, there may be, *other things being equal,* no more reason to demand that mystics validate their perceptions than that nonmystics validate theirs.

Of course, one can charge, as Russell does, that other things are *not* equal, that logic and science contradict the mystic's intuitions. Scientific facts, after all, are supposed to cohere systematically with other parts of our experience. Moreover, they are supposed to be intersubjectively verifiable. That is, other "normal" observers should be able to have similar perceptions under similar conditions.

However, as J. B. Pratt has pointed out,[2] it may well be that someday psychology will discover the conditions under which such "mystical" experiences *can* be reproduced. But this, argues Pratt, would still not by itself settle the issue as to whether or not such experiences have "cosmic" or metaphysical significance. A further consideration would then be the *sort* of conditions that would be jointly necessary and sufficient to reproduce such an experience. For example, according to Pratt, if it were found to be consistently reproducible by taking a certain psychotropic drug, such as lysergic acid (LSD), in a certain amount, then we might be less inclined to accord metaphysical status to the experience than we would, say, if it were found to be consistently reproducible after having undergone a certain rigorous moral and religious regimen of "soul purification."

It is notable, however, that James himself mentions having had a mystical experience, induced by inhaling nitrous oxide, to which he could not "help ascribing some metaphysical significance." According to James, the drug was able to dissolve "the filmiest of screens" which separate our "normal waking consciousness" from other entirely different states of consciousness.

Watts's "cosmic" experiences discussed by him in this chapter were not drug induced but rather arose in situations of "total extremity or despair" in which he found himself "without any alternative but to surrender himself entirely." But he has also reported in another article[3] having had experiences bearing some resemblance to the "cosmic" ones, while serving as a research subject for a psychiatric research group investigating the effects of LSD upon the production of experiences resembling those of the mystics. His own conclusion, drawn from these experiments (which resembles James's mentioned above), has been that it is possible that some uses of this chemical may "remove certain habitual and normal inhibitions of the mind and senses enabling us to see things as they would appear to us if we were not so chronically repressed."[4] Again, however, another obvious possibility—one of which Watts is also well aware—is that such chemicals simply serve to impair the normal functioning of one's nervous system.

In any event, the long history mystical experience has enjoyed, especially as a persistent element of organized religion, may make it difficult to dismiss *all* such experiences as mere hallucinations or as simply products of a malfunctioning nervous system. Moreover, as the essays by James, Russell, and Watts jointly make evident, such an unqualified rejection of mystical experience would hardly do justice to the complexity of the practical as well as metaphysical questions raised by such experiences.

NOTES

1. William James, "Pragmatism's Conception of Truth," *Pragmatism* (New York: New American Library, 1965), p. 145.
2. James Bisset Pratt, *Can We Keep the Faith?* (New Haven: Yale University Press, 1941).
3. Alan Watts, "The New Alchemy," in *This Is It* (New York: Random House, 1960).
4. Ibid., pp. 144–145.

ISSUES

WILLIAM JAMES

THE AUTHORITY OF
MYSTICAL EXPERIENCE

One may say truly, I think, that personal religious experience has its root and centre in mystical states of consciousness; so for us, who in these lectures are treating personal experience as the exclusive subject of our study, such states of consciousness ought to form the vital chapter from which the other chapters get their light. Whether my treatment of mystical states will shed more light or darkness, I do not know, for my own constitution shuts me out from their enjoyment almost entirely, and I can speak of them only at second hand. But though forced to look upon the subject so externally, I will be as objective and receptive as I can; and I think I shall at least succeed in convincing you of the reality of the states in question, and of the paramount importance of their function.

First of all, then, I ask, What does the expression "mystical states of consciousness" mean? How do we part off mystical states from other states? . . .

1. *Ineffability.*—The handiest of the marks by which I classify a state of mind as mystical is negative. The subject of it immediately says that it defies expression, that no adequate report of its contents can be given in words. It follows from this that its quality must be directly experienced; it cannot be imparted or transferred to others. In this peculiarity mystical states are more like states of feeling than like states of intellect. No one can make clear to another who has never had a certain feeling, in what the quality or worth of it consists. One must have musical ears to know the value of a symphony; one must have been in love one's self to understand a lover's state of mind. Lacking the heart or ear, we cannot interpret the musician or the lover justly, and are even likely to consider him weakminded or absurd. The mystic finds that most of us accord to his experiences an equally incompetent treatment.

2. *Noetic quality.*—Although so similar to states of feeling, mystical states seem to those who experience them to be also states of knowledge. They are states of insight into depths of truth unplumbed by the discursive intellect. They are illuminations, revelations, full of significance and importance, all inarticulate though they remain; and as a rule they carry with them a curious sense of authority for aftertime.

SOURCE: William James, *The Varieties of Religious Experience*, pp. 370–371, 378–379, 389–393, 397–398, 403–405, 407, 410, 413–415, 417–420.

These two characters will entitle any state to be called mystical, in the sense in which I use the word. . . .

Nitrous oxide and ether, especially nitrous oxide, when sufficiently diluted with air, stimulate the mystical consciousness in an extraordinary degree. Depth beyond depth of truth seems revealed to the inhaler. This truth fades out, however, or escapes, at the moment of coming to; and if any words remain over in which it seemed to clothe itself, they prove to be the veriest nonsense. Nevertheless, the sense of a profound meaning having been there persists; and I know more than one person who is persuaded that in the nitrous oxide trance we have a genuine metaphysical revelation.

Some years ago I myself made some observations on this aspect of nitrous oxide intoxication, and reported them in print. One conclusion was forced upon my mind at that time, and my impression of its truth has ever since remained unshaken. It is that our normal waking consciousness, rational consciousness as we call it, is but one special type of consciousness, whilst all about it, parted from it by the filmiest of screens, there lie potential forms of consciousness entirely different. We may go through life without suspecting their existence; but apply the requisite stimulus, and at a touch they are there in all their completeness, definite types of mentality which probably somewhere have their field of application and adaptation. No account of the universe in its totality can be final which leaves these other forms of consciousness quite disregarded. How to regard them is the question—for they are so discontinuous with ordinary consciousness. Yet they may determine attitudes though they cannot furnish formulas, and open a region though they fail to give a map. At any rate, they forbid a premature closing of our accounts with reality. Looking back on my own experiences, they all converge towards a kind of insight to which I cannot help ascribing some metaphysical significance. The keynote of it is invariably a reconciliation. It is as if the opposites of the world, whose contradictoriness and conflict make all our difficulties and troubles, were melted into unity. Not only do they, as contrasted species, belong to one and the same genus, but *one of the species,* the nobler and better one, *is itself the genus, and so soaks up and absorbs its opposite into itself.* This is a dark saying, I know, when thus expressed in terms of common logic, but I cannot wholly escape from its authority. . . .

Even the least mystical of you must by this time be convinced of the existence of mystical moments as states of consciousness of an entirely specific quality, and of the deep impression which they make on those who have them. A Canadian psychiatrist, Dr. R. M. Bucke, gives to the more distinctly characterized of these phenomena the name of cosmic consciousness. "Cosmic consciousness in its more striking instances is not," Dr. Bucke says, "simply an expansion or extension of the self-conscious mind with which we are all familiar, but the superaddition of a function as distinct from any possessed by the average man as *self*-consciousness is distinct from any function possessed by one of the higher animals."

The prime characteristic of cosmic consciousness is a consciousness of the cosmos, that is, of the life and order of the universe. Along with the consciousness of the cosmos there occurs an intellectual enlightenment which alone would place the individual on a new plane of existence—would make him almost a member of a new species. To this is added a state of moral exaltation, an indescribable feeling of elevation, elation, and joyousness, and a quickening of the moral sense, which is fully as striking, and more important than is the enhanced intellectual power. With these come what may be called a sense of immortality, a consciousness of eternal life, not a conviction that he shall have this, but the consciousness that he has it already.

We have now seen enough of this cosmic or mystic consciousness, as it comes sporadically. We must next pass to its methodical cultivation as an element of the religious life. Hindus, Buddhists, Mohammedans, and Christians all have cultivated it methodically.

In India, training in mystical insight has been known from time immemorial under the name of yoga. Yoga means the experimental union of the individual with the divine. It is based on persevering exercise; and the diet, posture, breathing, intellectual concentration, and moral discipline vary slightly in the different systems which teach it. The yogi, or disciple, who has by these means overcome the obscurations of his lower nature sufficiently, enters into the condition termed *samâdhi*, "and comes face to face with facts which no instinct or reason can ever know." . . .

The Buddhists used the word "samâdhi " as well as the Hindus; but "dhyâna" is their special word for higher states of contemplation. There seem to be four stages recognized in dhyâna. The first stage comes through concentration of the mind upon one point. It excludes desire, but not discernment or judgment: it is still intellectual. In the second stage the intellectual functions drop off, and the satisfied sense of unity remains. In the third stage the satisfaction departs, and indifference begins, along with memory and self-consciousness. In the fourth stage the indifference, memory, and self-consciousness are perfected. [Just what "memory" and "self-consciousness" mean in this connection is doubtful. They cannot be the faculties familiar to us in the lower life.] Higher stages still of contemplation are mentioned—a region where there exists nothing, and where the mediator says: "There exists absolutely nothing," and stops. Then he reaches another region where he says: "There are neither ideas nor absence of ideas," and stops again. Then another region where, "having reached the end of both idea and perception, he stops finally." This would seem to be, not yet Nirvâna, but as close an approach to it as this life affords. . . .

In the Christian church there have always been mystics. Although many of them have been viewed with suspicion, some have gained favor in the eyes of the authorities. The experiences of these have been treated as precedents, and a codified system of mystical theology has been based upon them, in which everything legitimate finds its place. The basis of the system is "orison" or meditation, the methodical elevation of the soul towards God. . . .

The first thing to be aimed at in orison is the mind's detachment from outer sensations, for these interfere with its concentration upon ideal things. Such manuals as Saint Ignatius's Spiritual Exercises recommend the disciple to expel sensation by a graduated series of efforts to imagine holy scenes. The acme of this kind of discipline would be a semi-hallucinatory mono-ideism—an imaginary figure of Christ, for example, coming fully to occupy the mind. Sensorial images of this sort, whether literal or symbolic, play an enormous part in mysticism. But in certain cases imagery may fall away entirely, and in the very highest raptures it tends to do so. The state of consciousness becomes then insusceptible of any verbal description. . . .

The deliciousness of some of these states seems to be beyond anything known in ordinary consciousness. It evidently involves organic sensibilities, for it is spoken of as something too extreme to be borne, and as verging on bodily pain. But it is too subtle and piercing a delight for ordinary words to denote. . . .

To the medical mind these ecstasies signify nothing but suggested and imitated hypnoid states, on an intellectual basis of superstition, and a corporeal one of degeneration and hysteria. Undoubtedly these pathological conditions have existed in many and possibly in all the cases, but that fact tells us nothing about the value for knowledge of the consciousness which they induce. To pass a spiritual judgment upon these states, we must not content ourselves with superficial medical talk, but inquire into their fruits for life.

Their fruits appear to have been various. Stupefaction, for one thing, seems not to have been altogether absent as a result. You may remember the helplessness in the kitchen and schoolroom of poor Margaret Mary Alacoque. Many other ecstatics would have perished but for the care taken of them by admiring followers. The "other-worldliness" encouraged by the mystical consciousness makes this over-abstraction from practical life peculiarly liable to befall mystics in whom the character is naturally passive and the intellect feeble; but in natively strong minds and characters we find quite opposite results. The great Spanish mystics, who carried the habit of ecstacy as far as it has often been carried, appear for the most part to have shown indomitable spirit and energy, and all the more so for the trances in which they indulged.

Saint Ignatius was a mystic, but his mysticism made him assuredly one of the most powerfully practical human engines that ever lived. Saint John of the Cross, writing of the intuitions and "touches" by which God reaches the substance of the soul, tells us that—

> They enrich it marvelously. A single one of them may be sufficient to abolish at a stroke certain imperfections of which the soul during its whole life had vainly tried to rid itself, and to leave it adorned with virtues and loaded with supernatural gifts. A single one of these intoxicating consolations may reward it for all the labors undergone in its life—even were they numberless. Invested with an invincible courage, filled with an impassioned desire to suffer for its God, the soul then is seized with a strange torment—that of not being allowed to suffer enough.

In spite of their repudiation of articulate self-description, mystical states in general assert a pretty distinct theoretic drift. It is possible to give the outcome of the majority of them in terms that point in definite philosophical directions. One of these directions is optimism, and the other is monism. We pass into mystical states from out of ordinary consciousness as from a less into a more, as from a smallness into a vastness, and at the same time as from an unrest to a rest. We feel them as reconciling, unifying states. They appeal to the yes-function more than to the no-function in us. . . .

. . . In mystic states we both become one with the Absolute and we become aware of our oneness. This is the everlasting and triumphant mystical tradition, hardly altered by differences of clime or creed. In Hinduism, in Neoplatonism, in Sufism, in Christian mysticism, in Whitmanism, we find the same recurring note, so that there is about mystical utterances an eternal unanimity which ought to make a critic stop and think, and which brings it about that the mystical classics have, as has been said, neither birthday nor native land. Perpetually telling of the unity of man with God, their speech antedates languages, and they do not grow old. . . .

I have now sketched with extreme brevity and insufficiency, but as fairly as I am able in the time allowed, the general traits of the mystic range of consciousness. *It is on the whole pantheistic and optimistic, or at least the opposite of pessimistic. It is anti-naturalistic, and harmonizes best with twice-bornness and so-called other-worldly states of mind.*

My next task is to inquire whether we can invoke it as authoritative. Does it furnish any *warrant for the truth* of the twice-bornness and supernaturality and pantheism which it favors? I must give my answer to this question as concisely as I can.

In brief my answer is this—and I will divide it into three parts:—

(1) Mystical states, when well developed, usually are, and have the right to be, absolutely authoritative over the individuals to whom they come.

(2) No authority emanates from them which should make it a duty for those who stand outside of them to accept their revelations uncritically.

(3) They break down the authority of the non-mystical or rationalistic consciousness, based upon the understanding and the senses alone. They show it to be only one kind of consciousness. They open out the possibility of other orders of truth, in which, so far as anything in us vitally responds to them, we may freely continue to have faith.

I will take up these points one by one.

As a matter of psychological fact, mystical states of a well-pronounced and emphatic sort *are* usually authoritative over those who have them. They have been "there," and know. It is vain for rationalism to grumble about this. If the mystical truth that comes to a man proves to be a force that he can live by, what mandate have we of the majority to order him to live in another way? We can throw him into a prison or a madhouse, but we cannot change his mind—we commonly attach it only the more stubbornly to its beliefs. It mocks our utmost efforts, as a matter of fact, and in point of logic it absolutely escapes our jurisdiction. Our own more "rational" beliefs are based on evidence exactly similar in nature to that which mystics quote for theirs. Our senses, namely, have assured us of certain states of fact; but mystical experiences are as direct perceptions of fact for those who have them as any sensations ever were for us. The records show that even though the five senses be in abeyance in them, they are absolutely sensational in their epistemological quality, if I may be pardoned the barbarous expression—that is, they are face to face presentations of what seems immediately to exist.

The mystic is, in short, *invulnerable,* and must be left whether we relish it or not, in undisturbed enjoyment of his creed. Faith, says Tolstoy, is that by which men live. And faith-state and mystic-state are practically convertible terms.

But I now proceed to add that mystics have no right to claim that we ought to accept the deliverance of their peculiar experiences, if we are ourselves outsiders and feel no private call thereto. The utmost they can ever ask of us in this life is to admit that they establish a presumption. They form a consensus and have an unequivocal outcome; and it would be odd, mystics might say, if such a unanimous type of experience should prove to be altogether wrong. At bottom, however, this would only be an appeal to numbers, like the appeal of rationalism the other way; and the appeal to numbers has no logical force. If we acknowledge it, it is for "suggestive," not for logical, reasons: we follow the majority because to do so suits our life. . . .

So much for religious mysticism proper. But more remains to be told, for religious mysticism is only one half of mysticism. The other half has no accumulated traditions except those which the textbooks on insanity supply. Open any one of these, and you will find abundant cases in which "mystical ideas" are cited as characteristic symptoms of enfeebled or deluded states of mind. In delusional insanity, paranoia, as they sometimes call it, we may have a *diabolical* mysticism, a sort of religious mysticism turned upside down. The same sense of ineffable importance in the smallest events, the same texts and words coming with new meanings, the same voices and visions and leadings and missions, the same controlling by extraneous powers; only this time the emotion is pessimistic: instead of consolations we have desolations; the meanings are dreadful; and the powers are enemies to life. It is evident that from the point of view of their psychological mechanism, the classic mysticism and these lower mysticisms spring from the same mental level, from that great subliminal or transmarginal region of which science is beginning to admit the existence, but of which so little is really known. That region contains every kind of matter: "seraph and snake" abide there side by side. To come from thence is no infallible credential. What comes must be sifted and tested, and run the gauntlet of confrontation with the total context of experience, just like what comes from the outer world of sense. Its value must be ascertained by empirical methods, so long as we are not mystics ourselves.

Once more, then, I repeat that non-mystics are under no obligation to acknowledge in mystical states a superior authority conferred on them by their intrinsic nature.

Yet, I repeat once more, the existence of mystical states absolutely overthrows the pretension of non-mystical states to be the sole and ultimate dictators of what we may believe. As a rule, mystical states merely add a supersensuous meaning to the ordinary outward data of consciousness. They are excitements like the emotions of love or ambition, gifts to our spirit by means of which facts already objectively before us fall into a new expressiveness and make a new connection with our active life. They do not contradict these facts as such, or deny anything that our senses have immediately seized. It is the rationalistic critic rather who plays the part of denier in the controversy, and his denials have no strength, for there never can be a state of facts to which new meaning may not truthfully be added, provided the mind ascend to a more enveloping point of view. It must always remain an open question whether mystical states may not possibly be such superior points of view, windows through which the mind looks out upon a more extensive and inclusive world. The difference of the views seen from the different mystical windows need not prevent us from entertaining this supposition. The wider world would in that case prove to have a mixed constitution like that of this world, that is all. It would have its celestial and its infernal regions, its tempting and its saving moments, its valid experiences and its counterfeit ones, just as our world has them; but it would be a wider world all the same. We should have to use its experiences by selecting and subordinating and substituting just as is our custom in this ordinary naturalistic world; we should be liable to error just as we are now; yet the counting in of that wider world of meanings, and the serious dealing with it, might, in spite of all the perplexity, be indispensable stages in our approach to the final fullness of the truth.

In this shape, I think, we have to leave the subject. Mystical states indeed wield no authority due simply to their being mystical states. But the higher ones among them point in directions to which the religious sentiments even of non-mystical men incline. They tell of the supremacy of the ideal, of vastness, of union, of safety, and of rest. They offer us *hypotheses*, hypotheses which we may voluntarily ignore, but which as thinkers we cannot possibly upset. The supernaturalism and optimism to which they would persuade us may, interpreted in one way or another, be after all the truest of insights into the meaning of this life.

BERTRAND RUSSELL

MYSTICISM AS
METAPHYSICALLY MISTAKEN

Mystical philosophy, in all ages and in all parts of the world, is characterized by certain beliefs which are illustrated by the doctrines we have been considering.

There is, first, the belief in insight as against discursive analytic knowledge: the belief in a way of wisdom, sudden, penetrating, coercive, which is contrasted with the slow and fallible study of outward appearance by a science relying wholly upon the senses. . . .

The first and most direct outcome of the moment of illumination is belief in the possibility of a way of knowledge which may be called revelation or insight or intuition, as contrasted with sense, reason, and analysis, which are regarded as blind guides leading to the morass of illusion. Closely connected with this belief is the conception of a Reality behind the world of appearance and utterly different from it. This Reality is regarded with an admiration often amounting to worship; it is felt to be always and everywhere close at hand, thinly veiled by the shows of sense, ready, for the receptive mind, to shine in its glory even through the apparent folly and wickedness of Man. The poet, the artist, and the lover are seekers after that glory: the haunting beauty that they pursue is the faint reflection of its sun. But the mystic lives in the full light of the vision: what others dimly seek he knows, with a knowledge beside which all other knowledge is ignorance.

The second characteristic of mysticism is its belief in unity, and its refusal to admit opposition or division anywhere. We found Heraclitus saying "good and ill are one"; and again he says, "the way up and the way down is one and the same." The same attitude appears in the simultaneous assertion of contradictory propositions, such as: "We step and do not step into the same rivers; we are and are not." The assertion of Parmenides, that reality is one and indivisible, comes from the same impulse towards unity. In Plato, this impulse is less prominent, being held in check by his theory of ideas; but it reappears, so far as his logic permits, in the doctrine of the primacy of the Good.

A third mark of almost all mystical metaphysics is the denial of the reality of Time. This is an outcome of the denial of division; if all is one, the distinction of past and future must be illusory. . . .

The last of the doctrines of mysticism which we have to consider is its belief that all evil is mere appearance, an illusion produced by the divisions and oppositions of the analytic intellect. Mysticism does not maintain that such things

SOURCE: Bertrand Russell, *Mysticism and Logic* (New York: Barnes and Noble, 1971), pp. 14–17, 20–23, 26–27. Reprinted by permission of Barnes and Noble Books, Totowa, N.J.

as cruelty, for example, are good, but it denies that they are real: they belong to that lower world of phantoms from which we are to be liberated by the insight of the vision. Sometimes—for example in Hegel, and at least verbally in Spinoza—not only evil, but good also, is regarded as illusory, though nevertheless the emotional attitude towards what is held to be Reality is such as would naturally be associated with the belief that Reality is good. What is, in all cases, ethically characteristic of mysticism is absence of indignation or protest, acceptance with joy, disbelief in the ultimate truth of the division into two hostile camps, the good and the bad. This attitude is a direct outcome of the nature of the mystical experience: with its sense of unity is associated a feeling of infinite peace. Indeed it may be suspected that the feeling of peace produces, as feelings do in dreams, the whole system of associated beliefs which make up the body of mystic doctrine. But this is a difficult question, and one on which it cannot be hoped that mankind will reach agreement.

Four questions thus arise in considering the truth or falsehood of mysticism, namely:

I. Are there two ways of knowing, which may be called respectively reason and intuition? And if so, is either to be preferred to the other?
II. Is all plurality and division illusory?
III. Is time unreal?
IV. What kind of reality belongs to good and evil?

On all four of these questions, while fully developed mysticism seems to me mistaken, I yet believe that, by sufficient restraint, there is an element of wisdom to be learned from the mystical way of feeling, which does not seem to be attainable in any other manner. If this is the truth, mysticism is to be commended as an attitude towards life, not as a creed about the world. The metaphysical creed, I shall maintain, is a mistaken outcome of the emotion, although this emotion, as colouring and informing all other thoughts and feelings, is the inspirer of whatever is best in Man. . . .

I. REASON AND INTUITION

Of the reality or unreality of the mystic's world I know nothing. I have no wish to deny it, nor even to declare that the insight which reveals it is not a genuine insight. What I do wish to maintain—and it is here that the scientific attitude becomes imperative—is that insight, untested and unsupported, is an insufficient guarantee of truth, in spite of the fact that much of the most important truth is first suggested by its means. . . .

. . . Instinct, intuition or insight is what first leads to the beliefs which subsequent reason confirms or confutes; but the confirmation, where it is possible, consists, in the last analysis, of agreement with other beliefs no less instinctive. Reason is a harmonizing, controlling force rather than a creative one. Even in the most purely logical realm, it is insight that first arrives at what is new.

Where instinct and reason do sometimes conflict is in regard to single be-liefs, held instinctively, and held with such determination that no degree of in-consistency with other beliefs leads to their abandonment. Instinct, like all human faculties, is liable to error. Those in whom reason is weak are often un-willing to admit this as regards themselves, though all admit it in regard to oth-ers. Where instinct is least liable to error is in practical matters as to which right judgment is a help to survival: friendship and hostility in others, for instance, are often felt with extraordinary discrimination through very careful disguises. But even in such matters a wrong impression may be given by reserve or flat-tery; and in matters less directly practical, such as philosophy deals with, very strong instinctive beliefs are sometimes wholly mistaken, as we may come to know through their perceived inconsistency with other equally strong beliefs. It is such considerations that necessitate the harmonizing mediation of reason, which tests our beliefs by their mutual compatibility, and examines, in doubt-ful cases, the possible sources of error on the one side and on the other. In this there is no opposition to instinct as a whole, but only to blind reliance upon some one interesting aspect of instinct to the exclusion of other more common-place but not less trustworthy aspects. It is such one-sidedness, not instinct it-self, that reason aims at correcting.

In advocating the scientific restraint and balance, as against the self-assertion of a confident reliance upon intuition, we are only urging, in the sphere of knowledge, that largeness of contemplation, that impersonal disin-terestedness, and that freedom from practical preoccupations which have been inculcated by all the great religions of the world. Thus our conclusion, however it may conflict with the explicit beliefs of many mystics, is, in essence, not con-trary to the spirit which inspires those beliefs, but rather the outcome of this very spirit as applied in the realm of thought.

II. UNITY AND PLURALITY

One of the most convincing aspects of the mystic illumination is the apparent revelation of the oneness of all things, giving rise to pantheism in religion and to monism in philosophy. . . .

Belief in a reality quite different from what appears to the senses arises with irresistible force in certain moods, which are the source of most mysticism, and of most metaphysics. While such a mood is dominant, the need of logic is not felt, and accordingly the more thorough-going mystics do not employ logic, but appeal directly to the immediate deliverance of their insight. But such fully de-veloped mysticism is rare in the West. When the intensity of emotional convic-tion subsides, a man who is in the habit of reasoning will search for logical grounds in favour of the belief which he finds in himself. But since the belief al-ready exists, he will be very hospitable to any ground that suggests itself. The paradoxes apparently proved by his logic are really the paradoxes of mysticism, and are the goal which he feels his logic must reach if it is to be in accordance with insight. The resulting logic has rendered most philosophers incapable of giving any account of the world of science and daily life. If they had been anxious to give such an account, they would probably have discovered the errors of their logic; but most of them were less anxious to understand the world of science and daily life than to convict it of unreality in the interests of a supersensible 'real' world.

It is in this way that logic has been pursued by those of the great philosophers who were mystics. But since they usually took for granted the supposed insight of the mystic emotion, their logical doctrines were presented with a certain dryness, and were believed by their disciples to be quite independent of the sudden illumination from which they sprang. Nevertheless their origin clung to them, and they remained—to borrow a useful word from Mr. Santayana—'malicious' in regard to the world of science and common sense. It is only so that we can account for the complacency with which philosophers have accepted the inconsistency of their doctrines with all the common and scientific facts which seem best established and most worthy of belief.

The logic of mysticism shows, as is natural, the defects which are inherent in anything malicious. The impulse to logic, not felt while the mystic mood is dominant, reasserts itself as the mood fades, but with a desire to retain the vanishing insight, or at least to prove that it *was* insight, and that what seems to contradict it is illusion. The logic which thus arises is not quite disinterested or candid, and is inspired by a certain hatred of the daily world to which it is applied. Such an attitude naturally does not tend to the best results. Everyone knows that to read an author simply in order to refute him is not the way to understand him; and to read the book of Nature with a conviction that it is all illusion is just as unlikely to lead to understanding. If our logic is to find the common world intelligible, it must not be hostile, but must be inspired by a genuine acceptance such as is not usually to be found among metaphysicians.

III. TIME

. . . It is difficult to disentangle the truth and the error in this view. The arguments for the contention that time is unreal and that the world of sense is illusory must, I think, be regarded as fallacious. Nevertheless there is some sense—easier to feel than to state—in which time is an unimportant and superficial characteristic of reality. Past and future must be acknowledged to be as real as the present, and a certain emancipation from slavery to time is essential to philosophic thought. The importance of time is rather practical than theoretical, rather in relation to our desires than in relation to truth. A truer image of the world, I think, is obtained by picturing things as entering into the stream of time from an eternal world outside, than from a view which regards time as the devouring tyrant of all that is. Both in thought and in feeling, even though time be real, to realize the unimportance of time is the gate of wisdom.

That this is the case may be seen at once by asking ourselves why our feelings towards the past are so different from our feelings towards the future. The reason for this difference is wholly practical: our wishes can affect the future but not the past, the future is to some extent subject to our power, while the past is unalterably fixed. But every future will some day be past: if we see the past truly now, it must, when it was still future, have been just what we now see it to be, and what is now future must be just what we shall see it to be when it has become past. The felt difference of quality between past and future, therefore, is not an intrinsic difference, but only a difference in relation to us: to impartial contemplation, it ceases to exist. And impartiality of contemplation is, in the intellectual sphere, that very same virtue of disinterestedness which, in the sphere of action, appears as justice and unselfishness. Whoever wishes to see the world truly, to rise in thought above the tyranny of practical desires, must learn to overcome the difference of attitude towards past and future, and to survey the whole stream of time in one comprehensive vision.

IV. GOOD AND EVIL

Mysticism maintains that all evil is illusory, and sometimes maintains the same view as regards good, but more often holds that all Reality is good. . . .

It is difficult to give a logically tenable account of this position without recognizing that good and evil are subjective, that what is good is merely that towards which we have one kind of feeling, and what is evil is merely that towards which we have another kind of feeling. In our active life, where we have to exercise choice, and to prefer this to that of two possible acts, it is necessary to have a distinction of good and evil, or at least of better and worse. But this distinction, like everything pertaining to action, belongs to what mysticism regards as the world of illusion, if only because it is essentially concerned with time. In our contemplative life, where action is not called for, it is possible to be impartial, and to overcome the ethical dualism which action requires. So long as we remain *merely* impartial, we may be content to say that both the good and the evil of action are illusions. But if, as we must do if we have the mystic vision, we find the whole world worthy of love and worship, if we see

> The earth, and every common sight . . .
> Apparell'd in celestial light,

we shall say that there is a higher good than that of action, and that this higher good belongs to the whole world as it is in reality. In this way the twofold attitude and the apparent vacillation of mysticism are explained and justified.

The possibility of this universal love and joy in all that exists is of supreme importance for the conduct and happiness of life, and gives inestimable value to the mystic emotion, apart from any creeds which may be built upon it. But if we are not to be led into false beliefs, it is necessary to realize exactly *what* the mystic emotion reveals. It reveals a possibility of human nature—a possibility of a nobler, happier, freer life than any that can be otherwise achieved. But it does not reveal anything about the nonhuman, or about the nature of the universe in general. Good and bad, and even the higher good that mysticism finds everywhere, are the reflections of our own emotions on other things, not part of the substance of things as they are in themselves. And therefore an impartial contemplation, freed from all preoccupations with Self, will not judge things good or bad, although it is very easily combined with that feeling of universal love which leads the mystic to say that the whole world is good. . . .

PRACTICE

ALAN W. WATTS

THE PHILOSOPHER AS MYSTIC: EXPERIENCING AND INTERPRETING COSMIC CONSCIOUSNESS

The most impressive fact in man's spiritual, intellectual, and poetic experience has always been, for me, the universal prevalence of those astonishing moments of insight which Richard Bucke called "cosmic consciousness." . . . [F]rom all historical times and cultures we have reports of this same unmistakable sensation emerging, as a rule, quite suddenly and unexpectedly and from no clearly understood cause.

The central core of the experience seems to be the conviction, or insight, that the immediate *now*, whatever its nature, is the goal and fulfillment of all living. Surrounding and flowing from this insight is an emotional ecstasy, a sense of intense relief, freedom, and lightness, and often of almost unbearable love for the world, which is, however, secondary. Often, the pleasure of the experience is confused with the experience and the insight lost in the ecstasy, so that in trying to retain the secondary effects of the experience the individual misses its point—that the immediate *now* is complete even when it is not ecstatic. For ecstasy is a necessarily impermanent contrast in the constant fluctuation of our feelings. But insight, when clear enough, persists; having once understood a particular skill, the facility tends to remain.

The terms in which a man interprets this experience are naturally drawn from the religious and philosophical ideas of his culture, and their differences often conceal its basic identity. . . . To a theist this will naturally seem to be a glimpse of the presence of God . . . and to a Buddhist this will just as naturally

SOURCE: Alan W. Watts, *This Is it and Other Essays on Zen and Spiritual Experience* (New York: Pantheon, 1958). Copyright © 1958, 1960 by Alan W. Watts. Reprinted by permission of Pantheon books, a Division of Random House, Inc.

Alan W. Watts (1915–1973) was born in Chislehurst, England, and received his education at King's School, Canterbury. He spent a lively career as a writer, teacher, lecturer, and broadcaster on philosophical issues of comparative religion and psychology. He is well-noted for his interpretations of Buddhist thought and for the popularization of Eastern religious thought in America. Among his many books are *The Way of Zen* and *This Is It*.

call to mind the doctrine of reality as the ungraspable, indefinable Void (*sunyata*). . . .

Rarely is the experience described without metaphors that might be misleading if taken literally. But in reading Bernard Berenson's *Sketch for a Self-Portrait* I came across a passage which is one of the simplest and "cleanest" accounts of it I have ever seen.

> It was a morning in early summer. A silver haze shimmered and trembled over the lime trees. The air was laden with their fragrance. The temperature was like a caress. I remember—I need not recall—that I climbed up a tree stump and felt suddenly immersed in Itness. I did not call it by that name. I had no need for words. It and I were one.

Just "It"—as when we use the word to denote the superlative, or the exact point, or intense reality, or what we were always looking for. Not the neuter sense of the mere object, but something still more alive and far wider than the personal, and for which we use this simplest of words because we have no word for it. . . .

. . . The experience has a tendency to arise in situations of total extremity or despair, when the individual finds himself without any alternative but to surrender himself entirely.

Something of this kind came to me in a dream when I was about eight years old. I was sick at the time and almost delirious with fever, and in the dream I found myself attached face-downward and spread-eagled to an immense ball of steel which was spinning about the earth. I knew in this dream with complete certainty that I was doomed to be spun in this sickening and terrifying whirl forever and ever, and the conviction was so intense that there was nothing for it but to give up—for this was hell itself and nothing lay before me but a literal everlastingness of pain. But in the moment when I surrendered, the ball seemed to strike against a mountain and disintegrate, and the next thing I knew was that I was sitting on a stretch of warm sand with nothing left of the ball except crumpled fragments of sheet-metal scattered around me. This was not, of course, the experience of "cosmic consciousness," but simply of the fact that release in extremity lies through and not away from the problem.

That other experience came much later, twice with intensity, and other times with what might be called more of a glow than a brilliant flash. Shortly after I had first begun to study Indian and Chinese philosophy, I was sitting one night by the fire, trying to make out what was the right attitude of mind for meditation as it is practiced in Hindu and Buddhist disciplines. It seemed to me that several attitudes were possible, but as they appeared mutually exclusive and contradictory I was trying to fit them into one—all to no purpose. Finally, in sheer disgust, I decided to reject them all and to have no special attitude of mind whatsoever. In the force of throwing them away it seemed that I threw myself away as well, for quite suddenly the weight of my own body disappeared. I felt that I owned nothing, not even a self, and that nothing owned me. The whole world became as transparent and unobstructed as my own mind; the "problem of life" simply ceased to exist, and for about eighteen hours I and everything around me felt like the wind blowing leaves across a field on an autumn day.

The second time, a few years later, came after a period when I had been attempting to practice what Buddhists call "recollection" (*smriti*) or constant awareness of the immediate present, as distinct from the usual distracted rambling of reminiscence and anticipation. But, in discussing it one evening, someone said to me, "But why *try* to live in the present? Surely we are always completely *in* the present even when we're thinking about the past or the future?" This, actually quite obvious, remark again brought on the sudden sensation of having no weight. At the same time, the present seemed to become a kind of moving stillness, an eternal stream from which neither I nor anything could deviate. I saw that everything, just as it is now, is IT—is the whole point of there being life and a universe. I saw that when the *Upanishads* said, "That art thou!" or "All this world is Brahman," they meant just exactly what they said. Each thing, each event, each experience in its inescapable nowness and in all its own particular individuality was precisely what it should be, and so much so that it acquired a divine authority and originality. It struck me with the fullest clarity that none of this depended on my seeing it to be so; that was the way things were, whether I understood it or not, and if I did not understand, that was IT too. Furthermore, I felt that I now understood what Christianity might mean by the love of God—namely, that despite the commonsensical imperfection of things, they were nonetheless loved by God just as they are, and that this loving of them was at the same time the godding of them. This time the vivid sensation of lightness and clarity lasted a full week.

These experiences, reinforced by others that have followed, have been the enlivening force of all my work in writing and in philosophy since that time, though I have come to realize that how I *feel,* whether the actual sensation of freedom and clarity is present or not, is not the point—for, again, to feel heavy or restricted is also IT. But with this point of departure a philosopher is faced with a strange problem of communication, especially to the degree that his philosophy seems to have some affinity with religion. People appear to be under the fixed impression that one speaks or writes of these things in order to improve them or do them some good, assuming, too, that the speaker has himself been improved and is able to speak with authority. In other words, the philosopher is forced into the role of preacher, and is in turn expected to practice what he preaches. . . .

In the span of one lifetime it is, of course, possible for almost every human being to improve himself—within limits set by energy, time, temperament, and the level from which he begins. Obviously, then, there is a proper place for preachers and other technical advisers in the disciplines of human betterment. But the limits within which such improvements may be made are small in comparison with the vast aspects of our nature and our circumstances which remain the same, and which will be very difficult to improve even were it desirable to do so. I am saying, therefore, that while there is a place for bettering oneself and others, solving problems and coping with situations is by no means the only or even the chief business of life. Nor is it the principal work of philosophy.

Human purposes are pursued within an immense circling universe which does not seem to me to have purpose, in our sense, at all. Nature is much more playful than purposeful, and the probability that it has no special goals for the future need not strike one as a defect. On the contrary, the processes of nature as we see them both in the surrounding world and in the involuntary aspects of our own organisms are much more like art than like business, politics, or religion. They are especially like the arts of music and dancing, which unfold themselves without aiming at future destinations. No one imagines that a symphony is supposed to improve in quality as it goes along, or that the whole object of playing it is to reach the finale. The point of music is discovered in every moment of playing and listening to it. It is the same, I feel, with the greater part of our lives, and if we are unduly absorbed in improving them we may forget altogether to live them. The musician whose chief concern is to make every performance better than the last may so fail to participate and delight in his own music that he will impress his audience only with the anxious rigor of his technique.

Thus it is by no means the main work of a philosopher to be classed with the moralists and reformers. There is such a thing as philosophy, the love of wisdom, in the spirit of the artist. Such philosophy will not preach or advocate practices leading to improvement. As I understand it, the work of the philoso-pher as artist is to reveal and celebrate the eternal and purposeless background of human life. Out of simple exuberance or wonder he wants to tell others of the point of view from which the world is unimaginably good as it is, with people just as they are. . . .

This may sound like a purpose, like a desire to improve, to those who in-sist upon seeing all human activity in terms of goal-seeking. The trouble is that our Western common sense is firmly Aristotelian, and we therefore believe that the will never acts except for some good or pleasure. But upon analysis this turns out to say no more than that we do what we do, for if we always do what pleases us—even in committing suicide—there is no means of showing what pleases us apart from what we do. In using such logic I am only throw-ing a stone back to the glass house from which it came, for I am well aware that expressions of mystical experience will not stand the test of logic. But, un-like the Aristotelian, the mystic does not claim to be logical. His sphere of ex-perience is the unspeakable. Yet this need mean no more than that it is the sphere of physical nature, of all that is not simply conceptions, numbers, or words.

If the experience of "cosmic consciousness" is unspeakable, it is true that in trying to utter it in words one is not "saying" anything in the sense of con-veying information or making a proposition. The speech expressing such an ex-perience is more like an exclamation. Or better, it is the speech of poetry rather than logic, though not poetry in the impoverished sense of the logical positivist, the sense of decorative and beautiful nonsense.

. . . It is nothing "spiritual" in the usual sense of abstract or ideational. It is concretely physical, yet for this very reason ineffable (or unspeakable) and indefinable. "Cosmic" consciousness is a release from self-consciousness, that is to say from the fixed belief and feeling that one's organism is an absolute and separate thing, as distinct from a convenient unit of perception. For if it be-comes clear that our use of the lines and surfaces of nature to divide the world into units is only a matter of convenience, then all that I have called myself is actually inseparable from everything. This is exactly what one experiences in these extraordinary moments. It is not that the outlines and shapes which we *call* things and use to delineate things disappear into some sort of luminous void. It simply becomes obvious that though they may be used as divisions they do not really divide. However much I may be impressed by the difference be-tween a star and the dark space around it, I must not forget that I can see the two only in relation to each other, and that this relation is inseparable.

The most astonishing feature of this experience is, however, the conviction that this entire unspeakable world is "right," so right that our normal anxieties become ludicrous, that if only men could see it they would go wild with joy. . . .

. . . For the experience makes it perfectly clear that the whole universe is through and through the playing of love in every shade of the word's use, from animal lust to divine charity. Somehow this includes even the holocaust of the biological world, where every creature lives by feeding on others. Our usual picture of this world is reversed so that every victim is seen as offering itself in sacrifice.

If we are to ask whether this vision is true, we may first answer that there are no such things as truths by themselves: a truth is always in relation to a point of view. Fire is hot in relation to skin. The structure of the world appears as it does in relation to our organs of sense and our brains. Therefore certain alterations in the human organism may turn it into the sort of percipient for which the world *is* as it is seen in this vision. But, in the same way, other alterations will give us the truth of the world as it appears to the schizophrenic, or to the mind in black depression.

There is, however, a possible argument for the superior truth of the "cosmic" experience. Its basis is simply that no energy system can be completely self-controlling without ceasing to move. Control is restraint upon movement, and because complete control would be complete restraint, control must always be subordinate to motion if there is to be motion at all. In human terms, total restraint of movement is the equivalent of total doubt, of refusal to trust one's senses or feelings in any respect, and perhaps its embodiment is the extreme catatonic who refuses every motion or communication. On the other hand, movement and the release of restraint are the equivalent of faith, of committing oneself to the uncontrolled and unknown. In an extreme form this would mean the abandonment of oneself to utter caprice, and at first sight a life of such indiscriminate faith might seem to correspond to a vision of the world in which "everything is right." Yet this point of view would exclude all control as wrong, and thus there would be no place in it for the rightness of restraint. An essential part of the "cosmic" experience is, however, that the normal restriction of consciousness to the ego-feeling is also right, but only and always because it is subordinate to absence of restriction, to movement and faith.

The point is simply that, if there is to be any life and movement at all, the attitude of faith must be basic—the final and fundamental attitude—and the attitude of doubt secondary and subordinate. This is another way of saying that toward the vast and all-encompassing background of human life, with which the philosopher as artist is concerned, there must be total affirmation and acceptance. Otherwise there is no basis at all for caution and control with respect to details in the foreground. But it is all too easy to become so absorbed in these details that all sense of proportion is lost, and for man to make himself mad by trying to bring everything under his control. We become insane, unsound, and without foundation when we lose consciousness of and faith in the uncontrolled and ungraspable background world which is ultimately what we ourselves are. And there is a very slight distinction, if any, between complete, conscious faith and love.

DISCUSSION QUESTIONS

1. What two characteristics of mystical experience does James use to distinguish it from other experiences? Do you think his criteria are adequate? Defend your answer.

2. What, according to Russell, is the main problem with the mystic's reliance upon intuition or instinct?

3. How does the mystic view the concept of time? What is Russell's criticism of the mystic?

4. How does the mystic view such notions as division and opposition or contradictoriness? What logical mistake does the mystic make, according to Russell?

5. How does the mystic view the concept of evil? What is Russell's criticism of the mystic's position?

6. What similarities, if any, do you think exist between Buber's *I-Thou* relation (as discussed in the previous chapter) and mystical experience? What differences, if any, do you think exist?

7. Compare Plato's view of ultimate reality with that characterized through mystical experience.

8. In your estimation, is the Christian belief in heaven and hell consistent with the mystic's view of reality as unity? Is the Christian distinction between God and his created universe consistent with the mystic's view of reality as unity? Defend your answers.

9. According to James, is the mystic justified in believing in the "truth" or "authority" of his or her own mystical experiences? Do you agree with James's reasoning? Defend your answer.

10. Compare Watts's response to the question of whether mystical experiences are "true" to that provided by James.

11. What, according to Watts, is the proper role of a philosopher like himself who has had "cosmic consciousness"? Do you agree with Watts? Defend your answer.

12. What significance, if any, do you attach to the fact that Watts's mystical experiences, as discussed in his article, arose in situations of complete "surrender"?

13. Why does Watts think "cosmic" experience is "unspeakable"?

14. Do you think that experiences like that of Watts ever provide genuine insights? Under what conditions would you be convinced about the veracity of such experience? Defend your answer.

15. In your own life, have you ever had an experience which you would be inclined to characterize as communion with God? If so, what similarities and/or differences did it bear to those experiences discussed by Watts? Has this experience(s) had any *practical* significance for your life? If you have *not* ever had any such experience, has this lack of direct encounter with the divine had any bearing upon your religious attitude? Explain your answer.

GLOSSARY

aesthetics The area of philosophy which studies the nature and value of art.

androgyny A social state in which gender distinctions such as between male and female roles, personality traits, modes of dress, and the like are not recognized.

a posteriori Pertains to knowledge or reasoning that is dependent upon experience; in contrast to that which is *a priori*.

a priori Pertains to knowledge or reasoning that is independent of experience.

argument In logic, a group of statements one of which, called the conclusion, is held to follow from, and to be justified by, the others, called the premises.

Artificial Intelligence (AI) A branch of computer science that investigates and devises methods for building expert systems such as information retrieval systems and natural language processors, and simulating human intelligence.

autonomy The state of being self-determining or of possessing the right of self-determination.

axiology The area of philosophy dealing with the general theory of value.

behaviorism, metaphysical A form of materialism according to which the human mind has no existence apart from human behavior and is in fact definable in terms of the latter.

behaviorism, methodological A methodological approach to psychology which limits the primary data of psychology to human behavior.

capitalism An economic system characterized by private ownership of property and free enterprise; in contrast to *communism*.

categorical imperative For Kant, the ultimate standard of morality. In one formulation it requires that we act only in ways that any rational being could consistently accept as universally binding. In another formulation it requires that we treat humanity as an end in itself and never as a mere means. In still another formulation it requires that we rationally and autonomously (freely) choose the universal laws that prescribe our actions.

categorical proposition In logic, a statement that asserts or denies a relation between two classes or terms; as, for instance, in the statements "All humans are mortal" (universal affirmative), "No humans are mortal" (universal negative), "Some humans are mortal" (particular affirmative), "Some humans are not mortal" (particular negative).

coherence theory of truth The theory of truth which holds a belief to be true (false) if, and only if, it coheres (does not cohere) with other beliefs in a coherent system of beliefs.

communism   As advanced by Marx and Engels, the economic theory taking as its central thesis the abolition of private property as a response to bourgeoise exploitation of the working class inherent in a capitalist economy.

compound statement   In logic, a statement composed of other statements as, for instance, in the cases of conjunctions, disjunctions, and hypothetical statements.

congruence   The condition exhibited when the counselor acts in accordance with his or her own feelings and attitudes and does not hide behind a professional facade.

conjunction   In logic, a statement having the form "p and q."

contradictories   In logic, two statements such that both cannot be true and both cannot be false.

contraries   In logic, two statements such that both cannot be true but both can be false.

correspondence theory of truth   The theory of truth which holds a belief to be true (false) if, and only if, it corresponds (does not correspond) to objective reality or fact.

cosmic consciousness   The name given to certain mystical experiences by the Canadian psychiatrist R. M. Bucke, the prime characterization of which is a consciousness of "the life and order of the universe." See also *mysticism.*

deductive argument   A logical argument whose conclusion follows *necessarily* from its premises; that is, it is impossible that all of its premises are true and its conclusion is false; in contrast to *inductive argument.*

democracy   A form of government in which the ultimate power is vested (directly or indirectly) in the people; which, as defended by Locke, consists in rule by the majority.

determinism   The thesis which holds that every event in the universe, including all human behavior, is entirely explainable and predictable according to causal laws; in contrast to *existentialism.*

deterrence theory of punishment   A utilitarian theory of punishment according to which the punishment of an offender is justified according to its tendency to deter others (general deterrence) as well as the offender himself or herself (particular deterrence) from committing the same offense in the future.

dictatorship   As defended by Hobbes, a form of government in which absolute power of government is vested in one man or in an assembly of men.

disjunction   In logic, a statement having the form "p or q."

doubt, methodic   As employed by Descartes, the systematic doubting of anything that can be doubted for purposes of finding something which cannot be doubted.

dualism, mind-body   The view that mind and body are two distinct items; in contrast to *mind-body monism.*

ego state   According to Berne, any one of three conditions of mind in which a person may operate at any given time. The ego states are known as the Parent, the Adult, and the Child.

empathy   As characterized by Rogers, the therapist's understanding of the client's feelings as if those feelings were his or her own without ever losing the "as if" quality.

epiphenomenalism   The view that mental phenomena are causally powerless byproducts of bodily processes and that, therefore, all changes in the universe can have only physical explanations.

epistemology   The area of philosophy which studies the nature, sources, scope, and validity of knowledge.

empiricism   The view that all of our (meaningful) ideas are ultimately derived from experience.

essence   The purpose or function of a

thing which uniquely defines it; that without which it would not be what it is.

ethical theory A theory which sets forth and defends some general principle(s) or standard(s) for distinguishing between morally right and wrong conduct; for instance, utilitarianism and Kantian ethics. Also, the area of philosophy that studies such theories.

ethics The study of morality, which can be divided into the anthropological study of morality (descriptive ethics) and the philosophical study of morality (philosophical ethics).

ethics, care A form of philosophical ethics that emphasizes the importance of concrete interpersonal relationships and the care of persons by and for persons.

ethics, Kantian The philosophical ethics of Immanuel Kant which proposes that we act according to a rational principle (or set of principles) of human conduct called the *categorical imperative*.

ethics, rule A form of philosophical ethics that formulates and defends certain rules or standards of moral conduct, for example, (*rule* or *act*) *utilitarianism* and *Kantian ethics*.

ethics, virtue A form of philosophical ethics that emphasizes the development of moral character. Compare *rule ethics*.

existentialism As defended by Sartre, the view that emphasizes human beings' freedom, responsibility, and authenticity in confronting human choices and in defining the meanings and purposes in life through concrete actions; in contrast to *determinism*.

hedonism The theory of value incorporated by Bentham into his utilitarianism according to which the only item having intrinsic value is pleasure, whereas the only item having intrinsic *dis*value is pain.

hypothesis A tentative or provisional explanation of a set of facts, which is

more or less probable in relation to those facts.

hypothetical statement In logic, a conditional statement, that is, one having the form "If p then q."

idealism, epistemological The view held by Berkeley according to which physical objects have no existence apart from their being perceived.

identity theory A form of materialism according to which mental states are identical with, one and the same thing as, brain states.

inductive argument A logical argument such that, if all of its premises are true, then its conclusion is *probably*, although not necessarily, true; in contrast to *deductive argument*.

interactionist theory As defended by Descartes, a theory of the mind-body relation according to which minds and bodies are two distinct entities that causally interact with each other. Also called *Cartesian dualism*.

logic The area of philosophy which studies rules and methods for distinguishing correct logical arguments from incorrect ones.

logical positivism As held by Ayer, the view that a proposition is factually significant if, and only if, it is, at least in principle, empirically verifiable. See also *verifiability*.

materialism The view that the only reality is matter, to which all else, including mind, is reducible.

metaphysics The general area of philosophy concerned with the nature of reality.

monism, mind-body The view that there is just one substance, either mind or body, to which the other is reducible. Materialism and epistemological idealism are monistic theories, in contrast to *mind-body dualism*.

mysticism A philosophical outlook characterized by belief in the possibility of direct, nondiscursive experience of cosmic reality; and in its unity, timelessness, and goodness as revealed through such consciousness. See also *cosmic consciousness*.

operational definition A definition in terms of observable behavior or conditions. For example, according to Herbert Simon, the term "intuition" is to be defined as "rapid solution and inability to report a sequence of steps leading up to the solution" rather than in terms of the language of subjective mental state or processes. See also *behaviorism, methodological,* and *pragmatism.*

pantheism The view that God and the universe are one and the same thing. According to William James, the range of mystical experience or cosmic consciousness can be characterized as pantheistic.

parallelism The view that mental and physical states form two causally independent series of events which nevertheless occur in harmony with one another.

particular affirmative statement In logic, a statement of the form "Some S is P."

particular negative statement In logic, a statement of the form "Some S is not P."

person-centered therapy A counseling modality characterized by a nondirective facilitator who possesses and exhibits certain qualities, especially those of congruence, unconditional positive regard, and empathy.

philosophy, applied Philosophy that addresses practical problems.

philosophy, pure Philosophy that addresses intellectual problems.

Platonic forms According to Plato, extrasensible, eternal, and immutable realities which provide objective standards of knowledge and truth.

pragmatism An American school of philosophy founded by Charles Pierce that views the truth (or falsity) of any idea in terms of the concrete difference it will or can make in anyone's actual life. According to William James, a ma-

jor exponent of pragmatism, a true idea is "true because it is useful" or "it is useful because it is true."

primary qualities According to Locke, properties of objects such as extension, figure, number, and motion which are inherent in the objects themselves. In contrast to *secondary qualities*.

Rational-Emotive Behavior Therapy A directive and cognitive approach to counseling incorporating elements of behaviorism, and based on the premise that change can be accomplished by identifying and challenging a client's irrational beliefs.

rationalism The view that human reason, as distinct from sense perception, is itself a significant source of human knowledge.

relativism The view that there are no absolute standards of truth; that such standards instead vary according to different times, cultures, or individual circumstances. As applied to moral standards, this view is called *ethical relativism*.

retributive theory of punishment The theory of punishment according to which a punishment is justified if, and only if, it is equal or approximately equal in magnitude to the wrong perpetrated by the offender; in contrast to the *deterrence theory of punishment*.

right, instrumental A right justified on grounds of social utility. The sort of right defended by utilitarians such as Mill.

right, intrinsic A right attaching to a person *qua* person irrespective of any considerations of utility or disutility, and which cannot be overridden by any such considerations. The sort of right defended by Kant.

secondary qualities According to Locke, properties which are nothing in the objects themselves but powers to produce certain sensations in us by means of their primary qualities; for instance, colors, sounds, tastes, and the like. In contrast to *primary qualities*.

solipsism   The view that the only things which can be known are one's own existence and one's own mental states.

square of opposition   In Aristotle's logic, a diagram for representing the logical relations between the four standard-form categorical propositions.

state of nature   As employed by Hobbes, Locke, and other social contract theorists, the condition of humanity without government or civil society.

stroke   A term used in Transactional Analysis which, according to Berne, can be defined as a verbal or nonverbal action "implying recognition of another's presence."

syllogism   A deductive argument having two premises and a conclusion.

tautology   In logic, a statement that is true by virtue of its logical form; for instance, "All red dogs are red."

teleology   The study or analysis of things in terms of ends, purposes, or consequences.

theodicy   An attempt to justify God's goodness given the existence of evil. (derived from Greek, *theo*: God, and *dike*: righteous).

transaction   In Transactional Analysis, a term used to describe an exchange of strokes.

Transactional Analysis   A counseling perspective, containing cognitive, rational, and behavioral elements, which is based on the premise that present-day decisions people make are rooted in childhood decisions and beliefs that are no longer viable in adult life.

truth function   In logic, a compound statement whose truth or falsehood is entirely a function of the truth status of its component statements.

unconditional positive regard   According to Rogers's person-centered approach to counseling, the therapist's warm caring for, and acceptance of, the client as a person regardless of what the client feels, expresses, or ex-periences. The therapist does not attempt to criticize, evaluate, or impose his or her own values upon the client.

universal affirmative statement   In logic, a statement of the form "All S is P."

universal negative statement   In logic, a statement of the form "No S is P."

utilitarianism, act   The ethical theory according to which an act is morally justified if, and only if, its performance is calculated to maximize human happiness.

utilitarianism, rule   The ethical theory according to which an act is morally justified if, and only if, its performance is required by a rule or policy the general adherence to which will, at least in the long run, maximize human happiness.

valid argument   A deductive argument having a logical form or skeleton such that any substitution instances which make all of its premises true must also make its conclusion true.

value, instrumental   The value a thing possesses by virtue of its ability to bring about or cause something else of value; in contrast to *intrinsic value*.

value, intrinsic   The value a thing possesses *in itself*; that is, quite apart from any ability it may have to bring about or cause anything else of value.

verifiability, strong-sense   According to Ayer, a proposition is verifiable in the strong sense if, and only if, its truth is *conclusively* empirically verifiable.

verifiability, weak-sense   According to Ayer, a proposition is verifiable in the weak sense if, and only if, experience can make it *probable*. The sense of verifiability accepted by Ayer.

victim mentality   A mindset in which a person feels, contrary to fact, responsible for his or her negative treatment by others, and allows this treatment to perpetuate itself. As characterized by Mill, women having such a mindset are "willing slaves."

CPSIA information can be obtained
at www.ICGtesting.com
Printed in the USA
FFOW03n0028010813
1502FF

9 780155 055599